Anonymus

The Irish Ecclesiastical Record

Vol. 11 XI, January to June, 1902

Anonymus

The Irish Ecclesiastical Record
Vol. 11 XI, January to June, 1902

ISBN/EAN: 9783742810410

Manufactured in Europe, USA, Canada, Australia, Japa

Cover: Foto ©Suzi / pixelio.de

Manufactured and distributed by brebook publishing software
(www.brebook.com)

TABLE OF CONTENTS

"Ut Christiani ita et Romani sitis." " As you are children of Christ, so be you children of Rome."
Ex Dictis S. Patricii. In Libro Armacano, fol. 9.

The Irish Ecclesiastical Record

A Monthly Journal, under Episcopal Sanction.

Thirty-fifth Year]   JANUARY, 1902.   [Fourth Series
No. 409.   Vol. XI.

Nihil Obstat.
GIRALDUS MOLLOY, S.T.D.
   Censor Dep.
Imprimatur.
  ✠ GULIELMUS,
    Archiep. Dublin.,
    Hibernias Prim

BROWNE & NOLAN, Limited
Publishers and Printers, 24 & 25
NASSAU STREET, DUBLIN.

. . PRICE ONE SHILLING . .
SUBSCRIPTION: Twelve Shillings per Annum, Post Free, payable in advance

FÉNELON [1]

IT is remarkable that two English writers, neither of them a Catholic, should at the same time bring out serious studies of the life and writings of Fénelon. The famous Archbishop of Cambrai has, indeed, been always somewhat of a favourite, even outside his own country and his own creed; and the reason of this is not far to seek. He has been represented as a mild and gentle character, opposed alike to the tyranny and intolerance of Louis XIV. and the savage orthodoxy of Bossuet. His mystical and ascetical writings have commended him to the Evangelicals, and even to the Quakers; and when we add that these writings were condemned by Rome we need no further explanation of his popularity. Unfortunately his admirers, both in France and here in England, have been much more anxious to construct an ideal hero than to set before us the real man. Of late years, however, he has met with more judicial treatment, and now we are able to see that, without possessing every virtue under heaven, he was an honourable and enlightened man, a brilliant *littérateur*, a devout and zealous ecclesiastic, a sympathetic, if not always wise, director of souls, and a great archbishop.

[1] *François de Fénelon*, by Viscount St. Cyres (Methuen, 1901); *Fénelon: his Friends and his Enemies*, by E. K. Sanders (Longmans, 1901); *Fénelon, par Paul Janet* (Hachette, 1892).

The materials for the following article are derived largely,
though not exclusively, from the two books just mentioned.
Both are well worth reading; but the palm must be given
to Lord St. Cyres for his knowledge of his subject and for
the truly Catholic spirit in which he generally writes.
Miss Sanders is frankly Protestant, and has no pretension
to any familiarity with Catholic doctrines and practices.[1]
Nevertheless she writes with an ease and grace which are
decidedly lacking in Lord St. Cyres' learned volume.

1. Francis de Salagnac de Lamothe Fénelon was born
in Périgord on August 6th, 1651. Of his parents little is
known, save that they were of a noble though impoverished
stock. One would like to learn more about his early
training besides the mere facts that he was brought up in
the paternal château and afterwards spent some time at
the University of Cahors and the Collège Du Plessy. He
possessed a charm, a grace, and a worldliness (in the good
sense) not often displayed by those whose training has been
wholly ecclesiastical. The Greek and Latin classics were
his inseparable companions all through life: allusions to
them constantly flow from his pen. His father's brother, the
Marquis de Fénelon, who had lost his son at the siege of
Candia, took the boy under his protection. The Marquis
was a man of austere piety and had been on intimate terms
with M. Olier, the founder of Saint-Sulpice. Accordingly,
the young Fénelon was sent to that celebrated seminary
at Paris. There seems to be no doubt that in his case
this step was taken through no merely worldly motives.
He had a real vocation to the priesthood, and never in after
life did he regret that he had entered the ecclesiastical
state. Saint-Sulpice was at this time presided over by
M. Tronson, so well known to students by his Examination
of Conscience for Clerics. Fénelon became a devoted
admirer of the saintly superior and long continued to
submit himself to his direction. In due course he finished

---

[1] Fénelon 'was twenty-four when he received the tonsure [!], and for
three years longer he worked as one of the community of priests of the parish
of St. Sulpice' (Sanders, p. 14). This passage shows how small is her knowledge of matters ecclesiastical.

his theological studies and was ordained priest at the age of twenty-four. His first intention was to set out for the East to convert the Turks and instruct their Christian subjects. But just as St. Philip found his Indies in Rome, so Fénelon's missionary zeal was employed in the work of conversion in Paris itself. After three years' labour in the parish of Saint-Sulpice, he was appointed superior of the *Nouvelles Catholiques*, a position which exercised much influence on his career and his posthumous fame.

As soon as Louis XIV. had got into his own hands the reins of government he took steps to bring about religious union among his subjects. Terrible Huguenot wars had devastated France and had prevented her from occupying that commanding position among the nations which the Grand Monarque destined for her. At first he relied only on argument. At his bidding, Regulars and Seculars, Jesuits and Jansenists, vied with each other in entering into controversy with the heretics. The ablest of the Church's champions, it need hardly be said, was the great Bossuet. His *Exposition de la Doctrine Catholique*, written in 1668 and published in 1671, and his *Histoire des Variations*, published in 1688, are to this day the standard works on the questions at issue. To this same period belongs the well-known work *De la Perpétuité de la Foi*, composed by the solitaries of Port Royal. As a result of these discussions many conversions took place. A congregation of religious sisters was established for the education of young girls just received into the Church. This was the institution which became known under the name of the *Nouvelles Catholiques*.

No more congenial occupation could have been given to Fénelon than the care of these youthful converts. He was at this time (1678) twenty-seven years of age, full of sincere zeal for the propagation of the faith, and yet with a kind and gentle character which could not fail to win the hearts of those entrusted to him. And, on the other hand, the constant intercourse with refined ladies and tender children developed in him those fascinating qualities which gave him afterwards such influence with the gentler sex. He presided over the little congregation more than ten years. A part of the time, however, was spent away from Paris in missionary labours. Louis XIV. had now resorted to forcible means for converting those who still held out against the arguments of Bossuet and his followers. After the revocation of the Edict of Nantes (1685) dragoons were sent into the disaffected districts, and their rude violence was supplemented by the logic and oratory of eminent preachers :—

Father Bourdaloue [wrote Mme. de Sévigné] is going to preach at Montpellier, where so many have been converted without knowing why ; but the Father will explain it all, and will make good Catholics of them. Hitherto the dragoons have been excellent missionaries, but the clergy now to be sent will complete the work.

Fénelon's labours at the *Nouvelles Catholiques* naturally singled him out to be one of these preachers. So great was his reputation that he was sent to one of the worst districts —the neighbourhood of the notorious Protestant stronghold of La Rochelle. Thus his name became associated with the persecuting policy of Louis XIV., and his opinions and conduct in this difficult situation have been misunderstood and distorted both by friends and foes.

In the eighteenth century it was the custom to hold up Fénelon as the advocate of toleration and the rights of man, contending strenuously against the bullying bigotry of Bossuet. La Harpe's *Eloge de Fénelon*, a work crowned by the Académie Française, is written entirely in this spirit. La Harpe's unsuccessful rival, on this occasion, the Abbé (afterwards Cardinal) Maury, gave a far more accurate account of Fénelon. It was not until our own day that this legend of Fénelon's tolerance was demolished by the publication of M. Onésime Douen's *L'Intolérance de Fénelon* (1872). We now have also his own letters, giving an account of his missionary labours. What do we gather from these ? First, nowhere in any of his letters, or in any other of his writings, is there a single word condemning the revocation of the Edict ; on the contrary, he approves of the use of force. The Government should take care, he says, ' to combine with Christian persuasion vigilance against desertions

and penalties (*la rigueur des peines*) against deserters.'
Moreover, he himself actively joined in the persecution ; he
denounced to the Secretary of State the would-be fugitives
to foreign lands ; he recommended that some of the leaders
should be transported to Canada ; and he complained of the
remissness of the convert officials. Nevertheless there was
some ground for the view that in his heart he believed that
force was no remedy. In the same letters in which he
approves of force he also recommends gentleness and
patience :—

It would be easy enough [he says] to make them all go to
Confession and Communion ; but what a show to make people
confess who do not yet believe in the true Church, or in her power
to forgive sins ! And how are we to administer Jesus Christ to
those who do not believe that they receive Him ? I know very
well that, when missionaries and soldiers are combined, the new
converts go together to Holy Communion. These stern, obstinate
spirits, embittered against our religion, are, for all that, cowardly
and with an eye to their worldly interests. At the least pressure
they will commit sacrileges without number ; but the only result
will be to drive them to despair or utter indifference to all religion.
We should bring down upon ourselves a horrible curse if we
contented ourselves with hurrying on a work with no real
foundation, and brilliant only to those who viewed it from afar.

Accordingly he begged for certain graces from the Government. ' Their clergy must be equal in capacity and learning
to the ejected pastors ; the State must furnish supplies and
competent teachers for their schools ; there must be free
distribution of New Testaments and books of Catholic piety,
printed in large type ; alms should be given to the well
disposed, according to the excellent system of the Consis-
tories. And Fénelon even brought down suspicion on his
head by leaving out of his sermons the customary Invocation to the Virgin, and by proposing that some special
prayers and Bible-reading should be added to the religious
services attended by the heretics.' [1] Fénelon's mission lasted
from December, 1685, to July, 1686, and was renewed for a
few months in the next year, 1687.

---

[1] St. Cyres, p. 27.

2. In this year, 1687, Fénelon published his first work. Though it had some connection with his labours at the *Nouvelles Catholiques*, it did not deal with any of the religious questions of the day. His friends, the Duke and Duchess of Beauvillier, had a large family of daughters. In their anxiety to bring them up well, they applied to Fénelon for guidance. The rules which he laid down for them grew into a treatise, which is now known to us under the title *De l'Education des Filles*.

To estimate this book at its just value we must bear in mind that the most enlightened thinkers of that age maintained that a woman's education should embrace nothing more than her catechism, sewing, singing, dancing and deportment, and correct speech. Their view was based on the inferiority of her sex : her whole duty consisted in keeping house and doing her husband's bidding. Fénelon contends that even these occupations require intelligence and training. To parody a later saying, he insists that we must educate our mothers. If we devote so much attention to the education of boys in order to fit them for the important work which they have to do in the world, how can we neglect the education of the women to whose care they are entrusted in their tenderest and most impressionable years? It is no argument to say that the feminine mind is naturally weak : all the more reason for making it strong. But Fénelon takes higher ground. He is a firm believer in the dignity of woman, and he considers that the frivolity, vanity, and affectation of which she is constantly accused, and is so often guilty, are the result, not merely of her sex,'but of her training. Give her a fair chance, such as, at least, her young brothers get, and she will no longer be a doll or a drudge, but a help meet for man.

The first part of his little work is devoted to early education generally—whether of boys or of girls. It will be sufficient here to remark that he insists on the importance of making lessons pleasant. They must be short, with frequent intervals of play : the actual things about which the children are learning must be brought before their eyes and put into their hands (object-lessons) ; the books must be nicely printed and bound, with plenty of beautiful pictures. Above all, the teacher must be kind and gentle, so as to win the pupils' confidence and love.

Next he deals with the teaching of girls in particular. He observes that the great aim should be to strengthen their character—to correct their many little weaknesses.

They are born actresses: tears cost them nothing: their emotions are lively, their intelligence narrow. . . . They are excited about their dress: a hat, a ribbon, a look of hair a bit higher or a bit lower—these are serious matters in their eyes. . . . They should be taught that it is a much greater honour to be good than to have nice hair and nice frocks.

Beauty, in fact, is of little use, 'except for the purpose of marriage'! Not that Fénelon despised attractions. He even lays down rules for dress, which he would have designed on the lines of the drapery of the ancient statues: simplicity and dignity should be the dominant notes. The programme of studies which he drew up, though far in advance of those days, may seem to us meagre enough. Spanish and Italian are forbidden, because the books written in those languages are dangerous and unsuitable for women. But he permits the study of Greek and Roman history, and 'even the history of France, which also has its beauties.' Works of poetry and eloquence are recommended, but great care is to taken in the choice of them. A little law should also be taught—for instance, the difference between a will and a deed of gift, the nature of contracts, what goods are movable and what immovable—but nothing that would encourage chicanery, to which women are so prone.

On the whole, we may conclude that Fénelon did much for the education of women, though he did not do all.

He stood far ahead of all other contemporary reformers. . . . Gaps there are, and contradictions and extravagances. Fénelon is open to the charge, so often brought against the Jansenists, of first teaching girls to think for themselves, and then forbidding them to express their thoughts. . . . Within his own lifetime, his correspondent and admirer, Mme. de Lambert, was already chafing at its narrowness. . . . And it was long before another disciple, Mme. de Rémusat, broadened his timid conception of a housewife, busied with much serving in the back ground, into the worthier ideal of a wife, whose glory it was to be the mother and the consort of a citizen, ready, though herself holding no cards in the game of life, to sit as a counsellor beside the players, to share in their victories, and console their defeats. Yet it was from the education of girls that these later reformers started ; from Fénelon they learned to turn ' all their knowledge into character, all their wisdom into virtue.'[1]

The Duke de Beauvillier was able to make an ample return for the excellent advice given to him in the *Education des Filles*. In 1689 he was nominated governor of the little Duke of Burgundy, grandson of Louis XIV., and his first action was to secure the appointment of Fénelon as preceptor.

It was indeed a great promotion from the *Nouvelles Catholiques* to the charge of the education of the heir to the throne. During the long years spent by Fénelon in the former task, he had not however neglected to make friends at Court. Besides the Duke and Duchess de Beauvillier, he had become acquainted with Madame de Maintenon whose influence was already supreme with the king and who was soon to become his wife. With Bossuet he was on most intimate terms ; and no one more highly approved of his selection than the great Bishop of Meaux. Louis XIV. is certainly deserving of high praise for his choice of two such men as Bossuet to teach his son, and Fénelon to teach his grandson. Yet in the former case the plan had resulted in utter failure. Bossuet had laid aside his sermons, his funeral orations, and his theological controversies, and had devoted himself entirely for ten long years to the instruction of the dauphin. But the pupil was not worthy of the master. The intellectual distance between them was too great to be bridged over. No doubt it would have been wiser to have selected some commoner type of mind to train up the sluggish and vulgar son of the great king. Fénelon was more fortunate in his pupil, and the pupil, too, more fortunate in his master. The Duke of Burgundy was a far superior character to his father. He was, indeed, of a fierce

---

[1] St. Oyres, p. 70.

and even savage disposition; his temper was violent and he was obstinate, but on the other hand his intelligence was of a high order, his memory was excellent, and he had a lively sense of the ridiculous. It was by appealing to this last, as well as by real kindness, that Fénelon was able to obtain control over his young charge; and he also took care to make the prince see at once the relative position of teacher and pupil. The result was soon perceptible. Burgundy made rapid progress in his studies, and what was better still, he became gentle and affable. A tender affection grew up between the two which lasted until the younger was so prematurely cut off. Indeed Fénelon ultimately came to have too much influence over the duke, who depended more and more on his 'Mentor' for spiritual and even political direction.

In 1695, Fénelon was nominated to the Archbishopric of Cambrai. He had, therefore, sacrificed only half the time devoted by Bossuet to the education of the dauphin. We must bear in mind that Burgundy was still a mere boy when his dear preceptor was taken from him. It is not fair to lay upon Fénelon the blame of the failure which followed. Early in 1702 the duke was sent to the army in Flanders. On his road he called at Cambrai, and, to his great delight, was allowed to see the archbishop. But the king had given orders that the interview should not be in private. 'To-day, after five years of separation,' wrote Fénelon, ' I have seen my lord Duke of Burgundy, but God has seasoned this blessing with very great bitterness.' The prince went through the indecisive campaigns of 1702 and 1703 with some credit. Then for five years he was kept at the Court. His position there was a difficult one. His father, the dauphin, was completely in the hands of a set of profligate favourites, at the head of whom was the infamous Vendôme. Burgundy's gloomy disposition and austere manners continually annoyed this cabal, who did their best to undermine his popularity. Strangely enough, their conduct does not seem to have reached the ears of the king. When, after the terrible defeats of Blenheim (1704) and Ramilies (1706), he resolved to make a supreme effort to restore the prestige of France, he appointed Burgundy commander-in-chief of the forces in Flanders. Marlborough and Eugene were the generals against whom the young prince was to contend. Some experienced leader, it was felt, should be sent as his adviser, and the king's choice fell upon Vendôme. Once more Burgundy had an opportunity of visiting his exiled master, but once again the king insisted on the same conditions as before. Some letters, however, have been preserved, which show how intimate were their relations more than ten years after they had been parted.[1]

The campaign, which followed, was most disastrous. Vendôme thwarted the duke in every way; the young officers sneered at his manners and devotions; even the common soldiers nicknamed him 'Télémaque.' The decisive defeat of Oudenarde and the loss of the great stronghold of Lille put an end for ever to his military career. Fénelon was heart-broken at the failure. He felt that he himself would be blamed. He wrote a manly, straightforward letter to the prince, pointing out the causes of the disaster, and at the same time holding out encouragement for further efforts.[2] But the king put no further trust in his grandson—it was not he, but Villars who fought the glorious defeat of Malplaquet in the following year. And now we must leave the Duke of Burgundy for a while, and turn to Fénelon's literary activity.

3. Most of us have made our first acquaintance with Fénelon as the author of *Télémaque*. It was his custom, while teaching the young prince, to throw some of his lessons into the form of fables. Though these were not meant for the public eye, they have been preserved, and they give us ample proof of his shrewdness and humour, and power of striking the imagination. They are naturally adapted to the special circumstances of his royal charge; hence they deal with the dangers of life at court, the evils of tyranny and

---

[1] *Correspondence de Fénelon*, i. 76; i. 89.

[2] I wish I could give the letter in full. It is an admirable example of paternal correction. Part of it may be found in Sanders, p. 275, *seq*.

bad faith, the worthlessness of wealth and high station without virtue.[1]

As the prince grew older, his preceptor gave these moral lessons in a more serious and ambitious form. We have seen how thoroughly Fénelon's mind was steeped in the classics. Accordingly, he wrote for his pupil a classical romance. His own account of it is given in a letter to Père le Tellier :—

> *Télémaque* is a fabulous narrative in the form of a heroic poem, like those of Homer or Virgil, in which I have set down the truths most necessary to be known by one who is about to reign ; there also are described the faults that cling most closely to sovereign power. But I have borrowed from no real persons. I have sketched no characters of our own time ; my book was written at odd moments hurriedly, bit by bit. It was sent to the press by a faithless copyist, and was never intended for publication.[2]

There seems no reason to doubt his sincerity in this matter. Indeed the appearance of the book shattered all hope of any reconciliation with Louis XIV.[3] It was impossible to convey any useful lesson without pointing out the defects of the existing ruler and his government ; and Fénelon's temperament no doubt caused him to do this in a form which looks rather like satire. But it was one thing to write for the prince's eye and quite another to hold up Louis to the ridicule of his subjects :—

> I wrote it [he says] at a time when I was overwhelmed by evidence of the confidence and kindness of the king. I should have shown myself to be not only the most ungrateful but the most reckless of men if I had attempted to take satirical and insolent examples ; I shrink from the very thought of such a thing.

Nevertheless the public insisted on taking it as a satire, and as such it had a prodigious success. The year of its

---

[1] Here is an example. As the young Bacchus was one day learning to read, an old Faun kept laughing at his blunders. 'How dare you make game of Jupiter's son ?' exclaimed the proud little god in a rage. The Faun replied calmly : 'How dare Jupiter's son make mistakes ?' This fable referred to an occasion when the young prince had rebelled against Fénelon's authority.

[2] *Œuvres*, vii., p. 665.

[3] Lord St. Cyres' printer has here played him a little joke. 'The existence of *Télémaque* first became known in the autumn of 1698, just when the Quietest controversy was at its fiercest.'—Page 179.

publication (1699) was a time when Louis XIV. and his
Court were the objects of hatred and jealousy to the rest of
Europe, and when even in France there was considerable
opposition to his despotic rule.   No wonder that such
passages as the following were read with delight by all the
enemies of the Grand Monarque :—

A king should have no advantage over others, except what is
necessary either to help him in his arduous duties or to exact
from the people the respect due to the representative of law and
order.   Moreover, the king should be more sober, less prone to
indolence, freer from arrogance and pride than others.   He must
not have a larger share of riches and pleasures, but of wisdom, of
virtue, and of renown.   He must be the defender of his country
and the leader of his armies abroad, and at home the ruler of the
people, who wins them goodness and wisdom and happiness.   The
gods did not make him a king for himself, but that he might
belong to the people.   All his time, all his care, all his love, is due
to the people, and he is only worthy of royalty inasmuch as he
forgets himself to devote himself to the public good. . . .
When kings allow themselves to recognise no law but their
own sovereign will, and put no curb upon their passions, they can
do what they please ; but by doing as they please they undermine
the foundations of their power ; they have absolute laws no
longer, nor traditions of government ; everyone will compete to
flatter them ; they will not have a people ; there will be none but
slaves remaining to them, and those will grow fewer daily.[1]

Fénelon's countless readers insisted that Idomeneus was
meant for Louis ; Boccharis was the Dauphin ; Louvois,
Protesilas ; Mme. de Montespan, Astarbe ; and William of
Orange, Adrastus.   Tyre was evidently Holland, and the
League of Augsburg against Louis was represented by the
coalition against Idomeneus.   Telemachus is, of course, the
Duke of Burgundy, and Mentor, Fénelon.   Read in this light,
the book will always be of interest.   But it must be confessed that the characters themselves are utterly wanting in
reality ; they are not beings of flesh and blood.   As to its
style, French critics are, of course, the best judges :—

The characteristic of Fénelon's style [says M. Paul Janet],
especially in *Télémaque*, is grace.   No French writer equals him
in this respect ; no one else has so depicted all that is sweet and
lovable and natural.   When he describes nature it is always under

---

[1] Liv. v. ; Liv. xvii.   See also Liv. xiv.   Sanders, pp. 162-4.

the simplest and most familiar aspects. . . . Besides grace, there is in Fénelon much imagination, not, as in Bossuet, grand, sublime, profound, Hebraic, but lively, brilliant, coloured, Greek. His narrative, in the finest passages (*e.g.*, battles, struggles, shipwrecks) is rapid, made up of lifelike, forcible strokes. Grace does not exclude strength (*e.g.*, the combat between Adrastus and Telemachus), or pathos (Idomeneus' sacrifice), or terror (the death of Boccharis). Yet he is at his best in depicting what is noble, delicate, and pure. In contrast to other poets he has succeeded better in his description of Paradise than of hell. [1]

As a critic of other writers Fénelon stands in the first rank. In his *Lettre à l'Académie Française*, written in 1714, just before his death, he enters into the famous controversy concerning the comparative merits of the ancients and the moderns. Though he speaks with caution, for fear of hurting the feelings of his literary friends, he is decidedly in favour of the ancients. He reproaches the moderns with being studied and stilted, unreal, continually straining after effect; whereas in the ancients all is natural, simple, and easy. [2] He is especially severe on French poetry, and justly points out that rhyme, which is considered so essential to it, is in reality its stumbling-block. Then, again, he deplores the excessive importance which the passion of love occupies in modern tragedies. Æschylus and Sophocles he would place above Corneille and Racine. One is not surprised to find him disapproving of modern comedy; but this does not prevent him from giving the highest praise to Molière—

We must admit [he says] that Molière is a great comic poet. I do not fear to say that he has gone even further than Terence;

---

[1] *Fénelon*, pp. 131-2.

[2] Lord St. Cyres aptly quotes Cardinal Newman: ' Passages which to a boy are but rhetorical commonplaces . . . at length come home to him, when long years have passed and he has had experience of life, and pierce him, as if he had never before known them, with their sad earnestness and vivid exactness. Then he comes to understand how it is that lines, the birth of some chance morning or evening at an Ionian festival or among the Sabine Hills, have lasted, generation after generation, for thousands of years, with a power over the mind and a charm which the current literature of his own day, with all its obvious advantages, is utterly unable to rival. Perhaps this is the reason of the mediæval opinion about Virgil, as if a prophet or magician; his single words and phrases, his pathetic half lines, giving utterance to the voice of nature itself, to that pain and weariness, yet hope of better things, which is the experience of her children in every time.'—*Grammar of Assent*, pp. 78, 79.

he has embraced a greater variety of subjects; he has painted
in strong colours all that is exaggerated and ridiculous; he has
opened up an entirely new road. Once more I find him great.

It was something for an archbishop to speak in such
glowing terms of a writer of comedies, after Bossuet's
denunciations in the *Maximes et Réflexions sur la Comédie*.
One of the last chapters of the *Lettre à l'Académie* is devoted
to history. While insisting that a historian must be truthful and thoroughly impartial, he requires him also to be an
artist. 'I prefer an inexact historian who bungles over
names, but yet paints with *naïveté* all the details, as, for
example, Froissart, to all the chroniclers of Charlemagne.'
But he must not be an embroiderer; he must give us a
faithful as well as lifelike picture of the past. He must not
confine his attention to wars and the intrigues of courts :
great importance should be attached to the history of
institutions of all kinds. Herein Fénelon was anticipating
the studies which, under the name of *Histoire de la
Civilization (Kulturgeschichte)*, have been cultivated with
such success in our own day.

Eloquence is duly treated of in the *Lettre*; but Fénelon
has also dealt with this subject in a special work entitled
Dialogues sur l'Eloquence. Here we are chiefly interested in
his views on preaching. The rival styles of the day were
represented by Bossuet and Bourdaloue; and, strange as it
may seem to us, Bourdaloue was the general favourite. It
was against this popular judgment¸that Fénelon set his face.
He contrasts the cold monotonous delivery, the elaborate
divisions, the minute analysis of character, the long
quotations and trains of reasoning of the great Jesuit, with
the simple and yet sublime and majestic, because Scriptural,
eloquence of Bossuet. He is strongly opposed to written
sermons learnt by heart :—

A man who does not learn by heart is master of himself; he
speaks naturally, his matter flows directly from its source, his
expressions are full of life and movement; his very excitement
provides him with phrases and figures which he could never have
found in his study. All that comes in the heat of delivery is full
of feeling and is natural—it has an air of being unstudied and

not being artificial. Moreover, a skilful orator regulates his materials according to the impression produced upon his audience.

This does not, of course, mean that the preacher should give no care to preparation. Fénelon insists on preparation, and even allows that certain brilliant passages and striking images might be elaborated beforehand. His own practice was in exact accordance with what he here lays down. We have only a few elaborate discourses from his pen ; and yet, both as a young priest and much more afterwards as archbishop, he possessed—

The secret of that purely Christian eloquence whose only law is sympathy, that speaks to the people not sternly as a prophet, but with the tenderness of a fellow-bondsman, who does not separate his lot from theirs ; and has himself first reached the spiritual haven into which he beseeches them to enter.[1]

Next to *Télémaque*, Fénelon's best known work is his *Traité de l'Existence de Dieu*. It consists of two parts : the first, popular and literary ; the second, scientific and metaphysical. It begins with the argument from design, and goes on to what is now known as the ontological argument ; then the nature of God is discussed at great length. The book is not likely to appeal much to English readers of the present day. In Paley's *Natural Theology* the argument from design is far more skilfully handled. There is, indeed, in Fénelon much subtle thought and fine writing about the nature of God—Who is ' Being,' without any sort of qualification, from Whom any sort of plurality or multiplication is absolutely excluded. But all this part savours of Neoplatonism, and is quite out of the orthodox beaten track.[2] As M. Paul Janet observes, ' his metaphysics and his theology border on heresy, in spite of his sincere desired to keep far from it.' But Fénelon's theological opinions and their tragic consequences must be reserved for a future article.

T. B. SCANNELL.

---

[1] St. Cyres, p. 40.
[2] Lord St. Cyres has a very learned chapter on ' Fénelon among the Philosophers,' dealing especially with his relation to Descartes and Malebranche. Page 248, *seq.*

THE RISE AND PROGRESS OF HIGHER CRITICISM

II.—THE FRAGMENT-HYPOTHESIS

IT is so-called, because it denies the essential unity of scope and purpose in the five books of Moses, and contends that they are made up of a number of originally unconnected fragments. This theory, too, is, sad to say, the invention of a Catholic, and a priest. His name was Geddes.[1] It is worthy of remark that he and Astruc were the only Catholics that contributed to the development of Higher Criticism, for Jahn, almost the only other Catholic writer of note that was imbued with its principles, contented himself with reproducing some of Eichhorn's ideas. The same is true of the ex-Catholic, Addis, in respect of contemporary critics. Geddes was original. While Astruc and Ilgen confined their speculations to Genesis, Geddes extended the critical analysis to the rest of the Pentateuch and to the Book of Josue. What is more, he carried the process of disintegration to a degree of which neither they nor even Eichhorn had ever dreamed. There is a radical difference between the Document and the Fragment-

---

[1] Alexander Geddes was born in Bannfshire, in 1737, the son of an honest farmer. Like his elder brother, who subsequently became a bishop, he made his ecclesiastical studies in the Scots' College, Paris, where he gave proofs of rare ability. On his return home in 1764, he was ordained priest and entrusted with the charge of a mission in Dundee, and afterwards of one in Bannfshire. Owing, however, to his lax opinions and his unclerical behaviour he incurred the displeasure of Bishop Hay, who, finding repeated remonstrances of no avail, at length threatened to suspend him. Geddes then left the Lowland district, and in 1779 he settled in London. For a few months he acted as chaplain to the Austrian Embassy until the chaplaincy was suppressed by Joseph II. In 1782 Geddes ceased to officiate as a priest, and devoted himself exclusively to literature and to Biblical studies. He was a good Hebraist, and only too well acquainted with the work of the German rationalists, Rosenmüller, Dathe, etc., but especially with those of Eichhorn and Michaelis, from which he imbibed his notions about the Pentateuch. One good thing he did should be mentioned. He refuted Priestley's intolerable assertions about our Lord. But Priestley, in his reply, says that he doubts 'whether such a man as Geddes, who believes so little and concedes so much, can be a Christian.' Geddes may have still preserved some shreds of faith, but the levity and profaneness of his conversation could not pass unnoticed. Indeed, this had been the case even before he left Scotland. As his friend and biographer, the Unitarian, John Mason Good, says, 'he could ridicule the infallibility of the Pope, and laugh at

hypothesis. The latter is supported mainly by arguments drawn from the middle books (Exodus, Leviticus, Numbers). It does not assume that the only documents in the Pentateuch are documents used by Moses, or that any connected narratives are to be found in it. On the contrary it maintains that even the so-called E and J passages may be of a very composite nature. The only connecting links between the fragments are those supplied by the compiler.[1] Sometimes he forgets to join the fragments. Strack[2] gives the following as instances. The command to make the golden candlestick is found in Exodus xxv.; the description of its manufacture ten chapters further on. Again in Leviticus xxiv. there are three verses about the supply of olive oil for the lamps of the golden candlestick, there is a solitary verse about the same subject in Exodus xxvii., and there are three verses about lighting the lamps, and one verse containing a description of the candlestick in Numbers viii. The Pentateuch is, when carefully analysed, found to be a heap of similar incoherent heterogeneous fragments, many of which are mutually contradictory. Such, in a few words, was the blasphemous theory put forward by Geddes in the preface to his work—

images and relics, at rosaries, scapulars, Agnus Deis, blessed medals, indulgences, obits and dirges, as much as the most inveterate Protestant in the neighbourhood.' When in 1792 the first volume of his projected translation of the Bible appeared (Pentateuch and Josue), it was at once prohibited by three Vicars Apostolic, and the only result of a protest on his part was that the Vicar of the London district, Bishop Douglas, suspended him from all priestly functions. Geddes is said to have asked for absolution the day before his death (20th February, 1806). A French *émigré* priest, the Abbé Saint-Martin, attended him, but could not say whether he was still conscious. Bishop Douglas would not allow Mass to be publicly offered for his soul. Such was the melancholy end of the founder of the Fragment-hypothesis. Of course Protestants, and especially the higher critics, regard him as a martyr for exegesis, and extoll his memory.

Addis has the hardihood to speak thus of Geddes:—'He was a man of blameless life and a sincere Christian, but his countrymen could not or would not understand him. His works, despite their faults of style, show real learning, and he understood far better than the dry rationalists, who then ruled in the German Universities, the spontaneous origin and the native simplicity o f Hebrew myth and legend.'—*The Documents of the Hexateuch*, by W. E. Addis, p. xxxv., note,

N.B.—While a Catholic, Addis was co-editor of *A Catholic Dictionary*.

[1] In this hypothesis, the compiler or the ' Redactor ' appears on the scene for the first time.

[2] *Einleitung in das A. T.*, p. 34.

' *The Holy Bible*, or the Books accounted Sacred by Jews
and Christians : otherwise called the Books of the Old and
New Covenants; faithfully translated from the originals, with
various readings, explanatory notes and critical remarks.
Vol. I. (Pentateuch and Josue). London, 1792.' His notions
about the authorship of Genesis, etc., will best be given in
his own words :—

It has been well observed by Michaelis that all external testimony here is of little avail ; it is from intrinsic evidence only that
we must derive our proofs. Now, from intrinsic evidence,
three things, to me, seem indubitable. (1) The Pentateuch in its
present form was not written by Moses. (2) It was written in
the land of Chanaan, and most probably at Jerusalem. (3) It
could not be written before the reign of David, nor after that of
Hezekiah. The long pacific reign of Solomon (the Augustan age
of Judea) is the period to which I would refer it; yet 1 confess
there are some marks of a posterior date, or at least of posterior
interpolation. But though I am inclined to believe that the
Pentateuch was reduced into its present form in the reign of
Solomon, I am fully persuaded that it was compiled from ancient
documents, some of which were coeval with Moses, and some even
anterior to Moses. Whether all these were written records, or
many of them only oral traditions, it would be rash to determine.[1]

Geddes ridicules the history of creation, the fall of
man, etc., the miracles recorded in Exodus, etc. He denied
also the inspiration of the Pentateuch. Here, again, it may
be more satisfactory to quote one of his remarks :—

I will not pretend to say that its history is entirely unmixed
with the leaven of the heroic ages. Let the father of Hebrew be
tried by the same rules of criticism as the father of Greek history.
Why might not the Hebrews have had their mythology as well as
other nations? And why might not their mythologists contrive
or improve a system of cosmogony as well as those of Chaldea, or
Egypt, or Greece, or Italy, or Persia, or Hindostan?

No wonder that his edition of the Pentateuch was prohibited. We shall now consider him in another character ;
not that of the vulgar scoffer, but that of the would-be
savant. In his preface he says :—

To the Pentateuch I have joined the Book of Joshua, both
because I conceive it to have been compiled by the same author
and because it is a necessary appendix to the history contained in
the former books.'

---

[1] Preface, p. viii.   [2] Page xxi.

Now, everyone knows the immediate relation which the
Book of Josue has to the Pentateuch,[1] the simple reason
of which is obvious to even the youngest member of a Bible-
history class. Josue completed the work begun by Moses,
hence the histories of their own times, which they respectively wrote, are intimately connected. But Geddes, and
after him all the higher critics who accept as much of
that history as pleases them, and no more, have their own
theory to account for the connection, similarity of expressions, etc. The connection is due to the man who combined
the fragments or the documents. The 'Hexateuch' is,
among critics at the present day, the accepted title of this
compilation.

So far as we know, the fashionable name was invented
by Wellhausen; or, at least, owes it currency to its being
used by him. There is a purpose in the name. In
the mouths of the critics it connotes their rejection of the
traditional authorship of the five books, by tacitly identifying
their origin with that of a book, which Moses could not have
written. As a contemporary critic[2] says :—

The object of the change of name is to show that the six,
rather than the five, form a complete literary whole, and may be
looked upon as one book in six parts.

---

[1] The division into five books dates from time immemorial, and is, we may
be sure, as old as Moses himself. The Jews employ the first word or words of
each book (Bereshith, Vealle Shemoth, etc.) as the name, just as, for example,
we do in the case of Papal documents : 'Unam Sanctam,' 'Ascendente
Domino,' 'Romani Pontifices.' The names indicative of the contents that we give
to the five books, i.e., Genesis, Exodus, etc., originated with the Septuagint.
But neither prefixed to this version, nor to the original Hebrew, was there any
collective name. We do, however, find one in the Peshitta (K'thaba durjatha
d'Mushe n'bia=the book of the law of the prophet Moses) ; and in the New
Testament we meet frequently with νομος, which is the translation of the
Old Testament name 'Torah.' The name in the Talmud and in the Rabbinical
books is rather peculiar ; it means 'five-fifths of the law.'
The oldest writings extant in which the name 'Pentateuch' is found, are
those of Origen (Commentary on St. John's Gospel), and of St. Hippolytus.
St. Epiphanius used the word habitually, indeed he divides the Old Testament
into four Pentateuchs. It is not, however, the only collective title. Cardinal Pitra
has published in his Analecta Sacra an ancient Greek list in which Genesis-
Ruth are ο Οκτατευχος. And St. Ambrose speaks of the 'Heptateuch': 'inveni
Heptateuchum, inveni regnorum libros,' etc. The same mode of reckoning is
found in the Cheltenham Canon (drawn up in A.D. 359) : after 'liber judioum,'
it has the remark 'fiunt libri vii.'
[2] Woods, in Hastings' Bible Dictionary.

And he proceeds thus :—

It is not intended by the title either to exclude the possibility
that the Hexateuch, like the rest of the Old Testament, was
subject to constant revision, or to imply that the sources out of
which it was compiled are necessarily to be found only in these
books. A century ago it was a matter of common belief that the
Pentateuch was written by Moses ; but this belief never rested on
anything but tradition, and will not bear examination. It will be
shown that, in fact, these books are the result of complicated
literary processes extending over a long period. As the Mosaic
authorship will thus be disproved at the very outset, it requires
no separate discussion.

Assuming, therefore, the late origin of the five books as
a matter beyond dispute, the critics proceed to justify their
pet appellation, or their watchword—for such ' Hexateuch '
is—by proving to their own satisfaction that these five
books are in reality only part of the first historical work in
Jewish literature. This is their argument, in a condensed
form.[1] It has, of course, been improved since Geddes' time :—

The so-called Pentateuch (which is certainly the product of a
comparatively recent period, i.e., B.C. fifth century, after the
return from the captivity) professes to contain the history of the
ancient Hebrew people. Now, it does not give a complete description of their origin, for it does not inform us when the national
existence began. It does not reach to the one event in which all
the preceding occurrences converged and culminated. There is
not a single word about the conquest of Palestine proper (i.e.,
western), and the settlement there of nine and a-half tribes.
Yet this is the supremely important fact of the first period.
Surely if what had happened on the east of the Jordan, a
comparatively insignificant incident, is narrated ; a fortiori, what
was accomplished on the western side of the river should have
been recorded. Now, this is not done in the Pentateuch, but it is
in Joshua, therefore the sixth book is an integral part, or rather
the fitting and indispensable conclusion, of the first work on
Hebrew history.

The argument is thus enforced :—

The promises made to the Patriarchs referred to the possession
of Palestine by their descendants. Beside the predictions of
prosperity, there is the announcement to Abram (xv. 13) of the
future bondage in Egypt ; and we may and must assume that the

---

[1] Holzinger, *Einleitung*, p. 7.

same law holds good for the Biblical description of both. Now the announcement of the oppression in Genesis is accompanied by a description of it in Exodus, therefore the fulfilment of the promises should be recorded in the same work. The 'higher unities,' in fact all the laws of literary composition demand it. But this is done in Joshua, and only in Joshua. We are therefore led to the same conclusion as before. The Pentateuch without the book of Joshua is only a torso.

Obviously, this is very flimsy reasoning, but it is apparently the best that the critics have to offer. We need only observe that if the critics understood and believed the Bible, they would know that the national existence of the Israelites began at the Exodus,[1] and was ratified immediately before their entrance into the promised land.[2] As regards the remainder of their argument, the sophism it contains is obvious. The Pentateuch does not profess to continue the history down to what the critics are pleased to regard (in opposition to Scripture) as the origin of the Hebrew nation. It ends with the death of Moses, who was not permitted to enter the promised land. It could not describe the conquest of Palestine historically unless it was written after the event : for their own purpose consequently the critics assume, contrary to all proof, that it was written centuries later, and then they say it is incomplete ! The *petitio principii* involved in their second argument is equally glaring. They assume the very point at issue—namely, that an analogy exists between the predictions of weal and of woe within the limits of one historical work.

We all know that Macaulay wrote a *History of England*

---

[1] See Exodus vi. 6, 7, xxix. 46 ; Ps. cxiii. 1, 2 ; Osee xi. 1.

[2] Deut. xxvi. 18, xxvii. 9. It appears that the critics are not in the least disconcerted by the fact, that the great feast of the Pasch was the commemoration of the Exodus, and that the other two feasts, Pentecost and Tabernacles, were respectively instituted in honour of events that took place *before* the entrance into the Promised Land. Moses evidently did not take the same view of it as the critics do, else he ought to have established *(by anticipation)* a feast for what the critics are pleased to entitle 'the great event.' Solomon, too, is to blame, for though he made a feast at the dedication of his temple, he quite neglected 'the supremely important fact of the first period.' But the unkindest cut of all is, that in the post-exilic period, when *the Pentateuch was being compiled ;* when, to speak seriously, no less than seven new feasts (Purim, Encœnia, etc.) were added, none was instituted to commemorate Josue's conquest of Palestine, with which the national existence began!

and MacCarthy a *History of our Own Times*. But, perhaps, in the distant future some very supe:ior critic (not the New Zealander) will say that both these productions were compiled from fragments by some individual belonging to the twenty-ninth century; then finding that the *History of England* does not contain a single word about the death of Lord Palmerston, or the result of Earl Beaconsfield's foreign policy, and discovering that the *History of our Own Times* does mention these events, our learned friend will conclude that in its detached state the *History of England* is incomplete, a torso in fact; so that he is certain that it and the *History of our Own Times* originally were parts of one and the same compilation. The 'higher unities,' in fact all the laws of literary composition demand it. Perhaps he will go on to say :—

A century ago it was a matter of common belief that one of these then divided books was written by Macaulay, and the other by MacCarthy : but this belief never rested on anything but tradition, and will not bear examination. It will be shown that, in fact, these books are the result of complicated literary processes extending over a long period. As the reputed authorship will thus be disproved at the very outset, it requires no separate discussion.

Enough by way of illustration, so to resume our description. Vater, in his *Commentar über den Pentateuch* (Halle, 1802-1805,[1]) brought Geddes' new theory under the notice of his fellow-rationalists in Germany. Indeed, it may be said with truth that what Eichhorn did for Astruc's hypothesis, Vater did for that of Geddes. The two Germans developed with the most perverse ingenuity and amazing perseverance what they received only sketched in outline. The authors of the *Oxford Hexateuch* say that :—

Vater carried out the Fragment-hypothesis to its fullest extent, and regarded the Pentateuch as a huge aggregate of separate compositions, varying naturally in extent, but not capable of classification into groups or of union into single wholes.

---

[1] The full title is 'Commentar über den Pentateuch, mit Enleitungen zu den einzelnen Abschnitten der eingeschalteten Uebersetzung von Dr. A. Geddes' merkwürdigeren critischen und exegetischen Anmerkungen, und einer Abhandlung über Moses und die Vorfasser des Pentateuchs.'

He held that there were thirty-eight fragments in Genesis, which in detail he treated as a conglomerate of incompatible statements. To quote the sympathetic *Oxford Hexateuch* again :—

Even Deuteronomy, which presented 'most appearance of unity,' did not escape his dissection. He pointed, with penetrating insight, to the different titles traceable in i. 1-4, iv. 15-49, and xii. 1 ; he insisted that i.-iv. 40 was not written by the author of iv. 45-xi. ; he declared that xii.-xxvi. was a piece by itself, subsequently united with the preceding discourses by xi. 32 ; he even affirmed that within this collection duplicates might again be discovered, such as xii. 13-16 and xii. 20-24 ; while xxxi. 1-8, 9-12, formed a parallel to xiii. 14-23, 24.[1]

To the objection that it was difficult to conceive so many disconnected compositions as circulating in a written form throughout Palestine, Vater replied :—

Difficult, to be sure, it is ; but it is a difficulty inherent in the subject ; that is, in the form of the Pentateuch as it now appears. And it is far less difficult and a great deal less artificial than the theory of two documents covering the same ground, the parts of which have been patched together to make up Genesis.'

Vater would grant that Moses was probably the author of some of the fragments now imbedded in the Pentateuch, but not that he was the compiler. As regards the time when these products of many minds were put together, Vater was inclined to assign a latter date than Geddes had done. He would say that from the period of David and Solomon a *corpus juris* was extant, which now forms part of Deuteronomy.

This is the 'law,' which was found in the temple in the

---

[1] To quote now a Protestant writer on the other side, R. Sinker, D.D., Fellow of Trinity College, Cambridge :—' One of the leading representatives of this view [*i.e.*, Fragment-hypothesis] was J. S. Vater, who, in his *Commentary on the Pentateuch*, reduces Genesis to thirty-eight fragments of various lengths, and treats the other four books in similar style. This theory has well been called the Document Theory run mad. It is not necessary to enter into any discussion of it ; it was long ago refuted and cast aside by the critics, who were themselves in turn to be the victims of their successors, *velut unda supervenit undam.* The essential fallacy of such a theory is at once seen if we are content to deal with a plain fact and not?a mass of subjective fancies.' —*Higher Criticism: What is it, and where does it lead us ?*' 1899. Page 35.

[2] *Commentar*, p. 514.

reign of Josiah, but it was gradually enlarged during the reigns of his successors by the insertion of numerous passages, both legal and historical. It attained its present dimensions a short time before the kingdom of Judah came to an end. Vater was led to make this unreasonable hypothesis, in order to account for the apparent contradiction between the existence of a code of legislation, and that non-observance of it which forms so painful a feature in the history of Israel. He says :—

In later times we find the most important laws of the Mosaic constitution either unknown or at least unobserved, so that the conclusion may be drawn therefrom that either the Pentateuch was not there, or at least not yet in its present extent the book on religion that was regarded as generally obligatory, which it must have been if it had been esteemed as such from the time of Moses.

De Wette is the next rationalist that claims our attention. He was of opinion that the fragments had been so unskilfully patched together, as to make it impossible to discover which of them were originally connected. Antecedently speaking, it is of course conceivable that a connection did at one time exist between some of them, but it is quite useless now to attempt to restore order and sequence, as Eichhorn and Ilgen would fain have done, for who can any longer tell what has been omitted by the author of the present compilation? Moreover, in primitive compositions such as these, written by uncultured men, there are no characteristics of style, no sure marks to guide the literary critic in his investigations. Not even the constant diversity in the use of the Divine names will serve as a criterion, for instead of being a clue to the existence of two writers, it rather indicates different periods of history, or different schools of religious thought.[1] Lastly, even though they were all that the literary critics postulate, who can guarantee that either Elohim or Jehova was respectively written in all the places, and only in the places, where it now appears?

---

[1] The admitted fact that in several passages the preferential use of either name could be satisfactorily explained by the context, had induced Vater to oppose the Document Theory. See the great Catholic *savant*, Kaulen (Professor in Bonn). *Einleitung*, p. 200. The question of the divine names, a fundamental one, will find a more fitting place for discussion, in the account of the Supplement-hypothesis.

It is evident from these few samples, that De Wette's system differed considerably from those of his predecessors, even from that of Eichhorn and Paulus, though these two professors had great influence over him while he was at Jena. The fundamental reason of this disagreement is to be found in his disregard of literary criticism. The conclusion he arrived at was, that the Pentateuch is from beginning to end one mass of myths and sagas. Besides the mythological element which enters so largely into the composition of the Pentateuch, there is a great deal of folk-lore made up of worthless and contradictory legends. Statements that indubitably bear the mark of having been derived from true traditions, must be regarded as non-Mosaic, but at any rate they are so disfigured by myths that they no longer possess any historical value. The so-called 'laws of Moses' belong to a comparatively late period, and the proper name for them would be 'the myths of the jurists.' To sum up, the Pentateuch may be of some interest as a literary curiosity, but it is not a reliable source of information.

Now let us see how some of these blasphemies are endorsed by the *Oxford Hexateuch*, and others suppressed, presumably because England has not advanced so far as Germany on the downward path of Rationalism.

The main strength of his work lay on the historical side. Putting aside the literary questions which had been raised concerning Genesis, De Wette turned to the examination of the institutions implied or described in the Pentateuchal codes. How far were these institutions, he asked in effect, consistent with each other, and how far did the history of Israel show evidence of their existence? Like another young student sixty years later, Graf, he opened his inquiry with an investigation of the differences between the Books of Chronicles and Kings; which ended in the rejection of the former as evidence for the religious usages of Israel under the early monarchy. The real testimony was to be found in the unconscious witness supplied by the indications of Judges, Samuel, and Kings. When these proved that the requirements of the Pentateuch were continually ignored or violated by the responsible leaders of the nation, did not such neglect or violation constitute good grounds for believing that the requirements in question had not yet been definitely imposed?

For example, the cultus enjoined at the Dwelling[1] assumed that sacrifice could be offered only in one place. That was also the fundamental law of Deuteronomy xii. Yet the whole history after the age of Joshua was one continuous demonstration that this principle had in no way controlled the religious practice of the nation. The Book of Judges showed that Mizpah, Bethel, and Shilo were all of them accredited sanctuaries. Samuel and the first kings had not been at all confined to a single altar. Mizpah, Bethel, Zuph,[2] Gilgal, Bethlehem, Nob, Hebron, Gibeon, each witnessed again and again the sacred acts which the law permitted on one spot alone. Even after the erection of the temple this freedom was still maintained. The worship of the royal sanctuary was in fact a court function, and by no means superseded that of the ancient centres of hallowed tradition. So far indeed as the description of the Levitical Dwelling was concerned, Exodus xxv., it could not be reconciled with that of the Tent of Meeting in xxxiii. 7 ; and it was plainly modelled on the edifice in Jerusalem. But with it was inseparably connected the Aaronic priesthood and the entire corpus of the Levitical law. That was indeed the product of a long development ; the history of the removal of the ark in 2 Samuel vi. showed how free and even lawless (from the later point of view) were the proceedings of David. The Pentateuch, then, contained within itself indications of the successive development of legislation ; and a comparison with history was the only satisfactory basis for conjectures concerning the origins of its different codes. In laying down this principle De Wette flung out a number of brilliant suggestions which were then little more than clever and courageous guesses, but have since become widely accepted.

The fundamental error in this assertion has been sufficiently refuted in the I. E. RECORD[3] : it is quite consistent with De Wette's canon of exegesis, viz., that Moses was to be interpreted as Homer is. De Wette's explanation of the origin of Genesis was equally irreverent. Genesis and Exodus was the national epic of the theocracy. It was concerned with the national religion, and its ceremonial expression. Leviticus is a comparatively recent collection of laws, authority for which was sought by boldly asserting that they had been given to Moses on Mount Sinai. Numbers is nothing more than an artless continuation of

---

[1] Exod. xxv.-xxx., and Leviticus, *passim*.
[2] 1 Sam. ix. 12.
[3] December, 1901, p. 571:

the preceding three books. Deuteronomy is a body of laws enacted at a still later period. As, however, the myth about Mount Sinai was too well known to bear repetition, and the character of the Deuteronomic legislation was quite different from that contained in Leviticus, the jurists of the time invented another origin for it; they gave out that it was a second code of laws made by Moses just before his death. De Wette is especially honoured by the critics as the discoverer of the all-important fact that Deuteronomy was written in the reign of Josias. To quote the *Oxford Hexateuch* again :—

In a striking chapter he argued that the law of the unity of sanctuary in ch. xii. certainly referred to Jerusalem ; before the temple there was no trace of a general national centre of religious worship. The book, therefore, belonged to the monarchy, and this was confirmed by its express sanction of the royal power, xvii. 14.—De Wette, then, assigned the book without hesitation to the seventh century, and by this result the majority of critics still to-day abide.[1]

This was his view at one time, but according to

---

[1] The *Encyclopedia Biblica* (1901) speaks in the same strain. It sounds his praises thus :—De Wette's chief concern, however, was not with the literary but with the historical criticism of the Pentateuch, and in the latter he made an epoch.

In his *Dissertatio critica* of 1805, he placed the composition of Deuteronomy in the time of King Josiah (arguing from a comparison of 2 Kings xxii. with Deut. xii.), and pronounced it to be the most recent stratum of the Pentateuch, not, as had been previously supposed, the oldest.

In his *Kritischer Versuch über die Glaubwürdigkeit der Bücher der Chronik* (1805), he showed that the laws of Moses are unknown to the post-Mosaic history ; this he did by instituting a close comparison of Samuel and Kings with Chronicles, from which it appeared that the variations of the latter are to be explained not by the use of other sources, but solely by the desire of the Jewish scribes to shape the history in conformity with the law, and to give the law that place in history which, to their surprise, had not been conceded to it by the older historical books.

Finally, in his *Kritik der Mosaischen Geschichte* (1807), De Wette attacked the method then prevalent in Germany of eliminating all miracles and prophecies from the Bible by explaining them away, and then rationalizing what remained into a dry prosaic pragmatism. De Wette refuses to find any history in the Pentateuch ; all is legend and poetry. The Pentateuch is an authority not for the history of the time it deals with, but only for the time in which it was written ; it is, he says, the conditions of this much later time which the author idealizes and throws back into the past, whether in the form of narrative or of law.

De Wette's brilliant *debut*, which made his reputation for the rest of his life, exercised a powerful influence on his contemporaries. For several *decennia*, all who were at all open to critical ideas stood under his influence.

Holzinger, in the third edition of his *Einleitung* De Wette
was inclined to agree with Gesenius that the composition of
Deuteronomy and the final revision of the Pentateuch was
to be assigned to the time of the exile. De Wette was the
first to observe that there is a radical difference of style
between the preceding ;books and Deuteronomy, and this
peculiarity may have suggested the notion that it must
belong to a somewhat later date. In conclusion, we may
remark that, like many other critics, De Wette subsequently
gave up the Fragment-hypothesis, and accepted, as we shall
see, the Supplement-hypothesis. But he remained to the
end the strenuous advocate of real criticism, or of the attack
on Scripture based not on linguistic considerations, but on
alleged contradictions.

Before we leave this theory and pass on to a further
development of the Fragment-hypothesis, we must mention
that the first assault on the genuineness of the laws and the
history of the Paschal feast was made by De Wette. He
attempts to discredit the history by irreverent and impertinent remarks such as these :—

> The whole ceremony is in one place represented as a protection
> against the death of the first born ; in another it is said to be
> commemorative of their deliverance. The Israelites were com-
> manded (Exod. xii. 11) to eat the lamb in haste, in readiness for
> departure ; yet in v. 39 they are said to have been taken unawares
> and to have made no other preparations for their journey. Moses
> could not possibly have found time then to enact laws for the
> future observance of the Passover, indeed it would have been
> absurd to do so, for how could the people in the desert procure
> lambs sufficient for the feast ?

After flinging out a number of brilliant suggestions (to
use the language of the *Oxford Hexateuch*), De Wette
majestically proceeds, like Calpurnius, the oracular philosopher in *Fabiola*, to give *his* explanation of the origin of
the Pasch :

> It was at first, you perceive, only a family custom. In course
> of time, however, it came to be observed with elaborate ceremonial
> in the many sanctuaries which, as you are doubtless aware, were
> scattered all over the land. I refer to Mizpah, Gibeon, etc. The
> fictitious command to keep it ' in one place which the Lord shall

choose' was given for the first time in Deuteronomy, a book which, I may be permitted to observe, I have discovered to be a literary forgery of the time of King Josiah.

This is pre-eminently one of De Wette's 'clever and courageous guesses which have since become widely accepted.' It has, of course, been developed to a very high degree by Wellhausen in his theory of the festal legislation contained in the D and P Codes. One cannot, however, but regret that the writers of the *Oxford Hexateuch* believe in De Wette and Wellhausen. There is a great deal of truth in what Sayce, the Oxford Professor of Assyriology, says :—

The ' critics' who reject the authority of tradition and of the Church, display nevertheless a most remarkable respect for authority of another kind. Ancient tradition, the teaching of the Christian Church and its Founder, the facts which the Oriental archælogist ventures to put forward, all count for nothing, but to the authority of a few scholars of the nineteenth century, mostly of the German race, we are bidden unreservedly to submit ourselves. Graf and Wellhausen, or Ewald and Dillmann, are the gods of the new Israel. So far as I can gather from the articles I have been reading, the mere statement that a particular view of the Old Testament writings and history has been promulgated by one learned professor and accepted by another, is considered sufficient to settle the matter. I confess that if we are to have a Pope, I should prefer the successor of St. Peter to a bevy of German professors.[1]

Berthold is the next prominent figure among the supporters of the Fragment-hypothesis. Although he maintained that the Pentateuch itself is nothing more than a *répertoire* of pieces which were put together long after the death of Moses, nevertheless he admitted that in Exodus some fragments were written either by the Hebrew legislator himself or by one of his contemporaries, while in Genesis fragments were preserved that dated from an even earlier age. The Erlangen professor's fondness for purely imaginary arrangements of chronology and for explanations of facts appears perhaps still more prominently in his attempt to determine the period in which the Pentateuch received its present form. Before he begins, however, to construct his hypothesis, he mentions some well known facts which it

---

[1] *Contemporary Review.*, November, 1896 : 'Biblical Critics on the Warpath,' page 720.

may be said, *en passant*, have no connection whatever with
his subjective edifice. He observes that Moses laid the book of
the law by the side of the ark as a witness to the covenant
(Deut. xxxi. 26), that Joshua added to it a record of the
renewal of the covenant at Shechem (xxiv. 26), and that
Samuel wrote the law of the kingdom 'and laid it up before
the Lord' (1 Sam. x. 25).[1] Berthold accepts these statements
simply because it suits his theory; if they created any
difficulty, they would summarily be condemned as fictions.
It would be in vain to ask him to prove that either Josue's
or Samuel's compositions were ever regarded as part of the
Pentateuch or attributed to Moses. But the man who got
a chair of theology for his essay written to show that the
Book of Daniel was the work of several authors, was not to
be restrained by considerations such as these.[2] Instead of
attempting to make good his supposition, Berthold goes on
to assert that this practice of adding to the law was quite
unknown in the time of the kings, when, however, legislation still continued to be made. Now, here again we may

---

[1] The law (*mishpat*) of the kingdom seems to be identical with the law of
the king (*mishpat hammelech*), eight verses long, viii. 11-18.   It is true that
Hummelauer in his *Commentary on Deuteronomy*, p. 296, gives very ingenious
reasons in order to induce his readers to accept his own opinion that *mishpat*
in v. 11 means only the practice of the king: (it has this meaning of ' practice '
in Judges xiii. 12, and 2 Kings i. 7 : see Gesenius *Thesaurus*, p. 1465), and
that in x. 25, *mishmat* means the provisional enactment made for the kingdom,
which enactment Hummelauer holds to be none other than Deut. xii. 1 xxvi. 15,
a passage which according to him Samuel inserted into the law. Hence a
large part of his *Commentary*, pp. 279-426, treats of what he calls the
' Collectaneum Samuelis,' and he gives for the most part, in agreement with
Driver, elaborate tables of ' Leges et Novellae.' Driver, however, thinks that
the relation of the Deuteronomic to the JE, P, and H Codes, shows with
certainty that Deuteronomy is a work of the seventh century. Whatever may
be thought of Hummelauer's theory, it is necessary to bear in mind that it
differs in this respect from Driver's, and that it is maintained by arguments
very different from those of Berthold. It is almost needless to remark that it
is diametrically opposed to the theory which Cornill and Wellhausen have
made so popular among the critics—viz., that ch. xii.-xxvi. are the original
Deuteronomy, or the real nucleus of the composite book which goes by that
name.

[2] Berthold maintained that the book consisted of nine fragments, written
by as many authors. This was considered a great advance on Eichhorn, who
was unable to discover more than five. Both critics started from the study of
the ' contradictions' in the book. The ' unity of authorship' has been denied
since their time by Reuss and Lagarde, but on the whole 'the critics' are
favourable to it. What they deny at present is the traditional authorship and
date. See a popular description of the state of the question in Anderson's
interesting work *Daniel in the Critics' Den.*

remark that there is not the slightest warrant for saying positively that during the royal period no prophet did what Josue and Samuel had previously done. For all we know, Elias may have been inspired to make an addition, distinct from the law. All that can be safely affirmed is that Scripture does not record any further instance, but its silence cannot justly be considered as coincident with Berthold's confident *dictum*, much less be regarded as an antecedent approval of his theory. Like other critics, he was sorely in need of a course of logic. The second part of his adventurous statement is still more faulty. Not only is there nothing in Scripture that could be construed into a tacit *nil obstat* of the statement that Pentateuchal legislation was made in the kingly period, but on the contrary the whole authority of Scripture is against it. If anything is made plain in the sacred books, not only in those of Kings, but in all from Josue to Machabees (or to Malachias, when discussing the matter with a critic), it is that the law was given by Moses, once for all.

According to Berthold, as long as the practice of adding enactments continued, the Pentateuch, such as we now have it, could not exist. This is obvious, but Berthold's inference is not obvious. He concludes that the Pentateuchal collection is not older than the period of the kings ; while, on the other hand, since it is received by the Samaritans, it cannot have been made at a date posterior to that of the schism of the ten tribes. The latter statement may pass. Therefore, says Berthold, the Pentateuch was compiled some time between the beginning of Saul's reign and the end of Solomon's. He is inclined to think that the work of putting the numerous fragments together was done about the commencement of Saul's reign, partly by the prophet Samuel and partly under his direction. And he would see a promise to undertake the task in the prophet's words to the people, ' I will teach you the good and right way.' Here we have an example of how little satisfies a higher critic who is looking out for a support for his fanciful theory. It is also deserving of attention that Berthold refers to Samuel as to an authority, when it suits him. Nevertheless the meaning he puts on the aged prophet's words is not admissible. The good and right way of which Samuel, the first great reformer, speaks, is the law of Moses. He had been reared in the service of the tabernacle established by Moses, and now, at the end of his days, it is to the provisions of the Mosaic law he refers in his speech of self-defence.[1] Moreover, the incident narrated in 1 Kings (1 Samuel) xv. shows that he regarded Exodus xvii. 14 and Deuteronomy xxv. 17-19, as obligatory. But without dwelling on such incidents, the whole tenor of Samuel's mission makes it evident that all his energies were directed to promote the observance of a law which he looked upon as ancient and as well known to the people.

But Berthold has not done with the Pentateuch yet. His study of the intrinsic character of Genesis i.-iv. lead him to regard it as of post-Mosaic origin : v.-xxxiii. he held to have been put together by Moses or by one of his contemporaries : xxxiv.-xlviii., xl, to be post-Mosaic, as is evident from the language, and from the allusions which they contain : while xlix. was inserted by the compiler of Genesis.

As regards the four other books, they were from the beginning four distinct collections, but it does not follow that they owe their existence to one person. Rather it would appear that the fragments which now constitute Exodus and Numbers—with the exception of Numbers i.-vi.—were gathered by one man, and that another put together the fragments that we call Leviticus. For if one individual had made the entire collection, he would certainly have incorporated Numbers i.-vi. into Leviticus, as an appendix. Lastly, Deuteronomy, which is so distinct in character from the preceding books, must be the work of another collector. In opposition to De Wette's view that Deuteronomy was written at a late period, and that it had no connection with the other books, Berthold held that unity of plan was visible throughout the Pentateuch, even though Deuteronomy contained for the most part only post-Mosaic, or revised and

---

[1] *Cf.* xii. 3 with Exod. xxiii. 4, 5 and Deut. xxii. 1.

enlarged Mosaic laws and speeches. To sum up: there were four or five collectors—three respectively, of Exodus-Numbers, of Leviticus, and of Deuteronomy, of whom two at least belonged to the school of prophets [1] that existed under Samuel's presidency.[2] Besides these Moses put together what is now Genesis v.-xxxiii.; so there were four collectors, and if the collector of the other part of Genesis be distinct

---

[1] The phrase, 'school of the prophets,' is a favourite expression of the earlier critics. They use it for their own purpose, e.g., to imply that prophecy was not supernatural, that—whatever it was—it could be taught, that the prophets who inculcated the spirit of the law were opposed to the priests whose interests lay in the material worship of the temple, etc. The expression itself is a harmless one, but it must be borne in mind that there is no Scriptural authority for it. The word 'school' does not occur even once in the Old Testament. Kennedy says with truth (Hastings' *Bibl. Dict.*, s. v. Education): 'A single word must suffice for the *schools of the prophets* (an expression with no Scriptural authority) of which so much was made by the scholars of former days. All that the Scripture warrants us in holding is that in a few centres, such as Bethel, Jericho, and Gilgal, men of prophetic spirit formed associations or brotherhoods, for the purpose of stimulating their devotion to Jehovah, through the common life of these schools. Edification, not education, was the main purpose of these so-called schools.'

In the first place where mention is made of a company of prophets such as is contemplated (1 Kings x. 5, 10; *Hebrew*, 'hebel'; *Sept.*, χορος; *Vulg.*, 'grex,' 'cuneus') it is quite evident that they formed a choir. Indeed, though the verb 'naba' (from which 'nabi,' prophet, is derived) usually means to foretell, to speak through inspiration, in 1 Par. xxv. 1-3 it signifies to chant the divine praises with a musical accompaniment (perhaps through inspiration), and it is possible that it has this connotation in what is related of Saul, who was filled with extraordinary devotion and fervour. Mangenot remarks:—'Nous pouvons en conclure légitimement que ces prophetes prophétisaient, non pas en prédisant l'avenir, mais en parlant et en chantant sous une impulsion surnaturelle et avec accompagnement musical.' The prophets spoken of here could be called a 'schola,' in the sense only of a 'schola cantorum.' In the second place where they are spoken of (in 1 Kings xix. 20), they are collectively designated as 'lahaqah,' εκκλησια, cuneus (here they are under the presidency of Samuel).

When they reappear in the third and fourth books of Kings, they are called the 'sons of the prophets'=prophets, or belonging to the prophetical order. To quote Mangenot again:—'Quant aux manifestations extraordinaires, qui se produisaient au milieu des chants et des louanges divines, et sur la nature desquelles nous sommes peu renseignés, elles n'avaient rien de commun avec la manie des devins antiques ni avec la névrose; c'etaient de charismes, analogues à ceux dont l'Esprit Saint favorisa les premiers Chrétiens.'—'Ils se proposaient un but pratique, celui de former de véritables adorateurs de Dieu, des observateurs fidèles de la loi mosaïque, qui par leurs exemples agiraient, sur la foule, arrêteraient les progrès de l'idolâtrie et ramenèraient leurs frères au culte de vrai Dieu.' (Vigouroux *Dict. de la Bible*, s. v. Ecoles de prophètes). Kaulen takes the same view. He says in the *Kirchenlexicon*:—'Da aber der Regel nach bestimmte natürliche Fähigkeiten voraussetzte, so sammelten die Propheten seit Samuel auch Schüler um sich und bereiteten diese auf die mögliche Berufung zum Prophetenamt vor. So entstanden Prophetenschulen, in welchen ein heiligmässiges, abgetödtetes Leben geführt, die Kenntniss des Gesetzes vertieft und die heilige Tonkunst geübt wurde.'

[2] 1 Kings xix. 24.

C

from the collector of Exodus-Numbers (which Berthold leaves an open question) there is a possible fifth.

Our readers will have noticed the gradual advance in error made by these four critics—Geddes, Vater, De Wette, Berthold. The denial of the Mosaic authorship of the Pentateuch has by this time become a necessary condition of scholarship. An indispensable qualification for critical fame consists in attributing Deuteronomy to a compiler that lived at a comparatively late period of Jewish history. But even Berthold was, as might have been anticipated, soon surpassed by other adherents of the Fragment-hypothesis, whose erroneous views will form the subject of a succeeding article.

[To be continued.]   REGINALD WALSH, O.P.

DR. SALMON'S 'INFALLIBILITY'

DR. SALMON is a theologian of unlimited resources, and this is shown conspicuously by his triumphant vindication of his rule of faith. It has been already shown, and on the clearest evidence, that the rule begets contradictory creeds almost without number; but, in this somewhat discouraging fact, the Doctor actually finds a proof of its divine origin.

The fact is [he says], what the existence of variations of belief among Christians really proves is, that our Master, Christ, has not done what Roman Catholic theory requires He should have done, namely, provided His people with means of such full and certain information on all points on which controversy can be raised, that there shall be no room for difference of opinion among them. But it is ridiculous to build on these variations an argument for the superiority of one sect over another.—(Page 87.)

The Doctor is quite correct in this last remark. ' It is ridiculous' to infer from these variations that one sect is better than another, for all are equally bad, all alike are blind leaders of the blind, and tend to the same abyss. The Church of God alone is the ark of salvation. She alone is proof against the gates of hell,—unchanged and unchangeable as a teacher and guardian of divine truth.

So anxious was our Blessed Lord Himself for unity of faith amongst men, that He prayed to His Eternal Father that His disciples should be one, even as He and the Father are one; and He established His Church and endowed it with supernatural attributes to generate and preserve that unity. ' He gave some apostles, and some prophets, and others some evangelists, and others pastors and doctors, for the perfecting of the saints, and for the edifying of the body of Christ, until we all meet in the unity of faith and of the knowledge of the Son of God . . . that henceforth we be no more children tossed to-and-fro, and carried about with every wind of doctrine.'[1] His Apostles exhorted their followers to

---

[1] Ephes. iv. 11-14.

'preserve the unity of Spirit in the bond of peace.' They
preached 'One Lord, one faith, one baptism, and specially
warned their followers against schisms. But Dr. Salmon
is a man of accomplished facts. In his theology 'whatever is,
is right' (except, of course, the Catholic Church, which must
be wrong in every hypothesis). He sees around him creeds,
whose name is legion, diametrically opposed on the most
vital doctrines of Christianity, and in this very fact he finds
a vindication of the rule which has generated, and which
explains them all. Our Lord and His Apostles, no doubt,
insist on unity of faith, and in the clearest possible language,
but Dr. Salmon holds that they did not mean it, as is clearly
shown by the almost numberless variations of existing sects.

This is a most convenient system of theology. It cannot
be assailed, and so it need not be defended. Its variability
enables it to assume different forms when seriously attacked,
and thus it evades the grasp of logic as well as of common
sense. It is a series of dissolving views. And as Dr. Salmon
enjoys such unrestricted freedom of belief or disbelief, it is
natural that he should sympathise with us, as victims of
'Roman bondage,' who are forced to surrender our liberty,
our 'most deep-rooted beliefs . . . solely in deference to
external authority . . . . though unable to see any flaw in
the arguments' for these beliefs (page 24). According to
Dr. Salmon, we make an irrational surrender of our liberty,
and in his great charity he is moved to pity us. But charity
is said to begin at home; and now, what about the Doctor's
own liberty? He does not tell us what articles of the
Christian faith he believes; but he tells us that they are
contained in the Bible, and that he has satisfied himself
that they are so contained. He must then have discovered,
for certain, the meaning of those texts of Scripture in which
his articles of faith are revealed. And if he have discovered
for certain, the meaning of certain Scripture texts, he is no
more free to reject that meaning than Catholics are to reject
the teaching of the Church; he is as much bound to that
meaning as we are to doctrines defined by the Church.
There can be no liberty to reject the known truth. And
what, then, becomes of his boasted liberty? He is free only

when he is ignorant. If he know the meaning of the text
he is not free to reject it. If he have definite knowledge
derived from Scripture he surrenders his liberty quite as
much as a Catholic. But he surrenders to a human authority
—to himself; whereas a Catholic surrenders his liberty in
deference to an authority that is divine. Dr. Salmon, then, can
claim the liberty of which he boasts only by the awkward
admission, that he does not know for certain the meaning
of a single text in his Bible. Such is the liberty which
Dr. Salmon and his theologians enjoy ; and such being the
case the Bible is to them a very useful rule of faith. It enab''
the Doctor, and men like him, to profess belief in the Christ   1
faith in general, without binding themselves to any particulat
dogma. With his theologians it serves its purpose as a war
cry against us ;—they could not, and their professor did not,
analyse it. And the result of this liberty is apparent in every
statement of so-called Protestant doctrine. They are vague,
meaningless platitudes—the natural, the necessary result
of the rule from which they come. Mr. Capes, whom
Dr. Salmon quotes as a friendly witness (page 62), says of
his Church :—

> To speak of the Church of England, therefore, as constituting
> a realization of the apostolical ideal of Christian communion is,
> in my opinion, entirely to misconceive its real character. In reality,
> the Establishment is a vast anomaly, both in its origin as a creation
> of the law, and in the totally contradictory doctrines which it
> allows to be taught within its pale.

And after describing the internal confusion of the
Establishment, Mr. Capes adds :—

> In the midst of this confusion it is not to be doubted that the
> Church of England, which is the very embodiment of the idea of
> Christian dissensions, has proved itself a working institution on an
> immense scale.

And so enamoured is Mr. Capes of this theological
bedlam that, like Dr. Salmon, he sees in its dissensions ' a
startling proof that, for the present, at any rate, the
apparent anomaly has a foundation in real unity.' [1] This
is the fruit of Dr. Salmon's rule of faith, in the words of his

---

[1] Capes' *Reasons*, pp. 187-190.

own chosen witness. Those who follow such spiritual guides
do not show much private judgment or discretion.

Now, as Dr. Salmon's rule enables him to put on the
Bible any sense at all he pleases, it is only natural that he
should make the following statement :—

There is no difficulty in an individual using Scripture as his
rule of faith, for he can learn, without much difficulty, what the
statements of the Bible on any subject are; and on most subjects
these statments are easy to be understood.—(Pages 130, 131.)

But as this statement is made in the face of facts, and
in direct contradiction to the testimony of St. Peter,
Dr. Salmon els ewhere qualifies it thus :—

But we say that the revelation God has given us is, in essential
matters, easy to be understood. Roman Catholics dwell much on
the difficulty of understanding the Scriptures, and quote St. Peter's
saying that the Scriptures contain many things difficult and ' hard
to be understood, which they that are unlearned and unstable
wrest to their own destruction.' But we say that the obscurities
of Scripture do not hide those vital points, the knowledge of which
is necessary to salvation.—(Page 90.)

It must be satisfactory to his students to see how easily
Dr. Salmon disposes of St. Peter. The saint said Scripture
is, in some parts, so difficult that 'the unlearned and unstable
wrest it to their own destruction.' But whatever may be
the conviction of St. Peter, Dr. Salmon says that 'the
obscurities of Scripture do not hide those vital points, the
knowledge of which is necessary to salvation.' Now it is
only a mistake as to ' those vital points ' that could lead to
spiritual ruin ; and since St. Peter says that some persons
did interpret Scripture to their own ruin, these persons,
then, must have mistaken those very ' vital points,' which,
according to Dr. Salmon, are so clear that no one can mistake them at all. ' Vital points ' may be mistaken, for they
have been mistaken, says St. Peter. No, replies Dr. Salmon,
' vital points ' cannot be mistaken, so clearly are they
contained in Scripture. Of course, the Trinity theologians
accept the statement of Dr. Salmon. It would be against
all the traditions of their Church and College to take the
teaching of a Pope in preference to that of a Protestant
professor.

Dr. Salmon frequently refers to those vital points, ' the knowledge of which we count necessary to salvation' (page 74). And with regard to them he says, again and again, that Scripture is sufficiently clear. This is the common Protestant theory of Fundamentals; and, like other Protestant teachers, Dr. Salmon is very careful not to tell us what these ' vital points,' these fundamental doctrines are. To bind himself down to any definite statement would be to surrender the liberty which his rule secures to him. But when he speaks of ' essential matters,' 'vital points,' h₁ clearly must mean that there are some doctrines which m ι be believed, though he does not state their number or defiu them. And here again, his rule of faith comes to relieve him of any undue dogmatic burthens, and acts as a safeguard to his liberty. For, whatever the ' vital points ' be, they must be contained in Scripture, and provable from it by the 'individual Christian.' Thus the 'individual Christian' is to judge for himself what the ' vital points ' for himself are ; and the inevitable result is, almost as many lists of ' fundamental articles ' as there are individuals. Now, Dr. Salmon professes, at least, to rest his faith on Scripture alone, and where can he find a trace of authority in Scripture for dividing revealed doctrines into articles which must be believed, and articles which may be disbelieved ? When he speaks of ' essential matters,' 'vital points,' he distinctly implies that there are matters that are not essential, points that are not vital. And where is his Scripture authority for this distinction ? He has none. The question here is not at all as to that minimum of explicit faith which, in all circumstances, and for all persons, is absolutely necessary as a means of salvation ; that has already been discussed.[1] Dr. Salmon is here discussing the rule of faith—the rule whereby men are to interpret God's revelation, and to find out what they are, not in extraordinary and exceptional circumstances, but in general and in ordinary circumstances, to believe. And Dr. Salmon, applying his rule, declares that amongst revealed doctrines,

---

[1] I. E. RECORD, July, 1901.

some are 'vital,' 'essential,' and must be believed; others
are not vital, nor essential, and may, therefore, be disbelieved. This is Dr. Salmon's theory. But our Lord's
own theory, unmistakably laid down by Himself, is very
different : ' He that believeth, and is baptised, shall be saved,
but he that believeth not shall be condemned.'¹ 'Going
therefore, teach all nations : . . to observe all things whatsoever I have commanded you.'² Here our Lord distinctly,
and without exception, states that he that believeth not
shall be condemned, and that we are to believe all that He
has commanded. He makes no distinction between truths
of faith, as vital and non-vital. He gives no liberty to reject
anything that He has revealed. And whoever rejects any
such truth shall, He says, be condemned. This is our
Lord's teaching. But the Regius Professor thinks this
' a hard saying ; ' and he tells his students that their
obligation of belief is limited to ' vital points,' which,
for their further comfort, they are at liberty to determine for themselves. Our Lord's words clearly leave
no room for the distinction ; but Dr. Salmon is a
' prayerful man,' and he knows that our Lord did not really
mean what He so distinctly and emphatically said. Revelation is all God's Word, and we believe it on His authority.
That authority is just as good for believing any one revealed
truth as any other. Everything that God has revealed is
an object of faith, to be believed, at least, implicitly. All of
it that is sufficiently proposed to us, we must believe explicitly. To reject any portion of it would be to refuse to
believe Him, to make Him a liar, to make a shipwreck of
the faith.

Thus Dr. Salmon's theory of ' vital ' and non-vital
articles is an outrage on reason, as well as a palpable
contradiction of our Lord's own express declaration. If ' the
revelation which God has given us is, in essential matters,
easy to be understood,' how is it that for three hundred
years Protestants have not been able even once to agree as
to what these ' essential matters ' are ? The Trinity, the

¹ Mark xvi. 16.   ² Matt. xxviii. 19, 20.

Incarnation, Baptismal Regeneration, the Sacramental System, the Inspiration of Scripture—these, surely, ought to be regarded as ' vital points ' of Christian faith ; ar ⟨ vet they are, one and all, held and denied by memb ⟨⟨ of Dr. Salmon's Church, who, all alike, appeal, to the Bible as a rule of faith, and all justify their denials by appealing to Dr. Salmon's distinction of essential and non-essential articles. Mr. Palmer, in his *Treatise on the Church*,' gives a number of theories of fundamentals held by Protestant theologians. He shows the state of hopeless confusion to which the discussion leads them, and he gives his own opinion in language that is very far from complimentary to those who hold the opinions expressed by Dr. Salmon. He says :—

Whatever foundation there may be for the notion that some doctrines are more important in themselves than others, it cannot be supposed that any doctrine certainly revealed by Christ is unimportant to us, or that it may be safely disbelieved, or that we may recognise as Christians those who obstinately disbelieve such a doctrine.'

St. Paul said to the Corinthians : 'I beseech you, brethren, by the name of our Lord Jesus Christ, that you all speak the same thing, and that there be no schisms among you, but that you be perfect in the same mind and in the same judgment.' The Apostle would have appealed in vain to men like Dr. Salmon. The result of the Doctor's teaching, the fruit of the rule which he maintains, is that men do not and shall not speak the same thing ; that there are schisms without number, and every day increasing in number ; that scarcely any two persons give the same judgment, even on the most vital Christian dogmas ; and that Dr. Salmon's Church is (to use the very candid description of his friend Mr. Capes) ' the very embodiment of the idea of Christian dissensions,' and ' that almost every existing school of Christian (?) theology can find a home within its boundaries.' The Gospel according to Dr. Salmon is not the Gospel according to Mr. Palmer, and the Gospel according to

---

¹ Vol. i., pp. 102-106.   ³ 1 Cor. i. 10.
³ Page 106.   ⁴ Pages 185-7.

Dean Farrar has little affinity with either, though all spring from the same prolific source of error—the Bible, and the Bible only, as a rule of faith. And in the Doctor's theology the rule reaches the climax of impious absurdity. For in his system the 'individual Christian is the supreme judge of "vital points,"' and, is, therefore, at liberty to say that any doctrine, no matter how clearly revealed, is still not 'a vital point,'—is not one of those 'the knowledge of which *we* count necessary to salvation,' (page 74), and may, therefore, be rejected as unnecessary. And thus the 'individual Christian' may, on Dr. Salmon's theory, reject every single article of the Christian creed, and the Broad Church section has actually done so. The rule which begets such religious chaos, such soul-destroying error, stands condemned.

Dr. Salmon's idea of the Catholic rule of faith reminds one forcibly of Mr. Pott's work on Chinese metaphysics. A criticism of this profoundly learned work appeared in the *Eatanswill Gazette*, and strangely enough had escaped the notice of Mr. Bob Sawyer, and even of Mr. Pickwick himself. When the last-named gentleman was questioned by Mr. Pott as to his opinion of the criticism, he said in his embarrassment : ' An abstruse subject, I should conceive.' ' Very, sir,' responded Pott, looking intensely sage. 'He crammed for it, to use a technical but expressive term ; he read up for the subject at my desire in the *Encyclopædia Britannica*.' ' Indeed ! ' said Mr. Pickwick. ' I was not aware that that valuable work contained any information on Chinese Metaphysics.' ' He read, sir,' rejoined Mr. Pott, laying his hand on Mr. Pickwick's knee, and looking round, with a smile of intellectual superiority, ' he read for metaphysics under the letter M, and for China under the letter C, and combined his information, sir ! ' Dr. Salmon must have done something of the same sort. He must have studied for Faith under the letter F, and for Rule under the letter R, and combined his information. ' And looking round with a smile of intellectual superiority,' not even second to Mr. Pott, he imparted his combined information to his admiring students who must have been more than ever convinced of ' the baselessness of the Roman claims.' He informed them

that no ' other proof is necessary, of the modernness of the
Roman rule of faith than the very complicated form it
assumes' (page 129). Now Chinese metaphysics are older
than the Catholic rule of faith, and certainly more complicated ; and hence a thing may be complicated and old at the
same time. The Doctor's logic then is not good. But here
is his 'explanation,' which is worthy of Mr. Pott when at
the zenith of his fame :—

But the true explanation why Roman Catholic controversialists
state their rule of faith in this complicated form is, that Christians
began by taking Scripture as their guide, and then when practices
were found current which could not be defended out of the Bible,
tradition was invoked to supplement the deficiencies of Scripture.
Last of all, when no proof could be made out either from Scripture
or antiquity for Roman Catholic doctrines and practices, the
authority of the Church was introduced to silence all opposition.
—-(Page 130).

This is combined information of the genuine Mr. Pott type.
Now, Dr. Salmon was not an eye-witness of the interesting
changes he has here recorded. Where, then, did he get his
information ? It must have come from some source as
reliable as Taylor's *Dissuasive* ; unless, indeed, it be a
private revelation to the Doctor himself. ' Christians
began,' he says, ' by taking Scripture as their guide.' No ;
they had not the Scripture to take as a guide when they
began. They began by taking the teaching of a divinely-
commissioned body—the *Ecclesia Docens*—as their guide ;
they had no other. ' And when practices were found
current which could not be defended out of the
Bible, tradition was invoked.' No ; tradition came before
Scripture, not after it ; and Dr. Salmon does not say what
the indefensible practices were. ' Last of all . . . . the
authority of the Church was introduced to silence all
objections.' No ; *first of all*, the authority of the Church
was introduced, when our Lord said to His Apostles, ' going
therefore teach all nations.' Not a line of the New Testament was written for many years after the giving of this
commission, which established Church authority, and is its
charter. This, then, is not a ' modern foundation,' as the

Doctor describes it; it is as old as Christianity. The
version then of our rule of faith, supplied by Dr. Salmon,
is a specimen of 'combined information,' quite on a par
in the Chinese metaphysics of Mr. Pott's critic, and the
young men who took in his Pickwickian theology are likely
to become enlightened guides of the rising generation of
Protestants.

He informed them, furthermore, that the Catholic
Church was so intolerant, so domineering, that she 'expects
to be believed on her bare word ; she does not condescend to
offer proofs' (page 128). Now, it is an average specimen of
the Doctor's consistency, that just seven lines lower down
than the above he admits, she does condescend to 'offer
proofs.' 'And if that Church condescends to offer proof of
her doctrine [which is an admission that she does], she
claims to be the sole judge whether what she offers are
proofs or not.' This is a serious, a grave charge against the
Catholic Church. 'She expects to be believed on her bare
word.' Yes, and the Doctor might have made his case
stronger; for, she not only 'expects,' but she insists on
'being believed on her bare word.' She holds her commission from God Himself; she will not, therefore, allow
Dr. Salmon, or his 'individual Christian,' to sit in judgment
on her. Had she done so, she would be in the same position
as the Doctor's town-clock Church ;—false to her commission, unreliable as a guide, and unworthy of obedience.
The Doctor's damaging attack on the Church is, then, merely
an argument of her divine origin. He is a profound logician,
this Regius Professor ; or, can it be, that he is a Jesuit in
disguise, who is knowingly putting forward arguments
against the Catholic Church, that can have but one result,
to bring ridicule on the cause he professes to advocate. On
such teaching his controversialists have a brilliant future
before them.

The Doctor has another grave charge against us, to
which we are prepared to plead guilty. 'What I want to
point out,' he says, 'is, that in the Roman Catholic controversy, this question about the rule of faith is altogether
subordinate to the question as to the judge of controversies,

or in other words, the question as to the infallibility of the Church' (page 127). And he repeats this at page 129. Now, if he had read, with any care, any of our dogmatic theologians on the subject of his lectures, he would find them speaking of a *remote* and of a *proximate* rule of faith. The *remote* rule is the Word of God, contained in Scripture and tradition ; it is thus a name for the source whence the Church takes her teaching. The *proximate* rule is the living voice of the teaching Church, which explains God's Word to us. The Word of God is in the keeping of the *Ecclesia Docens*, and is therefore subordinate to it. God has made it so, for he has made the teaching Church its guardian and interpreter. Dr. Salmon could have easily learned this from our theologians, and he should have learned it somewhere, before he set about confusing his students as to our teaching. But he does not seem to have sufficiently considered even his own position ; for he, too, holds that there is a judge of controversies to which his rule of faith (the Bible) is subordinate. The 'individual Christian' is, according to the Doctor, to decide whether the Church's teaching is in accordance with Scripture. The Doctor himself, therefore, is a judge of controversies, but *only for himself ;* and so, in his system, is each individual Christian to the same extent. And, such being the case, what becomes of the Doctor's position as Regius Professor ? Why is he dictating to his controversialists if each is a divinely consti-tuted judge of the contents of the Bible ? The main differ-ence between the Doctor and us, in this matter, is that he has a judge of controversy—himself, admittedly, notoriously fallible—a judge which cannot decide ; and we have a judge of controversy—the teaching Church—to which God has expressly promised Infallibility, whose decrees, therefore, must be final, because they must be true. It is not at all, as Dr. Salmon told his theologians, a question of the Bible against the Church, for the Church adopts the Bible ; it is her Bible ; it is a question of the individual against the Church. The Catholic judge of controversies has a commission from God ; the Protestant judge has no commission. It is a wearying task to follow Dr. Salmon through his illogical blunderings,

and it is anything but a favourable index of the educational
standard at Trinity, that its leading light should be so hopelessly bad a logician, that in his own special, chosen department, he should be unable to rise above the level of a street
preacher, and that its most advanced students should take
in their Professor's crude lucubrations, with as much awe
'and reverence as Mr. Pickwick displayed when swallowing
the Chinese metaphysics of Mr. Pott.

The Catholic rule of faith is not the caricature which
Dr. Salmon sets before his students. It has God for its
author. His wisdom designed it, and His power maintains
it. It is, therefore, adapted to its purposes and adequate to
the attainment of its end. In order to have divine faith we
must have God's Word, and we must know its meaning;
that is, we must have a witness to the fact of revelation,
and an interpreter of its true sense. And since faith is an
absolutely necessary means for salvation, the witness and
interpreter must be always present, living, testifying, teaching. For, if in any age since its institution, the witness or
interpreter had been wanting, then, in that age faith would
have been impossible, and salvation impossible also. And,
moreover, this witness and interpreter must be infallible.
If the witness were fallible, it might testify that God had
spoken when He had not spoken; and if the interpreter
were fallible, it might assign a meaning to God's Word which
is not His meaning. In either case we may be deceived,
and may not be believing God's words, but man's speculations. And if we may be deceived, our assent would be, at
best, doubtful, hesitating; and a doubtful, hesitating assent
is not faith, it is only opinion. To have divine faith, therefore, we must have a witness and interpreter that will
exclude doubt, that cannot err; that is, the witness and
interpreter must be infallible; and that infallible witness
and interpreter God has mercifully given us in the *Ecclesia
Docens*—the teaching Church, whose living, never-failing,
never-changing voice is the Catholic rule of faith. The authority of the teaching Church has been already stated and
proved in the I. E. RECORD for May, 1901,[1] and it is

---

[1] Pages 418-424.

unnecessary to make more than a brief reference to it
here :—

> This body [the *Ecclesia Docens*] is the infallible guardian,
> interpreter and teacher of the entire deposit of faith, and of all
> that appertains to faith and morals, and the infallible judge of
> every controversy in which faith or morals are involved. . . .
> As custodian of the faith, the Church preserves her precious
> charge from all admixture of error. . . . It is the shepherd's
> duty not merely to feed his flock, but to ward off the wolf from
> the fold.

This, as explained there, is the clear meaning of our
Lord's commission to His Apostles, and of His promise to
be with them in their teaching till the end of time. And
ever since, that teaching the Church has faithfully fulfilled
her mission as teacher and guardian of revealed truth.
'Their sound hath gone out to every land, and their voice
to the ends of the earth.' Animated and enlightened by
God's Holy Spirit, sustained by His promise, she has continued to teach in every age, and without interruption. She
has been found equal to every emergency that has arisen
during her extraordinary career. When tyrants sought to
drown her voice in the blood of her children, these children
bore noble testimony to her teaching. Her apologists put
pagan philosophy to shame, by contrasting it with her
heavenly doctrines : and heresies as they arose were condemned, and cast out when judged by the same rule of
truth. This has been her history, her working for the
nineteen centuries of her existence ; and it will be her
history for all the centuries, few or many, that are to come.

The Catholic Church is not a mere aggregate of
individuals, but a personality, living on through these
centuries, supernaturally endowed, and infallibly directed.
Her memory goes back to the days of her divine Founder's
earthly sojourn. At no time have her faculties been
impaired, or her divine protection diminished : she has been
always conscious of her supernatural guidance, and she
knows the meaning, and the extent of her commission. She
is, therefore, a competent reliable witness to the fact of
revelation, and a competent reliable interpreter of the sense

which the revelation bore. If, therefore, a doubt arises as to
any truth of faith, she can remove the doubt, and restate
the truth correctly; for, she heard it from the Founder's
lips, or the Holy Ghost communicated its meaning to her.
She is thus at all times able to teach the truths of faith with
the same authority as she first promulgated them; and any
truth once promulgated by her remains a part of her teaching
for ever. She is able also to state the fuller meaning of
those truths, and to show the relation in which they stand
to natural knowledge, or to any errors that time may bring.
All this follows necessarily from the divine commission to
the Church, and from the divine promise accompanying
that commission. The proof of this has been already
briefly considered,[1] and Dr. Salmon will find it fully stated
and vindicated in most of our dogmatic treatises.

This rule of faith, the living voice of the teaching
Church designed by God, and alone worthy of His wisdom.
is adequate to its end, and available to all. ' God wishes all
men to be saved and to come to a knowledge of the truth.'[2]
And since this wish is sincere, and efficacious, there must be
means divinely given and certainly sufficient to attain the
end desired. The first, the most necessary, the root and
foundation of all the means, is divine, supernatural faith,
and this we cannot have without certain knowledge of what
God has revealed. The rule of faith, therefore, if it come
from God, must be able to give us this certain knowledge
of saving truth. And the Catholic rule of faith does so, and
it alone does so. The voice of the living Church is the voice
of God speaking through her in accordance with His own
promise. She heard our Redeemer's teaching, she witnessed
His miracles, she saw the miracle of the first Pentecost, she
herself received the entire body of revealed truths, to her
alone were revealed in their fulness the conditions of man's
salvation, and in teaching all this to man she is guaranteed
against error by our Lord's special promise. And since His
pledged word shall not pass away, the teaching of the
Church must be always true; a sure, certain guide to all

---

[1] I. E. RECORD, May, 1901.   [2] 1 Tim. ii. 4.

that follow it, and all are bound to follow it. Dr. Salmon's Church is not a witness to the fact of revelation; she came fifteen hundred years too late; and she is completely discredited as an interpreter by the contradictory doctrines to which she stands pledged. And as for the Doctor himself, and his 'individual Christian,' they come later still; and even though the Doctor were a sort of Wandering Jew, who could trace back his career to the scene on Calvary, his reliability as a witness is completely shattered by his own lectures. Neither the Doctor, then, nor his Church can witness to the fact of revelation, nor tell its sense without grave risk of error, and therefore neither can be a guide in the important matter of faith.

Again, the Catholic rule of faith is available to all who seek it with ordinary prudence and in sincerity. The living voice, for the very reason that it is living, is readily taken up by the hearer. It is not like a book, often obscure and unintelligible, or to be understood only by the learned, and often after much study, and careful, thoughtful consideration. The living voice is accommodated to the capacities of all hearers, the least as well as the best educated. If there be anything obscure, the teacher is present to explain it; and since the teacher is divinely guaranteed against error, only the wilfully blind can fail to take in from it the truths of faith. There may be persons of weak intellect, who cannot be taught, or perverse persons, who will not be taught; but the efficacy of the rule cannot be called in question, because of such persons. This rule exemplifies in its full details the system, which, according to St. Paul, our Lord Himself instituted: 'And He gave some apostles, and some prophets, and other some evangelists, and other some pastors, and doctors, for the perfecting of the saints, for the work of the ministry . . . . . until we all meet in the unity of faith.'[1] This is the *Ecclesia Docens*— an organised hierarchy—a body of teachers spread all the world over, in communion with one another, and in subordination to their Head. From this divinely-constituted body

---

[1] Ephes. iv. 7-12.

the truths of faith are conveyed, through various grades of teachers, to the faithful. The priests, who are the immediate teachers of the people, are in strict subordination to their bishops, and under strict episcopal supervision, just as the bishops themselves are in strict subordination to the Pope, and under his supervision. Thus the channels through which the teaching of the faith reaches the people are so jealousy guarded, that every Catholic, no matter how little educated, has the highest moral certainty that the teaching he receives is the teaching of the Church. He has learned it from his Catechism; his knowledge has been repeatedly tested in his preparation for the Sacraments; it has been tested pretty severely by the bishop at the time of his confirmation. He has heard it explained, Sunday after Sunday, in the public instruction given to the people, and by different priests, and he finds them all agreeing in their teaching. He finds it stated in books, if he can read them, and if he happen to go to any foreign country he finds there the Catholic faith, embracing the very same truths he was taught at home. Thus the Catholic has abundant evidence —the highest moral certainty—that his faith is the faith of the Catholic Church. And he believes it, not on the authority of the priest who taught him, but on the authority of the wide-world infallible Church, whose teaching he knows it to be.

Thus the voice of the teaching Church reaches the most obscure of her children; and the rule of faith guides and enlightens him. It would not help Dr. Salmon to say that this rule is not made available to the ordinary faithful with sufficient certainty, since it reaches them only through a priest, who may be ignorant or perverse, and who, therefore, may teach heresy instead of divine truth. For even though it were granted that a priest may preach heresy to his people, the consequence above insinuated would not follow. On the contrary, if such an incident were to occur, it would only illustrate more forcibly the practical efficacy of the Catholic rule of faith. For if a priest, even in the most obscure and remote district in the country were, from the altar on Sunday, to deny any doctrine taught by the

Church—the Real Presence, the Supremacy or Infallibility of the Pope, the Immaculate Conception, or any other such doctrine of the Church—his flock would at once notice the novelty, would take the alarm, and convey the intelligence to the bishop, and not many days would pass before the delinquent would have to choose between a public retraction of his false teaching or expulsion from the Catholic Church.

Whatever may be Dr. Salmon's theory, this would most certainly be the actual fact. And thus the Catholic rule is available to all the children of the Catholic Church; and it is equally available even for those who are not of the Church. Her voice reaches them also, unless they refuse to listen to her. It removes misconception, it explains difficulties; the grace of prayer remains with them, and if they hear the Church's message to them, with the sincere desire of learning the truth, and with a sincere determination of embracing the truth when known, and if they pray for light and help, they shall find the Church's motives of credibility abundantly sufficient as an argument to trust to her guidance, to submit to her authority, and if they so submit, her voice will guide and enlighten them, too, into all supernatural truth. And thus the Catholic rule of faith is available for all.

But Dr. Salmon's rule is not available for all, nor reliable for anyone. For nearly four hundred years it was absolutely impossible as a rule; for fourteen hundred years it was morally impossible. It is only available even now for scholars of very considerable learning, and for all it is a source of most contradictory doctrine. It cannot, therefore, be from God.

Again, the Catholic rule of faith—the voice of the living Church—is alone a competent judge of religious controversies, and alone capable of deciding them; and her commission covers the whole extent of revealed truth. As already stated and proved,[1] the Church is the divinely-appointed teacher and custodian of all revealed truth. As teacher it is her duty to explain its meaning, and as custodian it is her

---

[1] I. E. RECORD, May, 1901.

duty to maintain it in its integrity, to exclude from it all
admixture of error. Many of the truths of faith are so clear
that one should think they could not become matters of
controversy; but history shows that even revealed truths
that are apparently plainest have been doubted and denied.
Again, many revealed truths are obscure; their full meaning
is not on the surface; and on such truths controversy will,
as a matter of necessity, arise, and there must be a judge
to decide such controversies, if the faith is to be preserved.
Now, it is the living voice of the divinely-commissioned
teaching body that can decide such controversies with
authority and with certainty. And as such controversies
may arise at any time, and do arise frequently, a voice
always living and active, always present to decide, and
infallible in its decisions, is the only competent judge. This
is the voice of the ever-living, teaching Church, which
originated with the Apostles, and has been the organ of
divine truth ever since their time, and shall continue to be
such till time ends. Its authority is in its divine commission, and its perpetual activity is in the fact that it cannot
discharge its commission without existing as a teacher ' till
the consummation of the world.' As teacher it speaks only
with reference to the deposit of faith, and as custodian of
that deposit, it speaks also on matters from which detriment
to the sacred deposit may arise. Moreover, the Church
speaks with the authority, and after the manner of one, who,
living still, lived also when our Redeemer lived, saw the
facts of His life, and with a mind supernaturally enlightened
took in His teaching in its true sense, and who, still more,
with a memory supernaturally aided, has preserved that
teaching, and with an infallible judgment tells us now what
it is. And the Church could not tell us with certainty what
our Lord's teaching is unless she knew with equal certainty,
what is not His teaching. This, and nothing else, is the
meaning of our Lord's commission to His Church, and of
the promise accompanying the commission. The voice,
therefore, of this Church is competent to decide any controversy on faith or morals that may arise, and is always
available for that purpose. She knows the extent of her

commission, she knows its limits, she will not go beyond these limits. Within it, her voice is final. It is the rule of faith.

Now, Dr. Salmon's rule is not competent to decide religious controversies. It has had a three-hundred years trial, and it has decided nothing except its own worthlessness. It has generated sects almost innumerable, professing most contradictory creeds, or rather not knowing what to profess. It set out by professing what it could not prove, that the Bible is God's Word; and now, at the bidding of the 'higher criticism,' it has come to hold that God's Word is somewhere in the Bible, but it cannot tell where. Such a rule cannot be from God. Dr. Salmon led his students to believe that he had disposed of the Catholic rule of faith, when he held up for their ridicule a caricature formed of some misquotations of Dr. Milner, supplemented by some not very ingenious inventions of his own. He told them that Dr. Milner 'demanded that God should miraculously secure men from error of any kind' (page 97). And his version of the Catholic rule is, 'I know that I am right and you are wrong, because I have a divinely-inspired certainty that I am in the right in my opinion' (page 82). It was no doubt very pleasant to them to be assured, on such high authority, that their task as controversialists was so easy, as Catholics were so very irrational and so absurd, but it would have been much better to have told them the truth.

And, having disposed of the Catholic rule, to his own satisfaction, the Doctor proceeds to lay the axe to the root of the whole Roman system, addressing his learned audience thus : 'I propose to lay before you such evidence as will show you that, whether there be anywhere an infallible church or not the Church of Rome certainly is not' (page 169) And the 'evidence' is supplied by the following facts (?) :—
(1.) 'Romish advocates seldom offer any proof' of the infallibility of the Church ; (2.) ' The Church of Rome has shrunk with the greatest timidity from exercising this gift of Infallibility on any question, which had not already settled itself without her help' (page 172) ; (3.) ' The Church of Rome herself does not believe in the Infallibility which she

claims' (page 173).   Now, the first of these statements is so
notoriously, so manifestly opposed to fact, that it is amazing
how even Dr. Salmon could have made it.   There is not a
dogmatic theologian, from Bellarmine to Dr. Murray, who
has written on the Church, that has not proved this very
doctrine which Dr. Salmon says they 'seldom' attempt to
prove at all !   And they prove it, not in the illogical manner
suggested by Dr. Salmon.   They prove, first, that the Church
of Christ is infallible, and then, by the application of the
notes of the true Church, they prove that the Church of
Christ is that one which Dr. Salmon calls the Church of
Rome.   The Doctor can misrepresent these arguments, but
he cannot refute them.   His second statement is, 'The
Church of Rome has shrunk with the greatest timidity,' etc.,
and hence he infers she is not infallible, and she knows it.
Here, again, we have a specimen of the Doctor's consistency.
He has frequently stated that the Church's definitions are
always new doctrines, and here he tells us that she 'shrinks'
from defining anything that had 'not already settled itself
without her help.'   If the matter be doctrine before the
definition, then, the definition does not impose a new
doctrine.

But his logic is even worse than his consistency.   His
conclusion does not at all follow from his premises.   The
Apostles were individually infallible, and yet, in order to
decide whether circumcision was, or was not necessary, they
assembled a council at Jerusalem, and it was only after 'much
discussion' that St. Peter delivered the infallible decision of
the Apostolic body.   Now, as the Apostles were individually
infallible, each of them could have at once decided this
question as it came before him, and without any discussion ;
yet they waited and discussed the matter fully in council.
Will Dr. Salmon make their hesitation an argument against
their infallibility, individually or collectively ?   His argument
is as good against the Apostles as against the Church, and
as bad against the Church as against the Apostles.   The
Church hesitates, therefore, she is fallible ; the Apostles
hesitated, therefore, they were fallible.   If Dr. Salmon
insists on the first, he must hold the second, and if the

Apostles were fallible, as the Doctor's logic proves, what is the worth to him of his rule of faith—the Bible? Simply nothing. This is the outcome of the Doctor's logic.

Now, it is proved that the Church is infallible in her teaching, and the hesitations alleged by Dr. Salmon (even if all were granted) are no disproof of that doctrine, however they are to be explained. And the explanation is very easy. For surely it is not a charge against the Church, that in the exercise of her high office she exhibits the prudence and caution which the supernatural character of her work demands. If she had rushed headlong to a decision, had shown the simplicity of the dove without the prudence of the serpent, the Doctor would, no doubt, quote Scripture to condemn her; but that she is prudent and cautious in her decisions ought to be regarded as a proof that she has a due appreciation of the sacredness of her office and of the eternal interests at stake. The obligation of using due caution and prudence is implied in her commission, and she is always sure to comply with the obligation; but it is not a necessary condition of the truth of her teaching. Whenever the Church defines, her teaching is infallibly true, whether the preparation be long or short. Her Founder's promise secures her in her teaching, and insures also the prudence and the wisdom of her decisions. But Dr. Salmon has, as usual, completely misrepresented the action of the Church. Whenever the truths of faith that are necessary to be explicitly believed have been assailed, the Church has made no undue delay in vindicating them and in condemning their assailants. Arians, Eutychians, Monophysites, Monothelites, Lutherans, Jansenists have been condemned with the promptitude and decisiveness which the interests of souls demanded. But there have been in the Church domestic controversies regarding matters, not dogmas of faith necessary to be explicitly believed, in which, therefore, the interests of souls were not concerned, and in such cases the Church, under the guidance of the Holy Ghost, has awaited the acceptable time. The controversies to which Dr. Salmon refers are of this latter class. And even in such cases, when the controversy reaches a stage, in which the interests of souls require

that a definitive judgment should be given, the Church
speaks, and with no uncertain sound. And this prudence
ought to be regarded, rather as a proof of the Church's
fidelity to her commission than as an argument against her ;
for ' verily the finger of God is here.'

But Dr. Salmon ' will argue still.' He says : ' Let us
examine by the evidence of facts whether the Church of
Rome believes her own claim to infallibility' (page 172) ;
and after his wonted manner of examining he concludes
(page 173) that she ' does not believe' her claim. Now, if
she claim it without believing it she is a hypocrite ; and, as
this is a very grave charge, it should not be made without
conclusive evidence to sustain it. But, before convicting
her, Dr. Salmon offers some very interesting evidence to
show that she does not claim it at all. And his witnesses
are quite worthy of him. There is, first, a Mr. Seymour,
author of a precious production called *Mornings with the
Jesuits*, in which he relates for the admiration of enlightened Protestants how he bearded the Jesuits in their
own stronghold at Rome. ' He asked them for proof that
the Church of Rome ever claimed infallibility' (page 173),
and then this veritable Baron Munchausen ' described the
consternation and perplexity into which the Jesuits were
thrown by his assertion that the Trent decrees contained
no claim to infallibility.' And of this wonderful story, which
seems at first to have staggered Dr. Salmon, he got full
confirmation from his friend, Mr. Capes, who subsequently
met in England ' one of Mr. Seymour's two antagonists
. . . an excellent specimen of a well instructed Jesuit. . . .
And he told Mr. Capes that it was quite true,' etc.
(page 174). Very likely !   A well instructed Jesuit ignorant
of the decrees of the Council of Trent ! A well instructed
Jesuit, or any Jesuit, not aware that to claim under penalty
of anathema, the internal assent of the faithful to truths of
faith, does not presuppose the infallibility of the claimant !
Of course Messrs. Seymour and Capes gave no names or
dates of this extraordinary occurrence. Such minutiæ would
be altogether out of place, and would only tend to defeat
the ends of Mr. Seymour & Co.

But let us hear another of Dr. Salmon's witnesses: Mr. Ffoulkes, who, like Mr. Capes, 'made the journey to Rome and back, states that he was never asked to accept this doctrine when he joined the Church of Rome' (page 174). Now, almost in the same breath, we are told by Mr. Ffoulkes that he made the following profession: 'Sanctam Catholicam et Apostolicam Romanam Ecclesiam, omnium Ecclesiarum matrem et magistram agnosco.' Now, *magistram* is not a mistress who owns, but a mistress who teaches, as his dictionary would have told Mr. Ffoulkes. He himself, therefore, said, 'when he joined the Church of Rome': 'I acknowledge the Holy Catholic and Apostolic Roman Church to be the mother and teacher of all Churches,' the clearest possible profession of Infallibility. Therefore, from his own lips, we have it that he actually professed and proclaimed that identical doctrine which he says was never proposed to him at all! If Mr. Ffoulkes had given such evidence in a court of justice, the presiding judge would quickly cut him short by saying: 'You may go down, sir.' So much for Dr. Salmon's witnesses. The Doctor's own theory is that, though Rome claims Infallibility now, she did not claim it till recently. 'There are more things in heaven and earth, Horatio, than are dreamt of in your philosophy.' There are many other ways besides a formal definition in which the Church speaks her mind. She has not formally defined her infallibility; but she has always acted as one who cannot err. She has never tolerated any denial of her teaching. Whenever false doctrines appeared she condemned them; when the dogmas of faith were assailed she vindicated them, and condemned their assailants. 'Acting is the test of belief,' according to Dr. Salmon himself. In the First General Council the Church anathematized the doctrine of Arius, and excommunicated those who held it. In the Second Council she anathematized the doctrines of Macedonius, and excommunicated those who maintained them. She acted in like manner towards Nestorius and his followers at Ephesus, and towards Eutyches and his followers at Chalcedon; and so on, down along the chain of ecclesiastical history, we find the Church anathematizing heretics

and heresies as they arise. Dr. Salmon, who knows so
much about the Council of Trent, does not need to be
reminded of the very emphatic condemnation of the errors
of Luther and his associates at that council; and his own
memory enables him to see how closely the example of the
earlier councils was followed by that of the Vatican. And,
as this action of the teaching Church has been accepted by
the body of the faithful, then, judging by Dr. Salmon's own
test : 'Acting is the test of belief,' the Church has always
claimed to be infallible, and the faithful have always
admitted her claim. What, then, becomes of the Doctor's
assertion that she neither claimed it nor believed it ? The
test which he himself has supplied proves his statement to
be false.

But the Doctor's ingenuity is not yet exhausted. ' I
may, however, say a few words now . . . about the disputes
which have raged within the Roman communion for centuries . . . as to the organ of the Church's infallibility. Does
the gift reside in the Church diffusive, or only in its Head ?'
(page 175). To assert the existence of a controversy on
this question is a demonstration of the want of knowledge
or want of sincerity of him who makes the assertion. The
statement implies that one of the parties to the controversy
denied the infallibility of the ' Church diffusive.' There
was never any such controversy in the Catholic Church.
Catholics hold, and have always held, as an article of faith,
unanimously, that the Universal Church, the ' Church diffusive,' can never believe or profess any false doctrine. Again,
' does the gift reside in a General Council, or in Pope and
Council together ?' (page 175). There can be no General
Council without the Pope, and we hold, and always have
held, that a General Council, confirmed by the Pope, is
infallible in its teaching ; and Catholics, furthermore, hold
unanimously that the teaching Church (that is, the bishops
in union and in communion with their head) is infallible in
its teaching. On these questions there never was a controversy in the Catholic Church, though Dr. Salmon told his
students that it had ' raged for centuries.' So far, then, ' the
organ of the Church's infallibility' was well known, was

fixed and certain, available to all, and sufficient to decide all religious controversies. Whether, moreover, the Pope, in his official capacity, was infallible was a subject of controversy, though the controversy was more theoretical than practical; but it has been settled by the infallible voice of the *Ecclesia Docens*, and there is controversy on it no more. This practical efficacy of the Catholic rule of faith is unintelligible to men like Dr. Salmon, whose Church has never decided, and never can decide, a religious controversy, being, as Mr. Capes truly said, 'the very embodiment of the idea of Christian dissensions.' And no wonder, since, if men are to think and decide for themselves in matters of faith, they will think for themselves, and each individual Christian becomes a rule of faith, but to himself only.

'But we have no such custom, neither has the Church of God.'[1] In that Church we recognise our divinely-commissioned teacher. Her voice, ever living, reaches us in all our spiritual needs, and is a sure guide in all our religious controversies—our rule of faith, always available, sufficient, secure and applicable to the whole body of revealed truth. The teaching authority of the Church is determined by her commission. That commission is to teach all nations all the truths entrusted to her. What precisely that is we must learn from the Church herself. She is the only surviving earthly witness to the commission, and God's Word is pledged that she shall always declare it truthfully. If, therefore, we want to learn the sphere within which she is an infallible teacher, we must take her own word for it. By using her powers she tells us what they are. If we find her claiming to teach infallibly on any subject, we must either admit that her claim is good, or that her Founder has not kept His Word. This, then, which is the very alphabet of Catholic teaching, enables us to see how the rule of faith, designed by God, contrasts with clumsy human counterfeits of it. The authority of the Church applies directly and immediately to all that is contained in the deposit of faith; that is to all the truths that are formally, that is, in themselves, either explicitly or implicitly revealed,

---

[1] 1 Cor. xi. 16.

and in teaching and explaining all this the Church is infallible. All this constitutes the direct object matter of her
commission. Some of these truths, like the Incarnation, the
Real Presence, are contained in Scripture. Some, like the
Inspiration of Scripture, are only in tradition. Again, some
are clearly and explicitly revealed ; some only obscurely and
implicitly revealed; some are speculative truths to be
believed ; some are moral principles to regulate our conduct ;
but all alike being revealed, constitute the object matter on
which the Church's infallibile authority is exercised, and on
all her voice is the infallible rule of faith and conduct.
Whenever, therefore, the Church proposes to us a truth of
faith, or any rule for our moral guidance, we are bound to
regard her teaching as the voice of God speaking to us
through an organ which He Himself has appointed and
commissioned, and if we refuse to hear her we refuse to hear
Him. At the Vatican Council as well as at the Council of
Jerusalem, in the twentieth century as well as in the first,
the voice is the same, the security is the same, the obligation of belief and of submission is the same, equally
imperative and stringent. And the fuller explanation of
any truth, which time may bring, is only an explanation of
an old truth, not the announcement of a new one.

But besides being a divinely-commissioned teacher, the
Church is also a divinely-appointed guardian of revealed
truths ; and as such she must be able to ward off anything
that may impair the integrity of her charge. The defence
of a fortress is a forlorn hope when all the outworks are in
the hands of the enemy ; and so, too, it is with the Church
in the exercise of her commission. Besides the truths that
are formally revealed, and are thus directly, and on their
own account, within the sphere of her authority, there are
many other matters not revealed at all, but which stand in
such relation to revealed truth as brings them indirectly
within the range of the Church's authority. The Church,
for instance, declares a certain version of Scripture to be
authentic, and unless such a declaration be warranted by
her commission, then all she could do is to declare that the
original Scriptures, long since lost, were authentic; an item

of information of no possible use to us. So, too, she tells
us that certain words, such as Homoousion and Transubstantiation, properly and accurately express vital points of
Catholic doctrine, and unless she be warranted in so doing,
then she may propose orthodox doctrine by a heterodox
formula, and thus lead her children astray, and falsify her
Founder's promise.

Again, we find opinions prevalent frequently, which,
though not directly heretical, are yet calculated to undermine some truth of faith—to generate, if they do not contain,
the poison of heresy. Such opinions are, in some degree,
in opposition to truths of faith, and, therefore, false so far.
But the falsehood is not contained in revelation ; and yet, if
the Church be not warranted by her commission to detect
that falsehood, and pronounce an infallible judgment upon
it, she cannot discharge her duty as guardian of the faith.
But she does not pass judgment on such matters on their
own account, but on account of the revealed truths on which
they infringe. Reason is God's gift, as well as faith, and,
therefore, between truths known by faith, and truths known
by reason acting rightly within its own province, there can
be no conflict. Philosophy, and the natural sciences, are
grounded on natural truths, and are drawn from those truths
by sound logical reasoning ; and as long as they are so drawn,
the Church is not concerned with them. But very often the
reasoning is unsound, and often also false premises are
assumed, and as a result, conclusions are deduced that come
into collision with the truths of faith, and the Church, in
virtue of her office as guardian of revelation, must be able
to detect such opposition, and to warn her children against
error in the dangerous guise of truth. It is well for scientists
to recollect that the highest truth is God's truth, and that
whatever contradicts it is not truth at all.

Again, there are educational and political theories that
infringe on the moral law, and it is clearly the duty, and
the right of the Church, as guardian of faith and morals, to
pronounce judgment on them, and to warn her children
against them. This opens up a very wide field for the
exercise of the authority of the Church. But the field is

defined by her divine Founder. He has determined its
boundaries; He has given the commission; He insures its
due execution. This truth is very clearly laid down by the
Vatican Council : [1] 'The Church which, with the apostolic
office of teaching, has got also the commission of guarding
the deposit of faith, has the right and the duty from God, of
condemning science, falsely so-called, lest any one may be
deceived by philosophy and vain deceit.' And towards the
close of the same session we are reminded that 'it is not
sufficient to avoid heretical depravity unless we avoid also
those errors that approach more or less closely to it.' And
long before St. Paul said the same to the Colossians :
'Beware, lest any man cheat you by philosophy and vain
deceit.' [2]

The truths of faiths that are formally revealed are in
the Church's keeping and always present to her mind. But
as guardian of the faith she must be ever vigilant to detect
errors that are daily springing up, which, if allowed to
circulate in the guise of truth, would subvert the faith in
the souls of her children. The current literature is often
simply saturated with dangerous, immoral, anti-Catholic,
and often anti-Christian theories. 'The slime of the serpent
is on them,' and, if allowed to circulate unchecked, they
would act as poison to souls. Now, if souls are to be saved
there must be an antidote for such poison, and power must
be inherent in the commission of the Church to detect the
poison and to apply the antidote. Whatever contradicts
her teaching must be against God's Word and against His
Will. A divine commission carries with it necessarily an
assurance of its due discharge, and in this case we have,
moreover, God's explicit promise for the due discharge of
the commission. It is clear, therefore, that the Church
must have from her Founder authority to pronounce an
infallible judgment on such errors of fact or speculation as
cross her path in the discharge of her duty, in the exercise
of her divine commission. And all such errors she pursues
through all their subtle ramifications till she casts them

[1] S. 3, c. 4.   [2] Col. ii. 8.

forth, branded with her anathema, as poison, which her children are bound on peril of their souls to avoid.

Now, as errors of this sort are usually consigned to writing, it follows that to determine the true sense of such writings, and thus to detect the error, is one of the most important departments to which the indirect authority of the Church extends. Bad books are being multiplied almost daily, and they are a most powerful means, in the hands of the evil one, for the ruin of souls; and hence the Church would be seriously obstructed in the discharge of her office, as guardian of faith and morals, if she were unable to detect and condemn the errors against faith and morals contained in such books. Were she to condemn as heretical a book that is really sound in doctrine, or to recommend as orthodox a heretical or immoral book, by the very fact she would become a teacher of false doctrine, and her Founder's promise would have failed. From the very nature of the office and commission of the Church, then, it follows that she has authority to determine the true sense of such books, and she has always exercised this authority; and her right to do so was not called in question until comparatively recent times. It is one phase of the great question of dogmatic facts, and a few words on it will serve to explain and to vindicate the action of the Church in this most important department of her office.

The condemnation of a doctrine by the Church presupposes a standard of comparison, and a judgment declaring that the condemned doctrine is not in agreement with the standard. The Church's sole standard is the deposit of faith, including, of course, the moral law, and her condemnation of any doctrine is a decision that the doctrine is at variance with her standard. And sometimes the Church tells not only that the condemned doctrine is opposed to the deposit of faith, but she tells also the degree, the measure of the opposition. This she does by attaching to the condemned doctrine certain notes or marks of theological censure, such as heretical, erroneous, proximate to heresy, savouring of, or suspected of heresy, offensive to pious ears, blasphemous, impious, scandalous, etc. A doctrine that is condemned as heretical, is in direct contradiction to an article of Catholic faith. An erroneous doctrine is one which directly contradicts what is called a theological conclusion, a truth deduced from two propositions, one of which is revealed and the other certain from reason. A doctrine is proximate to heresy when it contradicts a doctrine commonly held by theologians to be *de fide*, though not defined or proposed as such by the Church. Again, there are equivocal propositions which would be orthodox in the mouth of a Catholic, but which may also be used to convey or insinuate heresy. And when such propositions are used by heretics there is a presumption that the heretical sense is intended. Such propositions would be condemned as suspected or savouring of heresy. With regard to most of the other notes of censure, offensive to pious ears, *temerarius*, blasphemous, etc., the technical meaning is substantially the same as the ordinary meaning of the words.

Now, the Church issues all such condemnations in the exercise of her divine commission; that commission is her warrant and her safeguard; and it imposes on us a strict obligation of rejecting what she condemns just as readily as we accept what she teaches. For in reality this is one of her methods of teaching, and a most important one, and nothing can give us a more exalted idea of the efficacy and the security of the Catholic rule of faith than the super-natural instinct with which the Church pursues heresy through all its windings, and the minute accuracy of detail with which she detects and condemns it. It is the voice of the Good Shepherd speaking through His Church, inviting His flocks to wholesome pasture, and warning them against that in which the secret poison is concealed.

As already stated, the Church has always exercised this authority, and it is necessarily included in her commission. The exclusion of apocryphal books from the Canon of Scripture is a conspicuous instance of the [exercise of this authority. At the Council of Nicæa the writings of Arius, his letters to Alexander of Alexandria, and his *Thalia*, written against St. Athanasius, were condemned as heretical, and anathema to Arius became a watch-word of orthodoxy.

Five of the bishops present refused to subscribe to the condemnation of Arius, and were deposed. Two of them, Eusebius of Nicomedia, and Theognis of Nicæa, repented, and wrote a joint letter to the Fathers, in which they condemned the errors attributed to Arius, but declared that they believed him innocent. This looks somewhat akin to the Jansenist distinction of ' right ' and ' fact ' with, however, this very important difference, that they did not ground their favourable opinion of Arius on any quibble about his condemned writings, but on sermons delivered by him in their own presence and on private letters to themselves. It is evident that the Church claimed, in this case, to decide infallibly the sense of the writings of Arius, for it would be intolerable tyranny to sentence bishops to deposition and exile for refusing to assent to a declaration that may be false.

The writings of Nestorius were condemned at Ephesus; those of Eutyches were condemned at Chalcedon. The books of the Manichees were condemned by Leo I., and the errors of Pelagius by Innocent I. The ' Three Chapters ' were condemned at the Fifth General Council; and later on we find the same discipline enforced whenever the occasion for it arose. The condemnations of Gotteschalc, Berengarius, Jerome of Prague, Huss, Wickliff, are some of the many instances of the exercise of this authority. And as ' acting is the test of belief,' the Church, therefore, must have believed that the right to condemn heretical and bad books was included in her commission. And the right remained unquestioned till the rise of that subtle heresy which took its name from Jansenius of Ypres.

In the whole history of the Church there is no stranger phenomenon than the narrow-minded heresy first embodied in the now too-famous *Augustinus*. Whether Jansenius, in his last moments, retracted his error, or died obstinately attached to them, is now known only to the Searcher of Hearts. Certain it is, however, that he left to posterity a legacy of discord in that ill-starred book. The history of Jansenism presents to us the strange, sad spectacle of a number of men—some of them very able men—leagued together with the settled purpose of perverting the doctrine, and subverting the discipline of the Catholic Church, and striving, at the same time, by most dishonest means, to have themselves still regarded as loyal children of that Church. The *Augustinus* was published in A.D. 1640, shortly after the death of its author. As it was passing through the press, the Louvain Jesuits obtained from one of the printers copies of the proof-sheets. They studied the doctrine of the book, and had it denounced on the very day of its publication. Between Jesuits and Jansenists a fierce controversy arose. The Jesuits sent the book to Rome, and it was condemned by the Inquisition, not yet, however, as heretical, but as published in disobedience to the Decree of Paul V. on the controversy *De Auxiliis*. In the following year Urban VIII. condemned the doctrine of the book. St. Cyran and Arnauld defended Jansenius and his doctrine in writings apparently aimed at the Jesuits, but, in reality, directed against the Church. Cornet, the Syndic of the Sorbonne, presented Seven Propositions for examination to the Doctors of the University. Professedly they were the theses of some students applying for degrees, but, in reality, they were taken from the *Augustinus*. The theological faculty reduced them to five, and condemned them. Against this condemnation the Jansenists appealed, not to the *Ecclesia Docens*, but to the Parliament of Paris. The French bishops sent the Propositions to Rome, with the censure of the Sorbonne. The Pope appointed a commission of five cardinals, with thirteen consulting theologians, to examine the *Augustinus*. It held thirty-six congregations, at the last ten of which the Pope himself presided. St. Amour and other leading Jansenists were permitted to appear in defence of their views.

The result of all was that Innocent X., in A.D. 1653, formally condemned the Five Propositions, and attached to each its special censures. And now the real duplicity of the Jansenists began to show itself. They admitted that the Propositions were rightly condemned, and admitted also the Pope's right to condemn them, but they denied vehemently that Jansenius had held the Propositions, or that they were contained in the *Augustinus*. Against this subterfuge Alexander VII. issued the Constitution *cum ad S. Petri Sedem*, declaring that the Propositions were taken from the book of Jansenius, and were condemned in the sense of the author. Pascal, the wit of the party, now set to work. In the *Provincial Letters*, in a tone of bitter sarcasm, he ridiculed the teaching of the Jesuits, and the condemnation of his party by the Church. He admitted the right of the Church to decide infallibly all doctrinal matters, and admitted, accordingly, that the Five Propositions were heretical and properly condemned, but he denied to the Church the right to decide infallibly the concrete fact whether these Five Propositions were or were not a fair, accurate expression of the doctrine of the *Augustinus*. This, he held, was essentially a human fact, not contained in the deposit of faith, nor deducible from it ; determinable only by a critical examination of the book. Let the Church, he said, confine herself to faith and morals ; they cover the whole extent of her commission ; but let her not claim infallibility in a purely critical investigation. This is the substance of Pascal's diatribe, which was taken up eagerly by the party. It is the well-known distinction of 'right' and 'fact,' the 'right' being the truth or falsehod of the Propositions, and the 'fact' whether they were or were not contained in the book. The Jansenists then condemned the Five Propositions, but since they said the Church and Pope may err in attributing them to the *Augustinus*, they maintained that, in reference to that fact, a 'respectful silence,' was all that could be expected from them, and this they would observe in deference to the Pope, as supreme legislator of the Church. This further evasion was met by the formulary of Alexander VII. in A.D. 1664, and still more pointedly by the *Vineam Domini* of Clement XI., A.D. 1705. The error lingered on in various disguises, doing much mischief in Church and State, until after twenty distinct condemnations it got its death blow from the 'Unigenitus,' in A.D. 1713. This is a brief summary of the history of this subtle heresy.

Now, that the authors of this revolt against the Church should be described by Dr. Salmon as 'devout Catholics' (page 221), is not surprising, considering the general character of his book. The statement can deceive no one. But at page 416, in a note, he has a statement that is well calculated to deceive. In speaking of the Constitution of Alexander VII., he says, ' it was expressly stated that Jansen had asserted them (the Propositions) in the heretical sense.' Now, the insinuation here, as the context shows, is that the Pope decided, not merely the sense of the *Augustinus*, but what was actually in the mind of Jansenius when he wrote it ; that Jansenius actually entertained the heretical sense and intended to express it in his book. Now, this is completely to misrepresent the action of the Church, and the language of such doctrinal condemnation.

As Dr. Salmon has shown so little acquaintance with the theology of his own Church, it is no wonder that he should blunder on questions of Catholic theology. The language of such documents is technical, and Dr. Salmon should have sought out its real meaning before he undertook to explain it to others. And any Catholic theologian would have informed him that in condemning a book ' in the sense of the author,' the Church does not at all intend to pry into the mind of the writer, and tell what he was thinking of ; she does not say what his subjective meaning was ; she deals with the objective sense—that is, with the actual sense expressed in the book of which he is supposed to be the author. As long as the error is shut up in the mind of the writer it cannot affect the deposit of faith, for which the Church is concerned. Now, this is clearly stated in the *Vineam Domini* of Clement XI., dealing with those identical errors of Jansenius. The Pope says : ' The sense condemned in the Five Propositions of Jansenius is that which the words of these Propositions convey.' Thus, then, the Church, by the expression, ' sense of the author,' does not mean to define who is the author of a book. She takes this as a historical fact, generally admitted, but its truth or falsehood in no way affects her position as guardian of the faith. Neither does the Church, by the expression, ' sense of the author,' mean to define that the supposed author actually held the doctrines contained in the book, nor does she mean to say that

it is a fair statement of what he intended to express. The
writer may be an ignorant person, who used language
incorrectly, or a madman, who wrote at random, or a rogue
who concealed his real sentiments.

With all this the Church is not concerned. She is
concerned with the book itself, from which, and not from
the mental thoughts of the writer, detriment may come to
the deposit of faith. She supposes the writer to have used
language, as men ordinarily do use it, and to have intended
what he really said; she takes the book itself; she examines
its words and phrases, and compares its various parts, and
thus arrives at its true genuine meaning. It is this true
genuine meaning that she either approves or condemns;
and her commission as guardian and teacher of faith and
morals, supposes, and guarantees, the correctness of the
decision to which she comes. The author of a book as such
is the author only of what the book contains; it is this the
Church either condemns or approves, and, therefore, the
expression 'sense of the author' is strictly and critically
correct, and not at all open to Dr. Salmon's quibble. The
Doctor may consider the Catholic Church tyrannical and
intolerant; she is just as intolerant as God has made her—
neither more nor less. And if he had sincerely and candidly
examined even this Jansenist controversy it would have
taught him a very salutary lesson. Here we have a subtle
and most insidious heresy, on a most abstruse doctrine,
maintained, too, by men of great ability. Wit, eloquence,
satire, intrigue, are employed unsparingly and unscrupulously
in the interest of the heresy, yet, the Church is never
moved from her divinely-appointed course. She pursues
the heresy with unerring accuracy through all its ser-
pentine windings, through all its evasions and subter-
fuges, detecting it, exposing it, condemning it at every
stage; and ultimately casting it out lest it should taint her
sacred deposit or defile the souls of her children. 'Verily
the finger of God is here.'

Let the Doctor contrast all this with the manner in
which controversies are conducted in his own Church. He
says: 'In several doctrinal questions which have come

before the Privy Council [his *Ecclesia Docens*], it was found
to be easier by far to ascertain what the doctrine of the
Church of England was, than whether the impeached
clergyman had contravened it ' (page 222).

Is the Doctor serious ? No one has been ever able to
ascertain what the ' doctrine ' of his Church of England is,
and she herself is unable to say what it is. And no wonder :
for, as long as she has to bear the incubus of the ' individual
Christian ' sitting in judgment on her, the doctrine is his,
not hers; and hence it is that in all doctrinal controversies
she very properly observes the most profound and edifying
' religious silence.' Will the Doctor say when she has
broken this ' silence ' by a plain unequivocal statement
of her doctrine ?

There have been controversies about ' lights,' ' incense,'
' vestments,' position at the altar, etc., matters of rubric,
regulated by what may be called the bye-laws of Dr. Salmon's
Church. On such matters decisions have been sometimes
given, though they have generally given little satisfaction,
and have never been obeyed. A board of guardians can make
bye-laws and enforce them quite as effectually. But when
has Dr. Salmon's Church decided a question of doctrine ?
Does Baptism confer, or not confer, regenerating grace ?
Rev. Mr. Gorham held that it did not ; his bishop,
Dr. Philpotts, held that it did. The Court of Arches
agreed with the bishop, and condemned Mr. Gorham ; but
the Privy Council reversed the condemnation on the ground
that the Church of England did not say, and, no doubt, did
not know, whether Baptism did, or did not, give the grace
of regeneration. And her ' Irish Sister ' in this matter
exhibits the ' ingenious Catholicity,' already pointed out,[1]
by giving her children their choice of three doctrines, each
of which is incompatible with the other two. Is marriage
indissoluble? The Rev. Mr. Black says it is ; and he has a
large following who say that such is the doctrine of the
Church of England. But his archbishop, and most of the
bishops of his Church, hold the contradictory view, and issue

---

[1] I. E. RECORD, November, 1901.

licenses for the re-marriage of divorced persons. And his Church looks on, while her spiritual rulers, according to Dr. Lee, say practically: 'Believe nothing and preach anything.'[1] Is our Lord really and truly present in the Blessed Eucharist? Mr. Carter, Mr. Bennett, and Mr. Mackonochie say yes; Dean Farrar and Dr. Salmon say no. Each has a numerous following, and the Church looks on in helpless indifference. Are there real priests and a real sacrifice? The Ritualists, and some High Churchmen, like Dr. Gore and Dr. Moberly, say yes. Dr. Lightfoot said, however, that the Church 'has no sacerdotal system;' and Mr. Kensitt and his brother Protestants hold that every Christian is a priest, and Mr. Kensitt showed his sincerity by actually celebrating ' the Lord's Supper ' himself.

Again the Church looks on; she does not say, for she does not know, on which side is the true doctrine. And many other instances of this 'religious silence' could be here quoted. It is only necessary to mention the names of Bennett, Mackonochie, Purchas; to refer to the *Essays and Reviews*, the *Athanasian Creed*, or the controversy on Orders, to see how utterly powerless Dr. Salmon's Church is to decide any dogmatic controversy, and how helpless is any attempt to find out her ' doctrine.' Let Dr. Salmon contrast the inaction of his Church regarding these controversies with the action of the Catholic Church in the Jansenist controversy alone, and if he is unable to see on which side ' the finger of God ' is, he is past teaching. Whatever revealed doctrines Protestants hold they owe to the Catholic Church. Their own Church gives them nothing of her own but denials of Catholic doctrine, negations, that is, nothings. The Catholic Church, on the other hand, has spoken through all the ages of her existence with the same power, the same truth, the same definiteness, as on the first Pentecost. Her voice has never wavered; it is the voice of God, the infallible rule of faith, the infallible guide of conduct for all men and for all time.

[To be continued.]   J. MURPHY, D.D.

---

[1] *Eccl. Situation*, p. 45.

Notes and Queries

LITURGY

OFFICE OF THE DEAD AND STATIONS OF THE CROSS BEFORE BLESSED SACRAMENT EXPOSED

REV. DEAR SIR,—Kindly answer the following points in the next number of the I. E. RECORD :—

In a convent chapel, where the nuns keep up Perpetual Adoration before the Blessed Sacrament exposed in the remonstrance, is it lawful for the said nuns—(1) To recite the Office of the Dead; (2) To go round the Stations of the Cross collectively or individually?

SACERDOS.

I. It is not lawful to recite the office of the Dead in presence of the Blessed Sacrament exposed :—

'Dubium II. Num, durante expositione Augustissimi Sacramenti, officium pro defunctis recitari vel cantari liceat in choro?
'Ad II. Negative.
'Die 8 Februarii, 1879.' [1]

Therefore the Office of the Dead should be recited in some place other than the chapel; or the Blessed Sacrament should be replaced in the tabernacle during the recitation.

II. There is no decree to settle the point raised in the second query, nor have we seen the point treated in any author. We must, therefore, rely on certain established principles.

The principle that excludes the Office of the Dead would seem to be that it is of its nature unsuitable as a service before the Blessed Sacrament exposed, just as black is considered an unsuitable colour. But there is another principle, namely, that nothing is to be done which, though suitable in itself, would yet attract the attention of the faithful to itself and draw it off from the adoration of the individual consecrated Host exposed in the monstrance. It

[1] Decr. Auth. S.R.C.n. 3479.

is for this reason that Mass is not, as a rule, allowed to be said at the altar of Exposition; that Communion should not be distributed at the same altar; that a sermon, except it be a short *fervorino*, should not be preached; that palms and candles should not be blessed; that statues are not to be exposed, particularly during Quarant' Ore and Perpetual Adoration : ' Eo quod,' says De Herdt, ' SS. Sacramenti cultus harum orationum praecipuus et unicus sit finis, et omnia igitur ita disponenda sint ut populus totus sit in adoranda Eucharistia intentus.'

We think that according to this principle, the *Via Crucis*, whether gone through by a body or an individual, is not a suitable service in the presence of the Blessed Sacrament exposed. Because, for the proper performance of the *Via Crucis*, it is necessary, at least when there is no hindrance, to visit each Station in particular,[1] and meditate on the Passion of Christ. To this we see the same objection as that raised to the functions mentioned.—' Attentionem ad se attrahunt et a SS. Sacramento abducunt.' [2]

THE PRAYER 'EN EGO'

Rev. Dear Sir,—Would you be so kind as to indicate which is the correct form to use in the above prayer towards the end— ' Quod in ore ponebat *Tuo*,' or ' quod in ore ponebat *suo*.' I always made use of the latter form, or a translation of it, until I saw the the translation which is given in the prayer book issued by the Irish Catholic Truth Society. I thought at first it was a misprint, but I find it the same in the *New Raccolta*. On consulting different editions of the Breviary I find in some *Tuo*, in others *suo*, making, of course, altogether different sense in each case. I hope the gaining of the Indulgence does not depend on the use of *Tuo*.

In many of the translations the particular force of the particle *En* seems to be lost. The *Raccolta* brings it out fully : ' Look down upon me,' etc. In other respects, however, the *Raccolta* translation does not appear to be altogether perfect.

S.

There can be no doubt now that the correct word is ' *Tuo*.'

---

[1] Decr. Auth. S.C. Indulg. n. 287.   [2] De Herdt, vol. ii. n. 25.

Besides the authorities cited by our correspondent, there are the following :—

Beringer has ' *Tuo*.' [1]   The Roman review, *Ephemerides Liturgicae* says :—

' In oratione *En ego, O bone*, etc., post verba 'quod in ore ponebat' non *suo* dicendum est, sed *Tuo*.'

The writer gives three reasons, the most convincing of which is, 'quia in Libello Indulgentiarum *Raccolta di orazioni*, etc., *Tuo* habetur, non *suo*.' [2]

The I. E. RECORD of July, 1894, quotes from the *Analecta Ecclesiastica* of April, 1894, a decree of the Congregation of Indulgences.   The same decree appears in the *Acta Sanctae Sedis*, vol. xxvi., p. 702:—

'. . . Qaeritur igitur ab hac S. Congregatione Indulg.

' I. Utrum dicendum sit in oratione praefata " *ore Tuo* " an vero " *suo*."

' II. Utrum sit indifferens ad luorandam Indulgentiam " *suo* " vel " *Tuo*."

' S. Congr. relatis dubiis respondit.

' Ad I. Standum omnio textui collectionis authenticae, editae Romae anno 1886 ex decreto hujus S. Congregationis diei 24 Maii 1886.

' Ad II. Provisum in I.

' Datum Romae ex Secret. ejusd. S. Congr. die 29 Martii, 1894.' [3]

The ' Collectio ' referred to is that which is mentioned in the exposition of the questions, and the text of which has ' *Tuo*.'

We cannot decide for certain whether the gaining of the Indulgence depends on the use of ' *Tuo*.' From the answer ' Ad II.' in the decree just given, it would seem that it is, at least, endangered—unless the form, 'in ore ponebat *Tuo*.' be strictly adhered to.

As regards translation, all that is required is that it be faithful, and declared so by some one of the Ordinaries of the place, the language of which is that of the translated prayer. [4]

---

[1] Vol. i. p. 167, 2ieme Ed.
[2] April, 1901, p. 233.
[3] We have quoted from the I. E. RECORD only so much of the decree as we consider necessary.
[4] Decr. Auth. S.C. Indulg. n. 415.

CANDLES WITH ONLY 60 PER CENT. OF BEES' WAX

REV. DEAR SIR,—The Sacred Liturgy prescribes pure bees' wax candles for the offices, services, and ceremonies in our churches, but especially for the celebration of Holy Mass. Some places, as poor parishes, have got an Indult to use candles which contain only 60 per cent. of bees' wax.

Now, may I ask the Liturgist of the I. E. RECORD to give an answer to the following question : —

Is there any general Indult for Ireland to use, at the Holy Sacrifice of the Mass, wax candles containing only 60 per cent. of pure bees' wax ?

If *affirmative*, I can assure any person that of all the candles sold as *pure wax*, and manufactured in Ireland, most do not contain even 60 per cent. of pure bees' wax, and, therefore, the Sacred Liturgy cannot be observed.

If *negative*, the matter is still worse, because we buy candles given as *pure bees' wax* and they are far from being so, since there is just a little more than 50 per cent. of wax in them, and some of them have even a lesser quantity. The Sacred Liturgy suffers and the buyers also.

Now, I must say that real bees' wax candles would cost a little more than the present ones, although in other countries, in France, for instance, the pure wax candles are not so dear as the adulterated candles in England and Ireland.

Moreover, I have used both candles, and can state the following : Two candles, *all pure bees' wax*, have lasted for thirty-four Masses ; two candles, of same dimension, *mixed wax*, sold in Dublin by a chandler as pure wax, have lasted only for twenty-six Masses.

Therefore, I think that if we could get the Irish candle manufacturers to make *pure bees' wax candles* for the sacred use of Holy Mass, the prescriptions of the Liturgy would be observed, and the buyers would spare a little of their money.

REGULAR.

There is no special Indult for Ireland in the matter of wax candles.

It is clear that a certain number of the candles [1] ordered

---

[1] For the number required and various other questions regarding wax candles see I. E. RECORD, February, 1882 ; August, 1882 ; April, 1883 ; February, 1890, and December, 1895.

by the Church for the Holy Sacrifice and other Sacred Functions, should be made of bees' wax. The General Rubrics of the Missal T. XX. require 'ut ab eadem parte Epistolae paretur *cereus.*' It is a defect *in ministerio* 'si non adsint luminaria *cerea.*'[1] The *Caeremoniale Episcoporum*[2] speaks of *cerei* accensi 'qui solent fieri ex *cera communi.*' In the blessing of the Paschal Candle occur the 'phrases '*de operibus apum,*' '*apis mater* eduxit,' and in the first prayer for the blessing of the candles on the Feast of the Purification, '*per opera apum.*'

We certainly condemn the practice of selling as candles of *pure bees' wax* candles that contain only 60, 50, or less per cent. of that material. And we hope, for the sake of the good name of Irish and English manufacturers of candles for the Sacred Functions, that the information of our correspondent is not accurate.

But the question may be raised, and is raised, whether the candles required to be of bees' wax, must be *entirely* of this material; and, if not, whether a proportion of 50 per cent. or even more of vegetable or other suitable substance may be mixed with it, without making the candles unrubrical. We have not space to deal with this question in the present number of the I. E. RECORD ; we shall do so in the next.

P. O'LEARY.

---

[1] *De defect.* T. X. n. l.   [2] Lib. ii. cap. x. n. 4.

DOCUMENTS

PURE WINE AND BREAD FOR THE ALTAR
INSTRUCTION OF THE HOLY OFFICE TO THE BISHOPS OF THE UNIVERSAL CHURCH

DE SANCTISSIMAE EUCHARISTIAE SPECIERUM GENUINITATE ET CONSERVATIONE CURANDA AD REVMOS. DD. LOCORUM ORDINARIOS

EME. AC RME. DOMINE,

Pluries et variis ex locisSupremae huic Congregationi S. Officii dubia proposita sunt circa materiam (panem et vinum) SSmi. Eucharistici Sacramenti. Cum enim inhonestorum quorumdam mercatorum eo iam malitia pervenerit, ut farinas triticeas aliarum tum vegetalium tum etiam mineralium substantiarum admixtione adulterare, vinaque vel ex toto vel ex parte haud ex genimine vitis conficere passim non vereantur, cumque non raro difficile admodum sit, vel ipsis chimicis peritis huiusmodi fraudes agnoscere; non immerito dubitatum est, num ad licitam, imo et validam consecrationem farinae vel hostiae vinaque quae sunt in commercio, tuto adhiberi valeant.

Cum res, ut patet, maximi sit momenti et, ceterum, de farinarum vinorumque frequentibus adulterationibus dubitari nequeat; Emi. DD. Cardinales una mecum Inquisitores Generales pastoralem Rmorum. DD. Ordinariorum sollicitudinem excitandam censuerunt ut, accuratis institutis investigationibus, si quos abusus irrepsisse compererint, funditus, convellere satagant, ac diligenter caveant ne quid in posterum in propriis ditionibus fiat quod a latis nedum circa naturam sed et circa conservationem Sacrarum Specierum dispositionibus, quae a probatis auctoribus traduntur quaeque praesertim in Rubricis Missali Romano praepositis continentur, quomodocumque sit absonum. Quoties vero de venalium farinarum vel hostiarum vinorumque genuinitate rationabile adsit dubium, Sacerdotes sibi subditos ab eorum usu in conficiendo SSmo. Altaris Sacramento omnino prohibeant, eosque practicam rationem doceant genuinam materiam sibi comparandi. Quod demum, spectat ad Missas dubia materia antehac forte celebratas, ad S. Congregationem recurrant.

Quae quidem omnia dum, ut mei muneris est, cum Emtia. Tua communico, libenter occasionem nactus, fausta quaeque ac felicia Tibi precor a Domino.

Datum Romae ex S. O. die 30 Aug. 1901.

Addictissimus obsequentissimus famulus verus,

L. M. Card. PAROCCHI.

THE PRIVILEGES OF CERTAIN ABBOTS

SUPPLICATIO ABBATUM QUOAD EORUMDEM INTERVENTIONEM IN CONSISTORIIS SEMIPUBLICIS BEATORUM CANONIZATIONI PRAEVIIS

Rmi. Abbates Ordinarii Nullius Montis Cassini, S. Pauli de Urbe et SSmae. Trinitatis Caven. a Sanctissimo Domino Nostro Leone Papa XIII humillime efflagitarunt, ut sibi suisque successoribus confirmare in perpetuum dignaretur ius interveniendi suffragiumque ferendi in Consistoriis semipublicis Beatorum Canonizationi praeviis: eo vel magis quod ipsi auctoritate Ordinaria conficere possunt Processus informativos in Causis Beatificationis et Canonizationis, atque eorum antecessoribus intimatio pro supradictis Consistoriis semel atque iterum facta fuit, ipsique revera interfuerunt et votum dederunt. Placuit vero Eidem Sanctissimo Domino Nostro huiusmodi negotium Sacrorum Rituum Congregationi examinandum et discutiendum committere. Quae Summi Pontificis mandato obtemperans, praehabitis una cum informatione suffragiis, etiam praelo impressis, tum alterius ex Iuris Canonici Professoribus, tum Apostolicis Caeremoniis Praefecti, tum demum Commissionis Liturgicae, in Ordinario Coetu, subsignata die ad Vaticanum coacto, praefatam quaestionem, ab infrascripto Cardinali Sacrorum eidem Rituum Congregationi Praefecto propositam atque accurato examine discussam atque perpensam, ita resolvendam esse censuit: ' Consulendum Sanctissimo pro concessione privilegii singulis petentibus.' Die 5 Februarii, 1901.

Facta postmodum de his omnibus Sanctissimo Domino Nostro Leoni Papae XIII per ipsum infrascriptum Cardinalem relatione, Sanctitas Sua resolutionem Sacrae ipsius Congregationis ratam habens, privilegium abstandi suffragiumque ferendi in praedictis Consistoriis semipublicis, non solum tribus Abbatibus Oratoribus, sed etiam aliis Abbatibus Nullius singulatim petentibus indulgere dignata est. Die 9 Februarii, 1901.

DOMINICUS Card. FERRATA, Sacr. Rit. Congr. Praef.

L. ✠ S.

✠ DIOMEDES PANICI, Archiep. Laodicen. Secr.

LETTER OF HIS HOLINESS POPE LEO XIII. TO THE SUPERIORS-
GENERAL OF RELIGIOUS ORDERS IN FRANCE

LITTERAE SSMI. D. N. LEONIS XIII AD SUPERIORES GENERALES
ORDINUM ET INSTITUTORUM RELIGIOSORUM

Chers Fils salut et Bénédiction Apostolique

En tout temps les familles religieuses ont reçu de ce Siège
Apostolique des témoignages particuliers de sollicitude affectueuse
et prévoyante, soit quand elles jouissaient des bienfaits de la paix,
soit surtout dans les jours de dures épreuves comme ceux que
vous traversez en ce moment.

Les graves attaques qui dans quelques pays ont été récemment
dirigées contre les Ordres et les Instituts soumis à votre autorité,
Nous causent une douleur profonde. La sainte Eglise en gémit
parce qu'elle se sent tout à la fois blessée au vif dans ses droits et
sérieusement entravée dans son action qui, pour se déployer librement, a besoin du concours des deux clergés, séculier et régulier :
en vérité, qui touche à ses prêtres ou à ses religieux la touche à la
prunelle de l'oeil. Pour Notre part, vous le savez, Nous avons
essayé de tous les moyens pour détourner de vous une persécution si indigne en même temps que pour épargner à ces pays
des malheurs aussi grands qu'immérités. C'est pourquoi dans
plusieurs occasions Nous avons plaidé votre cause de tout notre
pouvoir au nom de la religion, de la justice et de la civilisation.
Mais Nous espérions en vain que Nos remontrances seraient
entendues. Voici, en effet, que dans ces jours-ci, chez une nation
singulièrement féconde en vocations religieuses, que Nous avions
toujours entourée de soins très particuliers, les pouvoirs publics
ont approuvé et promulgué des lois d'exception à propos desquelles
Nous avions, il y a peu de mois, élevé la voix dans l'espérance de
les conjurer.

Nous souvenant de Nos devoirs sacrés et suivant l'exemple de
Nos illustres prédécesseurs, Nous réprouvons hautement de telles
lois parce qu'elles sont contraires au droit naturel et évangélique,
confirmé par une tradition constante, de s'associer pour mener un
genre de vie non seulement honnête en lui-même, mais particulièrement saint ; contraires également au droit absolu que
l'Eglise a de fonder des Instituts religieux exclusivement soumis à
son autorité, pour l'aider dans l'accomplissement de sa mission
divine, tout en produisant les plus grands bienfaits d'ordre
religieux et civil, à l'avantage particulier de cette très-noble nation
elle-même.

Et maintenant Nous nous sentons intérieurement poussé à vous ouvrir Notre cœur paternel, dans le désir de vous donner et de recevoir de vous quelque consolation sainte et en même temps pour vous adresser des enseignements opportuns afin que demeurant plus fermes encore dans l'épreuve, vous en recueilliez des mérites abondants devant Dieu et devant les hommes.

Parmi les nombreux motifs de courage qui naissent de la foi, rappelez-vous, chers fils, cette parole solennelle des Jésus-Christ : 'Vous serez heureux lors qu'on vous maudira et qu'on vous persécutera et qu'on mentira de toute manière contre vous à cause de moi.'¹ Reproches, calomnies, vexations fondront sur vous à 'cause de moi ; alors vous serez heureux.' On a beau, en effet, multiplier contre vous les prétextes d'accustion pour vous abaisser : la triste réalité n'en éclate pas moins à tous les yeux. La véritable raison de vous poursuivre c'est la haine capitale du monde contre la 'Cité de Dieu,' qui est l'Eglise catholique. La véritable intention c'est de chasser, si c'est possible, de la société l'action restauratrice du Christ, si universellement bienfaisante et salutaire. Personne n'ignore que les Religieux de l'un et de l'autre sexe forment une élite dans la Cité de Dieu : ce sont eux, qui représentent particulièrement l'esprit et la mortification de Jésus-Christ ; eux, qui par l'observation des conseils évangéliques tendent à porter les vertus chrétiennes au comble de la perfection ; eux, qui de bien des manières secondent puissamment l'action de l'Eglise. Dès lors il n'est pas étonnant qu'aujourd'hui, comme dans d'autres temps sous d'autres formes iniques, la 'Cité du monde' s'insurge contre eux, surtout les hommes qui par des pactes sacrilèges sont plus étroitement liés et plus servilement soumis au 'Prince du monde lui-même.'

Il est clair qu'ils considèrent la dissolution et l'extinction des Ordres religieux comme une manœuvre habile pour réaliser leur dessein préconçu de pousser les Nations catholiques dans la voie de l'apostasie et de la rupture avec Jésus-Christ. Mais s'il en est ainsi, on peut dire de vous en toute vérité : 'Vous êtes heureux,' parce que vous n'êtes haïs et poursuivis qu'à cause du genre de vie que vous avez librement choisi par attachement pour le Christ.

Si vous suiviez les maximes et les volentés du monde, il ne vous inquiéterait pas et vous comblerait même de ses faveurs. 'Si vous étiez du monde, le monde aimerait ce qui est à lui,' mais parce que vous marchez dans des voies opposées aux siennes,

---

¹ Matt. v. 11.

vous êtes exposés aux insultes et à la guerre. 'A cause de cela le monde vous hait.'[1] Le Christ lui-même vous l'a prédit. Aussi vous regarde-t-il avec d'autant plus de complaisance et de prédilection qu'il vous voit plus conformes à lui-même quand vous souffrez pour la justice. Et vous, 'participant aux souffrances du Christ, réjouissez-vous.'[2] Aspirez au corage de ces héros qui 's'en allaient joyeux à la vue de l'assemblée parce qu'ils avaient été jugés dignes de souffrir pour Jésus Christ.'[3]

A cette glorie qui vient du témoignage de votre conscience,[4] se joignent, sans que vous les recherchiez, les bénédictions de tous les honnêtes gens. Tous ceux qui s'intéressent vraiment à la paix et à la prosperité du pays, estiment qu'il n'y a pas de citoyens plus honnêtes, plus dévoués et plus utiles à leur patrie que les membres des Congrégations religieuses : et ils tremblent à la pensée de perdre, en vous perdant, tant de biens précieux qui tiennent à votre existence. C'est une multitude d'indigents, de délaissés, de malheureux, au profit desquels vous avez fondé et vous soutenez toutes sortes d'établissements avec une intelligence et une charité admirables. Ce sont les pères de famille qui vous ont confié leurs fils et qui jusqu'à présent comptaient sur vous pour leur donner l'éducation morale et religieuse, cette éducation saine, vigoureuse et féconde en fortes vertus qui ne fut jamais plus necessaire qu'à notre époque ! Ce sont les prêtres qui trouvent en vous d'excellents auxiliaires de leur important et laborieux ministère. Ce sont les hommes de tout rang qui, par ce temps de perversion, trouvent des directions utiles et des encouragements au bien dans vos conseils, autorisés par l'intégrité de votre vie. Ce sont surtout les Pasteurs sacrés qui vous honorent de leur confiance, qui vous considèrent comme les instituteurs expérimentés du jeune clergé et reconnaissent en vous ces 'vrais amis de leurs frères et du peuple'[5] qui offrent pour eux à la clémence divine des prières et des expiations incessantes.

Mais personne ne peut apprécier les mérites insignes des Ordres religieux avec plus justice que Nous, qui du haut de ce Siège devons veiller aux besoins de l'Eglise universelle.

Déjà dans d'autres actes Nous en avons fait une mention particulière. Qu'il Nous suffise en ce moment de louer la grande ordeur avec laquelle ils suivent non seulement les directions, mais les moindres désirs du Vicaire de Jésus-Christ, entreprenant

[1] Ioann. xv. 19.
[2] I. Petr. iv. 13.
[3] Act. v. 41.
[4] II. Cor. i. 12.
[5] II. Machab. xv. 14.

toutes les œuvres d'utilité chrétienne et sociale qu'il leur indique, s'en allant sur les plages les plus inhospitalières, bravant toutes les souffrances et la mort elle-même, comme plusieurs l'ont glorieusement prouvé dans la dernière révolution de la Chine.

Si, parmi les plus chers souvenirs de Notre long pontificat, Nous comptons d'avoir élevé par Notre autorité un grand nombre de serviteurs de Dieu aux honneurs des autels, ce souvenir Nous est d'autant plus doux qu'ils appartiennent en majorité aux Instituts réguliers à titre de Fondateurs ou de simples religieux.

Nous voulons rappeler encore pour votre consolation, que parmi les hommes du monde distingués par leur situation et par leurs connaissances des néccessités sociales, il ne manque pas d'esprits droits et impartiaux, qui se lèvent pour louer vos œuvres, pour défendre votre droit inviolable de citoyens et votre liberté encore plus inviolable de catholiques. Certes il suffit de n'être pas aveuglé par la passion pour voir combien c'est montrer peu de prévoyance et de noblesse que de frapper des hommes qui sans rien espérer et sans rien demander pour euxmêmes se dépensent tout entiers au service de la société. Que l'on considère seulement avec quel zèle ils s'appliquent à développer chez les enfants du peuple les germes de bonté naturelle qui autrement saraient étouffés, à leur détriment et au détriment d'autrui. Semences précieuses que, la grâce aidant, les religieux cultivent patiemment assidûment, préservent de toute atteinte mortelle et conduisent à maturité. C'est ainsi que sous leur influence s'épanouissent comme des fruits magnifiques l'amour éclairé de la vérité, l'honnêteté, le sentiment du devoir, la fermeté du caractère et la générosité dans le sacrifice. Et quoi de plus propre à assurer l'ordre et la prospérité des Etats ?

Cependant, chers fils, puisque la malignité du monde vous poursuit au point de prétendre faire œuvre utile et louable en foulant aux pieds dans vos personnes les droits les plus sacrés, et qu'elle croit ainsi 'rendre hommage à Dieu '[1]; adorez avec une humilité confiante les desseins de Dieu. S'il laisse parfois le droit succomber sous la violence, il ne le permet que dans des vues supérieures de plus grand bien, en outre c'est sa coutume de secourir efficacement et par des voies imprévues ceux qui souffrent pour lui et se confient à lui.

S'il place des obstacles et des contradictions sur la route de

---

[1] Ioann. xvi. 2.

ceux qui professent par état la perfection chrétienne, c'est afin d'éprouver et de fortifier leur vertu, c'est plus particulièrement pour affermir et retremper leurs âmes exposées à s'affaiblir dans une longue paix.

Tâchez donc de correspondre à ces vues paternelles de Dieu. Adonnez-vous avec un redoublement d'ardeur à une vie de foi, de prière et d'œuvres saintes. Faites régner parmi vous la discipline régulière, l'union fraternelle des cœurs, l'obéissance humble et empressée l'austérité du détachement et l'ardeur pieuse pour la louange divine. Que vos pensées soient hautes, vos résolutions généreuses et votre zélé infatigable pour la gloire de Dieu et l'extension de son regne ! Puisque, parle malheur des temps, vous vous trouvez ou déjà frappés ou menacés par des lois funestes de dispersion, vous reconnaîtrez que les circonstances vous imposent le devoir de défendre avec plus de zèle que jamais l'intégrité de votre esprit religieux contre le contact dissipant du monde, et de vous tenir toujours prêts et aguerris contre toute épreuve.

Sur ce point Nous vous rappelons que diverses instructions ont été adressées aux Réguliers par ce Siège Apostolique et que d'autres prescriptions sont émanées des Supérieurs euxmêmes. Il faut que les unes et les autres gardent leur pleine vigueur et soient observées en conscience.

Et maintenant, religieux de tout âge, jeunes ou vieux, levez les yeux vers vos illustres Fondateurs ! Leurs maximes vous parlent, leurs status vous guident, leurs exemples vous précèdent ! Que votre application la plus douce et la plus sainte soit de les écouter, de les suivre, de les imiter ! C'est ainsi qu'ont agi un grand nombre de vos aînés dans les temps les plus durs. C'est ainsi qu'ils vous ont transmis un riche héritage de courage invincible et de vertus sublimes. Montrez-vous dignes de tels pères et de tels frères afin que vous puissiez dire tous, en vous glorifiant justement : ' Nous sommes le fils et les frères des saints !' C'est ainsi que vous obtiendrez les plus grands avantages pour vousmêmes pour l'Eglise et pour la société. En vous efforçant d'atteindre le dergé de sainteté auquel Dieu vous a applés, vous mériterez les récompenses surabondantes qu'il vous a promises. L'Eglise, cette mère si tendre qui a comblé vos Instituts de ses faveurs, obtiendra de vous, en échange, une coopération plus fidèle et plus efficace que jamais à sa mission de paix et de salut. La paix, le salut, voilà les deux besoins urgents de la société

actuelle travaillée par tant de causes de corruption et d'affaiblisse-
ment.   Pour la secouer, pour la soulever, pour la ramener
repentante aux pieds de ce très miséricordieux Rédempteur, il faut
des hommes de vertu supérieure, de parole vive, de cœur apostolique, qui aient, en même temps, la puissance médiatrice d'attirer
les grâces célestes. Vous serez de ces hommes. Nous n'en
doutons pas, et vous deviendrez ainsi les bienfaiteurs les plus
opportuns et les plus insignes de la société.

Chers fils, la charité du Seigneur Nous inspire une dernière
parole pour raffermir en vous les sentiments dont vous êtes
animés envers tous ceux qui attaquent vos Instituts et veulent
entraver votre action.

Autant par conscience vous devez garder une attitude ferme
et digne, autant par profession vous devez vous montrer toujours
doux et indulgents, parce que c'est dans le Religieux que doit
particulièrement resplendir la perfection de cette vraie charité
qui se laisse toucher par la commisération, mais qui ne connait
point la colère. Sans doute à vous voir ainsi payés d'ingratitude,
à vous voir ainsi repoussés, la nature s'attriste, mais, cher fils,
que la foi vons réconforte par ses oracles ! Elle vous rappelle
l'exhortation sublime : 'Triomphez du mal par le bien.'[1] Elle
vous met sous les yeux l'incomparable magnanimité de l'Apôtre :
' On nous maudit et nous bénissons ; on nous persécute et nous
supportons ; on blasphème contre nous, et nous bénissons.'[2] Par
dessus tout elle vous invite à répéter la supplication du Bien-
faiteur suprême du genre humain, Jésus, suspendu sur la croix :
' Père, pardonnez-leur ! '

Donc, chers fils, ' fortifiez-vous dans le Seigneur.'[3] Vous
avez avec vous le Vicaire de Jésus-Christ, vous avez avec vous
tout la monde catholique qui vous regarde avec affection, respect
et reconnaissance.

Du haut du ciel vos glorieux pères, vos glorieux frères vous
encouragent.   Votre chef souverain, Jésus-Christ, vous ceint de
sa force et vous couvre de sa vertu.

Fils bien-aimés, adressez-vous à son Cœur divin avec une
confiance filiale et de ferventes prières. Vous y trouverez toute
la force necessaire pour vaincre les plus furieuses colères du
monde. Il y a une parole qui retentit à travers les siècles, toujours vivante, toujours pleine de consolation : ' Ayez confiance,
j'ai vaincu le monde.'[4]

1 Rom. xii. 21.   3 Eph. v. 10.
2 Cor. iv. 12, 13.   4 Ioann. xvi. 33.

Puissiez-vous trouver encore quelque consolation dans notre
Bénédiction qu'en ce jour, consacré à la mémoire triomphante des
Princes des Apôtres, Nous sommes heureux d'accorder dans toute
sa plénitude à chacun de vous et à toutes et chacune de vos
Familles, qui Nous sont très chères dans le Seigneur.

Donné à Rome près Saint Pierre le 29 Juin de l'année, 1901,
vingtquatrième de Notre Pontificat.

LEON XIII PAPE.

PAPAL EULOGY OF URSULINE NUNS

LEO XIII PIAS MULIERES SOCIETATIS S. URSULAE LAUDAT ET APL.
BENED. RECREAT

LEO PP. XIII

AD FUTURAM REI MEMORIAM

Romanorum Pontificum Decessorum Nostrorum vestigiis
insistentes erga pias sanctarum virginum Congregationes, quae
ad pietatis et charitatis opera exercenda institutae, potissimum
tam gravibus Ecclesiae temporibus optime de christiana re mereri,
sibi gloriae ducunt, grato quidem ac sollicito studio, curas cogi-
tationesque nostras convertimus. Has inter frugiferas, quibus
Ecclesia Christi laetatur, Congregationes, minime Nos latet iure
et merito arcessendam esse piam mulierum unionem, quam sancta
Angela Mericia sub titulo Societatis S. Ursulae, primum instituit;
fel. rec. Paulus PP. III, datis sub plumbo Litteris quinto idus
Iunii anno Incarnationis Domini MDXXXIV probavit; Sanctus
Karolus Borromaeus confirmavit; Decessor Noster Pius PP. IX
rec. mem. meritis laudibus est prosequutus; tandem a.
MDCCCLXVI Hieronymus Verzeri Brixiensis Antistes nonnullis
innovatis articulis ad pristinam formam restituit. Haec enim
societas in aedificationem familiarum et ad effundendum late per
mundum bonum Christi Jesu odorem erecta, uberrimos iugiter in
Ecclesiae Dei emolumentum protulit fructus. Et sane virgines
dictam in societatem adlectae tum Brixia tum Mediolani, tum
Bononiae, tum Ianuae, tum etiam in hac alma Urbe Nostra, atque
in longo terrarum marisque spatio dissitis Africae regionibus iuxta
instituti tabulas, tam doctrinae christianae tradendae, quam pluribus catholicis pietatis charitatisque operibus vacant. Hae pueros
ac puellas ad S. Synaxim prima vice properantes, praemissis piis
exercitationibus instruunt, hae Filiarum Mariae Unionibus, scholis
festivis, infantium asylis, societatibus mutui inter operarias auxilii

praesunt, advigilant; hae aegrotantibus assident; indumenta ac
sacra supellectilia Ecclesiis pauperibus comparant; hae bonorum
in vulgus diffusionem librorum curant; hae precibus, verbo ac
vitae innocentis exemplo et devios ad virtutis semitas revocant, et
innumeras prorsus animas Christo lucrifaciunt. Quae cum ita
sint Nos precibus annuentes Emi. Mediolanensis Antistitis S.R.E.
Cardinalis Ferrari, et Episcopi Brixiensis, aliorumque Longo-
bardiae Episcoporum, nec non dilectarum in Christo filiarum
Magdalenae Girelli ac Iuliae Vismara dictae Societatis Moderatri-
cium Generalium tum Brixiae cum Mediolani ipsas virgines
hortantes, ut in inceptis insistant, neque unquam a primaeva
Regula deflectant, quam ipsa Sancta Angela tradidit illique piae
unioni veluti testamento reliquit, omnibus et singulis filiabus
Sanctae Angelae Mericiae actu existentibus, quae integre servantes
Regulam uti supra diximus a Paulo Papa III. approbatam et
nuperrime in pristinum restitutam ab Hieronymo Verzeri Episcopo naviter incumbunt ad propriam ac proximorum salutem
industrio studio procurandam. ut meritis praemium nanciscantur,
et novum ad potiora capessenda stimulum coelestium munerum
auspicem, Nostraeque voluntatis ac benevolentiae pignus, Apostolicam per praesentes Benedictionem peramanter impertimur.
Volumus vero ut praesentium Litterarum transumptis seu exemplis, etiam impressis manu alicuius Notarii publici subscriptis et
sigillo personae in ecclesiastica dignitate constitutae munitis, eadem
prorsus fides adhibeatur, quae adhiberetur ipsis praesentibus, si
forent exhibitae vel ostensae.

. Datum Romae apud S. Petrum sub anulo Piscatoris die XII
Iulii MCMI, Pontificatus Nostri anno vigesimoquarto.

ALOIS. Card. MACCHI.

NOTICES OF BOOKS

L'ACTION DU CLERGÉ DANS LA REFORME SOCIALE. Par Paul Lapeyre. Paris: Lethielleux, 10, Rue Cassette. Price, 3 fr. 50 c.

THIS is the work of a French layman, who understands his country, who desires to serve the Church, and who appeals to the clergy to come out from their seclusion and wield the full power they hold to rescue France from the peril that threatens her. M. Lapeyre understands thoroughly the difficulties they have to contend with. He does not indulge, like Mr. Michael Davitt, in sweeping generalizations and dogmatic assertions, based on utterly untrustworthy and misleading information.

If there is one thing remarkable about the clergy of France during the past ten or fifteen years it is the wonderful unanimity with which they have followed the advice of Leo XIII. There were no more strenuous supporters of the monarchy in former days than the people of Brittany; yet when a vacancy occurred in one of the constituencies there, not many years ago, the clergy fought a stirring battle against the Comte de Blois, the Monarchical candidate, an excellent Catholic, and a man of the highest character, and returned by a big majority the Abbé Gayraud, who was pledged to support the Republic against all attacks. The writer of this note happened to be in France at the time and to meet a good many of the clergy, both secular and regular, in different parts of the country. They were almost unanimous in support of the action of the clergy of Brest. The religious were particularly emphatic in their support of the policy of the Pope. A few of the older curés still held out in private; but they did not seek to influence anyone with their opinions.

The clergy generally were thoroughly alive to the necessity of changing the character of the Republic; but in order to do that they felt that the only course for them to follow was to accept honestly and absolutely the Republican form of government. But the men who have captured the government of France are like the British Jingoes who denounce as pro-Boers all who differ from them on the subject of the war; if you do not see eye to eye with the Rousseaus and the Bourgeois, the

Millerands and the Brissons, you are an enemy of the Republic and an agent of the Monarchy, and men are to be got in foreign countries to take them at their word and to brand the poor Carmelites and Capuchins, the Benedictines and Trappists, who are hunted like malefactors from their country, as enemies of the Republic!

Why, one of the commonest charges made against the Bishops of France by Monarchists and Imperialists is that they are the slaves of the Republic and that they have pressed their clergy into the service in the most high-handed fashion. And as for the Religious Orders, they are more directly under the control of the Pope than the secular clergy and if they had not obeyed his directions in the spirit as well as in the letter they would very soon have felt the pressure of his authority. That they inculcated monarchical principles in their schools is a thing that may be asserted with impunity over here ; but it would be received with a rather grim smile where people know how much truth there is in it. Probably the assertion was intended more as a lesson to the clergy of Ireland than as a satisfactory explanation of the expulsion of the Religious Orders from France. We should be the very last to object to such a lesson when it is founded on knowledge or on authority, and Mr. Davitt is a man whose disinterestedness and sincerity we should never think of calling into question. But we think that in this matter he has not drawn his information from trustworthy sources. We think he can safely be defied to produce any proof that the Religious Orders of France, the Pope's own Body Guard, as they are sometimes called, disobeyed the instructions of the Holy See and inculcated monarchical principles and opposition to the Republic in their schools. They have indeed inculcated opposition to Freemasonry, to the secret power of the lodges, to anti-Christian legislation, to the infamies of De Lanessan, to the wholesale banishment of religion from the public schools ; all this, of course, is opposition to the Republic and is the work of traitors and conspirators.

In a great many respects the antidote to false notions of this kind will be found in the little work mentioned at the head of these observations. It deals with a problem that requires great skill and delicacy of treatment, and it has gone more deeply than one might be inclined to believe into the nature of the disease from which the Republic suffers, and of the remedies that many people consider necessary. We do not say that the work is very profound or very original; but for a *livre de circonstance*, and a popular treatise on a popular question, it is exceedingly clever and interesting.

J. F. H.

St. ANDREW THE APOSTLE, PATRON OF SCOTLAND. By the Rev. Gerald Stack. Catholic Truth Society of Scotland, 52 Sauchiehall-street, Glasgow.

IT is not easy to write a biography of one of the saints of the New Testament. With the exception of the Blessed Virgin, St. Joseph, St. John the Baptist, St. Peter, St. Paul, and St. Mary Magdalen, the details known are of the scantiest. If, therefore, one wishes to produce a sketch of any of the less known of the Apostles a good deal of filling has to be done in the way of description either of scenery or of the ways and habits of life that prevailed in the life-time of the Apostles. Father Stack has adopted this method in his admirable sketch of St. Andrew. He has made the most of the few facts that are narrated of St. Andrew by the four Evangelists and the other sacred writers. He has filled up the narrative of these events with a very interesting account of the 'Home Teaching,' the 'School Life,' and the 'Peasant Life' of Palestine in the days of the Apostles.

Perhaps the most interesting part of Father Stack's sketch is that in which he tells how St. Andrew became Patron of Scotland. For the sake of those of our readers who may not come across the pamphlet, we give this interesting sketch in Father Stack's own words :—

'The legendary accounts which were once current, and which represented the relics of St. Andrew as having been brought to Scotland directly from Patrae or from Constantinople, are now generally rejected. In consequence of the researches of Dr. Skene, it may now be regarded as certain that the devotion to St. Andrew was introduced into this country from England. The following is a brief statement of the events which led to St. Andrew being adopted as the national patron. It has been already stated that on the translation of St. Andrew's body from Patrae to Rome, portions of the Saint's relics found their way to several of the important cities of the Roman Empire. It was natural that Rome should be among the number of the cities thus favoured. St. Wilfrid, the great champion of Roman discipline, who had been chiefly instrumental in converting king Oswy and the

Northumbrians into Roman usage, had made several journeys to Rome, and when, in A.D. 674, he founded the church of Hexham, he dedicated it to Saint Andrew, towards whom he entertained a special devotion. Bishop Acca, who, in A.D. 709, succeeded St. Wilfrid in the See of Hexham, obtained certain relics of St. Andrew, with which he enriched the church that had been founded by his saintly predecessor. Acca was forced to retire from his diocese in A.D. 732, and during his exile spent some time in Fife. These events explain how a portion of the relics of St. Andrew were brought into Scotland.

‘At the time when Bishop Acca took refuge in Fife, the Pictish monarchy was ruled by Angus MacFergus, who reigned from A.D. 731 to A.D. 761, and who was, perhaps, the most powerful king that ever sat upon the Pictish throne. In A.D. 736 he completely subdued the Scots of Dalriada. The crowning victory gained by the king's arms in this campaign against the Scots was attributed by him to the protection of St. Andrew, whose relics had lately been brought into his dominions, and whose patronage had been specially invoked in his behalf. Gratitude prompted the victorious monarch to erect and richly endow a church in honour of his patron at a place formerly known as Kilrymont, but which was destined ever after to be known by the name of St. Andrews. Some years later, in conjunction with the Anglic kingdom of Mercia, he inflicted severe losses on the kingdom of Northumbria, and these new successes seemed to have confirmed his devotion to his patron St. Andrew, and to have prompted him to make new endowments in honour of that Apostle.

‘In A.D. 756 Angus further extended his conquests. In alliance with his former enemy, Eadberct, king of Northumbria, he marched against the Strathclyde Britons and put an end to a contest which had lasted some twelve years, by subduing their capital Alclyde, or Dumbarton. Thus, before his death, in 761, the northern monarch had elevated the Pictish kingdom to a certain supremacy extending, more or less, over all the territory now comprised in Scotland, and the solid establishment of the veneration of St. Andrew in the Pictish dominions, and his adoption as the special patron of the Pictish monarchy, prepared the way for his ultimate reception as patron of the Scottish nation.

‘In A.D. 844 the Pictish and Scottish kingdoms were finally united in the person of Kenneth MacAlpin, king of Dalriada; and Malcolm III. (A.D. 1005-1034) completed the unification of the territory of Scotland by the acquisition of Strathclyde and Bernicia. From this time forward the consolidation of the kingdom of Scotland was gradually completed, and St. Andrew, the chosen patron of the Pictish power, became ultimately recognized as the patron of the Scottish monarchy, of the Scottish people, and of the Scottish Church.’

We noticed only one printer's error, but that is a rather inconvenient one—'Sottish monarchy,' p. 25. On the whole the pamphlet is admirable, and well suited to excite the devotion of the people to their patron saint. That was the main object of the author in contributing so valuable a work to the Catholic Truth Society of Scotland.

J. B.

'BUT THY LOVE AND THY GRACE.' By Francis J. Finn, S.J., author of *Percy Wynn, Tom Playfair*, etc. New York : Benziger Brothers.

WE were, we believe, the very first, on this side of the Atlantic, to call attention to the remarkable stories of Father Finn, and to recommend them to all schools and colleges as elevating and, at the same time, stimulating reading for boys. Father Finn seems now to have turned his thoughts from the school, and to have given them to the active and busy life of the world. The heroine, as we may truly call her, of the present story, Regina O'Connell, is a poor girl who goes to confession every week, and who finds in her devotion to religion, not only the compensation for many trials and afflictions, but the strength to bear them with a joyful heart. The story is short; it is well told; and no one who begins to read it is likely to leave it down unfinished. There is just, perhaps, a little excess of melancholy, a superabundance of affliction, a tone of predominating grief, that we should like to see reduced to more common standards of experience; but, on the whole, the story promises well for Father Finn's new departure, and we wish him as great a measure of success with his new class of readers as he has won in the schools.

There is one word of criticism that we must be permitted to indulge in. Father Finn gives Irish names to nearly all the characters in this work, particularly to the lowly and the humble, and we are glad of it; but why give English names— " Percy Wynn," " Tom Playfair," etc.—to all his school heroes ? Is there not a touch of snobbishness in all this ? But it is scarcely fair to blame Father Finn for a fault which is just as characteristic of some of our own countrymen, who cry very loudly for the Irish language, and yet, when they wish to depict a respectable character, take care to give him an English name. All such people ought to be discountenanced.

J. B.

THE CATHOLIC CHURCH FROM WITHIN. With Preface by
the Cardinal Archbishop of Westminster. London:
Longmans, Green, & Co. 1901. Price, 6s. 6d. net.

WE gather from Cardinal Vaughan's preface that the author
of this sketch is a member of the laity, and we quite subscribe
to the idea that it has many advantages over one drawn by
a priest. It is freer, says the Cardinal, and perhaps more actual.
It does not pretend to be professional. It is not authoritative :—

'The book is written by a member of the laity ; by one who
has lived for years—from childhood—among men and women of
the world ; who has mixed freely with Protestants ; who has
travelled much, and has also lived much at home, occupied with
books as well as with the discharge of many and diverse duties.'

Such a writer, having at the same time the deeply religious
sense and an acute mind, is particularly well qualified to turn out
a book that should prove a guide and a help to many persons
concerned about their souls. The deep interest taken in the work
by Cardinal Vaughan shows what importance he attaches to it,
and he has touched off in the preface the features of the volume
that are most likely to commend it to the public, whether Catholic
or non-Catholic :—

'There is something' [writes His Eminence] 'that certainly
differentiates the intimacy of Catholic life from other forms of life
that may be domestic, beautiful, tender and affectionate, but are
not also Catholic. People hear of Catholic views, Catholic
feelings and instincts—of ways and practices that are peculiarly
and distinctively Catholic. They come across them now and
then ; they get glimpses and touches of them in Catholic homes.
But generally they get no systematic presentation of them, unless
they live on very intimate terms with Catholic friends ; and even
then the presentations of them is often but fragmentary and
disconnected. The author of this book sketches for the reader
many and various phases of Catholic life so that at last he may
get a very fair and complete picture of the whole. The outsider,
therefore, may feel pretty confident, when he has gone through
the book, that he has penetrated a Catholic home of the educated
class, and this without the trouble of introductions, and subjection
to the many inane formalities of society in a strange house.'

A work so highly praised by a member of the Sacred College
needs no commendation from us. At the same time we are
happy to call attention to some special merits of the work on
which His Eminence does not dwell. There are towards the end

of the book two or three chapters—those on 'Giving and Taking Scandal,' 'The Cultivation of Catholic Instincts,' 'Marriage and the Bringing up of Children,' 'Vocations and Religious Orders '— that seem to us to present Catholic doctrines and ideas in a language so fresh and unconventional, that we think they ought of themselves ensure the success of the book.

J. B.

CORAM SANCTISSIMO. London : Sands & Co.

THIS is another work from the pen of Mother M. Loyola. It contains forty visits to the Blessed Sacrament. These show that Mother M. Loyola is as much at home when depicting the trials, the aspirations, and the consolations of adults as in leading little children along the road of true penance. Each visit seizes, generally with thrilling vivacity, *one* idea ; the subject is weighed in the presence of our Lord, the conclusions are always practical. Take, for example, 'The Visit XL. *Life*.' It opens : ' Life is a school, neither more nor less. *Not more*. Therefore we must not expect to find satisfaction. . . . . *Not less*. Therefore we must beware of squandering the time given us for our final state. . . . . Let me be schooled by the tasks and trials, the little joys and sorrows and passing brightness of this life. . . . . And when my school days are over and my lessons here are learned dear Father, take me home.' In like manner we have *Praise*, ' *Possumus*,' *Changes*, *Darkness*, *Responsibility*, etc. All speak to the mind and heart.

J. M.

DE SACRAMENTIS. Auctore H. Noldin, S.J., S. Theologiae Professore in Universitate Oenipontana, Sumptibus Ranch. (Pustet). 1901.

THIS volume of Moral Theology deals with the Sacraments in general, Baptism, Confirmation, Eucharist, Penance, Extreme Unction and Holy Orders. Father Noldin does not profess to treat these subjects with all the fulness of the larger works which are useful principally for professors and priests who desire to study profoundly the many interesting and practical questions which abound in Moral Theology. He professes to write a work for the use of schools in which the varied course of theological learning prevents a very deep examination of any particular branch of divinity.

Though Father Noldin's work is limited by the end in view it deserves the attention of all theologians. It serves admirably for the end primarily in view. Its clearness makes it a very welcome companion for the hard-worked student. Its comparative completeness renders it sufficiently ample in dimensions for all practical purposes. Its practical nature makes it a very useful book not only for the student in the seminary but also for the missionary priest who cannot always devote as much time to the study of theology as he may desire.

It would be too much to expect that we could agree with all Father Noldin's opinions. We find no opinion, however, in the book which has not eminent supporters. Some of his views, nevertheless, in our opinion border on laxity. We may mention specially in this connection the opinion which is put forward in page 287, n. 270. Father Noldin holds, in that place, that a mortal sin not yet directly remitted by the absolution of the priest is validly confessed even if it be confessed as a sin already directly remitted in the Sacrament of Penance. Though this view has some modern upholders we think it intrinsically improbable. The priest in the Sacrament of Penance is a necessary judge of every cause that demands reconciliation with God. He must then know, as far as possible, whether or not his penitent necessarily requires reconciliation with the Almighty. He cannot know this unless the penitent explains whether his mortal sins were committed before or after his last valid confession. No doubt the sin in itself is the same whether it be already remitted or not but it is not the same in its present relations to God. These are the relations of which the priest is appointed judge in the tribunal of Penance. Again, it is the duty of the priest to impose a suitable penance on his penitent. Now a mortal sin already remitted deserves only a light penance whilst a mortal sin not already remitted demands a grave penance. How can the priest then fulfil this duty of imposing a suitable penance unless he knows whether or not the mortal sin confessed has been already remitted in the Sacrament of Penance.

On page 263, n. 245b., Father Noldin says that contrition must be supernatural 'ratione motivi.' He explains this to mean that the contrition must have some relation to God and must not be from a merely temporal motive such as health, fame, etc.

He rejects the view that the motive of contrition must be known by revelation through the *lumen fidei*. We quite agree with Father Noldin in this latter point though we would add that inasmuch as there is question of the validity of the Sacrament the view rejected by him must be upheld in practice since it is a probable opinion. We think, however, that Father Noldin's first statement is not sound as expressed by him. We do not see how a relation to God from a merely natural point of view can be called a supernatural motive. Father Noldin does not explain how faith is necessary in his view for an effective act of contrition. We presume that he does admit the necessity of faith in some way.

We do not wish to speak of other opinions of Father Noldin. Though we may differ from some of them none of them are rashly held by him. We recommend his book very strongly. It is very suitable as a class book for theological students. It is very useful for the missionary priest. We hope that other volumes will proceed from the pen of the learned author.

J. M. H.

DE GEMINO PROBABILISMO LICITO. DISSERTATIO CRITICO-PRACTICA EXARATA CONCILIATIONIS GRATIA. Auctore D. Majolo De Caigny, O.S.B. Brugis Typis Désclee, De Brouwer et Soc. 1901.

THIS interesting little volume is an attempt to reconcile Aequi-probabilism with Probabilism. Some years ago the author wrote a Dissertation in favour of Aequiprobabilism. The conclusions put forward in that book lead logically, in the author's opinion, to the mode of reconciliation which he at present suggests. He is prepared to accept the principle of Probabilists : *lex dubia non obligat*. He gives his interpretation of this saying. When one opinion is certainly more probable than another opposing view then it is practically certain. Consequently if it be in favour of the law the law is no longer in practical doubt and must, therefore, be followed. If neither opinion be clearly the more probable, then the law is doubtful and consequently the opinion which favours liberty can be followed with a safe conscience. This is, *a fortiori*, true if the opinion which favours liberty be certainly the more probable. Father De Caigny thinks that all reasonable Aequiprobabilists and Probabilists will admit these conclusions.

We have always thought that there is very little difference, in practice, between Aequiprobabilism and Probabilism as explained by the moderate upholders of both systems. We think, however, that in theory it is not easy to reconcile both views. We fear that Father De Caigny leaves untouched a very important portion of the opinions of Probabilists. We fear that Probabilists will not admit that an opinion always ceases to be solidly probable when the opposing view is clearly more probable. As long as an opinion remains solidly probable the opposing opinion cannot be free from reasonable practical doubt though it may be favoured with a greater degree of probability. A Probabilist will in those circumstances apply his principle ; *lex dubia non obligat.* Thus, theoretically, no common resting ground can be found for the two systems. J. M. H.

"*Ut Christiani ita et Romani sitis.*" "As you are children of Christ, so be you children of Rome."
Ex Dictis S. Patricii, In Libro Armacano, fol. 9.

The Irish Ecclesiastical Record

A Monthly Journal, under Episcopal Sanction.

Thirty-fifth Year]
No. 410.

FEBRUARY, 1902.

[**Fourth Series**
Vol. XI.

The Catholic University School of Medicine.
Right Rev. Monsignor Molloy, D.D., Dublin.

Ireland and America.
Rev. M. F. Skinnors, O.M.I., Dublin.

The Rise and Progress of Higher Criticism.
Rev. Reginald Walsh, O.P., Maynooth College.

'Luke Delmege.'
The Editor.

Trinity College and the University of Dublin.
His Grace the Archbishop of Dublin.

Notes and Queries.

THEOLOGY. *Rev. D. Mannix, D.D., Maynooth College.*
Questions Regarding the Confession and Absolution of Reserved Cases. Application of the Mass in case of Duplication.

LITURGY. *Rev. P. O'Leary, D.D., Maynooth College.*
Must the Wax Candles Required by the Rubrics be entirely of Bees' Wax? The Grains of Incense for the Paschal Candle.

Documents.
Roman Authorities again call attention to the Form of Correspondence. The Foundation of New Religious Houses—Rules laid down by Propaganda.

Nihil Obstat.
GERALDUS MOLLOY, S.T.D.
Censor Dep.
Imprimatur.
✠ GULIELMUS,
*Archiep. Dublin.,
Hiberniae Primas*

BROWNE & NOLAN, Limited
Publishers and Printers, 24 & 25
NASSAU STREET, DUBLIN.

. . PRICE ONE SHILLING . .

THE CATHOLIC UNIVERSITY SCHOOL OF MEDICINE

THE present position of the Catholic University School of Medicine is, I think, only imperfectly understood, even by the friends and supporters of the University. During the past few years, the School has advanced by leaps and bounds, both as regards the efficiency of its work, and the number of its students. It has lately fallen to my lot, to give a short account of this progress, before the Royal Commission now sitting on Irish University Education ; and I frankly confess that the facts which it was my pleasant duty to collect and set forth, were a surprise even to myself.

The success which the School has achieved, is largely due to the hearty support it has received from the Catholic clergy and people of Ireland. And the idea has occurred to me, that the publication of my statement, in the I. E. RECORD, would be gratifying to our friends, and would help to secure for the School a continuance of their sympathy and support. I have accordingly prepared it for publication, from my notes ; and it appears in the following pages pretty nearly as it was spoken before the Commission.

I.—CONSTITUTION OF THE GOVERNING BODY.

At the outset, it is well to explain that the Catholic University School of Medicine stands on a somewhat different footing from that of University College in St. Stephen's

Green. It is managed by a Board of Governors, created by an Order of the Lord Lieutenant in Council under the Educational Endowments (Ireland) Act of 1885. This Board of Governors is a Body Corporate, with perpetual succession and a common seal; and it has power to acquire and hold property, real and personal, for the purposes of the School. Thus the School has a legal position in the eyes of the State, comparable with that of the other Medical Schools in Ireland, governed by chartered bodies. I propose to tell the Commissioners very briefly how this has come about.

The School was founded by the Catholic Bishops of Ireland, in the year 1855. The buildings were purchased and equipped out of monies collected from the people, who were just then reccvering from the effects of the great famine. The teaching staff were paid, for many years, by means of an annual collection made for the purpose; and the cost of maintenance was met, partly out of the same annual collection, and partly out of capital. But, about twenty years ago, the capital fund of the University was exhausted, and it was found no longer possible to continue the annual collection. Since then, the Professors have received no salaries, and the cost of maintaining the buildings and equipments, has been a first charge on the fees paid by the students. What remains of the fees, after this charge is defrayed, is divided between the Professors and Lecturers, according to a Scheme arranged by the Faculty of the School.

In the year 1891, the Bishops gave their consent that the School, and its endowments, should be dealt with by the Educational Endowments Commission, constituted under the Act of 1885. A Scheme was accordingly prepared by the Commissioners, for the future government and management of the School; and this Scheme, after passing through the various stages provided by the Act, was finally approved by the Lord Lieutenant in Council, on the twenty-fourth of May, 1892. The endowments transferred to the new Governing Body were : (1) The buildings and equipment of the School ; (2) A sum of £1,000, part of a bequest at the time in the hands of the Bishops, for the purposes of the Catholic University; and (3) £500 Bank of Ireland Stock, another bequest, yielding about £55 a year. This was the sum total of the endowments with which the School was launched on its new career.

The sum of £1,000, just mentioned, together with a further sum of £3,000, which was soon afterwards acquired from another source, was spent almost immediately, by the new governors, in improving the buildings and equipment of the School; and the income of the Bank of Ireland Stock was allocated to Prizes for the students. Accordingly, the buildings and equipment, as they now stand, and the small income of £55 a year, constitute at present the whole endowment of the School.

It is provided by the Scheme of the Educational Endowments Commission that the Governing Body shall consist of four *ex-officio* members; three representatives of the Faculty of Medicine in the School; three representatives of medical science outside the School; and one representative of the Bishops. The following is a list of the Governors, at the present time.

Ex-Officio Members.

1. Most Rev. William J. Walsh, D.D., Archbishop of Dublin, Chairman.
2. Right Rev. Gerald Molloy, D.D., D.Sc., Rector of the Catholic University, Vice-Chairman.
3. Sir Christopher Nixon, LL.D., M.D., F.R.C.P.I., Dean of Faculty.
4. Very Rev. Robert Carbery, Dean of Residence.

Representatives of the Faculty.

5. Patrick J. Hayes, M.D., F.R.C.S.E., F.R.U.I.
6. Ambrose Birmingham, M.D., F.R.U.I., F.R.C.S.I.
7. D. J. Coffey, M.A., M.B., F.R.U.I.

Representatives of Medical Science.

8. Thomas More Madden, M.D., F.R.C.S.E.
9. Richard F. Tobin, F.R.C.S.I.
10. Joseph F. O'Carroll, M.D., F.R.C.P.I.

Representative of the Bishops.

11. Most Rev. John Healy, D.D., Bishop of Clonfert.

II.—No Share in Public Endowments.

In order to understand fully the position occupied by the Catholic University Medical School, it is important to bear in mind that there are six Medical Schools in Ireland, and six only: three in Dublin, and three in the provinces. The three Medical Schools in Dublin are, the School of Trinity College, the School of the College of Surgeons, and the School of the Catholic University. In the provinces, the three Schools are those of Queen's College, Belfast, Queen's College, Cork, and Queen's College, Galway. All these Schools, with the single exception of the Catholic University School, have received large endowments from public funds.

The Schools of the three Queen's Colleges, with which the School of the Catholic University is brought into direct competition, under the Royal University, were all built and equipped out of public money ; the salaries of the Professors are paid by the Imperial Treasury ; and from the same source, an annual grant is made for the working expenses and maintenance of the Schools. Moreover, special grants are made, from time to time, for additions and improvements, as occasion requires. Thus, for example, in the three years 1891-1894, Belfast received special grants amounting to £7,842, chiefly for its chemical department. The Catholic University School, and it alone, has received nothing from the State.

III.—Progress of the School.

The number of students in the School has been rapidly increasing of late years, especially since the creation of the new Governing Body, in 1892 ; and I am informed that it is now the largest of all the Medical Schools in Ireland. I have asked for returns showing the progress of the School, in this respect, as compared with the other Medical Schools. It appears that the most authentic evidence on this point, applicable to all the Schools, is furnished by the number of new students, from each School, registered each year by the General Medical Council. Accordingly I have prepared a Table showing how this register stands, for the last five years, in the case of all the Irish Schools. It will be seen that, whereas in the first year of the period, the Catholic

University stands only fourth on the list, as regards the number of new students, in the last year of the period, it stands first.

TABLE I.

SHOWING THE NUMBER OF NEW STUDENTS REGISTERED FROM EACH OF THE IRISH MEDICAL SCHOOLS, IN EACH YEAR FROM 1896 TO 1900 INCLUSIVE.

	Catholic Univ.	Trinity College [1]	Coll. of Surgeons	Belfast	Cork	Galway	Total
1896	43	64	59	47	42	9	264
1897	45	47	38	49	22	8	209
1898	55	56	35	38	37	10	231
1899	50	57	50	50	38	13	258
1900	72	48	43	46	32	10	251
Total,	265	272	225	230	171	50	1213

Another kind of evidence bearing on this subject, is furnished by the number of students returned by each School, as being engaged each year in practical anatomy, commonly called 'Dissections.' This return is available for the Dublin Schools only ; and it is shown in the following Table for the last five years. Here again, we can see the progress of the Catholic University School. In the first years of the period, it stands lower than the other two Dublin Schools, whereas in the last year it stands higher.

TABLE II.

SHOWING THE NUMBER OF STUDENTS 'RETURNED FOR DISSECTIONS,' IN EACH OF THE DUBLIN MEDICAL SCHOOLS, IN EACH YEAR FROM 1896 TO 1901 INCLUSIVE.

	Catholic University	Trinity College [2]	College of Surgeons
1896-7	118	185	170
1897-8	115	188	150
1898-9	113	181	141
1899-00	123	170	130
1900-01	156	141	125

[1] In my evidence before the Commissioners, the return for Trinity College was left out, as Trinity College is excluded from their inquiry.
[2] In my evidence before the Commission, Trinity College was left out, as before.

It will be observed that, in the year 1900-1901, there was a sudden rise in the number of students 'returned for Dissections' from the Catholic University School, while there was rather a falling off in the other two Schools. I was anxious to ascertain whether this rise might not be due to some temporary or accidental circumstance; and accordingly I thought it well to obtain the return for the current year, 1901-1902. This return was furnished to me just before the sitting of the Commission, and shows the numbers as follows : Catholic University, 162 ; Trinity College, 115 ; College of Surgeons, 13C. Thus it appears that the great rise of last year has been fully maintained in the present year.

The most direct evidence of the size of a school, is to be found in the actual number of students attending lectures from year to year. This evidence we have not got either for Trinity College or for the College of Surgeons. We have it, however, for the three Queen's Colleges, and for the Catholic University School ; and as it enables us to trace the progress of each of these Schools from year to year, I thought it would be interesting to give the record for a somewhat lengthened period, say for fifteen years, from 1886-1887 to 1900-1901.

TABLE III.

SHOWING THE NUMBER OF STUDENTS ATTENDING LECTURES IN THE MEDICAL SCHOOLS OF THE CATHOLIC UNIVERSITY, AND EACH OF THE THREE QUEEN'S COLLEGES, IN EACH YEAR FROM 1886-1887 TO 1900-1901.

——	Catholic University	Belfast	Cork	Galway	Total
1886-7 -	105	240	176	45	566
1887-8 -	108	227	177	40	552
1888-9 -	120	222	172	42	556
1899-90 -	153	250	167	46	616
1890-1 -	158	229	180	37	604
1891-2 -	183	270	190	38	690
1892-3 -	158	243	200	41	642
1893-4 -	201	248	195	46	690
1894-5 -	203	212	172	54	641
1895-6 -	195	228	168	34	625
1896-7 -	200	227	164	32	623
1897-8 -	195	223	138	20	576
1898-9 -	210	206	137	29	582
1899-00 -	203	214	135	39	591
1900-01 -	260	226	130	29	645

A glance at this Table will show that the Catholic University School has been steadily advancing during the whole period under review. At the beginning of the period, it was far below both Belfast and Cork; about the middle of the period, it passed Cork, and has ever since remained ahead of it; while towards the end of the period, it closed up on Belfast, and eventually passed it. Again, it will be seen that the numbers of the Catholic University School have more than doubled within the period, while those of all the other Schools have fallen off. It is interesting also to note that a sudden increase of students in the Catholic University School, came in the year 1893-1894, and has since been steadily maintained. This was the first year after the management of the School had been handed over to the new Governing Body.

IV.—Efficiency as a Teaching Institution.

I have dwelt with some minuteness on these details, because it seems to me that the remarkable growth of our School, without the aid of public endowments, is a proof that it enjoys the confidence of a large section of the people of this country. I now pass on to show that it deserves that confidence, by reason of its efficiency as a teaching institution. There are two ways in which this efficiency may be tested : First, by the qualifications of the teaching staff; and Secondly, by the success of the students, in open competition with the students of other Schools.

As regards the teaching staff, I submit a list of the Professors and Assistant Teachers, in the various departments, with a statement of their qualifications, as they are usually set forth in the Programme of our School. The senior members of the staff are all men of established reputation, whose names speak for themselves. Of the junior members, whose names are not yet so well known to fame, I may say generally that they have nearly all passed through the Royal University, and have obtained the highest Honours and Prizes, both during their medical Course, and after taking out their degree.

THE TEACHING STAFF.

ANATOMICAL DEPARTMENT.

A. Birmingham, M.D., B.Ch., B.A.O., R.U.I., F.R.C.S.I., L.R.C.P.I. ; Fellow and Examiner in Anatomy, Royal University, Ireland ; Examiner in Anatomy, University of Cambridge, and Royal College of Surgeons and Conjoint Board, R.C.P. and R.C.S., Ireland ; Past President, Anatomical and Physiological Section, Royal Academy of Medicine, Ireland ; Past Vice-President and Secretary, Anatomical Society of Great Britain and Ireland.

Demonstrators of Anatomy.

P. J. Fagan, F.R.C.S.I. ; Surgeon to St. Vincent's Hospital, Extern Department.

George M. Keating, B.A. (in Biology), R.U.I., M.B., B.Ch., B.A.O., R.U.I., F.R.C.S.I.

PHYSIOLOGICAL DEPARTMENT.

Emeritus Professor.

Charles Coppinger, F.R.C.S.I., M.D., M.Ch. (*Hon. Causa*), R.U.I. ; Surgeon to the Mater Misericordiæ Hospital ; Consulting Surgeon to St. Michael's Hospital, Kingstown ; Examiner in Physiology, Royal College of Surgeons, Ireland.

Professor.

Denis J. Coffey, M.A., M.B., B.Ch., B.A.O. ; Fellow and Examiner in Physiology, Royal University, Ireland ; Lecturer on Physiology and Biology, St. Patrick's College, Maynooth.

Demonstrator of Histology.

Michael Curran, M.A., M.B., B.Ch., B.A.O., R.U.I.

DEPARTMENT OF CHEMISTRY.

Hugh Ryan, M.A., D.Sc. ; Fellow, and Examiner in Chemistry, Royal University of Ireland.

Assistant to the Professor.

George Ebrill, B.A. (in Chemistry and Physics), R.U.I.

DEPARTMENT OF SURGERY.

Patrick J. Hayes, F.R.C.S.E., M.D., M.Ch. (*Hon. Causa*), R.U.I. ; Senior Surgeon, Mater Misericordiæ Hospital ; Consulting Surgeon, St. Michael's Hospital, Kingstown ; Visiting Surgeon, St. Patrick's College, Maynooth ; Fellow and Examiner in Surgery, Royal University of Ireland.

Assistant to the Professor.

John S. M'Ardle, F.R.C.S.I. ; Surgeon to St. Vincent's Hospital ; Member of Council R.C.S.I.

MEDICINE.

Sir Christopher Nixon, M.D. (*Hon. Causa*), R.U.I., A.B., M.B., LL.D., Univ. Dub.; Fellow, R.C.P.I.; Licentiate, R.C.S.I.; Senior Physician to the Mater Misericordiæ Hospital; Member of Senate of Royal University of Ireland; Member of General Medical Council; Visiting Physician to St. Patrick's College, Maynooth.

MIDWIFERY AND DISEASES OF WOMEN.

Alfred J. Smith, M.B., M.CH., M.A.O. (Irel.), F.R.C.S.I., L.M.R.C.P.I.; Examiner in Midwifery, &c., Royal University of Ireland; Gynæcologist, St. Vincent's Hospital, Stephen's-green; Fellow and Member of Council, British Gynæcological Society, London.

DEPARTMENT OF PATHOLOGY AND BACTERIOLOGY.

Edmond J. M'Weeney, M.A., M.D., M.CH., M.A.O., M.R.C.P.I.; Examiner in Pathology, Royal University of Ireland; Pathologist to the Mater Misericordiæ Hospital; Bacteriologist to the Local Government Board, Ireland; President of the Pathological Section of the Royal Academy of Medicine, Ireland.

DEPARTMENT OF MATERIA MEDICA AND PHARMACY.

Martin J. Dempsey, B.A., M.D. (with Gold Medal), B.CH., B.A.O., R.U.I.; Fellow, Royal College of Physicians, Ireland; Examiner in Materia Medica, Royal University; Physician, Mater Misericordiæ Hospital.

Assistant to the Professor.

Lewis More-O'Ferrall, F.R.C.S.I., L. and L.M.R.C.P.I.; Physician to the Children's Hospital, Dublin.

DEPARTMENT OF MEDICAL JURISPRUDENCE AND HYGIENE.

Antony Roche, M.R.C.P., L.M., L.R.C.S.I.; Fellow of the Sanitary Institute of London; Member of the Society of Public Analysts; Examiner in Medical Jurisprudence and Hygiene, Royal University of Ireland.

DEPARTMENT OF OPHTHALMOLOGY.

Louis Werner, B.A., M.B., B.CH., F.R.C.S.I.; Ophthalmic Surgeon, Mater Misericordiæ Hospital; Examiner in Ophthalmic and Aural Surgery, Royal University; Assistant Surgeon, National Eye and Ear Infirmary.

DEPARTMENT OF BIOLOGY.

Biology.

George Sigerson, M.D., M.CH., F.R.U.I., L.R.C.P.I., M.R.I.A.; Examiner in Biology, Royal University of Ireland; Fellow of the Linnean Society, London.

Practical Biology (R.U.I. Course).

Alexander J. Blayney, M.A., M.B., B.Ch., B.A.O. (with First Place, First Honours, and First Exhibition), F.R.C.S.I.; Examiner in Biology, Royal University of Ireland; Assistant Surgeon to the Mater Misericordiæ Hospital.

Elementary Biology.

Denis J. Coffey, M.A. (in Biology), M.B., B.Ch., B.A.O.; Winner of University Studentship, R.U.I.; Lecturer on Biology, St. Patrick's College, Maynooth.

DEPARTMENT OF PHYSICS.

Natural Philosophy (R.U.I. Course).

J. A. M'Clelland, M.A., Royal University, B.Sc., Cambridge (for research work); Fellow and Examiner in Natural Philosophy, Royal University of Ireland.

Elementary Physics.

P. J. Fagan, Fellow and Licentiate, R.C.S.I., L. and L.M.R.C.P.I.; Surgeon to St. Vincent's Hospital, Dublin (Extern Department).

DEPARTMENT OF DENTISTRY.

Kevin E. O'Duffy, L.D.S., R.C.S.E.; Dental Surgeon to St. Vincent's Hospital, Dublin; Lecturer on Mechanical Dentistry, and Assistant Dental Surgeon, Dental Hospital, Ireland; President, Dental Students' Society of Ireland.

With respect to the students of the School, it is well to point out that they are free to present themselves either for the Conjoint examinations of the College of Physicians and the College of Surgeons, or for the examinations of the Royal University. In the one case, the successful candidates get a Licence to practice; in the other, they get a medical Degree. The Conjoint examinations offer the more easy approach to the medical profession; partly, because the examinations of the Royal University are of a higher standard of difficulty; and partly, because the Royal University requires a student to pass the Matriculation examination, and the First University examination in Arts, before he is allowed to present himself for his first examination in Medicine. Hence the Conjoint examinations are the more popular with students; especially with those who wish to reach their profession in the shortest time, and with the least trouble to themselves.

I find that, for the last eight or ten years, on the average, about 40 per cent. of the students of our School go up for the examinations of the Royal University, and 60 per cent. for the Conjoint examinations. There is no room for competition at the Conjoint examinations, as no Prizes are offered. But the Royal University offers, each year, to competition a small number of Exhibitions and other Prizes, in connection with their medical examinations. Taking the returns of the last eight years, I have made out the following Table of the Exhibitions gained, in that time, by the students of our School, and of the other Medical Schools that enter into the competition. I have also set down, for the purpose of comparison, the number of students, from each School, who have passed the examinations in the same time.

TABLE IV.

SHOWING THE NUMBER OF EXHIBITIONS GAINED BY THE STUDENTS OF THE CATHOLIC UNIVERSITY SCHOOL OF MEDICINE, AND THE SCHOOLS OF THE THREE QUEEN'S COLLEGES, AT THE MEDICAL EXAMINATIONS OF THE ROYAL UNIVERSITY, IN THE YEARS 1893-1900.

—	Catholic Univ.	Belfast	Cork	Galway	Total
First Class Exhibitions -	17	13	6	2	38
Second Class Exhibitions -	15	22	13	4	54
Total, - -	32	35	19	6	92
Number of Passes in the same time, - -	422	859	396	144	1,821

This Table shows that our School gained one Exhibition for every 13.2 students that passed the examinations; Belfast, one for every 24.5 students; Cork, one for every 21 students; and Galway, one for every 24 students. It is only fair, however, to take into account that the students who go up to the examinations of the Royal University, from our School, are only 40 per cent. of the whole, and that they are presumably a better class, taken all round, than those who go up for the Conjoint examinations; whereas, in the Queen's Colleges, a much larger proportion go up for the Royal University examinations. All I want to urge is, that our students are well able to hold their own, in fair and open competition, against the students of the endowed medical schools. And in this connection, I may be allowed to observe that we have gained a larger number of First Class Exhibitions than any other school.   Therefore, putting the best against the best, we stand absolutely first.

The Senate of the Royal University offers, each year, to competition, a Travelling Medical Scholarship of £100, subject to the condition that the successful candidate must go to some foreign school of medicine, and study there for a period of six months. Since 1893, four such Scholarships have been awarded, and one of these has been gained by a student of our School. A still higher Prize is the Medical Studentship, which is worth £200 a year, for two years. This Studentship was first established in 1893; and since then, five have been awarded altogether, of which students from our School have gained two.   Two Studentships in Biology, and only two, have been awarded since the foundation of the University; and both of these have been gained by students of our School. Lastly, it is the practice of the Senate, from time to time, to award a Gold Medal, in the case of highly distinguished answering, at the M.D. examination. Since 1893, six Gold Medals have been thus awarded; and of these, students from our School have gained four.

V.—Material Resources: Claim for Endowment.

It remains for me to give some account of the material resources of the School. I have already mentioned that the Governing Body expended all their available funds—about £4,000—in the year 1892, on the improvement of the buildings and equipment. But this was only a temporary makeshift. All that we could do with £4,000 was to add a little to the buildings; to provide some necessary apparatus; and generally, to put the School into decent working order, while waiting for better things. A sum of £4,000 is very small compared to the requirements, at the present day, of a well-equipped medical school for two hundred and sixty students. Moreover, I should tell the Commissioners that the School buildings, originally intended for about a hundred students, are totally inadequate, even with the additions recently made, to afford accommodation for the immense numbers now crowded into them. One unfortunate result of this deficiency of accommodation, is that it doubles the labours, in some cases, of our teaching staff; some of our Professors being obliged to divide their classes into two sections, and give every lecture twice over, first to one section and then to the other.

It appears to me that one of the most urgent needs connected with University education in Ireland, at the present moment, is to provide this School with buildings and equipment, together with an endowment for maintenance, worthy of the work it is doing, and such as will enable it to carry on that work more efficiently, and under more favourable conditions. I submit that we are entitled to such a provision on the ground of justice. We are also entitled to it on the ground of public policy. Our School is the largest medical school in Ireland; we have an efficient teaching staff; our students gain the highest prizes in open competition with the students of the endowed schools; they are destined to fill posts of great responsibility in the public service—in the army, in the navy, in workhouse hospitals, in county infirmaries, in dispensaries. Surely it is the interest of the State that these men should get their training in well-appointed and spacious halls, and that the teaching staff, which is charged with their education, should be provided with all the resources that modern science can supply.

If the case that I have made, on behalf of the Catholic University School of Medicine, should commend itself to the Commission as fair and reasonable, it is easy to point out the remedy, or, in the words of the warrant, 'the reform,' that is desirable in order to render the condition of this School, so far as its scope extends, 'adequate to the needs of the Irish people.' None of the difficulties that are said to surround the general University question have any bearing on the Medical School. Here, we have in existence a Governing Body, created by an Order of the Lord Lieutenant in Council, under an Act of the Imperial Parliament ; and all that is needed is to furnish that Body with a capital sum sufficient to provide the necessary buildings and equipment, together with an annual grant for maintenance, and for the salaries of the teaching staff, on a scale commensurate with that which is adopted in the medical schools already endowed by the State.

VI.—ORIGINAL RESEARCH.

I should like, if I may, to add a few words on the subject of original research. It is the business of a medical school, not only to teach what is already known, but also to extend the bounds of human knowledge, in the various branches of medical science. Great progress is made, from day to day, in Physiology, Pathology, Bacteriology, Anatomy, Chemistry ; and I submit that it is the duty of every medical school to take part in this progress. Some of the Commissioners will, perhaps, remember how strongly this principle was urged by the late Professor Huxley, during the last twenty years of his life ; and it is now, I think, generally accepted, almost as an axiom, by the highest authorities on the subject. I would, therefore, suggest that, in the reforms they may recommend, the Commissioners should not lose sight of original investigation. I feel confident that there is in Ireland a great store of intellectual power available for the work of research, if only the means and the opportunity were afforded for its development.

I do not confine this claim to medical schools. What I say with respect to original investigation in the various branches of medical science, I would say likewise for every other department of University work. But the case of medical schools comes vividly before me, at the present moment, because we have just now, in our own School, several men who have every qualification for carrying out original research, and who lack only the material resources necessary for doing it. Perhaps I may be allowed to give some evidence on this point.

I will take three typical examples. Among the subjects that lend themselves most readily to original research, in a medical school, are certainly included Pathology, Bacteriology, Physiology, and Chemistry. Now, in each of these departments, we are fortunate enough to have at present, among the younger members of our staff, a Professor specially prepared and equipped for original investigation. I will sketch very briefly the training which each of them has had.

To begin with the Professor of Pathology and Bacteriology. He read a complete course of Arts, and a complete course of Medicine, in the Royal University; getting the M.A. Degree in Arts, in 1887, and the M.D. Degree in Medicine, in 1891. During his course in Arts, he obtained a Studentship in Modern Languages, worth £100 a year for five years. Having a bent for research, he took advantage of his Studentship to go to the University of Vienna, in 1888, to study Pathology; and, in 1889, he went to Berlin, to work at Bacteriology, under Professor Koch. After his return, he took out his Degree of M.D., and was appointed professor of Pathology and Bacteriology in our School; this being, I understand, the first appointment of a special professor, in these subjects, made in any Irish medical school. I may say, he is now recognised as one of the leading authorities on Bacteriology in this country; and his lectures are attended not only by medical students, but by a considerable number of qualified professional men. He devotes a good deal of his time to original investigation, but he is greatly hampered in his work for want of space.

Next in order comes the Professor of Physiology. He also read a course of Arts and a course of Medicine, in the Royal University; getting his B.A. Degree in 1886, and his M.B. in 1888. He afterwards took out his M.A. in 1897. He got a Studentship in Biology, in 1889, which was worth £100 a year for three years; and, in 1890, he was appointed Assistant to the Professor of Physiology in our School. Wishing to make himself acquainted with the methods of teaching, and to put himself in touch with the work done, in other universities, he went to Louvain for three months

in the summer of 1894, and worked at Histology under
Professor Gilsen ; in 1896, he went for six weeks to Leipzig ;
in 1897, for six weeks to Marburg ; in 1899, for two months
to Munich, where he worked in the laboratory of Von
Kupfer, chiefly at the histology of the nervous system ; in
1900, he went again to Leipzig—this time for three months
—and worked, at the same subject, in the laboratory of
Professor His ; and, lastly, in the summer of 1901, he went
for three months to Madrid, and worked in the laboratory
of Professor Ramon y Cajal, who I am informed is the
highest authority in Europe on this particular branch of
Histology. All this time, this laborious student was doing
hard work in our School, first as Assistant to the Professor
of Physiology, afterwards as Lecturer in the subject, from
1893, and finally as full Professor from 1897. It would be
difficult, I think, to find anywhere a more striking example
than this of a keen desire for original investigation, combined
with great devotion to work:

My third example is our Professor of Chemistry. He
read a full course of Arts in the Royal University, taking his
B.A. Degree in 1895, and his M.A. in 1897, both with First
Class Honours, in Chemistry and Experimental Physics. At
the M.A. examination, he was awarded a Gold Medal for
highly distinguished answering in these subjects. In 1898, he
got a Studentship in the same subjects, which was worth
£100 a year for three years. He was also awarded, about
the same time, a Scholarship, by the Commissioners of the
great Exhibition of 1881. By the aid of these Prizes, he
was able to spend two years in the laboratory of Professor
Fischer of Berlin, devoting himself largely to original
research. On his return to Ireland, he got the Degree of
D.Sc. in the Royal University, and afterwards a Fellowship.
A vacancy having occurred, about the same time, in the
Chair of Chemistry, in our School, he was appointed to fill
it. Since his appointment, he has devoted the greater part
of his fees to the improvement of the chemical equipment
of the School, and to the maintenance of his department.

Now, it seems to me that these men—and I put them
forward only as examples, we have others of the same

stamp—have given abundant evidence of the qualities that go to make up the successful investigator: capacity, devotion to their work, trained skill, and, permeating all, the magnetic influence of the great masters at whose feet they have sat. But, under the present conditions of our School, original investigation is practically impossible to them. They have no space to work in ; the equipment at hand is deficient for research ; and their time is wholly absorbed in teaching. What they need is not much, but it is essential. In the first place, more room ; next, assistance in carrying on the teaching work of the School, so as to leave them more leisure for original work ; thirdly, improved equipment ; and lastly, a modest competence to enable them to live.

Just one word more. There are certain favoured spots dotted over the Globe, which supply gold for the use of the whole civilized world. In Ireland, there is a gold-mine of intellect, which once was the wonder of Europe, but which for centuries has been little worked, owing to the unhappy circumstances of her history. But the mine is still there ; and it needs only a comprehensive Scheme of University Education to make it available for the use of the nation, and of the world. Such a scheme of education has long been the dream of enthusiasts. It depends largely on the work of this Commission, whether or no it is now, at last, to become a reality.

GERALD MOLLOY.

IRELAND AND AMERICA

SOME NOTES OF A MISSION TOUR IN THE UNITED STATES

I

ON landing in New York I realized for the first time that America was a foreign country. I had always been accustomed to look on the United States as an expansion of Ireland and Great Britain, especially of Ireland. I was speedily undeceived. In numberless instances I found the sharpest contrasts between the new country and the old. The character of the people, their features, their habits, their tastes, their amusements, their manners—all, with the exception of their language, made me think that America resembled Ireland much less than does France or Italy or Germany. Indeed for a while I felt as if I had been wafted away into quite another sphere of existence and as if my voyage across the ocean had been an aerial journey to Mars or Mercury. This feeling of strangeness and isolation, however, soon wore off and I felt myself akin to the world around me.

I expected much from New York and, as usual in cases of great expectations, I was somewhat disappointed. My first impressions of the great city were decidedly unfavourable. The sight that thrust itself most aggressively upon me was that of the huge ugly overgrown ' stores ' and hotels, which shot abruptly up into the sky, looking down with contempt on the mere ten or twelve-storey buildings which flanked them on either side. I could not help imagining that the streets had been suddenly run up while the city architect was enjoying his holiday in Coney Island, or that they had been planned by him in some hideous nightmare.

Not of course that there are not magnificent buildings in New York, and very many of them, too, buildings that vie in splendour and in beauty with any to be found in London, or Paris, or Berlin. I need only instance St. Patrick's Cathedral, which crowns Madison-avenue, and which is undoubtedly the chief architectural glory of the city. Still I cannot help feeling that on the whole New York lacks grace and symmetry and picturesqueness. As a city I should prefer Boston with its stately mansions, its magnificent parks and boulevards, its splendid library, its broad open streets and its unique underground tramway system. Washington and Buffalo, too, impressed me as being more beautiful than New York; but I think Chicago sins infinitely more than the latter place against the canons of civic architecture as well (so it is said) as against certain other canons of much greater moment.

Perhaps, in fairness, I ought to add that my first impressions of New York might have been tinged by some little personal disappointments. There was some excuse for the bias if it did exist. I landed on the coldest, dreariest and wettest day that I experienced in America; I was charged 2½ dollars (10s.) for a two-mile drive in a cab (what would cost only 75 cents. in any other American city). Worse still, the entire male and female population seemed to be worked up to a state of the wildest patriotic excitement. Such shouting and hand-shaking, such cheering and laughing, such streamers and bunting, such triumphal arches and triumphal greetings! The Stars and Stripes of course floating from every house and waved by every hand, and thrust into every face, and depicted in every broach and button and pin. Everybody seemed to be stricken with an acute attack of neurotic insanity.

It was all for Dewey, who was to arrive the next day—Dewey the ' hero ' of Manilla ; the conqueror of the Spanish eastern flotilla ; the greatest Admiral, you were gravely informed, that ever commanded a vessel since the days of Noah! I was due in Boston in three days to take part in my first mission in America, and being in deadly terror of the Dewey fever I thought it better to cut short my visit to New York and to set out at once for the Puritan capital. For if the eve of the festival was such as I have intimated, what might not one have expected when the great day itself was ushered in amidst the booming of cannon and the beating of drums and the brazen defiance of military bands

and the deep loud huzzas of the millions of men and women
who thronged the streets ?

And here I may ask leave to say a word about myself
personally in order to explain the genesis of these 'notes.'
Late in the autumn of 1899 I was sent, with three other
Oblate Fathers of Inchicore, to preach a series of missions
in the United States. Usually we do not undertake missions
in Ireland during the winter months (except in towns and
cities) whereas it is only during winter that missions can be
given in America. If one had physical endurance enough,
therefore, he could labour at missions in America during
winter and spend the remainder of the year at the same
work in Ireland.   From my experience I would not advise
anyone to try it.   To try it once, I think, would obviate a
second attempt.   We intended to be back for our home
missions in five months, but so great was the pressure
brought to bear on us that the five months became eight,
and we left America only when the excessive heat made it
impossible for us to undertake any further engagements.

Apart from the duties that I was sent to discharge in
America, I valued very highly the privilege of being able to
visit a land in which, in common with all Irishmen, I had
always felt the keenest interest.   America, indeed, is a
country that must rivet the attention of all other countries,
and must compel the admiration of every race. The great
Republic is as yet a mere youth amongst the nations. It
suffers, perhaps, from some of the excesses and follies of
youth, but with these I am not now concerned.   The
vastness of its territory, the extent and variety of its
industries, its boundless material resources, its enormous
wealth, its fearless enterprise, its insatiable activity, its grim
fixed determination to keep ahead of all other nations in the
arts of peace and war—all these things unite in making the
States one of the greatest, if not the very greatest, of all the
Powers that ever ruled the destinies of men.   Irishmen
may be allowed to indulge in a little national pride as they
remember that in the building of this great social and
political fabric Irish hands and brains and blood have been
a chief factor.

A word as to the missions generally which formed the object of our visit to America. I say generally, for all the missions were conducted on the same lines, and what is said of one is true of all. Mission work is considerably harder in the States than at home. This is on account of the early and late hours and of the frightful severity of the weather. The mission is in full swing at 5 o'clock every morning. Whilst one of the Fathers celebrates Mass, the others are engaged in the confessionals. At the end of Mass there is a short instruction, and the service must be over at 5.45 to allow workmen and others to repair to their various employments. At 8 o'clock there is another Mass, followed by a sermon. At 3.30 p.m. the Church is filled with children gathered as well from the State schools as from those under the management of the clergy. At this service there is, of course, an instruction, and usually some very good singing by the children and their teachers. All American children are taught to sing, and all seem eager to display their vocal powers in church. In the evening at 7 o'clock, there is the usual mission service of Rosary, Sermon, and Benediction. Confessions are heard throughout the day, except from mid-day to 3 p.m.; but the great majority of the people prefer to discharge their duty in this respect either very early in the morning or from 7 to 11 at night. This gives the missioners little time for sleep; but it is the custom to retire to rest, and, if possible, to sleep for an hour or two after dinner, the usual time for dinner being about mid-day.

As a rule, our missions lasted a month; but this gave only a week to each section of the people. The first week was exclusively for married women, the second for women unmarried, the third for married, and the fourth for unmarried men.

There is a manifest drawback in this arrangement—the shortness of time allowed to each section. In the course of a week you can thunder with effect on the great truths of religion; you can, with the grace of God, soften hearts that were hardened, and give hope to souls that were despondent; you can bring sinners to the sacraments and to the beginning of a good Christian life; you can stir up pious and salutary emotions, and emotionalism, no doubt, has its uses in religion.

But it is not the 'fireworks,' as a venerable parish priest once said to me, that do the real work of a mission. It is not the powerful, vehement, impassioned discourses on the great truths that produce the lasting effects. I would depend much more on the clear, sound, solid instructions on doctrine and morals, delivered morning after morning for three or four weeks—instructions which convey to the minds of the people a correct if elementary knowledge on the chief points of dogmatic and moral theology. Religious emotionalism passes away; religious knowledge remains.

This, I will take leave to add, is worthy the attention of our good parish priests in Ireland. With us, too, the week for women and the week for men seems to be gradually supplanting the good old three or four weeks' mission, during which you had time to impart to the people a body of religious doctrine in a way that they were not likely soon to forget.

In America there are priests who regret the mere week mission, but who are seemingly powerless to remedy the defect. If we did not divide our people, they say, into four sections, the Church would be always inconveniently crowded, and hundreds could not find even standing room. The people, they will tell you, moreover, are so enthralled with their worldly affairs that they could not be induced to give more than one week's attendance to the spiritual exercises of a mission. I think that both these statements are unquestionable as far as America is concerned.

The attendance at missions in the States is quite as good as at home. Our missions were nearly altogether amongst Catholics of Irish birth or blood. Naturally they were glad to see missioners fresh from the old country, and they received us everywhere with a truly Irish welcome. Better still, our countrymen and countrywomen everywhere gave us proofs undeniable that in leaving the shores of Ireland they brought with them all the vigour of their Irish faith and all the sweetness of their Irish piety. As I shall have occasion to remark later on, many, very many, even amongst Irish-born Catholics, give up the practices of religion almost as soon as they arrive in America, and drift gradually into the ranks of indifferentism and unbelief. This we gathered from those who were able to speak with knowledge on the subject ; but from all that we, strangers, could see with our own eyes, our people in America are as full of faith and fervour as if they still lived in their own homes. Every morning we saw them in their hundreds, trooping into the church at five o'clock, with a long and hard day's work before them, and with the thermometer often some degrees below zero. In the evening the church, however spacious, was crowded to its fullest capacity, all being manifestly eager to profit of the message that was brought to them. It was gratifying to see the men almost as assiduous in their attendance at the mission exercises as the women. Indeed, in one church (at Springfield, Mass.) it was remarked that the number of men's confessions exceeded that of the women's.

I mentioned, incidentally, that during the mission confessions are heard during the hours of the public service. There is no difficulty in this, as in every church there is a crypt or basement. This crypt is for every-day use, while the church proper is reserved for Sunday services and other solemn occasions. Whilst sermon, or Mass, or Benediction goes on in the church, therefore, confessions are heard in the basement, and it is only in the basement that confessionals are placed.

The basement is also used for the children's Sunday Mass and Sunday-school. Indeed it may be called the children's own church. Nowhere more than in America are bishops and priests more fully alive to the vital necessity of planting in the child's mind a thorough knowledge of Christian doctrine, and nowhere is the Sunday-school system brought to a higher perfection. I have often seen over one thousand children assembled for catechism on the Sunday all settling down to work with the grimmest earnestness and ruled in their work by the strictest discipline. A priest is always present as general superintendent, but the teaching is done

by lay people who are chosen from amongst the best
educated and the most intelligent men and women in the
parish, and who regard it as a very great honour to be
entrusted with so noble a duty. Regularity of attendance
is ensured by a frequent and judicious distribution of prizes,
by the award of medals, of certificates of merit and proficiency, and above all by the constant vigilance of the
Rev. Director of the school. After catechism there is, of
course, Benediction, and the whole service is made bright
and attractive by music and singing. The children, indeed,
seem to need very little pressure to secure their attendance,
and their parents, however careless and indifferent themselves, will generally insist on their children going to the
Sunday Mass and the Sunday-school.

In the Sunday-school, as in the church, the American
priest is remarkable for method, order, and punctuality.
Indeed the whole parochial machinery works with clock-
like regularity. The pastor is in his ' office ' every morning
at a fixed hour for the transaction of business—arranging
about baptism, marriages, school attendance, funerals, or
Requiem Masses. By the way, there is always a *Missa
Cantata* if not a solemn High Mass *corpore presente* on the
occasion of the funeral even of the poorest parishioner.
Sick calls, too, are given before a certain hour in the
morning, and are always attended to before mid-day. The
priest, in fact, very properly imitates the business habits of
the country in the discharge of his sacred duties, and the
duties are made easier by order and punctuality.

The clergymen whom we met in the course of our mission
tour were chiefly American by birth and of Irish parentage.
There was a time when Ireland directly supplied the chief
portion of the English-speaking priests of the States. In
the various dioceses which we passed through the local
supply of clergymen was quite equal to the demand, and in
one or two instances we found that there were as many as
fifty or sixty priests lent to other dioceses. In some of the
Western States, however, bishops have still to depend mainly
upon Ireland for their clerical recruiting ground, whilst in
every diocese you are sure to meet a sprinkling of priests

who were born, educated, and ordained in Ireland. As to the high dignitaries of the American Church such names as Gibbons, Corrigan, Feehan, Riordan, Ryan, Williams, Kane, Brady, Burke, Byrne, Donohoe, Phelan, Fitzgerald, Foley, O'Dea, O'Gorman, O'Hara, M'Quaid, sufficiently bear witness to their nationality.

As to the progress of Catholicity in the States it has been in one way as rapid and as marvellous as any growth of faith that we find in the Church's history. The Church in the States has been, like the mustard seed of the Gospel, 'at first, indeed, the least of all seeds, but when it is grown the greatest among herbs and becometh a tree so that the birds of the air come and lodge in the branches thereof.' One hundred and fifty years ago there was but a handful of Catholics in Maryland and Pennsylvania—the only two colonies in which Catholics were allowed to exist, but in which also existence for them was made so irksome as to be almost intolerable. About a score of priests moved about amongst them, carefully concealing their sacred profession from those outside the Church ; Holy Mass was offered secretly in private houses, and in some few places openly, in log cabins which were dignified with the title of chapels. There was no real Church government in the country—all the thirteen English Colonies being nominally under the jurisdiction of the Vicar Apostolic of London. It is only one hundred and ten years since our illustrious countryman, the Most Rev. John Carroll, was consecrated the first bishop in the States, which, in breaking the British yoke, had established freedom of worship for Catholics and Protestants alike. At that time the Catholics could not have been more than forty or fifty thousand, and though emancipated, they still bore the marks of the chains, which they had worn so long. They had about twenty-five chapels of very modest dimensions, some few mission stations, and thirty-five priests. What a contrast between the American Church' of 1790 and the American Church of to-day ! To-day the Catholic Church is unquestionably the greatest religious power in the country. It has an Apostolic Delegate, a Cardinal, 14 Archbishops, 80 Bishops, 3 Vicars

Apostolic, 1 Prefect Apostolic, and about 12,000 priests. There is no religious census taken by the state in America, but we have it on various authorities, Protestant as well as Catholic, that in the States there are now at least 10,000,000 Catholics.

The Church in America, too, is fully equipped in every respect for the accomplishment of her divine mission. She has her great Catholic University at Washington, still, indeed, in its infancy, but already showing signs of intellectual activity and vigour. She has 7 other Universities of lesser note, but all of them centres of learning and religion. She has over 100 seminaries with a total of 5,000 students, 191 colleges for boys and 655 for girls, 4,000 parochial schools, 251 orphanages, 554 other charitable homes, and she reckons in round numbers a total of 1,000,000 children in her various institutions.

The American Hierarchy, recognizing the vast amount of good that can be accomplished, by a sound, healthy Press, gives every encouragement to the diffusion of Catholic literature. We find in the States the gratifying number of five hundred and fifty Catholic newspapers or periodicals. Most of these are in English, but there is a goodly number also in German, French, Polish, Slavonic, Magyar, Indian, or other languages. Many of these are under the immediate supervision of the Bishop, in whose diocese they are published, and some of them are regarded as the Bishops' official organs. It would be impossible to tell the good effects wrought throughout the length and breadth of the country by this great network of Catholic publications. This is one of the things certainly in which our kin across the seas are ahead of us in Ireland.

True to its Apostolic mission, the Church in America not only guards its own flock with zeal and love, but labours hard and labours successfully to gather other sheep into the one fold of the one Shepherd. Missions to non-Catholics, conducted chiefly by the Paulist Fathers, are now very general throughout the country. I was told that at many of these missions the church was crowded with Protestants, who came in an earnest and reverent spirit to weigh the arguments set before them on the claims of Catholicity. In almost every parish in which we ourselves gave missions, we found that there was constantly a certain number of Protestants preparing, by reading and instruction, for admission into the Church. We were not, therefore, surprised to learn that year by year thousands of Protestants seek and find peace and rest in the bosom of the Catholic faith. The holy war against infidelity and heresy is waged actively in every diocese and in every parish; and if Protestants are not always converted by the arguments addressed to them, their prejudices against Catholicity are very much modified if not utterly destroyed. Wherever you go, indeed, in America, you behold clear signs of activity and zeal. From one extremity to the other of the great Republic, the Church throbs with life and vigour, and its pulsations are felt through the whole social and political body of the country.

But we must look at the reverse side of the medal. The population of the States has been increasing by leaps and bounds. Has the Church increased her membership in the same ratio? The answer must, unfortunately, be a decided negative. There are many converts, but there are many more apostates. Large numbers are rescued from infidelity or heresy, but larger numbers lapse into indifferentism and irreligion. They begin by being bad Catholics and they end in agnosticism. It is very hard to give even an approximate guess at the number of these deserters, but it is, alas! too evident that they may be counted by the million. During the last sixty years, I think, it is no exaggeration to say, that as many as 4,500,000 men and women of the Irish race emigrated to America. Of these nearly all were Catholics, and nearly all left their homes in the prime of youth or in the full strength of early manhood. With the proverbial fertility of the Irish race is it too much to say that, at present, there ought to be as many as 10,000,000 Catholics of Irish birth or blood in the United States? But beside these you have to reckon some millions of Catholics from other countries, from Germany, Poland, Italy, France, Austria, and Canada. I do not think, therefore, that I am very wrong in asserting that if all emigrants and their children had remained faithful to the Church, we should to-day have in America a population of 20,000,000 Catholics. In other words the leakage of the past sixty years must have amounted to more than half the Catholic population, as account must be taken of the large numbers of converts that I have alluded to.

One out of every two lost to the Church. Ten out of twenty millions gone in the way of unbelief and perdition! The figures are appalling. To say that we have in the States ten million less Catholics than we ought to have is not, of course, to assert that there have been so many actual deserters from the Church, but only that there are so many unbelievers or religious waifs and strays, most of whom would be Catholics but for the apostasy or the religious indifference of their parents.

And let us always bear in mind that those who so fall away not only renounce the Catholic faith, but, as a rule, fling away belief in every form of Christianity, and reject every idea of the supernatural. In these latter times you hardly ever hear of a Catholic going over to any one of the numberless sects in the country. They become atheists and materialists pure and simple. Their only God is the dollar, their only heaven a luxurious home, their only hell a life of poverty or privation. They think no more of a future state than the ox or the ass.

What is the proportion of Irish Catholics who are thus swallowed up in the dark abyss of unbelief? One cannot conjecture with anything like accuracy, but there is no doubt that the proportion is large. Indeed, there are reasons to fear that the great majority of the apostates are of Irish extraction, and not a few of Irish birth. For the Irish seem to get much more easily Americanized than other people and to be Americanized (I use the word, of course, in an obvious sense) is to be dechristianized. Other immigrants, such as Germans and Canadians, keep up their own language, and their ignorance of the language of the country is a protection for their faith. The Irish unfortunately have not a language of their own to preserve, and the consequence is that they plunge at once into the habits and manners and modes of speech of those around them; they become a few months after their arrival more American than the Americans themselves; they are caught many of them by the spirit of irreligion that breathes everywhere around them, and if they do not formally give up the faith they become careless and indifferent, and by and by they bring up their children without any knowledge of God or of His Church.

This, I think, is one of the most mournful facts in our mournful history. The people who would gladly die like their fathers for the faith at home, deliberately give up this precious treasure in America as a sacrifice to the unbelieving spirit of the country. In the mind of the priest, in the mind of any true Catholic, can there be a stronger argument against emigration? Our heart grows sick or our blood takes fire, as we read of the thousands upon thousands of our race who died of fever fifty or more years ago in their passage across the Atlantic, and whose uncoffined bones lie at this moment in the depths of the ocean. From a Christian standpoint, was not their fate enviable when compared with that of the Irish emigrant of to-day who flies across the waters in one of our palace steamers, only to lose his faith and lose his soul at the other side?

Since my short tour in America I have been more than ever saddened by the sight of our departing emigrants, for I could not help looking on them as rushing to their own spiritual destruction. How heart-breaking this constant procession of our people to Queenstown or Liverpool for New York, this unceasing stream of the life-blood of a nation that deserves to live, but that day by day comes nearer to death. See that crowd of fine young men full of faith, full of piety, showing in their faces the candour, the honesty, the courage, the hope, the manly purity within their souls. What will they be after a few years amid the corrupting influences of one of America's great cities? Still sadder is it to see our beautiful Irish girls, true children of Mary Immaculate, pictures of sweetness, grace and innocence, hurrying away unconsciously to their ruin, both temporal and eternal!

Much better than we at home can American priests and bishops understand the awful perils that encompass the Irish emigrant in America, and they appeal to us in language the most earnest and the most vehement to keep our people in their own land. From Cardinal Gibbons, from Archbishop Corrigan, from Archbishop Ryan, from every American ecclesiastic that takes an interest in our Catholic nation, comes the constant cry to the Irish Hierarchy and clergy : Stop the tide of emigration. Save your flocks from the American wolf. Sacrifice not your faithful children to Moloch. For your people, America is the road to hell!

Would that this cry rang in the ear and in the soul and conscience of every priest in Ireland ! For I believe that to our priests more than to any other class of men it belongs to apply a styptic to this wound through which the nation's blood is flowing. Could there be any more useful subject for the pastoral discourse on Sunday than the perils of emigration? Could not priests use their great influence to create and foster a healthy public opinion on the subject? Could they not do much to tear away the glamour that surrounds American labour and American citizenship with a false splendour and to exhibit the Irish emigrant in the States, as alas ! what he is too often found to be—Godless, faithless, hopeless, sunk into depths of social misery and spiritual debasement from which there is no arising.

I have much more to say on this subject, and with the kind permission of the Editor, I shall continue my notes in some future numbers of the I. E. RECORD.

M. F. SHINNORS, O.M.I.

THE RISE AND PROGRESS OF HIGHER CRITICISM

III.—THE FRAGMENT-HYPOTHESIS—(CONTINUED)

AS we saw in the January number, the extravagances of Vater and De Wette caused their respective theories to be opposed by Bertheau, even though he held that the Pentateuch was a collection of fragments. This is true also of Bleek, who had been a pupil of De Wette's in Berlin. He rejected some of the assertions we have read, and, as was to be expected, gave to those he accepted quite a new character. This is presumably due in some measure to the great influence exerted on himself by two other of the Berlin professors, Schleiermacher in philosophy and Neander in history.

While Bleek rejected *a priori* the traditional authorship of the Pentateuch, he was nevertheless of opinion that considerable portions were written by Moses. Bleek says of himself, ' I am one of those who with all their suscepti- bilities to the teaching of revelation, refuse to identify the word of God with Holy Scripture, and regard it as their primary object to discern the word of God in Holy Scripture.' (This is a new application of the Fragment- hypothesis ; some parts of Scripture are to be regarded as merely human.) His views on the origin of the Pentateuch are contained in two essays written respectively in 1822 and in 1831. In the former he maintained that besides the passages in Exodus which are expressly attributed to Moses, the poems in Numbers xxi. 18-20, 27-30, and the laws in Leviticus i., vii., xvi., Numbers xxix., and probably Leviticus xiii. which presupposes a sojourn in the wilderness, were also his. In the second essay, Bleek gave his reasons for ascribing more passages to the Hebrew legislator. Not only was Leviticus xiii. certainly his, but Leviticus xvii. and apparently xi. and xv. also. Moreover the laws referring to the tabernacle[1] are

---

[1] Exod. xxv.-xxxi. 11.

also Mosaic, because they do not mention priests, but speak of Aaron and his sons! As regards the veracity of these books, the views of Bleek and of De Wette are diametrically opposed. The master taught that they contain myths, the pupil says they possess real historical worth. Equally marked is the difference between their respective opinions regarding the date of the compilation of the Pentateuch. Whilst De Wette and Gesenius assign it to the Babylonian captivity, Bleek believes it was much earlier, and believes, moreover, that there were two recensions or editions. He makes Deuteronomy the starting point of the investigation. According to him, it is of much later date than the other four books and in no sense Mosaic.[1] No credence whatever is to be given to the passages wherein it is stated that they were written by Moses; apart from their ambiguity, how could Moses have penned the statement about the preservation of the book? Again, in their intrinsic character respectively, there is a notable difference between Deuteronomy and the other books. It is no conglomerate, no fortuitous result of a crowd of fragments, but a literary composition, written so to speak at one sitting, even though its author made use of existing material. In tone and style it resembles the writing of the exilic prophets, of Jeremias especially, but its contents show that kings still reigned in Judah.

When this point has been proved to his own satisfaction, Bleek turns to the question of the 'five books.' Here in common with Geddes and Vater, whose view he had adopted in 1824, Bleek says that the narrative of the death of Moses is not the proper close of the history begun in Genesis, that Genesis requires the description of the occupation

---

[1] Cheyne (Professor of Scripture, Oriel College, Oxford—a very advanced critic) speaks thus of Bleek, etc. 'Meantime a reaction was rising which sought to direct criticism towards positive rather than negative results. The chief representatives of this positive criticism, which now took up a distinct attitude of opposition to the negative criticism of De Wette, were Bleek, Ewald, Movers, and Hitzig. By giving up certain parts of the Pentateuch, especially Deuteronomy, they thought themselves able to vindicate other parts as beyond doubt genuinely Mosaic, just in the same way as they threw over the Davidic authorship of certain psalms in order to strengthen the claim of others to bear his name.'

of Palestine, consequently that the Book of Josue is
its inseparable sequel and that we should never say ' five
books,' but ' six books.' It is not however to be inferred
that the compiler of Genesis put together the following
four books, as we have them at present. The date of
Deuteronomy would point to the closing years of the
kingdom of Judah as the period in which such a combination
was made, but the supposition is excluded by the fact that
in Exodus, leave is given to offer sacrifice anywhere—on the
sites of Theophanies, especially. This does not tally with
the history of the time. The only way to explain the
paradox is to admit two recensions.

The first was made by the compiler of Genesis, in the
time of the still undivided monarchy. The work treated of
events down to the time of Joshua's death, and was derived
partly from written copies of poems, tales, and laws, partly
from tradition. The visible unity of plan shows that the
editor was no mere compiler, even though he preserved as
far as possible the words of the originals. The peculiarity
of the recension consisted in this ; it was unauthoritative,
or, as we should say, intended only for private circulation.
The final and official edition was made by the author of
Deuteronomy some short time before the downfall of Judah
(586 A.C.) Not only did he insert Deuteronomy, but here and
there in the other books, Josue particularly, he made changes
and additions : e.g., in Leviticus xvii. the introduction
of the law about the one place of worship (this unwarranted
conjecture was afterwards retracted), and in Leviticus xxvi.
3-45. It was this second edition of the Hexateuch, and not
Deuteronomy alone—which never existed in a separate
form—that was found in the temple in the eighteenth year
of Josias, and that was declared canonical because it was
regarded as the work of Moses. At some subsequent
period the Book of Josue was detached from it.

As regards the date of the compilation of the first five
books, it is, according to Bleek, a mistake to refer to the
Samaritan Pentateuch, as if it dated from before the schism
of the ten tribes, for Bleek maintains with De Wette and
Gesenius against Berthold, that the Samaritans received the

Pentateuch from the Jews only after the return from Babylon.

This is a desperate assertion. It is scarcely necessary to observe that imagination is the sole source of Bleek's contribution to the Fragment-hypothesis. It had, however, the result of making De Wette change a part of his equally groundless theory. He granted now that Deuteronomy was composed in the reign of Josias, and that the Pentateuch was in existence before the exile, because it was known to the compiler of the Books of Kings, who lived about 586 A.O. Nevertheless, the first indication of the Pentateuch's existence is the finding of the book of the law in the reign of Josias, and the laws themselves are, with some exceptions, of non-Mosaic origin. In conclusion, De Wette granted that the poems in Numbers xxi. were really written by Moses. Professor Briggs, of New York, who is a leading critic himself, says in his *Higher Criticism of the Hexateuch* (1893), page 61, that Bleek was the first to give shape to what has been called the Supplementary-hypothesis. He made the Elohist original and fundamental, the Jehovist the supplementer. This is now an axiom among the rationalists, and its 'discovery' by Bleek may be a reason why Wellhausen did him the great honour of re-editing his *Einleitung*. However this may be, the origin of the 'Supplement-hypothesis' is, as we shall see, still a disputed question. It might have seemed at the time that Bleek's developments and De Wette's concessions would restore peace among the critics, but a new one who was an uncompromising defender of the Fragment-hypothesis now appeared on the scene.

This was Hartmann, who, like Vatke, carried the analysis almost to the point of annihilation. After his examination scarcely a Mosaic fragment remained in the Pentateuch. He observed that in proportion as we read down through the lives of the kings after Solomon, so do we find the number of references to the historical part of the Pentateuch increase and the exercise of divine worship become more like what is alleged to have been commanded by Moses. In the period of the last kings, written collections of laws become more numerous, so we may take it that by the time of Jeremias and Ezechiel the more important parts of the Pentateuch were already in existence. They were, however, not yet put into their present order, and they had to receive some expansions. Everything tends to show that the Pentateuch as we have it was compiled during the exile : as regards the respective age of the constituent parts of the gradually growing conglomerate, nothing can be known with certainty. It is useless to attempt to determine their relative antiquity by means of the historical books, because it is not possible to separate from the genuine parts of these, the fragments that were incorporated sooner or later.   (N.B.—This is the Fragment Theory with a vengeance.) The Israelites learned the art of writing in the age of the Judges, it is impossible to believe that Moses could write. At any rate, the Egyptian alphabet would have been incapable of representing Semitic sounds, and, therefore, when the Israelites got an alphabet, it was from the Phœnicians.[1] The style of the Pentateuch is the same as that of confessedly late books, and the anachronisms it contains show only too plainly that it is of recent date. Finally, with regard to the alleged archaic character of the five books, and the acquaintance with Egypt and Egyptian customs, etc., which Exodus is said to manifest, Hartmann answers that the archaisms could be put into a work written long after the time of Moses, and that it is exceedingly improbable that Moses could retain an accurate and expedite knowledge of Egyptian affairs. The disregard in general of literary criticism, or of the comparative study of words, passages, etc., which Hartmann manifests, is not peculiar to him ; it is characteristic, more or less, of all the supporters of the Fragment-hypothesis.[2] If it is so prominent

---

[1] Most of our readers know that some of the cuneiform tablets found in 1887 at Tel-el-Amarna were written more than a century before Moses was born, and that there are other Semitic inscriptions of a far earlier date. The Sippara tablet is thought to be as old as 4000 A.C. Again, the recent discoveries in Egypt show the accuracy of the descriptions in the Book of Exodus. Of course, our faith in the absolute veracity of Scripture does not need tablets, etc. Its sole rule is the infallible Catholic Church.

[2] Yet he could on occasion, when arguing against the traditional antiquity of Deuteronomy, and attempting to make out that it was written in

in Hartmann's treatment of the Pentateuch, it is because,
as Cornill says, he was the last energetic and logical
representative of this school.

Again, however, there was a change in its fortunes, and
it attained the most flourishing period of its whole career.
This time a philosophical element was introduced into the
discussion, which, owing apparently to its ultra-radical and
destructive tendencies, had ceased to be attractive. Gramberg,
and still more Vatke and George, brought this about. In
his *Critical History of the Religious Ideas of the Old
Testament*, Berlin, 1829, Gramberg attempted to show the
slow development of the priesthood, place of worship, sacrifices, feasts,[1] and religious customs amongst the ancient
Israelites. To do so he distinguished seven periods of
Hebrew literature. In the first, which extended from
David to Hezekiah, Genesis, Exodus, and Judges were
compiled from written and unwritten sources by some
unknown individual. Leviticus, Numbers, and Jeremias
belong to the fourth period, which coincides with the
beginning of the exile ; while in the fifth period, or towards
the end of the exile, there is evidence of the existence of
the following books :—Kings, Isaias, Deuteronomy (which

the age of the exile, descend to literary criticism. He gives a list of alleged
modern words, which [Archbishop] Smith calls classical. The list is long ;
but the great Catholic *savant* goes through it, and exposes the futility of all
Hartmann's objections. (See Smith, *The Pentateuch*, pp. 537-550.)

In his *Hebrew Feasts*, Prof. Green, Princeton, New Jersey, thus describes
this part of the system :—' Gramberg's *Critical History of the Religious Ideas
of the Old Testament* was published in 1829, in which he undertakes to give
an elaborate treatment of the whole subject. His strong rationalistic bias,
however, which he is at no pains to conceal, incapacites him for any real
apprehension of the religion, with which he deals in a purely formal and
mechanical manner, and which he seeks to explain upon the theory of priest-
craft. The various books of the Pentateuch are assigned to separate dates,
from the reign of David to the close of the Babylonish exile, and their institutions or enactments are compared with the statements or allusions
found in the historical and prophetical books of the corresponding period.
His conclusion is that worship was originally free and subject to no statutory
regulations. There were no fixed feasts, except such as were of a domestic
nature, and involved no great amount of sacrifices, such as the weekly Sabbath
and harvest festival, whose recurrence was determined by the season.
Jeroboam's opposition to the worship at Jerusalem first led the priests to
think of concentrating all the services of religion at this sanctuary ; and with
this view they invented new feasts and multiplied the rites connected
with them. Subsequently the poets who wrote Exodus and the rest of the
Pentateuch referred these ordinances, which the priests had instituted, to the

is made up of fragments of a date later than that of Josias), and Josue, which refers to Deuteronomy. We need not pause to refute this impertinent disarrangement of books and events, by means of which they are made, in spite of themselves, to fit a theory which bids defiance to tradition. Holzinger is right in saying that in one respect Gramberg is a forerunner of Wellhausen, though, of course, he intends this for praise.

Vatke applied the methods of Hegelian philosophy to the solution of the problem: Whence has the Pentateuch come? To understand his theory, we need to remember that Hegel's system of absolute Idealism and evolutionary Pantheism induced Hegel himself to place the Old Testament worship in the second [1] stage of religious development, that, namely, of the 'religions of spiritual individuality,' in which God is regarded as a thinking subject. Among the religions of this class, the Grecian represented the highest form of beauty, the Roman was conspicuous for practical utility, and the Israelite surpassed them both in sublimity !

---

higher authority of Moses; and, finally, the poetic author of Chronicles recast the history of the kingdom, so as to create the impression that the Levitical ordinances were then already obeyed. The people may have had feasts in honour of Jehovah from their first settlement in Canaan; but there is no certainty that even the most important of them were Mosaic, and, at any rate, they were not observed in accordance with the Mosaic requirements until the days of Josiah; and all the feasts prescribed in the Pentateuch were not in existence even then. The account of the origin of the Passover given in Exodus is self-contradictory and purely mythical. It could not have been instituted in view of their expected departure from Egypt, for Pharaoh had not given them permission to leave; and this permission could not have been foreseen. Exodus was the book of the law found in the temple in the reign of Josias, and the observance of the Passover dates from this time. The Passover, which was celebrated on a single night, and the Feast of Unleavened Bread, which lasted seven days, were at first distinct; but they are blended in Leviticus and Numbers, which show a great advance in the development of the *cultus*. The Feast of Weeks was plainly an invention of the priests, that they might obtain an early supply of the first fruits. Tabernacles, which in previous laws was located indefinitely at the end of the year, and was simply the feast of ingathering, came to be fixed on a particular day of the month, and to be regarded as commemorative of the march through the Wilderness.' Professor Green has, although he is not a Catholic, sufficient respect for the Bible, and sufficient common sense, to make him reject this folly.

[1] The first or lowest stage was that occupied by the ancient religions of the East. Their beliefs and rites were all gross and sensual, and they regarded God as the inherent force everywhere present in nature, in comparison to which the finite, or individual, sinks into nothingness. The third and last stage of religious development was Christianity or—Hegelianism !

The religion of pagan Rome appears to have made the most favourable impression on Vatke. With notions such as these he devoted all his energies to the defence and development of the Fragment-hypothesis; hence it is no wonder that he arrived at the following conclusions.

The true idea of government is not found in the constitution which Moses is said to have established. Even the most cursory examination of the political groundwork of the so-called Mosaic state reveals its abstract, unreal nature. So far from being a great legislator, he had not even the most rudimentary notions of political economy. The Hebrew commonwealth never existed, indeed a Hebrew nationality could never exist but by means of a governmental department, for which the boasted legislator made not the slightest provision. The case stands thus : Of the three indispensable departments of every polity, the legal, the judicial, the executive; in the Mosaic system, the last is utterly wanting, and the other two are imperfectly organized. Moses made no arrangement for the continuance of a legislative body, and to make up for it there is only one casual allusion to a prophet. There are, it is true some rules laid down for the guidance of judicial assemblies, however it must be admitted that for the most part they are obscure and ambiguous. But instead of precise regulations for the executive, as we have a right to expect, we find nothing. We do see, however, in superfluity, what we do not want, a confused mass of *minutiæ* about worship, income of priests, etc.

The Mosaic legislation has, therefore, no connection with the unity of a real political organization or state. It was never intended to be the constitution of a nation. ' Dem mosaischen Staat fehlt mit dem Begriff der wirklichen Herrschaft zugleich die höhere Einheit und die ganze Sphäre des offentlichen Rechts.' The boasted ' unity of the Pentateuch ' arises from the fact that its sphere of influence is confined to the abstract theocratic principle, and to that principle's necessary consequences. Its laws are simply concerned with the improvement of the religious and moral aspects of life, they have nothing to do with the establishment or with the preservation of civil and political relations. The Pentateuch was, therefore, compiled at a time when the Hebrew people had already attained a certain degree of development. It could have been formed only in the midst of a nation having fixed religious ideas and practices, and its origin is consequently analogous to that of canon law.[1]

Vatke's intention in all this was to re-establish the original theory of De Wette whose concessions to Bleek did not meet with his approval. He would not admit that there was any convincing proof of the Mosaic authorship of the poems in Numbers xxi., nor any reliable tradition to show that Moses promulgated the Decalogue. As regards the relative age of the parts that now make up the Pentateuch, Vatke had his own opinions. The book of the law found in the reign of Josias contained the substance of the older legislation, which, with slight alterations, is to be found in Exodus xiii., xix.-xxiv., xxxii.-xxxiv. Deuteronomy belongs to the time of Jeremias; it was written after the reform introduced by Josias. The last parts of the so-called

---

[1] Our readers will find a relief in turning from all this impious raving to look at a work of divine mercy. It is the conversion of Daumer, apparently the only rationalistic interpreter of Scripture at the time that got the grace. G. F. Daumer was one of Hegel's own pupils in philosophy. He became one of the bitterest enemies of Christianity. Though he was a good linguist and poet, some of his notions were remarkably puerile. The Garden of Eden was in Australia, and the Book of Numbers described the first emigration thence to America, and across Behring Straits to Asia! Daumer was so proud of this specimen of exegesis or ' discovery,' that he actually wrote :—' My new system of geography and ethnology is to history what the Copernican system is to astronomy.' With such folly a great deal of wickedness was combined. He maintained that Jehova, the God of the Hebrews, was identical with the Phœnician deity, Moloch ; that human sacrifices were commanded in the Old Testament, and also practised until the defeat of the Jehovist party ; that the Christian mysteries were infamous ; that our countryman, St. Malachy of Armagh, St. Bernard, St. Francis of Assisi, were three cannibals ; that Mahommedanism was superior to Christianity, etc. While uttering blasphemies such as these, just a year before his work on *Moloch-worship Among the Ancient Hebrews* appeared, by some mysterious influence he published a book of a very different nature : *The Glories of the Blessed Virgin.* (*Die Glorie der heiligen Jungfrau Maria.* Nuremberg, 1841). It finally led to his conversion on the Feast of the Assumption, 1858, as he often said. His death (December 14, 1875) was most edifying.

Cheyne remarks in his *Founders of Old Testament Criticism* :—' Vatke and George agree in affirming the late composition of the Pentateuch, in denying to Moses any participation in it all, and also in considering the contents as little better than mythical, taking Deuteronomy as the earliest of the several books and probably belonging to the age of Josias and the other books as later still.'

Pentateuchal legislation belong to the period of the exile. It seemed to Vatke impossible ' that a whole nation should suddenly sink from a high stage of religious development to a lower one, as is asserted to have been so often the case in the times of the Judges and the Kings.' It was in this way that the Hegelian critic manipulated the Word of God.[1] We may note in passing that Vatke gave up all this afterwards, just as easily as he had invented it—and adopted another theory.

George, another Hegelian, is the last critic of note that the Fragment school produced. He paid special attention

[1] Cheyne in his *Founders of Old Testament Criticism*, page 133, has the following eulogistic notice of Vatke:—' But beyond question his dominant interest was in Hegel (not in Schleiermacher, be it observed), and it is a noteworthy fact that directly he had mastered Hegel's system, the Old Testament began to appear to him in a new light. Starting from De Wette's conclusions he went with intuitive certainty far beyond his teacher, and his clue to the labyrinth of critical problems he derived from Hegel'; and page 136—'The step he was now about to take in the constructive criticism of the Old Testament could have been taken only by a thorough Hegelian; no other critic of his time would so intuitively have discerned order in the midst of conflicting phenomena.'

It is significant that in proportion as the critics talk about the conflicting phenomena of the Old Testament, they tend to deny the existence of the great historical personages, the saints of God, whose lives it narrates, and to reduce these holy men to mere shadowy mythological concepts. Cheyne's own views on this point may be learned from his article in the current number of the *Nineteenth Century*, ' A Turning Point in Old Testament Study.' It is a qualified encomium of Winckler, one of the foremost rationalists of the present day, who, in his *Geschichte Israels*, attempts to make out that Abraham, Isaac, and Jacob, are 'lunar heroes.' A few sentences will show what is the treatment of the Inspired Word which Cheyne has to a great extent approved of. It will be well to quote also some of Cheyne's words of praise. He says : 'The work before us is a perfect specimen of that free, disinterested treatment of things so much dearer to Matthew Arnold in 1864 than Colenzo's mixture of the practical and the scientific spirit. Of revolutionary or even reforming ecclesiastical designs Winckler is absolutely innocent. He appeals to a public which simply aims at a nearer approximation to the truth. It would, indeed, be too optimistic to assert that our popular theology has become historical, but even among practical Churchmen it is at least a tolerated opinion that Abraham was not an historical personage, either in the sense supposed by the older orthodoxy, or in the sense which is winning much favour among more recent theologians. Winckler thinks it right to treat Abraham, Isaac, and Jacob, and even Moses, Joshua, the Judges, Saul, David, and Solomon in a perfectly disinterested spirit, from the point of view of a criticism founded upon the facts of a comparative study of the legends of the East.' . . . ' Abraham, Isaac, and Jacob then, are lunar heroes. In the case of Abraham this is, according to Winckler, doubly certain. His father Terah comes from Ur in Chaldeah, the city of the south Babylonian Moon-worship (Nannar), but in order to reach Canaan, he must halt at Harran, which is the second great centre of lunar worship, in the region of the Euphratean civilization, &c., &c. Thus Winckler makes contributions not merely to

to what he considered the relative age of the constituent parts of the Pentateuch, and by applying the doctrines of Hegel and of Schleiermacher to the *soi-disant* history of the Hebrews he obtained the following results. In the Old Testament, three stages of development are distinctly visible. In the initial or rudimentary one, we meet with historical passages in Genesis and also certain parts of Exodus and Numbers, as is evident from their poetical and mythical character, though on the other hand there are parts which have been retouched or which belong to a later date. The next period of development was that of the

---

archæology but to geography, and if it be said that his geographical proposals are arbitrary, I deny that.' . . . ' And how comes Sarah to be at once Abraham's sister and his wife? Because Sarah, being the counterpart of Istar, has a double *rôle*. She is the daughter of the Moon-god, and therefore Abraham's sister; she is the wife of Tammuz, and therefore Abraham's wife. For Abraham too, according to Winckler, has a double *rôle*; he is the son of the Moon-god, but he is also the heroic reflection of Tammuz. Of Isaac, little is recorded; he dwells at Beersheba, the "well of the Seven-god, that is the Moon-god." Jacob, however, is much more definitely described. His father-in-law, Laban, reminds us by his very name of Lebena, the moon, and Laban's two daughters, Leah and Rachel, represent respectively the new moon and the full moon. Dinah, Leah's daughter, represents Istar, the daughter of the Moon-god, and with her six brothers makes up the number of the days of the week, one of which in fact (*Dies Veneris*, Friday) has a female deity. The respective numbers of the descendants of the two wives (excluding Joseph as a solar hero) are also significant for the calendar.'

' Joseph is a hero second in importance to none : his name is not properly that of a tribe ; Ephraim and Manasses are the tribes which he impersonates. In a larger sense, however, he impersonates all the tribes which subsequently formed the kingdom of Northern Israel, and of whom he may also be regarded as the patron deity. The key to his divine character lies in Genesis xxxvii. 10, where Joseph dreams that the sun, the moon, and the eleven stars did homage to him. The interpretation given in verse 10 is "I (Jacob), thy mother and thy brethren." But the mother has no place in an act of homage, and it is in the South Arabian mythology, not in the Babylonian, that the sun is feminine. In the original story, then, it was the Moon-god (Jacob), with his children, who bowed down before the Sun-god (Joseph), his son. The rest of the story of Joseph now becomes clear. The lunar heroes, Abraham and Jacob, fetched their spouses from the land of Moon-worship ; the solar hero Joseph goes to Egypt, the land of Sun-worship, to obtain for his wife the daughter of a priest of Heliopolis. But, like Abraham, Joseph also represents Tammuz, the sun of spring-tide, who dies and passes into the underworld, whither Istar descends to bring him back to earth. This is why he is cast into the pit, and again raised out of it. Hence another reason for Joseph's going to Egypt, for Egypt represents the southern region of the sky, in which the sun stands in the winter when Tammuz is dead. That the tribes of Israel (necessarily twelve, because of the signs of the Zodiac), together with their ancestors, are connected with an astral myth is not a new idea, but it has been worked out by Winckler with greater fulness of knowledge than by any previous writer.'

Our readers are by this time in all probability tired of this arrant nonsense, and have no desire to know how Winckler transforms Saul and Jonathan,

poets and prophets, during which reason was relegated to the second place and feeling or sentiment, reigned supreme. Internal evidence shows that Deuteronomy was composed about the end of this period, and under the influence of the prophets. The third and final period witnessed the full development of reason. It was then that the last books of the Old Testament were written, they are eminently rational and reflect faithfully the spirit of their time. It was the age of the hierarchy, particularly as this was developed after the return from Babylon. Leviticus was written at this time, with parts of Exodus and of Numbers. The development of the theocratic principle naturally led to a corresponding evolution in all other religious ideas, and consequently to an expansion of the law. We see the first signs of this religious movement in Deuteronomy ; we see its complete results in Leviticus.

It is quite plain that the last two systems contain the germ of the Graf-Wellhausen theory. Lest, however, some readers might think that these systems were quite obsolete and possessed at present only a paleological interest,[1] it may

David and Solomon, into solar, lunar and astral heroes, so we shall spare them further quotation. When reading the blasphemous utterances of the higher critics, there comes over one's mind the fear that ' tradidit illos Deus in reprobum sensum.' Cheyne almost ends his article with the words : ' The correctness of Winckler's solutions largely depends on the soundness of his textual criticism. I have often strong objections to make to these solutions, but if scholars, after undergoing a long and patient training, should agree with Winckler's textual criticism more nearly than with my own, I shall no doubt accept the verdict, for by that time I shall certainly have gone over to that bold critic myself.'

[1] We may be permitted a further remark. It is on the necessity of ever keeping in mind the underlying, essential connexion that exists between all these rationalist systems of Pentateuchal exegesis. In opposition to the truth, they are one. Much as they may vary among themselves, still these differences are only external and accidental. Wellhausen's theory is but the logical development of a long series of untrue statements. To understand thoroughly the latest phase of Higher Criticism, and to know what Wellhausen has done, it is necessary to begin at the beginning. And Wellhausen's popularity at present would not have been possible but for his predecessors. Not only did they prepare a reading public for him, but they made ' the brilliant remarks and courageous guesses' which he has since formulated into a system. The isolated utterances of every Pentateuchal critic in hostility to revelation, have been combined by him into an organic whole. In fact, the solidarity that exists among critics, is one of the things on which they plume themselves. And this unity is well described in the following words of one of their greatest living opponents. In a reply to some of them, Sayce writes thus :—' The forefront of my offending seems to be that I have spoken of the

be as well to quote once more the *Encyclopædia Biblica*, 1901. The passage will show what esteem and influence among critics Vatke and George possess at the present day.[1] It is as follows :—

TRUE METHOD.—Meanwhile, two Hegelian writers, starting from the original position of De Wette, and moving on lines apart from the beaten track of criticism, had actually effected the solution of the most important problem in the whole sphere of Old Testament study. Vatke and George have the honour of being the first by whom the question of the historical sequence of the several stages of the law was attacked on a sound method, with full mastery over the available evidence, and with a clear insight into the far-reaching scope of the problem.

We shall have occasion to treat of this in the history of the Development-hypothesis. Here, in conclusion, it need only be said that the follies of the Fragment-hypothesis caused it to fall into disrepute. It started by asserting that the repetitions in the Pentateuch, and the want of sequence in its parts, showed that it was made up of numerous fragments. But there is evidence of unity and order, of which the

---

critics as a body, without pointing out that whereas Professor X. is disposed to admit that the Israelites were once in Egypt, Professor Y. refuses to make any such admission at all. But I have nothing to do with these distinctions, or with the rival theories of critics within their own microcosm. They all start from the same principles, follow the same method, and agree in their general conclusions. ¶ It is against their method and principles, that I have raised a protest, and it is their general conclusions with which I have endeavoured to show that archæological discovery is irreconcilable. It is quite indifferent to me, whether Dillmann rejects the Grafian hypothesis, or whether Kittel is blamed by his fellow-workers for making too ample concessions to traditional views. Professor Cheyne's reply to Professor Driver's article in the *Contemporary Review* for March, 1894, seems to be quite unanswerable; 'for a few feet forward, more or less, does not matter much, when one is in a bog.'—' Biblical Critics on the Warpath,' *Contemporary Review*, Nov. 1896.

[1] On the other hand it is amusing to read in the *Studien und Kritiken* (1837) De Wette's estimate of the theory of 'these three young critics' as he calls Vatke, George and Von Bohlen. He suggests that there was a reason for their new hypothesis, viz., that the criticism of the Pentateuch might go the entire round of possible conjectures. And he sarcastically observes that 'the only thing wanting to make it attractive is truth,' and says truly enough 'whether from a dread of individualism inspired by the Hegelian philosophy, a cacoethes for development, or a love of paradox, they have joined the history of the Hebrews not to the grand creations of Moses, but have suspended its origin in airy nothing.'

Fragment-hypothesis has no explanation to give. As Strack says in Herzog's *Bibl. Encycl.* (art. Hexateuch):—

Der Engländer A. Geddes, J. S. Vater, und T. Hartmann liessen, hauptsächlich Mangel an Zusammenhang und Wiederholungen als Gründe angebend, den Pentateuch aus einer grossen Anzahl einzelner Fragmente enstanden sein. Diese Ansicht erwies sich dadurch als unhaltbar, dass ordnende Hand sowohl im Grossen als auch in vielen Einzelheiten unverkennbar ist; auch half sie zu keiner Einsicht in das Werden des Pentateuchs.

The so-called orthodox Protestants, as Hengstenberg, Hävernick, and Ranke, made the Pentateuchal question a test of belief or unbelief: against which proceeding George entered a vehement protest, just as his successors do. He was at the same time attacked on the other side by some of his fellow-rationalists, viz., Bertheau, Bleek, and Stähelin. Bertheau's contention was that the middle books could and should be divided into seven groups, each consisting of seven classes of Decalogues (490 commandments in all), which, beyond all doubt, were given by Moses, even though he possibly did not write them down. The other enactments were added subsequently, and at a still later period the historical passages. (Like other critics that are so dogmatic for a season, Bertheau retracted all this afterwards.) The two other opponents of George, Bleek and Stähelin, took up again the literary criticism, and in this way contributed to the introduction of the Supplement-hypothesis, which, with the permission of our readers, will be treated of in another article.

But, meanwhile, one specimen of the critical objections to the authenticity of the Pentateuch may be of interest. As we saw above, the supporters of the Fragment-hypothesis do not, as a rule, employ verbal criticism; they do not reckon up the number of times a part of speech occurs, or insist on peculiarities of style, but they rely on real criticism, whether the source of the objection be a geographical, historical, or archæological difficulty. And these objections are as long-lived as the other innumerable calumnies directed against the Catholic Church and all that she holds dear. It is not unusual to see some that were put forward by Bleek, etc., and answered by Catholic scholars (*e.g.*, Welte, Smith,

Vigouroux, Cornely) re-appear unblushing as ever in the pages of leading critics at the present day. (Strack, Holzinger, etc.) This is the case with the following objection.

The first 'geographical' difficulty is due to the fact that the expression *beeber hajjarden*, generally translated 'beyond the Jordan,' is often used in Deuteronomy to denote the country lying to the east of that river. It is quite obvious, say the critics, that we have here a convincing proof of non-Mosaic authorship. He who led the people out of Egypt did not cross the Jordan; whereas the man that wrote *beeber hajjarden*, in reference to the eastern desert and to the land of Moab, must have written in Canaan. Take, for instance, Deuteronomy i. 1: 'These are the words which Moses spoke to all Israel beyond the Jordan in the wilderness'; and *ib*. v. 5: 'Beyond the Jordan, in the land of Moab.' These examples are relied on by Bleek, and afterwards by Colenso.

But this apparently formidable objection admits of a perfectly satisfactory answer. *Beeber hajjarden* is, no doubt, used to denote the country on the other side of the Jordan in reference to the speaker; *e.g.*, in the unfulfilled desire of Moses: [1] 'I will pass over, therefore, and will see this excellent land beyond the Jordan.' But, paradoxical as it may be at first sight, it denotes also the country on the speaker's side of that river. It is employed by a trans-Jordanic speaker to designate trans-Jordanic territory, and by a cis-Jordanic writer to designate cis-Jordanic territory.

As regards the first usage, in the course of the very speech our opponents refer to,[2] Moses, who never crossed the Jordan, says:[3] 'And we took at that time the land out of the hand of the two kings of the Amorrhites, *beeber hajjarden* [virtually equivalent to 'on this side of Jordan'— if it means 'beyond,' it does so in a purely conventional sense, as will be explained further on], from the torrent Arnon unto the mount Hermon.'[4] Everyone knows

---

[1] Deut. iii. 25.   [2] Deut. i. 6; iv 40.   [3] Deut. iii. 8.

[4] The Vulgate has here: 'Tulimusque illo in tempore terram de manu duorum regum Amorrhaorum, qui erant trans Jordanem: a torrente Arnon usque ad montem Hermon.' Lest, however, its words, ' qui erant,' should

that the Arnon and Mount Hermon, and the land of the
Amorrhites that Moses took, are east of the Jordan ; therefore, *beeber hajjarden* has here a trans-Jordanic significance.
The whole speech is given in *oratio directa*, just as it fell
from the lips of Moses, and is, moreover, reported by himself. But a writer in the newest Hebrew lexicon (Clarendon
Press), apparently in the interests of higher criticism, makes
the sapient remark that 'the writer (D) ascribes his own
standpoint to Moses.' This is higher criticism ! On the
assumption that the words in question were used by Moses,
the chimerical cis-Jordanic writer in the seventh century
B.C. is invoked by the critics to put from his own standpoint
into the mouth of Moses, addressing the Israelites on the
east of the Jordan a thousand years before, a meaning
which would be not only quite irrelevant, but which is
incompatible with the context. Why do not the critics at
once put Arnon and Hermon into Western Palestine, and
say that Moses meant 'beyond the Jordan'? No ; in
Deuteronomy iii. 8 it is plain that he referred to the side of
the Jordan he was on, and also in i. 1-5, the two passages
which Bleek and Colenso misinterpret.

Now, for an example of the opposite usage ; *i.e.*, a cis-
Jordanic writer applying *beeber hajjarden* to cis-Jordanic
territory. We have it in Josue ix. 1 : ' Now, when all these
things were heard of, all the kings *beeber hajjarden* [*i.e.*, on
the west of the Jordan] that dwelt in the places near the
sea and on the coasts of the great sea ' ; *i.e.*, the Mediterra-
nean. This, surely, is intelligible ; but the Clarendon Press
Hebrew Lexicon remarks here, ' (D) from standpoint of those
just crossed.' Really, a very hard task is imposed on the poor
Deuteronomist : First, he had to go over the Jordan in order
to ascribe his own standpoint to Moses, and now he has to
come back in order to qualify himself for writing history
from the standpoint of those who have just crossed. This
is more higher criticism ! Why cannot Moses and Josue be

create a difficulty for some of our readers, it may be observed that in the
Hebrew there is nothing to correspond to them: The substantive verb is not
used and the passage reads exactly as translated into English above.

let alone, and why may we not learn Hebrew idiom from them? [1]

Lastly comes the best example of all; a passage in which *meeber lajjarden* is used of both trans-Jordanic and cis-Jordanic territories. It is Numbers xxxii. 19. 'We will not inherit with them on yonder side of the Jordan [*meeber lajjarden*], or forward; because our inheritance is fallen to us on this side of the Jordan [*meeber hajjarden*], eastward.' In each clause respectively, an adverb determining the relative position is added, in order to remove the ambiguity of the expression. This is often done also in the case of *beeber hajjarden :* ' towards the sunrise ' is added in Deuteronomy iv. 41, 47, 49; Josue i. 15; xii. 1; xiii. 8, 32; xviii. 7; xx. 8; 1 Paralipomenon vi. 63; in order to make it clear that the east of the Jordan is meant: and for a similar reason, where there is reference to the west side, ' seawards ' is added in Josue v. 1; xii. 7; xxii. 7; and ' towards the sunset ' in Deuteronomy xi. 30.

Our readers may very well ask what they are to think of this Protean expression 'beyond the Jordan' which has opposite meanings at the speaker's will, and which if it is ever to get an independent and fixed signification of its own, needs to be determined by an adjunct. One of the greatest authorities on the subject, the late (Archbishop) Smith explains it thus in his work on the *Pentateuch*, page 433 :—

Its proper signification, when used of a river, is bank, margin, side, river-land. This is equivalently admitted by Gesenius in his

---

[1] This usage may be illustrated by an example taken from a much later date, and referring to another river. In 1 (3) Kings iv. 24 Solomon's kingdom, which extended to the western bank of the Euphrates (in the Old Testament the river *par excellence*), is said to be *eber hannahar* (Vulgate, *trans fumen*), but the Authorised Version, correctly, ' on this side the river.' Nevertheless the *Oxford Lexicon* has ' beyond the river,' because this Book of Kings was written in Babylonia! Higher criticism again; and Professor Driver, the writer of the article in the *Lexicon*, refers to his own *Introduction to the Literature of the Old Testament*, p. 191, where we read as follows : 'The intermediary verses, iv. 20-26, interrupt the connection, and seem to be an insertion, which the expression in v. 24—' beyond the river ' (i.e., the Euphrates)—applied to the country west of the Euphrates, and implying, consequently, a Babylonian standpoint (see Ezra iv. 10), shows, cannot be earlier than the period of the exile.' Again in 1 Esd. iv. 10 the meaning of *eber hannahar* is ' this side of the river.' The true explanation is, that a man writing in Judea is speaking of Samaria.

Thesaurus, and amply justified by Fürst in his *Lexicon*. From this definition it is clear that, of itself, the word does not imply the other side, more than this side : and that it is, after all, the immediate context that is to determine its exact bearing.

Nevertheless, seeing that in Arabic, *abar* signifies 'to cross over, and that in Assyrian, the twin-dialect of Hebrew, *ebru* signifies 'the region beyond,' it may very well be that the Hebrew *eber* means 'beyond.' The verbal stem *abar*, from which it is derived, certainly means to cross. And this agrees with what Smith himself says, on page 430, namely that *beeber hajjarden* would have been used by Abraham and his immediate descendants in Canaan to denote the country lying to the east of the Jordan, that the expression like other similar ones was retained by the people during the sojourn in Egypt, and that it was quite intelligible to them and caused no surprise, whatever,[1] when Moses used it in the land of Moab. And the Archbishop points to the fact that in after-ages Peraea (Περαν του Ιορδανου) was the proper name of the north-east provinces.

[To be continued.]   REGINALD WALSH, O.P.

---

[1] This may be made more intelligible by examples. The name 'Trastevere,' which means 'beyond the Tiber,' dates from the time when the whole of the imperial city lay on the eastern bank of the river. Hence it cannot be used in accordance with its original and proper signification, except by one who is on the same side as are the seven hills. But the name is employed by everyone quite irrespectively of the bank of the Tiber on which one happens to be. You hear it on both sides of the Ponte Sisto, and though you hear it in the Lungara, there is not the least danger of mistake, because 'Trastevere' has become the inalienable appellation of the district that begins at the foot of the Janiculum, or Montorio. The word 'Alsace' affords another good example of the limitation of a name to designate a particular locality exclusively, so that in course of time a common noun has become a proper one, and has lost its relative significance to gain an absolute one. Alsace virtually means 'the other side,' it comes from the mediæval Latin *Alisatia* and the Old High German *Elisazzo*, which mean 'incola peregrinus,' 'Bewohner des andern Rheinufers'='a foreigner from the other side of the Rhine.' (See Kluge's *Etymologisches Wörterbuch der deutschen Sprache*, s. v. Eland.) But at the present day 'Alsace' is, to many nations, on *this* side of the Rhine.

'LUKE DELMEGE'[1]

WE have once again to offer our hearty congratulations to Father Sheehan. His new novel, *Luke Delmege*, though not in all respects up to the standard of *My New Curate*, is still a book of uncommon interest. The phases of clerical life with which it deals are touched by the hand of an expert. The humour and the pathos of the story will bring smiles and tears to many a fireside in Ireland and beyond the seas. Irishmen of all classes, layman and priest, merchant and manufacturer, the reformer of antiquated methods in agriculture and industry, the pioneer of technical education, the zealot and the *doctrinaire*, will all find food for reflection in the book. It will help them, if they need help, to realize the difficulties of their task. It will do but little, we fear, to enable them to solve the riddle that puzzles so many theoretical philanthropists.

The deep note of religious faith echoes through the book from beginning to end, but the light note of humour tingles on the surface. The development of this latter vein, since the days of *Geoffrey Austen* is quite remarkable, and to a great extent accounts for the widespread popularity of Father Sheehan's recent works.

Humour that takes the critical turn is a dangerous possession; but Father Sheehan has kept his gift well in control; and there is not a sally of his wit or a gleam of his comic descriptions that any critic could seriously find fault with.

Lightly, sparingly, and with a sympathy begotten of intimate acquaintance, does he depict the foibles, the peculiarities, the eccentricities of his brethren. No one assuredly could do it more mildly and write a novel. We have heard, no doubt, the cry of ' Wolf ! Wolf ! ' It is hard to write anything nowadays without someone shouting

---

[1] *Luke Delmege*. By the Rev. P. A. Sheehan, Author of *My New Curate*, etc. London: Longmans, Green, & Co. 1901. 6s.

'Wolf' from behind his anonymous hedge. The man must, however, be badly off, indeed, for a wolf who seeks one in the author of *Luke Delmege* and *My New Curate.*

At a time when we are all talking so loudly of the havoc wrought by the corrupt literature that pours into our country from across the channel we cannot but feel deeply grateful to one who has done a man's part, and done it so effectively, to stem the tide. Father Sheehan's novel may have its defects; it may not be all that we might wish; we shall not conceal our dislike for many of its features; but in substance it is a good book; and should it find a place alongside *My New Curate* in every Irish cottage the home will be the richer and the better for its possession.

Maynooth, we observe, has come in for its share of the author's sly and pungent criticism; but Maynooth has with stood the shock of far more wicked assaults with comparative equanimity. She was not much affected by the caricatures of Lever or of Carleton. The satire of Thackeray and Carlyle left her undisturbed. Now, that she is putting on the coat of her second century, she is not likely to become more sensitive than she used to be to the shafts of humorists and of novel-writers. They are all welcome to try their hand. If they have any suggestion to make for her good that is practical and sound, a thing that rarely occurs, we have no doubt it will get due consideration. If not, those responsible for the College will probably listen to their babble whilst they follow their own guiding star.

It must not be thought that Maynooth is the only college in the world that sends out a 'first of first' man with a good conceit of himself. The author of *Luke Delmege* has possibly heard of the Cambridge Senior Wrangler who, with his academic honours thick and fresh upon him, went up to London and drove to the theatre. Just as he made his appearance a great outburst of cheering arose from the assembly, and he immediately proceeded to bow in all directions, acknowledging the cheers. To his great disgust, however, he soon learned that the cheers were intended, not for himself, but for King George IV., who was just then entering his box.

Maynooth also shares with many other colleges the privilege of sending out into the world men whose knowledge is, for the time being at all events, crude and ill-digested. We ourselves had the privilege of meeting, some years ago, a distinguished Oxford graduate, who had just carried away the prize of his university in Modern History, but was, nevertheless, under the impression that Daniel O'Connell was a Protestant. We had great difficulty in persuading him that he was mistaken.

Luke Delmege combines the defects of these representatives of Oxford and Cambridge. He goes forth from Maynooth with his head turned; he is elated by success, carried away by his worldly hopes. Still worse, he is utterly ignorant of the manners of the drawing-room; he does not know when it is his duty to open the door for the ladies; he has not seen the most recent numbers of the *Lancet* and the *Medical Press;* he is not able to hold his own in the illuminating conversation of the Sumners and the Louis Wilsons; he dare not go to the piano to sing: he shouts his ballad from the chimney-piece; he has not read Gabriele d'Annunzio's last; he has never even heard of Guy de Maupassant: terrible drawbacks of Maynooth education, to which the attention of the Trustees ought to be called at the earliest possible moment. They might surely be expected to get up a drawing-room in Maynooth in which those of their students who have no drawing-rooms at home, and who know not how to profit by the instructions of Valuy or the ' Manual of Etiquette,' might be taught how to stand at a piano and to hand around tea. At this hour of the day young clerics might at least be supplied with an up-to-date library that would bring them into line with the age, and enable them to speak with authority of Zola and of Ouida to those intellectual giants, the Sumners and Louis Wilsons, of our country towns and villages.

A mere knowledge of scholastic philosophy is not, it appears, after all, the best equipment for a man who has to face the philosophies of the world. Leo XIII. may think otherwise; but then Leo XIII. has a good deal to learn from young men with progressive views. Rusty weapons dug up from the saw-pits of the middle ages are expected to stand against the instruments of precision brought to bear upon them by modern science. As well might you put the effigy of a knight in doublet and breastplate in front of a Maxim gun. Just fancy your *Sic argumentaris, Domine*, applied to the reasoning of a Huxley or a Mallock? Why it would go to pieces in your hands before the dialectics of the new woman, to say nothing of the new man? Only think of the Maynooth stripling who has been immersed for six or seven years in the mere theoretical study of Christian principles, and who has not devoted more than a single year to the department of ethics and sociology, presuming to have an opinion on questions of politics and economics in the presence of Mr. Taper and Mr. Tadpole, of those thoughtful experts, graduates, perhaps, of a University, who have been ruminating on such questions all their lives ; or in face of practical men of the world, trained to business habits and comprehensive views, in the public-houses and pawn-shops of the country !

At least if the juvenile cleric wishes to rise above his immediate surroundings, and to take an intelligent interest, even though he take no active part, in the great movements of thought that agitate the world, let him not go forth without having grappled with the antagonists of his time. Let him make an honest endeavour to grasp the principles of Kant and of Spencer, of Comte and of Haeckel, of Lasalle and of Karl Marx. Let him do it at first hand and not through the pauperizing medium of a text-book. This certainly has a fine sound. But we wonder what the professors of *Higher Philosophy* have been doing in Maynooth for the past ten or fifteen years. Luke Delmege had, we believe, left the College just before they came. In so far we sympathize with him. But it is not the philosophical faculty alone that is responsible for his outfit. He is the product of the College as a whole. He must have had the advantage of being trained in the theological school and in the school of character and discipline by some of the greatest churchmen of the century. That between them they should have turned out the blundering 'idiot' their 'first of first' man proves himself to be could not be regarded as very complimentary, if there was any evidence of an intention on the part of the author to represent Luke Delmege as the best that they could educate. But, in our opinion, there is no such evidence. The hero is from the start a strange and peculiar personage. As such he is treated all along the line. Foreigners and others may, no doubt, regard him as representative of Maynooth education. But after all what great matter does it make how they regard him?

We have heard of persons who think that in all this Father Sheehan has dealt an unnatural blow at the reputation of his *Alma Mater*. There are few, we imagine, so narrow-minded as to share in this view. We prefer to think that the interest of the author of *Luke Delmege* in his own college is not the less warm and sincere because he has spoken so freely of what he regards as some of her short-comings. Whether he is justified in his strictures is a matter that we should like to leave to others to decide. All we can say is that to us they appear supremely ridiculous. It is but natural that those who are jealous of the fair name of the College should object to see her held up to the scoffs of Englishmen and Americans. But then, of course, everything depends on the intention of the writer and on the importance that need be attached to the opinion of those who generalize and conclude from the specimens presented to them. If she has turned out a 'Luke Delmege,' has she not also turned out a parish priest of Doneraile? The greatest tribute to her position in the ecclesiastical world is that so many persons should be concerned about her merits and defects. She has in hand, in truth, an undertaking that is serious and weighty enough not to trouble herself about trifles. So great is the variety of her interests and activities that she may safely welcome criticism on many details of her work. Minds of a worldly tinge may not be able to judge her methods without bias. Enough for her if she attains with the great mass of the young men she sends out into the world the standard of St. Bonaventure, *Incedunt securius, resistunt fortius*.

It must not be forgotten, moreover, that at Maynooth there was planted in the innermost recesses of Luke's heart a seedling that never entirely failed, but ultimately took root and came to a fruitful and happy maturity. It was on the day of his ordination that he first became fully conscious of its presence.

How paltry every human ambition seemed then ; how ragged the tinsel of kings, how cheap and worthless the pinchbeck of earthly thrones ! How his soul burned to emulate the heroism of saints—to go abroad and be forgotten by the world and remembered only by Christ—to live and die amongst the lepers and the insane—to pass by one swift stroke of the dull sword of the executioner in China or Japan to his immortal crown !

Compare these early sentiments with those of the chastened and toilworn priest at the end of his short career, and after all you have the key to his education and his character.

It has been remarked, we believe, that Father Sheehan's clerical personages are, on the whole, not typical of the Irish priesthood. To a certain extent there are grounds for the criticism ; but, then, it is not necessary, for the purposes of a novel, that they should be typical of the whole body. It is enough that they should be either representative of a class or that they should be painted from life ; and that there are in the country specimens of the kind described, few, we think, would venture to deny. After all, poets and novel-writers seldom lay hold of characters that are genuinely typical. In the commonplace, work-a-day representatives of any calling or profession they take, as a rule, but little interest. They are attracted, perhaps through the influence of some subtle affinity, by the oddities of genius ; they revel in the company of strange comrades ; they require someone with distinctive traits, with salient features, with some natural characteristics unusually developed. If they do not find the personage they are looking for, they invent him, or they exaggerate and dress up such material as they discover. By such devices, by such intermingling of fact and of fiction, they manage to instruct and to amuse. One touch of nature makes the whole world kin, and the amusement derived from the foibles, the weaknesses, the eccentricities of individuals, held up to nature's mirror, contributes no small share to the general stock of common sense. No one, for instance, would take the curate whose aesthetic taste finds adequate satisfaction in the picture of 'Elliman's Embrocation' as typical of any but the rarest and most outlandish. Yet, Father Sheehan's joke is not, to say the least, calculated to provide him with imitators.

It is also put forth that these descriptions of clerical life are liable to convey to the laity, to those outside the Church and to those outside the country, a false impression of the Irish clergy, and possibly to shock the finer feelings of those for whose perversion the millstone is the penalty. We confess that we have heard this charge brought against the book with mingled feelings. On the whole, we would say that the good opinion of people who are capable of being shocked at these descriptions is of very paltry value. A little criticism that is not malignant is good for all men who are not hypocrites or fools. We distrust the piety of Tartufe and the professions of Mr. Pecksniff. We are not all perfect, and, if we think the laity imagine that we are, we must be living in a paradise of our own creation. The Irish clergy are loved by the people for their all-redeeming qualities, and, perhaps, not a little also for those very human characteristics which Father Sheehan has reproduced. They bring them nearer to the popular heart ; they establish connecting links with the faithful which are stronger than any 'hoops of steel.' Rarely, indeed, do they offer umbrage even to the weaklings ; they are held in awe before *unum de pusillis istis.*

There are in the book a few things, perhaps, on the verge of propriety that might well have been omitted. Members of the parochial clergy are not numerous, we imagine, who would suggest to a young priest, fresh from his ordination, that he might violate or ignore the diocesan statutes. There are also many polite attentions of society that are quite becoming in lay people, but are out of place in an ecclesiastic, particularly in a priest—attentions, too, that are least expected by those who are best educated and most refined.

It is probable that in the future, as in the past, the Irish clergy will look for the ideal in such matters to St. Charles Borromeo and St. Vincent de Paul, to Jean Jacques Olier and the Council of Trent, rather than to the lofty personages created to give them hints and suggestions by the author of *Luke Delmege*.

As for those outside the Church, there are many things in the book that ought to attract them; and they are more likely to be impressed by a picture drawn from nature, however imperfect it may be, than by one evolved from the recesses of the imagination. If they are still dissatified let them look nearer home and see what they have to find. In the case of foreigners, there are, no doubt, some grounds for thinking that they may draw conclusions that are not justified from Father Sheehan's book. *Videbitur infra*.

As far as we are concerned, the faults we have to find with *Luke Delmege* are faults of manner and of method rather than of motive or of delineation.

The action of the story seems to us not to be well maintained. The connection of the various incidents with the main subject of the narrative and with one another is often involved in a sort of nebulous haze. It would look as if there were too many characters introduced to allow the interest to be fixed on any but a few. One might drop the book at the end of any chapter without feeling irresistibly drawn to follow it to the end.

Again, the author is much too fond, in our opinion, of throwing at the heads of his readers the names of foreign writers. It may look learned, but it can scarcely escape the note of pedantry. They come, in all his books, in a regular procession—Goethe, Kant, Klopstock, Novalis, Richter, Wieland, etc. That the author is deeply read in German philosophy and German poetry we are quite willing to believe. We should, however, credit it with no less freedom did he not obtrude the evidences of his knowledge so very persistently.

If foreign words must be introduced it would be as well to have them spelled correctly. Such words as ' Commissionaire ' (page 291), ' bonhommie ' (page 357),

'Dame de St. Esprit' (page 376), 'denouement' (page 550), would require revision. We are pretty sure also that Charcot does not speak of an 'idée fixée,' although, of course, it would be grammatically correct. Then a '*pfennig*' (page 291) is not the hundredth part of a franc, but the hundredth part of a mark. No one on earth could mistake a pfennig for a franc. There is, however, a nickel coin of ten pfennigs that might easily be mistaken for a franc. There is no one more liable to overlook errors and misprints than the person who first committed them to paper.

We saw not long ago a very strong and patriotic pronouncement of the author of *Luke Delmege* on the Irish language and its claims upon Irishmen of the present day. We are quite sure the pronouncement was sincere; but we are somewhat astonished that the author of such popular sentiments can scarcely find an Irish name for any of his heroes or heroines. Geoffrey Austen, Charlie Travers, Gwendoline Oliver, Hubert Deane, Helen Bellamy, Bittra Campion, Father Letheby, Mr. Ormsby, Dr. Calthrop Mrs. Wenham, Luke Delmege, Barbara Wilson, Amiel Lefevril, Canon Murray, have no very Celtic sound about them. From an enthusiast about the tongue of the Gael we should have expected something more distinctly Irish. Is it impossible to associate distinction with a Carroll, or a Sullivan, or an O'Connell? We thought the McCarthys were good for something besides 'welting the flure.' The most despicable character in the book bears the name of Fitzgerald. We refer to the friend of the Prince of Wales. 'Wire me, Fitzgerald.' 'Say Fitzgerald recommended it.'

Perhaps Father Sheehan knows best what his public likes. He may have taken his Irish readers at their own estimate, knowing the weakness of so many amongst them for the style and title of people whom they regard as their betters. But then we should not quite expect that a seer and a prophet would allow himself to be influenced by the vitiated taste of the public. Is not his mission to educate and reform? Has he not proclaimed from the house-tops that Irish speech and Irish sentiment, and the ideal of

Irish saints and sages and scholars, constitute the only lever
that can bring back the race to a sense of its dignity, the
only barrier that can save it from destruction and guide it
along the path congenial to its progress ? When we think
of this, and when we see that all the English clerics are
models in their line, and that all the Irish ones, though
good enough in their way, are still replete with deficiencies, bred in imperfection, and when we meet with an
O'Shaughnessy and a Fitzgerald only to laugh them to scorn,
whilst the Sheldons and the Drysdales and the Godfreys
are intended to excite envy and admiration, we find ourselves face to face with a curious problem and we make
our own reflections on the value of some of the pronouncements we hear about 'our grand old tongue,' about the
pressing claims of Celtic civilization and ' the undying spirit
of the Gael.'

Father Sheehan, no doubt, wrote for English and
American readers, as well as for the people of Ireland.
He is the very last person, we are quite sure, to whom the
intention could be imputed of holding up his own countrymen to the ridicule of foreigners; and yet we can scarcely
deny that some things at least in his book, whether he wished
it or not, are calculated to leave the impression that he has
done so on the mind.

Far be it from us to minimize the importance of
refinement, of a gentlemanly bearing, of a knowledge of
the art of life, of an acquaintance with the rules of propriety, of correctness of speech and precision of thought.
If amongst the Irish clergy there are some who attach
but little value to such things, in that they do not stand
alone. They have brethren in every country in the world.
Perhaps if in Ireland they had turned their backs upon
the people who stood by them in evil days as they
stand by them now, and had sought more refined and
cultivated company, they might be greater adepts in the
world's ways, and might even hold their own with the
Sheldons and the Drysdales; but then, perhaps, too, another
side of the picture might not be quite so pleasant to contemplate.

It is self-evident that the man who in his own person represents the two greatest moving forces in the world—religion and education—ought to seek to elevate others to his own standard rather than allow himself to sink to theirs. But then on the bleak mountain side and in the sequestered valley, by the storm-tossed ocean and over the desolate moor, the veneer of conventionality meets with considerable friction. That some of it should be rubbed off in the turmoil of life is easily intelligible. Meantime the well-spring of kindness and charity often becomes purer and more abundant where nature rules in her lonely majesty, and its vivifying streams flow out more profusely over the fields for which Providence intended them. Where we have the essential we need not complain too much at the absence of the accessory. In the great majority of cases we have both. The one is usually the result, the natural embellishment of the other. No individual character in Father Sheehan's book would, perhaps, indicate anything to the contrary. But taking them all in all they would seem to make the balance incline to the other side.

If we have spoken thus plainly about what we regard as some of the defects of Father Sheehan's work, it is certainly not because we are blind to its merits or insensible to its beauty. On the contrary, we should like to do the fullest justice to its many admirable qualities—to its quaint humour, its bright and lifelike pictures, its easy yet vivid style, its evidence of sympathy, of penetration, and of insight.

We can forgive a good deal for the sake of Father Meade and Father Tracey, of the excellent Canon and of Miss Barbara Wilson. An intimate knowledge of all that is homely and genial in Irish life has seldom been more remarkably displayed. In reproducing the peculiar turns of thought and speech that are prevalent in our day, the author has become an adept. There is something of the terseness of epigram in his phrases and a flavour of poetry in many of his sentences. He has gone for his English to its living source among the poets and prose writers of its best days. In his scrutiny of character, its developments and the influences that have shaped it, he has made his

way far beneath the surface. This indeed is one of the great
merits of his book.

Father Sheehan, as things appear to us, has looked with
a more intuitive glance, and has seen deeper into the elusive
nature of the Celt, and of that variety of the race that
flourishes in his native land, than almost any other man
of his time. He has caught, as it were in snapshots,
phases of its life that had never yet been secured by
any other artist; he has wrought into fiction features
that have been evolved from legend and from myth,
from temperament and from history, from the tragedies
and comedies of other days; and through them he has
enabled us to scrutinize at leisure the soul that gives
them life. We see it enveloped in the mist of centuries; we
watch its countless changes, its innumerable contrarieties,
its ever-fitful efforts; we witness the perpetual struggle that
goes on within it between the dream and the reality, the
beauty of ideas and the tyranny of facts. It escapes from
our view in a sort of mystic light, unwearied only in the
pursuit of its everlasting destiny.

And yet he has not done all that we would wish, nor all
that we might expect. He has been for the most part a
psychologist, who has noted the phenomena, but has done
little to indicate their value. He has probed our wounds,
but, with one exception, has suggested no remedy; he has
laid bare our weaknesses, and he has also left us under the
impression that they are inherent and incurable. If not a
fatalist, he makes upon us the impression of one whom
Christianity alone has saved from being a pessimist. There
is an element of irony in the reflection that his message
should recall to us the memorable words of a philosopher of
his own creation: ' *Cui bono* ? 'Twill be all the same in a
hundred years.' In these days of storm and stress, of sifting
and of change, of great projects and of sanguine hopes, we
might have expected something less calculated to damp our
spirits.

It would not, we admit, be consonant with the principles
of his art that he should undertake the work of a benevolent
society or of the Department of Agriculture. But at least

we might expect him to direct to those complicated problems of life, so lightly skimmed over in his book, some share at least of that attention which he represents as distracted by futilities and wasted in fruitless speculation. He might have helped to make his countrymen conscious of the forces which their carelessness has left to slumber in such unproductive lethargy. He might have shown them, under the concentrated light of his own intelligence, the results of their waywardness and caprice. He might have pointed to some exit from the maze in which their energies seem fettered. He has preferred to remain a passive moralist. He has chosen to adopt too much of what we regard as the vicious principle of 'art for the sake of art,' describing things as they are and allowing them to tell their own tale. On the higher plane of religious life he has contrasted in the priest the value of learning and of piety, to the detriment of the former, an error that goes far to spoil the book, and is opposed to the teaching of the best spiritual guides.

The part of the work that is not religious will, on the other hand, have no more direct or practical effect than to interest and amuse the present generation and reflect to posterity the ways and manners of our time. And yet we are thankful, indeed, for what we have received. It is not perfect. It is not a classic. It is not a masterpiece. It is full of absurdities and of stilted nonsense. It is like a speech of Lord Rosebery, leaving us oftentimes in doubt as to which side it takes. It is hopeless and helpless where both hope and help are needed. But in spite of these defects, and of others that we need not mention, it is, taking it all in all, a fascinating book, a clever, an instructive, and a good one.

J. F. HOGAN, D.D.

TRINITY COLLEGE AND THE UNIVERSITY OF DUBLIN

IN a letter recently published in some Dublin newspapers a startling paradox has been propounded. There is, we are informed, no distinction between Trinity College and the University of Dublin : Trinity College is the University of Dublin, and the University of Dublin is Trinity College.

The statement thus made is of so extraordinary a character that it may be well for me to transcribe it in the very words in which it has been made. The author of it says :—

I can confidently assert that *no such entity as a University of Dublin, distinct from Trinity College, or independent of it, or outside it, or in any way apart or separate from it, exists, or ever did exist, legally, constitutionally, or in fact.*

Again :—

The College is thus the University in every particular.

And again, after a quotation from the Act of Union :—

These words are repeated three times in Article Eight, showing that constitutionally *the University* of Trinity College *and the College* of the Holy Trinity of Dublin are *one and the same thing, perfectly identical.*

As a member of the Catholic Episcopacy of Ireland, and more especially as Archbishop of Dublin, I feel called upon to protest against these statements. I do so, primarily, in discharge of the duty that I owe to the memory of an illustrious predecessor of mine in the See of Dublin, Cardinal Cullen,—a duty, let me add, that all Irish Catholics owe to the memory of that great prelate, of whom it can be said, without fear of contradiction, that to him, more than to any other Irishman, living or dead, the credit is due that there is a University question, alive, and clamouring for settlement on the line of absolute equality for Catholics, in Ireland to-day.

In personal writings of Cardinal Cullen, as well as in resolutions of the assembled Episcopacy of Ireland—resolutions not only cordially and publicly approved by his Eminence, but, we cannot doubt, largely inspired, in the framing of them, by his wisdom,—there was a proposal more than once put forward as covering everything that was needed to place within the reach of the Catholics of Ireland, on terms of perfect equality, the degrees, the endowments, and the other Collegiate and University advantages enjoyed by our fellow-countrymen of other creeds.   It was a proposal put forward only in the supposition that a Catholic University,—meaning by this, a Catholic University in the proper sense of the words,—was not to be established. The proposal was, that there should be established in Dublin a new College, in every respect equal to Trinity College, and, like Trinity College, a College of the University of Dublin.

Hence it is that I have to protest against the slur cast,—inadvertently, I am sure,—not only upon my predecessor, Cardinal Cullen, but upon our whole Episcopal body, by the statements now given to the public as indisputable statements of the law of the case.   Those statements simply amount to this, that the distinction upon which the proposal that I have mentioned is essentially based,—the distinction between Trinity College and the University of Dublin,—is wholly groundless.

Undoubtedly if, as is now alleged, 'no such entity as a University of Dublin, distinct from Trinity College, exists, or ever did exist, legally, constitutionally, or in fact,'—if, ' in every particular, the College is the University,'—if ' the University ' and ' the College ' are ' one and the same thing, perfectly identical,'—then, obviously, the proposal so formally enunciated by the assembled Catholic Episcopacy of Ireland, that another College, equal to Trinity College, should be established as a College of the University of Dublin, is not only irreconcileable with law, but is mere nonsense.

In connection with a similar matter, I had occasion some short time ago to remark that a confusion of ideas as

between a College and a University is not unnatural in
Dublin. It is not unnatural at least in the case of those of
our fellow-citizens who have not had the opportunity
of visiting Oxford, with its 24 Colleges, or Cambridge,
with its 19 or 20 Colleges,—University towns in which the
distinction between College and College, and between
College and University, is plain even to the little children
in the streets. But that surely is no reason why those of us
who have a perfectly clear idea of the distinction between
Trinity College and the University of Dublin should be
charged with ignorance, either of the facts or of the law of
the case, by persons who themselves proclaim that they
are ignorant of the existence of the distinction, and who
appear to be unable even to see it when it is pointed out by
others.

So far, then, for the legal theory recently sought to be
set up, in its relation to the published resolutions of the
Irish Catholic Episcopacy. I have now to touch upon
another aspect of the case.

It is, I must say, a marvel to me that, long before this,
some prominent member of the Irish Bar has not, on a
ground quite different from mine, come forward to make the
protest that I am making now. It is possible, no doubt,
that in this country, unhappily of short-lived memory, the
services rendered to his Catholic fellow-countrymen by Isaac
Butt, in his advocacy of their claims in the matter of
University education, are already beginning to be forgotten.
But there must still be members of the Irish Bar by whom
those services have not been forgotten. In the statements quoted at the beginning of this paper, the distinction
which was the very foundation upon which Mr. Butt
rested so much of his labour in this special field
of public work,—the distinction between Trinity College
and the University of Dublin,—is treated as a thing
utterly at variance with every legal principle that has
a bearing upon the point. It is treated in fact, as a thing
scarcely worthy of serious refutation. I am at a loss to
understand how it is that so many of those who in their
early days at the bar were his contemporaries, have submitted

in silence to see such a reflection cast upon the memory of the great lawyer who was once looked up to by them as the brilliant leader with whom it was their pride to be associated in any case, great or small.

Anyone who chooses to do so is free, of course, to say that Cardinal Cullen knew nothing of English law. My great predecessor—eminent as, on a memorable occasion, he showed himself to be as a canonist,—would, I have no doubt, in his humility, have disclaimed all pretension to an accurate acquaintance with any branch of the law that is administered in our civil courts. But, however that may be, it amazes me to find that amongst the practising lawyers of our day even one could be found who would care to commit himself to a statement amounting equivalently to this, that in reference to the legal, constitutional, and actual relation of Trinity College to the University of Dublin, Isaac Butt is to be set down as nothing better than an ignoramus.

The issue raised by the statements quoted at the beginning of this paper is the very simple one: Is the University of Dublin identical with Trinity College, or is it not?

In dealing with the issue thus raised, I may begin by expressing my satisfaction that it is not necessary for me again to set forth the long series of quotations from Acts of Parliament, from Royal Letters Patent, and from other authoritative documents, which I recently had occasion to cite [1] in connection with a point—in itself of comparative insignificance—as to the name by which the University of Dublin may be designated. I am happily not further concerned with the statement that it is 'inaccurate' to speak of that University as the 'University of Dublin.' I have shown that this very name is given to that University in no fewer than eleven Acts of Parliament— twice in five of them, three times in another, six times in another—and, again, in nine Royal Letters Patent—twice in one of these, three times in another, and five times in

---

[1] I refer to a letter of mine published in the *Freeman's Journal* of the 6th of January, in the present year.

a third. I may safely regard the statement about the 'inaccuracy' of the designation, as amply disposed of.

But *prius est esse quam denominari.* The statement by which anyone who feels himself called upon to vindicate the resolutions of the Irish Episcopacy from the stigma of inaccuracy,—and not merely of inaccuracy, but of nonsense,—now finds himself challenged, is the unqualified denial that, as distinct from Trinity College, such a thing as a University of Dublin, no matter by what name it may be designated, exists at all!

From the way in which this grave matter has been dealt with, bandied about as it has been for the last few weeks, in letters, and speeches, and newspaper articles, a person uninformed as to the facts never could have supposed that the case stands as it really does. Who, for instance, not otherwise informed as to the facts, could have supposed that the very point now so flippantly discoursed about had been, in the past, the subject of most careful consideration, in all its legal bearings, by eminent lawyers of the highest judicial rank? Who could have supposed that one Vice-Chancellor of the University of Dublin, Lord Chancellor Blackburne, had communicated to the Senate of the University, so far back as the year 1858, a 'formal and deliberate opinion,' upon it? Or that another lawyer, of the very highest reputation, an ex-Chancellor of Ireland, Sir Joseph Napier, when Vice-Chancellor of the University, finding a view somewhat at variance with the considered opinion of his predecessor, Lord Chancellor Blackburne, propounded by a non-legal Fellow of Trinity College, in a published work, had applied himself to a further and most minute examination of the case in all its bearings? Or that a long and detailed statement of the conclusions at which Sir Joseph Napier then arrived,—fully confirmatory as they were of the view put before the University Senate by his predecessor in 1858,—was communicated by him, as he himself expresses it, 'to *the governing body of the College*, and to the *Senate of the University*,' in 1871? Or that this erudite exposition of the whole question, first published in a pamphlet in 1871, has since been republished as an introduction to a well-known volume,[1] brought out in Dublin by the publishers to the University so recently as 1896 ? Or that,—to bring to a close this long series of references,—the conclusion arrived at and established, without qualification of any kind, by those two eminent lawyers is, that Trinity College and the University of Dublin are not only two distinct bodies, but are two distinct corporations, in the strictly legal sense of the word.

At this point, it will be convenient to go back a little, to trace matters up from an earlier time.[2]

In the Dublin University Calendar for 1833,—which, I think, will be found to have been the first issue of the Calendar,—there was published an interesting historical account of the foundation of the College and University. In that account, reference was made by the learned editor of the Calendar, the late Dr. Todd, in terms of unqualified approval, to a pamphlet published in 1804, by the Rev. George Miller, D.D., then a Fellow of Trinity College.[3] Dr. Todd refers to this pamphlet ' for a complete and satisfactory discussion of the question about the distinction between the College and the University.'

Dr. Miller, as is obvious from the title of his pamphlet, was a fore-runner of those theorists of the present day who maintain that the distinction between the University of Dublin and Trinity College is only a 'supposed' one. Dr. Todd, in 1833, was clearly in agreement with Dr. Miller on the point. He says that Dr. Miller ' has clearly shown that the opinion about the necessity of a distinction between

---

[1] *A Catalogue of Graduates of the University of Dublin*, vol. ii. (Second Edition). Dublin : Hodges, Figgis, & Co., 1896.

[2] To avoid an otherwise confusing multiplicity of quotation marks and footnote references, I may here state, once for all, that, in the remainder of this paper I adhere as closely as possible to the words of Sir Joseph Napier's learned exposition of the subject when dealing with any of the matters with which he has dealt.

I shall not formally quote from that exposition except in those cases in which I may consider it advisable to adduce the authority of Sir Joseph Napier in support of some particular statement.

[3] *An Examination of the Charters and Statutes of Trinity College, Dublin, in regard to the supposed distinction between the College and the University.* By the Rev. George Miller, D.D., F.T.C.D.

the University and the College originated in the prejudices
of our early Provosts, who were all educated at Cambridge.'[1]
But Dr. Todd afterwards came to see that the denial of
the distinction between the College and the University
was quite untenable.   In his learned and singularly
interesting Introduction to another volume[2] published by
him many years afterwards,[3] he again referred to Dr.
Miller's pamphlet, no longer, however in terms of approval, but for
the purpose of confuting more than one of the positions on
which Dr. Miller had relied in endeavouring to prove that
the University was not distinct from the College.

Working out a train of reasoning, in the strangeness
of its logic almost worthy of some of Alice's acquaintances
in Wonderland, Dr. Miller took for his starting-point
the often-quoted expression, *Mater Universitatis*, which, in
Queen Elizabeth's Charter of Foundation, is applied to
Trinity College. He set about explaining that expression
in several ways, and then proceeded to argue that, in whatever way it was to be understood, it required that the
College, 'in its actual circumstances,'—that is, so long as
it continued to be the only College on the foundation,—
'should be considered as *the same with the University*.'[4]
But, to quote the common-sense criticism of Dr. Todd :—

Is it not a most strange mode of expressing this [that the
College is the same with the University] to say that the
College is the mother of the University? . . . Is a mother
identical with her children? . . . It is true Trinity College is

[1] *Dublin University Calendar*, 1833, Introduction, page 56, footnote (e).
[2] *Catalogue of Graduates* (Dublin, 1869).
[3] A graceful and touching reference to Dr. Todd, made by Cardinal
Cullen in an address delivered by His Eminence at the Catholic University,
on the 2nd of July, 1869, the day of Dr. Todd's funeral, may appropriately be transcribed here. It will be observed that the occasion of the
Cardinal's reference to Dr. Todd was his quoting from the volume mentioned
in the text above. The passage is as follows :—
    'I might refer to many Catholic writers for the proof of the facts I have
now narrated, but I wish rather to refer you to the Preface of the " List of
Graduates of Trinity College," by Dr. Todd, the last work which proceeded
from the pen of that distinguished scholar, whose lamented demise has cast a
gloom over all who prize the remnants of Celtic literature, and whose remains
were this morning, to the grief of all our citizens, borne to their long resting
place.' (*The Writings of Cardinal Cullen*, Dublin, 1882, vol. 3, p. 234.)
[4] Dr. Miller's Pamphlet, pages 8, 9.

the only College in the University, but this does not make it the same with the University ; nor does it explain, in either of the interpretations proposed by Dr. Miller, in what intelligible sense she is the ' Mother of the University.'[1]

Dr. Todd's own explanation of the phrase is that—

The College was to be the parent of the University, to bring up and nourish in all sound learning, as a mother gives nourishment to her children, those who were afterwards to become graduates and members of the University.[2]

But the precise sense in which the expression *Mater Universitatis* is to be understood is a matter of but secondary importance. Sir Joseph Napier adopts an· explanation somewhat similar to Dr. Todd's, adding, as a further point, that—

The prescribing of the preliminaries and conditions of graduation, the appointment of University officers (except the first Chancellor), and the making of regulations for conferring Degrees. were confided to the governing body of the College.[3]

He disposes, as summarily as Dr. Todd did, of the odd theory set up by Dr. Miller, that the expression *Mater Universitatis* requires us to consider ' the College as *the same* with the University.' As Sir Joseph Napier puts it—

It would be strange, if not absurd, to have designated the College as ' *Mater Universitatis* ' if the University was not to be regarded as *distinct from the College.*[4]

For a reason not at all difficult to understand, there seems to have always been in Trinity College itself an unwillingness to give but scant recognition to the distinction between the College and the University, and, indeed, as far as possible, to ignore that distinction altogether. From the fact that Trinity College has for centuries been the only College of the University, the distinction has never, of course, come into very practical effect. But that is no reason for denying the existence of the distinction. As Dr. Mahaffy,[5] whose words I have

---

[1] *Catalogue of Graduates* (1869), Introduction, page xvi., footnote.
[2] *Ibid.*, Introduction, pages xv., xvi.
[3] *Catalogue of Graduates* (1896), Introduction, pages vi., vii.
[4] *Ibid.*, Introduction, page x.
[5] *The Book of Trinity College, Dublin* (Belfast, 1892), chap. i., p. 17.

not many opportunities of quoting with so near an approach to full concurrence, says, in reference to it :—

> In the first place we may name the distinction between University and College, one often attempted by theorists, and which may any day become of serious importance if a new College were founded under the University, but one which has practically had no influence in the history of Trinity College.
> We even find such hybrid titles as Fellow of the University[1] . . . used by people who ought to have known the impropriety.

An attempt has recently been made to attach very exceptional importance to a statement in the Report of a Royal Commission of 1851, which was 'appointed,' we are informed, ' to inquire into the state of Dublin University.' It may not be altogether unimportant to note, for the sake of greater accuracy, that the subject of the inquiry for which that Commission really was appointed, was, in the words of the Queen's letter appointing it, to inquire 'into the State, Discipline, Studies, and Revenues of Our University of Dublin, *and the College of the Holy and Undivided Trinity therein,* and of all and singular the Colleges and Schools in Our said University.'[2]

In the Report of that Commission, Trinity College is described as ' a College with complete University powers of granting Degrees in all arts and faculties, and of electing University officers.' The Report adds that 'those powers were conferred by Charter on Trinity College, without any provision being made to give other Colleges, when founded, a share in the government of the University,' and that ' the

---

[1] The reference is to a window erected in the College Chapel set up as a memorial of Bishop Berkeley, which calls him ' a Fellow of this University.' The following sentence in the footnote in which that reference is explained is worth quoting :—' I need not point out how this blunder has been exalted into an official title by the Examining Body called the Royal University of Ireland, which has no Professors for its University, and no College for its Fellows.' (*The Book of Trinity College*, page 17, footnote 2).

[2] The only practical outcome of the insertion of the last clause of the reference to the Commission was a statement, in one of the replies received from Trinity College, to the effect that a ' Hall, called Trinity Hall,' established in 1617, was converted in 1660 into a Hall for medical students, and ultimately became the College of Physicians. ' But,' it is added, ' the present King and Queen's College of Physicians has since obtained a distinct Charter, and, though "connected with" the University by the School of Physic Act (40 Geo. III. cap. 84) can no longer be considered a College in the University.'

constitution of Dublin University, as being a College with University powers, has never been changed since its foundation.'

Now to quote such things in the way they have been quoted, borders upon trifling with the public. It would be interesting to know by what conceivable process, or on what conceivable ground the constitution of Dublin University could have been changed, in the sense of giving 'other Colleges a share in the government of the University,' so long as Trinity College continues to be the only College of the University.

But, to go a little deeper into the matter, it is well to look to the evidence on which those statements quoted from the Report of the Commission rest, keeping in view at the same time the somewhat peculiar way in which the Commission conducted its inquiry.

I take this latter point first. From the beginning to the end of its proceedings, the Commission of 1851 never orally examined a single witness. An important section of the inquiry was conducted simply by sending a number of printed questions to certain persons, or classes of persons, connected with the College, or with the University. These questions were to be replied to in writing. There was no sifting of the evidence, such as is usual in the examination of witnesses on whose evidence the Report of a Commission is to be based. No step was taken to elicit any further information in reference to any matter, stated, no matter how jejunely, in the carefully-worded written replies to the questions of the query sheet. Naturally, then, there was little chance of any information reaching the Commission that might be in any way out of harmony with what then was, and has since, to a large extent, continued to be, the Trinity College view of the relation between that College and the University of Dublin.

The queries as to the relation between the College and the University seem to have been sent only to the Provost and Senior Fellows. In justice to those College dignitaries it should be added that there is not in any part of their reply, which is a joint one, the faintest suggestion that,

in describing the authority vested in them in relation to the
affairs of the University, they meant to do more than state
the facts of the case as it actually stood. There is, I mean,
nothing whatever in their reply to suggest that, in their view,
the enlargement of the University,—if it were enlarged by
the establishment in it of other Colleges,—would not involve
such a modification of the constitution of the University
as would place those other Colleges, so established, on a
footing of equality with Trinity College in reference to all
University matters. Naturally, they had not this point in
contemplation at all

In connection with all this, I may here refer to an interesting pamphlet, published fifteen years after the date of
the Report of the Commission.

The pamphlet, as is stated in its Preface, was published
from Trinity College, in May, 1868. It was, I am informed,
very generally believed in Dublin at the time that the author
of it was Dr. Lloyd, then Provost of the College. In connection with a plan of University reform outlined in the
pamphlet, based upon the establishment of a new College in
the University, the following passage occurs. I quote it, not
at all in view of the imputed authorship of the pamphlet,
but solely on account of its usefully supplementing the very
meagre statement on the subject of the relations between
the College and the University, officially forwarded to
the Commission of 1851 by the Provost and Senior Fellows
of that day. The passage is as follows :—

The University of Dublin is a University with a single
College. . . . The non-existence of a plurality of Colleges has
made it unnecessary to draw a definite line to distinguish its two
offices ; and the fusion of the two has been rendered more complete
by the act of the founder, which vested the supreme power in the
Provost and Senior Fellows of the College.

*This doubtless was meant to be but provisional, and to last only
until other Colleges were affiliated.* Still, however, Trinity College
has remained the sole College in the University of Dublin to this day.

Here then is suggested an obvious mode of carrying out the
measure referred to. Little more is needed than to draw a well-
defined line between the University and the College . . .

The Provost and Senior Fellows of Trinity College. . . .
possess by Charter the right of the initiative in all ' Graces'

brought before the Senate. *The privilege* thus given to Trinity College *should of course be resigned*, so that all affiliated Colleges might *stand on an equal footing.*

This extract is especially useful in showing up the misleading character of an attempt that has been made in more than one quarter to set the public astray as to the nature of the proposal so definitely put forward by the Irish Bishops,— for the first time, I think, in 1869, the year after the appearance of the noteworthy pamphlet to which I have just referred. It is nothing but an outrage upon the Bishops of that time to suggest that they contemplated, or would have in any way countenanced, the placing of a Catholic College of the University of Dublin in a position [in that University inferior in any respect to the position, which, as a logical consequence of the circumstances of the case, has been held in the University, down to the present day, by Trinity College alone.

Another document should be here referred to—a document, to which, on some ground, to me, I must confess, unintelligible, it has been sought to attach extraordinary importance.

It is a petition from some thousands of graduates, presented to Parliament in 1868, for the maintenance unimpaired of ' the Protestant Constitution of the University of Dublin.' This document is quoted as—

The unanimous declaration of *the College and University,* which are *one inseparable institution,* affirming its own constitutional and legal title, and then giving the words 'of Dublin' as local designation at the end of the document.

As to the question of the ' constitutional and legal title ' of the University, I must be excused for saying that I fail to see how the mere signatures of 6,000, or of 60,000 graduates of the University of Dublin could be supposed to establish the ' inaccuracy ' of a title, which, as I have already shown, —if I may repeat what I have said upon this point in an earlier part of this paper,—is given to the University of Dublin in eleven Acts of Parliament, twice in five of them, three times in another, six times in another, and, again, in ten Royal Letters Patent, occurring twice in one

of these, three times in another, and five times in a
third. In a volume published five years ago,[1] I myself
called attention to the fact that the title 'University of
Trinity College' is given to the University of Dublin in
one solitary Act of Parliament, the Act of Union,—a fact
to which that eminent lawyer, who in his time was Lord
Chancellor of Ireland, and was for many years member of
Parliament for the University, the late Dr. Ball, directs
attention in his volume on Irish Legislative Systems,
dismissing it with the significant remark that it is
'singular' that the University should have been ' called " the
University of Trinity College," and not "the University of
Dublin." [2]

In face of the paradoxical denial, with which we are now
confronted, of even the existence of the University of Dublin
as distinct, in any particular, from Trinity College, the
question of the name by which that University may be
designated is a question plainly of very little moment.
Besides, it is a question that I have dealt with quite
sufficiently elsewhere.[3] But as I have at all touched upon
it here, I may mention that Sir Joseph Napier, dealing
with the whole question in its broader aspect, incidentally
refers as follows to one of the numerous Royal Letters
Patent in which the University is designated the University
of Dublin :—

In the Letters Patent of 1 George III., where the University
of Oxford is described as *celeberrima Academia Oxoniensis*, the
University of Dublin is described as *Academia illustrissima
Dubliniensis*.[4]

He calls attention also to a number of the Acts of Parliament, and of the other Letters Patent, in which this title is
repeatedly used.[5] Noticing the fact that in the Act of
Union, the University is called the ' University of Trinity
College,' he describes this, I would presume to say, very
felicitously, as the 'maternal' name of the University.

---

[1] *The Irish University Question,* (Dublin, 1897), page 27.
[2] *Irish Legislative Systems.* By the Right Hon. J. T. Ball. LL.D., D.C.L.
(London, Dublin, 1880), page 179.
[3] In the letter already referred to, page 161, footnote 1.
[4] *Catalogue of Graduates* (1896). Introduction, page xvi., footnote.
[5] *Ibid,* pages xv., xvi.

It is almost superfluous to add that nowhere throughout his elaborate dissertation, which extends over 28 pages, is there to be found even the faintest suggestion that the the title ' University of Dublin,' is ' inaccurate,' or that the title of ' University of Trinity College,' so ' singularly ' [1] used in the Act of Union, has any claim to be regarded as ' the legal and constitutional title,' of the University.

As a final comment upon the use so strangely made of the graduates' petition, I direct attention to the words in which I find that petition described as ' the declaration of the College and University, which are *one inseparable institution.*' For this statement,—if it is to be taken as affirming, or suggesting, that the graduates' petition describes the College and the University as ' one institution,' whether separable or inseparable,—I have only to say that it has not in the document a particle of foundation to sustain it.

The text of the document has been quoted. It speaks for itself. But even if the document itself could not be referred to, the fact that Sir Joseph Napier's name is signed to it is sufficient evidence that no such legal solecism as the assertion that Trinity College and the University are ' one inseparable institution ' was to be found in it. The suggestion that this document, the first signature to which is that of Sir Joseph Napier, Vice-Chancellor of the University, sustains the denial of the distinction between the College and the University,—or sustains the assertion that it is ' inaccurate ' to speak of the University as ' the University of Dublin,' and that its ' legal ' ' constitutional ' title is ' the University of Trinity College,'—could assuredly have been put forward only in the absence of all knowledge of the existence of the learned and exhaustive legal paper in which Sir Joseph Napier has so lucidly stated his views upon both the points now so curiously called in question.

I may now give, in outline, Sir Joseph Napier's

---

[1] See Dr. Ball's *Irish Legislative Systems*, page 172.

interesting statement,—deduced from the Charters and all other documents bearing upon the matter,—of the distinction that exists, 'legally,' 'constitutionally,' and 'in fact,' between Trinity College and the University of Dublin.

Trinity College, as is well known, was established by Queen Elizabeth in 1592. The College was established as the 'mother of a University,' which it was to supply with 'studiosi,' who were to be admitted to take degrees; and for the conferring of those degrees the authorities of the College were empowered to make all necessary regulations.[1]

Although, under the Charter of Elizabeth, the actual creation of the University was only effected through the instrumentality of the College, it does not follow, says Sir Joseph Napier, that the University is not to be considered as having been founded by Elizabeth:—

What was done in pursuance of the Charter was done by the Queen's authority, and is deemed in law to have been done by herself. The distinction between the founding of the College and the founding of the University should be clearly understood. There were available means of completing the foundation of the College at once and directly; but the case was different as to the University, for although by legal intendment it was founded by the Charter, it had afterwards to be brought forth by the College as its 'mater.' [2]

He then points out—and the observation apparently is a very relevant one—that unless the matter is duly considered in its integrity, the Charter of Queen Elizabeth

Is likely to be (and it often has been) *misunderstood* to have merely founded *a College with University privileges.*[3]

And he adds:—

When the whole matter is duly considered, it will be seen that the University designed by this Charter, and constituted under it, was intended to be, and was, *a distinct incorporation.*[4]

---

[1] *Catalogue of Graduates* (1896), pages iv.-vii.
[2] *Ibid.*, page vii.
[3] *Ibid.*
[4] *Ibid.*

Under the powers granted by the Charter, a code of regulations for the conferring of degrees was drawn up, a Senate was formed, and, seven years after the foundation of the College, the first 'Commencements,' or conferring of degrees, took place. As Sir Joseph Napier puts it,—

The 'Universitas' designed by the Charter of Elizabeth had been constituted by the Provost and Fellows of the College under its provisions. . . . A period of gestation (if I might say so) had been required before the University could thus have been brought to the birth.

As the design was that it should come from the womb of the College, privileges had been conferred on the *studiosi*, and powers were given to the Provost and Fellows of the College, by which provision was made for the constitution and continuance of a proper staff of University officers, and of a body of accredited teachers. *It may therefore be said that the College was adorned or invested with the privileges of a University.*

But after the holding of Commencements [the conferring of Degrees], which first took place A.D. 1600, *juxta tempus idoneum*,[1] *i.e.*, seven years after the foundation of the College, the University was brought to the birth, and thenceforth it was distinct from, although dependent on, its ' mater '—the College.

' Distinct from the College.' How sadly ignorant of law Sir Joseph Napier—to say nothing of poor Isaac Butt—must have been !

We now come to the Charter of Charles I. It is dated A.D. 1637. By that time, the University was in full working order. There is an ancient collection of University regulations, entitled ' Consuetudines seu Regulae Universitatis Dubliniensis pro solenniore collatione graduum,' the precise date of which is uncertain, but which, there is reason to believe, was drawn up [2] before the date of the Charter of Charles I.

Sir Joseph Napier calls attention to an interesting indication of the fact that the University, which at the time of the Elizabethan Charter existed only ' in intendment

<hr />

[1] Words used in the Charter of Queen Elizabeth (see *Catalogue of Graduates*, 1896, Introduction, page v.).

[2] See the Introduction to the *Dublin University Calendar* for 1869. See also an interesting note in reference to those ' Customs or Rules,' in Dr. Todd's Introduction (page xxxiii., footnote) to the *Catalogue of Graduates*, published in 1869.

and consideration of law,' as a future outcome of the
College, was in existence and in working order when the
Charter of Charles I. was issued. In the Charter of
Elizabeth, the Chancellor,—in the first instance appointed
by the Queen, afterwards to be elected by the Provost and
Senior Fellows,—is called Chancellor of the College, 'ut
posthac idoneam hujusmodi personam . . . pro *hujus
Collegii Cancellario* eligant.' But now, in the later Charter
of Charles I., the Chancellor is designated Chancellor of
the University—' Cancellario *Academiae sive Universitatis
praedictae.*' [1]

In the ancient collection of Rules for the conferring of
Degrees, already referred to, the Senate—*Senatus Academicus*
—is mentioned and its functions are defined. The Senate,
as may be seen by reference to any recent issue of the
University Calendar,[2] is the public Congregation of the
University. It consists of the Chancellor of the University,
the Doctors in the several Faculties, and the Masters of
Arts.

It is well perhaps here to explain that the name Senate,
in the case of the University of Dublin, is used in a sense
wholly different from that in which it is applied to the
Governing Body of the institution known as the Royal
University of Ireland. The Senate of the University of
Dublin is not a Governing Body at all. It has nothing to
do with the drawing up of programmes, the appointment of
Fellows or Professors of the College, or anything of the
kind. It in no way interferes with the academic freedom of
Trinity College. Consisting, as it does, of those who
may be presumed to have at heart the honour of
the University of which they are Doctors or Masters, it
confers the Degrees of the University upon those who are
presented to it, by the College, with the testimony of the
College that they are worthy of the academic rank proposed
be conferred upon them.

A Degree of the University of Dublin can be conferred

[1] *Catalogue of Graduates* (1896), Introduction, pages vii.-ix.
[2] See the *University Calendar* for 1901. Vol. 2, page 9.

only by the Senate of the University, that is, by the voice of the majority of the Senate:—

In concessione gratiae in domo congregationis, pars major semper habeat ratione totius, ac proinde quicquid majori parti placeat, omnino ratum esto.[1]

But, whilst the Senate of the University may refuse a Degree, it cannot confer one on its own motion. The intended graduate must in all cases be presented by the College, represented by its Provost and a majority of its Senior Fellows:—

Nemini publica Senatus academici gratia concedatur, nisi privatâ gratiâ Praepositi et majoris partis Sociorum Seniorum antea commendato.

Though not needed for the pointing out of the distinction between the University and the College, it may, for the sake of completeness of statement, be added here, that there is in the Senate a further authority of a very important kind in reference to the conferring of Degrees.

The headship of the University Senate is vested in three of its specially representative members: the Vice-Chancellor,[3] representing the University; the Provost of Trinity College, representing the College; and the Senior Master non-Regent, duly elected,[4] representing the body of graduates of the University. These three members of the Senate constitute the *Caput Senatus Academici;* and the concurrence, not only of the *Caput* as a whole, but of each of its three individual members, is necessary before a Degree can be conferred:—

Si quae petitio ad gradum offeratur, esto in potestate tum Vice-Cancellarii, tum Praepositi, tum Magistri senioris non Regentis qui in Collegio degat, impedire quominus reliquo Senatui proponatur.[6]

Quite independently of the authority of the eminent lawyers who have specially applied themselves to the study of the matter, the mere statement of the arrangements thus

---

[1] *Consuetudines seu Regulae*, Cap. IV.
[2] *Ibid.*
[3] The Vice-Chancellor is mentioned as it is he who usually attends. Of course, he attends as the substitute of the Chancellor of the University.
[4] Each Master of Arts is styled 'Regent' for three years after taking his degree; after the third year, he becomes 'non-Regent.'
[5] See the *University Calendar* for 1901. Vol. 2, page 10, n. 5.
[6] *Consuetudines seu Regulae*, Cap. II.

made for the conferring of the Degrees of the University is, in itself, sufficient to show very plainly the distinction between the College and the University.

As to legal authority, we have the clear statement of Sir Joseph Napier:—

The intention is manifest that the University should be a *distinct*, but not an independent, body.

Sir Joseph Napier then goes on to deal with the furth question, whether the University is a body, not only distinct from the College, but so broadly distinguishable from it that the College and the University are two distinct corporations in the legal sense of the word.

As to this, there seemed, at least at one time, to have been some difference of opinion. Early in the year 1858, a very eminent lawyer, Mr. Francis A. Fitzgerald, afterwards, as Baron of the Exchequer, a universally respected Judge, gave it as his opinion that the University was not a corporation.[2]

After this, in the December of the same year, Lord Chancellor Blackburne, then Vice-Chancellor of the University, communicated to the Senate of the University ' a formal and deliberate opinion,'[3] in which, amongst other things bearing upon the point, he said :—

In addition to these and other considerations of a similar kind, it was to be kept in mind that the Legislature and the Crown, from the earliest period down to the time of the last Charter (21 Vict.), had recognised and treated the University as a body corporate; but what was directly to the purpose was that the Charter of the Queen [the Charter of 21 Vict., A.D. 1857] recognises and perpetuates all the functions and duties of the University, and its means of exercising them in their full integrity.[4]

I may incidentally remark that one of the provisions of the Charter of 1857, here referred to, is as follows :—

The Senate of the University shall be, and continue to be, a body corporate, and have a common seal, and shall have power under the said seal to do all such acts . . . (in conformity . . . with the Charter and Statutes of Trinity College, AND with the Statutes, Laws, and By-laws OF THE UNIVERSITY), under the

---

[1] *Catalogue of Graduates* (1896), Introduction, page xl.
[2] See a portion of this opinion in Dr. Todd's Introduction to the *Catalogue of Graduates* (1869), pages xxiii.-xxv. footnote.
[3] See the *Catalogue of Graduates* (1896), Introduction, page xl.
[4] *Ibid.*

name, style, and title of the Chancellor, Doctors, and Masters of the UNIVERSITY OF DUBLIN.[1]

Sir Joseph Napier, after quoting the words of ex-Chancellor Blackburne, his predecessor in the Vice-Chancellorship of the University, points out that the opinion previously given by so eminent a lawyer as Baron Fitzgerald was before the ex-Lord Chancellor, when he arrived at the opposite conclusion and publicly communicated his opinion to the Senate. Until he had himself become Vice-Chancellor of the University, Sir Joseph Napier,—on the authority, as he says, of so eminent a Judge,—had accepted as final the opinion of his predecessor, given, as it was, in the circumstances mentioned. But, finding it stated more than once by Dr. Todd, in his learned Introduction to the *Catalogue of Graduates*, published in 1869, that the University was not a corporate body, he thought it his duty, as Vice-Chancellor of the University, to apply himself to a special study of the question.[2]

Those who wish to follow this matter out in detail will find a full and clear exposition of it in Sir Joseph Napier's elaborate legal dissertation on the case, in which he states the conclusions at which he arrived, both upon this particular point and upon some others as to which Dr. Todd ' had impugned the received opinion as to the import of certain parts of the Charter of Queen Elizabeth.'[3]   It is sufficient here to state that the first and second of the conclusions thus arrived at are:—

1. That the College has certain University privileges which have been conferred on its *studiosi* and on its governing body.[4]

2. That the University (properly so called) is *a distinct corporate body.*[5]

I, of course, am not in any way concerned with the question as to the two distinct corporations. That is a lawyers' question, pure and simple. And as to the distinction that unquestionably exists between Trinity College and

[1] See the *University Calendar* for 1901, Vol. ii., Introduction, page 11.
[2] *Catalogue of Graduates* (1896), Introduction, page xi.
[3] *Ibid.*, pages xi., xii.
[4] See *ante*, page 173.
[5] *Catalogue of Graduates* (1896), page xxiii.

the University of Dublin, I am concerned with it simply upon the ground indicated at the beginning of this paper. The declaration of the Catholic Episcopacy of Ireland, to which I there referred, is as follows:—

Since the Protestants of this country have had a Protestant University with rich endowments for three hundred years, and have it still,[1] the Catholic people of Ireland clearly have a right to a Catholic University.

But should Her Majesty's Government be unwilling t⟩ increase the number of Universities in this country, *religious equality cannot be realised* unless *the degrees, endowments, and other privileges*, enjoyed by our fellow-subjects of a different religion, *be placed within the reach of Catholics on terms of perfect equality.*

Attempts have, from time to time, been made to bring the Bishops of Ireland into odium with our Catholic people by falsely representing that this emphatic assertion of the rightful claim of the Catholics of Ireland to a settlement of the University question on the basis of perfect equality, was in some way undermined by the declaration of the Bishops that a satisfactory settlement of that question could be effected by the establishment, either of a National University of Ireland, or of a second College of the University of Dublin. And grotesque descriptions have been given of the state of degrading subjection in which the Catholics of Ireland would be placed if their one place of higher education in Ireland were to be a College of that University, the constitution of which, as is notorious, at present works out in the complete dependence of the University upon Trinity College.

In the course of this paper quite enough has been said to show that, on this particular line of settlement of the University question, an essential condition of any arrangement that could be contemplated as admissable would be that,—in words which I have already quoted,— the position of privilege hitherto held by Trinity College in the University of Dublin ' should be resigned,' so that each College of the University should ' stand on an equal footing.'[2]

---

[1] This was first published in 1869, and was republished in 1871, before the passing of the ' University of Dublin Tests Act,' of 1873. It is unnecessary here to point out in detail to how trifling an extent the passing of that Act has affected the existing state of things either in Trinity College or in the University of Dublin.

[2] See *ante*, page 169.

And this precisely is what the Irish Bishops have said in
their declaration, the first part of which I have already transcribed. In that declaration, they set forth, as an essential
condition of the establishment of 'religious equality,'
that in connection with whatever University system a
College to be established for Catholics might be placed,
that College should 'fully participate' in 'the privileges
enjoyed by other Colleges of whatsoever denomination or
character.'

I shall be told, no doubt, that no equitable settlement
could be worked out through the establishment of a
second College in the University of Dublin, without a very
substantial modification of the constitution of that University. This surely is no new discovery. It was all clearly
before the minds of the Bishops when framing their historic
declaration on the subject. That is plain from the terms of
the declaration itself. After laying down the essential conditions of equality,—by which, it should be noted, they
meant, to use their own words, 'religious equality,'—they
go on to say :—

All this can, we believe, be attained BY MODIFYING THE CONSTI-
TUTION OF THE UNIVERSITY OF DUBLIN, so as to admit the
establishment of a second College within it,[1] IN EVERY RESPECT

---

[1] One of the worst of the numerous misrepresentations which, if allowed to
pass without exposure, could not fail to place the action of the Bishops in a
very false light before the Catholics of Ireland, has reference to the site of
the new College, on the supposition of an additional College being established
within the University of Dublin. The suggestion has been represented
as if it involved the building of a College in some corner of the Park of
Trinity College. Mr. Butt, who devoted so much time and thought to the
working out of a plan of settlement on the basis of a new College in the
University of Dublin, has even been quoted as the authority for this view
of the locality of the College.

I prefer to take my view of Mr. Butt's proposal, and of what it involved,
from Mr. Butt himself. Speaking in the House of Commons, when introducing
his University Bill on the 16th of May, 1876, he said, in reference to this
branch of the subject :—

'It will be, of course, *for the authorities of the College* to determine the
most convenient site, either in their present situation [St. Stephen's Green]
or *in any other*, within a certain distance of the centre of the City of Dublin,
which I propose to fix at *three miles*. I would prefer they should be placed
in the immediate vicinity of Trinity College, and the Bill gives power to the
governing body of Trinity to sell or lease for this purpose a portion of their
ground, *if the authorities of the new College should be desirous* of that site.
But this is *a matter entirely for the College itself.*'

I have transcribed this extract from a pamphlet containing a verbatim
report of the speech, brought out by Mr. Butt himself.

EQUAL TO TRINITY COLLEGE, and conducted on purely Catholic principles, in which your Bishops shall have full control *in all things regarding faith and morals*, securing thereby the spiritual interests of your children, and placing, at the same time, Catholics ON A FOOTING OF PERFECT EQUALITY with Protestants, as to DEGREES, EMOLUMENTS, AND ALL OTHER ADVANTAGES.

It is under these conditions, and under these conditions only, that the Bishops have ever stated that the essential requirements of an equitable settlement of the Irish University question could be effected through the establishment of a second College in the University of Dublin.

I may be asked, whether I think it possible that Trinity College, its governing body, and its numerous array of sympathisers and supporters throughout the country, would ever consent to an arrangement involving the resignation of its privileged position in the University of Dublin? I can only reply that with that question I have nothing to do.

It must be remembered that the Irish Bishops have never themselves claimed to have the University question settled on this line. Our position in the matter is clear and unmistakable. If the statesmen who have the responsibility and the duty of constructing a satisfactory system of University education for Ireland, see any insuperable difficulty in the way of the establishment of a new University, we have to remind them that the establishment of a Catholic University is the policy, and the only policy, which we, Bishops, have at any time positively advocated. Then, if, on any ground, those statesmen wish, in preference, to construct a plan of settlement based on the establishment of a new College in the University of Dublin, we have said to them without reserve that, in our opinion, the thing can be done. But we have added, as, in the discharge of our duty to the Catholic body in Ireland, it was our duty to add, that there are certain conditions without which, equality,—meaning by this, religious equality, surely an indispensable condition of any equitable settlement in this matter,—cannot be secured.

For some reason or other—presumably on some abstruse rule of legal interpretation,—the aspect of the University question dealt with in the preceding paragraphs seems to be regarded as lying outside the limits of the inquiry with the carrying out of which the Royal Commission now sitting has been charged. It has, however, come rather prominently before the public within the last few months, and I can only repeat what I have frequently said in reference to it in years past. If the feeling prevalent in Trinity College is to be allowed to stand in the way of the Catholics of Ireland being dealt with on lines of equality within the University of Dublin, then surely the Catholic claim to be dealt with on lines of equality in the only other conceivable way in which equality can be reached,— through the establishment of a new University for Catholics,—becomes simply irresistible.

On whatever line it may be found most feasible to do justice to the long-suffering Catholic people of Ireland, one thing, it is to be hoped, will, on all hands, be conceded as indisputable. We have to be extricated, without further unnecessary delay, from the humiliating position in which we have so long been forced to stand. Our Protestant fellow-countrymen are in the enjoyment of every educational advantage that the State provides for its most favoured subjects. For us, there is nothing better placed within our reach than the miserable system of examinations, and of College and school work carried on solely with the view of preparing for those examinations,—the system, educationally ruinous instead of advantageous, that is administered by the examining body officially designated the Royal 'University.'

To bring this unduly long paper to a close, I transcribe the following interesting passage from the work of an old French writer. I find it quoted in a footnote to Dr. Todd's Introduction to the Catalogue of Graduates of the University of Dublin, the volume so frequently referred to in the preceding pages :—

'Depuis plus de huit cens ans,' says the learned Pioles, avocat au Parlement, 'qu'il y a des écoles publiques et générales dans le royaume, il n' étoit encore venu dans l'esprit de personne de croire qu'une Université put être divisée de telle sorte qu'elle fût en partie dans une ville, et en partie dans une autre. Au contraire, et les illustres fondateurs, a qui les Universités doivent leur naissance, et les augustes protecteurs, a qui elles doivent leur conservation, princes, rois, prélats, souverains pontifes, tous ont été persuadés qu'il étoit essentiel a ces Universités, que chaqu'une d'elles fût toute entiére dans un seul et unique endroit.' [1]

But, apart from the authority of any writer, the present outburst of feeling in educational circles in England, antagonistic to the continued maintenance of the Victoria 'University,' with its scattered Colleges in Manchester, Leeds, and Liverpool, must of itself suffice to render impossible the further subjection of the Catholics of Ireland to the discredited system embodied in the Royal 'University' of Ireland.

✠ W. J. W.

---

[1] See the *Catalogue of Graduates* (1869), Introduction, page xv., footnote *b*.

Notes and Queries

THEOLOGY

QUESTIONS REGARDING THE CONFESSION AND ABSOLUTION OF RESERVED CASES

REV. DEAR SIR,—I. When a person has incurred a reserved censure, and there is no time to get faculties to absolve from the Bishop, and there is some pressing necessity to receive Communion, is a penitent bound to confess his sins to an ordinary confessor who has no power over the reserved case? Or, will it be sufficient to elicit an act of perfect contrition before Communion?

II. Again, if a penitent has been absolved, in case of necessity, by the faculties granted in 1886, must he always write to Rome within a month? If so, must the penitent's name be mentioned? Would it be enough to write to the Bishop or a confessor who happens to have faculties to deal with the case?

CENSURA.

I. The reason for doubt in regard to the first question is, of course, that it seems useless to confess a sin, over which the confessor has no jurisdiction. Moreover, a penitent should not be obliged to confess his sins twice over. But, if you bind the penitent, in the case contemplated, to confess his reserved sin to a confessor who has no power to absolve from that sin directly, he will still remain bound to confess that same sin afterwards to a confessor having special faculties to deal with the reservation.

In replying to this question of our correspondent, it is necessary to distinguish between papal and episcopal cases. If the reserved censure be a papal censure the penitent is certainly bound to confess before receiving Communion. The reason is evident. Since 1886 any ordinary confessor can, in case of urgent necessity, absolve directly from papal censures. An obligation will, indeed, remain of writing to Rome within a month. But the obligation of *confession*, with its inherent difficulty, is altogether removed. Since 1886 there is, therefore, in regard to papal cases, no reason, to excuse a penitent in the circumstances named from a full confession to any ordinary confessor available.

If there be question of an episcopal censure, then, either the Bishop has adopted the Roman procedure regarding absolution from reserved cases or he has not. If the Bishop has applied the Roman procedure to his own reservations, then, of course, for the reason given above, a full confession must be made before Communion. If, on the other hand, the Bishop has not adopted the new procedure introduced in 1886, it is at least probable that the penitent would not be bound to confess, to an ordinary confessor, a sin over which that confessor has no direct jurisdiction. It would, therefore, be sufficient, if he elicited an act of perfect contrition before going to Communion. It should be noted, however, that if he cannot elicit an act of perfect contrition, he is bound to confess some unreserved sin with attrition, and so obtain indirectly the remission of the mortal sin with which we suppose his soul to be burdened. Again, it is, of course, manifest, that if the penitent had, in addition, to the reserved sin, an unreserved mortal sin, he would certainly be bound to confess the unreserved sin.

II. When a penitent has, in case of urgent necessity, been absolved from a papal case, in virtue of the extraordinary faculties granted in 1886, he is bound, *sub grave*, and under pain of falling back into that censure--if any--from which he has been absolved, to write to Rome within a month. The case may be referred to Rome either by the confessor who gave the absolution or by another confessor, or even by the penitent himself. Usually the confessor who absolves will undertake the duty of writing to Rome. He will use some such form as the following given by Fr. Noldin [1] :—

EMINENTISSIME PRINCEPS,
    Titius contraxit censuram speciali (ordinario) modo Romano Pontifici reservatam propter lectionem librorum prohibitorum (propter patratum duellum). Cum ipse nec ad confessarium privilegiatum accedere nec sine absolutione dimitti potuerit et ceteroquin rite despositus videretur, absolutionem recepit. Nunc vero ad obediendum ecclesiae praescriptis hisce litteris per me infrascriptum confessarium ad S. Sedem recurrit ad accipienda mandata paratus implere poenitentiam, quam in poenam delicti. Eminentiae vestrae praescribere dignabitur.   N. N.

---

[1] *Vid. De Sacramentis,* p. 388.

The real name of the penitent is not to be used, but the confessor should, of course, give his own name and address, so that the reply may be sent to him. On the outside the letter should be addressed—Eminentissimo Principi Cardinali Poenitentiario Majori, Palazzo della Cancellaria Apostolica, Roma.

It often happens that the Bishop, the Vicar-General, and other confessors have special delegated faculties to absolve from papal reserved cases. Would it be sufficient, for the penitent, our correspondent asks, instead of writing to Rome, to write to some confessor who happens to have the delegated faculties? It would be sufficient to write to the Bishop or to the Vicar-General, when they have the requisite faculties. It would not suffice to write to any other confessor.[1] It is needless to add, of course, that if the penitent is not deterred by the difficulty of repeating his confession of the reserved case in the ordinary way, that, instead of writing to Rome or to the Bishop, or to the Vicar-General, he may be absolved and freed from all further obligation by *any* confessor, who has special faculties to deal with his reserved case. In other words, when a penitent is absolved, in virtue of the faculties of 1886, the obligation of writing to Rome (or to the Bishop or the Vicar-General) is merely conditional—he must either write to Rome (or to the Bishop, etc.), or he must *de novo* confess in the ordinary way to a duly authorised confessor and receive absolution.

APPLICATION OF THE MASS IN CASE OF DUPLICATION

Rev. Dear Sir,—Kindly answer the following question :— There is a rule in this diocese, that each priest has to say three Masses for a deceased priest. When a priest duplicates, can he say the second Mass for the deceased priest?   Sacerdos.

Yes, a priest of that diocese who legitimately duplicates, may take a stipend for his first Mass, and offer the second Mass for one of his deceased brethren, in discharge of his obligation under the diocesan arrangement.[2]

D. Mannix.

---

[1] See reply S. C. Inquis. 21 Dec., 1900, in I. E. Record, May, 1901, p. 472.
[2] Conf. resp. S.C.C. 14 Sept. 1878.

LITURGY

MUST THE WAX CANDLES REQUIRED BY THE RUBRICS BE ENTIRELY OF BEES' WAX?

WE promised to deal with this question in the present issue of the I. E. RECORD.

The only treatment of the question that we have at hand is a *Suffragium* submitted to the Sacred Congregation of Rites by Father Calcedonius Mancini, C.M., one of the Consultors of the said Congregation. It is published in the *Ephemerides Liturgicae* of June, 1901. Though by no means of the same value as a decision of the Sacred Congregation of Rites it is deserving of very great respect, as expressing the opinion of one whose position proves him to be well versed in Sacred Liturgy.

We think it worth while to give *in extenso* that part of the *Suffragium* which directly answers the question.

It will be seen that it is the Consultor's opinion :—

(1.) That, whilst it is desirable that the candles in question should be entirely of bees' wax, yet ' if a notable part of the candles be of bees' wax, the liturgical law is observed.'

(2.) That, even when the quantity of bees' wax is a ' pars satis minor, ut ne notabilis quidem dici queat,' the Rubrics are still substantially, though somewhat imperfectly, observed.

(3.) That, for certain reasons, it is better that the Congregation should not define the proportion required.

The *Ephemerides* states that the Congregation had not given a decision up to June, 1901. As far as we are aware, it has not done so yet.

SUPER CERA IN SACRA LITURGIA SUFFRAGIUM

EMI. PATRES,

Pluribus abhinc annis quaestio agitatur super cera in functionibus sacris adhibenda : an scilicet cera apum necessario adhiberi debeat, quamvis cum aliqua extranea substantia, minori tamen proportione, possit esse commixta, an permissa necne dicenda sit cera ex alia materia pro maiori parte composita, seu cera apum quasi ex integro exclusa. . . . . .

At nunc mihi inquirendum est, utrum ad Rubricarum, quae

retulimus, observantiam, necesse sit omnino, ut *totae* candelae sint ex cera apum. Cui quaesito negative certo certius reponendum est; quia si pars candelarum, saltem notabilis, ex cera apum sit, lex liturgica observatur, et Orationes Ecclesiae suum habent obiectum comprobatum : quod per se patet et demonstratione non eget. Quid autem iudicandum, si pars satis minor, ut ne notabilis quidem dici queat, inveniatur tantum in candelis Liturgiae inservientibus? Audeo pariter reponere, et per has candelas observari, licet minus perfecte, Rubricas, et Orationes liturgicas finem suum attingere.

Dixi *minus perfecte*, et iure, quod nemo negabit ; quia lex eiusque spiritus, cum dicunt candelas, nonnisi id omne intelligere possunt, ex quo candelae constant : in casu autem, haud omne, sed pars tantum et satis minor est ex apum cera, ut minus proinde perfecte Rubrica observetur. Observatur tamen ; quia si ad totum non potest lex referri, refertur nihilominus ad partem, quam ex cera apum vere supponimus. Similiter finem suum liturgice Orationes assequuntur, quia cera apum, esto in minori parte, in candelis non deest. Quid autem vetat, ut pars pro toto accipiatur ? Non enim de sacramentis agitur, sed de sacramentalibus.

De hac agendi ratione exempla plura in sacra Liturgia non desunt : adeo ut verba quae proferuntur haud perfecte iis quae fiunt respondeant. Ex. gr. Baptizato, ex antiquo neophitorum more, qui vestem albam induebant post baptisma receptum, nunc quoque dicitur : *Accipe vestem candidam, etc.* Sed notat Rituale pro *veste candida* imponendum infanti *Linteolum* (*tit. II. cap.* 2, *n.* 2). Rubrica Missalis (*ad Sabb. Sanct.*) dicit : ' Excutitur ignis de lapide . . . et accenduntur carbones.' Antiquitus comprobabatur perfecte Rubrica, cum alius ignorabatur modus excitandi ignem. Sed impraesenti alius adhibetur modus aut carbones deferuntur accensi, ut Rubrica perfecte non comprobetur, et Oratio nonnisi imperfecte scopum suum coassequatur. Nonne calvo tonsura prima confertur, et Oratio verba facit de comis capitis deponendis ? Nonne si Acolytho tradatur Breviarium pro libro Epistolarum, valida est Ordinatio, cum nihilominus dicat Pontifex ; *Accipe librum Epistolarum ?* Atque ita de aliis pluribus. Consequenter haud nimis insistendum hac in ratione, quam ex aliis exemplis atque ex sensu liturgico nihili faciendam esse censeo.

Aliquid nunc super Decretis, sed breviori calamo, mihi dicendum est. Plura citantur etiam ab A. Lavergne, sed eius, ne rigoris excessum dicam, zelum liturgicarum legum probare non valent. Et imprimis notandum, Decretum primum ab illo citatum a nova Collectione exulasse, aliudque exuli fuisse suffectum. Hoc autem prohibet tantum lumina ex oleo nutrita, mensae altaris imminentia, et sacrificii tempore ardentia (*Romana* n. 4035 *ad VI*). Aliud affertur Decretum in *Massilien.* n. 2865

(4975) ; sed loquitur explicite de cera stearina, super qua respondet : *Consulantur Rubricae.* De eadem cera loquitur Decretum *Divionen.*, uti ait praecitatus cl. Lavergne, et super illa S. R. C. respondisset : *Nihil innovetur :* Dies inscripta dicti Decreti esset 7 Sept. 1850, sed in nova Collectione non legitur : utcumque res se habeat, de cera stearica semper verba faceret. Affertur et Decretum in *Caronopolitana*, num. 3063 (5255), quod dicit eliminandum abusum *adhibendi candelas ex sevo.* Aliquod autem Decretum candelas praefatas prohibitas ex sola necessitate S. R. C. permittit. Porro animadverto, citata Decreta ad rem non facere, quia agunt de candelis ex stearina aut sevo exclusive, quas et ipsemet improbo et repudio seu ob foetorem, quem redolent, seu ob indecentiam. Eiusmodi vero non sunt candelae, quas ego adhiberi posse teneo.

Silendum esse censeo de auctoribus, qui vix de candelis ex pura apum cera adhibendis verba faciunt : excludunt tamen, saltem, super altaria, lumina ex stearina, ex sevo, ex oleo. Refert cl. Lavergne notam quamdam, excerptam ex Ephemeridibus Liturgicis, quas ipse moderor ; et gratias illi refero, quod simplicem notam Redactoris in S. R. Cognis Decretum commutavit. Ceterum haec nota ait tantum, commixtionem alterius materiae in cera pro functionibus liturgicis nullo pacto esse prohibitam (1894, *pag.* 537).

Sive ergo Rubricae, sive Decreta, sive auctores consulantur, asseri iure nequit, candelas partim ex cera apum, licet minus notabili proportione ; partim ex aliis materiis confectas, esse prohibitas : quamvis vetitae sint aliae, quae ex stearina, ex sevo aut adipe exclusive conficiuntur.

Nunc ad symbolismum. In cereis esse verum symbolismum, utpote ab Ecclesiae sapientia admissum, nemo catholicorum ambigit. Cereus repraesentat Christum, apis repraesentat almam Virginem : Christus est mel, mel apis mater educit : Virgo mater genuit Christum : cera apum purissima est, et virgo nuncupatur ; sed et virgo est apis, quae eam generat : Virgo est Maria, quae genuit Christum repraesentatum a cera, etc. etc. Haec, ut de lumine sileam, quod et ex oleo producitur. Hoc symbolismum admittit Ecclesia, uti constat ex Missali Romano et Gotico, ex Sacramentario S. R. Ecclesiae, e Ruperto Abbate, et generatim ex Patribus.

At nonne symbolismum istud in candelis habebitur, dummodo in iis apum cera non desit, in modica licet quantitate ? Nec deesse quoque poterit symbolismum luminis quod in cera semper ostenditur. Ergo et symbolismum manebit, quamvis candelae ex mera apum cera confecta non fuerint.

Ceterum et hoc breviter animadvertam. Cera primitus, uti oleum, adhibita ne in Ecclesia fuit ob symbolismum, an symbolismum, post cerae usum adinventum fuit ? Hoc unum pro

certo habeo, symbola, figuras, mysticasque significationes
sine fine excogitatas fuisse semper in ritibus et caeremoniis
Ecclesiae: ut vix ritus aliquis, vix aliqua caeremonia insti-
tuta fuit, statim devotae mentes et animi reconditos in illis
sensus detexerint. Excogitare num futurae aetati (quidni et
praesenti)? non licebit symbolismum novum in candelis ex cera
apum, cum vegetali vel animali commixta? Etiam, arbitror.
Immo addam quod mihi subit in mentem, haec scribenti. Si
cera apum purissima repraesentat Christum, cerea pars vegetalis
aut animalis depurata, primaeque commixta, nonne optime
repraesentare homines poterit, qui in Christo purificantur, atque
in ipso, Apostolo docente, efficiuntur iustitia Dei, et cum Christo
capite unum corpus mysticum tanquam membra efformant, ut
fiant lux in Domino? En optimum symbolismum, puto : quod si
ceterum non arrideat, perspicaciores non deerunt spiritus, qui
aliud perfectius excogitabunt.

Praeterea si primaevi Christifideles omnia possedissent naturae
artisque subsidia ad candelas conficiendas, quae in praesenti
aetate noscuntur, putandum ne, illos ea omnia repudiasse
propter praefati symbolismi defectum, an potius iisdem ulla sine
difficultate usi fuissent, symbolismo neglecto quod ceterum
adinvenire nullius momenti negotium constituit? Hoc ipse ab
omnibus edoceor, Ecclesiam quidquid do usibus, nec ritibus
exceptis, profanisque consuetudinibus gentilium accipere potuit,
accepisse, sanctumque fecisse. Atque in praesenti videmus
eamdem Ecclesiam, alterius generis lumina, quae ignorabat anti-
quitas, adoptasse sibi, licet extra cultum, in templis, uti ceram
vegetalem, animalemque, gas, acetilene, electricum ; aliaque
fortasse adoptabit, si excogitari poterit hominis ingenium.

Haec dicta sint, ne nimia symbolismo vis tribuatur, cum
Ecclesia pro sua sapientia ingenii progressum nequaquam spernat,
sed ritus ac caeremonias temporum adinventis aptare semper
solemne habuit, habebitque.

Ex hucusque dictis ac discussis liquido, ni fallor, profluit,
candelas altarium esse posse ex cera, quam apes non educunt,
dummodo cera apum in commixtione non desit. Huiusce autem
cerae apum quantitatem determinare lex posset quidem, sed non
deberet.

(a) Quia venalitas dominatur in fabricatoribus : adeo ut lege
abuterentur ad maiori illam pretio venumdandam.

(b) Quia in commixtione, cerae apum quantitatem mensurare
memo posset : ut fabricatoribus fides sit adhibenda, qui tamen,
generaliter loquimur, mendaces sunt.

(c) Quia non arbitror imponendam legem, quae urgeri nonnisi
maxima cum difficultate potest.

Ut finem dicendi faciam censeo necessarium esse, ut S. R. C.
pro sua sapientia statuat, ceram apum in candelis pro cultu

inservientibus omnino requiri, quin tamen excludi absolute debeat alterius naturae, seu vegetalis, quae praeferenda est, seu animalis cera, quam, attentis rerum, temporum, locorumque adiunctis, S. R. C. permittit, aut tolerat. Hinc opinor, dubium iam propositum, et pro modulo meo resolutum, alia seu sequenti ratione posse exprimi :

'An candelae super altaribus ponendae, omnino et integre ex cera apum esse debeant, an esse possint cum alia materia seu vegetali seu animali commixtae, ita tamen ut aliqua, saltem notabilis, pars cerae apum in illis omnino nunquam desit?'

Resp. *Negative* ad primam partem : *Affirmative* ad secundam.

Quae omnia dicta sint sub censura Eminentiarum Vestrarum.

CALCEDONIUS MANCINI, P.C.M.

Sacr. Rit. Congr. Consult. Commiss. Liturg. Secret·

THE GRAINS OF INCENSE FOR THE PASCHAL CANDLE

REV. DEAR SIR,—A clerical customer of ours, who has ordered a Paschal candlestick and set of incense grains, has raised a point, whether it is rubrical to use ornamental brass incense grains or not.

These brass incense grains are made like a small case with a screw cover, into which the grains proper are put.

We shall be very pleased if you will kindly inform us through the medium of the I. E. RECORD on this point. Thanking you in anticipation and trusting we are not troubling too much.—Yours sincerely,   JOHN SMYTH & SONS.

The rubrics of the Missal speak only of 'quinque grana incensi.' They do not prescribe any special form. Neither does the Sacred Congregation of Rites. Merati,[1] quoting Bauldry *verbatim,* says :—

Quinque grana incensi novi . . . pulchre elaborata in modum nucis pineae ferreisque clavis suffulta, et in extremitate inaurata, modo tamen plus thuris appareat quam alterius rei.

This is the only description we have seen—grains made (1) like a pine cone ; (2) with an iron nail ; (3) gilt, only at the top, so that more incense than gilding appears.

But as the cases described by our correspondent are not directly against the rubrics or decrees of the Sacred Congregation of Rites, and as they are extensively used and very convenient, we would be slow to condemn them.

P. O'LEARY.

---

[1] In *Gavantum,* Pars iv., tit. x., n. 1.

DOCUMENTS

ROMAN AUTHORITIES AGAIN CALL ATTENTION TO THE FORM OF CORRESPONDENCE

EME. AC RME. DOMINE,

Haud raro accidit, ut ad SS. Romanas Congregationes, hac Suprema S. Officii non excepta, a RR. Curiarum Episcopalium negotiorum Romae Procuratoribus (italice ' Agenti Ecclesiastici ') documenta, de rebus etiam gravissimis et maxima observatione dignis, plane resignata atque omnium oculis patentia exhibeantur ; eadem vero nonnunquam adeo parvulis atque exiguis chartulis neglectaque forma exarata sunt, ut et erga S. Sedem non parum indecentia atque ad positiones, quas vocant, efformandas minus apta inveniantur.

Haec omnia iure merito lamentantes Emi. Domini Cardinales una mecum Inquisitores Generales, in Congregatione Generali habita fer. IV, die 24 Aprilis anni currentis omnibus Episcopalibus Curiis significandum mandarunt, ut in posterum huiusmodi documenta, in folio communis Romae dimensionis conscripta, vel directim per publica epistolarum diribitoria vel, si quidem rationabili ex causa Procuratorum opera uti velint, ita clausa et sigillo munita transmittant, ut nullus ex parte ipsorum Procuratorum clandestinae aperitioni locus esse queat.

Quae dum, ut mei muneris est, ad Em. Tuae notitiam defero, lubenter capta occasione, fausta quaeque ac felicia Tibi precor a Domino.

Datum Romae ex S. O. die 23 Aug., 1901.

Addictissimus obsequentissimus famulus verus,

L. M. Card. PAROCCHI.

THE FOUNDATION OF NEW RELIGIOUS HOUSES—RULES LAID DOWN BY PROPAGANDA

ILLME. AC RME. DOMINE,

Quamvis probe sciat haec S. Congregatio de Propaganda Fide, ingentem provenire missionibus utilitatem ex ministerio Regularium : ita ut maxime in votis sit videre eorum domus ubique institui : curandum tamen est, ut res ordinate et ad praestitutae disciplinae normam peragantur. Quamobrem duxit S. Congregatio per praesentes litteras in memoriam Ordinariorum locorum a se dependentium revocare sententiam, quam ut communem hodie et cui favet passim rerum iudicatarum auctoritas, tradit Constitutio SSmi. D. N. LeonisXIII. quae incipit 'Romanos Pontifices': nempe: non licere Regularibus, tam intra quam extra Italiam, nova monasteria aut conventus sive collegia fundare, sola Episcopi venia, sed indultam quoque a Sede Apostolica facultatem requiri. Cui legi cum aut semper aut ubique obtemperatum non fuisse videatur, ideo eius observantiam voluit S. Congregatio per praesentes urgere. Diligenter ergo in posterum abstineant Ordinarii omnes Sacrae Congregationi subiecti a licentia danda religiosis Institutis domum aperiendi in territorio propriae iurisdictionis, absque venia prius a praefata S. Congregatione obtenta. Quod vero attinet ad domus religiosas huc usque in iisdem territoriis, S. Congregatione inconsulta, forte erectas, etsi haec, Ordinariis flagitantibus, singulisque ponderatis casibus, propensa omnino sit ad legitimas habendas huiusmodi fundationes : tamen mandat ut de praedictis si quae existant domibus, distinctus ab Ordinariis exhibeatur elenchus, ac simul pro iisdem canonica ratihabitio per supplicem libellum petatur.

Interim Deum precor ut Te diu sospitet.

Datum Romae ex Aedibus S. C. de Propaganda Fide die 7 Decembris, 1901.

Amplitudinis Tuae

Addictissimus Servus

MIECISLAUS Card. LEDÓCHOWSKI, *Praefectus*,
ALOYSIUS VECCIA, *Secretarius*.

"*Ut Christiani da et Romani ritu.*'   · As you are children of Christ, so be you children of Rome."
Ex Dictis S. Patricii, In Libro Armacano, fol. 9.

The Irish
Ecclesiastical Record

𝔄 𝔐𝔬𝔫𝔱𝔥𝔩𝔶 𝔍𝔬𝔲𝔯𝔫𝔞𝔩, 𝔲𝔫𝔡𝔢𝔯 𝔈𝔭𝔦𝔰𝔠𝔬𝔭𝔞𝔩 𝔖𝔞𝔫𝔠𝔱𝔦𝔬𝔫.

𝔗𝔥𝔦𝔯𝔱𝔶-𝔣𝔦𝔣𝔱𝔥 𝔜𝔢𝔞𝔯 ⎤
No. 411.   ⎦   **MARCH, 1902.**   ⎡ 𝔉𝔬𝔲𝔯𝔱𝔥 𝔖𝔢𝔯𝔦𝔢𝔰
                                    ⎣ Vol. XI.

Nihil Obstat.
>   GIRALDUS MOLLOY, S.T.D.,
>   *Censor Dep.*

𝔦𝔪𝔭𝔯𝔦𝔪𝔞𝔱𝔲𝔯.
>   ✠ GULIELMUS,
>   *Archiep. Dublin.,*
>   *Hibernae Primas*

BROWNE & NOLAN, Limited

Publishers and Printers, 24 & 25

NASSAU STREET, DUBLIN.

. . PRICE ONE SHILLING . .

'THE IRISH COLLEGE IN PARIS, 1578-1901'

GLEANINGS—LANGUAGE

IN a book recently published, the present writer has given an account of the Irish College in Paris, from its origin to the present time. In that work the relations of the College with the University of Paris, and the course of studies in theology and philosophy, received due notice. One point, however, as being of secondary importance, was not dwelt upon, viz., the language in use amongst the students. The language of the schools was Latin; the language of the country was French. The Irish students were obliged to make use of these. But they were Irishmen; and what was the language of their daily life? This is a question not without interest, and in the present paper the writer purposes to examine—(1) Whether, assuming that the English language was spoken, the Irish language was also in use in the College; (2) What attention was paid to the study of Irish; (3) What was done by the College for the diffusion of Irish literature and for the preservation of the language; and (4) to add a few words on the proficiency of the students in the French language.

I

That the Irish language was in use in the Irish College in Paris in the eighteenth century does not admit of doubt. That College was a national establishment in the fullest

sense of the word. Some of the Irish colleges in France
educated priests for particular provinces. The College at
Lille, for instance, was reserved for the education of Leinster-
men. Oliver Plunket, Archbishop of Armagh, in a letter
addressed to Propaganda on 13th May, 1671, laments that
no students were admitted in the Irish colleges at Bordeaux
and Toulouse except those from Munster. In his zeal for
the welfare of the Church in Ireland the saintly Primate
desired a truly national college. The Irish College in Paris
had been already in existence for nearly a century. In their
protest against Jansenism, in 1651, its students declared
that the number of Irishmen studying in Paris was greater
than in any other city in the world. In 1672 the Bishops
of Ireland, with Dr. Plunket at their head, desired to
give to the College still further development; and they
deputed Dr. Molony, Bishop of Killaloe, to proceed to
Paris for the purpose of negotiations with the authorities
in France. Writing to Propaganda, in 1672, to ask permission for Dr. Molony to absent himself from his diocese,
Dr. Plunket speaks thus of the College :—

It will be a great seminary for the missions of this kingdom,
being in a city so rich, so desirous of procuring the propagation
of the faith, as their charity sufficiently proved during the late
persecution of Cromwell, when the Parisians supported hundreds
and hundreds of ecclesiastics and students exiled during that
tempest. It is certain that the Bishop of Killaloe will do more
good by procuring for us that College than he would do did he
remain in his diocese during his whole lifetime.[1]

In the College archives there is no mention of Dr.
Molony's mission in 1672. But no doubt Dr. Maginn and
Dr. Kelly were acting by authority of the Bishops when
they obtained possession of the Lombard College.

A similar omission occurred in more recent times respecting the visit of Dr. Hussey to Paris, to solicit permission
to re-open the Irish College in that city after the
revolution. This visit is thus recorded in a manuscript
note by Dr. Walsh, which we have been fortunate enough to
find at the Archives Nationales.[2]

Aussitot que le traité d'Amiens permit aux Evêques d'Irlande

[1] Moran, *Life of Oliver Plunket*, pp. 110, 112, 113, 114.
[2] Arch. Nat. H³, 2561.

d'envoyer un deputé, ils choisirent M. l'Evêque de Waterford parceque ce Prélat était en même temps aumonier et agent accrédité de S. M. Catholique dàns les trois royaumes insulaires. Ce deputé fut presenté par l'ambassadeur d'Espagne ; il sollicita et obtint l'arrêté du 19 fructidor an. 9, dont l'article 10 est ainsi conçu. 'Le Ministre de l'Interieur est chargé de l'execution du present arrêt, qui sera inséré au Bulletin des Lois.'[1]

It is a pleasing duty to record the services rendered to the College by the accomplished Bishop of Waterford, the zealous Bishop of Killaloe, and the heroic martyred Primate of Ireland. But to return to our subject, the Irish College in Paris was open to students from all the provinces of Ireland, and they must have brought with them the language then prevailing in the country. That such was the fact is evident from authentic records. But first let us see what was the condition of the language, and what was the extent to which it prevailed in Ireland.

As to the state of the Irish language in the eighteenth century, two of the Superiors of the College, Rev. Andrew Donlevy, and Rev. David Henegan, furnish reliable information. In the elements of the Irish language appended to his *Catechism*,[2] Father Donlevy[3] laments the incorrect forms which had crept into the language in the following terms :—

Poets, not the ancient and skilful, who took pains to render their poems sententious and pithy without much clipping, but the modern makers of doggerel rhymes and ballads, to save time and labour, introduced the custom of clipping and joining words together in order to fit them to the measure of their verses. Others who wrote in prose, have either in imitation of the poets, or through ignorance or want of judgment, strangely clipped and spelled and huddled them together as they are pronounced, let their pronunciation be never so irregular and defective ; not reflecting that a poetical licence, even when justifiable, is not

---

[1] By this decree the Bureau referred to in the *History of the Irish College, Paris*, 1578-1901, pp. 67 and 70, was established.

[2] Donlevy's *English-Irish Catechism*. Paris: 1742; pp. 506-507.

[3] In Ware's *Antiquities of Ireland*, vol. ii., p. 254, Harris refers to Father Donlevy as follows :—'The present Prefect of this Seminary (Irish College, Paris), is Dr. Andrew Donlevy, titular Dean of Raphoe, and author of a work of Christian instruction in catechetical method, English and Irish, printed in Paris, 1742. I take occasion to mention him here out of gratitude for many favours I received from him, particularly by his transmitting to me from time to time several useful collections out of the King's and other libraries in Paris.'

imitable in prose, or that writing as people speak or pronounce is
to maim the language, to destroy the etymology, and confound the
propriety and orthography ; for not only the several provinces of
Ireland have a different way of pronouncing, but also the very
counties, and even some baronies in one and the same county, do
differ in the pronunciation; nay, some counties pronounce so
oddly that the natural sound of both vowels and consonants
whereof, even according to themselves the words consist, is utterly
lost in their mouths. . . . It is no wonder then that a
language of neither court, nor city, nor Bar, nor business, ever
since the beginning of James the First's reign should have suffered
alterations and corruptions, and be now on the brink of utter
decay, as it really is, to the great dishonour and shame of our
natives, who shall always pass everywhere for Irishmen, although
Irishmen without Irish is an incongruity and a great bull. Besides
the Irish language is undeniably a very ancient mother language,
and one of the smoothest in Europe, no way abounding with
monosyllables nor clogged with rugged consonants which make a
harsh sound upon the ear.   And there is still extant a great
number of old valuable Irish manuscripts both in publick and
private hands which would, if translated, give great light into the
antiquities of the country, and furnish some able pen with
materials to write a compleat history of the kingdom.   What a
discredit then it must be to a whole nation to let such a language
go to wrack?

Rev. David Henegan, in an article on Keating in the
Grand Dictionnaire de Moreri, edited by Drouet, in 1759,
writes thus (we translate from the French) :—

The Irish language, which Keating made use of in his works,
is the purest dialect existing of the Celtic tongue.   The Breton
and the Welsh being much mixed with barbarisms and foreign
terms on account of the intimate and necessary commerce of those
two nations with the Romans, the French, the Saxons, and other
nations.   Whereas the Irish and the northern Scotch, who are
only a colony of the former, living in some degree separated from
the rest of Europe, were easily able to preserve the purity of their
language, which they cultivated with great care, as may be easily
seen by the order, the case, and the clearness which reign in their
poetry and their tales, which surpass in this respect all the best
compositions of the period in the other vulgar tongues of Europe.
But this advantage is already beginning to disappear by the mixture which the too frequent use of English has introduced insen-
sibly, so that soon men of literary education will be the only
persons who can flatter themselves that they speak that language
with correctness and purity.

So much for the state of the language itself. To what extent was it spoken? Mr. Lecky in his *History of Ireland in the Eighteenth Century* writes as follows [1] :—

A very competent authority, in 1738 states that not more than one person in twenty was ignorant of English ; and another writer, who described the County of Down a few years later, declared that Irish was there only prevelant among the poorer Catholics, and that they showed a strong desire that their children should learn English.

Yet Irish continued to be spoken through nearly the whole of Ireland down to the end of the eighteenth century. Townsend, in his *Survey of Cork,*[2] speaks thus of Catholics: ' The greater part derive no eventual advantage from their school-days ; for, being recalled at an early age, and mixing with a family who speak only Irish, even the little smattering of English they had acquired is soon lost.' Wakefield, who visited Ireland in 1808, says :[3] ' The Irish language is so much spoken among the common people in the city of Cork and its neighbourhood that an Englishman is apt to forget where he is, and to consider himself in a foreign city. In the county Wexford,' he writes, ' although the Catholic is the prevailing religion, the language everywhere spoken is the English.'

Another Englishman, John Carr, Esq., in his account of his tour in Ireland in 1805, writes thus :—

It [the Irish language] is remarkable for the variety of its powers ; it is affecting, sweet, dignified, energetic, and sublime. In the county Meath, which borders on the Metropolis, it has been said, a justice of the peace must understand Irish or keep an interpreter. In the north-west and south-west counties the English language is scarcely known. In the county of Wexford English customs and habits prevail, and the English language is quite forgotten.[4]

From the foregoing testimonies it is evident that, though deteriorating, the Irish language was prevalent amongst

---

[1] *History of Ireland in the Eighteenth Century,* vol. i. p. 331.
[2] Addenda, p. 60. See Wakefield, *Ireland, Political and Social.* London, 1812, vol. ii. p. 582.
[3] Vol. ii. pp. 582 and 766.
[4] *The Stranger in Ireland, or a Tour in the Southern and Western parts of the Country in 1805,* by John Carr, Esq. London, 1806, p. 399.

Catholics in Ireland. The Irish students in Paris, coming
as they did from all the provinces of Ireland, must have
brought with them the language of the country. But here
we are not left to inferences only. Documents bearing on
the subject are still extant.

In 1734 a controversy arose with reference to the
propriety of sending young men to study in Paris, who had
already been ordained priests at home. The priests
of the Lombard College drew up a memorandum in their
own defence,[1] and in it the language question was
introduced. The junior students, they stated,[2] had greater
facility in acquiring a perfect mastery of the French
language. It was a kind of necessity for them to learn
it, as they were more dependant on charity than the
priests. Many of them acquired such proficiency in it that
they forgot their native tongue. The priests, on the other
hand, coming to France later in life never acquired a perfect
French accent. They were, therefore, less inclined to remain
in France. They preserved their mother tongue, and were
therefore better fitted than the juniors for the work of the
mission in Ireland. 'L'experience l'a demontré et a fait
voir,' says the Memorandum, 'que la plupart des ecoliers
ne pouvaient être employés á la mission faute d'avoir
conservé l'usage de la langue irlandaise.'

Here, then, there is evidence of the use of the Irish
language in the daily life of the students. But there
are other proofs also. By his will, dated 1764, the Most
Rev. John O'Brien, Bishop of Cloyne, founded burses
in the College, and he laid it down as a condition that
candidates, to be eligible to them, should be able to speak
and read Irish.

Again, we have evidence on the same point so late as

---

[1] See *Irish College in Paris from* 1598 *to* 1901, p. 36.
[2] A l'égard de la precaution qu'on prend d'obliger les jeunes Irlandais
a parler leur langue maternelle, on sait que cela n'est praticable ni de la part
des superieurs qui ont assez d'autres soins, ni de celle des Ecoliers qui ne
peuvent trop parler la langue française avec laquelle ils pourvoient à leur
subsistence.   Il y a plus ces prêtres sortis de leur pays dans un âge mûr con-
servent la connaissance de toute la plus utile, c'est a dire celle de leur langue
maternelle, les ecoliers au contraire l'oublient et sont forcés de l'oublier.
—*Memoire pour les Pretres, imprimé,* Arch. Nat., M. 147.

1774. About that time the Irish burses at Poitiers were transferred to Paris. A decree was prepared sanctioning the transfer, with the limitation that no particular college should have an exclusive right to the burses. In reference to this draft scheme it was argued that the Irish College was the establishment to which they should be allocated.

As the draft rule [it was said[1]], has not yet been ratified, it seems proper to observe, that inasmuch as one of the principal motives for which the burses have been withdrawn from the Poitiers College, has doubtless been to prevent the bursars from losing the use of the Irish language, a knowledge of which is absolutely necessary for the mission in that country, nothing can be more opposed to that motive than the first article of the aforesaid scheme; which says, that no college or house of the university shall have a particular right to the said funds. From the moment that these burses were founded for persons destined to the mission in Ireland, the Irish seminary seems to be the place where they ought to be educated to the exclusion of all others. . . . . However respectable are the seminaries of St. Nicholas de Chardonnet, and of the Trente-Trois, where several of those bursars have hitherto been placed, they cannot make up for the want of the Irish and English languages, which are indispensable to missioners.

A further testimony bearing on the same point is found in a letter of Dr. Kearney, rector of the College, to the Bishop of Meath in 1788. Speaking of one of the students, he says :—'He applies close to his duty, of which one proof is that he knew no Irish some months ago ; he has now got to be able to get the whole Irish Catechism by heart.'[2]

From all this it is manifest that the Irish language continued to exist as a living language in the Irish College in Paris throughout the eighteenth century. Let us now proceed to consider what provision was made for instruction in Irish, and for practice in the literary use of the language.

II

Not only was Irish spoken, it was also taught in class. We have evidence of this in the foundation made by

---

[1] *Etat des Revenues fait par ordre de l'archevêque de Paris, superieur majeur*, MS. 1788.

[2] Cogan, *Diocese of Meath*, vol. iii. p. 125.

M. Philip Joseph Perrotin, lord of Barmon and Knight of the Order of St. Michael. That excellent French gentleman, having learned how necessary a knowledge of the Irish language was for missioners in Ireland, made a donation of three hundred livres a year to promote the study of that tongue. Two of the clauses of the donation were to the following effect :—

1. There shall be in perpetuity a class of Irish for the advantage of those who cannot read or write that language. . . . .
4. There shall be given four prizes each year, two for such as shall be best in Irish composition, and two in favour of those who shall know the catechism best in the same tongue. The two former shall be of ten livres each, and the two latter of five livres.[1]

But it was not by conversation and by instruction in class only, that a knowledge of the Irish language was promoted. The students were taught to preach in Irish. To encourage them in this exercise, prizes were awarded to the most successful. A generous benefactor of the College, Bartholomew Murry, M.D., amongst many other donations, made one for this purpose. By the act of donation, dated 1764, he gave—

One hundred livres a year also in perpetuity, from the death of the said donor, in the form of prizes, to the deacons and priests of the said community of Irish clerics, who shall have preached best in Irish and in English, to wit : Sixty livres to the person who shall have preached the two best sermons of his own composition in Irish ; and forty livres to whoever shall have preached best two sermons of his own composition in English, and the same person may obtain both prizes if he surpass all others in preaching in both languages.

It is plain, then, that the Irish language held a prominent place in the course of studies, and that a literary knowledge of it was encouraged.

III

While the Irish language was thus cultivated, provision was also made for printing and circulating Irish books ; and the superiors of the College co-operated in the

---

[1] He modified this clause at a later date, making the first premium in each case ten livres, and the second five livres.

production of works destined to preserve the language. One of the effects of the persecution of Catholics in the seventeenth century was to deprive them of the means, and of the liberty to print religious books in the Irish language in Ireland. The dearth of books of religious instruction moved zealous Irishmen resident on the Continent to do what in them lay for the instruction of their countrymen at home. In this good work, says the Abbé Henegan, the Irish Franciscans led the way :—

C'est a Louvain surtout qu'on a composé et publié le plus de cette éspéce de livre par les soins des Religeux Observantins du Convent du Saint Antoine de Padoue ; dont plusieurs se sont extrêmement distingués par leur capacité et leur zéle a maintenir la foi Catholique dans leur patrie.'

The Irish Franciscans of the Convent of St. Antony, at Louvain, had catechisms printed in Irish for distribution among the people.[2]

In Rome, too, Irish books were printed at the Propaganda Press. There Father Francis O'Mulloy published a work of religious instruction in the Irish language, entitled *Lucerna Fidelium*, in 1676 ;[3] and in 1677 his Latin-Irish Grammar issued from the same press.[4]

---

[1] *Dictionnaire de Moreri.* A.D. 1759, art. Keating, by Henegan.

[2] A copy of one of these catechisms, printed at Louvain in 1663, is to be seen at the Bibliothèque de l'Arsenal, in Paris. It has the following approbation : ' Visa attestatione duorum Sacrae Theologiae professorum idiomatis Hibernici bene peritorum, ac omni exceptione majorum, quâ testantur hunc catechismum, auctore, R. admo. et sapentiss. D.D., G.T., S.S., T.D.. &c., compositum, plane consentire principiis fidei Catholicae, apostolicae et Romanae, necnon puritati Vitae Christianae, hinc, censeo, posse, imo debere imprimi ad juventutis Hibernicae instructionem et animarum salutem. Datum Lovanii hac 18 Octobris MDCLXIII. Antonius Dave, Sacrae Theologiae doctor et professor regius, librorum censor apostolicus et archiep. Mechlinensis.' This little book has had its odyssey. It bears the mark : ' Ex libris Congregationis Missionis domus St. Lazari Parisiensis.' Inside the cover it has the following words written in English : ' Lord, have mercy on me. Patrick O'Bryan is my name, and with my pen I write the same.' The same is repeated, with the signature James Kehoe—a frail monument, but, in this case, *aere perennius*. The catechism contains the manner of serving Mass, but without the *De Profundis*.

[3] ' Lucerna fidelium seu fasciculus discerptus ab authoribus magis versatis qui tractaverunt de doctrina Christiana, divisus in tres partes, authore P. Francisco O'Molloy, Hibernio Midensi. Romae, 1676.'

[4] ' Grammatica Latino-Hibernica nunc compendiata, authore R. P. Francisco O'Molloy, Ord. Min. Strict. Observantiae, in Collegio Sti Isidori S. Theologiae Professore Primario, Lectore Jubilato, et Provinciae Hiberniae in curiâ Romanâ, Agente Generali. Romae ex typographia S. Cong. de Propaganda Fide, A.D. 1677.'

But in the beginning of the eighteenth century the books printed in Louvain had become scarce. To supply the want of Irish books, writes the Abbé Henegan in the article above referred to, an Irish priest resident in Paris, the Abbé Begley,[1] had Irish type cast in that city in 1730. He then invited Hugh M'Curtin, who had already published. at Louvain, his *Elements of the Irish Language*,[2] to come to Paris, and enabled him to publish there his well-known *Anglo-Irish Dictionary*.[3]

A few years later Rev. Andrew Donlevy, Licentiate of Laws and Prefect of the clerics at the Lombard College, availed himself of the opportunity of printing Irish books in Paris, and in 1742 he published his Irish-English catechism.[4]

Donlevy's *Catechism* forms an octavo volume of 518 pages, with the Irish and English texts on opposite pages. In the appendix there is an abridgment of the Christian Doctrine in Irish and in rhyme, by Father Bonaventure O'Heoghusa [O'Hussey], O.S.F, and a short treatise on the elements of the Irish language.

At the beginning of the book are printed certificates of approval by Bishops O'Gara, Gallagher and M'Donough; by Rev. F. J. Duany, O.E.S.A., and Rev. T. B. Kelly, O.S.F., both doctors of the Sorbonne; and by Dr. Corr, and Dr. M'Kenna, Provisors; by Father Hennessy, Licentiate; and by Rev. Richard Devereux, Principal of the Lombard College, the latter certifying for the English text only.

The printing of this book was a real *tour de force*, and is thus referred to in the preface : ' An absence of upwards of thirty-one years from one's native country, and the profound ignorance of the printer, who understood not one word of either language, will be a sufficient apology for the

---

[1] In the deed of the Foundation M'Carthy Rabagh, dated 1729, mention is made of a Father Begley as follows : ' Thadee Begley prêtre, docteur en Theologie de la Sorbonne, prêtre habitué de la paroisse de St. Germain l'Auxerrois.' He is, no doubt, the person referred to above.

[2] Louvain, 1728.

[3] *Anglo-Irish Dictionary*, by Hugh M'Curtin. Paris, 1732.

[4] The title of the English part is *The Catechism ; or, Christian Doctrine by way of Question and Answer, drawn chiefly from the Word of God and other pure sources.* Paris, 1742.

faults of both the languages and of the press.' The expense
of printing was defrayed, it is added, 'by a very worthy
gentleman, Philip Joseph Perrot,[1] Lord of the Manor of
Barmon and other territories, and Knight of the Royal Order
of St. Michael, and who of a long time is well affected to
the Irish Nation, and has often given proofs of his affection
to several of them, and without whose concurrence this
little work could never have come to light.' The instruction
contained in Donlevy's *Catechism* is simple, clear, and full,
as will be seen from the extracts printed below.[2]

M. de Perrotin's benefits did not end with the publication
of Donlevy's *Catechism*. As has been stated above he made
a donation, producing an annual revenue of three hundred
livres, to promote the study of Irish. A portion of the
revenue was destined for the Professor of Irish, a portion for
prizes, and a portion was to be set apart for printing in
Irish. The following are the terms of the act of donation:

---

[1] The name in the original document is Perrotin.

[2] The following is an extract from the chapter on Meditation in Donlevy's
Catechism, pp. 451, 485 :—

Question : What is that prayer which you call meditation or mental
prayer ?

Answer : Meditation or mental prayer is a serious and frequent reflection
which is made in the presence of God, and by the assistance of His grace, on the
truths of salvation, to know them well, to love them, and to put them in
practice.

Q. Is this prayer of great benefit ?

A. It is of very great benefit, for by practising it we learn to know solidly
the truths of salvation, to love them warmly, and to put them in practice
faithfully. These are the three effects of meditation, which can hardly be
sufficiently esteemed, because they comprehend all that is necessary for
salvation. Moreover, meditation teaches us to speak to God and to hear God.
We speak to God when we pray, God speaks to us when He enlightens our
understanding by good thoughts, excites our will by holy inspirations, and
animates us to put them in execution, etc., etc.

Q. Doth it not belong only to recluses, or people who have quitted the
world, to use this prayer ?

A. Not only to them, but also to others. It is the business of everybody
to learn well the truths of salvation, to love them, and to put them in
practice.

Q. Who is the author of meditation or mental prayer ?

A. God Himself, for when He gave the law to His chosen people He commanded them to meditate on it continually, saying : 'The things which I
command thee this day shall be in thy heart, and thou shalt teach them to
thy children, and thou shalt meditate on them whether sitting in thy house
or walking on thy way, lying down, and rising up; and thou shalt have them
in thy hand, and they shall be before thy eyes.' Deut. vi. 6, 7, 8, &c., &c.

Q. Is not meditation or mental prayer a difficult exercise ?

A. It is not, as it can be easily made manifest. But it is very strange

' There shall be printed from time to time catechisms and
other little books of piety in the Irish language, which shall
be given gratis to the students and ecclesiastics returning
to Ireland, to be by them distributed to persons capable of
instructing the young.'[1]

In an *Etat des Revenus*, made by order of the Archbishop of Paris in 1788, the following observation is found
with reference to M. Perrotin's foundation :—

This foundation is invaluable. The Irish language is a dialect
of the Celtic and altogether different from English. The policy of
the Government has introduced the latter into all public acts,
debates in Parliament, the pulpit, pleadings in the courts, so that
the Irish language is no longer in use except amongst the country
people, who are almost all Catholics. In order to withdraw them
from their religion, the Government has established a chair of
Irish for the country ministers. It is, therefore, essential that
Catholic missionaries should be acquainted with it, in order to

---

that men should account that hard which is performed daily in all sorts of
business except that of salvation. What merchant is there that doth not
seriously, and often think on the affairs of his traffick ? Who is it that has a
process or suit at law, and doth not daily cast up in his mind the means to
gain it ? And that not lightly and hastily, but seriously, with attention, and
with affection, and putting in execution all the means he finds. To act in
this manner in the affairs of salvation is what we understand by meditation,
etc.

Q. Can we not easily work out our salvation without meditation or mental
prayer ?

A. Not easily, indeed ; for seeing meditation or mental prayer is nothing
else but a serious and frequent reflection upon the truths of salvation, to know
them, to love them, and to practice them ; it is certain that it is a very difficult thing to effect our salvation without meditation, as it is very hard to
practice the truths of the same salvation without knowing them, to know
them without thinking seriously and frequently on them, and without often
and humbly demanding of God the grace to know them, to love them, and to
practise them, etc., etc.

SACRAMENT OF HOLY ORDERS.

Q. Is it sufficient that his parents design him for the Church ?

A. No, for parents are often as worldly, and as vain as their children ;
moreover, they are commonly ignorant of the obligations of clergymen, and
of the dangers of that high calling ; so that as our Saviour said to the children
of Zebedee, and to their mother, they know not what they ask. St. Matt. xx. 22.
Con. Burdig. 1624.

If they have a mind that any of their children should be clergymen,
they ought to present to God the most worthy. the most pious, the most
studious, for it is not pleasing to God, or the Church, to offer them the dull-
witted, the impious, the maimed, the infirm, or the refuse of their children.
Lev. xxi. 18. Decr. Greg. IX., lib. 1.

[1] This foundation, like all the others, was reduced by two-thirds at the
great Revolution, and has been further reduced by *Conversions des Rentes*
from five to three per cent. 300 livres are equivalent to £12.

combat successfully the efforts of the ministers; and that they should be able to supplement their oral instruction by books such as catechisms. It is to be regretted that the revenues of the foundation are so small.

The accuracy of the statements here made are borne out by the testimony of Lecky in his *History of Ireland in the Eighteenth Century*.[1] Having stated that Irish was prevalent only among the poorer Catholics, he continues:—

In the preceding century, Bedell and Boyle had clearly seen that to translate the Bible and to spread the doctrines of Protestantism in the native language was the true method of encountering Catholicism in Ireland. The Lower House of Convocation in 1703 passed a resolution desiring the appointment of an Irish-speaking minister in every parish. Archbishop King supported the plan. Trinity College made arrangements for teaching Irish to students. The English Society for the Promotion of Christian Knowledge gave some assistance, and two or three clergymen devoted themselves with eminent success to preaching to the people in their own language. The Government, however, which desired to eradicate the language discountenanced their efforts.

The necessity for instruction in Irish was, therefore, a very real one, and it is a pleasure to record the efforts made by the national college in Paris to prepare its students for this important work.

Nor were the services rendered to Irish literature limited to teaching, and to the printing of books of piety. The College had also a share in giving to the world two other works of interest to Irish scholars. The first of these was O'Brien's *Foca Loir, or Anglo-Irish Dictionary*.[2] That work was written in Ireland in 1767, and was sent to Paris to be printed. It was examined, and certified for publication, by the Abbé Henegan, one of the Superiors of the Irish College, and published in 1768. This work contains a dedication by the author, to his Eminence Cardinal Castelli, Prefect of the Propaganda. After stating in the letter of dedication,

---

[1] Lecky's *History of Ireland*, etc., vol. i. pp. 331, 332.
[2] *Foca Loir, or Anglo-Irish Dictionary*, by J. O'Brien. Paris, 1768. The author is believed by many to have been the Most Rev. John O'Brien, Bishop of Cloyne. The dedication to Cardinal Castelli is in favour of this view. See also preface to O'Reilly's *Irish Dictionary* by O'Donovan, and, *Dictionary of National Biography*, art. O'Brien, John.

that not more than one-seventh of the population of Ireland
was non-Catholic, the author speaks as follows of the Irish
language :—

Non immerito, sane, dixerim, nativo hujusce gentis idiomati
divinam Providentiam alligasse odium quasi innatum erga novas
omnes in rebus fidei molitiones, quippe cum in confesso est apud
nostrates universos, nullum hominem, cui hâc solummodo linguâ
uti datum erat, ab orthodoxâ Christi fide unquam extorrem esse
factum.   Non igitur injuria linguae sanctae nomenclatura sibi
arrogaret.   Haec, tamen, cum talis sit, tam efficax ad fideles
nostros in recto veritatis tramite continendos, ad interitum pro-
pediem esset ruitura, nisi Eminentissima Dominatio Vestra eam
potentissimo suo patrocinio, suâque munificentia, sublevasset,
eique etiam vitam imo et perennitatem asseruisset.

The second work which the College had a share in giving
to Irish literature was the *Book of Lecain*.[1]   That valuable
and ancient manuscript had long been in possession of the
Lombard College; and O'Curry[2] attributes the chief excellence of Mageoghegan's *History of Ireland* to the fact that
he had an opportunity of consulting it.

Towards the end of the eighteenth century the Royal
Dublin Society established a committee of men interested in
the literature and antiquities of Ireland.   That committee
deputed the Chevalier Thomas O'Gorman to apply to the
Lombard College, and such other bodies as he might have
an opportunity of visiting, for copies of manuscripts and
ancient records illustrating the history and antiquities of
Ireland.   Rev. Charles O'Neil, Principal of the College, and
Rev. Laurence Kelly,[3] Prefect of the Clerics, responded to
the appeal made by the Chevalier O'Gorman.   In consequence a meeting was convened at the Lombard College on
11th of March, 1773, of persons interested in Irish literature
and antiquities.   The Most Rev. Richard Dillon, Archbishop
of Narbonne, himself of Irish origin, presided.   A branch
committee was established in Paris, and the Superiors of
the Lombard College promised to furnish to the Society a

---

[1] The *Book of Lecain*, of 600 pages, small folio, is to be seen in the Library,
Royal Academy.   *Dict. of Nat. Biography*, art. MacFirbis.
[2] O'Curry's *Lectures*, p. 442.
[3] Dr. Kelly was a priest of the Diocese of Armagh.

copy of the *Book of Lecain*, the only valuable manuscript in their possession.

A few years later, in 1787, the Royal Irish Academy received from the Abbé Kearney, Superior of the Irish College in Paris, the original manuscript of the *Book of Lecain*, and that body still preserves it as one of its most valued treasures. [1]

Thus did the Irish College in Paris co-operate all through the eighteenth century in promoting the study of Irish and in preserving Irish literature. The names of Begly and Perrotin, and Murry and Donlevy and Henegan ought not to be forgotten. And they might not unreasonably say :—

> Si Pergama dextrâ
> Defendi possent, etiam hâc defensa fuissent. [2]

IV

Whilst the Irish language was thus cultivated, the French language was not neglected. Irish was the mother tongue of the students ; French was the language of their place of exile, and they could not be ignorant of it. The priests who came to France late in life acquired, indeed, a knowledge of the language ; but they admitted that they always retained their own accent. The junior students acquired greater proficiency. Many of them came at an early age and attended the classes in grammar and rhetoric at the University. They were sometimes obliged to appeal to the charitable for means of support, and, hence, a knowledge of French was a necessity for them. Some of them looked forward to a career in France. In consequence several of them acquired great proficiency in French. A contemporary document speaks as follows :—

Les écoliers Irlandais viennent en France dans un age peu avancé, age au l'on apprend, et l'on oublie facilement, ce qui est du ressort de la memoire. Ils ont besoin de parler la langue française pour se procurer du secours, pour aller audevant pour les solliciter. Ils apprennent cette langue et negligent la leur. Imperceptiblement ils l'oublient. Cela est naturel et l'experience l'a demontré. [3]

---

[1] Gilbert's *History of Dublin*, vol. iii. pp. 223 and 235.
[2] *Aenid*, lib. ii. 293.
[3] *Memoire pour les Pretres*, A.D. 1736. Aux Archives Nationales, M. 147.

Many Irish ecclesiastics, educated in Paris, acquired such proficiency in the use of the French language that they were found qualified to perform the various duties of the sacred ministry in France. In the seventeenth century Rev. John Lee, the Founder of the Irish College in Paris, was attached to the Church of St. Severin, and was sought after as a confessor by the *élite* of Paris. Dempster made the popularity of Lee the occasion for his satire. And the author of the *Vindiciae Hiberniae*, etc., thus defends him :—

Joannem in primis Ley venerandae senectutis atque irreprehensibilis vitae hominem, scurriliter mordes quod, nihil aliud nòrit quam edentulas, ad D. Severini, vetulas captare. Sic tu sacrorum irrisor assiduam optimi viri in moderandis conscientiis operam (cujus in hoc munere singulare donum eum principibus viris valde reddit acceptum) impia dicacitate prosequeris.[1]

Dr. Tyrell could not have been the agent of the Confederation of Kilkenny at the French Court, nor Dr. Malachy Kelly, the Councillor of Louis XIV., without an intimate knowledge of the French language. Dr. Michael Moore had such a command of French that he delivered with eloquence an oration in honour of Louis XIV., on 16th May, 1702, in the College of Navarre. The circumstance is thus recorded in the *Gazette de France*, 20th May, 1702, No. 20, page 338 :—

Le meme jour le Sieur Morus, Recteur de l'Université de Paris, et cydevant President du Collegé de Dublin, prononça avec beaucoup d'eloquence le panegyrique du Roy, fondé par la Ville, qui s'y trouva en Corps avec un grand nombre de personnes, de qualité.[2]

During the eighteenth century many Irishmen held parishes and canonries in France. Dr. Moylan, afterwards Bishop of Cork, was a curé in Paris before his appointment to that see.

But not only were Irishmen connected with the College able to speak the language, some of them published works

---

[1] *Vindiciae Hiberniae*, etc., a G. F. Veridico Hiberno. Antwerp, 1621. p. 44.

[2] Gilbert's *History of Dublin*, vol. i., p. 329. *Registre de la Nation d'Allemagne*, No. 40.

in French. In 1726, Rev. M. E. Fennell, Dean of Killaloe, published in Paris, and in the French language, a dissertation on the validity of Anglican Orders in reply to Le Courrayer.[1] In 1758, Abbé Mageoghegan,[2] published his *History of Ireland*, in French. The Abbé Right, mentioned in the correspondence with Dr. Plunket,[3] wrote in that language an ode dedicated to the officers of the Irish Brigade, from which we quote the following lines :—

Fiers Irlandais : ainsi votre audace indocile
Du fond de votre exile, sous un ciel etranger.
Sut combattre et mourir, et vaincre et se venger,

.   .   .   .

Des rives du Veser aux plaines de l'Asie.
Vous servez votre Dieu, votre Roi et votre patrie.
Vous qui animoient jadis la gloire et la vengeance
Clare, Routh, et Lucan, les fastes de la France
Ont assez consacré l'honneur de vos travaux,
Et vous Dilons, et vous dignes fils d'un heros.
Intrepides guerriers, &c., &c.

In this respect, too, the Abbé Henegan, deserves special mention. That learned man might justly be styled, *Docte sermones utriusque linguae.*[4] His co-operation in the publication of *O'Brien's Dictionary* proves him to have been a scholar in Irish. He was also a master of the French language. A large number of articles in the edition of *Moreri's Dictionary*, published by Drouet in 1759, are from

---

[1] 'Memoires ou Dissertation sur la validite des ordinations des Anglais et sur la succession des Evêques Anglicans, pour servir de response au Rev. P. Le Courrayer,' par M. E. Fennell, Doyen de Leon en Irlande. Paris, 1726. 1st part, pp. 1-340 ; 2nd part, pp. 1-220. Probably he is the E. Fennell mentioned in the University Register as present at the meeting of the masters of the Natio Constantissima in 1684. See *Irish College in Paris from 1578 to 1901*, page 198.

The Abbé Gould, a Cork man and a student at Poitiers, preached in French with great success, and published several works in that language. His work on the *Veritable Croyance de l'église Catholique* (Paris, 1720), in which he treats the question of the validity of Anglican Orders, merited the eulogium of the Abbé Renaudot.

[2] Two Paris students who did not take orders became distinguished as historians. Sylvester O'Hallaran, M.D., is the author of a *General History of Ireland, from the earliest accounts to the close of the twelfth century.* London, 1778. Martin Haverty, author of a *History of Ireland, ancient and modern* (Dublin, 1860), entered the Irish College in 1831, and left in 1834.

[3] Cogan's *Meath*, etc., vol. iii., p. 46.

[4] Horace, *Odes*, III., 7.

the pen of the Abbé Henegan. Amongst them may be mentioned the articles on Keating, Lynch, Molyneau, and Nary, and in particular an article on Ireland, extending over thirty folio pages. These articles prove him to have been a scholar, and the fact that he was invited to contribute to that great work shows the esteem in which he was held in Paris. His name ought not to be forgotten in Ireland, and especially in his native diocese, Cork.

In the nineteenth century, too, many of those connected with the College were well versed in the French language. Dr. Long, who was rector from 1814 to 1819, had filled the office of curé, in the diocese of Laon, for many years. Rev. Timothy Gillooly, sometime Professor in the College, spent several years in clerical work at Argentan. Rev. James O'Hallaran, having filled for some time the office of Econome, went to the diocese of Perigord, where he died curé of Thiviers. Rev. Michael Hogan,[1] who was Professor of Moral Theology about 1854, became at a later date curé in the diocese of Perigueux. Of the two last mentioned the former was an uncle and the latter a brother of the late lamented and distinguished Sulpician, Very Rev. John Baptist Hogan, D.D., a man eminent amongst the eminent theologians of St. Sulpice. Nor was the Irish language neglected in the nineteenth century. Dr. M'Hale, nephew of the Archbishop of ¡Tuam, and Dr. (now Cardinal) Logue, were Professors of Irish in the College after 1850.

The example of the students of the eighteenth century, and their success in both languages are a lesson and an encouragement to those of the present time to apply themselves to such studies as may be useful in the twentieth century.

PATRICK BOYLE, C.M.

---

[1] [Father Michael Hogan acted for some years as Military Chaplain at Farmoy, the Curragh and Aldershot. He died at Arcachon and was buried in the cemetery outside that town in the year 1863. His brother, who died on the 30th of last September, is laid to rest in the Sulpician vault in the cemetery of Mont-Parnasse in Paris. *Requiescant in pace.*—ED. I. E. RECORD.]

'THE IRISH PRIVILEGE OF ANTICIPATION OF MATINS AND LAUDS'

IT is regrettable that the original or copy of Indult in favour of the above privilege has not been found, as was expected, in some diocesan archives. In considering its extension we have to fall back on its substance as embodied in the Synodal Statutes of Cashel ; and the Indult as there found grants the privilege of anticipating the time for the recitation of the Divine Office then and for ever to the secular and regular clergy of Ireland. The non-use or disuse of the Indult by the clergy did not cut off their successors from its use ; nor was the Indult given merely to the Orders existing in Ireland at the time of the grant, but, as I conceive, was given to every Order of the clergy in Ireland for all time to come. The privilege, as not given merely to individuals or existing generations, could not be cut off by them from their successors.[1]

There is some reason for thinking that the privilege extended not only to the private recitation of the Office but to the choir ; and in order to help us in forming an opinion on the matter it is well to consider—(a) the text of the Indult as made known to us, (b) the immediate context, and (c) the historical context.

(a) The Indult ran thus :—

Sciant sacerdotes nostri quod obtentum sit pro illis et pro omnibus sacerdotibus hujus regni tam secularibus quam regularibus privilegium a sanctae memoriae Pio Papa VI. inchoandi Matutinum cum Laudibus hora secunda pomeridiana pro sequenti die toto anni decursu.

The privilege is given without limitation as to place or manner of recitation. It is reasonable to suppose that the privilege was given for the Office as usually read, and it is presumable that it was read by the religious in choir, and sometimes, perhaps, by a secular with a companion.

---

[1] Ballerini, *Opus Theologicum Morale*, vol. i., p. 433.

The Indult ought to be interpreted according to the plain
meaning of the words (' verba Indulti intelligi prout jacent,')
and as the Indult makes no distinction between the private
and public recitation of the Office we have no warrant for so
doing.

1. It may be said that a departure from common law is
odious and that a dispensation in it should be strictly interpreted. Yes, when there is a doubt or obscurity; but the
words of the privilege are plain.

2. An exception lies against strict interpretation when
there is question of a pious or religious end,[1] and surely a
regard for the duties of the Irish mission was essentially a
case of religion.

3. An exception against strict interpretation lies in
favour of religious Orders.[2]

4. An exception lies when there is question of Papal
Indults, which should be liberally interpreted. (' Indulta
Pontificia late interpretanda.')[3]

5. A Papal privilege is to prevail not only against the
common law but the convenience of a third party in order
to prevent a privilege from being nugatory.[4] We know
that the appointment of religious to the care of souls, as
being incompatible with the rule of religious life, was only
provisional in Ireland. (' Quotiescunque desint presbyteri
seculares instituant ad interim ipsorum loco et per modum
provisionis Regulares.)[5]

If then religious, after having been for some time on the
mission, had retired to their convents and observed the
choral service, the indulgence of the Pope which was granted
for all time would, on the supposition of Indult being
applicable only to the private office, have been nugatory.
(*Glossa :* ' debet aliquid conferre alias delusoria esset
indulgentia.)

(b) But an objection is grounded on the context of the

---

[1] Reiffenstuel, lib. 1, Decr. tit. 3, de Rescriptis.
[2] *Ibid.* Ballerini, p. 430, vol. i.
[3] Bened. XIV. *de Synodo*, ch. xi. n. xiv. and p. 562.
[4] Reiffenstuel, lib. 1, tit. 3.
[5] *Hib. Dominicana*, p. 180.

Indult, or rather on the two paragraphs which succeed it.
They run thus :—

Quoad spectat ad tempus quo horae canonicae dicendae sunt
pro Officio publico, hoc est in choro, servanda est consuetudo
recepta.   In Officio privato magis etiam expedit ut *quantum fieri
potest* singulae horae suis respective temporibus per intervalla
dicantur.

Prima potest inchoari immediate post ortum solis,
tertia, sexta, et *nona* possunt etiam tunc legi, vel alia quacumque
hora ante duodecimam pomeridianam.   Et Vespere et Comple-
torium possunt dici post meridiem.   Et Matutinum cum Laudibus
ut antea diximus, etc.

A learned writer in the I. E. Record grounds a proof
against the extension of the Indult to the choir on saying :
'That the regulation for the Office *in choro* ends with the
word *recepta,* and that the words *in Officio privato* cover all
that follows the second paragraph specifying *sua respective
tempora* of the first' (paragraph).

Now, firstly, the statement as to the time for the choral
recitation—that the received custom may be observed—does
not prove that the Indult regarded only the private recitation.   The Synodal Statute does not draw a distinction
between the time for beginning Matins in choir and out of
choir.   If there were to be a distinction we may presume it
would have been expressed as in a preceding paragraph.   In
that paragraph the Archbishop, in describing the matter of
the Office, distinguished between the matter of the private
from that of the public Office, which was more lengthy.   But
no such distinction is made in reference to the time.   Here
I may observe that under the word *time* was included every
hour besides Matins at which each division of the Office was
begun till it was ended, that probably the interval between
each such hour was principally in the mind of the writer,
and that in point of fact reference to time was made, as had
been to every other point about the Office, on the general
principles of law.

Secondly, it was not quite correct to state that the
'second paragraph specified *sua respective tempora* of the
first' (paragraph).   For in the beginning of the chapter on
the Office the Archbishop stated that it consisted of seven

parts, and, therefore, the simple division of time at mid-day for the small hours did not cover the seven divisions which are supposed by common law to be observed in choir.

The entire chapter was a tract devoted to an explanation of the Office on the principles of common law except the paragraph on the Indult. So far was it from referring solely to Ireland that the chapter made statements that could not refer to Ireland. Thus the *Beneficiati* are mentioned amongst those bound to the Office, but no such, apart from priests, were in Ireland. So, too, mention is made of the daily and nightly Office, but no nightly Office, as understood in the Pontifical law, prevailed in Ireland.

The twenty-seventh chapter of the Cashel Statutes as a liturgical tract treated of the order to be observed in reading the Office ; of the attention that it required ; of the character of the Breviary ; of the omission that would constitute a mortal sin ; of the causes that would exempt from the Office ; of the time for reading the Office, and of the suspension into which abuses in choir lead.

The remarks of the Archbishop on the time for the Office must have been of a general character, and included all the divisions of the Office and not Matins merely. Hence the heading of theological manuals on the hours of the Office is found as ' Quoad tempus debitum ad horas dicendas ' (Gury, Ballerini). Under this heading the several hours into which the Office may be divided and read without sin are given. In like manner the writer of the Cashel Statutes treated of the Office ' Quoad tempus.' If he had given the general law or recognised customs in regard to the choral recitation he would have to travel a vast and unfamiliar field. He should have to state the discipline of the Trappists, Cistercians, and others who preserved the primitive discipline by a division of the three Nocturns corresponding to the three watches, and by the application of Lauds to the fourth watch of the night.

Or, if he were to consider only the comparatively modern discipline, he should exhibit the secular canons as meeting at midnight according to Rubrics of the ' Juris Pontificii.' The Rubrics directed that the Office should begin after midnight so as to be ended before the day-spring : ' Profeta ait ; media nocte surgebam: "Ergo his temporibus laudes Creatori nostro referemus."'[1]

Nor was the difference between the primitive and modern discipline confined to the nightly Office. The primitive discipline reserved Vespers, or, as it was called, ' duodecima,' till the twelfth hour or six o'clock p.m., while the modern discipline pushed on the Vespers to three o'clock, and, of course, the hours of Sext and None earlier still: But the austere Orders, as was the case in our early Irish Church, have the several parts of the Office gone through at the times corresponding with the names of the hours, and suggestive of some stage of the Sacred Passion.[2]

Owing to this tedious variety the writer of the liturgical tract very wisely stated in general terms that each Church was to follow its approved custom in the choral service. In making this statement the Archbishop did not speak of particular privileges as being departures from the common law of which he was treating. But having stated that the received custom of recitation in choir ought to be followed, he added that it is more expedient to observe, as far as possible, in the private recitation, the several intervals between the several (7) hours. The synodal writer then laid down the common law or general opinion of theologians as to the lawful division in the private recitation. Every part of the Office could be said without sin, however inexpedient, from Prime to Vespers before mid-day, and Vespers and Compline after it. Then, instead of giving the common law for Matins, the writer referred to the Indult already given.

If the Archbishop had not treated of the time for the Office on general principles, as he had done in regard to its every other point, it would have been quite easy for him to say ' this is to be your practice in the private recitation of the Office in my diocese '—for he had no choral chapter— and as to the religious they, as the materials for a choir, did not live together. Thurles was the only town that contained two religious (Franciscans) ; and even though

---

they should have lived together they were not capable of
forming a choir.

Under the word *time*, Matins and Lauds, without an
interval were included, and the remarks of the Archbishop
on these as said in choir appear to me to have been made on
the principles of common law and referable only to the
universal Church. Following the recognized manuals,
especially Ferraris, the Archbishop states in regard to time
'in choro servanda est consuetudo recepta'; and
Ferraris, 'in choro servanda sunt tempora consueta sub
mortali, private non sub mortali tempora statuta singulis
horis.' The remarks, on Matins, were made with regard to
the general Church; but if we could suppose them made
in regard to the Irish discipline they were qualified by the
Indult previously given. But with regard to every other
hour said in choir, besides Matins, and included under the
word *time*, the remarks of the Archbishop could and did
refer to the Irish discipline. For there was choir service in
other parts of Ireland than in Cashel, and probable diversity
of practice as to the intervals from Prime to Compline. We
know that Compline did not necessarily follow immediately
Vespers. Thus, while in Lent we are allowed to read Vespers
after 9 o'clock, a.m., we are not allowed to read at once
Compline after them. In like manner Pius VII., in granting
leave to a certain bishop to have his canons go through all
the Office at a single meeting and Matins and Lauds on the
previous day after Vespers and Compline, conditioned that
Compline should not be said till after Noon.[1]

To this variety of practice as to the hours, without
speaking of Sext or None, that probably prevailed in
Ireland the Archbishop may have alluded, saying that each
established custom as to the hours should be followed. A
reference only to the daily hours in Ireland by the Archbishop was natural on the supposition of the Matins and
Lauds having been fixed by the Indult. This view is
rendered the more probable as, when he speaks of the
private Office he would have it, as to the intervals, modelled

---

[1] Gardellini, vol. i., p. 294.

on the public recitation, and accordingly began with his treatment of Prime and not of Matins. Thus the context affords additional proof that the text of the Indult did not limit its application to the private recitation of the Office.

(c) It is desirable to consider the attitude of the Irish Church to the choral service when the Indult was given to the Irish priests. We can well suppose that the conditions under which the Office was gone through in Ireland was known to the Propaganda, and that the chiefs of the Irish Church in asking for an Indult in regard to the Office made known the general mode of its recitation.

As regards the secular clergy there was no daily choral service in any cathedral, even where there was a nominal chapter. The Bishops, then, in applying for an Indult did not ask, we may presume, for its application to a canonical or choral recitation. A choral chapter was a thing in the very distant future.

But the same statement cannot be made in reference to the religious. Many, indeed, were employed as curates or parish priests on the mission, and as such had no opportunity or obligation of reciting the Office *in choro*. For there was scarcely a second curate in any parish at this time; and where there happened to be two together they were not religious. While the large number of one hundred and fifty were provisionally secularised and under the immediate and sole jurisdiction of the bishops a still larger number, one hundred and seventy-eight, lived in their convents. They were worthy successors of those who had suffered in Ireland privations of every sort and met death in every shape. And now that some measure of liberty was enjoyed we may presume they availed of it, and followed their holy rule in the recitation of the Office. This was expected from them even when the Irish Church was, humanly speaking, at a very low ebb. Even so early as the year 1751 the houses of religious were not to be regarded by the Propaganda as formal convents without observing community life. The instructions of the Cardinal Protector are clear on the point. They are given in one of the chapters of the Synodal Statutes of Cashel. (' Habeantur tanquam conventus formales illae tantum domus in quibus communem ducunt vitam Regularem.') The entire document, of which this is an extract, may be seen in *Hibernia Dominicana*, pages 180-2. The decrees of the Congregation insisted that the noviceship should be gone through in some Catholic country, but the Provincials in Ireland guaranteed that austere discipline and community life could be observed in Ireland as certainly as in any foreign Catholic country. The noviceship at the time was not allowed in Ireland. By and by, however, leave was granted for the establishment of noviceships in Ireland, but it was accompanied with the condition that the noviceships should be observed agreeably to the Pontifical decrees. The twentieth rule of the Decree of Clement VIII. directed that the novices should mix with the professed only ' during the time of choir-service, processions, and in refectory ' (' in caenaculo causa refectionis '). In some convents during Dr. Bray's episcopate the common table, owing to poverty, was kept only during the concluding portion of the noviceship.[1] And when an effort was made to observe the rule with regard to the common table, it is quite certain that the choral service as required was not neglected. Assuredly the good religious did not deserve the reproach addressed to the degenerate Greeks :—

> You have the Pyrrhic dance as yet,
>   Where is the Pyrrhic phalanx gone?
> Of two such lessons, why forget
>   The nobler and the manlier one?

During the Episcopate of Dr. Bray there were in Ireland 55 Dominicans in 14 houses ; 68 Franciscans in 18 houses ; 24 Augustinians in 8 houses ; 28 Carmelites in 10 houses ; and 10 Capuchins in 3 houses. I find no mention of how 7 Canons Regular were housed. Now, it is quite certain that in some, if not in all of these 53 houses, containing 187 religious, the Office was read *in choro*. Even in the 3 Capuchin houses, containing 10 residents, it could have been read in choir. For

---

[1] *Spicilegium Ossoriense*, vol. iii., p. 360.

according to law three persons, though only novices, could form a choir.[1]

And Gardellini[2] makes mention of a request preferred by and granted to a Jesuit, August 13, 1847, in connexion with the choir. He was allowed to begin Matins at twelve o'clock on the previous day even with a companion ('anche con compagno'), on account of missionary work. The privilege is given under the heading *in choro.*

Having seen that the Indult was obtained for all the religious in Ireland, we may be certain that their Superiors had joined the Bishops in requesting the Indult. The privilege was asked by the Provincials not for those who were secularised and withdrawn from their jurisdiction; and, therefore, we are led to infer it was asked for those who led a community life.

Furthermore, if the wants and welfare of the Irish Church were the chief motive for the Papal Indult, there was the same reason for granting it to the recitation of the Office in as well as out of choir; for in the year 1810, when the Indult appears to have been published for the first time, the population of Ireland was above four millions, and the difficulty then of supplying the spiritual wants of the faithful was enormously greater than at present. In the absence of public roads a priest then, in most parishes, had only a bridle-path, and had to wade through unbridged streams. The present facility of communication would enable a single priest to do as much as two at that time; and when we contrast the present educated state of the public mind even with that consequent on the six years' famine of 1845, devolving slow and painful work on the confessor, we can easily fancy the heavy work consequent on the penal laws during centuries, and aggravated by the Irish rebellion. All these causes combined, during the twenty-one years previous to the Synod in 1810. to make the Irish mission laborious indeed.

While the character of the country rendered the multiplication of priests doubly necessary, this, coupled with the

---

[1] Reiffenstuel, lib. 3, Decr. tit. 31 n. 116.   [2] Vol. i., p. 50.

mental condition of the masses, rendered a quadruple increase of priests necessary. But so far from having three or four priests to one at present, there was scarcely one then with probably a larger population to every three priests at present. The number of secular priests was then fourteen hundred, and this circumstance inferred the necessity of drawing on the services of the religious.

The antecedent probability of religious having been utilised for missionary work is supported by positive evidence. The Provincials of the Orders assure us that the duties of the mission and the calls of dying penitents interfered with the observance of community life. They state that sudden and importunate calls drew them even from the necessary bodily refreshment : ' Utpote refectionis hora decumbentes et in articulo mortis constitutos arcessiti sacramentalis absolutionis beneficium impendant.'[1] This was not an occasional occurrence; it was the recognised duty of the religious ; for the Provincials in advocating a noviceship in Ireland in preference to that in a foreign country stated that thus the novices would be more familiarised with the missionary work in Ireland, which was their destiny : ' Quia cum eorum singuli ob obeundas in hoc regno sacras missiones destinentur.'[2] Yes, each novice was destined, while observing as much as possible the discipline of his Order, practically to the work of the missionary priest. We are not to suppose, then, that the regulars, weighted with the work of the mission, were excluded from the benefit of the Indult.

Even in Dublin, where there ought to be less need of religious help, one would think, the duties of the secular priests had, according to the *Relatio* of Dr. Troy, to be supplied by the religious : ' Parochorum aliqui absque vicariis a regularibus vicinis in excipiendis confessionibus vivere coguntur.' To the same effect the Bishop of Waterford, in reference to the Franciscans there and in Clonmel, states ' they assist the pastors.' So, too, the Bishop of Ferns bears testimony to the missionary help of eight Franciscans

---

[1] *Hib. Dom.*, p. 182.   [2] *Ibid.*

in Wexford and of four Augustinians in Ross: 'They are
employed in preaching, catechising, and instructing the
people, attending the sick, and assisting the parochial
clergy occasionally in the administration of the Sacraments.'
Finally, among other testimonies, let us listen to that of
Archbishop Bray himself. Writing of the religious, he
stated : 'The resident friars or regulars not employed as
curates are supported by the charity of the Catholics, and
their assistance to the parish priests, in places where they
reside, is necessary to the sacred functions.'

The religious then, while endeavouring to act up to the
rules of their holy founders, were faithful to the missionary
work for which they were ordained; and I repeat, if the
necessities of the Irish mission were the motive of the
Indult there appears no reason for withholding it from the
religious. Nor was the Indult for the choir anything singular
or unnatural. On the contrary, it were to penalise discipline
and aspirations after what was perfect to grant to the
seculars, free comparatively, what was withheld from
the self-denying and doubly-weighted religious. Three or
four met in order to recite the Office in common. The
religious met, not in a church, for, without the encroach-
ment of a choir, there was only scanty room, and often
insecure, for their congregations. The meeting of the religious was so quiet and unceremonious, in some rickety
tenement, as scarcely to deserve the name of choir. Their
choir was quite different from that of secular canons. These
were so much bound to give edification that their choir
could not be moved from a fixed place in the church without
Papal dispensation. But even such canons, because of the
severity of winter or some other inconvenience, sometimes
got an Indult to read all the Office together, from Prime to
Compline, and begin Matins after mid-day the previous day.[1]
Benedict XIV.[2] makes mention of an Indult empowering a
bishop to allow his canons to begin Matins at three o'clock
p.m., rather than at midnight. We learn from Suarez
that it was a common practice through Spain to begin

---

[1] Gardellini, *Decret. Authen.*, vol. i., pp. 290-4.
[2] *Institutiones*, c. cvii., p. 21.

Matins in choir in winter at two o'clock p.m., and Ballerini [1] states that several religious Orders received the privilege of reciting Matins at two o'clock p.m.

To limit, then, without warrant, the Irish Indult to the mere private recitation of the Office would appear to be singular and, in the circumstances, unnatural. The Indult was not a very singular or extraordinary boon, and its unstinted extension was called for not by ostentation or mere convenience but by the necessities of a Church which lived through ages of persecution, under Providence, only by the indulgent care and annual financial support of the Sovereign Pontiffs. The probable inference then, from what I have stated is that the Indult extended to the Office in choir as read in Ireland.

SYLVESTER MALONE.

---

[1] Vol. iv., p. 307.

DR. SALMON'S INFALLIBILITY

VII

PETER PLYMLEY said to 'his brother in the country,' that he always thought him 'a bit of a goose.' The ground for this opinion was that Abraham held theological views precisely similar to those which Dr. Salmon is labouring to infuse into his young controversialists; and if they take in their professor's teaching they shall certainly be open to the very doubtful compliment paid to the Rev. Abraham Plymley by his shrewd and candid brother. The Doctor is setting before them an adversary of his own creation; he is hiding from them the real adversary they shall have to confront; he is continually attributing to the Catholic Church doctrines she does not hold, and arguments she does not use. He is labouring to perpetuate a false tradition, and is not scrupulous as to the means of doing so; his misquotation of fathers would wreck the reputation of any one presuming to be a scholar, and his history and his theology are alike worthy of Mr. Mark Twain. In one thing only is he consistent, in his hatred of the Catholic Church, and all through his lectures he has given expression to that hatred with an adroitness which shows considerable ability, but ability sadly misapplied. An opponent who makes a good fight is deserving of respect, but Dr. Salmon has not done so throughout his lectures. There is not a solitary instance of a scholarly attempt to refute any Catholic doctrine, though there is abundant matter well calculated to strengthen the prejudices of the ignorant. His students have been from their childhood taught that nothing good can come from Nazareth, and he is labouring to strengthen this conviction instead of imitating the Apostle by inviting them to 'come and see.'

The Infallibility of the Church has been proved, and Dr. Salmon has not even attempted to refute the reasoning by which that doctrine is established. He very properly told his students early in his lectures that 'the whole

Roman Catholic controversy turns on the decision of the one question—the Infallibility of the Church—and he proceeded to give his decision, that is, to prove that the Church is fallible. But he does not seem to have at all realized the nature of the difficulties he has to meet at the very outset. For, whatever is to be said of the Church, the Doctor himself rejects all infallibility in religious matters, and, therefore, his own decision in this matter must be fallible.

He undertakes to prove that the Church is fallible; but how is he to do so? In order to do so he must show conclusively that the Church teaches false doctrine on some matter in which she claims infallibility. But in order to show that any doctrine is false there must be a standard of comparison to test it, and that standard must be a doctrine infallibly true. If the standard were not such, then a doctrine may be out of harmony with it—may contradict it, and still be true. Now, by what authority does the Doctor set up his infallible standard to convict the Church of false teaching? Only an infallible authority can set up such a standard, and Dr. Salmon denies that there is any such. He has no authority but his own reason. 'The individual Christian' is his judge of controversies, his supreme arbiter. Dr. Salmon's reason may be very profound and reliable within its own sphere, that is, in the natural order; but the Church's doctrines lie in the supernatural order, and into that order the Doctor's reason cannot pry.

He, therefore, has no adequate standard to test the Church's doctrines, and thus, from the very nature of the case, he can pronounce no opinion on them that is not fallible. If the Church teach anything that contradicts reason, the Doctor's reason—his sole standard—can point out the contradiction, and by all means, let him do so; but let him not attempt the impossible task of measuring the supernatural by his natural reason. This would be like attempting to measure the sun's light by a farthing candle. He cannot show that the Church errs in her teaching unless he is able to declare infallibly what is the truth on the matter in question, and this he cannot do. And so all his loud boasting of 'beating us out of the open field,' comes to this that the very first step in his theological parade is an impossibility. His feet are fixed to the earth and he cannot move.

Lord Macaulay said that the Catholic Church was the most extraordinary work of human policy which the world ever saw; but if Dr. Salmon's description of her were true she would have been the greatest monument of human folly which the world has yet witnessed :—a Church with a creed so flatly, so frequently, refuted by her own acts ; and yet her continued existence through nineteen centuries would be one of the greatest miracles recorded in history. Infallible in theory, but, according to Dr. Salmon, most fallible in practice, this Church has lived through all the ages, beset with difficulties which she has surmounted, assailed by determined and powerful enemies whom she has conquered ; how does the Doctor explain this standing miracle ? The explanation is, she is not what the Doctor describes her ; she is ' the Church of the living God, the pillar, and the ground of truth,' secured by God's explicit promise against the ' gates of Hell.'

Dr. Salmon devotes three long lectures to a series of statements, the aim of which is to discredit the Church as a teacher. Under the headings of ' Hesitations of the Infallible Guide,' ' Modern Revelations,' and ' Blunders of the Infallible Guide,' he has brought together a mass of miscellaneous matter as a series of charges against the teaching authority of the Church. In the charges themselves, there is nothing new, and there is nothing new or striking in the Doctor's manner of presenting them ; and when he has said his last word the Church's authority remains untouched. The lectures must have been amusing to his students, but as part of their training for controversy they were simply waste of time. The Church did not decide the controversy *De Auxiliis ;* she does not ' publish an authorized commentary on Scripture' (page 188) ; ' she does not put the seal of her infallibility' to any of ' her catechisms or books of devotion ' (page 190) ; she does not tell us whether we are or are not bound to believe the extraordinary incidents recorded in the *Glories of Mary* and in the *Roman Breviary ;* she does not tells us what we are to believe about Loretto, Lourdes, or La Salette. On all these she has carried her caution to an extraordinary degree, lest she may compromise her infallibility, but by a just judgment on her she has completely shattered the claim by her condemnation of the scientific teaching of Galileo. This is the burden of Dr. Salmon's three long lectures. Now in all these charges, except the last, he is condemning the Church for what she has not done; and in the last he is charging her with having done what she never did at all. He admits himself that he is judging her by what she has not done. ' The complaint I made was,' he says, 'that the Church of Rome did not tell us whether we are to believe these things or not.' And he wants to know ' why she does not ' (page 215, note). The Doctor, in his capacity of *Judex Controversiarum*, is so much in the habit of sitting in judgment on his own Church—a Church made by men—that he fancies he can take the same liberty with the Catholic Church, founded by God. But she has her mission marked out for her, and she will not turn from her appointed course to accommodate even a Regius Professor. His duty is to hear her, not to judge her. He told his theologians that—

Romish teaching has constantly a double face. To those within the communion it is authoritive, positive, stamped with the seal of infallibility, which none may dispute without forfeiting his right to be counted a good Catholic. . . . She speaks differently to those who have the courage to impugn it, and bring it to the test.—(Page 187.)

Here is a grave charge, specific and direct; and as proof of it Dr. Salmon brings forward a number of subjects which, according to himself, the Church does not teach at all. There is a strange fatality about the Doctor's logic. The Church, he says, abandons her teaching on a number of subjects which, he says, she never taught at all. So the Doctor told his theologians who, no doubt, appreciated his logic. It shall be an evil day for the Catholic Church when Dr. Salmon's patent controversialists take the field against her. Now, the Doctor has a wide field open to him. Let him search through the history of the Church from the first Pentecost to the present day, from St. Peter to Leo XIII.,

and let him find out, if he can, a solitary instance in which
the Church permitted anyone, either in the Church or outside of it, to impugn a doctrine which she once taught. He
can find no such instance. For those who impugn or deny
her defined doctrine the Church has invariably one answer,
and that is final—*anathema sit.*

Dr. Salmon founds one of his charges on the controversy
De Auxiliis, on which he takes his information from Burnet's
Commentary on the Seventeenth Article. He has not studied
the folios of Levinus Meyer or Serry, or the modern works
of Schneeman, to say nothing of the voluminous writings
of those who actually carried on the controversy ; and the
result is that he seems to know as much about the controversy *De Auxiliis,* as he does of the Beatific vision. It is
amusing to hear one like Dr. Salmon giving his views so
confidently on a controversy which for years engaged the
talents of such men as Bannez and Alvarez and De Lemos
on one side, and Molina and Lessius and Bellarmine and
Gregory of Valentia on the other. A disputation on it by
Dr. Salmon's students, and under his own training, would
be better than a pantomime. It was essentially a scholastic
controversy—confined to the schools, and the body of the
faithful took no part in it ; they did not and could not enter
into its merits. No Catholic doctrine was affected by it ; the
necessity of grace was maintained by all the parties to the
controversy ; and so too was the existence of efficacious
grace and its co-existence with free will. The point of the
controversy was, what was the intrinsic nature of efficacious
grace—what precisely it is that makes grace efficacious.
This point was argued with a great deal of logical and theological subtilty on both sides, and, unfortunately, with a
good deal of the *odium theologicum* also. To check, to
repress this uncharitableness was the immediate, the
pressing necessity, and that was done by Paul V. commanding each school to abstain from attaching theological
censures to the opinions of the opposite school. But the
interests of souls called for no decision on the question as
to the intrinsic nature of efficacious grace, and no decision
was given on it. It was allowed to remain, and it still is

a matter for free discussion amongst theologians, due regard
being had to the requirements of charity.

Again, Dr. Salmon says: ' It might be expected that the
infallible guide would publish an authoritative commentary
on Scripture' (page 188). If the 'infallible guide' agreed
with Dr. Salmon that the Bible alone is the rule of faith,
then his suggestion may be valuable, though to make it
really so the guide should first 'teach all nations' to read.
But the 'Infallible Guide' does not agree with the fallible
Doctor; and a more than sufficient answer to his suggestion
is, that much as the Church prizes the Bible she does not
depend on it for her teaching; she taught for many years
before it came into existence, and she would have continued to
do so till the end of time, even though it had not been written.
Her Founder said to her: ' Teach all nations.' He did not
say to her: ' Write a book, and read it for all nations, or
give it to them to read for themselves.' Now, the Doctor
knows all this well, but he has introduced this matter in
order to have an opportunity of attacking the Church for
the Notes of the Rhemish New Testament. He gives a
number of these notes, which he professes to have taken
from Macnamara's Bible, and he clearly regards them as
most wicked in doctrine. Now, in the edition of Macnamara's
Bible, published in Cork in A.D. 1818, there is not a single
one of the notes quoted by Dr. Salmon, but they are the
Rhemish Notes all the same; and Dr. Salmon seeks to
make the Church responsible for them by quoting St. Augustine and St. Thomas as holding the doctrines which the
Notes contain; though he is sorry to find that St. Thomas ' is
able to quote St. Augustine for this doctrine.' The doctrine
of the Notes, confirmed by St. Augustine and St. Thomas, is
substantially this, that heresy is a grievous sin, and deserves
to be severely punished; and that in certain extreme circumstances it may deserve capital punishment. The Church,
however, whose aim is the conversion of the sinner, does
not, as St. Thomas says, hastily condemn, but only after a
first and second monition; but if the heretic continues
obstinate, the Church, despairing of his conversion, separates
him from her children by excommunication, and leaves him

to be dealt with by the civil tribunal. And St. Thomas argues, that as falsifiers of money and other criminals are severely punished, it is only just that even greater punishment should be inflicted on those who kill the soul. And, moreover, in the case of persons who have fallen away into heresy after baptism, the Notes say, with St. Thomas and St. Augustine, that such persons may be compelled to return to the Church, on the ground that they belong to her by baptism, and may, therefore, be compelled to keep the promises made by themselves in baptism or by their sponsors for them. A rebel does not cease to be a subject when he rises up against legitimate authority.

This is the doctrine of the Notes which has excited the virtuous indignation of the Professor, and, no doubt, of his students also. He made no attempt to deal with the doctrine on its merits ; and lest his students should be led to think that it had any foundation in Scripture, he conveniently omitted from the note to Luke ix. 55 the following sentence :—' Therefore St. Peter used his power on Ananias and Saphira, when he struck them both down to death for defrauding the Church.' He did not remind his students that St. John described heretics as ' deceivers and anti-Christs ' ; that St. Paul warned Timothy to avoid them, just as the Catholic Church says to her children to-day. There is more to be said for the Notes than the Doctor seems to think. The Church is a perfect society, supreme, and independent within her own sphere, established by God, for saving souls. She must, therefore, be able to make and enforce such laws as enable her to attain her end, and this power must be inherent in her ; must be contained in the charter of her institution. This is the unchangeable principle out of which grew the laws of the Church regarding heresy. The Church says that it is permitted, that it is not unlawful to punish heretics, as well as other evil-doers, with death, but she does not say that it is necessary or always expedient to do so, that it may be, not that it must be, so punished is all that follows from the condemnation by Leo X. of Luther's thirty-third proposition. The Church, as a matter of course, regarded heresy as a crime of the

greatest magnitude, directly destructive of souls; and it was
only natural that in the 'ages of faith' Christian society
should take up the same view, and that it should find
expression in the civil codes. And so it happened; and in
the early civil codes, drawn up under the influence of
Christian ideas, we find heresy classed with high treason,
and punished with equal severity. Indisputable evidence of
this is supplied by Hergenrother, *Church and State*, vol ii.,
pp. 304, 309, 316, 320, and also by Pollock and Maitland,
History of English Law, vol. ii., pp. 543, 544. Such laws
would, no doubt, in our time be regarded as extravagant in
their rigorous severity. But we must recollect that the
temper of the times is different. Now a crime against an
earthly king is punished with death, whilst blasphemy
against the King of Heaven is permitted to pass unnoticed.
The legislators of those early times thought differently, and
they often had before them, too, evidence of the ruin and
devastation brought on by heresy. The Church did not
inflict this punishment. She separated the obstinate heretic
from the communion of her children by excommunication,
and left him to be dealt with by the civil laws which
regarded heresy as a crime against the state; this is the
legislation which St. Thomas vindicates, and which is so
offensive to the humane orthodoxy of Dr. Salmon. Now, if
he regard the soul as more precious than the body or than
worldly goods, it is difficult to see how he can quarrel with
this legislation; and if, on the other hand, he considers the
loss of the soul by heresy a lesser evil than the loss of life
or property, it is difficult to see how he can claim to be a
Christian—a follower of Him who said: 'What shall it
profit one to gain the whole world if he suffer the loss of his
soul.'

Whilst Dr. Salmon was thus declaiming against the
intolerance of the Catholic Church, he could have seen from
his window the spot on which the Catholic Archbishop of
Cashel, Dr. O'Hurley, was put to a most cruel death—not
for heresy, but for his attachment to the true faith; and he
could have found in his own library evidence of how Loftus,
the Protestant Archbishop, was gloating over the sufferings

of the illustrious martyr. Has he no knowledge of the civil disabilities of his Catholic fellow-countrymen ; disabilities that are imposed on them solely because they are Catholics? Even the Duke of Norfolk cannot become Lord Lieutenant of Ireland as long as he remains a Catholic. Does he not see from the daily papers how even now, after seventy years of Catholic emancipation, Catholic jurors are told contemptuously to 'stand aside,' and for no other reason than that they are Catholics, and by insolent officials who own their positions to their Protestantism? Has he forgotten all this in his zeal to denounce St. Thomas and St. Augustine?

And here again Dr. Salmon seems to be quite unaware that the doctrine he is denouncing is actually taught by the leading divines of the Church to which he professes to belong. Pearson, *On the Creed*, art. 9, says : ' A man may not only passively and involuntarily be rejected, but may also by an act of his own, cast out or reject himself, not only by plain and complete apostasy, but by a defection from the unity of truth, falling into some damnable heresy.' Barrow says that a heretic ' in reality is no Christian, nor is to be assumed or treated as such, but is to be disclaimed, rejected, and shunned.'[1] Dr. Auliffe, in his *Parergon Juris Anglicani*, page 294, says that ' no man can doubt but that we may proceed with some severity' against heretics. Palmer, in his treatise on the Church, proves at great length that heretics may be excommunicated, as 'heresy is a most deadly sin.'[2] And[3] he details the punishments of heresy in a manner which shows how well his Church is able to copy from Catholic legislation. And Dr. Blunt, in his *Dictionary of Doctrinal and Historical Theology*, art. Heresy, has the same doctrine as Palmer, though he has to admit that ' Heresy has so completely evaporated as an ecclesiastical offence, that it is not even mentioned in modern books on ecclesiastical law.' Probably it is the evaporation that has acted on Dr. Salmon's memory, and that has made him forget the teaching of his brother

---

[1] Vol. ii., p. 762.   [2] Vol. i., p. 82.   [3] Vol. ii., p. 225.

theologians. And that this Protestant theology was not
allowed to remain a dead letter, the Catholics of this country
have learned from a prolonged and bitter experience. To
say nothing of the savage anti-Catholic legislation of
Elizabeth and James I., in the Acts 7th and 9th of
William III., s. 1, c. 3, and in 2nd Anne, s. 1, c. 3 and 6,
we can find specimens of the toleration extended to Irish
Catholics by the heads, in spirituals and temporals, of
Dr. Salmon's Church. And with this legislation known to
him (for he must know it), it is amazing that he should have
referred to the doctrine of the Rhemish Notes. In Howard's
*Special Cases on the Laws against the Further Growth of
Popery in Ireland,* published in Dublin in A.D. 1775, the
reader will find a record of religious intolerance as cruel as
anything recorded of pagan persecutors; and all these
unjust, iniquitous, inhuman laws were passed and put into
execution by the heads of Dr. Salmon's Church, and in
order to maintain the ascendancy of that Church.

And the zeal of Dr. Salmon's Church was not limited to
the punishment of Catholics, as the following will show :—
The Rev. Thomas Emlyn, a Presbyterian minister, was
tried for 'heresy and blasphemy' in the Court of Queen's
Bench, Dublin, on the 14th of June, 1703. The charge
against him was grounded on heterodox views on our Lord's
Divinity, which would now be regarded as ordinary specimens of the Higher Criticism. Some Protestant bishops,
amongst them Dr. Marsh, of Armagh, and Dr. King, of
Dublin, were present at the trial to testify their zeal for
orthodoxy; and though the evidence was anything but
strong, the jury found Mr. Emlyn guilty, and he was
sentenced to a fine of £1,000, and he was to be kept in jail
until the fine would have been paid. After the poor man
had been two years in prison the authorities began to realize
that the fine was excessive, or more likely, that its payment
was impossible, and it was reduced to £70. Then came the
point of the case that illustrates the zeal against heretics
that animated Dr. Salmon's spiritual fathers. The Primate,
Dr. Narcissus Marsh, a former Provost of Trinity College,
was by law entitled to a shilling in the pound on all such

fines, and this most rev. Shylock insisted that his share should be levied off the original thousand and not off the reduced sum of seventy; and it was only when he found that the full amount could not possibly be extracted from the unfortunate 'heretic,' that he consented to accept £20 as a compromise. This is a manifestation of zeal against heresy which Dr. Salmon will not find recommended in the Rhemish Notes, or sanctioned in the teachings of St. Augustine or St. Thomas.

Now, the Catholic Church can tell definitely what is heresy; the Protestant cannot do so. In the Catholic Church there is an authority set up by God to teach true faith; heresy is a rebellion against that authority, and, therefore, is justly punished. But in the Protestant Church the 'individual Christian' is the authority, and since the individual cannot rebel against himself, heresy is impossible, and, therefore, it is irrational to punish it. Or rather, perhaps, since heresy is the selection of one's own faith by one's own authority, and since each Protestant claims a right to select for himself, then all alike are heretics, and no one has a shadow of right to censure or punish another for his religious views. In this matter the Catholic Church has been always consistent; the Protestant Church has been always inconsistent.

Again, Dr. Salmon complains that though the Catholic Church 'has catechisms and other books of instruction . . . she has not ventured to put her seal of Infallibility to any of them' (page 190). And hence he says 'if we detect a catechism in manifest error, if we find a preacher or a book of devotion guilty of manifest extravagance, . . . the Church always leaves a loophole for disowning him.' And he adds: 'Does it not seem strange that a communion possessing the high attribute of Infallibility should make no use of it in the instruction of her people?' (page 191). Yes, it would 'seem strange' if it were a fact; but it is one of Dr. Salmon's fictions, and not a very clever or ingenious one. The Catholic Church is a teacher, and she is that precisely in virtue of her Infallibility. It is that which ensures that the ever-living voice shall always enunciate divine truth.

Catechisms and books of devotion are permitted to circulate amongst Catholics, and are used by them, provided they have proper ecclesiastical approbation. That approbation ensures that the books contain nothing opposed to faith or morals—no doctrinal error, no unsound principle of morality.

Now this approbation presupposes an infallible standard of faith and morals, whereby the doctrine of such books is tested. And hence, if such books have this approbation, the faithful who use them have ample security as to the orthodoxy of the doctrine, as far as the approbation goes. And, therefore, ' in the instruction of her people ' the Catholic Church always uses that very ' attribute of Infallibility ' which, according to Dr. Salmon, she never uses at all. The Doctor was speaking to his students when he made this extraordinary statement, and clearly he thought his logic good enough for them. But all his rhetoric here is leading up to what he evidently regards as a crushing case against the Catholic Church. ' I need take no other example,' he says, ' than the case I have already mentioned of Keenan's Catechism' (page 191). He had already quoted the Catechism at page 26 to convict the Catholic Church of a change of faith, and now he quotes it to show, moreover, ' that we, heretics, knew better what were the doctrines of the Roman Church than did its own priests ' (page 192). Now, assuming (and it is scarcely a safe assumption) the correctness of Dr. Salmon's extract from Keenan, what does it prove? According to the Doctor, Keenan said of Papal Infallibility, some fifty years ago : ' It is no article of Catholic faith.' This is, according to the Doctor and his friends, a false statement; they ' knew better what were the doctrines of the Roman Church than did its own priests.'

Now, in order that a doctrine be an article of Catholic faith, it must be revealed, and it must be proposed by the Church to the faithful. The Infallibility of the Pope was revealed in Christ's charge to St. Peter, and it has ever since been in the Church's keeping as part of the deposit of faith. But it was not proposed by the Church to the faithful until the Vatican Council, and, therefore, up to that time it was ' no article of Catholic faith.' And, therefore, Keenan's statement was true and the Doctor's statement is not true. Up to the time of the definition it was an article of divine faith to such as had considered the evidence of its revelation and are satisfied of its sufficiency—and there were very many such; but it was not an article of Catholic faith for anyone until it was taught by the Church. But see what the Doctor's logic comes to. At page 26 he introduced Keenan's statement to convict the Church of a change in faith. If there be a change of faith made by the definition of Papal Infallibility, then Keenan's statement must have been true; it was not an article of faith when he wrote. But if Keenan's statement be false (as Dr. Salmon says at page 192), then there was no change in doctrine caused by the definition. But the Doctor's memory is just as bad as his logic, for at page 26 he held Keenan's statement to be true; at page 192 he holds it to be false, and again he holds it to be true at page 269, where, in reference to the evidence of some Irish bishops before a Royal Commission, he says, 'they swore, as they then could with truth, that the doctrine of the Pope's personal Infallibility' was not an article of Catholic faith. The students are fortunate in their teacher! Now all this is so elementary, so frequently and so clearly stated by Catholic theologians, that it is difficult to fancy a Regius Professor ignorant of it; and yet it is only the plea of ignorance that can shield him from the charge of bearing false witness against his neighbours.

A great rock of scandal to Dr. Salmon is the Roman Breviary, and also the process of canonisation of saints. This ardent lover of truth is shocked at 'the number of lying legends . . . that are inserted in the Breviary by authority for the devotional reading of priests' (page 196). But the Church, with her wonted versatility, is prepared to repudiate them when called to account by theologians of the Dr. Salmon type. He says: 'If a Protestant hesitating to become a convert to Popery, should allege, as the ground of his hesitation, the number of lying legends proposed by the Church for his acceptance, he would be told that this is no obstacle at all, and that as a Roman Catholic he need not believe any of them' (page 196). The Doctor is here referring

to the brief histories of the saints that are generally given
in the lessons of the Second Nocturn of the Breviary.
And as he proclaims himself that Catholics are not bound to
accept these histories as truths of faith, it is difficult to
see what legitimate motive he can have in putting them
forward as arguments against the Church's Infallibility. As
the Church orders the Breviary to be read by priests, it can
contain nothing that is opposed to faith or morals; this is
all the Church guarantees. The intending 'convert' is
asked to accept the Catholic profession of faith, which com-
prises a number of truths originally revealed by God, and
proposed by the Church for the belief of the faithful. The
histories of the saints, given in the Breviary, were not
revealed, and are not put forward as such by the Church;
and, therefore, the intending convert is truly told that he is
not bound to accept them as truths of faith—for it is of
such truths that Dr. Salmon is speaking. But according to
the Doctor they are 'lying legends proposed by the Church.'
Now, the Doctor's word is not a substitute for proof, and he
has not even attempted to prove that any of the statements
referred to as 'lying legends' is really such. The Roman
Breviary was frequently revised, and the last general revision
of it was made under Urban VIII. by a congregation of
cardinals, amongst whom were Bellarmine and Baronius, and
they were assisted by a number of eminent scholars as consulting theologians, amongst whom were Gavantus, the
great writer on Ritual, and our own countryman, Father
Luke Wadding. Now, it is not a conclusive proof of the
Doctor's modesty, or even of his prudence, to find him
setting down as 'lying legends' statements which passed the
criticism of such scholars. The Regius Professor would
make a very sorry figure if he was for a while under
examination in history and theology by Bellarmine and
Baronius. But even on Dr. Salmon's own admission there is
much more to be said for the histories of the Breviary. He says
that many of them, at least, are taken from Bulls of Canonisation, and if he would only read one process of canonisation he
would be in a better position to judge of the character of
the evidence he is discussing so glibly. Let him but read

vol. v. of Moigno's *Splendeurs de la foi*, let him study the investigation there given, and he will be less confident in his assertion of 'lying legends.' The lying legends are those of Dr. Salmon, and of men like him, whose sole stock-in-trade they are. Such statements excite no surprise in Irish Church Mission teachers, but in a university professor they are lamentable.

In justification of his assertions Dr. Salmon quotes the case of the Holy House at Loretto, which he proves to be 'fictitious' on the high authority of his friend, Mr. Ffoulkes. Now, as Mr. Ffoulkes' reasons are not given, we have only his assertion repeated by Dr. Salmon, which, as a proof, amounts to nothing. Another of his arguments is from the case of St. Philumena—but the Doctor doctors the history of the saint in his own peculiar fashion. He says:—

We learn from the authorized history of her life that a good Neapolitan priest had carried home some bones out of the Roman catacombs, and was much distressed that his valuable relics should be anonymous. He was relieved from his embarrassment by a pious nun in his congregation, who, in a dream, had revealed to her the name of the saint and her whole history, etc. —(Page 197).

This history must have been 'authorised' by the Doctor himself. The real history, which he could have found in the Breviary, tells us that the relics were not 'anonymous' at all. They were discovered in the catacomb of St. Priscilla, on the 2nd of May, 1802. They were contained in an urn, and on a terra-cotta slab covering them was written: 'Philumena. Peace with thee.—Amen.' On the tomb also was found the lily, the symbol of virginity, also the palm, the blood-stained phial, the arrow, and other symbols of martyrdom. Dr. Salmon can see a fac-simile of the slab in Northcote and Brownlow's *Epitaphs of the Catacombs* (page 53). Now De Rossi, judging from the internal arrangement of this catacomb, and also from the inscriptions and symbolisms used, holds that it goes back to the second century of the Christian era. Here, then, we have a fact as strictly historical as anything recorded of the catacombs, showing that the relics in question are those of Philumena,

a virgin and a martyr, who must have suffered at a very
early period of Christian history. Now, whether the ' dream
of the pious nun,' alleged by Dr. Salmon, be real or unreal,
the historical fact which he has conveniently suppressed
reveals both the name and the character of the saint, and
supplies also abundant foundation for the devotion to
St. Philumena, which has so shocked the tender conscience
of this truth-loving theologian.

This case of Philumena leads the Doctor on to ' the subject of modern revelation as a foundation for new doctrines '
(page 199). He says: ' But these alleged revelations are
also the foundation of new doctrines, and the Pope's silence
concerning them affects the whole question of the rule of
faith' (page 200). And the new doctrines thus introduced
are, according to Dr. Salmon, ' Purgatory, Devotion to the
Sacred Heart, and the Immaculate Conception.' These
revelations are, according to Dr. Salmon, ' in plain English,
ghost stories,' and on such stories ' beliefs are being silently
built up in the Church ' to such an extent that the Church
really ' is a vast manufactory of beliefs to which additions
are being yearly made' (page 213). The sum of his charge
against the Church in this matter is that very many of her
doctrines are founded on ghost stories, and that, as she will
not tell us definitely what we are to think of these stories,
she is, therefore, shown to be fallible. Now, first, Infallibility
can be tested only by what the Church does teach, not by
what she does not teach ; and, hence, the Doctor's
instances cannot be a test at all. And, secondly, no article
of Catholic faith is founded, or can be founded, on any
revelation not contained in the original deposit of faith.
This is the Catholic theory, and Dr. Salmon is well aware of
it. Whether there have been revelations made to individuals
in later times is a matter to be determined by testimony, but
such revelations cannot enter into the deposit of faith, and
no article of Catholic faith can be grounded on them. And
of this, too, the Doctor is well aware. If there be in reality
any such modern revelations those to whom they were made
are bound to believe them, not, however, as articles of
Catholic faith (for such they cannot be), but as articles of

divine faith, for, in the supposition, God has spoken to them and they must believe Him. But others to whom the revelation was not made are not bound to believe it, for the simple reason that they have not sufficient evidence that God has spoken. Dr. Salmon says : ' If there be any one in the latter Church to whom God has made real revelations we are bound to receive the truths so disclosed with the same reverence and assent which we give to what was taught by the Apostles ' (page 214). He is here giving testimony unconsciously against himself. Unfortunately for him in his own theory the statement is quite true. He has no better means of knowing what the Apostles taught than he has of knowing whether a revelation was made to this or that individual in recent times. But in the Catholic theory —the true theory—the Doctor's statement is quite false; for the Catholic has the infallible authority of the Church to tell him what was taught by the Apostles, whilst in the case of modern revelation he has only the authority of the person to whom the revelation is alleged to have been made.

One of the doctrines alleged by Dr. Salmon to have been founded on modern revelation is that of the Immaculate Conception. Well, the doctrine was defined in 1854, and the alleged revelation, or rather apparition, took place in 1858. The doctrine thus came before the revelation, and consequently could not be founded on it. The Doctor first builds his house and then looks about for a foundation. This is genuine town-clock theology. Again, he regards the revelations made to Margaret Mary Alacoque as the foundation of devotion to the Sacred Heart, and he says : ' My object is to show that every one of these alleged revelations has a distinct bearing on doctrine ' (page 224). He holds that they give rise to the doctrine.

Now, devotion to the Sacred Heart is founded on the Incarnation, on the Hypostatic Union, and Dr. Salmon cannot well maintain that the doctrine has been in any way affected by the revelation said to have been made to Blessed Margaret Mary. Out of this doctrine devotion to the Sacred Heart grew, and though it has become much more general since Margaret Mary's time, it existed long before her time. There is an Act of Consecration to the Sacred Heart given in the *Divini Amoris Pharetra*, written by Lauspergus, and published A.D. 1572, fully a hundred years before Blessed Margaret Mary's time. The devotion is distinctly referred to in the *Vitis Mystica*, c. 3, n. 8, fully four hundred years before her time; and it is not difficult to trace it much farther back into Christian antiquity. It is thus very much more ancient than Dr. Salmon fancies, and it could not, by any effort of imagination, be said with truth to have been founded on the revelations said to have been made to Blessed Margaret Mary. But to the Doctor 'it is downright Nestorianism;' and he condemns it on the ground that in the Nestorian controversy 'it was distinctly condemned to make a separation between our Lord's Godhead and His Manhood' (page 223). This precisely is what the devotion does not do. It rests on the impossibility of such separation; it presupposes the inseparable union of 'our Lord's Godhead and His Manhood,' as the Doctor can see for himself, in any Catholic treatise on the subject, if he care to ascertain the truth. Of Blessed Margaret Mary herself he says: 'This poor nun was subject to what we heretics would call hysteric delusions.' This is his substitute for argument. He does not consider the evidence for the alleged revelations; that would be a tedious, a difficult process, and may perhaps lead him to an undeniable conclusions. Within his class-room he knew that his assertions would pass for argument, but for those outside, who may read his lectures, and calmly and patiently test his statements, to fancy that his mere assertion will carry much weight is one of the most supreme delusions of his life.

But, as might have been expected, the doctrine of Purgatory is Dr. Salmon's most fruitful source of argument against the Catholic Church. All through his lectures, there is a tone of levity when speaking of Catholic doctrines that is open to grave suspicion, but this is most noticeable in his references to Purgatory. 'The whole faith of the Church of Rome on this subject,' he says, 'has been built upon revelations, or, as we should call it in plain English, on ghost stories. For hundreds of years the Church seems to

have known little or nothing on the subject' (page 206). The
Doctor himself seems certainly ' to know little or nothing'
of it when he speaks thus. The Catholic Church teaches
that ' there is a Purgatory, and that souls detained there are
helped by the suffrages of the faithful, but most particularly
by the acceptable sacrifice of the altar.' This is the defined
doctrine on which theologians are allowed to reason and
pious souls to meditate, so long only as their reasonings
and inferences do not infringe on this fixed truth. Where
this place or state of purgation is : what the precise nature
of the sufferings there endured : how long they are to last
for anyone, the Church does not say : though there is a
strong tendency of Catholic teaching to lead one to believe
that the pains are severe. And much unauthorised speculation on these questions in popular instructions is distinctly
discouraged by the Council of Trent. Now the supreme and
sufficient argument for this or any other Catholic doctrine
is the teaching of the infallible Church. The doctrine is
necessarily involved in the doctrine and practice of prayer
for the dead which the Church has always taught and maintained. If it be well to pray for the dead, if our prayers
help them, then there must be some of them in such a state
as to need our help. The saints in heaven do not need our
prayers or help, and to the lost souls in hell our prayers can
do no good. The souls, therefore, who can be served by our
prayers must be in some intermediate state, in some state of
purgation or expiation, where our prayers can procure for
them the succour they need. This place or state Catholics
call Purgatory. This is the substance of the doctrine on
Purgatory which the Church has always taught, though
Dr. Salmon told his theologians that for hundreds of years
she seems to have known little or nothing of it.

Now, in the face of this confident assertion stands the
indisputable fact that the doctrine was taught and believed
by God's chosen people long before the Catholic Church
came into existence at all. Dr. Salmon is, of course,
familiar with the well-known text, 2 Machabees xii. 43, 44,
which records that Judas Machabeus made certain provision
' for sacrifices to be offered for the sins of the dead, thinking

well and religiously concerning the resurrection,' etc. This clearly cannot be set down as the personal opinion of Judas. He is giving expression to the belief which must have been held by all those who co-operated with him in that act of mercy; by all who believed in the resurrection. They must have believed that it was not 'superfluous and vain to pray for the dead.' Now, if it was not 'superfluous,' then some of the dead must stand in need of prayers ; and if it be not 'vain,' then the prayers must be useful to the departed souls. No wonder, then, holding this doctrine, that he should say, ' It is, therefore, a holy and a salutary thought to pray for the dead, that they may be loosed from their sins.'

It will avail the Doctor nothing to say that the book is not canonical; for (to say nothing of the conclusive evidence against this statement) the text supplies historical proof, that the Jews at that time prayed for the dead ; and believed that departed souls were succoured by the prayers of the living. It is then absolutely certain that the doctrine was believed and acted on by the Jews in our Lord's own time, and there is no trace of any protest from Him or from the Apostles against it. On the contrary, there are texts in the New Testament which seem to presuppose the doctrine, and the force of such texts becomes much stronger when taken in connexion with the comments and teaching of early fathers. Doellenger, whom Dr. Salmon frequently quotes as an authority, shows that several texts of the New Testament were understood in early times as referring to the state of the departed souls and to make special comment on 2 Tim. i. 16-18.[1] Tertullian [2] says ' we make annual sacrifices for the dead,' and in the opening sentence of the next chapter (iv.) he says : ' Of this and other such customs if you ask the Scripture authority, you shall not find it. Tradition hands it down to you, custom confirms it, faith secures its observance.' And in his book, *De Exhortatione Castitatis,* he argues against second marriages

---

[1] *First Age of the Church,* vol. ii., pp. 64-70.
[2] *De Corona Mil.,* c. iii., No. 79.

on the ground that the husband has still a religious
affection for the deceased wife, 'for whose soul,' he says,
' you pray, for whom you offer up annual sacrifices.'[1] St.
Cyprian in his sixty-sixth letter *Ad Clerum* refers to a previous synod which forbade priests from becoming executors,
and he now orders that anyone who violates that law shall
not have the sacrifice offered for him when dead. St. Cyril of
Jerusalem[2] says that after ' Commemorating patriarchs, and
prophets, and apostles, and martyrs, that God may through
their intercession receive our prayers, we then pray for . . .
all those who have died amongst us believing that it shall be
the greatest help to their souls for whom prayers are offered
while the holy and august victim is present.' It is quite
unnecessary to multiply texts from the early fathers, this
doctrine is the teaching of them all. Most readers will
recollect the feeling language of the dying St. Monica to her
son, St. Augustine, asking to remember her at the altar.
St. Ambrose, St. Chrysostom Epiphanius, St. Gregory the
Great, all teach this doctrine in the most unmistakable
language. Again in all the ancient liturgies there are prayers
for the dead,[3] and the same cry for mercy goes up from the
tombs of the catacombs. Moreover, in several early councils
we find canons regulating oblations for the dead. Against
all this teaching it is alleged that the prayers referred to are
only commemorations such as we find made of persons
departed who certainly do not need our prayers. We often
find the Blessed Virgin and the Apostles so commemorated.

A glance at the texts and prayers will however dissipate
this delusion. In the text given from St. Cyril a clear distinction is made between those whom we commemorate to
honour, to gain their intercession, and those whom we commemorate as an act of charity to obtain mercy for them.
And this distinction is clearly laid down in the writings of
other fathers, and is as clearly embodied in the ancient
liturgies, as it is in the Roman Missal of this day. Honourable
mention, such as distinguished soldiers get in military

---

[1] Cap. xi.
[2] *Cat. v. Myst.*, No. 9.
[3] See Renaudot, *Observationes*, vol. ii. p. 103. Ed, London, 1843.

despatches, will not satisfy this. And from these original fountains of Apostolic teaching, the doctrine has come down through fathers and councils to our own time. Now, are all these testimonies ghost stories? In the face of this chain of evidence the Doctor told his theologians that for many hundreds of years the Church seemed to have known little or nothing of the doctrine!

And in this, as in other matters, Dr. Salmon seems to know as little of the teaching of his own theologians, as of that of ours. The very latest commentator on the Articles, the Rev. E. Tyrrell Greene, M.A., says, while explaining Article 21 :—' There is abundant evidence which goes to prove that the practice of prayer for the dead prevailed in the Primitive Church ' (page 148) ; and he proves his assertion from the ancient liturgies and from inscriptions in the catacombs. Dr. Luckock, Dean of Lichfield, says :—' It seems almost impossible to form any other conclusion than that the souls of the departed pass through some purifying process, between death and judgment.' [1] And Dr. M. MacColl, Canon of Ripon, in his *Reformation Settlement,* after a long and appropriate quotation from Jeremy Taylor, says :—

I will now assume that I have established these three statements :—(1) that the Church of England has nowhere refused her sanction to prayers for the dead ; (2) that such prayers have been sanctioned by the Christian Church from the beginning ; (3) that the Christian Church inherited them with our Lord's tacit sanction from the Jewish Church.—(Page 318.)

And that Dr. MacColl is correct in his reference to the Church of England, was clearly proved by the decision of the Court of Arches in the case of Breeks *v.* Woolfrey, Nov. 19th, 1838. In that year a Catholic, John Woolfrey, died at Carisbrooke, in the Isle of Wight. He was buried in the local cemetery, and his wife erected a tombstone to his remains with the following inscription :—

Pray for the soul of J. WOOLFREY.
It is a holy and a wholesome thought to pray for the dead.
—2 Ma. xii. 46.

---

[1] *Intermediate State,* c. vii. 62.

This prayer was too distasteful to the orthodoxy of the local parson, Rev. J. Breeks, who cited Mrs. Woolfrey before the court of the Bishop Winchester, in order to have the tombstone and inscription removed. From this court it was sent to the Court of Arches, of Canterbury, where a decision was given on the day above-named by Sir Herbert Jenner Fust. The charge is a most elaborate survey of the ecclesiastical law bearing on this question; but the outcome brought very little consolation to the wounded feelings of the Rev. John Breeks. The tombstone, with its prayer, was to remain. The rev. gentleman was much more orthodox than his Church. He may inhibit prayers for the dead, but there is no evidence that the Church of England ever did so. And, as if to make matters worse for Mr. Breeks, the judge had the cruel taste of quoting the epitaph, composed by Bishop Barrow, for his own tomb; which can still be read in the Cathedral of St. Asaph, and which is quite as Roman as the prayer for poor J. Woolfrey. All these men too, of course, based their opinions on 'ghost stories.' Surely if Dr. Salmon had been aware that divines of high standing, scholars of high reputation, had made, after mature examination, the statements given above, he would have been less reckless in addressing an audience even such as his was.

Instead of setting before his students the real foundation of our doctrine, he entertained them with the recital of a number of stories well calculated to bring ridicule on it. He took from Father Faber, and from the Abbé Louvet, a number of alleged revelations as to the general character of Purgatory, and the state of the souls therein, and on these 'ghost stories' he told them 'the whole faith of the Church of Rome' on this matter rests. He has not even attempted to disprove any one of the 'stories.' And even though he had disproved them all, the Catholic doctrines on Purgatory and on Prayers for the Dead would remain just what they are. From Father Faber's *All for Jesus* he quotes a number of such expressions as ' Our Lord said to St. Gertrude,' or ' to St. Teresa,' which he clearly regards as too silly to need refutation. Now, Father Faber must have believed that there was evidence for these statements, and must have believed them. He does not give them as arguments for doctrine. In fact, only one of the passages quoted by Dr. Salmon refers to Purgatory ; and Dr. Salmon draws from them the following conclusion :—' A number of new things about Purgatory are stated on this authority . . . for instance, that the Blessed Virgin is Queen of Purgatory, that St. Michael is her Prime Minister,' etc. (page 205). This is very witty, and must have been amusing to Dr. Salmon's theologians, but Father Faber is not to blame for the Doctor's profane levity. He believed the revelations quoted by him, just as he was free to disbelieve them if he thought the evidence unsatisfactory. And anyone who reads his work, and knows his history, must feel that he possesses the critical faculty quite as much as Dr. Salmon, though he has used it in a different way, and with far different results. And certainly Dr. Salmon, as revealed in those lectures, is not the man to give a decisive opinion on the dealings of God with favoured souls as St. Gertrude or St. Teresa.

But Dr. Salmon's favourite author on this subject is the French Abbé Louvet. This priest seems, from his book, to be a pious man, not overburthened with judgment, and he wrote in circumstances of special difficulty. ' I have formed a very high opinion both of the piety of the Abbé and of his literary honesty,' says Dr. Salmon (page 205). And no wonder, for he supplies the Doctor with some valuable material for his lecture. He gives, for instance, and fully believes the history of St. Patrick's Purgatory as told by Count Ramon, and, furthermore, he actually regards it as in some way connected with the real Purgatory of the departed souls. No wonder that Dr. Salmon should admire so learned, so reliable an authority. But, to do the good Abbé justice, he does not claim such high authority himself. In his Preface he apologises for the many imperfections of his book. He is a hard-working missionary in China, and he says that the book was written during a period of illness, away in his distant mission many thousand leagues from any library, from notes taken long before, and from memory. To expect a reliable or valuable work on a difficult subject from one so

circumstanced is out of the question. And the Abbé's
memory failed him on one very vital matter. According to
the law of the Catholic Church such a book should not be
issued without proper ecclesiastical approbation, and the
Abbé's book has none ; and it is certainly quite characteristic of Dr. Salmon, as a controversialist, that he should
quote as a high authority on Catholic doctrine a book
written in violation of the law of the Catholic Church.
There are recorded in Scripture visions and revelations
quite as wonderful as any recorded by the Abbé Louvet.
Those recorded by him then are possible, and for all that
Dr. Salmon has said they may be true. They are not to be
disposed of by notes of exclamation. As long as statements
like those of Abbé Louvet do not infringe on faith or
morals, the Catholic Church is just as much, and just as
little, concerned with them as Dr. Salmon himself, and he
is quite aware that this is so. And yet he makes on it the
following characteristic comment :—

> To people of their own community they assert things as
> positive facts, which they run away from defending the moment
> an opponent grapples with them. It would seem as if their
> maxim was, ' We need not be particular about the truth of what
> we say if no one is present who can contradict us.'—(Page 216,
> note.)

Et tu Brute ! Such a statement implies an unusual
amount of hardihood, considering the character of his own
lectures !

The 'Gallican theory' is, according to Dr. Salmon, fatal
to the Infallibility of the Church. 'That theory,' he says,
' places the Infallibility in the Church diffusive' (page 262).
The Doctor's language here is equivocal. It would apply
either to passive infallibility of the body of believers, or to
the active infallibility of the teaching Church. And as his
aim here is to assail ' infallibility in teaching,' let it be
supposed that he is more logical than his language indicates, and that by 'the Church diffusive' he means the body
of bishops diffused throughout the Church, and including,
of course, the Pope. The Gallicans held that this body was
infallible in its teaching, and this doctrine has been already

proved. They disbelieved in the Infallibility of the Pope; and it is a curious thing about Dr. Salmon's logic that his arguments against the doctrine which the Gallicans held are arguments in favour of the doctrine which they denied, and which he himself denies and denounces most vehemently. 'One thing is plain,' he says, 'namely, that if this is the nature of the gift of infallibility Christ has bestowed on His Church, the gift is absolutely useless for the determination of controversies' (page 269). 'We can see thus that the Gallican method of ascribing Infallibility to the Church diffusive does not satisfy any of the *apriori* supposed proofs for the necessity of a judge of controversies' (page 271). Thus, whilst arguing against one Catholic doctrine he is, no doubt, unconsciously proving another; his argument against the infallibility of the Church tends very strongly to prove the Infallibility of the Pope. The General Synod should look to the Doctor's logic. As Dr. O'Hanlon used to say, 'such teaching deserves a note.'

Now, the Gallicans held the Infallibility of the Church, how then can they be quoted as witnessing against that doctrine? The Doctor has not explained the intricate process which led him to this discovery. How far Gallicanism can be regarded as an argument against Papal Infallibility will be considered when that doctrine comes on for discussion. Dr. Salmon is well aware, for he says so, that the Declaration of 1682 was forced on the French Church by the tyranny of Louis XIV.

I believe [he says] that, but for court pressure, Bossuet and his colleagues would not have engaged in the controversy with Rome, which the act of formulating these propositions involved. . . . I have my doubts whether these hangers-on of the court of Louis XIV. really carried the religious mind of the nation with him.—(Page 266.)

And yet, strange to say, in the very same page he says: 'The four Gallican propositions expressed, as I believe, the real opinion of the French Church!' They did not express the real opinion of the venerable French Church, and of this there is now conclusive evidence. They were forced on by the unscrupulous tyranny of the king and his ministers; and were accepted only by time-serving prelates who were ready to give to Cæsar what belonged to God. M. Charles Gérin, in his *History of the Assembly of* 1682, has accumulated from sources hitherto unpublished, a mass of information on the proceedings of the assembly ; and has put in its true light the conduct of its leading spirits. It was a packed assembly. Its members were really chosen by the king's agents. Only thirty-four out of one hundred and thirty bishops were present, and these were selected, not for their learning or their piety, but for their well-known servility ; and M. Gérin has produced letters of very many of them which show how fully they expected to be rewarded for their services. Such an assembly could have no moral weight, and its decision was forced on the French Church by the most absolute tyranny. In his fifteenth chapter M. Gérin shows what were the feelings of the French Church at the time, and the means adopted to crush those feelings. Colbert, the king's unscrupulous minister, had his spies in the University to note how the articles were likely to be received, and the secret reports supplied to him are brought to light by M. Gérin. Of one hundred and sixty doctors of the Sorbonne 'all, but six or seven,' are reputed as opposed to the articles; in the College of Navarre 'all, but one,' opposed; at St. Sulpice and the Foreign Missions Colleges 'all, but four or five'; and among the orders 'all.' And a month after the assembly Colbert, himself, writes that nearly all the bishops who signed the declaration would willingly retract the next day if they could. This is the evidence of facts, as adduced by M. Gérin, and it completely disproves Dr. Salmon's statement that the 'four articles expressed the real opinion of the French Church.' And it is clear, therefore, that even as a difficulty against Papal Infallibility, Gallicanism breaks down hopelessly.

In speaking of General Councils Dr. Salmon has surpassed himself. Here his real controversial tact is conspicuous ; and if his students carry away from his lectures any respect for early General Councils, the fault is not attributable to their Professor. He told them that the authority of General

Councils had now practically ceased to be matter of controversy, because that Catholics 'who claim that prerogative for the Pope, and whose ascendancy was completely established at the Vatican Council of 1870, have been quite as anxious, as we can be, that no rival claim for councils should be allowed to establish itself' (page 281). The Doctor is here drawing on his imagination. Catholics can never give up any doctrine once taught by the Church. There have been several dogmatic treatises written on the Church since the Vatican Council; and he will find in each one of them this doctrine stated and vindicated, though he told his students it was practically set aside. This doctrine is included in the ordinary proof of the Infallibility of the *Ecclesia Docens* which Dr. Salmon has not considered. But having laid down the above extraordinary premises, he proceeds to discredit General Councils on Catholic authority. 'I am trying to prove no more,' he says, 'than has been asserted by eminent Roman Catholic divines as, for example, by Cardinal Newman' (page 282). Now it must be borne in mind that there is question only of General Councils, for to such only do Catholics attribute Infallibility. And Newman's testimony against them, he says, is that ' Cardinal Newman describes the fourth century Councils ' (Nicæa and first of Constantinople being of the number), ' as a scandal to the Christian name.'

It appears absolutely useless to look for a fair quotation in Dr. Salmon's book. This quotation is from Newman's *Historical Sketches*, vol. iii. p. 335, and is as follows :—
' Arianism came into the Church with Constantine, and the Councils which it convoked and made its tools were a scandal to the Christian name.' Dr. Salmon omitted all except the concluding words of the sentence, and applied these words in a sense openly and expressly excluded by the text. According to Newman, certain Arian Councils were ' a scandal to the Christian name,' and, therefore, says Dr. Salmon to his students, we have Newman teaching that all the fourth century Councils, Nicæa, and the first of Constantinople amongst the number, were ' a scandal to the Christian name.' Now, Dr. Salmon could not have mistaken

Newman's meaning in the passage, for besides his specially naming the Arian Councils, he added, in the very next sentence, ' the Council of Nicæa, which preceded them, was by right final on the controversy, but this Constantine's successor, Constantius, and his court bishops would not allow.' And yet Dr. Salmon quotes Cardinal Newman as teaching that even this Council of Nicæa was ' a scandal to the Christian name '!

On the strength of his misquotation of Newman, Dr. Salmon proceeds to show that the Ecumenical Councils of the fifth century were quite as much discredited as those which preceded them, and selects specially the Council of Ephesus. His argument against this Council is founded altogether on the personal character of St. Cyril of Alexandria, whom he paints in the very blackest of colours indeed. After referring to a number of Cyril's alleged misdeeds, he again quotes Cardinal Newman :—' Cardinal Newman here gives up Cyril, "Cyril, I know, is a saint, but it does not follow that he was a saint in the year 412"' (page 307). Now, to say that a man is a saint does not look like giving him up; and Newman, moreover, says of him, after referring to the charges made against him :—

Thoughts such as these . . . were a great injustice to Cyril. Cyril was a clear-headed constructive theologian. He saw what Theodoret did not see. He was not content with anathematising Nestorius; he laid down a positive view of the Incarnation which the Universal Church accepted, and holds to this day, as the very truth of Revelation. It is this insight into and grasp of the Adorable mystery which constitutes his claim to take his seat among the Doctors of Holy Church.'

But the question is not at all what was the personal character of Cyril, but was the Council infallible : and Cardinal Newman, in the very page quoted by Dr. Salmon, has given his answer which is the answer of all Catholic antiquity : ' There was a greater Presence in the midst of them than John, Theodoret, or Cyril, and He carried out His truth and His will in spite of the rebellious natures of His chosen ones.' [2]

---

[1] *Hist Sketches*, vol. iii., p. 345.   [2] *Ibid.*, vol. iii., p. 353.

Cardinal Newman here asserts, what no Catholic ever thought of questioning, that the authority of General Councils is due to the over-ruling guidance of the Holy Ghost, and not to the personal character of those who compose them. And at a time when heretical bishops were intruded in several sees by the civil power, and laboured by the most violent means to diffuse the poison of their heresy, it is not much matter for surprise that one like St. Cyril, of strong temper, and of stern, unbending orthodoxy, should, in dealing with them, have sometimes forgotten the principles of politeness. But, in the eyes of Dr. Salmon, St. Cyril's unpardonable sin is that he was the Pope's Legate at the Council.

Dr. Salmon quotes a well-known text of St. Gregory Nazianzen against the authority of General Councils. It is from the opening of letter forty-two to Procopius : ' If I must write the truth, I am disposed to avoid any assembly of bishops, for of no synod have I seen a profitable end, but rather an addition to, than a diminution, of evils ' (page 297). Now, there is nothing more notorious about the text than that it does not refer to General Councils at all. The only General Council held before this letter was written was that of Nicæa ; and in his twenty-first oration on St. Athanasius he speaks in most enthusiastic terms of that ' Holy Council held at Nicæa, and of the three hundred and eighteen most select men whom the Holy Spirit brought together there.' Surely, then, it is trifling, even with his students, to quote St. Gregory against that Council. Now, the letter was written before the second General Council, the first of Constantinople, and consequently could not refer to that Council either. There are some Protestant writers who say that Gregory's letter was in reply to an intimation to attend the second General Council, and they continue with a strange perversity to quote his letter against it. But, even though this were granted (and it is not granted, for it is not true), the letter could have no reference to General Councils, for the second General Council became general only *in exitu*. No one regarded it as a General Council at its opening. And, therefore, even though Gregory's letter actually referred to it, it would be no evidence against the authority of General Councils. St. Gregory was speaking of a number of synods held in his time, in which the violence of heretical bishops rendered calm discussion impossible, and from which, therefore, no good result could be anticipated. And Dr. Salmon himself supplies abundant proof that St. Gregory was complaining of such synods, and that he had ample cause.

At page 295, he quotes even St. Augustine against the infallible authority of councils. But it is perfectly clear, even from the extract given by Dr. Salmon, that the saint is only anxious to bring his Arian opponent to argue on the common ground of Holy Scriptures ; and hence he says, ' I shall not quote Nicæa against you, for you reject it ; nor you quote Rimini against me, for I reject it ; let us argue on the Scriptures which we both accept.' The extract is from *Liber Contra Man. Ar.*, Lib. 2, c. 14, n. 3, and the opening sentence of the section shows how fully St. Augustine maintained the doctrine which Dr. Salmon told his students he denied !

But Dr. Salmon puts the climax to his arguments against the Infallibility of General Councils, when he compares them to meetings of the Protestant Synod ! ' When an assembly of ourselves meet,' he says, ' together to consult on questions affecting the interests of the Church . . . we do not expect any such assembly to be free from error' (page 285). After this very modest disclaimer on the part of the Doctor, it is difficult to see how General Councils can survive the blow. It is ' the most unkindest cut of all.' As already stated the Infallibility of General Councils *rests* not on the personal character and merits of those who compose them, though very many learned and holy men are always among them, it rests on God's promise to be with His Church in her teaching. Dr. Salmon accepts the doctrine of the early General Councils, not, however, because the Councils were infallible, but because he knows that the doctrine is true. But how does he know this ? The answer is not far to seek, it is the old story, General Councils are not infallible but the Doctor is.

[*To be continued.*]   J. MURPHY.

TRINITY COLLEGE AND THE UNIVERSITY OF DUBLIN

IN the February number of the I. E. RECORD,[1] I dealt at considerable length with some statements, recently made, in which it was denied that there is a distinction of any kind between Trinity College and the University of Dublin. The statements [2] were as follows :—

I can confidently assert that *no such entity as a University of Dublin, distinct from Trinity College,* or independent of it, or outside it, or in any way apart or separate from it, *exists, or ever did exist, legally, constitutionally, or in fact.*

Again :—

The College is thus the University in every particular.

And again, after a quotation from the Act of Union :—

These words are repeated three times in Article Eight, showing that constitutionally *the University* of Trinity College *and the College* of the Holy Trinity of Dublin *are one and the same thing, perfectly identical.*

It would almost seem that the trouble taken, not merely to establish the existence of the distinction between Trinity College and the University of Dublin, but to point out the precise nature of the distinction between them, was taken in vain. Not more than a day or two after the appearance of the article in which all this had been done, the statement was again put forward, and no less emphatically than before,—

That Trinity College is the University of Dublin in every particular, and that the University of Dublin is Trinity College.

Furthermore, it was now alleged that, so far from the assertion of the absolute identity of Trinity College with the University of Dublin being in any way inaccurate, or

---

[1] See I. E. RECORD, Vol. xi., no. 2, Feb. 1902, pages 158-182.
[2] Throughout this paper, the italics in the passages quoted are mine.

indeed in any way open to question, it was a matter definitely established by a solemn judicial decision :—

This assertion is not open to argument or doubt, as *it has been solemnly decided by a court of justice.*

And, as if in final confirmation of the conclusive character of the judicial decision thus brought to bear upon the point,—a decision given by one of the most eminent members of the Irish Judicature, the present Master of the Rolls,—the public were informed that the decision—

Was never appealed from, and now places the matter *beyond argument or criticism.*

As to all this, I do not think it proper, in the circumstances, to content myself with a merely general assurance that the assertion—' Trinity College is the University of Dublin, and the University of Dublin is Trinity College,'— often as it may be reiterated, is simply untenable; that every word written in the February issue of the RECORD in refutation of it stands good; and that, as to the additional assertion now made—that the identity of Trinity College with the University of Dublin is a matter not open even to argument or doubt, a matter solemnly affirmed in a court of justice, by a judicial decision, never appealed from, and consequently placing it beyond argument or criticism,—the attempt thus made to sustain the denial of the existence of a distinction between Trinity College and the University of Dublin is as completely out of joint with fact as I have shown the denial itself to be.

I do not, as I have said, think it proper, in the circumstances, to rest satisfied with this mere broad general statement. The readers of the RECORD have, I feel, a claim upon me to go a step further, and put them in a position to see for themselves how the case really stands as regards the bearing upon it of the judicial decision referred to. I proceed therefore to do so.

At the outset, I may state at once that the judicial decision in question is one that does not in the most remote degree conflict with any statement of mine. It has

nothing whatever to do with any matter ever dealt with
by me. To make this plain, nothing more will be needed
than to show, from the text of the judgment itself,
what the point decided by that judgment really was.

The judgment of the Master of the Rolls, out of which
so much capital has been sought to be made, has been
introduced to public notice in the following terms :—

An old graduate of Trinity College, named Reid, died in 1883,
having by his will bequeathed a large legacy to 'The Corporation
of the University of Dublin.' The question arose, to whom
should it be paid. The Corporation of Trinity College claimed it,
and *declared that they were entitled to it, because Trinity College
is the University of Dublin.*
An action was brought . . in the Court of the present Master
of the Rolls. The plaintiffs were :—' The Provost, Fellows, and
Scholars of Trinity College, Dublin ;' the defendants were . . .
' the Chancellor, Doctors, and Masters of the University of
Dublin.'
As THE PLEADINGS DISCLOSE, the plaintiffs claimed the money,
as being the University,—

Here, for the second time in the course of this short
quotation, we meet with the statement that 'the Provost,
Fellows, and Scholars of Trinity College,'—that is to say,
the Corporation of Trinity College,—claimed Mr. Reid's
bequest on the ground that ' Trinity College is the University of Dublin.' That is a very definite statement. It is
a statement made in a letter addressed to a public newspaper by a professional lawyer. The statement, moreover,
is coupled with a distinct assurance, given to the public
by the writer of the letter, that the claim which he
alleges to have been made on behalf of Trinity College
was made in a particular document,—one of the documents
technically designated ' the pleadings ' in the case.[1]

---

[1] I ought perhaps to explain that the word ' pleadings,' as thus used, has
reference, not to the speeches or other oral statements made by counsel, but
to certain written documents that are lodged in Court. One of these, put in
by the plaintiffs, is designated the ' statement of claim :' another, put in
by the defendants, is designated the ' statement of defence.' In the suit taken
with reference to Mr. Reid's bequest, these two documents constitute the
' pleadings.'
We shall see a good deal more about the pleadings in this case, a little
further on.

I cannot but apprehend that a statement coming before the public with credentials apparently so satisfactory,—especially in view of the volunteered citation of documentary evidence in proof of it,—may, if uncontradicted, be accepted as true. I am obliged, therefore, to say that the statement thus formally made is, nevertheless, quite at variance with fact.

No such assertion as that alleged to have been put forward by the representatives of Trinity College in the suit in question, was ever put forward by them. The documents so strangely referred to as documents in which it is to be found, contain no such assertion. The statement for which the gentleman who has put it forward was unfortunately induced to make himself responsible to the public, is a statement that could not have been made by any person of ordinary intelligence who had read with ordinary care the legal documents referred to.

I shall have something more to say upon this aspect of the case when I come to deal with it in detail. For the present, I resume the quotation :—

As the pleadings disclose, the plaintiffs claimed the money, *as being the University,* and the defendants claimed it on the ground that the University is distinct from the College, and that they represented the University.

The case was argued by eminent counsel on both sides, and on June 2, 1888, the Master of the Rolls delivered an elaborate judgment in which he reviewed the constitution of Trinity College and its University from its creation under the charter of Elizabeth to the date of the judgment . . .

Then his lordship decreed that *the money bequeathed to the University of Dublin must be paid to Trinity College, the two things being inseparable and indistinguishable* . . .

The judgment of the Master of the Rolls . . . never was appealed from, and now places the matter beyond argument or criticism . . .

The next literary critic who desires to prove that there is a University of Dublin distinct from Trinity College may save himself the trouble of reading ancient history by reading one of the most erudite judgments ever delivered at the Four Courts.

I have reserved for separate quotation the following further statement. It is a statement that could hardly fail to inspire full confidence in the accuracy of the account

given of the judgment of the Master of the Rolls in the
passages I have just quoted. Before transcribing it, I may,
however, state that it presents for consideration an aspect of
the whole case which, I have no doubt, will seem to
many readers of this paper somewhat peculiar, not to say
inexplicable. The statement is as follows :—

It [the judgment of the Master of the Rolls in the case
referred to] is *public property*, and *can be read by any person*. I
have given *the exact date*, to make it *easy of reference*.

All this might well seem,—as, I have to confess, it
seemed to me when I first read it,—somewhat superfluous.
It might fairly be assumed, one would think, that a judgment such as this judgment of the Master of the Rolls was
described to be, was not unlikely to be found where any
such judgment would naturally be looked for, namely,
in the *Law Reports* of the time. It was, we were
assured, an elaborate and erudite judgment. No important judgment of the eminent judge by whom
it was delivered, could fail to be so. Then, we were told,
it judicially decided a matter that unquestionably is of
singular interest, as well as of great public importance,—
the actual position of Trinity College in relation to the
University of Dublin, and of the University of Dublin
in relation to Trinity College. Furthermore, as was
alleged, it decided all this in such a way as to show
that the College and the University are not two things
but one,—so that all the supposed legal lore of at
least one great lawyer, Isaac Butt, to say nothing of
others, in regard to the distinction between the College
and the University, was nothing better than empty
folly. The decision, we were moreover assured, was of
such a nature as to place this matter, once for all, beyond
the reach of ' argument,' ' doubt,' or ' criticism.' The
volumes of the *Law Reports* for the time in question are so easy of access that the assurance elaborately
given, that a judgment of such exceptional importance was
' public property,' and could ' be read by any person,'
might well seem superfluous.

But, superfluous or not, the assurance was at all

events a welcome one. For, whatever might be obscure in the case, one thing was plain. No one who had even an elementary idea of the points to which, in a suit for the interpretation of a will such as that in question, a judge would naturally address himself, could read the statement I have quoted, as to the point decided by the judgment referred to, without desiring to have some further information on the subject. An offhand assertion that, in interpreting the will of an individual testator, a judge of great eminence undertook to decide, and actually decided, that Trinity College and the University of Dublin are one and the same thing,—even although the assertion was made by a lawyer, and was backed up, as the assertion in question was, by a distinct reference to specified legal documents,—could hardly claim to be entitled to acceptance until the documents thus specified, and the report of the judgment itself, had been examined.

The date of the judgment was considerately given, 'to make it easy of reference.' The testing of the correctness of the account given of the point at issue in the case, and of the decision given upon it, seemed then to be a very simple matter. Any reported judgment can be found with ease by means of the well-arranged Indexes of a volume or two of the *Reports*,—or, if necessary, in the last resort, by means of the Digests, in which the various items of the Indexes to the volumes of a series extending over a number of years are arranged in alphabetical order throughout.

I have here to touch upon a somewhat personal aspect of the case. I happen to be not unacquainted with the general arrangement of the *Reports*. Having taken it for granted that I should be able to find without difficulty the report of the important judgment in question, I thought it somewhat strange that an examination of the volume of the *Reports* for 1888, and subsequently a search through some later volumes of the series, failed to disclose the faintest indication that any question as to the relation of Trinity College to the University of Dublin, or as to their identity, or the distinction between them, had been decided, or had even come before an Irish Court for decision.

The explanation, however, of my failure,—an explanation arrived at with definite certainty only after reference to some legal friends of more than ordinary experience,—was simple enough. This judgment, represented as being of such rare interest, and of such exceptional importance, is not to be found in the *Reports* at all.

Further investigation led to the discovery that a printed report of the judgment is preserved in the Library of Trinity College. Other copies, I must presume, are to be found elsewhere: otherwise it would not be easy to see how the statement that the judgment is 'public property' and may be 'read by any person,' could have been made.

But, let this be as it may, it is hard to see how the mention of the date of the judgment, as the only clue given to facilitate reference to the report, was anything but misleading. A great deal of time and labour that might have been more profitably employed would have been spared if the plain statement had been made,—not that this judgment of the Master of the Rolls is 'public property,' or that it can be 'read by any person,' or that it was delivered on the 2nd of June, 1888, and so can easily be referred to,—but that a copy of the judgment is to be found, in whatever place, really accessible to the public, a copy of it is to be found in point of fact.

I am assuming—I trust not over-confidently—that the statement publicly made as to this judgment being 'public property,' is true. I am consequently assuming that a copy of the judgment is to be found in some place where it may be 'read by any person' who may not happen to have the privilege of admission to the Library of Trinity College. I may add, however, that, as I have ascertained on inquiry, nothing is known of this important judgment, or of any report of it, either at Messrs. Hodges, Figgis, and Co.'s, the publishers to the University, or in the

Library of King's Inns. or even in the National Library of Ireland

I have not been able to have the report of the judgment searched for elsewhere than in the places I have just now mentioned. My only means therefore of getting access to it was by having the twenty-six pages of the report of it that is preserved in the Library of Trinity College trans cribed for me there by two friends, who, with very great kindness, undertook the task. They did so in order that I might not be left without a copy of this judgment with which I was so plainly called upon to deal,—publicly stated, as it had been, that the judgment was legally con- clusive against all that I had written in the last issue of the RECORD, the public being at the same time informed that the judgment was 'public property,' and could be 'read by any person.'

At all events, I have a full transcript of the judgment before me now. Also, as 'the pleadings' in the case have been so confidently referred to, it is satisfactory to know that, although the case in question was decided more than thirteen years ago, the documents appealed to are not at all beyond the range of inspection. Every such document is placed on official record, and I have before me, as I write, an officially certified copy of 'the pleadings' at both sides in this case—the 'state- ment of claim' on the one hand, and the 'statement of defence' on the other. Thus I am in a position to show up in full detail the very peculiar and very question- able way in which the case, and the judgment given in it, have recently been put before the public.

We have seen that the suit brought into Court, was for the judicial interpretation of a will. The will was a very peculiar one. The testator, as it appeared, intended to leave a considerable amount of property to the authorities of Trinity College for certain specified purposes, including a gift of books to the Library, and the establishment of a Professorship and of some Sizarships. But in making his will, he mixed up 'the University of

Dublin.' 'the Corporation of the University of Dublin,'
'Trinity College, Dublin,' and 'the Board of the University,'
to such an extent that even the Master of the Rolls had no
little trouble in undoing the tangled knot.

1. There was a bequest of books to 'The Librarian for
the time being, of the University of Dublin,'—the books to be
divided by the Librarian, at his discretion, between 'The
Library of the University' and 'The lending Library of
Trinity College.'

2. There was a bequest to 'The Corporation of the
University of Dublin for the endowment of a Professorship,
the duties of which were to be assigned by 'the Board of the
University.'

3. There was another bequest to 'The Corporation of
the University of Dublin' for the establishment of certain
Sizarships in Trinity College,—the conditions to be determined by 'the Board of the said University,' and a portion
of the fund to be applied to rewarding schoolmasters for
preparing students 'for the Sizarship examinations of the
University.'

The point to be determined was to whom the second and
third of these bequests were to go. The question to be adjudicated upon, however, was not, whether the Library of
Trinity College is the Library of the College or the Library
of the University,—nor whether the Board of Trinity College,
consisting of the Provost of the College and the seven Senior
Fellows of the College, is the Board of the College or the
Board of the University,—nor whether the College examinations for Sizarships are College examinations or University
examinations,—nor whether the Corporation of Trinity
College is, or is not, the Corporation of the University of
Dublin,—nor whether Trinity College is, or is not, the
University of Dublin.

None of those questions arose in the case. The question
that arose in it was of a widely different nature. Mr.
Reid, the testator, whose executors awaited the judgment
of the Court, had used in his will the expression, 'the
Corporation of the University,' and the question was *what
body he, Mr. Reid, meant to designate by that expression.*

Mr. Reid's bequest was claimed, on the one hand, by the 'Provost, Fellows, and Scholars,'—in other words, the Corporation,—of Trinity College. It was claimed, on the other hand, by the Senate of the University of Dublin. To which of these bodies had Mr. Reid intended his bequest to go? That was the point to be decided in the case.

This may be the most convenient place to dispose of the extraordinary series of assertions already referred to,—that the case adjudicated upon by the Master of the Rolls was a case of a bequest to the University; that Trinity College claimed the money 'as being the University,' and that the Master of the Rolls upheld the claim of the College, judicially deciding that 'Trinity College is the University of Dublin in every particular.'

Now, in the first place, neither Trinity College, nor its legal representatives, took up any such position as that the College is the University of Dublin.

And, secondly, the Master of the Rolls—far from deciding that Trinity College is the University of Dublin—on the contrary, as we shall see, distinguished, in this very judgment, between the College and the University, in the clearest possible words.

For the present, I shall deal only with the first of these two points. Trinity College did not, as alleged, claim the bequest on the ground that the College was the University. It has, as we have seen, been publicly stated, not only that this claim was made, but that the claim is disclosed in the pleadings. That statement is wholly incorrect. No such claim was made. No such claim, therefore, is disclosed in the pleadings. On the contrary, the 'statement of claim' distinguishes clearly between the College and the University throughout.

The claim made by the College, as the 'statement of claim' itself shows, was not that Trinity College is the University of Dublin, or that the Board of Trinity College is the Board of the University. As set out in the pleadings, the claim was that, there being no such body, strictly speaking, as 'the Board of the University,' the words 'Board of the University'

in the will must be taken to refer to the Board of
Trinity College,—this being 'the only Body called or
known as "the Board," either in the College or in the
University.' And so on of the rest.

The 'statement of claim' put before the Court on behalf
of Trinity College is perfectly definite : as the following
summary of it shows, there is nothing stated in it that is
not indisputable fact. After setting out Mr. Reid's will,
a voluminous document, the statement recounts, in legal
terminology, the following facts :—

There is no such Body, strictly speaking, as ' the Board of the
University :' there is *the Board of Trinity College*, and there is
the Senate of the University.

Trinity College is *the only College in the University* : by Letters
Patent of Elizabeth and Charles I., the College is incorporated
under the name of the Provost, Fellows and Scholars of the College
of the Holy and Undivided Trinity of Queen Elizabeth, near
Dublin, the Plaintiffs in this action.

The Provost and Senior Fellows of the College constitute the
Governing Body of the College : they are known as the Board of
Trinity College. There is no other Body called or known as ' the
Board,' *either in the College or University*.

The defendants in the action, the Senate of the University,
were incorporated by Letters Patent of Queen Victoria, under the
title of the Chancellor, Doctors, and Masters of the University of
Dublin. These Letters Patent are dated 24th July, 1857.

The testator, Mr. Reid, was educated in Trinity College,
where he took his degree of M.A. : he was called to the Irish Bar.
He went to Bombay in 1853 [the date is important], and never
returned to Ireland.

All the endowments by which *the University of Dublin* is
sustained are vested in the Plaintiffs, and are *managed by the
Board of Trinity College*.

Until 1874, when a new Body, known as the Council, was
constituted by Letters Patent, the appointment of the Professors
in the University was vested in the Board. It is now, with
certain exceptions, vested in the Council, subject to the approval
of the Board. Certain other functions (specified), previously
discharged by the Board, require, since 1874, the sanction of
both Board and Council.

The Council, as constituted by the Letters Patent of 1874,
consists of the Provost, or the Vice-Provost, of Trinity College,
and sixteen other members elected out of the Members of the
Senate of the University.

The *Board of Trinity College elect* to all the existing *Sizarships, after the usual examination of candidates*.

Beyond the usual formal statements, as to the death of the testator, the grant of probate to his executors, the amount of property bequeathed, and so forth, the statement of claim contains nothing more.

This, I trust, sufficiently disposes of the unaccountable assertion that:—

As THE PLEADINGS DISCLOSE, the plaintiffs claimed the money, *as being the University.*

At the other side, the case of the defendants, the Senate of the University, came simply to this: that the Senate was incorporated under the title, ' The Chancellor, Doctors, and Masters of the University of Dublin;' and that the body thus incorporated was the one designated by Mr. Reid, ' The Corporation of the University of Dublin.'

The case thus lay between two corporate bodies, the Corporation of Trinity College and the Corporation of the Senate of the University, each claiming to be the Corporation to which Mr. Reid intended his bequest to go.

As the Master of the Rolls expressed it:—

This is a case of latent [1] ambiguity, and in such cases the rule is (when the fact of ambiguity is shown), first to see whether the other words of the will afford grounds sufficient to enable us to decide between the two conflicting bodies, and, if not, then to admit extrinsic evidence.

And again, towards the close of the judgment:—

In my opinion, treating the question as one *of intention,* the testator has clearly shown on the face of the will itself that *what he meant by ' The Corporation of the University of Dublin'* was the Corporation of Trinity College.

I am bound *to give effect to that intention* unless it is encountered by some rule of law.

At this point, it may be well, for the information of those who may not otherwise have an opportunity of making themselves acquainted with the provisions of the law

---

[1] It is fortunately unnecessary to enter upon an explanation of the technical distinction between 'latent' ambiguity and 'patent' ambiguity. It is sufficient to know that the ambiguity in Mr. Reid's bequests was an ambiguity that was to be dealt with by the Court in the manner so clearly expressed in the extract from the Master of the Rolls' judgment, quoted in the text above.

relating to such matters, to indicate, as briefly as possible, to what extent, and under what conditions, the personal intention of a testator is taken by a court of law as determining the true interpretation of his will.

The fundamental principle to be followed in the interpretation of a will is essentially different from that which regulates the interpretation, for instance, of a deed. In a deed, every phrase and every word has to be construed with technical accuracy, without reference to the personal intentions of the parties to the deed, however clearly ascertained those intentions may be. It is quite otherwise with a will. As to this, the common-sense rule of the common law is stated as follows in a manual of authority :—

> In construing wills, the Courts have always borne in mind that a testator may not have had the same opportunity of legal advice in drawing his will as he would have had in executing a deed. And the first great maxim of construction accordingly is, that the intention of the testator ought to be observed.[1]

This explains how it was that the principal point to be adjudicated upon in the suit in the Rolls Court between the Senate of the University of Dublin and the Board of Trinity College, was, whether, by the complicated phraseology which he employed in his will, Mr. Reid,— the testator whose will was in question—*meant to designate the College* or *meant to designate the University.*

There is, however, an important point to be noted here. It would be by no means correct to state without qualification that the ascertained intention of a testator is, in all cases, to determine the interpretation of his will. Such a statement, indeed, would be very far from the truth. The intention to which effect will be given must be one that can be gathered from the will itself. In other words, it must be an intention in some way expressed in the will,—that is to say, the will must be so worded as to be capable of bearing the meaning that has to be put upon it in order to give effect to the testator's ascertained intention.

---

[1] Williams. *Principles of the Law of Real Property* (17th edition). London, 1892, page 229.

Moreover, a Court is by no means left to its own uncontrolled discretion in deciding whether an expression in a will is capable of being construed so as to give effect to the ascertained intention of a testator. It would not, for instance, depend upon the merely personal view of a Judge whether such an expression as 'The Corporation of the University of Dublin,' could be taken by him as meaning 'The Corporation of Trinity College,' or whether such an expression as 'The Board of the University,' could be taken by him as meaning 'The Board of Trinity College,' on its being ascertained that those were the meanings which a testator personally intended to convey by the expressions in question. To quote again from the manual quoted from a few pages back—

The decisions of the Courts in pursuing this maxim [that the intention of the testator ought to be observed], have given rise to a number of subsidiary rules, to be applied in making out the testator's intention; and, when doubts occur, these rules are always made use of to determine the meaning; so that the true legal construction of a will is occasionally different from that which would occur to the mind of an unprofessional reader.[1]

As the same writer goes on to explain,—

Certainty cannot be obtained without uniformity, nor uniformity without rule. Rules, therefore, have been found to be absolutely necessary; and the indefinite maxim of observing the intention, is now largely qualified by the numerous decisions which have been made respecting all manner of doubtful points, each of which decisions forms and confirms a rule of construction, to be attended to whenever any similar difficulty occurs.[2]

Now it is a fundamental rule in this matter that an expression which, from usage or otherwise, has one definite meaning, and one definite meaning only, cannot have a different meaning put upon it by a Court for the sake of carrying out the ascertained intention of a testator. A bequest, for instance, made to St. Vincent's Hospital, Dublin, would not, in any circumstances, be awarded by a Court to the Mater Misericordiæ Hospital, Dublin. In such

---

[1] Williams. *Principles of the Law of Real Property* (17th edition). London, 1892, page 250.
[2] *Ibid.*

a case, evidence as to the intention of the testator,—evidence
for instance, that he named the one hospital instead of the
other, simply by mistake,—would not be admissible.

Thus, in a case in which a testator devised to certain
trustees all his estates in the County of Limerick, and it
was proved that he had no estates in that county, but
had estates in the adjoining County of Clare, it was
decided in the House of Lords by Lord Brougham, then
Lord Chancellor, assisted by Chief Justice Tindal, and by
Lord Lyndhurst, Chief Baron, that evidence to prove that
the testator intended to devise his Clare estates, and that
the word Limerick was inserted by mistake for Clare, was
not admissible.[1]

This rule, of course, determines the construction of a
bequest in which a word occurs which has, by statute, or
in any equivalent way, acquired a definite meaning. Thus,
for instance,—the word ' acre ' having a statutory meaning,—it has been decided that evidence was not admissible
to prove that a testator who devised forty-five acres of
land in Ireland, meant Irish, not statute, acres.[2]

In the case of Mr. Reid's bequests, there was, as we
shall see, no real room for doubt that by the words ' the
University of Dublin' he meant to designate Trinity
College. But before the Judge could go into any inquiry
as to what Mr. Reid's intentions were, he had to ascertain
whether there was room for any such inquiry, as there
certainly would not have been, if, in the case of
Trinity College and of the University of Dublin, the
expression 'the University' had been determined by
statute, or by unvaried usage, to designate only the
University, as distinct from the College. As is clearly
expressed in the passage already quoted from the judgment,[3]
it is only ' when the fact of ambiguity is shown,' that the
rule about seeking, in other parts of the will or elsewhere,
for evidence of the testator's intention can be applied.

---

[1] See Jarman on Wills (5th edition, London, 1893), vol. i. page 412.
[2] *Ibid.*, page 392, footnote (c).
[3] See *ante*, page 265.

Thus, as the Master of the Rolls pointed out in his judgment,—

> If the gift had been to 'the Senate,' or to 'the Chancellor, Doctors, or Masters,' there would have been no question, since, whatever belief one might have had of the intention of the testator, the body would have been unmistakably defined.

No one indeed could assert that, in the case of Trinity College and the University of Dublin, those two designations have been uniformly and consistently used to designate, respectively, the College and the University. I have had occasion elsewhere[1] to call attention to the fact that, whilst, in a number of Acts of Parliament, the College and the University are clearly and sharply distinguished, there is at least one Act in which the two expressions 'the College,' and 'the University,' are plainly used to designate the same body. A similar absence of uniformity in usage is to be observed,—as I have also had occasion to point out,—in the case of some of the Letters Patent or Charters referring to the College and the University.[2]

The looseness—to use the Master of the Rolls' expression—with which the expressions the 'College' and the 'University' have thus been used both by the Crown and by the Legislature, was clearly brought out by him in an elaborate analysis of the earlier College Charters, the Act of Union, and the Irish Reform Act of 1834.

The incorporation effected by the Letters Patent of 1857 was, in his opinion,—

> Not the incorporation of the University of Dublin, but of its Senate merely.

Still, as he expressed it,—

> There are two bodies in existence [the plaintiffs and the defendants in the case, the Corporation of Trinity College on the one hand, and the Corporation of the Senate of the University on

---

[1] In a letter published in the *Freeman's Journal* of the 6th of January, 1902.
[2] See the letter referred to in the preceding footnote.

the other] to either of which [in the will in question] the designation of ' Corporation of the University of Dublin ' may refer, and to one or other of which it must refer ; not with strict accuracy in either case perhaps, but *sufficiently clearly to enable a gift to take effect in favour of whichever is in fact meant.*

In other words, there was no such unvaried and consistent use of the expressions as would stand in the way of the carrying out of Mr. Reid's intention in favour of either body, if his intention as to which of the two he meant to make his legatee could be ascertained.

The question being thus reduced to a question as to the personal intention of Mr. Reid, the claims of the different bodies whom he might be supposed to have intended to designate had to be considered.

First, the Master of the Rolls dealt with the body known as 'the Council.' In the course of the proceedings in Court, it had been suggested that this might be taken to be the body which Mr. Reid had designated ' The Board of the University.'

' The Council' is a body of somewhat recent erection. It was brought into existence by Letters Patent of the late Queen, dated November 4, 1874. In relation to the distinction between the College and the University, these Letters Patent of 1874 are of considerable importance. They distinguish clearly between the two bodies, the College and the University. Having done so, they vest in a ' Council,' to be elected from amongst the members of the Senate of the University,—and, to a certain specified extent, by the members of the Senate, voting as members of it,—certain powers previously vested in the Board of Trinity College alone. The following extracts from the Letters Patent may usefully be transcribed here :—

Whereas the regulations of the Studies, Lectures, and Examinations *in our said College of the Holy and Undivided Trinity,* near Dublin, preliminary to obtaining Degrees in Arts or Faculties *in our University of Dublin,* and the appointment and election of Professors, have been vested in *the Provost and Senior Fellows of our said College.* . . .

And whereas it has been represented to us that it is desirable that a Council, to be constituted . . as hereafter mentioned, should . . have a share in the regulation of the Studies, Lectures, and Examinations of *our said College*, and in the appointment and election of Professors, and the regulation of the tenure of office and the duties of said Professors. . .

And whereas the Provost and Senior Fellows *of our said College* and the Senate *of our said University* have given their assent to the constitution . . of such Council, it is therefore our will and pleasure that a Council be constituted . . which shall consist of the following members.

The Letters Patent then go on to provide for the election of a Council, consisting of 'the Provost *of our said College*,' and of sixteen members. These members are—

To be elected out of the Members of the Senate *of our said University.*

Regulations for the holding of the first election were to be framed,—not by the Provost of the College, but by—

The Chancellor, or, in his absence, the Vice-Chancellor, *of our said University.*

Power was also given to 'the Provost and Senior Fellows and Council,' acting jointly, to alter the rules regarding the election of the Members of the Council, with, however, the proviso—

That no such . . variations shall have any force or efficacy until they shall have received the sanction of *the Senate of the University* in congregation lawfully assembled.

With certain specified exceptions, the nomination to all Professorships is then given to 'the Council,' subject to the approval of the Provost and Senior Fellows of the College. But the Provost and Senior Fellows cannot hinder the appointment of a Professor nominated by the Senate, except on grounds judged *by the Chancellor of the University* to be sufficient.

Before the establishment of the Council, the existence of the University, as distinct from the College, had, of course, been fully recognised by law. As distinct from the College, the University had, for instance, the capacity of receiving within it one or more Colleges,

other than Trinity College,—such as the 'other Colleges
or Halls,' contemplated by the Charter of James I.,—
the College, 'to be of the University of Dublin,' and
'to be called by the name of the King's College,' the
erection of which was provided for by the Act of 1667,—
and the College, to be 'a member of the University of
Dublin,' the erection of which was contemplated by the
Act of 1793.

But, distinct as Trinity College and the University of
Dublin undoubtedly were, there was, until a comparatively
recent time, but little that could be regarded as a visible
indication of the distinction between them. This was no
less so, as regards the students and other residents in the
College, than as regards the public outside. As—in speaking
of the state of things in the College when Mr. Reid was
a student there, 'long before the Senate was incorporated
or the Council heard of,'—the Master of the Rolls
felicitously expressed it, the College and the University
were, at that time, 'inseparably and indistinguishably
blended.'[1] But the establishment of the Council made a
striking change. The members of the Council are elected
exclusively from amongst the members of the Senate of the
University, and a specified section of them are elected
by the members of the Senate of the University, voting
as members of that Senate. Thus, through its Senate, the
University, as distinct from either the Corporation of Trinity
College, or the Board of Trinity College, became a tangible
reality in connection with the College and its educational
work.

The suggestion that the expression, 'The Board of the
University,' in Mr. Reid's will, might mean the Council,

---

[1] One of the strangest of the many strange statements recently made in
reference to the Master of the Rolls' judgment is that in which this felicitous
phrase, admirably expressive of the close combination of the two bodies, the
College and the University, is represented as a decision that the University
is the College, and that the College is the University!

Starting from the postulate that the description of one institution as
the parent of another, Collegium, Mater Universitatis, is only an expressive
way of saying that the two institutions are one and the same, we must, of
course, be prepared to find ourselves brought face to face with some eccentric
results.

was set aside by the Master of the Rolls as quite unten-able. Of the Council he said :—

I need not allude in detail to its constitution ; suffice it to say it is nowhere called the Board in any official document.

And again, towards the close of the judgment :—

'The Board' has a well-defined meaning in Trinity College. It means the Provost and Senior Fellows. It was contended . . that the word is synonymous with 'Council.' In my opinion the testator *did not mean* to designate *a body which was not consti-tuted till long after his connection with Trinity College ceased.* The contest here is between the College and the Senate.

In the second place, the Master of the Rolls took up the case of the defendants, 'the Chancellor, Doctors, and Masters of the University of Dublin,'—in other words, the Senate of the University.

The question being as to the testator's intention, the case of the Senate was an essentially weak one. The Senate,—as I explained in my paper in the last number of the RECORD,—was not incorporated until 1857, years after the testator had left the College and University. There was no reason to suppose that Mr. Reid, living, as he did, away in India, had ever even heard of the incorporation of the Senate. At all events, there was nothing whatever to support the view that the Senate was the body *which he meant to designate* by the expression, 'The Corporation of the University of Dublin.' Besides, as the Master of the Rolls pointed out, that was not even a technically correct designation of the Senate. Speaking of the Letters Patent of 1857, by which—

The Senate or Congregation of the University of Dublin, consisting of the Chancellor, Doctors in the several faculties, and Masters of Arts of the said University—

had been erected into a body corporate—

under the name, style, and title, of the Chancellor, Doctors, and Masters of the University of Dublin,—

the Master of the Rolls considered that this was an incorporation, not of the University of Dublin, but of its

Senate.[1] Neither on the ground, then, of strict legal accuracy in designation, nor on the ground that Mr. Reid, by the expression 'The Corporation of the University,' could be held to have meant to designate the Senate, could judgment be given in favour of that body.

The Senate of the University being thus excluded, the only remaining body that Mr. Reid could be supposed to have intended to designate by the expressions in his will was Trinity College. We are now nearing the close of this interesting judgment, and we reach the point at which, as I have mentioned in an earlier part of this paper, the Master of the Rolls, so far from having decided that Trinity College and the University of Dublin are 'inseparable and indistinguishable,' or—

That Trinity College is the University of Dublin in every particular, and that the University of Dublin is Trinity College,—

on the contrary, most formally and expressly distinguished between them.

I quote from the judgment. Coming to his final judicial interpretation of Mr. Reid's intention as expressed in the will, the Master of the Rolls said :—

In the words of the will itself are to be found indications which leave to my mind no doubt as to what his intention was . .
First, he bequeaths all the books which he may die possessed

---

[1] Although the point stands quite apart from any question dealt with either in this or in my former paper, it is interesting to note that, on the question described in my article in the February number of the RECORD (page 177) as a lawyers' question, pure and simple, with which I was not in any way concerned, the Master of the Rolls held that, prior to the Letters Patent of 1857, the Corporation of Trinity College was the only Corporation connected with either the College or the University.

This was the view taken also by that eminent lawyer, the late Baron Fitzgerald (see RECORD, ibid., page 176.) The Master of the Rolls, after expressing his view on this point, added :—'It cannot, therefore, admit of doubt that, prior to the Letters Patent of Queen Victoria [A.D. 1857], a gift to "The Corporation of the University of Dublin" would have meant a gift to Trinity College, Dublin, and could have meant nothing else.'

It may also be worth noting that, as is quite clear from several passages of the judgment itself, the attention of the Master of the Rolls, strange to say, was not called to the important legal opinion of Sir Joseph Napier.

of 'to the Librarian, for the time being, of the University of Dublin.'

There is no *Librarian of the University of Dublin*, or of the Senate of the University of Dublin. There is a *Librarian of Trinity College*.

No Librarian of the University of Dublin, and yet a Librarian of Trinity College! These strikingly definite statements, let it be remembered, occur in the judgment which, as the public have been most formally assured, decided—

That Trinity College is the University of Dublin in every particular, and the University of Dublin is Trinity College.

Notwithstanding Mr. Reid's obvious mistake in the designation of the person to whom he wished to bequeath his books in trust for the College Library,—notwithstanding even the fact that in the bequest itself he not merely called that Library 'the Library of the University,' but distinguished it by this designation from another library, the lending Library, which he properly designated 'of Trinity College,'—no question was raised, or could be raised, as to this bequest. *Falsa demonstratio non nocet cum de corpore constat.*

So much for the bequest to the Library. Then as to the bequest for the Professorship, the Master of the Rolls said:—

Secondly, the testator bequeaths his shares or stock . . . to his trustees for the purpose of paying the same to the Corporation of the University of Dublin, to endow in the said University a Professorship . . provided that it shall be lawful for the Board of the University to assign any other duties . . to be performed by the said Professor . .

The word Board has a well-defined meaning in Trinity College. It means the Provost and Senior Fellows. It was contended . . that the word is synonymous with Council. In my opinion the testator did not mean to designate a body which was not constituted till long after his connection with Trinity College ceased ; and his use of the words 'Board of the University' affords *a key to what he meant by* ' the Corporation of the University of Dublin.'

Here again, as we see, the question was, What body did Mr. Reid *mean* to designate when he *said* 'The Corporation of the University of Dublin.'

As to the bequest for the establishment of additional Sizarships, the words of the Master of the Rolls were especially pointed and emphatic. He said :—

> Thirdly, the testator bequeaths his Three per cent. Consolidated Bank Annuities to the Corporation of the University of Dublin, ' to found in Trinity College, Dublin, additional Sizarships . . and the Board of the said University shall determine the annual stipend to be allowed . . and I empower the same Board to apply the residue . . to such schoolmasters . . as [under certain conditions] shall undertake to prepare . . a certain number of boys . . for the Sizarship Examinations of the University . .
> There are *no Sizarships in the University*. They are *in the College*.
> There are *no Sizarship examinations of the University*. They are held *in, and by, Trinity College*.

No Sizarships in the University, and yet Sizarships in the College ! No Sizarship examinations of the University, and yet Sizarship examinations held in, and by, Trinity College ! And we find all this emphatically stated in the judgment which, it was sought to lead the public to believe, had decided—

> That Trinity College is the University of Dublin in every particular, and that the University of Dublin is Trinity College.

But this line of comment, necessary in the circumstances, is becoming monotonous. I will only add that it was immediately after the words just quoted, relating to Mr. Reid's expression, 'the Sizarship examinations of the University,' that the Master of the Rolls concluded his judgment with the following pithy summing up of the case, the two first sentences of which I have quoted in an earlier portion of this article, as a luminous introduction to all that was to follow :—

> In my opinion, treating the question as one of *intention*, the testator has clearly shown on the face of the will itself that *what he meant by the Corporation of the University of Dublin* was the Corporation of Trinity College.
> I am bound *to give effect to that intention* unless it is encountered by some rule of law.
> I have already shown,—at, I fear, too great length,—that the

phrase ' Corporation of the University of Dublin ' has *no such defined meaning* as, in a case like the present, *excluding all enquiry as to particular intention ;* and I have therefore no hesitation in pronouncing a decree for the plaintiffs.

And this is the end of the case in which the issue was represented to be, whether Trinity College is, or is not, the University of Dublin ! And this is the judgment which was represented as having decided that Trinity College is the University of Dublin in every particular, and that the University of Dublin is Trinity College !

The importance of the question dealt with in this paper is manifest. Just now, a determined effort is being made to secure for a temporising policy in the matter of University education in Ireland, whatever Catholic support can be secured for it. It ought, we are told, to be recommended to the Royal Commission now inquiring into the subject, that the Commission, as the outcome of its inquiry, should report in favour of the establishment of a College for Catholics in the so-called ' University,' known as the Royal University of Ireland.

In justification of the policy thus suggested, it is proclaimed that the establishment of a Catholic University, or the establishment even of what has come to be known as a ' University for Catholics,' is now quite out of the question. The Catholics of Ireland are told, then, that instead of looking for the establishment of a new University for themselves, or of looking for equality with their Protestant fellow-countrymen on any other line,—by means, for instance, of the foundation, in the University of Dublin, of a Catholic College equal in all respects to the present solitary College of that University, Trinity College,—they will better consult for their own interests if they meekly accept as inevitable a further postponement, for some indefinite time, of the establishment of religious equality in the matter of higher education in Ireland, and beg of the Royal Commission to report in favour of the establishment of a College for them, side by side with the Queen's Colleges, in the Royal ' University' !

To secure some foothold for this temporising policy, no stone is being left unturned. Thus the public have recently been told that one road to equality, hitherto supposed to have been open, is hopelessly blocked by a definite judgment of a court of law, solemnly deciding that there is no such thing as a University of Dublin distinct from Trinity College. If this were so, the idea of establishing in the University of Dublin a College for Catholics, distinct from Trinity College, and on a footing in the University in all respects equal to that of Trinity College, would be a mere chimera. There would be an end, then, of one possible project, as to which the Bishops of Ireland have publicly declared themselves satisfied that, under it, religious equality could be fully secured, and every religious interest fully safeguarded.

It seemed well worth taking the necessary pains to show the utter irrelevancy of the appeal to the judicial decision by which, as the public were led to believe, progress in that particular direction had been proved to be impossible. One thing has now been made plain. There is no judicial decision to the effect alleged.

Will, then, the attempt that has been made to represent that one particular line of settlement of the Irish University question on the basis of religious equality lies outside the sphere of legal possibility, be persisted in? If it be, some other method of furthering it will have to be tried than that of appealing to a judgment which, as has now been conclusively shown, decided nothing whatever as to the relation, whether of identity or of distinction, between Trinity College and the University of Dublin, and was simply a judicial interpretation of what a certain Mr. Reid meant by two or three puzzling expressions in some clumsily drafted clauses of his will.

✠ W. J. W.

𝕹otes and ℚueries

LITURGY

THE SEPARATE CONSECRATION OF CHALICE OR PATEN

REV. DEAR SIR,—Possibly you may find space to clear up a perplexity, which is mine to-day and to-morrow might be another's.

It has happened more than once that I have been obliged to get a chalice or paten re-gilt.

I am told that I ought not to ask a bishop to re-consecrate either of these articles separately, as the separate consecration of chalice only or paten only would involve a mutilated ceremony not contemplated by the rubrics of the Pontifical.

What am I to do? Should I be justified in sending for consecration the newly-gilt paten, together with a chalice already in use, which does not itself need consecration.—Yours faithfully,

γαμμα.

The section of the Pontifical which describes the ceremony of the consecration of the sacred vessels does not *expressly* arrange for the separate consecration of a chalice or a paten. The ceremony is, in substance, as follows :—

The bishop, having said the *Adjutorium nostrum*, etc., reads, for the consecration of the paten, an invitatory and prayer, and then anoints the paten with chrism, using the *form*. He next reads, for the consecration of the chalice, an invitatory and prayer, and anoints the chalice, using a form. Lastly, he says a single prayer over both, and sprinkles both with Holy Water.

It will be seen that the only thing common to the consecration of the two are the *Adjutorium*, the final prayer, and the sprinkling with Holy Water.

In case of the separate consecration of a chalice or paten, the procedure would be very simple :—

Say *Adjutorium*, observe the rite given above for the *one* sacred vessel to be consecrated, and sprinkle with Holy

Water after having said the final prayer with the necessary change. The only words that require a slight and obvious change are ' *Hoc vasculum et Patena sanctificentur* . . . . . *efficiantur.*'
Is this lawful ?

We think it is. The only alternative is that mentioned by our correspondent—to present, for re-consecration, with the unconsecrated vessel, a vessel which is already consecrated and which is not supposed to have lost its consecration. We can remember no precedent for this alternative in any part of the Liturgy, whereas such an arrangement as we have described is quite usual. One instance, which is perfectly analogous as regards the point under consideration, is the case of the blessing of Holy Water. The *Ordo ad Faciendam*, etc., prescribes the blessing of salt ; now the Sacred Congregation of Rites [1] declared that salt need not be blessed each time, but that salt blessed on a previous occasion may be used, of course without being re-blessed. In the same way, a chalice or paten may be consecrated separately ; though there is not an *express* Rubric to this effect, the Pontifical does *implicitly* contemplate it. The facility of separating the two ceremonies seems to indicate this intention.

Other examples may be adduced, such as the conferring of Orders in various combinations for which the Pontifical does not expressly provide, and for which, consequently, certain changes have to be made.

As regards practice, we have ascertained from a prelate that in some instances in which he was asked to consecrate a paten without a chalice, or a chalice without a paten, it never occurred to him to doubt that the ceremonies could be detached. The improbability of doubting is the only reason that we can suggest for the fact that this question is not even raised, as far as we can see, in any one of the many authors, who treat of the consecration of. chalices and patens.

---

[1] Dec. Auth., 8 Apr., 1713.

MASS ON HOLY THURSDAY, WITHOUT MASS ON GOOD
FRIDAY AND HOLY SATURDAY

REV. DEAR SIR,—You would very much oblige me by answering
the question : May a Priest say Mass on Holy Thursday, without
doing so on Good Friday and Holy Saturday?—Yours, etc.,
P. H.

The Sacred Congregation of Rites has decided this
question by the following Decree :—

Dubium 1. An Feria V. in Cœna Domini in Ecclesiis
Parochialibus aliisque non Parochialibus celebrari possit Missa
lecta vel cum cantu quin peragantur functiones Feriae VI. in
Parasceve et Sabbati Sancti.

Dubium II. An praedicta Missa legi vel decantari possit in
Ecclesiis et Oratoriis spectantibus ad Regulares, ad Seminaria et
ad Pias Communitates.

Ad 1. In Ecclesiis Parochialibus ubi adest Fons baptismalis,
serventur Rubricae Missalis et Decreta, adhibito Memoriali Rituum
Benedicti XIII., pro functionibus praescriptis, si extet defectus
sacrorum ministrorum et clericorum. In aliis vero Ecclesiis
non Parochialibus omitti potest functio Sabbati Sancti, non
tamen illa Feriae VI. in Parasceve ; et fiat sepulcrum : expetita
facultate pro usu dicti *Memorialis*, si idem sacrorum ministrorum
et clericorum defectus existat.

Ad II. Affirmative quoad Regulares proprie dictos juxta
Decretum sub n. 2799 diei 31 Augusti 1839 ; Negative quoad
Seminaria et Pias Communitates, nisi habeatur Apostolicum
Indultum.
9 Dec., 1899.

N. 2799 referred to runs thus :—

1. An in Ecclesiis ubi functiones majoris Hebdomadae fieri
nequeunt, Feria V. in Cœna Domini celebrari possit Missa lecta.

2. An si hujusmodi Ecclesiae sint Regularium, id liceat, ut
Superior communicare valeat suos Alumnos pro adimplemento
Paschalis praecepti.

Ad 1. ' Negative.'

Ad 2. Superior celebret in privato Oratorio ad ministrandam
Religiosis communionem : et si desit Oratorium, fiat in Ecclesia
ianuis clausis.

Hence (1) there is one case in which Mass may be said
on Holy Thursday without any function on Good Friday or
Holy Saturday, that in which Regulars, strictly so called,
cannot carry out the functions of Holy Week, and wish to

give the Paschal Communion to the Religious. Even in this case the Mass is to be said in a private oratory, or, if there be no oratory, in the church with closed doors.

(2) In parochial churches, where there is a baptismal font, there is no permission for Mass on Holy Thursday, unless the functions of the Triduum be carried out, at least according to the *Memoriale Rituum*.

(3) In non-parochial *churches*, Mass is allowed on Holy Thursday with the omission of the functions of Holy Saturday but not those of Good Friday.

(4) In all other cases—in Seminaries and Communities—Mass may not be celebrated on Holy Thursday without an Apostolic Indult, unless the functions of the Triduum be carried out. The omission of the function of Holy Saturday does not seem to be extended to these cases.

P. O'LEARY.

[283]

CORRESPONDENCE

FATHER FINN'S NOVELS

CINCINNATI, *February 5th,* 1902.

REV. DEAR SIR,—Your reviewer, J. B., in a very kind appreciation of my latest published story, seems to accuse me of a touch of snobbishness in giving *English* names to all my school-boy heroes. I am sure he will withdraw the charge when he has read the following explanation :—

I wrote *Tom Playfair* for the little boys I was teaching at the time, and did not dream of ever publishing the story. To designate Tom's character, I named him 'Playboy,' and Playboy he remained for years till there came question of publication. It was manifest that Playboy would be unsuitable ; at the same time I wanted the idea of a play-lover to be suggested by my hero's name. Playfair naturally suggested itself, and so Playfair it became, and I must confess it never occurred to me to ask myself whether the name were English or Irish. Next came Percy Wynne. I thought that Wynne was an Irish name. 'Percy' I chose as hinting at the girlishness of the character. Again, I never asked myself whether 'Percy' were English or Irish. Harry Dee, my next school hero, has an Irish name; so has Harry Archer ; so, too, Gerald O'Rourke.

And now for *Claude Lightfoot.* I wrote the entire story before I could settle upon that restless young gentleman's name. Intending to make the name of the hero the name of the book too, I wished for something that would hit off the character. It came, at last, with the last chapter. Again, I never asked myself whether the name were English or Irish.

You will observe, then, that when I wished to choose a name illustrative of the character, it was, from the nature of the case, an English name, not because it was English, but because it suggested a meaning.

I take this occasion to thank you for the kindly manner in which you have dealt with my little stories.—Yours sincerely,

F. J. FINN, S.J.

[On the first count in the charge—Tom Playfair—we are quite willing to acquit Father Finn. In the case of Percy

Wynne we begin to become unsettled. When we come to Harry Dee we are reluctantly compelled to convict, but with extenuating circumstances. We cannot, however, accept Claude Lightfoot. Claude is entirely too much for us.— J. B.]

FATHER MATHEW UNION

DONERAILE,
13th February, 1902.

DEAR REV. SIR,—May I once more make your hospitable columns the medium of communication with our members and the clergy generally, to inform them that our Council met for the first time on the 11th inst., in St. Finbarr's West Temperance Hall, Cork. In the unavoidable absence of Monsignor M'Swiney, the Venerable President of the ' Union,' the chair was filled by the Very Rev. Father Wogan, Guardian, O.F.M., Vice-President. There were also present :—Very Rev. Prior¡O'Quigley, O.P. ; Rev. Dr. MacCarthy, P.P.; Rev. Father Flynn, P.P.; Rev. Father Cregan, Adm.; Rev. Father O'Leary, C.C.; and the Secretary. Others wrote to say they could not come. The Very Rev. Father Nicholas, Vicar, O.S.F.C., and the Very Rev. Prior O'Leary, O.S.A., were placed on the Council.

After an interesting discussion, the first General Meeting was fixed to take place on the 3rd June next in Cork.

There are some who will say that Dublin would have been a better selection, being more central, and considering the location of many of the members. At any other time there would be much to be said in favour of that view ; in fact, one of those present suggested such an alteration of Rule VII. as would put that idea into practice. But this year the Grand National, or, rather, International, Exhibition will be held in Cork from May to November, and, doubtless, there are few of the clergy who will not patronise it ; therefore, they can ' kill two birds with one stone ' by so arranging that their visit to the Exhibition and to our Meeting shall synchronise.

The date, 3rd June, was fixed on (1) so that it should be as soon as possible, in order to shorten the long night of inactivity, (2) not to interfere with the Diocesan Retreats nor the big Meeting in Maynooth, (3) not to clash with the Vacation.

The ' Report ' has been in the hands of the Members for some time, and it will be seen by its pages that we have over 100 members, but we want 1,000, and now is the time for the other 900 to send in their names, so that they may play a part in the General Meeting. Especially would I appeal to those who have already made the sacrifice by taking the Pledge, of whom there is a goodly number scattered over the country ; they have done well in becoming Total Abstainers, they will do still better by joining the ' Union.' I would ask those who are already Members to help the poor Secretary by doing a little ' recruiting,' particularly at the approaching Retreats.

Any Member who wishes to read a Paper at the Meeting, or to propose any alteration in the Rules, or to make any suggestion, will please communicate with me, in order that I may prepare an Agenda.

The Council will have to be elected (or re-elected), according to Rule IV., the Members from each Diocese and Order selecting their own representative.

It has been suggested that there should be *four* Vice-Presidents, one from each Province, but such questions are for the Members to decide upon.

There are many plans for soberising Ireland. I believe that if the Irish Clergy joined this ' Union,' *as a body*, the problem would be solved. ' Happy above all,' says Cardinal Manning, ' are the Pastors who go before their flocks in the League of the Cross.'

Your faithful Servant,

WALTER O'BRIEN, c.c.,
Secretary.

DOCUMENT

PILGRIMS TO THE HOLY LAND DISPENSED FROM RECITATION OF THE BREVIARY

E SACRA CONGREGATIONE SUPER NEGOTIIS ECCLES. EXTRAORD.

INDULGETUR AD TRIENNIUM COMMUTATIO BREVIARII, PRO SACERDOTIBUS LOCA SANCTA PEREGRINATURIS

Très Saint-Père.—Le directeur des pèlerinages populaires de pénitence aux Lieux-Saints, humblement prosterné aux pieds de Votre Sainteté, expose que durant ces pélerinages il arrive souvent que des prêtres ne peuvent, à cause des fatigues et difficultés de ce voyage, réciter ni convenablement, ni commodément, l'office divin ; en conséquence il implore humblement de Votre Sainteté, qu'Elle daigne étendre à ces prêtres le privilège déjà accordé aux prêtres des pélerinages de la Société allemande de Terre-Sainte, par rescrit du 6 mars 1898, renouvelé le 26 février 1901, en vertu duquel il leur est accordé, pour le temps du pélerinage, de réciter le chapelet de cinq dizaines à la place de l'office divin, quand ils ne peuvent réciter celui-ci facilement.

Ex Aud. SSmi. Die 21 Julii 1901.

Ssmus. Dominus Noster Leo divina Providentia Papa XIII., referente me infrascripto S. Congr. Negotiis Ecclesiasticis extra-ordinariis praepositae Secretario, benigne annuit pro gratia, juxta preces, ad triennium proximum. Contrariis quibuscumque minime obfuturis. Datum Romae e Secretaria ejusdem S. C. Die, mense et anno praedictis.

✠ PETRUS, Arch. CAESARIENSIS, *Secretarius.*

NOTICES OF BOOKS

A Short History of the Hebrews to the Roman Period. By R. L. Ottley. Cambridge University Press.

This work is published, the author says, in order to furnish students with a manual which is consistent with the present state of knowledge. Care has evidently been taken with the chronology, even though no attempt is made to enter into the discussion of some vexed questions. We think, however, that it would have been to the advantage of students in general if Mr. Ottley had dealt with the Assyrian chronicles, eponym canons, etc. Tables of dates are given, however, the first of which, entitled 'Primitive History to Accession of Solomon,' must be accepted subject to the author's warning, 'the following dates are for the most part extremely uncertain.' The remaining five tables, in which the dates are more or less ascertained, mention some contemporary events in profane history, but, as we said, we should have been pleased to find a continual use made of at least the Assyrian chronology in the body of the work. The maps which Mr. Ottley gives are good, and well adapted to students ; especially the physical map of Palestine, which strikes one as being almost as useful as Smith's large map. The representation of the accompanying details displays considerable ingenuity. We wish that we could approve of the writer's own standpoint, but, unfortunately, it is that of the higher critic. At the same time it must be said that he has not, as so many others, made a history of the Hebrews the occasion for ventilating his theories and for constructing history in accordance with them. His own views are kept almost out of sight. They appear chiefly in an Appendix. In our opinion the value of the book would have been enhanced if mention of archæological discoveries, especially some recent ones, were more frequently made. The author's style is easy and flowing, so his *Short History* is very readable.   R. W.

Ceremonies and Processions of the Cathedral Church of Salisbury. By C. Wordsworth, M.A. Cambridge University Press.

Every publication that tends to throw light on ecclesiastical usages common in England before the Reformation is of great interest at the present day. We always find, as we anticipated, that in olden times Catholics had the same devotional practices as those we are accustomed to take part in. On this account, the ceremonies of a Cathedral church are full of instruction to every intelligent reader. Those of Salisbury, which were very elaborate, show what care had been bestowed on them, in order to ensure the beauty of Divine worship. A comparison between the ' Processions and Ceremonies ' now edited and the corresponding portions of the *Pontificale Romanum* would afford much pleasure to others, as it has done to the writer of this notice. The Sarum rite promulgated by St. Osmund for his own diocese in 1085 was very perfect. Other dioceses in the south of England and some in Scotland and in Ireland accepted it. We may mention here that words used in the marriage ceremony at the present day in this country are to be found in the ancient Sarum rite. What Maskell did for its Missal some years ago, Mr. Wordsworth has now done for its Processional. Some of the usages were almost peculiar to Salisbury, for instance, the custom of carrying three crosses in the procession on Christmas Day, and on Ascension Day of carrying a lion and a dragon. It would be impossible within our limits to mention even a tithe of the interesting things which this book contains. Students of liturgy will find that it contains a mine of information. It should be, if not in every priest's collection, at least in all our college libraries.

R. W.

"Ut Christiani ita et Romani sitis." "As you are children of Christ, so be you children of Rome."
Ex Dictis S. Patricii, In Libro Armacano, fol. 9.

The Irish, Ecclesiastical ·Record

𝔄 𝔐onthly 𝔍ournal, under 𝔈piscopal 𝔖anction.

𝔗hirty-fifth 𝔜ear]
No. 412.   APRIL, 1902.   [𝔉ourth 𝔖eries
        Vol. XI.

Nihil Obstat.
    GIRALDUS MOLLOY, S.T.D.
      Censor Dep.
Imprimatur.
    ✠ GULIELMUS,
      Archiep. Dublin.,
      Hiberniae Primas

BROWNE & NOLAN, Limited

Publishers and Printers, 24 & 25

NASSAU STREET, DUBLIN. ⎈

. . PRICE ONE SHILLING . .

SUBSCRIPTION : *Twelve Shillings per Annum, Post Free, payable in advance*

ST. ASSICUS

FIRST BISHOP AND PATRON OF THE DIOCESE OF ELPHIN

IT is the peculiar good fortune of Elphin, not alone that
the see was founded by the National Apostle, but that,
except the feast day, all the known facts respecting the
first bishop have been recorded in the two most
authentic memorials of native hagiography,—the *Tripartite
Life* and the Patrician Documents in the *Book of Armagh*.
St. Assicus was one of St. Patrick's earliest and most
remarkable disciples in Ireland and the first bishop of the
very ancient see of Elphin. St. Patrick in his missionary
tour through Connaught, which he entered by crossing the
Shannon at Drumboilan,[1] near Battle-bridge, in the parish
of Ardcarne, according to Usher in 434,[2] according to
Lanigan in 435,[3] came to the territory of Corcoghlan, in
which was situated the place now called Elphin.

The prince or chief of that territory, a noble druid
named Ona, or Ono, or Hono, of the royal Connacian race of
Hy-Briuin, gave land and afterwards his castle or fort to
St. Patrick to found a church and monastery. The place,
which had hitherto been called, from its owner's name,

---

[1] See *Irish Monthly*, vol. vii., p. 487, ' St. Patrick's Travels through
Elphin.' Right Rev. J. J. Kelly, D.D.
[2] *Index Chron.*, Works, vi., p. 569.
[3] See *History*, vol. i., p. 240.

Emlagh-Ona,' received the designation of Elphin, which
signifies *the Rock of the Clear* [*Spring*], from a large stone
raised by the saint from the well miraculously opened by
him in this land, and placed by him on its margin; and
from the copious stream of crystal water which flowed from
it and still flows through the street of Elphin.   There
St. Patrick built a church called through centuries *Tempull
Phadruig*, Patrick's Church, which he made ane piscopal
see, placing over it St. Assicus as bishop; and with him he
left Bitheus, son of the brother of Assicus, and Cipia,
mother of bishop Bitheus.   St. Patrick also founded at
Elphin an episcopal monastery or college, which is justly
considered one of the first monasteries founded by him, and
placed over it the holy bishop Assicus.

The site of the church built by St. Patrick was that at
present occupied by the Protestant church of Elphin.   The
town extends along the summit of a ridge, in a direction
nearly east and west.   The Church of St. Patrick was
situated on the eastern verge of this ridge.   It is unnecessary
to dwell on the dishonour and insult offered to the memories
of St. Patrick and St. Assicus, and to the faith and feelings
of their flock, by raising the temple of a new religion on the
ruins of their venerable cathedral.   This, however, is a
degradation to which many of our most august sanctuaries
have been subjected.   The new, beautiful, and commodious
Church of St. Patrick, built by the learned and patriotic
parish priest, Very Rev. Canon Mannion, on the opposite or
western end of the ridge on which Elphin is situated, holds

---

¹ Ab Erico Rubro (son of Briun) originem sumpserunt Kenal-mac-erca:
Erici ex Aenea filio tres nepotes Ida, Ono, et Dobtha; a quo Kinel-dobtha:
de quibus O'Hanly, et O'Brocnan in tractatu Corcachlandae in Roscomaniae
districtu inter Tir-Olillam ab Aquilone, et Bagnam montem a meridie:
S. Berachi (S. Berache or Barry) atavus idem Dobtha extitit.   Ida, et Ono Cor-
cholandae domini prof essione Druides erant.   Ono idem, ex quo Hy-onach regio,
et familia obtulit ultro suam arcem S. Patricio, Imleach-ona nuncupatur;
ubi Sanctus sedem episcopalem Oilfinensem erexit, quae usque in hunc
diem (1685) ita continuat a multis saeculis perampla ditione locupletata
Ecclesia autem haec nomen illud adepta fertur, ex eo quod in loco, in quo
extructa est, sit fons limpidus a S. Patricio de nocte productus e terra. Fionn,
i.e. lucidus, vel clarus appellatus, et ad ejus marginem ingens lapis ibi jam-
pridem erectus; nam *Oil* vel *Ail* prisca lingua Hibernica lapidem, vel saxum
denotat: unde Oilfinn idem sonat, quod saxum lucidi fontis.—*Ogygia*, pars. iii.,
cap. lxxix., p. 375.

the legitimate succession to the Church of St. Patrick and St. Assicus. Like so many of the towns of Ireland, the episcopal city of Elphin had its origin in the church and monastery which St. Patrick founded there, and over which he placed St. Assicus in the fifth century. The name of Emlagh-Ona is still preserved in the townland of Emlagh, which adjoins the town of Elphin. Emlagh-Ona was obviously so-called to distinguish it from this other Emlagh, coterminous with it and still retaining the name.

The first bishop of Elphin was a worker in metal. He is described in the *Book of Armagh* as a *cerd*, *i.e.*, a wright, the *faber aereus Patricii*, and he made altars, chalices, and patens, and metal book-covers, for the newly founded churches. Following the example of their master, the successors and spiritual children of St. Assicus founded a school of art and produced most beautiful objects of Celtic workmanship in the diocese of Elphin. Of these, some remain to the present day, objects of admiration to all who see them. The famous Cross of Cong, undoubtedly one of the finest specimens of its age in the western world, was, as an inscription on it testifies, the work of Maelisa Mac Egan, comarb of St. Finian of Clooncraff,[1] near Elphin, co. Roscommon, under the superintendence of Domhnall, son of Flanagan O'Duffy, at Roscommon, who was successor of Coman and Kiaran, abbots of Roscommon and Clonmacnoise, and bishop of Elphin. It is held that the exquisite Ardagh Chalice,[2] which was given to Clonmacnoise by Torlogh O'Conor, and was stolen thence, was made, if not by the same artist, in the same school at Roscommon. The Four Masters record A.D. 1166: The shrine of Manchan of Maothail (Mohill) was covered by Rory O'Conor, and an embroidering of gold was carried over it by him, in as good style as relic was ever covered in Ireland. It is, therefore,

---

[1] Cluain-cremha, *i.e.*, the meadow or lawn of the wild garlic, now Clooncraff, to the east of Elphin. The plunder of Cluain-cremha is recorded at A.D. 815 of the *Annals of Ulster*. Dr. B. MacCarthy, in his Introduction to the *Annals of Ulster*, just completed, shows that Dr. O'Conor took *Orgain* (pillaging) to signify *the taking away of the organs* and turned it into *direptio organorum*; subjoining an irrelevant dissertation to show the very ancient use of organs in the psalmody of the Western Church.

[2] So called from having been found at Ardagh, co. Limerick.

fair to conclude that this beautiful work was also executed
in the school of art founded by St. Assicus in the diocese of
Elphin.

Like our Divine Lord Himself, who ennobled and
sanctified the labour of the handicraftsman, like St. Paul,
who earned his livelihood by the work of his own hands,
the patron of Elphin, we have seen, was a worker in metal.
His was

> The nobility of labour, the long pedigree of toil.

He was clearly such a craftsman as a celebrated writer
of our time had in view when he wrote :—

> If the poor and humble toil that we have food, must not the
> high and glorious toil for him in return, that he may have Light,
> have Guidance, Freedom, Immortality. These two in all their
> degrees I honour : all else is chaff and dust, which let the wind
> blow whither it listeth. Unspeakably touching is it, however,
> when I find both dignities united ; and he that must toil out-
> wardly for the lowest of man's wants, is also toiling inwardly for
> the highest. Sublimer in this world know I nothing than a
> peasant saint, could such now anywhere be met with. Such a
> one will take thee back to Nazareth itself : thou wilt see the
> splendour of heaven spring forth from the humblest depths of
> earth, like a light shining in great darkness.[1]

About seven years before his death, St. Assicus, grieved
because some of the inhabitants of Magh-Ai, or Machaire-
Connaught, the plain in which Elphin lies, had falsely
given out that a lie had been told by him, seeking solitude,
desiring to be alone with God, secretly fled from Elphin
northward to Slieve League, a precipitous mountain in
Donegal. He spent seven years in seclusion on the island
of Rathlin, adjacent to Glencolumbkille. His monks sought
him, and at last, after great labour, found him in the
mountain glens. They sought to persuade him to return
with them to Elphin ; but he refused on account of the
falsehood which had been spoken of him there. The king
of the territory gave to him and to his monks after his
death the pasture of one hundred cows with their calves,
and of twenty oxen, as a perpetual offering. There the

---

[1] *Sartor Resartus.*

holy bishop died, and they buried him in the desert, far from Elphin, in Rathcunga, in Seirthe. Rathcunga is now locally called Racoon. It is a conical hill, the apex of which is entrenched like a rath, and contains an ancient cemetery, now disused, in the parish of Drumhome, county Donegal. In this sacred and celebrated place, St. Patrick had built a church and monastery, where had dwelt seven bishops: and in the same place, St. Bitheus, bishop, the nephew of St: Assicus, is buried. Their relics were held in the highest honour, and for many ages were religiously guarded by the monks and venerated by the people.

Of the church and monastery of Racoon, hallowed by the relics of the holy bishop and anchorite Assicus, and the holy bishop, Bitheus, and by the presence of St. Patrick and seven bishops, even the ruins have perished. But the children of St. Assicus, the first bishop and patron of Elphin, still, even to our age, have piously preserved his memory, and hold before their eyes his example of the union of labour and contemplation. St. Assicus probably died before the close of the fifth century. His feast is observed on the 27th of April, on which day he is honoured as patron of the diocese of Elphin, where his festival is celebrated as a double of the first class with an octave. It is a major double for the rest of Ireland.

Hennessy[1] identifies Bite with St. Beoaedh, bishop of Ardcarne, in the county of Roscommon. 'He was,' he says, 'nephew of St. Assicus, bishop of Elphin, who was also buried in Rathcunga. St. Beoaedh died on the 8th of March, 524, on which day he was venerated. The *Chronicon Scotorum* has his death at 518.' But Beoaedh (Vividus Hugo) of Ardcarne—Beoaedus de Ardcharna in Connacia, qui erat episcopus, obiit 523: *Mart. Dungall.*, *Mart. of Tallaght*, pp. xvii., 3—does not appear to have been identical with Bite, nephew of St. Assicus. Bite was a bishop and is often mentioned in the *Tripartite* and *Book of Armagh* with Essu and Tassach (Assic), as one of Patrick's *cerds*. He was left at Elphin with Cipia his mother, and, there can be little doubt,

---

[1] *Tripartite*, p. 434, n. 3. Beoaedh is also given in the *Calendar of Aenghus*, at March 8.

succeeded the founder, St. Assicus. There is a St. Biteus, abbot of Inis-cumhscraidhe, now Inishcoursy, co. Down, at the 29th of July. St. Biteus of Elphin is given in the list of St. Patrick's disciples furnished by Tirechan, Asacus (recte Assicus), Bitheus, Falertus (Felartus).[1] But the equation of Bite and Beo-Aed calls for no refutation. The latter died, according to the rectified chronology of the Annals of Ulster, in 524. He was seventh in descent from Lugnid Mac Con, king of Ireland, slain A.D. 207. Amongst the saints of Lugaid's sept mentioned in the versified Genealogies of Saints,[2] Bite is not included,—an omission which effectively disposes of the allegation that he was nephew of Beo-Aed.

Assertions have been made regarding St. Assicus which are not borne out by the ancient authorities, and serious mistakes have been committed by various writers in treating of him. It has been said that Elphin derives its name from a white rock or stone: that Assicus was a druid: that he was the husband of Cipia and father of bishop Bitheus: that he retired from Elphin through shame because he had told a lie there. There seems to be no warrant for these statements in the reliable sources of our knowledge respecting St. Assicus. To show this, I give the extracts regarding our saint from the Tripartite and Book of Armagh.

Tripartite Life[3]

It is there he (Patrick) founded Cell-mor of Magh-glass, and left therein two of his people, i.e., Conleng and Ercleng. Deinde venit in fines Corcu-ochland, on this side of Tirerrill (Ua-Ailella, ac. pl., MS.) and north of Baune (Ba[d]hgna MS.).[4] There were two brothers in that place,

---

[1] The Tripartite Life of St. Patrick, with other Documents relating to that Saint. Edited with Translations and Indexes by Whitley Stokes, D.C.L., LL.D., 1887, p. 304.
[2] Book of Ballymote, 232b, 233a.
[3] Part II., Stokes's ed., p. 94-6.
[4] Anciently Sliabh-baghna na d-Tuath [S.—b. of the territories], extending through the three districts called The Tuatha, from north to south, parallel with the Shannon. The western side of Sliabh-Baune (Corcoghlan) belonged to Mac Branan, descended from Ona; the eastern (Kinel-Dofa) to O'Hanly, descended from Erc the Ruddy. Caranadoe Bridge (Caradh na-dtuath; Calad na-d., by interchange of l and r: causeway of the Territories) still preserves the ancient name of the Tuathas.

i.e., Id and Hona (hOna MS.); druids (were) they. Dixit
hOno ad Patricium : What wilt thou give me for that land ?
Dixit Patricius : Vitam eternam. Ait hOno: Thou dost
possess gold; give it to me for it. Respondit Patricius :
I have given my gold to all (persons), but God will give
more. He came upon a mass of gold afterwards in the
enclosed place of the swine and Patrick gave that lump of
gold to him for the territory. Tir-in-brotha (*land of the
mass*) is its name. Tunc dixit Patricius : Nec rex eris, nec
de semine tuo regnabit in eternum. Illius vero lacrimis
misertus est Patricius dicens, he shall not be king whom
thou wilt not accept and ordain (*i.e.*, place over them
and maintain in power) : quod impletur. The race of
(Muircertach) son of Erc is the strongest and wealthiest
in Connaught, but they rule not as arch-kings.

Ono, son of Oengus, son of Erc the Ruddy, son of
Bron [Brian], de quo the Ui-Onach : he offered (presented :
obtulit = the Irish of the text) his dwelling to Patrick and
Imlech-Ononn (was) its name at that time ; Ail-find, however, to-day. From the rock that was raised from out the
well that was made by Patrick in the field and is over the
brink of the well nominatur locus *Ail- ; find* de aqua
noncupatur. Et dixit illi Patricius : Blessed shall be thy
seed and there shall be victory of laics and clerics from thee
to doom ; and with them shall be the heritage (coarbship)
of this place. Et posuit ibi Assicum et Bite[um], filium
fratris Assici[-cus, MS.], et ¡Cipiam, matrem Bitei episcopi.
Assicus, sanctus episcopus, faber ereus (erat) Patricii, and he
used to make altars and quadrangular dishes (patens) a:id
quadrangular book-keepers, in honour of Patrick. And
there was a quadrangular dish of them in Armagh, and
another in Elphin, and another in Domnach-mor of Magh-
Seolai, on the altar of Felart, the holy bishop (Felarti,
episcopi sancti, MS.), in Ui-Briuin-Seolai, far from Elphin
westward.

Assicus went afterwards in flight into the north, to
Sliabh-liac in Tir-Boghaine. He was seven years on an
island there, and his monks sought him out, and found him
after toil in the mountain glens, and they took him with

them thence. And he (*i.e.*, Assicus, gloss in text) died with them in the desert, and they buried him in Rath-Chunga in Serthi. Inde dicitur, *Time to fare to Serthi* (*i.e.*, it is time to be dead and buried : a local proverb). And the king of the territory gave to him and to his monks after his death the pasture of one hundred cows, cum vitulis suis and of twenty oxen, in offering perpetual. For he said himself that he would not go again into Magh-Ai,[1] because of the lie that was said there of him. His relics are in Rath-Chunga, and to Patrick belongs the church. (But) the community of Colum-cille and (that) of Ardstraw[2] occupied it (literally, has come upon it : the verb agreeing with the first subject ; it became a Columban abbey). . . .

He (Patrick) went after that, between Assaroe and the sea, into the territory of Conall (Tyrconnell), the place where Rathcunga is to-day. He marked out a place there, and said it would be a habitation and city for him (Patrick), cum septem episcopis. Et ubi [ibi] est Bite, filius fratris As[s]ici, from Elphin.[3]

Stokes reads (p. 148) and translates (p. 149) ' cathir docum vii. episcoporum : ' a city for seven bishops. He took *docum* to be an Irish genitive governing *episcoporum*. But Dr. MacCarthy showed that the reading was ' *do*, cum septem episcopis ': for him (the Irish *do*), with seven bishops. The whole text is a mixture of Irish and Latin. Stokes adopted what he admitted was a ' brilliant' emendation.[4]

---

[1] Magh Ai, now Machaire-Chonnacht, or the Maghery, a beautiful plain in the county of Roscommon, extending from near the town of Roscommon to the verge of the barony of Boyle, and from the bridge of Cloonfree, near Strokestown, westward to Castlerea.

[2] Ard-Srath,'Ardstraw, now a parish church, but formerly a cathedral, near Strabane, in the county Tyrone.

[3] Part II., Stokes, p. 148.

[4] The seven bishops of Racoon are invoked in the Litany of Aengus, in the *Book of Leinster* (lithographed edition, page 374a, l. 14).

See the Litany of Aengus Céile De published (with translation) from a MS. in the Archives of St. Isidore's, once portion of the *Book of Leinster*, by Dr. B. MacCarthy, M.R.I.A., I. E. RECORD, First Series, vol. iii., p. 471.

Book of Armagh—(Collectanea of Tirechan).[1]

Venierunt ad Campum Glais, et in illo posuit 'celolam magnam, quae sic vocatur, Cellula magna. [The Cell-mor of Magh-Glais of the *Tripartite.*] Et in illa reliquit duos barbaros [*i.e.*, not Roman subjects, but natives], Conleng et Ercleng, monachos sibi.

Deinde venit ad Assicum et Bitteum et ad magos qui fuerunt de genere Corcu-Chonluain, Hono et Ith, fratres. Alter suscepit Patricium et sanctos ejus cum gaudio et immolavit sibi domum suam et exiit ad Imbliuch-Hornon (*lege* Hononn). Et dixit illi Patricius: *Semen tuum erit benedictum, et de tuo semine erunt sacerdotes Domini et principes* (abbots) *digni, in mea elimossina* (subject to Armagh) *et in tua hereditate* (the coarbs or abbots to be of Hono's sept). Et posuit ibi Assicum et Betheum, filium fratris Assici, et Cipiam, matrem Bethei episcopi.

Assicus, sanctus episcopus, faber aereus erat Patricio et faciebat altaria [et] bibliothecas qua[drata]s. Faciebat in[super] patinos sanctus noster (sancti nostri, MS.) pro honore Patricii episcopi. Et de illis tres patinos quadratos vidi: id est, patinum in aeclessia Patricii in Arddmachae et alterum in aeclessia Alofind (gen. of Ail-find: Elphin), et tertium in aeclessia magna Saeoli, super altare Felarti, sancti episcopi.

As[s]icus iste fecit profugam in aquilonem regionis ad Montem-lapidis[-um] (Sliabh-liac).[2] Et fuit septem annis in insola quae vocatur Rochuil,[3] retro Montem-lapidum. Et quaerebant illum monachi sui et invenierunt eum in convallibus montanis, juxta laborum artificiorum (their toil in the search was like the labour of artizans). Et abstraxerunt eum monachi ejus. Et mortuus est apud illos in disertis montibus et sepilierunt eum irRaith-chungai hi Sertib (in Racoon in Serthi). Et dedit rex illi et monachis suis post mortem [ejus] foenum c. vaccarum cum vitulis suis et bovum xx.,—immolatio aeterna; quia dixit quod non reverte[re]tur in Campum-Ai, quia mendacium ab illo dixerunt. Et sunt

---

[1] Folio 11 c. d.
[2] Sliabh-liag, a precipitous mountain over the Atlantic, in the parish of Glencolumkille, barony of Bannagh, county of Donegal.
[3] Now called Rathlin O'Birne, adjacent to Glencolumkill, about fifty acres in extent.

ossa ejus in Campo-Sered, hirRaith-chungi (in Magh-Sered, in Rath-chunga). Monachus Patricii [erat], sed contenderunt eum familiae Columbae-cille et familia Airdd-eratha.[1] . . .

Patricius vero venit de fonte Alo-find (of Elphin) ad Dume-cham Nepotum-Ailello (Ui-Ailella : Tirerrili) et fundavit in illo loco aeclessiam, quae sic vocatur *Senella Cella Dumiche* usque [ad] hunc diem, in quo reliquit viros Sanctos Macet, et Cetgen, et Rodanum prespiterum.

Etiam intravit (Patricius) in Campum *Sereth* trans amnem [the Erne] inter Es-ruaid [Assaroe, co. Donegal] et mare, et fundavit aeclessiam hirRaith-argi (in Rath-argi) et castrame-tatus est in Campo-Sereth. Et iuvenit quendam virum bonum de genere Lathron et baptitzavit eum et filium tenerum cum eo, qui dicebatur Hinu, vel Ineus, quia posuit illum pater in fana (=linteum, a sheet) super collum ejus, quia natus est in via cum patre de monte veniens. Et baptitzavit Patricius filium et scripsit illi [patri] abgitorium[2] [elements of Christian Doctrine] et henedixit eum benedictione episcopi. Qui postea retenuit Assicum sanctum cum monachis suis in Ard-roissen,[3] id est, hirRaith-congi (in Racoon), in Campo-Sereth, in tempore reguru Fergusso et Fotbuid.[4]

---

[1] 'Recves (*Adamnan*, pp. 284-5) infers from this passage that the monks of Ardstraw were in dispute with Columban monks respecting Racoon, county Donegal. But the tenor of the Tract and the absence of *ad invicem* (*cf.* con-flinguentes (*sic*) *ad invicem* (*Book of Armagh*, fol. 13a) show that the contention (for the grazing of 100 cows with their calves and 20 oxen) was directed against Armagh, conjointly and successfully, by the monks of Ardstraw and the Columban monks. This is clear from the extract given above from the *Tripartite*. 'His (Assic's) remains are in Racoon and to Patrick belongs the church. [But] the community of Colum-cille and [that] of Ardstraw have seized it.'—*Annals of Ulster*, ed. MacCarthy, vol. iii., pp. 514-5.

[2] For the references to the *abgitoria* in the *Tripartite* and *Book of Armagh*, see Introduction to *Annals of Ulster*, p. cviii., note 6.

[3] Roshin, Tirhugh barony, Co. Donegal, on the road from Belleek to Ballintra. The corresponding place of the *Tripartite* shows that the final sentence (Qui postea, etc.,) is an addition. The value of it may be estimated from the equation of Roshin and Racoon, and the fact that Fergus and Fothud are not found as joint or successive kings in the regal succession. The rulers in question were Fergus and Domnall, kings of Ireland, A.D. 565-567. They are best known as victors with Dermot, king of Ireland, in the battle of Culdrevny (Cooladrummon, eight miles north-west of Sligo town), on behalf of their kinsman, St. Columba, in 561.

[4] *Book of Armagh*, fol. 15, a, b.

From these texts it is clear that Elphin does not mean a white stone or rock. Stokes (page 96) gives the text of the *Tripartite*: Nominatur locus Ailfind ; de aqua nuncupatur : and translates—The place is named *Ail-find* from the stone (*ail*) which was raised out of the well that was made by Patrick in the green, and which stands on the brink of the well : it is called from the water [*find* (fair)]. But Dr. MacCarthy, in his criticism in the *Academy*,[1] showed that this text and rendering were incorrect. For, he pertinently asked, if the place is named Ailfind from the *ail* or stone, what remains for it to be called from *aqua* ? It has to be borne in mind that the scribes did not understand their text ; and that, as can be seen in the facsimile prefixed to Stokes's edition, punctuation was confined to the full stop. Dr. MacCarthy amended it thus : From the *ail* (rock) . . . nominatur locus *ail ;* *find* de aqua nuncupatur. The place is named Ail from the *ail* and designated find (fair, clear, sparkling) from the water. In other words, Ailfinn is *petra purae* (aquae), or in Irish Ail-finn (uisci), rock of clear water. *Uisci* is masculine or neuter, and so has *finn* or *find* (pron. *feen*), not *finne* or *finde*, in the qualifying adjective. There is not a shred of authority for the statement that Assicus was a druid, or of the race of Ono.

According to the *Tripartite* and *Book of Armagh*, Bite was the nephew, not the son, of Assicus. The former has Bite, filius fratris Assici, and the latter, Et posuit ibi Assicum et Betheum, filium fratris Assici et Cipiam, matrem Betbei episcopi. In one MS. of the *Tripartite* the reading is filium Assici. Stokes adopted this, though he had in the other, and printed it himself at foot (page 96), filium fratris Assicus [-ci], and the same in the *Book of Armagh.* This Dr. MacCarthy[2] pointed out, and Stokes accepted the correction.

St. Assicus fled from Elphin, not because he had told a lie there, but (which is quite another thing) because a lie had been told there of him. In Stokes's *Tripartite* (page 96),

[1] See also *Trans. R.I.A.*, xxix., page 195.
[2] See *Trans. R.I.A.*, vol. xxix., part vi., page 195.

the sentence: 'For he said himself that he would not go again into Magh-ai,' is inserted between *Serthi* and *unde dicitur*, an unwarrantable tampering with the text of the two MSS., as the corresponding passage in the *Book of Armagh* proves. Stokes furthermore translates, in accordance with this schoolboy collocation : They buried him in Racoon, for he had declared that he would not go again into Magh-ai, on account of the falsehood which had been uttered by him there. But *roraided uad* does not mean ' which had been uttered by him,' but had been uttered as if from him ; *by him* (denoting agency) would be *lais*, and this is confirmed by the Latin of the *Book of Armagh* : quia mendacium ab illo dixerunt—the people of Magh-ai gave out a lie as coming from him. The local ruler of Baunagh gave to him and his monks after his death his princely offering through joy at having his bones in Racoon, instead of their being carried home to Elphin ; and St. Assicus would not have them brought to Elphin, because of the falsehood which had been given out there as if uttered by him, and his monks remained where the relics of their holy master rested.

The author of the Life of St. Patrick in the *Book of Armagh* says : The holy bishop Assicus was the goldsmith of Patrick, and he made altars, and quadrangular book-cases. Our saint also made patens in honour of Patrick the bishop ; and of them I have seen three quadrangular patens, that is, the paten in the church of Patrick in Armagh, and another in the church of Elphin, and the third in the great church of Saetli, on the altar of Felart, the holy bishop. The altar of Felart, on which was this beautiful paten of St. Assicus, was in the church founded by St. Patrick on Lough Sealga, called Domnagh-Mor of Magh Sealga, in the townland of Carns, near Tulsk and Rathcroghan, the royal residence of Connaught.

The *Tripartite* [1] tells us that from Oran (which is in the barony of Ballymoe, between Roscommon and Castlerea), where he had left bishop Cethec, St. Patrick directed his steps to another place not far from Oran, also very celebrated

---

[1] Stokes, pp. 106-8.

in pagan and Christian times, namely, to Magh-Selca, *i.e.*,
to Duma-Selca, where there were six young men, sons
of Brian [Briun], viz.—Bolcderc, Derthacht, Eichen, Crem-
than, Coelcharna, and Echaid.[1] And Patrick wrote three
names there on three stones, viz. : Jesus, Soter, Salvator.
Patrick blessed the Ui-Briuin from Dumha-Selca, and
Patrick's seat is there between the three stones, in quibus
scribsit literas, et nomina episcoporum qui cum illo illic
fuerunt, viz., Bronus episcopus [2] of Caisel-Irre, Sachellus of
Baislic-mor in Ciarraighe, Brocaid of Imlech-ech, brother
to Loman of Ath-truim, Bronachus, presbyter, Rodan,
Cassan, Benen, Patrick's successor, and Benen, brother of
Cethech, Felartus, bishop, and his sister, a nun there, and
another sister, quae sit in insola in mare Conmaicne, *i.e.*,
Croch-Culli-Conmacne.   And he founded a church on
Loch-Selca, *i.e.*, Domhnach-[mor] of Magh-Selca, in quo
babtizavit the Ui-Briuin et benedixit. Patrick went into
Gregraidhe, of Loch-Techet, and founded a church there.

Hennessy, in his version of the *Tripartite*,[3] says :
' Duma-Selca, or the mound of the chase, was the old name
of a mound which still exists in the townland of Carns, a
little to the south of the village of Tulsk, in the county of
Roscommon.   The mound or moat lies due east from the
celebrated mound of Carnfree.   Canon O'Hanlon, in his
Lives of the Irish Saints,[4] says : ' Magh-Selca, also called
Duma-Selca, is interpreted in English, the Mound of the
Chase.   This was the old name of a mound which still
exists in the townland of Carns, a little to the south of Tulsk
village, in the county of Roscommon.'   The place, we learn
from the *Dinnsenchus* (history of names of places) in the
Book of Ballymote (lithographed edition, page 386 b-7b) was

---

[1] *The Book of Ballymote*, in a genealogical tract, which Charles O'Conor
of Belanagare, has headed ' Of the Hy-Brune Heremonians,' states, (page 89a)
that there were 24 sons, who are named, the eldest of whom, Eichin, was king
at the coming of Patrick. All proved obstinate, except the youngest, Duach
the Valorous, who was converted by St. Patrick, and became the first Christian
king of Connaught.   To him and his seed the saint promised the kingship,
' and that was fulfilled.' The prophecy, needless to add, was made after the event !

[2] Stokes (p. 108) inserts [Biteus] and translates (p. 109) Bite of Casel-Irre,
although he gave before (p. 94), episcopus Bronus . . . qui est at Caisel-hIrroe.
So also at pp. 140, 319.

[3] *Ibid.*, p. 407, note.   [4] *Ibid.*, p. 592, note.

originally called Ard-cain (pleasant height),[1] and afterwards
Duma-selga (mound of chase), from the chase of the six
swine of Derbriu,[2] daughter of Eochy the Generous (King of
Ireland, B.C. 137). The names, various wanderings, and
deaths (the heads were brought to the mound) are set forth
in prose, and, more copiously, in twenty-seven quatrains.
Hennessy and Canon O'Hanlon, therefore, hold that Magh-
Selca, where Patrick baptized the sons of Briun was at the
present Carns, near Tulsk and Rathcroghan; yet, strange
to relate, both, following O'Flaherty, say that Domhnach-
mor of Magh-Selca, which occurs in connection with it, in
the same passage, is on the banks of Lough Hackett, county
Galway, and is now called Donagh-Patrick. O'Flaherty, in
his *Ogygia*,[3] states that the six sons of Brian [Briun] were
converted in Magh-Seola, on the banks of Lough Hackett,
[in the diocese of Tuam]; and Hardiman, in his edition of
O'Flaherty's *Iar Connaught*, says : ' Here also he built the
church of Domnach-mor, now called Domnach-Patruig, on
the banks of Loch Sealga (*recte* Loch Cime), in the barony
of Clare, county Galway.' [4]

This is all clearly wrong, as the *Tripartite* says that
St. Patrick came from Oran, which is in the vicinity of
Carns, and far away from Lough Hackett. It states that
Patrick blessed the Ui-Briuin from Dumha-Selga, and, in
immediate continuation, that 'he founded a church on Loch-
Selca ; *i.e.*, Domnach-mor of Magh-Selca—in quo baptizavit
Uu-Briuin et benedixit.' Therefore, Dumha-Sealga, Loch-
Sealga, and Domnach-mor of Magh-Sealga are in the
same place, namely, in the townland of Carns, to the
south of the village of Tulsk, south-east of Rathcroghan,
county of Roscommon, and not far from Oran, from which
St. Patrick went to it. The townland of Carns is so named
from the Dumha-Sealga and the celebrated Carnfree, the
tumulus or mound of Fraech, on which The O'Conor was

---

[1] There is still a village called Ardkeena, adjoining Tulsk.
[2] Derbriu.—This is the form in the poem on the names of celebrated
woman by Gilla-Modubta (*circa* A.D. 1172) in the *Book of Leinster* (p. 137b).
Drebriu, by metathesis of *e* and *r*, is the *Ballymote* word.
[3] Part III., cap. lxxix., p. 374, marginal notes.
[4] O'Flaherty's *West Connaught*, p. 148. Taken from the *Ogygia* (*loc. cit.*).

inaugurated, and which is so frequently mentioned in the Irish Annals.[1] It is in the parish of Ogulla, barony and county of Roscommon. Carnfree, originally called Cnoc na Dala (Hill of the Meeting), was so called from Fraech, the son of Fiodhach of the Red Hair, from whom also is named Cluain-Fraich, near Strokestown, a palace of the O'Conors down to the sixteenth century. The townland is still called Cloonfree Palace. 'They conveyed the body of Fraech,' says the *Dinnsenchus* of the *Book of Lecan*, 'to Cnoc na Dala, to the south-east of Cruachan, and interred him there; so that it is from him the Carn is named: unde dicitur Carn-Fraich;' *i.e.*, the Carn of Fraech. It is less than three miles south-east of Rathcroghan. Duma Sealga, *i.e.*, the Hunting Mound or Mound of the Chase, is the green hill to the east of Carnfree.

Carnfree is now usually called Carn-breac, the speckled carn, because it is composed of clay and large stones, which appear through the grass. It is not nearly so high as the Dumha-Sealga, which rises about thirty feet above the level of the surrounding fields, and seems to be entirely composed of earth. It is of sugar-loaf shape, and not more than two feet square on the top. 'The green moat to the east of Carnfree,' writes O'Donovan, who visited the place in 1837, 'is the Dumha-Sealga, so celebrated in the *Dinnsenchus* and Lives of St. Patrick.' The *Tripartite* tells us that at Dumha-Sealga, which was near the royal palace of Cruachan, Briun's six sons were living. It was here, then, that St. Patrick converted the Hy-Briuin and held his council. Here he founded the church called Domnach-mor of Magh-Sealga, 'in quo baptizavit Uu-Briuin et benedixit.' Colgan, in his paraphrase of the *Tripartite*, tells us that the saint went from Oran to Magh-Sealga, and there—in loco amaeno ubi circumfusa regio late conspicitur—in a pleasant place, where there is a wide prospect of the surrounding country, held his council. Now, as O'Donovan observed, the Dumha-Sealga and Carnfree are most conspicuous objects in the plain of Croghan. From them a wide prospect may

---

[1] See *Annals of the Four Masters*, 1225, 1407, 1461.

be had for miles around. Here, says the Latin *Tripartite*,
St. Patrick and his attendant bishops sat and deliberated
concerning the conversion of the people of the territory. It
adds : In supra memorato tractu de Dumha-Selga, ad
marginem lacus, qui vulgo Loch-Selga vocatur, extruxit
ecclesiam, quae *Dominica magna* nuncupatur : et in ea in
mysteriis fidei instruxit, lavacro regenerationis intinctos
Christi familiae aggregavit, suaque sacra benedictione
munivit filios [Briuin], gentemque de Hua-Briuni.[1] These
were the sons or relations of Briun, King of Connaught.
Their palace was hard by at Rathcroghan. Domnach-mor
of Magh-Sealga was, therefore, near Dumha-Sealga. There
was in ancient times a large lake called Loch-Sealga, or
Selca, extending from the present lake at Briarfield to the
Ardakillan Lough. The country has been thoroughly
drained; but in the Mona-Gran [2] and swallow-holes intervening there are distinct traces of the ancient lake. There is
no proof whatsoever, from the ancient and reliable authorities,
that Lough Cime or Lough Hackett was ever known as
Lough Sealga; while the part of the ancient Lough Sealga,
or Selca, which still remains at the place now called
Briarfield, near Carns, still retains the name of Shadlough.

From the Domnach-mor of Magh-Selca, in which he
baptized the Hy-Briuin and blessed them, St. Patrick
went into the Gregraide. The hill of Drum-Greagh-
raighe, and the church of Cell-Curcaighe, now Kilcorkey,
near Belanagare, and in the neighbourhood of Rathcroghan and Carns, are referred to in the Irish Annals as in
the territory of Greaghraighe : so that before and after he
founded Domnach-mor of Magh-Sealga, St. Patrick was in the
immediate neighbourhood of Carnfree and Cruchan-Ai, and
far away from Galway and Lough Hackett. The Domnach-
mor of Magh-Sealga stood a short distance north of Dumha-
Sealga. The foundations of an ancient church can still be
traced; there are still evident signs of the church-yard, and the
field is now called Church-park. A pass leading out of this

---

[1] *Triad Thaum. Septima Vita*, p. 136.
[2] Grean (gran) means the gravelly bed of a bog or stream ; hence, *mona
regan*, boggy gravel beds or gravel-bottomed bogs.

field is called *Stile an Aifrin*. Between it and the hill is another field called *Shan-baile, i.e.*, the old town, which doubtless grew around the church and monastery. This Dumha-Sealga of Magh-Ai, as we have seen in the *Dinnsenchus*, was celebrated even before the time of St. Patrick.

The church and monastic house founded by St. Patrick in Magh-Sealga, near Rathcroghan, were for ages held in the utmost reverence, and continued to be a retreat, whither the chiefs of the Hy-Briuin retired from the world to prepare for death. Thus, the Four Masters, at the year 1448, relate that Conor, son of John, son of Eachmarcach Mac Branan, lord of Corcachlan for a period of thirty-seven years, died at Dumha-Sealga on Magh-Ai, having resigned his lordship the year before, and was buried at Roscommon. Under the same year, the Annals of Duald Mac Firbis record his death thus : ' Conner, son to John ffits [son] Eachmarkagh, dux of Corcachlann for the space of thirty-seven years, died at Dumha Sealga on Magh-ay, after he had renounced his lordship a yeare afore that for God's sake, after receiving extreme unction and making penance, and was buried in Roscommon. God rest his soule.'

St. Felart, on whose altar one of the patens made by St. Assicus was used, was the bishop placed by St. Patrick over the Domnach-mor of Magh-Seola or Sealga. He was one of the bishops present with the saint at Dumha-Sealga : Felartus bishop, and his sister, a nun there, that is, at Dumha-Sealga.[1] She is distinguished from another sister in Galway : namely, the sister who is in an island in the sea of Conmacne (Connemara). Archdall, in his *Monasticon Hibernicum* [2] says a monastery named Domnachmor, was in Magh-seola, in the country of Hybruin-seola, in the county of Roscommon, where St. Felartus was bishop in the fifth century. Walsh, in his ecclesiastical history of Ireland, has Domnach-more of Magh-Sealga, in the territory of Hy-Briuin-Seola, county of Roscommon. St. Felartus, a disciple of St. Patrick, was bishop of this church. He attended the synod of Magh-Seola which St. Patrick held here. And

---

[1] *Tripartite*, Stokes's Edition, p. 109.
[2] Page 609, co. of Roscommon.

again, under the heading Co. Roscommon, ' Magh Selga or
Seola, Domnachmore of: In the Life of St. Patrick, by
St. Evin (*i.e.* the *Tripartite Life,*) it is stated that the
apostle, having come to this plain, near Elphin, found three
pillar stones.'

St. Patrick was accompanied to Ireland by some Gallic
missioners, who asked him to assign places of retirement to
them where they might serve God in seclusion:[1] From the
hill of Oran he pointed out to each of them his own place.
One of these was the Imge of Baslic [Baslick], between
Hy-Maine and Magh-Ai. Canon O'Hanlon[2] refers here to the
Gauls invoked by St. Aengus in his Litany of Irish Saints:
SS. Gallos de Magh-Salach, invoco in auxilium.   The
plain here referred to is not Magh-Sealga of Cruachan, but
Magh-Salach, *Sally-plain,* as is clear from the *Book of
Leinster.*[3]   After the Collectanea of Tirechan, in the *Book of
Armagh,* are three columns of notanda mainly indicating
parts of the *Tripartite* not included in the *Book of Armagh*
Patrician Documents.   The last but one (not in the *Tripar-
tite*) is: Gas, Mac Airt, in Campo Sailech: Gas, son of Art,
in Magh-Sailech.[4]   As Elphin and its neighbourhood are so
much in the *Tripartite* and *Book of Armagh,* there is little
doubt that Magh-Sailech is Sally-Field, at the northern end
of the peninsula running into Lough Boderg, in the parish of
Kilglass, barony of Ballintober North, diocese of Elphin.[5]
Near this is the *Rath of the Romans.*   The *Annals of the
Four Masters,* at the year 1248, have the entry: Felim, son
of Cathal Crovderg, gave by order of Teige O'Monahan,
Rath-na-Romhanach to the Canons of Kilmore, in the
honour of the Blessed Virgin Mary and St. Augustine. The
townland is now called Rathnarovanagh. It is probable
that some of the Romans invoked by Aengus dwelt here.

There is now no trace of the stones inscribed by
St. Patrick. O'Donovan tells us that he made every search
for the inauguration stone of the O'Conors, but could find
no such stone, nor tradition respecting it.   He thinks it

---

[1] *Tripartite,* Stokes, p. 104.
[2] *Lives of Irish Saints,* vol. iii., p. 592.
[3] *Book of Leinster,* 387a, line 39.
[4] Stokes, p. 351 ; Hogan, p. 116.
[5] Identified by Dr. MacCarthy.

probable that it was either destroyed or carried away several centuries since. There is still here a long standing-stone called *Cloch fhada na gcarn* (long stone of the cairns). There are a few other slabs standing, without any particular dressing or shape. At present no remains exist of any ecclesiastical buildings of stone at Dumha-Sealga or Carns. This cannot surprise us, when we recollect that, in the words of the Four Masters, the men of England broke down the monasteries and sold their roofs and bells and burned the images, shrines and relics of the saints.

There are some ruins at Killukin in the neighbourhood, which gives name to a parish in the diocese of Elphin. Among the miracles of St. Patrick are 'the consecrated residences not to be destroyed, namely, Rath-Airthir and Sen-domnach in Magh-Ai: *Eccur Sen-domnaig*, that is a proverb.'[1] It will be remembered that the *Tripartite* says the altar of Felartus was in Ui-Briuin-Seolai, far westward from Ailfind.[2] There were many Seolas: there was eastern Seola (Airther-Seola) and western Seola. Lanigan translates this from Colgan's *Tripartite*, 'at some distance from Elphin, to the west,' which corresponds to the situation of Carns; and says: 'Next we find him, Patrick, at Mag-Seola, at some distance from Elphin to the west, in which place he is said to have held a synod.'[3] And in a note: 'The situation of Mag-Seola is laid down somewhat precisely in the *Tripartite Life*, l. 2, c. 39, which places it in regione de Hybr[i]uiu, quae haud parum ab Ailfinia ad occidentem distat.' The Life in the *Book of Armagh*, which is more accurate than the *Tripartite*, has only: Et tertium in aeclessia magna Saeoli super altare Felarti, sancti episcopi.[4] This is strongly confirmed by Tirechan's account in the *Book of Armagh*: Venit vero Patricius ad Selcam [*i.e.*, Duma-Selca] in quo [fuerunt] filii Briuni, cum multitudine episcoporum sanctorum. Castrametati sunt in cacuminibus Selcae, et posuerunt sibi stratum et sedem inter lapides, in quibus

[1] Stokes's *Tripartite*, p. 251.
[2] *Ibid.*, p. 97.
[3] *Ecc. Hist.*, p. 244 and p. 247, note 92.
[4] Hogan's *Documenta*, etc., p. 69.

scripserunt manu sua literas quas hodie conspeximus oculis
nostris. Et cum illo fuerunt Bronus, episcopus, Sachellus.
. . . Felartus episcopus de genere Aillello [et ejus]
sorores ii.,—[una, monacha ejus; et altera, quae est in
insola] in mari Conmaicne, [quae] sic vocatur Croch Cuile.[1]
Et plantavit aeclessiam super stagnum Selcae *inscae* [*recte*,
insulae], et babtitzavit filios Broin[2] [Briuin]. We have here,
therefore, there can be little doubt, one of those glosses or
explanations of a scribe who did not know the localities.

The *Tripartite* tells us that Patrick came into the territory of Corcu-Ochland, on this side of Ui-Ailella (Tirerrill).
The *Book of Armagh* says that the druids, Hono and Ith,
fuerunt de genere Corcu-chonluain. They were of the royal
Ui-Briuin race of Connaught, Ono being the son of Erc the
Ruddy, son of Bron [Briun], de quo the Ui-Onach. Corcaghlan, Corcu-Ochland in the *Tripartite*, was one of the three
districts anciently called *Teora Tuatha*, the three Tuathas
or Territories. These were Tir-Briuin-na-Sinna, Kinel-Dofa,
and Corcaghlan. These territories extended from the
northern part of Lough Ree to Jamestown on the Shannon,
from Jamestown to Elphin, and thence again to Lough Ree.
Kinel-Dofa (or Doohy-Hanly) comprised the parishes of
Kilglass, Termonbarry, and Clontuskert, together with the
eastern part of Lisonoffy [*Fort of Ui-Dobhtha*, or *Ui-Dofa*]
parish, in the baronies of Ballintober North and South,
county Roscommon. Corcaghlan included the parishes of
Bumlin, Cloonfinlough, Kiltrustan, and the western part of
Lissonuffy, which was anciently called Templereagh. These
parishes now form part of the union of Strokestown. We
see from the *Tripartite* and *Book of Armagh* that in the
time of St. Patrick it extended to Elphin. The Kinel Mac
Erca were the Mac Branans and O'Hanlys, the ancient
chiefs of this territory. Mac Branan, Prince of Corcaghlan,
was descended from the noble Druid Ona, who presented

---

[1] This Island of Connemara is now called Crughnakeely, and sometimes
Deer Island.

[2] *Documenta de S. Patricio, ex Libro Armachano*, edidit E. Hogan, S.J.,
p. 76. 30. *The Tripartite Life of St. Patrick*, with other Documents relating
to that saint, edited by Whitley Stokes, D.C.L., LL.D. Tireohan's *Collections*,
p. 319.

Emlagh-Ona, now Elphin, to St. Patrick, and, therefore, through Erc the Red and Briun, King of Connaught, from Eochy Mughmeodain, Monarch of Ireland from A.D. 358 to 366. Eochy was father of the celebrated Niall of the Nine Hostages, whose eldest son, Laeghaire, was monarch at the time of the coming of St. Patrick. From Eochy's eldest son, Briun, king of Connaught, the O'Conors, O'Rourkes, Mac Dermots, Mac Geraghtys, O'Beirnes, and other ancient families of Connaught derive their descent. O'Donovan says that in 1837 the representative of the family of MacBranan was Hubert Branan, of Belmount, near Strokestown, brother of the late respected parish priest of Ahamlish, diocese of Elphin, the Rev. Malachy Brennan. Hubert Branan, as O'Donovan tells us, then enjoyed a small property of about fifty-six acres in Corcaghlan, one of the most ancient hereditary estates in the world.

[To be continued.]   J. J. KELLY.

SHALL WE RETURN TO PAGAN ETHICS?

THE question of morals is, at the present time, of paramount importance. Next to the dissemination of right
principles of morality nothing is more imperative than the
eradication of wrong ones. Not only must the true standard
of right and wrong be vigorously maintained, but false
standards must be peremptorily challenged. The well-being
of society demands this. Unsound principles are the parents
of insane deeds. Warped notions of right and wrong are
the greatest menace to the body politic. False systems of
ethics, established on unsound bases, soon collapse, and in
their fall overturn all that is best in our social institutions.

For this reason it seems to me that an article entitled
' The Relation of Ethics to Religion,' which was printed in
the September number of the I. E. RECORD, should not be
permitted to pass unchallenged. To be sure, the writer's
intention appears to be the best. He wishes to separate
morals from religion ; yet he trusts to religion to keep men
moral. His anxiety is about those who cast off religion.
For them he wishes to draw up a code of morals independent
of all religion—natural as well as supernatural. He is manifestly aware that he is treading on dangerous ground ; and,
hence, he proceeds apparently with the greatest caution.
He does not venture a single dangerous statement which he
docs not—sooner or later—modify, cancel, or wholly withdraw. He seems to have a dim consciousness of the moral
ruin which must inevitably follow a general adoption of his
principles ; but he looks to religion to ultimately repair the
moral chaos which their adoption would create.

Of the writer, Mr. W. Vesey Hague, I have no knowledge beyond what is furnished by his article. Judging from
that article, the writer would seem to belong to that peculiar
class of men who have come into being with the so-called
scientific movement of the last half century. These men do
not belong to the movement itself ; but they are completely

dazzled—in some instances, even blinded—by the false glare and glitter of modern ideas. They take the leaders of agnostic thought at their own lofty estimate of themselves. They are unable to distinguish between the mere tinsel and the real gold in our progress. And they believe that the agnostics and the speculative scientists, who have nothing to show but their empty negations and still more empty guesses, are the glory of our age; simply because agnostic and scientist are so loud-voiced in their own behalf. With this class the tendency is to decry everything Christian, and extol everything pagan. While still clinging to Christianity, they do not disguise their admiration of things agnostic. They adopt the ideas and opinions of their agnostic idols; they copy their mincing style and affected language; they lend an air of importance to common words by capitalizing the initial letter. In the tasks which they set themselves they seem to keep one eye on the task, and one ever on the agnostic model. Religion they treat with a species of condescending tolerance; but they never fail to let you understand that they regard it as a bore. It is something for which they find it necessary to be always apologizing. It might be tolerable if it kept its own place; but it insists, they remind you, in obtruding itself where it is not wanted. Christianity, they admit, is good for the restraining of the masses; but whenever it comes into conflict with modern ideas, the blame is, of course, to be placed upon religion.

The writer of the article in question seems to be a moderate disciple of this school. There is in his article the same ill-disguised impatience over the intermeddling on the part of religion; there is mild censure for the scholastic ethics; there is a sneer at what he calls 'the classic moralists' of the Church. 'Our modern Catholic system,' he complains, has so invaded the realm of morals that morals and religion are now intermingled in an almost hopeless state of confusion, which defies all attempt at disentanglement. Things have, indeed, come to such a pass that—

The morality of a Catholic is so much apart of his religion, and the natural ethical impulses are for him [the Catholic] so inseparably

associated with the dictates of a divine lawgiver, that it is
hardly possible for him to conceive of a morality which should rest
upon any other basis than that of a divine ordinance.

But this is not the worst. So far, in Mr. Hague's
opinion, has the evil progressed, so completely has religion
interwoven itself into the very texture of our morals, and
'the positive morality of Christian countries of to-day is
so much a purely religious affair that, were the hope of a
future state of existence suddenly blasted, it [the morality]
would inevitably disappear.' This state of things Mr. Hague
regards as exceedingly deplorable. 'The exclusive character
of such a view as this,' he tells us, 'must be patent to all
who take the trouble to think out the matter for themselves,'
and it 'is particularly regrettable just now when the continuous spread of agnosticism tends to render the recognition
of a non-religious ethic every day of more importance.'

Poor deluded Christians that we are. What mistaken
notions we have had of things! What a foolish complacency
we took in contemplating the beauty of Christian morality!
It was our vaunted boast that the true idea of morals—
man's primal notion of right and wrong being in a great
measure lost—came into the world with the Sinaitic code,
and that the spread of morality invariably followed the light
of the Gospel. Now it appears we were all wrong. Our
work was a Much Ado about Nothing. The proper application of our energies in the moral sphere would have been
shown in framing a code of ethics from which all notion of
law, obedience, duty, conscience, rewards and punishments,
merit and demerit—even freedom and responsibility—was
rigidly excluded; so that when the gigantic intellects of
agnosticism had succeeded in brushing aside for ever the
cobwebs of Christian sophistry—which had so long be-
clouded the minds of men—there might be still left some
influence to save those illustrious emancipators of thought
from lapsing into barbarism. It is quite an original and
novel notion that it is the duty of Christian moralists to
abandon their own sphere in order to codify moral regulations for our neo-pagans. A cynic might even suggest that
if the tendency of agnosticism is to upset morality, that

very fact should stand against the new cult as its severest
condemnation.   Mr. W. Vesey Hague, however, seems to
think otherwise.   Indeed he unhesitatingly throws the
blame on religion.   Religion has unblushingly entered into
an unholy alliance with morality.   This alliance was evil and
misleading from the outset.   Now it has created confusion
worse confounded ; and the sooner we recognise the necessity
of divorcing morals from religion the sooner the evil will be
remedied.   Back to paganism we must go if we are to
have ' an ethic' pure and uncontaminated by contact with
religion, if we wish to break up for ever the unhallowed
union.   The world has had enough of the preposterous
mistake of the ' attempt to found goodness upon duty, to
make morality submission to an absolute commandment, the
result of a law "shot out of a pistol" in the supra-mundane
regions,' and it will not be the fault of Mr. W. Vesey
Hague if this state of things should continue.   It is
true that his views as to how the deplorable evil is to be
remedied are not very definite.   Even such as they are, he
tells us they are only ' provisional.'   He admits that he is
' far from thinking that' he has ' been entirely successful in
solving the problem ;' but he hopes that some one will take.
up the matter and work it out ' with greater fulness of
detail and more fruitful results ' than he could presume to
attempt.   One thing, however, is fixed in his mind as
absolutely certain, viz. : that morality must be completely
secularized ; and further, he has concluded that the only
way to accomplish this is by a speedy return to pagan
ethics.

The attempt to secularize morals is not entirely new—
not even in our day ; although no Catholic before Mr. Hague
had, as far as I am aware, undertaken the attempt.   The
eudaemonism in which Mr. Hague would have us all take
refuge—though he tries to disguise it under the name of
Aristotelianism—is, in reality, nothing more than a vague
and undefined utilitarianism.   The greatest-happiness principle of Bentham and Mill reached the climax of absurdity
at the hands of Mr. Herbert Spencer, under whose fostering
care, the doctrine, it was hoped, had been ' cherished ' for

ever into everlasting peace and rest. In his efforts to
reconcile the conflicting interests of egoism and altruism,
so long the bane of the famous theory, Mr. Spencer found
the reconciliation and solution of the discordant claims in a
sublimated form of altruism, according to which—if practically carried out to its logical conclusion—a man's greatest
happiness should consist in planning how to surreptitiously
inflict injury on himself, in order to be thus rendered able
to afford others the altruistic satisfaction of relieving him.
One would suppose that absurdities of this nature would
put an end to the greatest-happiness principle for ever, and
with it the secularization of morals. It is, indeed, true that
Mr. Hague does not openly avow the utilitarian doctrine,
and that it is to ancient rather than to modern paganism he
appeals for a remedy; but that is neither here nor there,
for in his search for a secular basis of morals he makes
common cause with Mill and Spencer.

Mr. Hague's notion of what constitutes the ethical end
of human action is vagueness itself. He starts with the
assumption that 'the doctrine of eudaemonism is well
founded, and that happiness of some sort is the end and
aim of all human activity.' This indeterminate happiness
being assumed as the end, all actions are 'right' or
'reasonable,' according as they are 'conducive to, in
harmony with, or, at least, not opposed to, the ultimate
end.'

Now this might be all very well if we knew in what form
of happiness Mr. Hague makes the well-being of mankind
consist. But while he reminds us that 'in the interpretation given to the notion of happiness the widest possible
differences have prevailed,' he is singularly cautious about
committing himself to any particular interpretation of the
term, and in consequence we can make very little headway
as to what actions are right or wrong. If actions are moral
or immoral in proportion as they are conducive to an end,
it is quite manifest that we must know what that end is
before we can pass judgment on the morality or immorality
of the action. It will not do to say happiness is the end of
action. We must give some definite meaning to this term

happiness ; otherwise we may be liable to confound moral
with immoral actions. And as Mr. Hague himself says ' the
widest possible differences have prevailed ' regarding the
meaning of the term, it is all the more necessary for him to tell
us to which of those widely-differing significations the term
happiness is to be restricted. Is it the happiness of the
individual or the happiness of society? Is it the happiness
of the egoist or that of the altruist ? If the happiness of the
individual, is it his happiness in this life or in a future life ?
All these forms of happiness are so widely different that
actions which might be highly conducive to one of them
might be highly destructive of the other. St. Augustine
tells us that Varro, even in his time, enumerated as many
as two hundred and eighty-eight different forms of the
sovereign good or the well-being of man. The agnostic
moralists assume happiness as the basis of morals, and by
happiness they tell us they mean what gives pleasure. Now
the epicurean placed his happiness in sensual pleasures,
the stoic placed his happiness in virtue, while Plato and
Aristotle agreed in believing intellectual pleasure to be the
highest form of human happiness. It is quite manifest
then that if the right or reasonable in human action be what
leads to happiness, it is necessary to define at the outset
what we mean by happiness ; for few things are more
certain than that actions which conduce to virtue or to
intellectual enjoyment are by no means the actions that
lead to the sty of Epicurus. Consequently no system of
ethics can be based on a general notion of happiness ; and
to say that ' happiness of some sort is the end and aim of all
human activity,' and then to ' contend that on this assumption a complete and coherent system of Ethics may be
worked out,' is about as reasonable as to say that we can
build up a system of ethics on the Gulf Stream.

But Mr. Hague tells us that he is not concerned with
the ethical standard, ' but rather with the bare notions of
ethical right and wrong ' ; and although his notions of
right and wrong, as has been seen, must remain vague and
uncertain, he is determined, at all hazards, to effect a
complete and eternal separation of morals from religion.

'Ethics must hand over to religion the concepts she has borrowed, and of which she has made an illegitimate use, and religion on her side must recognise the independence and relative autonomy of ethics.' This is the treaty which he would draw up between the two rival powers, and which establishes for ever 'the independence and autonomy' of morals. The concepts which ethics has borrowed from religion are, as we have seen, the concepts of law, duty, obedience, conscience, and so forth. These being eliminated the dereligionization (or secularization) of morals is complete, and we are ready to return to the morality of the pagan. Since, however, we are asked to abandon our Christian view of morals, and go back to the Nicomachean ethics, it might be advisable to glance for a moment at what pagan ethics have really done for morality.

Investigation upon this point is not altogether reassuring. To be sure we have had various pagan systems—many fine words, and even some exalted notions of right living. But the real test is not in moral theories, but in the results which the applied theories give us. The enhancing beauty for Mr. Hague, of the Greek and Roman moralist was that 'he never imposed commands; he simply offered counsel.' The question, therefore, naturally arises : Were the counsels followed? What results did they produce? And history is not slow to give the answer. The depravity of morals, the degradation of human nature, the corruption of mankind, in those pagan times, is without a parallel in the history of the world. This is proved by indisputable and unquestioned evidence from all sides. Fathers of the Church, like St. Augustine ; pagan historians, like Sallust, Livy, and Tacitus ; poets and satirists, like Horace and Juvenal—all have left us pictures of Greek and Roman life, dark with the iniquity of those days. The people were steeped in vice and crime. To use the expressive phrase of Balmez, there was not a veil for even the greatest crimes. Such impure divinities as Adonis and Priapus, such temples of lewdness as those of Venus in Babylon and Corinth, such lascivious games as the Lupercalia and the Florealia, such inhuman spectacles as the gladiatorial combats, in one of

which, according to Tacitus, ten thousand people were put
to death, went hand in hand with the teachings of the Greek
and Roman moralists. St. Augustine tells us that not the
body only, but ' the mind itself, was drenched with iniquities.'
Seneca asserts that *Omnia sceleribus ac vitiis plena sunt.*
Juvenal tells us that, in spite of the teachings of the philosophers, the people had no higher ideals than *panem et
Circenses.* Even Lecky, in his work on morals, is forced to
admit that the moral doctrines of the philosophers were far
superior to the practices of the people ; that the people
were in a high degree corrupt ; and that the teachings of
their moralists were powerless to effect a moral elevation.
If these be the results which the pagan moralists could
effect by means of their counsels, it might be as well to
pause before exchanging our Christian for the Nicomachean
ethics.

And, if we examine into the systems themselves of the
pagan moralists, the prospect is not altogether encouraging.
Nothing can be more degrading than the views which these
moralists and philosophers take of human life and the dignity
of man. Aristotle himself maintained in his ethics that
utility and expediency are the measure of the means to be
employed in the pursuit of happiness. He advocated the
lawfulness of slavery, and held that no reasoning faculty
existed in the soul of a slave. Plato, in his ideal state,
would have women, like everything else, the common property of all. His praises of the god Eros was simply a
deification of the most degrading as well as the most revolt-
ing of vices ; and Aulus Gellius, according to St. Augustine,
makes mention of even the most shameful amatory verses
composed by no less a person than the renowned moralist—
the divine Plato himself ! Socrates, as is well known, gave
lessons to abandoned women as to how they should ensnare
their paramours ; while Epictetus—who is one of Mr. Hague's
ideals—allowed free scope to sexual intercourse. Such are,
in brief, some specimens of purely secular ethics, from
which all foreign notions of duty, obedience, conscience,
and law are rigidly excluded. I shall not insult Mr. Hague
by saying I hope they are to his liking.

It is not necessary, however, to go back to ancient paganism for the condemnation of secularized morality. One example from our neo-paganism—for which agnosticism is only another name—will be quite sufficient to show us what we may expect when all traces of duty and obligation are eliminated from our new science of ethics. The greatest moralist of agnosticism is pre-eminently George Eliot. She is the poet and high priestess of the new ethics. No Christian moralist has uttered more impassioned language on the subject of goodness, and none has given expression to more intense altruistic sentiments. She has held up some of the loftiest ideals to the gaze of mankind, and has preached, in striking and forcible language, high moral truths. Even ministers of the Gospel have for the while forgotten the pages of Holy Writ, and turned to hers instead for texts of highest morality. We all remember how soulfully she sang :—

> Of those immortal dead who live again
> In lives made better by their presence.

And how she extolled that

> . . . . . . beauteous order that controls
> With growing sway the growing life of man.

The world listened entranced as she sang of ' deeds of daring rectitude,' and as she uttered her fine ' scorn for miserable aims that end with self.' It hung upon her fervent accents in which she prayed that she might

> . . . . . . be to other souls
> A cup of strength in some great agony.

Words could hardly portray more beautifully the ideal of a noble life than those in which she longed to ' be the sweet presence of a good diffused.' And yet when the world came to examine the sweet beauties of that life, as exemplified in the preacher, it found—as, perhaps, Carlyle would phrase it—that the morality was nothing but ' ignominious ooze.' With all her beautiful altruism, with all the exalted sentiment of her soulful song, with all her lofty moral precepts, the example which her life has left the world was that of a woman who, in open defiance of public morality, in defiance of public opinion, and in defiance of public decency, gave herself up to the gratification of illicit love. The ' beauteous order ' of domestic life and social purity she trampled beneath her feet. For ' deeds of daring rectitude '—of which she sang so loftily—she substituted in practice deeds of daring turpitude. Her fine ' scorn for miserable aims that end in self ' was forgotten in the indulgence of her own fleshly inclinations. The ' cup of strength to other souls in some great agony,' which she proved to be, was that she became a barrier to the just claims of a lawful wife, whose place she brazenly usurped. And ' the sweet presence of a good diffused,' which she became, took the form of a moral plague-spot from contact with which, honest wives and mothers shrank in disgust and disdain.

All this is, of course, now forgotten. To genius, sooner or later, everything is condoned—and that George Eliot possessed genius of a high order no one in his senses will undertake to deny—but in expatiating on the beauties of agnosticism, and setting up an ideal of secularized morals for our admiration and example, it is well not to forget that the loftiest preacher of morals-divorced-from-religion, as well as the highest type of agnostic excellence, was one, about the most significant fact in whose life her biographer is discreetly silent ; and of whom another writer ventures the somewhat curious statement, that her union with George Henry Lewes ' could not be legalized by either Church or State, but it was sanctioned by the approval of a large circle of personal friends.' It is, of course, somewhat impolite to now recall these ugly facts; but the interests of sound morality demand the unpleasant repetition.

Here then is your highest type of neo-paganism—not a mere ignorant and unlettered rustic, but one possessing all the culture of her school—preaching and poetizing about the beauty of the moral life, especially in its altruistic relations, yet disregarding vital moral principles, and even braving public opinion in order to live according to her own inclinations. What then is the value of your pagan morality when divorced from all ideas of duty, obligation and conscience ? Much more of the same kind could be adduced in evidence, but for the sake of brevity let these suffice.

Having abolished all notions of duty and obedience from the science of ethics, the question naturally arises : How is the new moral code to obtain its sanction? And the answer, we are at once told, is that all sanctions are to be wholly abolished. The new ethics will have nought to do with compulsion ; they are to be purely optional. ' Ought,' we are told, is a term which ' from the ethical standpoint has no real meaning.' Again, we are informed that ' the moralist, if he is to remain true to his mission, must proceed by way of counsel and example. Prove to a man, if you will, that some actions are right, but leave him to perform them or not as he pleases, or you desert the region of ethics altogether.' ' Sweet reasonableness ' must be the talisman of all your persuasion. And when the new moralist is confronted with the question : ' Why is good action to be pursued, and evil action to be avoided? he has no complete answer to the question . . . and he is apt to appear at a loss when too closely pressed.' Further, Mr. Hague tells us that, ' speaking from the strictly ethical standpoint, no complete answer can be given to the question : Why ought I to be moral? There is really no " ought " about the matter.' The answer is simply : ' I " ought " to be moral because morality is reasonable.' And if we still persistently and unreasonably further inquire ' Why reasonable action is alone to be pursued?' the new moralist has no alternative but to answer : ' If you wish to be unreasonable, remember you can only do so at the cost of doing violence to your own nature as man; but, of course, if you are such a fool as to be unaffected by this consequence, and if the " good for man " has really no attractions for you, I am afraid there is no more to be said.'

Of course, Mr. Hague here forgets that in talking so magisterially he forgets entirely that he has not yet shown what he means by ' reasonable action,' inasmuch as he has not even pointed out what is to be the definite end of such action, and that unconsciously he feels justified in adopting this lofty strain about ' doing violence to your own nature as man ' simply because he gets his true concept of the ' good for man ' from religion. But he should not forget that religion and duty being excluded altogether, and the ' good for man ' being yet wholly undetermined, all his views regarding what is right or reasonable action can be nothing more than pure assumption. But let that pass— at least for the present.

What is worthy of notice here is the singular position of the neo-pagan morality. Wiser than an all-wise Being, the new moralist, knowing man's noble nature and his natural proneness to good, is perfectly satisfied that all that is necessary in order to induce him to practise virtue and shun vice is merely to point out to him the reasonableness of the one and the unreasonableness of the other, thus doing away at once with all pains and penalties, rewards and punishments; and such clumsy contrivances as laws, obligations, and duties.

Confidence in human goodness is surely to be commended, Optimism, however, can, on some points, be carried too far. Indeed, few things are more amusing than the way in which many well-meaning people go through life. They manage to close their eyes to the real world around them, and live in a fanciful dreamland of visionary perfection. They amuse themselves by spinning most beautiful theories of purest gossamer concerning imaginary Utopias which are utterly impossible of realization in this mundane sphere. They never take man as he is, but as they would have him be, which with them is equivalent to, as he must be. When they are brought face to face with the real state of things, they will admit that their views are mere theories, and that in the present state of human existence they are not apt to get them accomplished ; yet they persist in dreaming them all the same.

Of course, if the business of life is to theorize or build air castles, or amuse ourselves with blowing soap-bubbles, which are beautiful while they last, there is no more to be said. A beautiful science of ethics, fully fashioned, so as to captivate the most æsthetic taste, may be all very well; but, if no one will fashion their lives according to its dictates, it will be about as useful as so much bottled moonshine. The world in which we live is, however, a practical one, and likes to mingle the *utile* with the *dulce.*

Indeed, Mr. Hague himself admits that the new ethics will not be a very powerful aid to practical morality. He candidly confesses that ' it is not too much to say that, were it not for the help of the theologian, the moralist's counsels would remain for ever ineffective with the great mass of mankind.' This single admission, of course, cancels his entire contention ; but he has others of a similar nature.

He has told us that ' sweet reasonableness ' is the true note of ethical action—the real incentive to morality from the neo-pagan point of view. But he takes pains to tell us later that ' poor, weak humanity, however, stands in need of motives more powerful than the gentle allurements of reasonableness, " sweet," indeed, but often powerless amid the clash and conflict of uncontrollable impulses.' And a little later he adds : ' To follow right for righteousness' sake were, indeed, true wisdom; but it is the wisdom of angels rather than of men.' Now, if our poor, weak humanity stands in need of more powerful motives than the gentle allurements of 'sweet reasonableness' to draw it to the practice of moral good, what useful purpose can the neo-pagan science of ethics serve, since the only motive to the practice of goodness which it urges is that of ' sweet reasonableness'? And if the 'following of right for righteousness' sake' be the wisdom of angels rather than of men, it is quite manifest that Mr. Hague, in planning his new code of ethics, must contemplate a new system of morals not for mortal man at all, but for the angelic choirs, since in that code he makes 'for the sake of right ' the only motive to action—unless, indeed, he regards the disciples of negation, for whom the code is intended, as nothing short of ' angels ' in disguise. He will tell us, of course, that he expects his ethical creed to be supplemented by religion, and that both will work in harmony. But as his new ethics can be intended only for two classes of men—those who cling to religion and those who reject it—it is quite manifest that in the case of the former it would be superfluous, while in the case of the latter it would be absolutely worthless, inasmuch as the agnostics reject with scorn the supplementary aids of religion which Mr. Hague suggests, and without which, he

tells us, 'poor, weak humanity' is 'powerless.' For it must
not be forgotten that Mr. Hague's expulsion of religion is a
quite sweeping and comprehensive process, and includes not
only revealed but natural religion as well. He does not
hesitate to tell us that the notion of a natural law seems
to 'him' to be open to serious criticism from more than
one side, and he is quite sure that it is, moreover, a notion
'which finds its true place not in a system of ethics, but in
a system of natural theology.'

The new ethics seems to be blind to the fact that this
exclusion of all that makes morality intelligible leaves the
moralist on a boundless sea, without chart or compass to
guide him, and that when he undertakes to instruct his
disciples as to what constitutes morality, he is utterly
unable to give anything like a conclusive demonstration.
The moralist may insist that happiness is the end of
man; but his disciple is apt to enquire: What kind of
happiness? Happiness in a future life seems to be excluded
from Mr. Hague's court; for it is the 'continuous spread
of agnosticism' that renders 'the recognition of a non-
religious ethic' so pressing, and agnosticism scouts all
notion of a future existence. Hence our happiness—
whatever it may be—must be confined to the present life.

But putting aside Mr. Spencer's notion of the highest
happiness, viz., that of making ourselves miserable that
others may have the happiness of relieving us, there are
many other forms of pleasure—and the new school admits
that happiness consists in pleasurable feeling—that do not
outrage common sense to quite the same extent as
Mr. Spencer's. Even moral distortions of evil have
passed, and now pass, for happiness. We have already
seen what different views of ' the sovereign good' have been
maintained by philosophers in the past. The thief, the
gambler, the libertine, the drunkard, has each his own view
as to what constitutes happiness for him. At all times there
have been those who were of Hamlet's opinion, that 'there's
nothing, either good or bad, but thinking makes it so.'

As a matter of fact there is nothing more remarkable
than the different views men hold regarding right and

wrong action outside the realm of Christian morals. The Egyptian practices lying and deception; and he is said to regard the practice as praiseworthy, even when the lying and deception are the end as well as when they are the means. The Turcoman will make pilgrimages to the tombs of noted robbers, for the purpose of making offerings there. The Fiji islander looks upon murder as highly honorable, and is not quite at his ease until he has performed at least one such noble deed. How is the new moralist to convince these that his views of right and wrong and not theirs are the correct ones? Each man will have his own standard of happiness and there will be as many standards of right and wrong, in other words, as many moral codes, as there are individuals.

Hence in addition to the difficulty of compelling men to live up to your moral code, you have the further fundamental difficulty of convincing them that your moral code is the right one. They may object to your views of happiness altogether; to your notions of right and wrong in consequence; and thus to your entire moral code; and you are powerless to demonstrate the truth of your teachings. It is not here a question ' of compelling the vulgar to strive' for the realization of their ' sovereign good.' It is a question of convincing them that they should adopt your opinion as to what that good is. And the difficulty will not be confined to the vulgar. It is quite as likely to be met with among the moral philosophers themselves.

We have seen how George Eliot's practical standard of ethics was placed in what the world regards as baseness. In the same way life itself is regarded as good, since without life there can be no happiness; yet some of the greatest moralists have held opposite views of the value of life. Cicero regarded death as terrible; Socrates looked upon it with indifference; and Cato coveted death. Hence the new moralist in proposing his views is apt to be informed that at most the view we take of ethics is a matter of taste. Indeed, in point of fact John Stuart Mill classed ethics not as a science, but as an art, and regarded morality as a purely æsthetic achievement. Mr. Hague sees this difficulty, but he endeavours to meet it by telling us that ' the ethical end imposes itself upon our reason in a manner that admits no denial.' This, however, is a strange answer from one who has not ventured even to tell us what 'the ethical end' is, except in terms so vague and general as to be worth nothing. If 'the ethical end' imposes itself so undeniably upon our reason, why does not Mr. Hague boldly proclaim what it is? He must not forget that he is codifying morality for those who do not believe in a future life, and that he has boldly put natural law out of court altogether.

In spite of these facts, however, when he comes to prove his contention that 'the ethical end' imposes itself upon our reason in a manner that admits of no denial he is obliged to bring back both these discarded elements and appeal to them for support. Indeed without them it would be simply impossible for him to maintain that 'the ethical end' cannot be ignored by reason. Even with all the sanctions which religion has thrown around the moral Law, men have succeeded in blinding themselves to the true conception of morality. The couplet which tells us that

Vice is a monster of so frightful mien,
As, to be hated, need but to be seen,

is excellent poetry, and even a very near approach to truth, in communities where the Christian idea of morals has taken root. But in communities where the primitive notions of duty as well as the original conceptions of a divine Law-giver are completely lost, we find strange travesties of moral good and evil. As St. Paul says, the original notion of right and wrong becomes quickly obscured when we lose sight of the true basis of morals.

Mr. Hague falls into the error of all those who in latter times have undertaken the task of secularizing morals. They view our full-orbed Christian morality as a whole, but close their eyes to the sun of Christian teaching which has given it warmth and life. They would build up a system of ethics without religion, without God, without the notions of law, obligation, conscience, duty, obedience. As well might they undertake to give us the world with its trees and flowers and fruits without the sunshine which gives them life. Religion is the root, morality is the fruit, the flower if you will. As well hope to have the flower or the fruit without the plant as have morals thrive and flourish where the notions of God and religion are altogether obliterated. Fortunately for the world these notions cannot be wholly obliterated. Distorted reflections of the truth may indeed obtain, as among the Gentiles of old, of whom St. Paul speaks ; but the notions of good and evil, though obscured, will still remain. Mr. Hague, like Bentham, and Mill, and Spencer, simply takes the world as Christianity has leavened it. They all forget that the present condition of morality is due to Christian teaching ; and they foolishly imagine they can accomplish the same moral results with Christianity eliminated. They fondly but vainly imagine they can secure all the beauties of Christian morals without Christian teaching, without Christ, and without God.

This delusion has led Mr. Hague into many amusing inconsistencies and contradictions in the brief limits of his essay. For example, he sets out with the statement ' that religion arose, historically, quite independently of morality, and that, to a certain extent, the connection between them has always remained a precarious one ' ; and on page 217 he tells us, ' the ethical category is primary and fundamental, and in this sense it may be said that all true religion has its roots in ethical ground ' ; while yet again he has reversed the situation by telling us, on page 214, that :—

In the earliest types of religious thought, as in the latest and most developed, we meet with the concept of a Divine Will, conceived in a manner analogous to that of a human legislator or even a despot, in which all moral precepts have their roots, and from which they derive their constraining force.

This jumble of contradictions—in which religion and morality are first represented as independent of each other, next so closely related that religion has its roots in ethics, and lastly which tells us that all moral precepts have their roots in and derive their constraining force from religion— becomes doubly amusing, when we remember that these contradictions constitute a portion of the argument for the complete divorce of morals from religion.

Again Mr. Hague tells us (page 208), that, if he must speak his whole mind, he believes, that 'in the Nicomachean ethics of Aristotle is to be found the basis and substance of the only completely consistent and satisfactory body of ethical doctrine.' On the following page he informs us that he 'will assume that the doctrine of eudaemonism is well founded'; and he adds, 'I contend that on this assumption a complete and coherent system of ethics may be worked out.' Nevertheless a little further on (page 216), forgetful of all this, he writes:—' To be sure, I do not believe that there is any such thing possible as a complete system of ethics constructed dogmatically in advance.' And as though he feared he might miss the climax of absurdity in .his contentions he adds:—' And so it is only by looking to concrete human experiences, by viewing real men in their various complex relations, individual, social, political, and most of all by living for ourselves the moral life, that we can determine the final truth in ethics, or can reach the full and adequate comprehension of the good for man.' And he quotes William James to the effect that there can be no final truth in Ethics any more than in physics, until the last man has had his experience and said his say. Which of these contradictory statements are we to take as the convictions of Mr. W. Vesey Hague, if he has any?

These, however, are merely one or two of the absurdities in which Mr. Hague's article abounds. We meet with them on almost every page. ·The entire article from beginning to end is a tissue of inconsistencies which show the confusion that reigns supreme—not in the world of ethics—but in Mr. Hague's hazy conception of the relation between religion and morals. It is difficult to be patient with the simpering dilettantism of the shallow agnostic. With the Christian would-be-imitators of the agnostic, this dilettantism becomes absolutely nauseating.

It is to be feared that there is no hope for the agnostics, about whose moral interests Mr. Hague is so intensely anxious that he would upset all Christian morality to cater to their whims. The remedy assuredly cannot lie in applying the ploughshares of devastation to the field of morals

in order to cut out morality by the very roots—after the
fashion of the agnostics themselves in the region of faith.
Mr. Hague's energies would find far more useful employment in showing his agnostic friends the supreme absurdity
of their irrational position. Let Mr. Hague think the
matter over. And let us hope that when next he undertakes the task of ' setting down the results of some thinking
on the subject' the absence of sanity, consistency, and
Christianity from his contention, may not be quite so
conspicuous as in the article I have just been considering.

SIMON FITZSIMONS.

GOD: KNOWN OR UNKNOWN?

I

IN the March number of the *Fortnightly Review*, in an
article under the title ' The Unknown God ? '—mark the
note of interrogation—Sir Henry Thompson gives expression
to some thoughts on religion, which, he tells us (page 413),
have been taking shape within him for upwards of twenty
years. One cannot but sympathize with an earnest man
who has struggled so long in a tangle of religious
opinion such as confuses modern thought. His labour,
he goes on to say, has happily brought him its own reward,
' by conferring emancipation from the fetters of all the
creeds, and unshakeable confidence in the Power, the
Wisdom and the Beneficence which pervade and rule the
Universe.' It is not too much to presume that his object
in giving to the world a syllabus of the reasoning that
helped to strike off these fetters, is to aid other prisoners in
their efforts to attain the same happy freedom.

As Sir Henry's confidence in his new position—I dare
not call it a creed—is unshakeable, it is not any part of my
intention in writing this paper to submit considerations
which he might have overlooked, so as possibly to make
him doubt if it be real freedom which he enjoys. But as

some of us have not yet been able to emancipate ourselves, and—such being the habit of slaves—would like to look before taking such an important leap, we would beg Sir Henry to answer a few questions, so as to clear away certain suspicions, which, so strong is association, have somehow got fixedly rooted in our minds.

II

It is pleasant, to begin with, to find oneself in agreement with Sir Henry as to the lines on which an enquiry of this kind should be conducted :—' The one method alone that can throw light on the subject is a studious observation of the facts of nature and of the inferences which may be legitimately drawn from them' (page 406). I do not know what phase of thought may predominate in some of the many sects whose 'diametrically opposite claims' Sir Henry has tested in the course of his investigations. I can only speak as a 'devotee of that old Papal Church' which he represents (page 413) as 'denouncing the exercise of reason and inquiry in all matters connected with religion'; and as such I would ask him to consider whether this statement, viewed merely as one of fact, may not be just a little too strong. I am sure he will accept my word when I assure him that for more than thirty years I have been engaged in 'reasoning and inquiry into matters connected with religion,' having been commissioned and bound to do so by that same 'old Papal Church.' I know others who have been similarly engaged, under the same commission ; nor do I see any prospect of bringing these investigations to an end. Moreover, any educated fellow-devotee with whom I have become acquainted, whether personally or through writings, maintained that it was only fools who submitted to the papal or any other authority, without having first satisfied themselves by a study of facts that the claims to which they yielded were so well founded as to necessitate submission.

This, however, is by the way. Sir Henry will be glad to hear—and will, I hope, accept my word for it—that the 'devotees of the old Papal Church,' at least, profess to believe only as they are compelled by facts.

There are facts, however, and facts: and it is here that the devotees aforesaid may not be able to see eye to eye with Sir Henry. From their point of view one fact is just as much a fact as another—supernatural fact is as good as natural—nor do they see any reason why they should confine their observations to ' the facts of nature ' alone. Whatever order it belongs to, if it be a fact, it is not to be got over by any amount of *a priori* reasoning. The ' devotees ' think, moreover, that it is not only by the telescope, or the microscope, or the balance, that facts can be ascertained, but by history as well ; nor are they prepared to cast to the winds all the records of the race. except those which seem to tell only for one side. I regret to have to acknowledge a suspicion that, with all his devotion to fact, Sir Henry Thompson does not quite agree with us in this.

Take, for instance, the miracles which raise in the minds of Christians a suspicion, let us say, that, after all, some supernatural divine revelation may have taken place. The suspicion is entirely due to the historical evidence ; so many men say they saw these miracles, or that they had it directly from those who saw. There was, for example, a celebrated religious teacher—a ' devotee ' Sir Henry calls him also (page 397)—the facts of whose life fit in quite remarkably with predictions which were in existence, as cannot be denied, long before he was born. From his station in life he should have been an ignorant artisan ; yet he founded the most harmonious and powerful social and religious organisation the world has yet known. His death was one of the most public facts ever witnessed ; and yet he was afterwards seen alive. Of this last fact we have testimony so strong that it is almost ridiculous to conceive how his ideas should have spread, unless his friends were really convinced that they had seen him living after death.

It is all very well, as against this, to put in evidence the general principle that, as the operations of nature are uniform, such a fact cannot have occurred. The fact, if it be a fact, is worth a bushel of your principles ; and the historical evidence for the fact is so strong as to make it impossible to put away the suspicion that Sir Henry may not be so free as he thinks. It is the truth that sets one free.

How does this evidence strike him ? At the opening of the second part of his paper he claims to have 'demonstrated two important statements '—demonstrated them, of course, by the 'one method' already referred to.   The second of these statements so demonstrated runs :—

The authenticity of the ancient records, existing in every part of the world, made at different periods of men's history, and regarded as supernaturally or 'divinely' revealed, ... has never been substantiated, and is in fact unsupported by evidence.

Will the reader believe that the man who claims to have demonstrated this statement—by a 'studious observation of facts,' too—has not made the slightest reference to any one of the facts that have been alleged as supporting the Christian revelation.

He has passed in brief review the nebular hypothesis, the progress made in astronomy, chemistry, physics, geology, biology, physiology, palæontology.   He tells how people procured fire in olden times ; and in this connection refers to the origin of the lucifer match in the following sentence, as remarkable for its matter as for its style :—

For ages past the universal mode for procuring fire during the absence of sunlight, has been that still practised no longer ago than 1833, viz., by striking a smart blow on a piece of steel held in the left hand with a sharp flint held in the right, from whence the sparks falling upon some tinder (charred linen), and contained in a tin box, the tinder became ignited, to which a sulphur-tipped match being applied a flame was produced sufficient to light a candle.—(Page 401, note).

Of course he does not fail to refer to evolution; the anthropoid ape is exhibited once more, and we are told how exactly he grew to be the civilised man we know.

Curiously, however, in the recital of these 'facts,' one notices such expressions as 'man probably at first used food' of a certain kind ; 'probably excavated caverns, using perhaps for that purpose branches of trees,' of which 'he might construct rude huts'; and 'he would soon come to make' wooden spears. 'The process by which man acquired the first rudiments of speech must have been a very gradual one'; 'the rights of personal ownership must have been

recognised'; 'the builder of a hut would naturally be
entitled to regard it as belonging to him'; 'the discovery
of fire must have marked an epoch in history.' These are
some of the 'facts' that go to prove that 'revelation has
never been substantiated and is unsupported by evidence'—
to prove it, too, it is well to remember, according to 'the
one method that alone can throw light on the subject.'

Or is it that Sir Henry puts these things forward as
'inferences which may be legitimately drawn from' the
facts of nature? If so, his method of demonstration is
almost as old as the hills, nor was there ever a quack
philosopher who had not inferences of the kind to support
his theories.

III

Before taking leave of this aspect of the question—the
necessity of basing one's speculations on solid facts—I
would like to ask Sir Henry Thompson what he means
when he says that 'all knowledge is relative to the individual, and all the phenomena of Nature are known to us
only as facts of consciousness' (page 404, note). Professor
Huxley, indeed, said something similar, and the doctrine is
recognised almost as an axiom in Agnostic philosophy: but
what does it mean?

Take, for instance, the solar system. Sir Henry is
convinced, as we all are now, that the sun is the centre,
and that the stars are not set in a solid firmament revolv-
ing round the earth. This conviction, however, did not always
prevail, as he is careful to insist: he finds in the error or
ignorance of ancient times a conclusive proof that the writers
of books recognised by Christians as sacred, did not receive
any divine supernatural revelation. What, however, are the
'facts'—according to his own notion of facts? The only
true facts, apparently, are those of consciousness: 'the
phenomena of Nature'—such, for example, as the solar
system—'are known to us only as facts of consciousness':
and 'all knowledge'—even of the solar system—'is relative
to the individual.'

So we are assured. But, then, why blame those early
writers? Is it that they did not express what they felt

within themselves as 'facts of consciousness'? And if 'all
knowledge is relative to the individual,' were they not
individuals, with as good a right to their own relations and
forms of thought as Sir Henry Thompson has to his?

If we are to enter at all on 'the one method alone that
can throw light' on this or any other subject, the 'studious
observance of facts,' let them by all means be real objective
facts, not facts of consciousness; for no one ever lived
that could not prove any proposition whatsoever, were he
allowed to build his arguments on foundations of that kind.

IV

Let me not, however, be unjust to Sir Henry. Forgetful
of his 'facts of consciousness' he does give us later on
(page 410) a kind of negative objective fact, in proof of his
assertion that revelation has never been substantiated. It
is that 'the precious secret' of the power of anæsthetics
was not revealed. 'How evident is it,' he cries out, in
italics, 'that "Revelation" was no part of the plan.'
Enough, surely, to shake the faith of all but the most confirmed 'devotee.'

If, however, he does not give us facts, he treats us to
that other part of his method—'inferences': 'that all
events must follow the laws of nature, which are immutable'
(page 412); that as modern science has shown the astrono-
mical notions of the writer of the first chapter of Genesis
to be at fault, that document could not have formed part of
any supernatural communication; and that as the revelations which so many suppose to have been made to
Zoroaster, Gottama, and Mahomed, were not real, there
can be no reason for believing in any such communication
whatsoever. 'Facts,' indeed.

Sir Henry is an eminent surgeon, and, no doubt, esteems
his profession, with the allied one of medicine; but of the quack
surgeons and physicians that have been the name is legion;
shall we therefore conclude that all surgeons are quacks?
He believes, apparently, in the revelations made all through
nature by 'the Infinite and Eternal Energy from which all
things proceed'; and which 'will not ever remain wholly

unknown or unknowable'; and yet this great book has not been at all times rightly interpreted, and there still remain some errors to be shaken off. It would help his 'inferences' enormously if he could make it plain why ignorance and error should in one case be but the initial stage of the process through which we come to a knowledge of the revealed truth, whereas in another case they prove that no revelation could possibly have been made.

V

Although Sir Henry has 'emancipated himself from the fetters of all the creeds,' he is not without an 'unshakeable confidence in the Power, the Wisdom, and the Beneficence which pervade and rule the Universe'; nor without 'belief,' either, 'that the Infinite and Eternal Energy will not ever remain wholly unknown and unknowable.' Nay, he professes to 'live a life of faith' in the 'Source of the Infinite and Eternal Energy.' No wonder, then, that he should proclaim himself a religious man; not, indeed, a 'devotee' of any form of 'creed,' which 'might suggest the validity of prayer to a Deity'; his religion is one whose 'public or private service can suitably consist only in adoration of the grandeur and of the beneficence which pervade the universe' (pages 412-414). Needless to say he does not sanction the use of the term 'God' to denote 'the Supreme Power and Wisdom,' because this and similar terms 'have become so completely identified by long association of ideas with schemes of theological doctrine based on alleged' theophanies. In fact, to think of the Supreme Power as 'God' is a form of idolatry, making It out to be so contemptible a thing as a 'Personality' (page 395).

Sir Henry must pardon us if we do not quite follow his reasoning in this connection. There is a Something—be sure to spell with a capital S—which as Infinite and Eternal Energy pervades and rules the universe. It is Infinite in Power and Knowledge; and is, moreover, Beneficent—on the whole. It does not appear to be quite Infinite in Beneficence, since there are boons which Infinite Power and Knowledge might have given—as for instance the

removal of all pain—and which It has not granted.
Now you can call this Something a 'Source of Energy,'
or even an 'Energy,' a 'Power,' an 'Intelligence'; you
you may speak of Its 'Will,' 'Beneficence,' 'Tendencies,'
'Dispositions,' 'Purposes'—'applying these terms as we
should to human beings, an analogy which must be permitted to man's limited means of expression.' You must
not, however, call it a 'Being,' or a 'Person,' or 'God'—
these terms are so anthropomorphic and lowering ; and have
been, moreover—as the others have not been—debased by
long-continued evil associations.

Sir Henry, making allowance for 'man's limited means
of expression,' permits the use of 'analogous'—what one
might call 'morphic'—terms, whereby to denote the
Supreme Energy. We must, however, choose only from
the higher forms, such as 'Power' and 'Energy;' or if you
do become 'anthropomorphic,' you must not make use of
any word that has been current among the 'devotees' of the
'creeds'—Christians, for instance; but must be content
with such as 'Infinite,' 'Eternal,' 'Intelligence,' 'Beneficence,' 'Purpose,' and 'Design.' The wretched Christians
never thought of associating their superstitious theophanies
with these. You are to cry shame on anyone who ventures
to speak of God's 'right hand' or 'eye,' but may applaud
when you hear the Infinite Source spoken of as a 'Power'
or an 'Energy' —all such things being, of course, infinitely
elevated over hands and eyes and other organs.

VI

As for the Agnostic's claim to religious sentiment, what
do we find? Sir Henry Thompson will not use the term
'God,' because it has been so long associated with supersti-
tion; but is not the same true of the term 'religion'? It
was not Mr. Spencer or Professor Huxley that got this term
adopted into human language; the word is so old that the
question is mooted whether in one form or another it may
not be as ancient as the race itself. Anyhow, it is very
venerable, nor is anybody entitled to make use of it unless
in the sense in which it has been used traditionally, and

in which it is still understood by the people at large. It is but a pretence to say that one is honest, or merciful, or law-abiding, or chaste, except we attach to these terms the conventional meaning which everybody will take up. The same, of course, applies to 'religion.'

Now, Sir Henry Thompson describes his religion as 'one in which a priestly hierarchy has no place, nor are there any specified formularies of worship' (page 409). I do not object to this, since it is universally understood that priests and hierarchies and specified formularies are not necessary for the performance of truly religious acts; and I allow that a Deist may be religious. But when Sir Henry goes on to justify his assertion, quoting Huxley to the effect that 'religion ought to mean simply reverence and love for the ethical ideal, and the desire to realise that ideal in life,' I say: the question is, not what religion ought to mean, but what it does mean; and I add that Professor Huxley's 'love for the ethical ideal' may be excellent morality, but it surely is not what men commonly understand by religion.

Religion, indeed, is reverence; but reverence connotes a person reverenced. We do not reverence the sun, although it is a great source of energy—spelling this time without capitals—and has done us a deal of good. We do not reverence ideals: we may love them, or hate them, or follow them; but we do not reverence them. We reverence a person who has worth. To reverence is to honour; and honour connotes recognition, not merely of worth of any kind, but of personal worth. The sun, as I have said, has worth, and it is well for us that it has; but we do not honour it, much less reverence or adore it.

For, religion is that peculiar kind of honour which is paid to worth which is recognised as Infinite. This is the traditional meaning of the word; and an Agnostic who does not recognise the Personality as well as the Infinity of the Source of Energy, however truthful, just, temperate, or prudent he may be, cannot, by the very nature of his system, make the least claim to be regarded as religious,—unless he wishes to gain respect by decking himself out in the clothes of others. Think of bending down in adoration, not of One Who is grand and beneficent, but of 'the grandeur and beneficence which pervade the universe.'

VII

Sir Henry Thompson's article suggests so many puzzles that it is impossible to commemorate all, and it is not easy to make a selection: I must content myself with the following, in addition to those already proposed.

The first puzzle is suggested by the title of the article, 'The Unknown God?' Think of it coming from one who, in the very article under that title, refuses to ' adopt, for the purposes of designating the Supreme Cause of all things, any of the brief words which have been in general use, as " Jehovah," " Theos," " Jove," or " God,"' (page 394). Surely Sir Henry either forgot the title of his paper when he came to that sentence, or else he forgot the sentence when he came to choose the title.

Then, it is an ' Unknown God '—with a note of interrogation. Sir Henry 'states his belief that the subject of his paper, " The Unknown God? " may be regarded as in progress of solution'—whatever that may mean—' by following the process suggested, and that the " Infinite and Eternal Energy from which all things proceed " will not ever remain wholly unknown or " unknowable," but may be still further elucidated.' The subject, therefore, must be wholly unknown, else how could it be supposed to *remain* ever so? Yet, if it is wholly unknown, how can it be *still further* elucidated? And is it not wonderful how much Sir Henry has contrived to learn about this wholly unknown Source of Energy—that it exists, has power, intelligence, will, beneficence, purpose, design, and so on. With this before you, tell me, is it known or unknown to Sir Henry? No wonder he had recourse to that note of interrogation.

In the next place I notice that he insists that the Source of Energy is Infinite in Knowledge and Power ; but he does not tell us wherein this infinity is displayed. Not in creation, for there was no such thing—creation, in Mr. Spencer's words, is unthinkable. Things 'proceed

from the Eternal Energy,' indeed ; procession of one thing
from another distinct thing being, of course, thinkable by
the poorest mind.

What proceeds, however? Something infinite? But
who has given proof that the universe is such? It is very
large, no doubt ; but between a large thing and an infinite
there is a whole infinity of difference. If it should be only
something finite that ' proceeds,' after all, where is the
ground for regarding the source as infinite?

My third puzzle is the assertion which Sir Henry
repeats so often, that ' man acquired all his stores of natural
knowledge—in the widest sense—solely by his own unaided
efforts' (pages 399, 404. 405, 407). What! absolutely
without aid? Where, then, is the ' Infinite Energy from
which *all things* proceed'? Is this knowledge not a thing?
Or does not it also come from the Source of Eternal
Energy?

Finally, Sir Henry, greatly troubled about the beneficence of the ' Source,' seeing that the world which proceeds
from but is not created by It, is a weary world after all,
satisfies himself, like Leibnitz, that with all its defects it is
the best world possible. It has been so very perfect as an
educational machine. Man, being left ' to fight his own
way throughout'—'self-taught, not helped'—has become
' the efficient and highly endowed creature he is'; such as,
' it is next to certain,' he could not be ' if the human race
had at any time a revelation.' This, by the way, is one of
Sir Henry's proofs—on his own new method of studious
observance of facts.

Nay, but has man not received aid from the Source
' from which all things proceed'? His education, therefore,
has not been without help from the Master : no wonder that,
' efficient and highly endowed creature as he is,' he should
be so feeble. Better, one would think, to have given him
no help at all, or given all he stood in need of, even though
it might be necessary to throw in revelation. And, indeed,
when you come to think of it, what is the good of education
except to form character? And could not an Infinite and
Eternal Energy, if it wished to be as beneficent as was

possible for it, do this of itself, without submitting poor
man so often to the rod?

VIII

It must be that, in my case, the evolutionary process
has not been sufficiently advanced to allow me to regard all
knowledge as relative to the individual, or to be satisfied
that all the phenomena of nature are known to us only as
facts of consciousness. For no other reason could I have
failed to realize the force of Sir Henry Thompson's 'demonstration'—on the new positive method—that 'revelation is,
in fact, unsupported by evidence;' and it must also be due
to the same defect that I should hesitate about taking up
the new 'religion,' even though I might have a chance of
securing thereby 'complete liberty of thought and action.'
There are some things one almost does not want to be free
to do—to tamper with truth, or to bow down in adoration
before mere energies and sources of energy. I do not want
to become free to worship the sun, nor the ether—though
that, perhaps, is the great storehouse and source of all
material energies whatsoever. When I want to worship I
will select as object the highest that I can find, not the
lowest; and I will try to represent it to myself, if not
adequately, yet at least with the highest conceptions of
which I am capable, humbly confessing that when I have
done my best it is but wretchedly insufficient. Bad as it
may be, however, it shall be my best. Even when I think
of the 'Infinite and Eternal Source from which all things
proceed' —since to think at all, I must have recourse to
analogy, and clothe my concepts in forms taken from
material things—I will try to honour it by selecting the
best robes at my disposal. Not as a man, therefore, shall I
represent it; nor yet as a beast or a vegetable; still less as
a mere energy or power; my very best and highest form of
concept is that of a spiritual person; and it is under this
image that I shall try to think of and worship the 'Source
from which all things proceed.'

W. McDONALD, D.D.

Notes and Queries

LITURGY

THE IRISH PRIVILEGE OF ANTICIPATION OF MATINS AND LAUDS IN CHORO

We think it better to defer a complete reply to the learned article of the Very Rev. Sylvester Malone, V.G., on the above subject, in the last I. E. RECORD, until we have succeeded in discovering the Indult of Pius VI., or given up all hopes of discovering it. The search for the document has been going on. The archives of Armagh, Kilkenny and Dublin have been searched without success. It is unfortunate that only the first part of the 'Jus Pontificium de Propaganda Fide' is published. This first part contains only the Acts of Popes; the second part is to contain the Acts of the Congregation itself, and it is more than probable that the Indult we are looking for is an Act of the Congregation. We have taken steps to have the Propaganda archives searched.

We wish to remove a misconception of our opinion under which Dr. Malone seems to labour. He speaks of the case in which the Office might be read ' by a secular with a companion,'[1] and again of a case in which a Jesuit ' was allowed to begin Matins at twelve on the previous day, even with a companion,' this privilege being given ' under the heading *in choro*.'[2]

We do not deny—and never did—that by virtue of the Indult of Pius VI. a Secular priest in Ireland may begin Matins at 2 p.m., not only with one, but with any number of companions, and that any number of Regulars, who are excused from attendance at the *community* recitation, may do the same. This method of saying the Office, by which a

---

[1] Page 211.   [2] Page 219.

number *voluntarily* assemble to recite the Office, may come under the heading *in choro*, as contradistinguished from *individual* recitation; but it is not recitation *in choro*, as contradistinguished from the *private* recitation of the Office.

De Herdt speaks of this as the private recitation of the Office: ' In private officii recitatione cum uno aut pluribus sociis.'[1] The choral recitation which we have been discussing is that of the Synodal Statutes of 1810: ' Pro officio publico, hoc est in choro '—the *community* recitation to which a Chapter or Regular Order is *obliged*.

We are indebted to our Rev. correspondent, ' D: A. D.,' who first opened this question, for reference to a Rescript which ought to throw a good deal of light on it. The Rescript is published in Colgan's *Diocese of Meath*,[2] and is contained in a letter from ' The Rev. J. Connolly to Dr. Plunket.' The letter is as follows :—

Rome,
St. Clement's, July 6th, 1803.
Right Rev. and Dear Sir,
. . . The following is a true copy of the grant of the other petition I presented in your Lordship's name :—
Ex audientia SSmi. Dni. Nostri Domini Pii Divina Provida. P.P. VII. habita per me infrum S. Congnis. de Propaganda Fide Secretarium, die 30 Junii 1805. Sanctitas sua, justis ac rationalibus causis adducta benigne indulsit, ut a singulis e Clero tam Seculari quam Regulari Dioecesis Midensis in Hibernia quotidie recitari possit *privatim*[3] Matutinum cum Laudibus diei sequentis, statim elapsis duobis horis post meridiem. . . .
Datum Romae ex Oedibus dae. S. Congnis. die et anno, quibus supra. . . . .

The Indult of Pius VI. must have been granted before August 28, 1799, on which date that Pope died. Dr. Plunket had been Bishop of Meath from 1779, and surely he must have known of the existence of that Indult. It is evident that he was not satisfied with the extent of the privilege granted, as being only ' *pro sacerdotibus*,' and accordingly he applied to

---

[1] Vol. li., n. 389.
[2] Vol. iii., p. 348.
[3] The italics are ours.

have it enlarged '*pro clero.*' [1] But, whatever may have been his reason for asking for a modification of the privilege, his petition was: ' Ut . . . quotidie recitari possit *privatim,*' etc.; and this petition was granted. We think it utterly improbable that this petition would have been presented and granted in 1805, six years at least after the concession of the Indult of Pius VI., if the Indult of Pius VI. had granted the privilege for not only the *private*, but also for the *strictly choral* recitation of Matins at 2 p.m.

LICENTIA ORDINARII FOR BLESSING BEADS, &c.

REV. DEAR SIR,—I have heard it asserted frequently of late, and with a certain amount of assurance, that the 'licentia Ordinarii loci' is *now* required, if not for the *valid*, at least for the *lawful*, exercise of any special ' faculty ' one may have direct from Rome or from the Superior-General of a religious Order, duly authorized to delegate such faculty. I should feel obliged if you would state in an early number of the I. E. RECORD whether any *direction* requiring such a condition has been issued from Rome within recent years. What makes me particularly sceptical on this matter is the fact that *I* have quite recently obtained 'faculties' to enrol in the Confraternities of the *Brown* and *Blue* Scapulars, as well as in that of the Scapular of the Sacred Heart; to bless beads with what is known as the *Dominican blessing*; to bless Benedict medals, etc., and, strange, not a word about the Ordinary in any *pagella* forwarded me ! Is it possible to fancy this would be so if any legislation had taken place or direction given requiring the ' licentia Ordinarii loci ' ?

In reference to what, I think, used to be called the *Propaganda* blessing of religious objects, even by a sign of the cross ' nihil dicens,' and the attaching to beads the Brigittine indulgence, I find in a ' direction ' issued by the Congregation of Indulgences on 14th June, 1901, that for the *valid* exercise of the faculty ' the priest must be approved of for hearing confessions of men at least.' I should like to have your opinion as to whether this means ' approved of in one diocese ' or ' in each diocese ' where he wishes

---

[1] We are authoritatively informed that, by a liberal interpretation, *clerus* includes, under the circumstances, not only priests, deacons, subdeacons, and regular clerics, but even non-tonsured regulars bound to the recitation of the Office.

to use the faculty *validly*? In my opinion it is sufficient to be approved of in one diocese—say Dublin—to exercise the faculty *validly*, say throughout Ireland. The Congregation leaves no room for doubting that for the *lawful* exercise of the faculty the 'licentia Ordinarii' is necessary everywhere one finds himself.

Awaiting light and direction, I beg to subscribe myself yours, etc.,

S.

I. We shall first deal with the faculty of attaching to beads, etc., the *Apostolic* Indulgences.

This subject was treated in the I. E. RECORD of October, 1898; but more light has been thrown on it since by a decree of the Sacred Congregation of Indulgences, dated the 14th June, 1901, and published in the *Acta Sanctae Sedis* of September, 1901, p. 124 :—

Ad 1ᵐ *detur instructio.*

INSTRUCTIO

1. Convenit ut qui facultatem benedicendi Coronas, Cruces, Rosaria, Numismata, etc., cum applicatione Indulgentiarum Apostolicarum et S. Birgittae obtinere cupit. . . .

2. Ut valide praefata facultas exerceatur opus erit, ut Sacerdos ad excipiendas Sacramentales Confessiones, saltem virorum, sit approbatus.

3. Ad eam facultatem licite exercendam requiritur consensus Ordinarii loci in quo quis ea uti velit, firmo manente quoad Regulares exemptos, decreto, hujus S. C. diei 8 Junii, 1888.' Hic autem consensus optandum ut sit expressus ; sufficit tamen etiam tacitus vel implicitus, et in aliquo casu, quando practice aliter fieri nequeat, sufficit etiam consensus prudenter praesumptus.

Datum Romae ex Secretario ejusdem S. Congregationis die 14 Junii, 1901.

.   .   .   .

From this decree it is plain—

(1.) That for validity nothing more is required than that a priest should have approbation for hearing confessions—at least those of men.

But must he be approved in each d ocese in which he wishes to use the faculty validly, or will it suffice that he be approved in one? Our opinion agrees with that of our

---

¹ This is a mistake for 2 Januarii, 1888.

correspondent : it is sufficient that he be approved in one. It is evidently by design that the Sacred Congregation omits ' ab Ordinario loci in quo quis ea uti velit' in treating of the validity, whilst it inserts these words in treating of the lawfulness.

(2.) That for lawfulness the 'Consensus Ordinarii' is required.

(3.) That the Ordinary is the 'Ordinarius loci in quo quis ea uti velit.

(4.) That 'Regulares exempti' enjoy the privileges granted by the decree of 2nd January, 1888.[1] This privilege is that, if the faculty be exercised within the precincts of their monastery, convent, or houses of residence, it is sufficient for them to get the 'licentia superioris vera jurisdictione pollentis in suo Ordine, uti Abbas, Provincialis, vel Generalis totius Ordinis.' The consent of the Ordinary of the diocese is required only when the faculty is exercised outside the convent.

(5.) That, though the express consent is desirable, it is sufficient to have the tacit or implied consent, or even the prudently presumed consent, when no other can be obtained. For instance, 'it may be safely regarded that the bishop, in granting the other faculties for a mission or retreat, *ipso facto* (though implicitly) also accords this consent to exercise the above Papal Faculty.'[2]

II. We shall now consider other faculties that 'one may have direct from Rome or from the Superior-General of a religious Order.'

We are not aware that any direction has been issued on this question of the 'licentia Ordinarii,' in connection with these faculties, within recent years. The direction of the 5th of February, 1841, stills holds good :—

2° Utrum qui obtinet diversas facultates ab Apostolica Sede, scilicet altaris privilegiati personalis, erigendi stationes Viae Crucis, benedicendi cruces, numismata, etc., debeat exhibere dictas

---

[1] See I. E. RECORD, Jan., 1899, p. 86.
[2] *Ibid.* Oct., 1898, p. 372.

facultates Ordinario, etiamsi nulla mentio facta sit in concessionum Rescriptis.

. . . .

Sac. Congregatio die 5 Februarii, 1841, respondit . . . .

Ad 2^m : Affirmative quoad Viae Crucis erectionem : Negative relate ad alias facultates, nisi aliter disponatur in obtentis concessionibus.

The 'consensus Ordinarii' is certainly not required for the valid exercise of these faculties, whether mention be made of it in the Rescripts of Concession or not. This is deduced, in the case in which mention is made, from the parity of the faculty for the *Apostolic Indulgences.* There is an *a fortiori* case, if there be no mention of it. Even the exception made in the above response, in the case of the erection of the Stations of the Cross, does not affect the validity :—

Si l'on n'omettait que cette exhibition du pouvoir, l'erection du Chemin de la Croix ne serait pas nulle pour cela, puisque les decrets cités ne le disent pas.[1]

'Exhibere facultates Ordinario' and 'Episcopi assensum petere seu habere' have the same meaning.[2]

The 'consensus Ordinarii' is required for the lawful exercise of these faculties, if mention be made of it in the Rescripts of Concession ; otherwise it is not required, except in the single case of the erection of the Stations of the Cross.

Beringer, relying, as we presume, on the decree quoted above, says of the Carmelite faculties : ' Ceux qui ont obtenu ces pouvoirs n'ont pas besoin, pour en faire usage, de la permission episcopale.'[3] The same holds for faculties got from the Superior-General of any religious Order, duly authorized to delegate such faculties.

It may be objected that in the decree of February 5, 1841, there is mention only of faculties ' ab Apostolica Sede.' But those granted by the Superiors-General of any religious Orders are ' ab Apostolica Sede ' ; they could come from no other source.

---

[1] Beringer, vol. i., p. 272, note 1.
[2] Vermeersch, *Praelect Can.,* T. 1, p. 328, n. 525, ed 3,
[3] Vol. ii., p. 201, note 3.

THE LAST GOSPEL IN VOTIVE MASS OF HOLY GHOST DURING LENT

Rev. Dear Sir,—This is the 6th day of March, and according to the *Ordo* I have an option between the ferial Mass and the votive Mass of the Blessed Sacrament, but I prefer to take up the Votive Mass of the Holy Ghost because a friend requested me, at my convenience, to offer up that Mass for his intention.

I was perplexed as to what the Last Gospel should have been; because I knew, if I had taken the Votive Mass of the Blessed Sacrament, it should have been the Gospel of the ferial Mass; and because I saw in the *Ordo* under the Votive Mass of the Holy Ghost, page xxvi., ' In fine semper dicitur evangelium. In principio.'

Kindly direct me that I may not be perplexed again.

Sacerdos.

The Gospel ' In Principio.' etc., is the last Gospel for all Votive Masses that are strictly so called, *i.e.*, that are not in accordance with the Office.[1] The six Masses granted 5th July, 1883, and corresponding to the six Votive Offices, are plainly not Votive Masses strictly so called, if the Votive Offices be said : they are treated in every respect as ordinary semi-doubles, and, therefore, have as last Gospel the Gospel of the Feria.[2]

P. O'Leary.

---

[1] Gen. Miss. xii. 2.
[2] Rub. Miss. *ante* Miss. Vot. per an.   See also I. E. Record of May, 1884.

CORRESPONDENCE

ARCHBISHOP'S HOUSE,
DUBLIN, 18th March, 1902.

REV. AND DEAR SIR,—My paper on 'Trinity College and the University of Dublin,' published in the March number of the I. E. RECORD, dealt chiefly with two statements made by a member of the Irish Bar,—one, indeed, of his Majesty's Counsel,—in reference to a certain judgment of the present Master of the Rolls.

The Master of the Rolls was alleged to have judicially decided,—in a judgment which, it was furthermore alleged, was public property, and could be referred to by any person,—that between Trinity College and the University of Dublin there is no distinction whatever; that the University is the College; that the College is the University; and that neither differs from the other in any particular.

In the course of my paper I had occasion to state that,—notwithstanding the assurance thus given to the public as to the judgment referred to being 'public property,'—it was only by having a transcript of the judgment made from a volume which was not to be found except in the Library of Trinity College, that I was able to obtain a copy of it at all.

If the need for showing up the inaccuracy of the statement, unaccountably made on such authority, as to the purport of the Master of the Rolls' judgment in the case in question, had arisen only a few weeks later than it did, I could, as it now appears, have obtained a copy of the judgment without any difficulty. Within the last fortnight, a volume, printed at the University Press, containing a report of it, has been published.

The title of the volume is *Chartæ et Statuta Collegii Sanctæ et Individuæ Trinitatis Reginæ Elizabethæ, juxta Dublin.* Vol. II. Dublinii: Sumptibus Academicis, 1898.

The title-page, it will be observed, bears the date, 1898. The volume was edited by the late Dr. G. F. Shaw, S.F.T.C.D., and it has a preface signed by him. It evidently was printed in 1898, but for private use only. It has now, for the first time, been given to the public.

I may add that, as I am having my two papers, recently published in the I. E. RECORD, printed for publication in a pamphlet, I have thought it useful to publish with them *in extenso* the judgment of the Master of the Rolls, which,—whilst it is totally irrelevant to the matter in connection with which it has been very improperly dragged into public controversy,— is, in reference to the matter with which it really dealt, a judg-ment of very much more than common interest.

The forthcoming publication of it will enable those who are any longer interested in the recent controversy, to have at hand for reference, within the covers of the same pamphlet, every statement that I have made upon the subject, and— together with my statements—the report of the judgment by reference to which the accuracy of those statements will be found to be fully sustained.—I remain, Rev. and Dear Sir, your faithful servant,

✠ WILLIAM J. WALSH,
Archbishop of Dublin.

TRINITY COLLEGE AND THE UNIVERSITY OF DUBLIN

51, LOWER BAGGOT-STREET,
March 14, 1902.

REV. DEAR SIR,—Some time ago in a newspaper discussion of the Irish University Question, I stated that apart from Trinity College, there does not exist legally, constitutionally, or, in fact, any such entity as a University of Dublin.

This assertion having been controverted in the I. E. RECORD of February, I pointed out in a letter to the *Freeman's Journal* of February 8, that the identity of the University of Dublin with Trinity had been decided by a Court of Justice on the 2nd June, 1888, in the case of the ' Provost, Fellows, and Scholars of Trinity College *v.* The Chancellor, Doctors, and Masters of the University of Dublin.' In my letter I quoted portions of the judgment which declare this identity in the most unmistakeable terms. The greater part of the judgment is in fact an elaborate argument to demonstrate that identity. It shows that the phrases ' Trinity College, Dublin,' ' University of Dublin,' and ' University of Trinity College, Dublin,' are used interchangeably in Acts of Parliament, and in the Charters and Regulations. And that ' at the time of the Act of Settlement the Corporation of the College was the Corporation of the University. There was no other Corporation but that of the College, which, in the words of the Letters Patent of James I., was declared, and was held to be a University. ' Sit et habeatur Universitas.'

The Master of the Rolls closed the first part of his judgment with these emphatic words—' It cannot therefore admit of doubt that prior to the Letters Patent of Queen Victoria a gift to the Corporation of the University of Dublin would have meant a gift to Trinity College, Dublin, and could have meant nothing else.'

In the second part he proceeds to examine whether the Letters Patent of Queen Victoria made any change, by incorporating a University of Dublin, and he decides that they did nothing of the kind : that they merely incorporated a Senate with very limited powers. Accordingly he held that as ' it was to Trinity College and its University of Dublin, inseparably and undistinguishably blended with it, that the testator owed his training and his degree, and as he had in his will used the terms University and College as loosely as the Legislature had used them, it was evident that the body referred to was Trinity College.

The letter in which I referred to this judgment as establishing in law the identity of Trinity College and the University of Dublin was criticised in the last number of the I. E. RECORD, and it was declared that I had not accurately interpreted the meaning and scope of the judgment. In the absence of a full copy of the judgment any discussion of it in your pages could not be satisfactory. I beg to enclose a copy herewith for insertion in the I. E. RECORD. It is very clear and intelligible, and I am satisfied to leave it to the interpretation of your readers.

In the first seven[1] pages the purport of the pleadings, and their legal meaning and effect are set forth.

The important part of the judgment begins on page seven,[2] with the words :—' The principal question for decision therefore is,

---

What is the body which the testator designates as the Corporation of the University of Dublin ?'

Independently of this temporary controversy this judgment has a permanent interest, for the light it throws on the relation of Trinity College to 'its University of Dublin.' I fancy, therefore, your readers will deem it of sufficient value to warrant its being submitted to them in its entirety.

As my previous quotations will, on re-examination, be found to be perfectly accurate, I leave the question of the withdrawal of certain comments which you have published to your own sense of fairness and good taste.

I shall only add what I have often stated, that speaking as a Catholic layman, I believe the proper solution of the Irish University Question is that in which Irish Catholics will have an independent University of their own.—Yours, etc.,

M. DRUMMOND, K.C.

[We are happy to gratify Mr. Drummond's desire to the extent of publishing in our present issue the decision of the Master of the Rolls which he has been good enough to send us. Beyond this we fear that it is not possible for us to meet his wishes. Nor can we admit that Mr. Drummond had any strict right to expect us to insert this document. When he stated some time ago that the decision was public property and within the reach of anyone who wished to examine it, his statement was not strictly accurate. If it were made now it would be quite correct; for only a few days ago a volume was published containing the Statutes, Decrees, and Legal Decisions that refer to Trinity College and the University of Dublin [1] from the year 1846 to the year 1896. In this volume the decision of the Master of the Rolls is to be found at page 507. We might, therefore, consider ourselves dispensed from encumbering our own pages with the decision, and we might refer those of our readers who had any doubt as to its meaning

---

[1] *Chartæ et Statuta Collegii Sacrosanctæ et Individuæ Trinitatis Reginæ Elizabethæ juxta Dublin.* Vol. ii. Dublinii: Weldrick, MDCCCXCVIII. Although dated 1898 the volume was issued only in March, 1902.

to the volume we have mentioned. We prefer, however, not to give any one an excuse for charging us with injustice or partiality.

We think, at the same time, that if Mr. Drummond imagines the minds of our readers will be so confused by the legal technicalities and phraseology of this document, as not to be able to spell their way through its meaning, he has made a rather serious mistake. It is plain to any one that what the Master of the Rolls has decided is something entirely different from what Mr. Drummond contends he has decided. It is quite clear that the Plaintiffs are not the University of Dublin, nor do they claim to be. It is likewise clear that the Defendants are not the University of Dublin, but the incorporated Senate of the University. But where does it appear that the College and the University are identical? What evidently has led to so much confusion is the fact that in giving his decision on a totally different issue from that which Mr. Drummond thinks was involved in the case, and in reviewing the facts and arguments that led up to his judgment, the Master of the Rolls made certain statements and observations from which Mr. Drummond seems to us to have drawn an illogical conclusion.

Everyone knows that the connection between the University of Dublin and Trinity College was at all times, and is now exceedingly close. It could not have been otherwise seeing that there was but one College in the University. There was a period, as the Master of the Rolls has clearly shown, when the distinction between the two was scarcely perceptible. The framers of the Charter of James I. 'considered Trinity College and the University of Dublin as so inseparably connected that their titles are used throughout as synonymous terms.' Of course they were inseparably connected and they are inseparably connected now. What wonder that their titles should have been used as synonymous terms when there was but one College in the University? The very same Charter says that Trinity College was founded ' ad exemplum academiarum nostrarum Oxoniensis et Cantabrigiensis.' The Master of the Rolls does not think 'that the reference to them (Oxford and Cambridge) indicates an intention that Trinity College and the University of Dublin should be separate bodies.' They need not, of course, be separate bodies while there is only one College in the University. But what is to prevent the same body from acting in two different capacities? And while they need not be separate bodies where has the Master of the Rolls decided that they must be identical or that there was anything to prevent them from *becoming* separate? Both phrases, Trinity College, Dublin, and the University of Dublin, were used interchangeably as well in Acts of Parliament as in the Charters and Regulations. What wonder, seeing that the connection between the two was so intimate and that there was no necessity of any kind to draw the distinction? At this period, when the College and the University were so closely blended as to be indistinguishable the Master of the Rolls does not anywhere state that they were identical.

The Letters Patent of Queen Victoria in 1857 bring out the latent distinction between the two that was there from the beginning in a manner that leaves not a shadow of doubt as to its existence now and at all times. The testator had left the College and the University long before this distinction was made clear. It was to Trinity College he owed his training and his degree, both of which he received at a time when the College was inseparably and indistinguishably blended with the University. Therefore, according to the judge, the intention of the testator was to leave his money to the College and not to the University or its Senate, as there was nothing to show that he was aware of the circumstances which had brought out into the light of day the fundamental distinction between the two and left them no longer inseparably and indistinguishably blended.

Mr. Drummond leaves to our sense of fairness and good taste whether we ought not now to withdraw the charges of 'inaccurate quotation' that have been made against him in our pages. Mr. Drummond knows perfectly well that whatever charges were made against him in our pages were made,

much against his will, we are quite sure, by one to whom
as a Catholic layman Mr. Drummond owes a little deference
and respect. Yet nobody asks him for an apology.
Nobody, as far as we remember, has accused him of
'inaccurate quotation.' Attention has merely been called
in our pages to the evidently inaccurate and incorrect
interpretation that he has given of a legal decision. We do
not see how that can be withdrawn by us or by anyone. He
has committed himself and his reputation as a lawyer to the
statement that in the lawsuit in question Trinity College
claimed the money 'as being the University of Dublin.' He
has added, moreover, that 'the pleadings in the case' clearly
prove what he thus unequivocally asserts. Now it has been
clearly shown that the 'pleadings in the case' prove no such
thing. It has been clearly shown that no such position was
taken up by Trinity College in the dispute. It has been
clearly shown that no such case as he has represented was
ever submitted for decision to the Master of the Rolls. And
it has been clearly shown that no such decision as he insists
upon was ever given by the Master of the Rolls or by any
body else. How then can he expect us or others to withdraw
the charge of 'inaccuracy' that has been made against him?
What is charged is certainly not that Mr. Drummond
wilfully misrepresented the facts. Nothing of the kind has
even been suggested. What has been said, and what we fear
must stand, is that his statements were 'out of joint
with fact'; that he has been wrong in his interpretation of
the decision; that he has discovered in 'the pleadings in the
case' things that are not there at all; and that he has confounded things that are quite distinct from one another. All
that may happen to a very good and honourable man ; and
we do not say that it is entirely Mr. Drummond's fault if it
has happened to him. But we really cannot see how we are
called upon to apologize for it.

It is pleasant to turn from these contentious matters to
the last sentence in Mr. Drummond's letter, in which he
declares, 'as a Catholic layman, that the proper solution of
the University question is that in which Irish Catholics will
have an independent University of their own.' That is

certainly very satisfactory ; for it shows that Mr. Drummond
at all events does not regard the brand of denominationalism
as a brand of shame and of inferiority. We are aware,
however, that Mr. Drummond does not think we are yet ripe
for a Catholic University pure and simple, and that in his
opinion we might wait with advantage for some decades
until we have well trained men to put into it as teachers.
Now there are two advantages to be gained from a Catholic
University—the Catholic advantage and the intellectual one.
As regards the Catholic element we were probably much
better fitted for a Catholic University in Dr. Newman's
time than we are now, and we are certainly much better
fitted now than we can hope to be after twenty or thirty
more years of compromise, of programmes imposed by a half-
Protestant Senate, of mere grinding for degrees and of
mixed examination boards. As for the intellectual advantage, we may, indeed, hope, from an extension of the
present system and more money, for a considerable increase
in the number of graduates ; but what hope is there
of a better quality of education?   What advance in
intellectual progress has been made during the past twenty-
five years to justify a prolongation of the experiment?
The condition of the country is the most eloquent reply.
The fault is, of course, entirely in the system, and no
better results could be expected from it than have been
obtained.

We must not be understood to say that we would not
accept any solution which would give us a College in either
of the existing Universities that would be thoroughly national
and representative, that would have practical autonomy, a
separate corporate existence, the power of appointing its
own professors and arranging its own programme, and have
the same powers in regard to degrees as Trinity College, and
be adequately endowed.   We may have our own opinion as
to the University in which such a College would be the more
secure, enjoy the greater liberty, maintain the higher
standard of education, give the more valuable degree, and
win the larger share of the confidence and generosity of the
public.   But we reject nothing.   We merely hold ourselves

at liberty to judge of any scheme that is proposed upon its merits, adopting at the same time the words of the statement made by the Catholic Hierarchy in 1896, "with a sincere desire to remove rather than to aggravate difficulties.'

Our claim, of course, is for equality. We leave to others to say what instalment of their rights they would think it worth their while either to accept or to reject.— ED. I. E. RECORD.]

CANDLES FOR THE ALTAR

3, EUSTACE-STREET, DUBLIN,

February 24*th*, 1902.

REV. DEAR SIR,—We have read with great interest your articles in the recent numbers of the I. E. RECORD apropos of the quantity of beeswax that candles for the altar should contain.

We are only too anxious to comply with the requirements of mother Church in all things ecclesiastical, and if you would kindly give us some standard which is considered by competent authority to be the correct amount that should be used in the composition of beeswax candles we should be very pleased to have our beeswax candles composed with that standard.

The quality of beeswax candles is purely a question of price, and manufacturers would be, and are, only too glad to supply the pure article where their customers are prepared to pay the price, which is very little more than they have to pay for the inferior article.

Traders throughout the country are the principal cause of the deterioration in the quality of the beeswax candle in their anxiety to buy cheaply, and our travellers almost daily meet with the remarks of the traders to the effect that *they* ' don't care what the candles are made of provided they have the word " wax " stamped on the end.'

In this, as in most other cases, the best criterion that the pure article is being supplied is the price paid, and to our certain knowledge candles are being sold at such a price as to preclude the possibility of even a *decent* quantity of beeswax being included in their composition.—Yours faithfully,

HAYES & FINCH.

[We could not undertake to fix a standard. We must await an instruction from the Sacred Congregation of Rites. For the present, we must adopt the principle : ' Sinere res vadere ut vadunt.'—P. O'LEARY.]

DOCUMENTS

TRINITY COLLEGE, DUBLIN v. THE ATTORNEY-GENERAL AND OTHERS

JUDGMENT OF THE RIGHT HON. THE MASTER OF THE ROLLS, DECIDING THAT A REQUEST TO 'THE CORPORATION OF THE UNIVERSITY OF DUBLIN' VESTED IN TRINITY COLLEGE

(*June* 2, 1888)

This case comes before the Court on a motion by the plaintiffs on admissions in the pleadings. The plaintiffs are the Provost, Fellows, and Scholars of Trinity College, Dublin, and the defendants are the Attorney-General, the Chancellor, Doctors, and Masters of the University of Dublin, and the trustees and executors of the will of the late Richard Tuohill Reid, barrister-at-law, formerly of Killarney, in the County of Kerry, and afterwards of Bombay, in the East Indies.

The will of Mr. Reid is set out *in extenso* in the plaintiffs' statement of claim, except that in the will the testator describes himself as LL.D., without stating, however, of what university. The will bears date the 22nd of September, 1881. It commences by appointing the defendants, Sir George Christopher Molesworth Birdwood, Knight, M.D., of the India Office, and James Cornelius O'Dowd, Deputy Judge Advocate-General, and Barrister-at-Law, of No. 35, Great George's-street, Westminster, his executors.

The statement of claim alleges that the testator died on the 11th day of February, 1883, at Rome, without having revoked or altered his Will, which was duly proved in the Probate Division of Her Majesty's High Court of Justice in England by the defendants George Christopher Molesworth Birdwood and James Cornelius O'Dowd on the 25th day of April, 1883. The testator had no assets in Ireland.

Hannah Reid, the sister of the testator in his will mentioned, died before him, on the 9th day of February, 1883. Her life estate, therefore, never came into existence. The ready money and cash at the testator's bankers were sufficient for payment of his debts, funeral and testamentary expenses, and the other expenses connected with the administration of the estate.

The bequest in the will contained of all the testator's shares or stock in the Great Indian Peninsula Railway Company, and in the Bombay, Baroda, and Central India Railway Company, is, for the sake of convenience, referred to as the second bequest, and the bequest of all the testator's funds in Three per Cent. Consolidated Bank Annuities is referred to as the third bequest.

The testator was, at the time of his death, possessed of the sums of £2,800 Great Indian Peninsula Railway Company Guaranteed £5 per cent. Stock and £1,904 Bombay, Baroda, and Central India Railway Company Stock; which sums became vested in his executors, as trustees of his will, for the purposes of the second bequest; and he also died possessed of the sum of £6,089 13s. 4d. Consolidated £3 per Cent. Bank Annuities, transferrable at the Bank of England, which became vested for the purposes of the third bequest.

As to the second bequest, the plaintiffs say that there is no such body, strictly speaking, as the Board of the University. The defendants, the Senate of the University have been incorporated by Letters Patent, dated the 24th July, 1857, under the title of the Chancellor, Doctors, and Masters of the University of Dublin, and as such Corporation are, by the said Letters Patent, empowered to hold and acquire such property, real and personal, as may be given or bequeathed to them. Up to the present the defendants have not acquired, nor do they now hold, any property.

As to the third bequest, the plaintiffs say ' that Trinity College, Dublin, is the only College in the University and is incorporated by the Letters Patent or Charter of the 34th year of Queen Elizabeth, which was confirmed by the Letters Patent, or Charter of the 13th Charles I., under the name of the Provost, Fellows, and Scholars, of the College of the Holy and Undivided Trinity of Queen Elizabeth, near Dublin, who are the plaintiffs in this action. The Provost and Senior Fellows of the said College are by the said Charter and Statutes of the College constituted the Governing Body of the College, and are known as the Board of Trinity College, Dublin. There is no other body called or known as the Board either in the College or University.' That statement must be taken as uncontradicted.

The defendants, the executors, having been informed of the facts aforesaid, were advised that they could not safely give effect to the second and third bequests without the protection of the Court, and accordingly they lodged in the Chancery Division of

the High Court of Justice in England, to the following credit:—
' In the matter of the trusts of the bequest by the will of the late
Richard;Tuohill Reid, in favour of the Corporation of the University
of Dublin, in trust to found a Professorship of Penal Legislation '—
the said sum of £1,904, Bombay, Baroda, and Central India
Railway Company Stock, and the sum of £2,300, Great Indian
Peninsula Railway Company Guaranteed £5 per cent. Stock, part
of the said sum of £2,800 like stock; and £339 8s. 6d. cash,
representing the said second bequest, and the dividends that had
accrued in respect thereof up to the 1st July, 1884, less by a sum
of £702 16s. paid by the same defendants in respect of duty on
the capital of the second bequest; and £26 2s. for duty on the
income thereof, and £27 10s. being a moiety of the costs of and
incident to the lodgment in Court.

The defendants, the executors, also lodged in the Chancery
Division of the said High Court of Justice in England, to the
following credit:—' In the matter of the trusts of the bequest by
the will of the late Richard Tuohill Reid, in favour of the Corporation of the University of Dublin, in trust to found in Trinity
College, Dublin, additional Sizarships, Exhibitions, and for other
purposes '—the sum of £5,463 17s. 11d. Consolidated £3 per Cent.
Bank Annuities part of the said sum of £6,089 13s. 4d. like
annuities, and £217 4s. 8d. cash, representing the third bequest,
and the dividends that had accrued in respect thereof, up to the
5th July, 1884, less by a sum of £616 11s. 6d. paid by the same
defendants in respect of legacy duty on the capital of the third
bequest; and £16 9s. for duty on the income thereof, and £27 10s.
being the remaining moiety of the costs hereinbefore mentioned.

The result of this proceeding was the payment of 10 per cent.
legacy duty for both the second and third bequests, from which
duty they would probably have been free if lodged in this Court,
inasmuch as the law in England is different from that in this
country. Here no duty is payable on bequests for purposes
merely charitable in Ireland.

The statement of claim then states that the testator, who was
born in the County of Kerry, was educated in Trinity College,
Dublin, where he took the degree of Master of Arts. He was
fterwards called to the Irish Bar, and went to Bombay in the
year 1853, after which period he never returned to Ireland.

The statement of claim then avers that all the endowments
estates and property by which the University of Dublin is

sustained, including all endowments for special purposes, are vested in the plaintiffs, and managed by the Board of Trinity College. The appointment and election of the Professors in the University was also vested in the said Board up to the time when the Council was constituted by Letters Patent of the 4th day of November, 1874. By these Letters Patent the nomination to all professorships with certain specified exceptions, is now vested in the Council, subject to the approval of the Board; and since the constitution of the Council any proposed alterations in the rules and regulations respecting any studies, lectures, or examinations (not connected with the Divinity School), and also any proposed alterations in the rules and regulations respecting the qualifications, duties, and tenure of office of any professor (not connected with the Divinity School), require the approval both of the Board and of the Council. No new professorship can now be created or founded by the Board without the consent of the Council.

The Council consists of the Provost, or in his absence the Vice-Provost, of Trinity College, and sixteen other members elected out of the members of the Senate of the University.

The Board of Trinity College elect to all the existing Professorships after the usual examinations of candidates.

The statement of claim then states that the plaintiffs are desirous that a scheme or schemes may be settled and approved by the Court for the regulation and management of the said charitable bequests respectively, and for the application of the income of the said stocks and securities, pursuant to the trusts by the said Will declared with respect to the same respectively, and that the plaintiffs may be at liberty to apply in the Chancery Division in the High Court of Justice in England for the transfer to the credit of this action of the several securities and moneys standing to the credits respectively hereinbefore mentioned.

The plaintiffs claim :—

1. That the trusts of the Will of the testator Richard Tuohill Reid, with respect to the second and third bequests respectively, may be carried into execution under the direction of the Court.

2. That the plaintiffs may be at liberty to apply in the Chancery Division of the High Court of Justice in England in the said matter, under the Trustee Relief Act, for the transfer and payment into this Court, to the credit of this action, of the several securities and moneys which now are, or shall at any time hereafter be, standing to the said credits hereinbefore mentioned.

3. That a scheme or schemes may be approved by the Court, directing the regulation and management of the said charitable bequests respectively, and the application of the income of the said stocks and securities, pursuant to the trusts of the said will, declared with respect to the same respectively.

4. That for the purposes aforesaid all necessary accounts may be taken, inquiries made, and directions given, and

Such further relief as the case may require.

The Chancellor, Doctors, and Masters of the University of Dublin have filed a statement of defence, by which they admit the making of the will as set forth in the statement of claim, and the statements of fact and the documents in the statement of claim mentioned, and submit that they are the body designated as the Corporation of the University of Dublin in the will ; and that the stocks and funds which are in the statement of claim designated as the 2nd and 3rd legacy bequests respectively should be transferred and paid to them for the purposes of the will ; and state that they are desirous that a scheme or schemes directing the regulation and management of the said charitable bequests respectively, and the application of the income of the same may be settled and approved of by the Court as in the statement of claim is prayed.

The Attorney-General has delivered a statement of defence in which he states in substance that he has no knowledge of the several matters in dispute, but submits that the legacies are good charitable bequests.

The principal question for decision therefore is, What is the body which the testator designates as ' The Corporation of the University of Dublin ' ?

Trinity College, Dublin, was founded by Queen Elizabeth by a Charter dated A.D. 1592, in the 34th year of her reign. That Charter is of great importance in determining the constitution of Trinity College, and of the University of Dublin.

That Charter recites :—

' Cum dilectus subditus noster Henricus Ussher Archidiaconus Dubliniensis nobis humiliter supplicavit, nomine civitatis Dubliniensis, pro eo quod nullum Collegium pro Scholaribus in bonis literis et artibus erudiendis infra regnum nostrum Hiberniæ adhuc existit ; ut unum Collegium *matrem Universitatem* juxta civitatem

Dubliniensem ad meliorem educationem institutionem, et instructionem Scholarium et studentium in regno nostro praedicto erigere, fundare, et stabilire dignaremur '; and goes on to provide :—'quod de cætero sit, et erit, unum Collegium *mater Universitatis* in quodam loco vocato Allhallowes juxta Dublin praedictum, pro educatione, institutione, et instructione juvenum, et studentum in artibus et facultatibus, perpetuis futuris temporibus duraturum, et quod erit, et vocabitur COLLEGIUM SANCTAE ET INDIVIDUAE TRINITATIS JUXTA DUBLIN A SERENISSIMA REGINA ELIZABETH FUNDATUM. Ac illud Collegium de uno Praeposito et de tribus Sociis nomine plurium, et tribus Scholaribus nomine plurium, in perpetuum continuaturum erigmus, ordinamus, creamus, fundamus, et stabilimus firmiter per praesentes.'

Then, after nominating the first Provost, the Fellows, and Scholars, the Charter proceeds to incorporate them :—

'Per nomen PRAEPOSITI, SOCIORUM, ET SCHOLARIUM COLLEGII SANCTAE TRINITATIS ELIZABETHAE REGINAE JUXTA DUBLIN.'

Then follow directions as to the election in future of the Provost, Fellows, and Scholars who are empowered to acquire and hold manors, lands, tenements, and hereditaments for the maintenance of the College, and to sue and be sued by their corporate name ; and the Charter continues in these most important words :—

'Et cum gradus quosdam in artibus et facultatibus constitui literis fuisse adumento compertum sit, ordinamus per praesentes, ut studiosi in hoc Collegio sanctae et individuae Trinitatis Elizabethae Reginae juxta Dublin, libertatem et facultatem habeant, gradus tum Baccalaureatus, Magisterii, et Doctoratus, juxta tempus idoneum in omnibus artibus et facultatibus obtinendi.'

The 'tempus indoneum' here probably refers to the period at which the first Undergraduates would be ready to receive degrees. The Charter proceeds :—

'Hoc semper iterum proviso, ut cum hujus Collegii Socii septem integros annos post gradum Magisterii ibi assumptum adimpleverint, tum è Sociorum numero amoveantur, ut alii in eorum locum suffecti, pro hujus Regni et Ecclesiae beneficio, emolumentum habeant ; et ut INTRA SE pro hujusmodi gradibus assequendis habeant libertatem, omnia acta, et scholastica exercitia adimplendi, quemadmodum Praeposito, et majori parti Sociorum visum fuerit, ac ut omnes personas pro hujusmodi rebus melius promovendis eligere, creare, nominare, et ordinare possint, sive sit Procancellarius, Procurator, aut Procuratores, (nam Cancellarii dignitatem honoratissimo et fidelissimo Consiliario, nostro, Guilelmo, Cecillio, Domino Baroni de Burghley, totius Angliae Thesaurario, delegatam approbamus), et ut posthac idoneam hujusmodi personam, cum defuerit, pro hujus Collegii Cancellario Praepositus, et major pars Sociorum eligant, ordinamus.'

This Charter was granted in 1592, and no other Charter or Letters Patent were granted during Elizabeth's reign. In 1613 further Letters Patent were granted by King James I. An interval of twenty-one years therefore had elapsed between them and the Charter of Elizabeth ; and that Degrees must during that interval have been conferred on Students of the College appears to me to be beyond doubt. Therefore it must have been considered that the Charter of Elizabeth, *proprio vigore*, conferred upon the College power to grant degrees. Some body, duly authorized by the Crown, must have conferred them : since the granting of degrees is a Branch of the Royal prerogative, the Crown being the fountain of honour. The Chancellor, Vice-Chancellor, and Proctors, were not incorporated ; the Provost, Fellows, and Scholars were : and it follows that they must have conferred the degrees in the interval between the Charter of Elizabeth and that of James I., though, no doubt, in this the College acted through the Vice-Chancellor.

The Charter of James, after reciting the Charter of Elizabeth, proceeds :—

'CUMQUE DICTUM COLLEGIUM SIT ET HABEATUR UNIVERSITAS, AC HABEAT GAUDEAT, ET UTATUR OMNIBUS ET SINGULIS LIBERTATIBUS, PRIVILEGIIS, ET IMMUNITATIBUS AD UNIVERSITATEM SIVE ACADEMIAM PERTINENTIBUS SIVE SPECTANTIBUS . . . idcirco operae pretium et necessarium videtur, quod DICTUM COLLEGIUM ET UNIVERSITAS habeant plenam et absolutam potestatem duos Burgenses de seipsis eligendi, eosque mittendi ad supremam illam curiam Parliamenti in hoc regno nostro Hiberniae, de tempore in tempus, tenendi : in qua quidem curia hujusmodi Burgenses sic electi et missi, juxta formam universitatis Oxoniensis et Cantabrigiensis in Anglia usitatam, notum faciant verum statum dicti Collegi ac universitatis ibidem, ita ut nullum statutum aut actus generalis dicto Collegio ac universitati privatim, sine justa ac debita notitia et informatione in ea parte habita, praejudicit aut noceat SCIATIS quod nos, de gratia nostra speciali, . . . Voluimus et concessimus, ac per praesentes pro nobis haeredibus, et successoribus nostris, voluimus et consedimus, praefatis Praeposito, Sociis, et Scholaribus dicti Collegii, et successoribus suis, necnon ordinamus et stabilimus per praesentes, perpetuis futuris temporibus quod sint et erunt in dicto Collegio ac universitate juxta Dublin duo Burgenses Parliamenti nostri, haeredum, et successorum nostrorum.'

The words just quoted, such as ' Cumque dictum Collegium sit et habeatur universitas,' ' et utatur omnibus et singulis libertatibus privilegiis et immunitatibus ad universitatem pertinentibus,' ' Collegii et universitatis praedictae,' ' quod dictum collegium et universitas habeant '; again, the same words, ' dicti Collegii ac universitatis,' ' dicto Collegio ac universitate juxta Dublin,' show that the framers of the Charter considered Trinity College and the University of Dublin as so inseparably connected that their titles are used throughout as synonymous terms. To whom is the power of electing two members given? ' Praefatis Praeposito, Sociis et Scholaribus dicti Collegii.'

The Charter recites that Trinity College was founded by Queen Elizabeth, ' ad exemplum academiarum nostrarum Oxoniensis et Cantabrigiensis.' Oxford and Cambridge are, no doubt, in some respect analogous Universities. But they are essentially different in this, that they each contain several Colleges ; and I do not think that the reference to them in this Charter indicates an intention that Trinity College and the University of Dublin should be separate bodies.

The next Charter is that of 13 Charles I., which bears date in 1637. It recites the Charter of Elizabeth, and states that by it she granted ' quod deinceps esset unum Collegium mater Universitatis, in quodam loco vocato Allhallowes juxta Dublin.' It then recites the incorporation of the College; its power to acquire and hold lands for the maintenance of the College; its capacity of suing and being sued in actions, real, personal, and mixed; of having a common seal ; the power of the Provost and majority of the Fellows to make laws, statutes, and ordinances. for the government of the College ; and that ' eadem nuper regina per easdam literas suas patentes ordinaverit, ut studiosi in dicto Collegio libertatem et facultatem haberent gradus tum Baccalaureatus, Magisterii et Doctoratus, juxta tempus idoneum, in omnibus artibus et facultatibus obtinendi ; et ut intra se, pro hujusmodi gradibus assequendis haberent libertatem omnia acta et scholastica exercitia adimplendi, quemadmodum Praeposito, et majori parti Sociorum visum foret.' The Charter confirms the Charter of Elizabeth in respect of its above recited provisions, and provides, with the consent of the Provost, Fellows, and Scholars, that

Fellows should not be removed at the end of seven years, as provided by the Charter of Elizabeth : recalls the power of the Provost and Fellows to make statutes and ordinances, and reserves that power to the Crown ; repeals those already made, and substitutes an amended code.

In further Letters Patent of the same year (13 Charles I.) I find this recital after referring to the great advantage of schools and universities in England :—' Quod et reipsa fecit regina Elizabetha celebris memoriae Collegium Sanctae Trinitatis juxta urbem Dubliniensem extruendo ; quod etiam annuis reditibus dotavit et ACADEMIAE PRIVILEGIIS ORNAVIT.'

The Letters Patent then proceed to establish certain laws for the government of the College. The Provost and seven senior Fellows are to form a Board. The Board are to have the government of the College, the election of the Fellows, officials etc., and the conferring of degrees ' GRADUUMQUE COLLATIONES DEFINIANT, ET CONCLUDANT.' A more clear assertion that the College had the right of conferring degrees it is not easy to imagine.

The next Letters Patent which I have to refer to are those of the 34 George III. (A.D. 1794). They are addressed to the Provost and senior Fellows, and relate to the admission of Roman Catholic students to degrees and announce : . . . ' quod omnibus subditis nostris, qui religionem Pontificiam sive Romano-Catholicam profitentur, liceat et deinceps licebit in dictum Collegium admitti, atque gradus in dicta academia obtinere, praestitis prius omnibus exercitiis per leges et consuetudines academiae requisitis, aliquo statuto dicti Collegii, aut statuto, regula aut consuetudine quacunque dictae academiae in contrarium non obstante.'

Now, pausing here, if nothing else had happened, what was the position of the University of Dublin ? There was no separate incorporation of it. If there had been it must have been by Royal Charter by virtue of the prerogative of the Crown. There was no express creation of it apart from the College. The College had the power of electing the Chancellor and the other officers, and of ' defining and determining ' the conferring of degrees. The College was supreme ; and the University was a branch or department of it, if indeed the College itself was not more accurately the University. That it was so considered by the framers of the Charter of James I. appears from the expressions : ' sit et habeatur universitas,' ' academiae privilegiis ornavit,' and from the power of the College to confer degrees 'intra se.' It cannot therefore admit of doubt that prior to the Letters Patent of Queen Victoria a gift to the 'Corporation of the University of Dublin' would have meant a gift to Trinity College, Dublin, and could have meant nothing else.

Both phrases, Trinity College, Dublin, and University of Dublin, are used interchangeably, as well in Acts of Parliament as in the Charters and Regulations. The Fourth Article of the Act of Union of Great Britain and Ireland, 40 Geo. III. c. 38, is, 'that four lords spiritual, by rotation of sessions, and twenty-eight lords temporal elected for life by the peers of Ireland shall be the number to sit and vote on the part of Ireland, in the House of Lords of the United Kingdom ; and one hundred commoners (two for each county in Ireland, two for the City of Dublin, two for the City of Cork, *one for the University of Trinity College,* and one for each of the most considerable cities, towns, and boroughs) be the number to sit and vote, on the part of Ireland, in the House of Commons of the Parliament of the United Kingdom.'

By the Reform Act of 1832, 2 & 3 William IV. c. 88, section 11, it is (no doubt) enacted that 'the city of Limerick, the city of Waterford, the borough of Belfast, and *the University of Dublin* shall each respectively return one member to serve in such future Parliament, in addition to the member which each of the said places is now by law entitled to return.' But by sect. 70 it is provided 'that in addition to the persons now qualified to vote at the election of a member to serve in Parliament *for the University of Dublin,* every person being of the age of twenty-one years, who has obtained, or hereafter shall obtain, the degree of Master of Arts, or any higher degree, &c., *or a Scholarship or Fellowship in the said University,* shall be entitled to vote for the election of a member or members to serve in any future Parliament for the said University,' &c. By the University of Dublin in this context Trinity College must also be meant, since Scholarships and Fellowships belong to the College, and not to the University proper.

The Act of Settlement, too, speaks of the lands of the University, meaning obviously the lands of Trinity College, Dublin. The corporation of the College was at that time the corporation of the University. There was no other corporation but that of the College, which, in the words of the Letters Patent of James I., was declared, and was held to be, a University 'sit et habeatur universitas.'

There is nothing in this view, I think, opposed to the opinion of the late Mr. Blackburne, Vice-Chancellor of the University. He said :—

' It is now, for any practical purpose, not necessary to inquire whether the University was a corporate body before the late Charter. But I may observe that through the agency of the Chancellor, or the Vice-Chancellor, and other proper officers, for whose perpetual appointment the Crown made ample provision, the power to grant degrees was insured to continue for all time. So, and in like manner, the succession of members of the Senate was to be for ever supplied out of the members of another body expressly incorporated.'

Mr. Blackburne thus gives no positive opinion on the question. Nor is the view I have expressed opposed, in my opinion, to the fundamental idea of College and University. The Universities of Oxford and Cambridge are in some respects anomalous bodies, differing in constitution from nearly all, if not all, other ancient Universities.

In *The Attorney-General* v. *Lady Downing and others* (Wilmot's Ca. and Op. 14), Lord Chief Justice Wilmot says :—

' And, indeed, I think Universities and Colleges are within the proper and genuine sense and meaning of the words " Schools of learning." The places where the public exercises are performed are called the schools. An University is a great school, incorporated to instruct, by their Professors and regular exercises, all who come to study there, and by degrees to give their students rank and credit in the republic of letters, and which are qualifications for lucrative offices and employments in life. It is a public school of divinity, physic, law, and all arts and sciences. And colleges are schools of learning, furnishing scholars for the universal school, which is a combination of all those schools ; and in any other view than as schools of learning they are as useless to society as monasteries ; and, therefore, I think they are not only within the equity of the Act, but within the words of it. And I consider this devise as made for the further augmenting of the University : and for that reason the University, in its corporate capacity, is very properly made a relator in this information being materially and essentially interested in the benefaction. For though the University is not a corporation of Colleges, but of matriculated members, and all colleges are separate corporations, yet these colleges attract and furnish the members to be matriculated, and every new college enlarges the universal school, and by increasing the number of scholars adds weight, dignity and strength to the University.'

Generally speaking, a University and College are one body. The Universities of Bologna and Paris are both teaching Universities, and Trinity College in this respect appears to have resembled them.

We now come to the Letters Patent of the Queen (21 Vict., July 24th, 1857). In them we find the following recitals :—

' Whereas we are informed that the Senate or congregation of the University of Dublin, consisting of the Chancellor or Vice-Chancellor, Doctors in the several faculties and Masters of Arts in the said University, has heretofore for the last two hundred years and upwards been governed by certain rules or statutes entitled " Regulae seu Consuetudines Universitatis Dubliniensis pro solemniore graduum collatone." And whereas our right trusty and right entirely beloved Counsellor, John George Archbishop of Armagh, Primate of all Ireland, Chancellor of the said University ; our right trusty and well-beloved Counsellor, Francis Blackburne, Doctor of Laws, Vice-Chancellor of the said University ; and our trusty and well-beloved Provost and Senior Fellows of the College of the Holy and undivided Trinity, near Dublin, have humbly represented unto us that the said rules or statutes have, by lapse of time, become in many respects obsolete and unsuited to the present state of the said University and College, and doubts have been raised as to whether the Provost and Senior Fellows of the said College have power to alter and amend the same ; and the said Chancellor, Vice-Chancellor, Provost and Senior Fellows have therefore humbly supplicated us to remove the said doubts, and to grant unto the Provost and Senior Fellows of the said College, and also unto the Senate or Congregation of the said University, such further powers as will enable them to revise, alter, or repeal the said rules and usages relating to the conferring of degrees by the said University, and to enact other rules or regulations for the same purpose, to be binding and obligatory on all members of the University.'   .

Then the granting part of the Letters Patent is as follows :—

' We are graciously pleased to accede to their request. Know ye, therefore, that we, of our special grace, certain knowledge, and mere motion, by and with the advice and consent of our right trusty and well-beloved cousin and counsellor, George William Frederick Earl of Carlisle, our Lieutenant-General, and General Governor of Ireland, do, by these presents, for us, our heirs and successors, enact and confirm to the Provost and Senior Fellows of the College of the Holy and Undivided Trinity aforesaid, and unto the Chancellor or Vice-Chancellor, Doctors and Masters of the said University, all such powers, rights, and privileges, as by the Charters and Statutes of our royal predecessors to the Provost, Fellows, and Scholars of the College of the Holy and Undivided Trinity aforesaid, or to the University of Dublin aforesaid, have heretofore been given. granted or by usage and prescription possessed, without any alteration or diminution whatever as herein provided.

'And it is our will and pleasure that the Provost and Senior Fellows of our said College of the Holy and Undivided Trinity shall have power, if they shall think fit, to alter, amend and repeal all laws, rules or bye-laws heretofore existing, for the more solemn conferring of degrees by the Senate of the University aforesaid and to make, enact, and enforce, from time to time, such additional laws, rules, and bye-laws, to alter or vary the same for the like purpose as to them shall seem fit. Provided always that no such new laws, rules, or bye-laws, or emendations or alterations of such existing laws, rules, or bye-laws, shall be of force or binding upon the said University until they shall have received the sanction of the Senate of the same in congregation lawfully assembled.'

No law is to be proposed except by the Board. Then, the constitution, powers, and privileges of the Senate are defined and determined, and to carry out the objects in view the Senate is incorporated in these words :—

'And our will and pleasure further is, that the *Senate* of the said University shall be, and continue to be, a body corporate, and have a common seal to do all such acts as may be lawful for them to do (in conformity with the laws and statutes of the realm, and with the Charter and Statutes of the College of the Holy and Undivided Trinity, and with the Statutes, Laws and Bye-Laws made or to be made in pursuance of these our Royal Letters) under the name, style and title of the Chancellor, Doctors, and Masters of the University of Dublin.

'It shall be further lawful for the said Chancellor, Doctors, and Masters to apply the lands which may or shall belong to the said University Senate for the promotion of useful learning in the said University, subject to such regulations as the Provost and Senior Fellows of our said College shall approve of or subscribe.

'And it shall be lawful for the said Chancellor, Doctors, and Masters of the said University, in their corporate capacity as aforesaid, to have, hold, acquire and receive such lands, manors, tenements or other property, real or personal, as may from the date of these presents be given or bequeathed unto them, by any person whatsoever, for the encouragement of learning in the said

University. Provided also that such gift or bequest does not impose any condition or obligation inconsistent with the Statutes of the University in force at the time of such gift or bequest, or inconsistent with the Charters and Statutes of the College of the Holy and Undivided Trinity, near Dublin.'

It is on these Letters Patent and the incorporation therein contained of the Chancellor, Doctors, and Masters, that the claim of the Senate, who are the defendants, depends. In my opinion, that is not the incorporation of the University of Dublin, but of its Senate merely.

By another Charter of the same reign another University, the Queen's University, has been incorporated. The second Charter of the Queen's University (I have not the first one at hand) is in these words :—

'We do will, order, . . . and found a University, which shall be one body politic and corporate by the name of the Queen's University in Ireland.' . . . 'And we do further will and order that the said body politic shall consist of a Chancellor, Senators, Secretary, Professors, Graduates, and Students.'

Thus we find a Charter of the same reign, dated a few years after the Charter incorporating the Senate, by which a University was incorporated, consisting of a Chancellor, Senators, a Secretary, Graduates, and Students, and in it the persons precisely defined and described of which the University is to consist. This is not an accidental circumstance. The advisers of Queen Victoria knew how to incorporate a University when they meant to do so.

There is, however, another body, viz., the Council, which was established by Letters Patent of the 38 Vict. (November 4, 1874), and to which it is said the will of Mr. Reid refers when he speaks of the 'Board.' I need not allude in detail to its constitution, suffice it to say, it is nowhere called the Board in any official instrument. The contest here is between the College and the Senate.

There are, therefore, two bodies in existence, to either of which the designation of corporation of the University of Dublin may refer, and to one or other of which it must refer : not with strict accuracy in either case, perhaps, but sufficiently clearly to enable a gift to take effect in favour of whichever is in fact meant. If the gift had been to the 'Senate' or to the Chancellors, Doctors, and Masters, there would have been no question, since whatever belief one might have had of the intention of the testator, the body would have been unmistakably defined.

There is, of course, no reported case in point: *Mostyn* v. *Mostyn*, 5 H.L.C., 155; *Stringer* v. *Gardiner*, 27 Beav. 35, 4 De Gex and J. 468, are cases of gifts to known individuals where there is some inaccuracy in the name and the description connected with it. Nor have *Ellis* v. *Houstoun*, 10 Ch. Div. 236, or *Holmes* v. *Custance*, 12 Ves. 279, any intimate bearing upon it.

Kilvert's Trusts, L. R. Ch. 171, comes perhaps nearer to the present case than any of those which were cited. In that case a testatrix by a will made in 1868 gave a legacy to the 'treasurer for the time being of the fund for the relief of the widows and orphans of the clergy of the diocese of Worcester, to be applied by him in the benefit of the charity.' Two societies made a claim— one had been founded in 1777 for the relief of the widows and orphans of the clergy of the diocese, at which time the diocese comprised only the Archdeaconry of Worcester. In 1837 the Archdeaconry of Coventry was added to the diocese, and in 1848 the Worcester Society altered its title so as to show that its operations were restricted to the Archdeaconry of Worcester. The other Society had been founded in 1877 for the relief of widows and orphans of clergy in the Archdeaconry of Coventry. The father of the testatrix had been a subscriber to the Worcester Society till his death in 1817. His widow had continued the subscription till her death in 1860, and the testatrix had continued it from that time at an increased rate; but it did not appear that the testatrix or any of her family had subscribed to the Coventry Society; it was held by Vice-Chancellor Malins that the gift was to be treated as a gift to an object, not to a particular society, but must be apportioned between the two societies. But the Court of Appeal held that the gift was a gift to a particular society, with a slight inaccuracy of description, and that the Worcester Society was solely entitled. Lord Justice James said:—

'Parol evidence is admissible to show which of the two was meant. Evidence has always been admitted to show which of two societies the testator knew, and to which of them he subscribed. Such evidence is admissible to remove an ambiguity, if there has been sufficient ground laid to raise an ambiguity, and I am assuming against the appellant that the Coventry Society have raised an ambiguity. The fund must, in my opinion, be paid to the treasurer of the Worcester Society.'

Lord Justice Mellish: 'I am of the same opinion. The

language of the bequest shows that the testatrix had some particular society in her mind, and the question is, what society? There is no difference between the course to be adopted here and in any other case of finding who answers the description given in a will of a legatee. If there was no society answering the description sufficiently to enable it to claim the legacy, it might be that the Court would carry the gift into effect as a gift for the relief of the widows and orphans of the clergy of the diocese. Here, however, I think it clear that the appellants come near enough to the description to be entitled to the legacy, if there was no other society to compete with them. There is a description of the society by its old name; that name has been changed, but that object is precisely the same as at first, and the old name is wholly inapplicable to it. Then, assuming another society to come near enough to the description to have ground for a claim, parol evidence is admissable to remove the ambiguity, and the evidence given is decisive.'

This, in short, is a case of latent ambiguity, and in such cases the rule is (when the fact of ambiguity is shown) first to see whether the other words of the will afford grounds sufficient to enable us to decide between the two conflicting bodies, and if not, then to admit extrinsic evidence.

The extrinsic evidence in the case, or rather the extrinsic facts admitted without proof, are all the one way.

The testator had left the College and University long before the Senate was incorporated or the Council heard of. It was to Trinity College, and its University of Dublin inseparably and undistinguishably blended with it, that he owed his training and his degree.

But in the words of the will itself are to be found indications which leave to my mind no doubt as to what his intention was. He uses the words University and College as loosely as the Legislature and the Crown use them. First he bequeaths all the books which he may die possessed of ' to the Librarian for the time being of the University of Dublin.' There is no Librarian of the University of Dublin or of the Senate of the University of Dublin. There is a Librarian of Trinity College, Dublin.

Secondly, the testator bequeaths his shares or stock in the Great Indian Peninsula Railway Co., &c., to his trustees for the purpose of paying same to the Corporation of the University of Dublin, to endow in the said University a Professorship of Penal Legislation, provided that it shall be lawful for the *Board* of the

University to assign any other duties which they may consider
proper to be performed by said Professors so as to make the study
of Penal Legislation a regular branch of instruction in the Law
School of the University. And I empower the said Board to
award prizes annually for proficiency in the said branch of legal
science, &c. The word Board has a well-defined meaning in Trinity
College. It means the Provost and Senior Fellows. It was
contended by Mr. Twigg, on behalf of the defendants, that the
word is synonymous with Council. In my opinion the testator
did not mean to designate a body which was not constituted
till long after his connexion with Trinity College ceased, and his
use of the words 'Board of the University' affords a key to
what he meant by the Corporation of the University of
Dublin.

Thirdly, the testator bequeaths his three Per Cent. Consolidated
Bank Annuities to the Corporation of the University of Dublin,
'to found in Trinity College, Dublin, additional Sizarships,
or Exhibitions in the nature of Sizarships, not to exceed five
in number, open only to students of limited means, natives
of the County 'of Kerry, who, having failed to obtain the
ordinary Sizarship of the College, may be deemed to have
shown sufficient merit : such Exhibitions to be held on
conditions similar in all respects to those upon which ordinary
Sizarships are held in the said College, and not to preclude such
Exhibitioners from obtaining any other Exhibitions or Prizes to
which an ordinary Sizar would be eligible ; and the Board of the
said University shall determine the annual stipend to be allowed
to each such Exhibitioner, or the privileges in lieu of such stipend,
in such a way as to place him with respect to exemption from fees,
free commons, and free rooms, on a footing similar to that of ordinary Sizars.' What Board? Plainly the Board of the same Body—
the same Corporation to which he made the bequest, 'and I
empower the said Board to apply the residue of such income (if
any) in such manner as they may think best calculated to
encourage superior education in the said County, as, for instance,
by assigning from time to time stipends, to such schoolmasters as
may distinguish themselves in preparing students for the said
University, such stipends to be given on condition that such
master or masters shall undertake to prepare, free of expense, as
day scholars, a certain number of boys of limited means for the
Sizarship Examinations of the University, or in such other way

as to the said Board may seem most effectual and expedient for
the promotion of superior education in the said County.' There
are no Sizarships in the University; they are in the College.
There are no such Examinations as Sizarship Examinations of
the University. They are held in and by Trinity College. In my
opinion, treating the question as one of intention, the testator has
clearly shown on the face of the will itself that what he meant by
the Corporation of the University of Dublin was the Corporation
of Trinity College. I am bound to give effect to that intention
unless it is encountered by some rule of law. I have already
snown at, I fear, too great length, that the phrase ' Corporation
of the University of Dublin ' has no such defined meaning as in a
a case like the present, excluding all inquiry as to particular
intention ; and I have therefore no hesitation in pronouncing a
decree for the plaintiffs.

INSTRUCTION TO GERMAN CHAPTERS FROM PAPAL SECRE-
TARY OF STATE REGARDING THE ELECTION OF BISHOPS

E SECRETARIA STATUS

INSTRUCTIO PRO CAPITULIS GERMANIAE QUIBUS COMPETIT ELECTIO
EPISCOPORUM, CIRCA MODUM HOC MUNUS PERAGENDI

ILLME. AC RME. DOMINE,

Ad notitiam Sanctae Sedis pervenit, in electionibus Episcoporum, quae, in plerisque Germaniae partibus, speciali iuris
ordinatione, Capitulis commissae sunt, quandoque occurrere tum
libertati Ecclesiae et Apostolicae Sedis dignitati, tum pactis cum
loci Principe initis minus consentanea. Quum vero, ad religionis
incrementa, ad regni et sacerdotii concordiam, utiliorem episco-
palis muneris procurationem, summopere intersit distinctius
declarare, quae sint, hac in re, Capituli iura atque officia ;
Sanctissimus Dominus Noster Leo Papa XIII., pro Apostolica
Sua sollicitudine et paterna charitate, universis et singulis
earundem dioecesium Ordinariis ea quae sequuntur exponi iussit,
cum ipsis Capitulis communicanda atque ab omnibus diligenter
servanda et custodienda, ita ut, deinceps, quavis ambiguitate
sublata, amotisque iis, qui forte irrepserunt abusibus, Ecclesiae
libertas, pactorum fides et Sedis Apostolicae dignitas sartae
tectaeque maneant.

Illud est in primis animadvertendum, Constitutiones Apostolicas

' De salute animarum,'[1] 'Impensa Romanorum Pontificum,'[2] 'Ad Dominici gregis,'[3] Litterasque in forma Brevis 'Quoad de fidelium'[4] et ' Re sacra,'[5] ad normam conventionum cum Principibus initarum, a Romanis Pontificibus sa. me. Pio VII., et Leone XII. editas, Capitulis Metropolitanis et Cathedralibus Germaniae facultatem et officium attribuere, libere prorsus atque ad sacrorum Canonum praescriptum Archiepiscopos et Episcopos eligendi. Capitula nimirum id habent operis ac muneris, ut eiusmodi electionum libertatem, ab Apostolica Sede in tuto positam et a civili Regimine, initis respective pactis, admissam neque directe, neque indirecte, violari unquam sinant aut imminui.

Porro constans doctrina, a qua se recedere nec velle nec posse Sancta Sedes aperte semper declaravit, acatholicae potestatis interventum, hac in re, non admittit nisi negativum et qui libertatem canonicae electionis incolumem relinquat. Quam libertatem laederet profecto aut minueret positivus concursus vel influxus potestatis ipsius, sicut et illimitatum excludendi ius in negotio electionis Pastorum, quos 'Spiritus Sanctus posuit regere Ecclesiam Dei.'

Iam vero negativus interventus, Principi vel Regimini acatholico permissus, eo demum spectet, ut personae minus illi gratae non eligantur : unde Capituli partium est illos tantum adsciscere, quos, ante solemnem electionis actum, inter alias dotes, ad Ecclesiam instruendam, tuendam et pacifice gubernandam requisitas, prudentiae laude, publicae quietis ac fidelitatis studio praestare, ideoque Principi non esse minus gratos constet.

Meminerint insuper electores ac serio perpendant, quam grave et magni momenti sit illorum munus ; nihilque aliud ob oculos suos ponant, quam animarum salutem et Ecclesiae emolumenta, ut, omni deposito humano respectu, illi uni suffragium conferant, quem caeteris aptiorem et digniorem reputaverint.

Qui vero nonnisi digniores et Ecclesiae magis utiles promovendi sunt, tenentur electores candidatorum catalogo eos tantum inscribere, quos indicent omnibus qualitatibus ad Ecclesiam sancte sapienterque regendam necessariis reapse pollere. Si enim alios, de caetero bene meritos, sed ob provectiorem aetatem, vel

---

[1] Pro Regno Borussiae, 16 Julii 1821.
[2] Pro Regno Hannoverae, 21 Martii 1824.
[3] Pro ecclesiastica provincia Rheni Superioris, 10 April 1827.
[4] Ad Capitula Regni Borussici, 16 Iulii 1821.
[5] Ad Capitula provinciae Rheni Superioris, 28 Maii 1827.

adversam valetudinem, aut aliam ob causam, muneri impares, candidatis accenserent, Canonici periculo sese committerent ipsos demum inhabiles eligendi, cum summo Ecclesiae detrimento.

De Commissarii civilis interventu in electionibus, nihil iuris Gubernio attribuunt vel recognoscunt apostolicae Sedis acta et documenta, quae huc spectant. Quod si eiusmodi interventum plenae libertati electionum vel Ecclesiae dignitati quomodocumque officere contingat, Capitula id ferre nec possent nec deberent.

Speciatim, admittere nequit Apostolica Sedes, ut Canonici, dum electionem peractam Commissario significant, approbationem seu ratihabitionem quodammodo expostulent aut exquirere videantur civilis potestatis. Nec permitti potest, ut adstanti populo statim notificetur electio, velut completa et perfecta. Sed comitiorum exitus ita publicandus erit, ut simul declaretur capitularem actum suos canonicos effectus non sortiri, nisi quum a Summo Pontifice fuerit confirmatus. Proinde solemnis et publica gratiarum actio, pro electione facta omnino differenda est, usque dum Apostolicae confirmationis certum habeatur nuncium.

Mandat denique Sanctitas Sua, ut harum litterarum exemplar in tabulario cuiusque Capituli diligenter asservetur, itemque praecipit, ut sede episcopali vacante, antequam de electione peragenda Canonici capitulariter pertractent, haec mea epistola simulque Breve ' Quod de fidelium ' vel ' Re sacra ' (pro diversitate loci) religiose et ad integrum perlegantur.

Haec omnia Beatissimus Pater praedictis Germaniae Capitulis per Episcopos singulos significari iussit : eaque Sanctitati Suae de Capitularium integritate, prudentia ac fide est opinio, ut ipsos apprime mandata eiusmodi servaturos, commissoque munere naviter perfuncturos esse minime dubitet.

Erit igitur Amplitudinis Tuae, Summi Pontificis nomine haec de re certiores facere Capitulares tuae iurisdictioni subiectos ; dum sincerae aestimationis meae Tibi sensus ex animo profiteor.

Tuae Amplitudini
Romae, e Secretaria Status, die 20 Iulii 1900.
addictissimus
M. Card. RAMPOLLA.

NOTICES OF BOOKS

AN INTRODUCTION TO THE OLD TESTAMENT IN GREEK.
By H. B. Swete. Cambridge University Press, 1900.

THIS is an admirable work, worthy both of the author's high
reputation and of the great University to which he belongs. As a
guide to the nature and history of the Greek versions, the
Septuagint especially, it is far superior to many introductions that
need not be mentioned. Not only are all the newest and best
sources of information drawn upon here, but a vast amount of
erudition is given to the world for the first time. This, indeed,
was to be expected from a scholar of Dr. Swete's attainments.

The work before us may best be described as 'Prolegomena'
to his critical edition of the Septuagint (2nd ed., Cambridge,
1895-1899). In his opening chapter he gives a detailed and most
interesting narrative of the origin of this version. The story of
Aristeas is discussed, and put aside. As the learned author says,
page 19: 'Everything points to the conclusion that the version
arose out of the needs of the Alexandrian Jews. Whilst in
Palestine the Aramaic-speaking Jews were content with the
interpretation of the *Methurgeman,* at Alexandria the Hebrew
lesson was gladly exchanged for a lesson read from a Greek
translation, and the work of the interpreter was limited to
exegesis.' Where there is abundance of what is good, it is hard
to make a selection, but we may say that a section that will be
found to possess a special value is Part I., ch. v., which describes
the uncial and the cursive MSS. of the Septuagint. Part II., ch. ii.,
also cannot fail to be of great use to the student, containing, as it
does, an elaborate table (accompanied by explanations) of the chief
instances of 'difference of sequence ' in the Hebrew and Greek
Bibles respectively. This is followed by a division entitled
' Differences of Subject-matter.' In the succeeding chapter,
' Books not included in the Hebrew Canon,' occurs one of the
few blemishes to be found in the work. While treating of
2 Machabees, Dr. Swete says it is an 'inaccurate, and to some
extent mythical panegyric of the patriotic revolt,' page 278. That
an average non-Catholic should be under the erroneous impression that 2 Machabees was a merely human production, and of

the kind just alleged, might cause no surprise, but that a scholar
of Dr. Swete's fame should express himself in this way is contrary
to all our cherished anticipations. In several places of his book he
shows implicitly respect and kindly feeling for the Catholic Church.
and he knows that the Catholic Church venerates 2 Machabees
as divine. The deutero-canonicity of the book is evidence only of
either local or temporary doubts which in no way affected the
belief of the universal and perpetual Church. Her Tridentine
canon is the one that she received from the Apostles, and held
through all the intervening ages. Even from lists of the sacred
books in MSS., Fathers, and Synods, which Dr. Swete gives
(pages 201-214), it is plain that 2 Machabees was regarded as
inspired. Such is the power of the tradition, which Luther dared
to oppose, that to the present day schismatical bodies in the East,
though separated for centuries from the unity of the Church,
retain the book. See Vigouroux, *Dict. de la Bible*, s. v. 'Canon,'
or any similar work. On page 15, Dr. Swete speaks of ' the
confessedly fictitious correspondence between Philadelphus and
the Palestinian Jews in 2 and 3 Machabees.' The latter is one
of the apocryphal books, with which we have nothing to do : we
can only say that so far as we are aware, 2 Machabees contains
no correspondence whatever between Philadelphus and the
Palestine Jews, but if it did the correspondence could not be
fictitious. With regard to the remark made on pages 251, 252,
viz. :—' Ps. xiii. (xiv.) 3 s. c. This, the only long interpolation in the
Greek Psalter, is found, upon examination, to be made up of
Pss. v. 10b., cxxxix. (cxl.) 4b., ix. (x.) 17a., Isa. lix. 7, 8, Ps. xxxv.
(xxxvi.) 1a., all taken from the LXX version with slight variations.
That it never formed part of the Hebrew Psalm may be safely
affirmed, yet it is quoted continuously in Rom. iii. 13, 18, where it
follows without break upon an abridgment of Ps. xiii. (xiv.) 1, 3 ';
we may say that it was from the Epistle (in which St. Paul had
quoted continuously all these texts) that the combination was
inserted into the Septuagint Psalm. St. Jerome explains the
matter to his disciple, St. Eustochius, thus :—' Non tam Apos-
tolum de Ps. 13 sumsisse id quod in hebraico non habetur, quam
eos qui artem contexendarum inter se Scripturarum Apostoli
nesciebant, quaesisse aptum locum, ubi assumtum ab eo ponerent
testimonium, quod absque auctoritate in Scriptura positum non
putabant.' (In Isa. xvi., Prooem.). Nothing better in brief
compass could be desired on ' The Greek of the Septuagint,' than

Part II., ch. iv. (pages 289-314), and the same must be said of ch. v., 'The Septuagint as a Version.' Among the contents of Part III., we would direct especial attention to ch. ii., ' Quotations from the Septuagint in the New Testament.' The student of the Gospels and Epistles will do well to keep this list open on his desk, and the student of the Old Testament will derive considerable help from the chapter on ' The Greek Versions as a help to Biblical Study.'

In a short notice such as this it is impossible to point out all he excellencies of this *Introduction*, but the scope of these observations will be attained, if it has shown that Dr. Swete's book is indispensable to those who take up the study of the Septuagint. The Appendix, which contains a critical edition of the letter of Aristeas, with an introduction by H. St. G. Thackeray, will be welcome to all professors in our seminaries.

R. W.

THE HISTORY OF CONFESSION TO A.D. 1215. By C. M. Roberts Cambridge University Press, 1901.

THIS little book contains evidence of wide reading. The author has brought together many passages from Scripture, the Fathers, the Councils, and the Penitentials. But his inference from these texts is erroneous ; nor, indeed, is this to be wondered at, for, to understand the meaning and drift of some of them, an acquaintance with the technicalities of theology is required. The formulas of the Catholic Church, the witness to tradition found enshrined in the pages of her Doctors and Fathers, can be interpreted only by those who know the *mens et praxis Ecclesiæ*. Above all, where there is question of a sacrament of the Church, an Anglican is almost sure to make mistakes. This is the reason why the author has failed to see the meaning of other passages. Nevertheless, though his book is so faulty, it is consoling to find an Anglican writing on a subject about which, until recently, the body to which he belongs knew next to nothing. His thesis which was that of the Reformers, is that until the thirteenth century sacramental confession, or confession made to a priest duly empowered to forgive sin, was not obligatory. He imagines that the confession ' made to God,' to use the expression of some of the Fathers, differs from the confession made to God's priests, of which they so often speak. He imagines also that confession in private to a priest for the purpose of obtaining absolution was

purely voluntary, and that non-sacramental confession in public was what was ordinarily taught and practised. His error arises partly, as we have seen, from a misconception of the passages he quotes, and partly from his not mentioning and discussing some most relevant passages. For instance, St. John xx. 23, where our Lord says that He sends His Apostles (*all of them priests*), as He Himself had been sent, and gives them the power of forgiving sin. And the correlative obligation of confessing to the priests of the Church is taught in St. James v. 14-16, to which he makes no allusion. Specific confession of sin is necessary, else the grant of judicial power to the Apostles and their successors in the priesthood would be nugatory. Another passage which must refer to sacramental confession has not been noticed by the author. It occurs in the Διδαχη των Αποστολων xiv. 1. Κατα κυριακην δε κυριου συναχθεντες κλασατε αρτον και Ευχαριστησατε, προεξομολογησαμενοι τα παραπτωματα υμων, οπως καθαρα η υσια υμων η· Again, he fails to see that Origen, whom he quotes on page 33, is not speaking of 'voluntary confession before the Church,' and apparently, he is not aware that Origen (Hom. 2 in Lev. n. 4) explains St. James v. 16, of sacramental confession, and speaks too of the sinner not being ashamed to own his sin to the priest of God, and of thus obtaining pardon. The author does not mention Origen's first Homily on Psalm xxxvii., so we will give the words : 'Et ille quidem Christus αρχιατρος, qui posset curare omnem languorem et omnem infirmitatem, discipuli vero ejus, Petrus vel Paulus, sed et prophetæ, medici sunt, et hi omnes qui post Apostolos in ecclesia positi sunt quibusque curandorum vulnerum disciplina commissa est, quos voluit Deus in ecclesia sua esse medicos animarum.' So too, though he quotes some words of St. Cyprian, he does not give this important passage :—
'Confiteantur singuli, quaeso, fratres, delictum suum, dum adhuc qui deliquit in seculo est, dum admitti ejus confessio potest, dum satisfactio et remissio facta per sacerdotes apud Deum grata est.' Nor does he tell his readers about these words of St. Hilary though he speaks of the saint on page 68 : 'Ceterum extra veniam est, qui peccatum cognovit, nec cognitum confitetur ' (in Psalm cxxxv. 3), and 'Confitendum enim crimen est, ut obtineatur et venia ' (in Psalm cxviii.).

Nowhere will Mr. Roberts find it stated that the voluntary non-sacramental avowal of sin, to which he would fain refer many sayings of the Fathers, is stated to be capable of remitting guilt, and to be necessary for salvation. As he mentions with approval, near the end of his work (page 114), the erroneous opinion of Gratian and of Peter Lombard about 'confession made to God,' perhaps we cannot conclude this short notice more suitably than by quoting the words of the Church's greatest theologian, St. Thomas of Aquin : 'Quod ponitur hic pro opinione, heresis est. . . . In talibus, antequam determinetur per ecclesiam, quod ex eis sequitur aliquid contrarium fidei, non judicatur heresis esse, sed nunc post determinationem ecclesiae sub Innocentio III. factam, heresis reputanda est.'

R. W.

IRISH GRAMMAR. By the Christian Brothers. Dublin : M. H. Gill & Son.

THIS Grammar does much to smooth the path of learners of Irish. It is concise, clear, and simple, yet exhaustive in its treatment of the various grammatical rules. A valuable feature is its wealth of illustration, each section being copiously illustrated by examples, all drawn from living phrases current among native Irish speakers. It thus fulfils the purpose of a phrase-book as well as of a grammar, and affords the diligent student copious materials for familiar Irish conversation. It is based throughout on the modern usage, and rightly discards all grammatical forms which, though found in books and commonly inserted in other grammars, are no longer heard in the popular speech in any part of Ireland. We note with pleasure that the recognised standard of spelling is adhered to, for we know that the eccentric and widely different systems of spelling followed by some 'modern' Irish writers have been a fruitful source of discouragement to many unfortunate beginners.

The author departs, in some instances, from the teaching and phraseology of the older school of Irish grammarians, and in most of these departures, as, for example, in his treatment of the verbal noun, and the dependent form of verbs, is, we think, fully justified in the light of recent investigations. The new theory regarding what is called here the 'indefinite' form of the verb, as distinct from the passive, is, however, more doubtful. We are astonished at the novel doctrine laid down regarding the possessive pronouns, mo, vo, ▵, etc. The author states (page 74) that the term 'possessive pronouns' is 'incorrectly' applied to these words. His argument is singular : 'The possessives in Irish can never stand alone, hence they are not pronouns.' The same reasoning would exclude the corresponding English forms, *my*, *thy*, *her*, *our*, etc., from the category of pronouns. It is obvious, of course, that in Irish, as in English, these forms are used instead of the genitive case of the nouns to which they refer, and are, therefore, rightly called *pronouns*. The name of 'possesive pronouns' is given to the corresponding forms by grammarians in all languages, so far as we know.

We hope this book will have the large circulation which it deserves. The Christian Brothers, by producing it, have established an additional claim to the gratitude of Irishmen.

J. M.

A MANUAL OF ASCETICAL THEOLOGY. By the Rev. Arthur Devine, Passionist. London : R. & T. Washbourne, 4, Paternoster-row. New York : Benziger Brothers. Price, 7*s.* 6*d.*, nett.

THE alternative title, namely, 'The Supernatural Life of the Soul on Earth and in Heaven' would, in our opinion, be more appropriate, and better adapted to give a clue to the contents of Father Devine's latest contribution to the Theological Literature of the day than the name under which it is introduced to the public. Briefly, Mystical Theology may be described as the practical science of the Higher Spiritual Life. Now, in the book before us, there is, it appears to us, a little too much of the speculative and too little of the practical to satisfy this definition. To quarrel, however, over a mere title, its aptness or the reverse, is ungenerous in a critic, especially when passing from the title-page to consider and analyze the six hundred neatly printed pages of carefully-chosen and well-written matter that compose the volume, he finds less to find fault with and more to admire. For we can truly say that the present work is destined to enhance the already well-established reputation of its author for ripe scholarship and sound theological knowledge.

The aim of the writer as revealed to us by a perusal of the book is to give an exposition, simple yet intelligent, of the fundamental principles of sacred science that lie at the very root of the Spiritual Life, to explain the lines along which that life is nourished and strengthened, and to indicate the nature of its final and complete consummation. The work is, accordingly, divided into three parts. The first treats of the beginnings of the

Supernatural Life, the sources from which it is derived and the processes of its development, and here we are at once initiated into the mysteries of Grace, its nature, kinds and effects. From this we pass to the virtues by an easy and natural transition. Their functions and offices are clearly indicated, and their classification is accomplished in a manner that lacks nothing in clearness and adequateness. In the course of this section our author discusses, in a learned way, questions about the states of nature, the total and adequate cause of supernatural acts, the relations between charity and sanctifying grace and the indwelling of God in the souls of the just, which if not altogether devoid of interest for the mystic in search of the Higher Life will assuredly not fail to stimulate the curiosity of the student eager to gather information on the debateable points of Scholastic Theology.

In the second part of the work the author treats of the increase of the Supernatural Life, and here he has many beautiful things to say, and he says them well. The doctrine of merit is fully and exhaustively discussed, and the Sacraments, as means of increasing the supernatural within us, are adequately dealt with. We admired especially the chapters dealing with the Blessed Eucharist, and of these we would emphasize in a marked way that one in which are explained the effects of this most august Sacrament. The third part is conversant with the soul in the enjoyment of its last end, and here we are again presented with many interesting problems discussed by the Scholastics about the Beatitude of the Just, nature of the Beatific Vision, qualities of the Glorified Body, and the meaning of seeing God ' face to face.'

For this brief and inadequate *resumé* of the contents of Father Devine's book it will be seen that the volume bristles with delightful discussions on many matters freely debated by theologians. Let us assure our readers that everything touched upon is handled with deftness and dexterity. The issues are plainly put, and in arguing his case the author holds no brief for any school, but is concerned solely with the merits of each particular question. Every opinion advanced, if not the commonly received one, has at any rate the guarantee of respectable authority, quotations at great length being introduced at intervals to drive home an argument. Some of these, however, are very long, and in view of the easy and pleasing style which our author commands we would prefer in many instances to see the pith and marrow of an external statement given in his own free and forcible manner.

P. M.

THE LAST SUPPER. A Poem. By Rev. M. A. Murphy, C.C.,
Freshford, Kilkenny. Dublin : Browne & Nolan. 1902.

WE offer our sincere congratulations to Father Murphy on
having produced at this very appropriate season a poem well
worthy in its tender devotion, its pure and dignified verse, its
elevated style, of the most sacred theme with which it deals. It
required some courage to make the attempt in the rhyming
pentameters of Pope and Goldsmith ; but Father Murphy has
shown how suitably all measures can be utilised for sacred purposes. Although St. Thomas was anything but a professional
poet, yet it seems to us quite certain that no poet has ever
expressed so aptly in verse as he has done the doctrine of the
Church on the subject with which Father Murphy deals. Father
Murphy, however, has been, in our opinion, exceedingly happy in
his choice of words. And even though some of the expressions
might be improved, there is nothing in the whole poem that gives
the reader the least shock, or seems out of harmony with the
subject or the spirit in which it should be approached. Father
Murphy has dealt mainly with the historical aspect of the great
event, and has gone through all the scenes and motives with the
greatest care ; but his lines on the Eucharist itself at the end are
particularly sweet and well turned. It is long since we have read
any verses composed by a priest that have given us so much
pleasure.

J. F. H.

"Ut Christiani ita et Romani sitis." " As you are children of Christ, so be you children of Rome."
Ex Dictis S. Patricii, In Libro Armacano, fol. 9.

The Irish Ecclesiastical Record

𝔄 Monthly Journal, under Episcopal Sanction.

Thirty-fifth Year]   **MAY, 1902.**   [Fourth Series
No. 413.   Vol. XI

Nihil Obstat.
   GIRALDUS MOLLOY, S.T.D.
     Censor Dep.

Imprimatur.
   ✠ GULIELMUS,
     Archiep. Dublin.,
     Hibernae Primas

BROWNE & NOLAN, Limited

Publishers and Printers, 24 & 25

NASSAU STREET, DUBLIN.

. . PRICE ONE SHILLING . .

SUBSCRIPTION: Twelve Shillings per Annum, Post Free, payable in advance

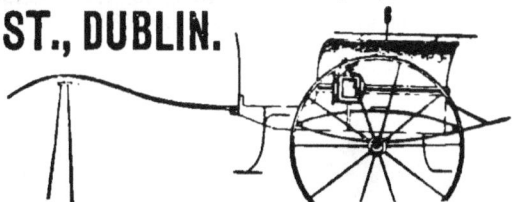

IRELAND AND AMERICA

NOTES OF A MISSION TOUR IN THE STATES

II

IN the February number of the I. E. RECORD I set down
the defections from the Church in America during
the last half-century as reaching the enormous figure
of 10,000,000. Since uttering this opinion, I have
received several friendly remonstrances, intimating, all of
them, that I had taken too gloomy a view of the subject, and
that I had over-stated a case which was surely bad enough
without any exaggeration.

I need hardly say that nothing could give me greater
pleasure than to find that these objections had something
solid to rest on. In all that has been said or written to me,
however, I cannot see any good reason for altering the
estimate I have given. It can hardly be necessary to repeat,
that I can form but a mere opinion in the matter, and that
it would [1] extremely presumptuous on my part to hazard
anything like a dogmatic statement on a subject which is
necessarily intricate and obscure. Americans who make a
special study of their religious statistics very often differ *toto
coelo* in their estimates both of the actual number of Catholics
in the country and of those who have been lost to the Church
during the period referred to. Lamentably large as my
estimate has been, some American Catholics have gone so far

as to double it, fixing the loss to the Church at 20,000,000. At the Catholic Congress held in Chicago in 1893 (in connection with the ' World's Parliament of Religions ') this was mentioned as a 'conservative estimate.' Mr. M. T. Elder, of New Orleans, was very outspoken on the subject, as well as on the condition of Catholicity generally in the States. Some of his remarks deserve to be quoted if only for the flavour and vigour of their characteristic American phraseology.

When I see [said he] how largely Catholicity is represented among our hoodlum element I feel in no spread-eagle mood. When I note how few Catholics are engaged in honestly tilling the soil, and how many Catholics are engaged in the liquor traffic. I cannot talk buncombe to anybody. When I reflect that out of the 70,000,000 of this nation, we number only 9,000,000, and that out of that 9,000,000 so large a proportion is made up of poor factory hands, poor mill and shop and mine and railroad employées, poor Government clerks, I still fail to find material for buncombe or spread-eagle or taffy-giving.

On the other hand, Dr. Gilmary Shea, a most conscientious and painstaking writer, would seem to reckon our losses for the last eighty years at only about 4,000,000.

No doubt in making calculations one is strongly, though, of course, unwittingly, biassed by one's surroundings. One priest will take a very roseate view of the Church in America, both actual and prospective, while another will tell you unhesitatingly that the present condition of Catholicity in the States is bad and the outlook a hundred times worse. Not unnaturally they argue from the particular to the general, and each one looks on his own parish as the entire country in miniature. And if priests and laymen who are Americans, and who live in America, take such widely divergent views on the religious condition and the religious statistics of the country, a foreigner would be guilty of gross impertinence if he were to write as one having special or exclusive information. He can only form his opinion honestly from what he has seen and heard and read, and then allow it to be taken for what it is worth. Accepting even the most favourable view of the matter, there is unfortunately no room for doubting that millions have been lost to the Church in America, a very large proportion of these millions being of Irish birth or blood.

Naturally we look for the causes of these alarming apostacies; and the inquiry, if we make it, will give us a further insight into the religious condition of America, and especially of Ireland in America. Here is a Church as perfectly organized as any in the world ; fully equipped in every way for its warfare against error and sin ; its universities, colleges, seminaries, orphanages, charitable homes, parochial schools, all in flourishing condition; its Press well and ably conducted ; its religious associations numerous and active ; its convents and monasteries all centres of light and piety ; its twelve thousand priests pious, learned, exemplary, zealous ; its one hundred archbishops and bishops, standing as faithful sentinels on the watch towers—ever ready to warn their flocks of the approach of the enemy, and to impede and bar his progress. How is it, that with great and powerful agencies like these, the outflow from the Church is so large and so continuous ?

The causes are manifold and are not far to seek. We have but to open our eyes to see them. First of all I would point out that the moral atmosphere of the country seems to be charged with influences that are anti-Catholic and un-Christian. Worldliness, mammonism, naturalism, materialism seem to be among the chief elements that enter into the life of the people. Many are uncompromising infidels, and are proud to proclaim it. The late Colonel Ingersoll, charlatan though he was, had his hundreds of thousands of blatant atheistic followers scattered all over the States. In some of the large cities he was often able to address an audience of three or four thousand men, who were always ready to applaud his coarse blasphemies with enthusiasm, and to re-echo his ribaldries within the circles of their own influence.

The majority of Americans do not formally reject the Christian revelation ; they regard it rather with a sort of mild approval. If their religion is Christianity, it is a Christianity very much diluted with scepticism ; or it might be more accurately described as a Deism slightly tinged with the teachings of the Gospel. The truth is, they trouble themselves very little about dogmas, or about the claims of the various sects in the country. They make up their minds that a man's religion is of little more account than the colour of his neck-tie or the cut of his frock coat. If they go to a place of worship on the Sunday it is usually to hear a smart discourse on some burning question of the hour, or on the depravity of some public man ; or to enjoy the epigrams of some fashionable preacher, whose theological doctrine is as vague and vapid as his eloquence is pointed and sparkling. ' Never mind priests and churches,' they say ; ' take no heed of the threats and promises of the preacher and the theologian ; laugh alike at their blazing hell-fire and their psalm-singing paradise. Be a good citizen ; a faithful husband, an affec- tionate father, a loyal friend, and then God will never trouble to inquire into your religious opinions.'

I do not know whether the independence and self- reliance engendered by republican institutions lead to freedom of thought in matters religious, but the American does seem to think that he ought to be quite as unfettered in theology as in politics ; and that he has as much right to choose his religion as he has to vote for his favourite politician.

We, Americans [you are told], are not to be ' bluffed ' into any form of religion, and we are not to be caught by any of the vener- able but incredible stories of your Scriptures. We are a smart people, sir. We test and we sift all things. We know what is false and we reject it : we cling to the true. We can tell at a glance the real coin of historic and religious truth, while we can just as easily detect the counterfeit that so often passes current in its stead. No, don't you try to make our countrymen believe what is unbelievable.

Yet, curious psychological fact, these very Americans, so smart and sharp and wide-awake and hard-headed and incredulous, often prove themselves the simplest and the most guileless people in the world in matters which are outside the range of revealed truth or of Church authority. America is pre-eminently the country of cheats and charlatans. They flourish there as they do nowhere else. During my stay in Boston the city was thrown into

unwonted excitement by a mountebank who had just
founded a new religion called 'The Holy Ghost and Us.'
(He might have spared himself the trouble, as there were
already about four hundred new religions in the country.)
He spoke every evening to the third Person of the Blessed
Trinity as to an intimate friend. He proclaimed that whatever he asked, be it a piano or an arm chair or a phonograph
or a Bible, the Holy Ghost was sure to hand it down 'right
away.' If we may credit the Boston newspapers of the day
this man was one of the most marvellous personalities of the
century, and one of the most successful. The *élite* of the
city, we were told, became his ardent disciples, and at the
night services held in a theatre ladies smothered him with
showers of dollars and gold pieces and pearls and diamonds.
As this happened two years ago, the new religion no doubt
is now dead and forgotten. While we were giving a Mission
in the same sanctimonious city, a 'reverend' faith-healer
was arrested by the police for swindling. His tactics were
simplicity itself. If you suffered from consumption or cancer
or a broken leg or a broken heart, you had simply to write
to him, telling him the nature of your complaint, promising
never to consult a doctor, and—enclosing one dollar. The
moment you received his formal acknowledgment you were
healed ! At the time of his arrest this modern thaumaturgus
was in the receipt of two thousand dollars a week. He
complained piteously to the Irish policeman who took him
into custody that he was in very bad health, and that
imprisonment would certainly be his death, receiving the
characteristic reply that he had only to write himself a letter
and that he would be all right on the instant. An adventurer
of a different character plied a very brief but successful trade
while I was in Brooklyn. He had discovered a marvellous
way of investing money, and offered 10 per cent. per week
to his clients. Will it be believed that streams of gold
flowed into his coffers at once, and that when he decamped
with 90 per cent. of his receipts he was richer by some
hundreds of thousands of dollars ?

Yet it is the dupes of glaring frauds like these who will
loftily inform you that the Christianity, whose historic

evidences and moral and doctrinal beauties captivated the intellects of such men as St. Augustin, St. Thomas of Aquin, Bossuet, Newton, Pascal or Newman, does not come up to the level of their requirements and does not satisfy their critical acumen.

A man may, by taking certain poisons in very minute quantities, succeed by-and-bye in drinking with impunity a dose which would be fatal to another. The Irish exile leaves his native shores full of faith in the word of God and in the teachings of His Church. As soon would he doubt that the sun shines in the firmament as question the truth of a single article of his religion. He first tastes poison in swallowing a large and deadly potion. He had never in his life heard a word uttered against the fundamental truths of Christianity, and he finds himself suddenly thrust in amongst a multitude of men who believe in nothing. They are men too, perhaps, who are his superiors in point of intelligence and education, and who are irreproachable in the matter of some of the coarser vices, such as drunkenness. These men assail his faith from every point; they laugh at him or express a supercilious pity for the fools who, like him, believe as eternal truths the fables which have so ably been held up to scorn by Robert Ingersoll and others. What is he to do? How is he to answer? Of course he learned his catechism in Ireland and understands all that the catechism teaches, but he is utterly unequipped for polemics of this sort. He could knock a man down that insulted his faith, but he is not fit to enter into the arena of argument with the trained athletes of atheism or agnosticism. He is beaten again and again in the wordy strife, and is driven from the field amid the jeers of the enemy. But the foundation of doubt has been laid within his soul. He has taken his first draught of poison. By-and-bye it will do its deadly work.

Indifferentism, too, is a great irreligious force in America, and one with which the Irish immigrant is very soon called on to do battle. The indifferentist is a more insidious, a more covert, and in this way a more dangerous foe than the open atheist. He fights religion behind a mask of religion.

He expresses very kindly his approval of Christianity, but his uncompromising hatred for all Christian sects or churches in particular, especially for the one Church which professes to have authority from God to enlighten men's minds and to curb the unruly desires of their hearts. ' Be anything you like,' he says, ' but a bigot, and a bigot is a man who has more faith in his own church than in any other. Above all things let us insist in this free country on complete religious freedom '—which in his mouth means complete freedom from religion.

It is easy to see how, in a country so very generally in the grasp of atheism and heresy, the Catholic runs a grave risk of being swept by the forces around him into the vortex of unbelief, or into a religious indifferentism which is little better than downright infidelity.

With the loss of faith disappears the purity of morals. Infidelity and immorality act and re-act one upon the other. It is not always easy to know which is the cause and which the effect. Sometimes infidelity leads to immorality, but very generally the case is reversed. What is a more effective sedative for an alarmed and troublesome conscience than to believe that neither here nor beyond the grave is there a Justice to punish the wicked and reward the good ?

I do not know whether America is better or worse in morals than certain countries of the Old World. Unfortunately, vice is a plant that is indigenous to every soil, and it is not always easy to tell where it strikes its roots deepest or spreads its branches widest. I will only state what is the general feeling in the country itself, and it is that the widespread immorality of American cities is something horrible. The casual observer does not see much to offend the eye. Outside of the slums and dens of infamy which are haunted only by the lowest and most abandoned of the criminal classes, everything seems decent and orderly. In the public streets of New York or Boston or Chicago, you meet with no such disgusting evidences of profligacy as you see in some of the best streets of London, and alas ! sometimes in some of the best streets of Dublin, too. In the state of Massachusetts, and, I believe, throughout New England generally, some of the old Puritan laws are still in full force and activity. The slightest familiarity amongst the sexes, for instance, is punished most rigorously, not by fine, but by imprisonment; and when I was in Boston a great, but unavailing outcry was raised in the Press because two school children, as they were called, had been sentenced to a month's imprisonment for having kissed each other playfully in the public street. In the same State, seduction, concubinage, drunkenness, and other irregularities are punished by long terms of imprisonment or penal servitude. The Sabbath must be observed with even more pharisaical strictness than it is, or rather has been, in Scotland; and woe to you if you sit down even in your own house to have a quiet game of chess or cards or billiards with the members of your own family. The prying policeman will hale you before a judge, and will have you punished as a law breaker and branded as a criminal.

Yet, these towns and cities, externally so decorous, are but ' whited sepulchres, which, indeed, appear beautiful outward, but within are full of dead men's bones and of all uncleanness.'

What is most lamentable in this is the precocious depravity of the young. Doctors and others conversant with the subject, will tell you that it is only too common to find lads of fifteen or sixteen years of age who have been initiated into some of the worst mysteries of iniquity. We hear much of the glorious independence of the American girl who needs no chaperon, who is able to take care of herself, and who scorns the platitudes of Mrs. Grundy. If mothers in Ireland knew what this ' independence ' means for their daughters how their hearts would ache, and how they would curse the causes, whether political or economic, that drove their innocent girls from under their roof.

I do not care to say more on this very delicate and unpleasant subject. My only reason for referring to it, is to point out that it is one of the causes of the defection of

Catholics from the Church. They know that it is useless to be Catholics in name if they are open rebels to the Church and her doctrines. They know that to be Catholics they must go to confession, and they know that confession necessarily means the fixed determination to lead a good, clean, Christian life. This resolution they are not prepared to take ; and to go on satisfying the lower instincts of their nature, they end by giving up their faith and ceasing to profess any sort of religious belief. Why should they not live like all those around them ? They are but eddies in the stream, and how can they struggle against the current that bears them on ?

Political corruption, too, plays a not insignificant part in the spiritual ruin of Catholics in the States. Fortunately or unfortunately, Irishmen are born politicians. In American cities they are far and away the sharpest and the ablest political organizers to be found. The mere Yankee is but a babe in their hands. Say what you will about Tammany Hall, for instance—and Tammany Hall, I think, is not half as black as it is painted—there is no doubt in the world that it has been, and still is, in spite of a recent check, the most perfect and the most powerful political association in the country.

But I fear that it would be very difficult to reconcile American politics, such as we find them, with the principles and practices of Catholics. It would not be true to say that every city politician in America is a knave, but one might safely assert that every knave is anxious to have something to say to city politics. In America politics are a game ; the rules are loose and the stakes are high. Every situation has its price. Without money you can no more become a street scavenger in Chicago than you can become a senator at Washington. In proportion, of course, to the emoluments of the office is the amount of money that you must hand over either to an individual or to the particular party that has favoured you. The bribe is called by other names, but a bribe it continues to be all the same. In New York and other places the Irish are adepts in carrying out these ' duties ' of citizenship, and the native Americans hate our countrymen only because they are unable to cope with their tactics. The institutions and customs of the country give occasion, if not encouragement, to this system of bribery. A Republican becomes mayor of a city, and he proceeds forthwith to clear all his political opponents out of their various offices. In a year or two a Democrat takes his place, and a similar process is repeated. At every election dollars are flying about thick as leaves in autumn, most of them falling to the share of the most dishonest and corrupt. If the confessional stands in the way of these practices, then the confessional must be set aside, and the Catholic who deliberately sets aside the confessional has taken one great and dangerous step towards the complete abandonment of his faith.

In my former paper, I mentioned incidentally that the Irishman falls very easily and speedily under the spell of American manners and habits. He goes out to America as to an El Dorado in every sense of the word. Not only is America a country teeming with wealth and pulsating with industrial activity, but it is, moreover, the land of the free, where no government will dare oppose the will of the people, and where landlord tyranny exists only as a bad dream. Whatever he sees in the great Republic he is ready to admire, and whatever he admires he is eager to imitate. One of his terrors is to be taken as a green stranger from beyond the Atlantic, and one of his ambitions is to be undistinguishable from the native population. I have met young men who had not been a year in America, and but for an occasional sweet note of their South of Ireland Doric I should have taken them to be typical Americans. Their gait, their manner, their physical appearance, their language, their gestures, their up-to-date American words and phrases—all showed how swiftly they had been absorbed by the population around them. It is like the limpid streams that rush down our Kerry hills only to be lost in the bitter waters of the ocean. As was remarked some time ago by a smart Dublin weekly review, the gastric juices of Uncle Sam are very powerful, and much as he swallows he is able to digest all. Every year some half-million of Europeans are swept

into his Gargantuan stomach, but he assimilates them all
and transmutes them into a new ethnic product which is
neither Irish, nor German, nor English, nor French, but
purely and simply American. There are exceptions. Some
do escape this Americanizing process. Even in the heart of
New York I met some Scottish Highlanders, as they loved
to call themselves, who, though natives of Nova Scotia or
Prince Edward Island, were just as Scottish as if they had
always trod their ancestral heath. They knew hardly a
word of English, but that did not seem to disconcert them in
the least, or to interfere with them in their daily avocations.

The French Canadians, too, have a most decided
objection to be Americanized. They are a people within a
people. They live their own lives and pursue their own
ideals. They have their own language as it was spoken in
the court of Louis le Grand, and they cling to it loyally and
fondly. Wherever they are in any considerable numbers,
they form a little Canada, living in the same locality,
working in the same mills or factories, having their own
churches, their own priests, their own schools ; and not a
word of English is spoken in church or school or home. I
noticed this especially in Lowell, Mass., where I spent some
considerable time. There are Canadian 'stores' in Lowell
where the shop assistants will condescend to answer a
question in English, never giving utterance in that tongue
to what is not commercially necessary. Some tradesmen
go so far even as to make an attempt at translating into
English the French wording of their projecting sign boards.
The effort is not always a brilliant success, and I remember
being struck especially with an advertisement board which
showed on one side the words, ' C. *Mangin, Réparateur des
tuyaux,*' and on the other, the laconic, if misleading, translation: '*C. Mangin, a Piper.*' In this city of Lowell, you
can see at a glance the contrast between the Canadians and
the Irish. There are about twenty-five thousand of each
race in the city, the Irish mostly of American birth. They
are all Catholics, and nearly all good practical Catholics,
too. The Canadians live in a section of the city which is
appropriately called *Little Canada* ; the Irish have no

special quarters of their own. The Canadians preserve intact their national individuality, the Irish are identified with the Americans. The Canadians are Republicans in politics, while the Irish are almost invariably Democrats. The Irish look down on the Canadians as poor, spiritless creatures, who know nothing of the dignity or the rights of labour, and who are always ready to turn every strike to advantage by doing the blackleg or the Chinaman. The Canadians retort that the Irish are a factious, blustering, discontented race, who cannot appreciate the advantage of a fair day's wages with continuous work. The Canadians have their eyes for ever turned beyond the waves of the St. Laurence, and dream of the day when they shall be able to return to their beloved Canada with sufficient money to purchase and to stock a farm; the Irish hardly ever think of settling down in Ireland. The Irish and the Canadians of Lowell seem, indeed, to agree only upon one point, and that is their dislike of the Anglo-Saxon. For Canadian loyalty to Great Britain, as far as I could discover, both in the States and in Canada, exists only in the imagination of the self-complacent Englishman. The Canadian hates equally the Englishman and his language.

As I have intimated, ignorance of English seems in no way to interfere with the Canadian's industrial or commercial pursuits, while the use of his own language exclusively is a grand safeguard both of his faith and of his patriotism. If Irish emigrants had only the common bond of their own beautiful tongue, they would be at once more Irish and more Catholic than they are. But I must not make an incursion into the kingdom of the Gaelic League; and as a set off to some of these language remarks, I may mention that in another city of Massachusetts (Salem), I learned that as late as the eighteenth century out of twenty women who were burned alive for witchcraft, there were three Irish ladies, the only evidence against whom was that they spoke in a tongue which they could have learned only from Satan! The knowledge of Irish had its occasional drawbacks in times gone by. At the present time I am quite satisfied that were the Irish in America to imitate the Canadians and others and speak only in the tongue of their fathers, they would not be a whit less prosperous in their temporal affairs, while they would gain immensely from a religious and moral point of view.

I might add from an Irish national point of view. We are inclined to boast sometimes of the Greater Ireland beyond the seas and of our ten or twenty million brethren who live and flourish under the folds of the Stars and Stripes. I fear that there is a considerable amount of delusion in the pride and hope that we love to centre in American Ireland. In the great body of the Irish born in America you will find very little Irish feeling or sentiment. Ireland is for them little more than a geographical sign. They know nothing of her history or of her ancient glories. They have heard of her only in connection with oppression and poverty and famine and begging. They regard her as the Cinderella of the nations, as condemned for ever to helpless misery and slavery. You meet O'Briens, O'Connors, O'Flahertys, O'Rorkes, who would feel it an insult to be called Irish. You will find a number of still more recreant Irishmen who try to hide every trace of their nationality under the veil of an American name and who drop their O's and their Mac's as light-heartedly as our friends across the Channel drop their h's. Thus it is not unusual to find that Joseph O'Reilly becomes Ebnezer Riley, that Andrew Power develops into Aaron Powell and that James O'Keeffe blossoms into Job Quaiffe.

I saw evidences in various ways of this lack of Irish sentiment amongst the Irish-Americans. I was present at concerts organized and conducted exclusively by Irish-American Catholics, and there was not a song or a tune to bring back the memory of the old country. Worse still, at some entertainments held in Catholic assembly rooms, I saw specimens of the stage Irishman that were fit to grace the boards of the low London music hall. I saw some monster processions passing through the streets of Chicago and Boston, in which there were some thirty or forty military and other bands, some of them bands of Irish regiments, and these bands regaled us with the music of every country but Ireland. As far as I could see the Ancient Order of Hibernians—much patronized by bishops and priests—and certain purely political associations which regard the overthrow of England as a necessary step to the relief of Ireland, seem to have a monopoly of Irish patriotism amongst the American-born Irish. The great body of the Irish in America entertain for their mother country at most but a feeling of Platonic benevolence. They all hate England to their hearts' core but that does not in all cases imply a passionate love for Ireland. Since the failure of Stephens, and still more since the downfall of Parnell and the consequent split of Irish Nationalists, they seem to have lost all practical interest in the old country. They are Americans and Americans without any hyphenic qualification. The man who first saw the light of day in a poor-house or a prison does not care to be reminded of his birthplace. I am afraid it is the feeling of the majority of the American Irish.

This attitude is, I think, rather encouraged than opposed by the clergy generally. ' We want no Irish here,' said a most estimable priest to me, himself the son of Irish parents, ' nor Dutchmen, nor Italians, nor Poles, nor Frenchmen. We want Americans and Americans only. It is the first civic duty of every immigrant to our shores to become an American.' I have heard some Irish-born priests express the same conviction in language much more emphatic and rather less flattering to Ireland. Now with all respect for those who hold such opinions, I differ from them entirely as far as Irish immigrants are concerned—and I deal in these papers only with Irish immigrants. The Irishman who has no love for his country has very little for his Church. Get an Irishman to deny his country to-day and he will deny his faith to-morrow. In his mind Ireland and Catholicity have always been in some way identified. To despise one is to undervalue the other. I have noticed the fact repeatedly not only in America, but in England and Scotland. Whenever I heard an Irishman making little of his own country, and apologising as it were for his birthplace ;

or whenever I saw him spelling his name Morphy instead
of Murphy or Daniel instead of O'Donnell I always
concluded that if he was a bad Irishman he was a worse
Catholic; and I do not know that I was ever mistaken.
I dissent with some diffidence on this point from most of
my clerical brethren in America, but I believe that those
who best understand the genius and character of our people
will say that my disagreement is not without a good and
solid foundation.

No doubt the Irish immigrant must be thoroughly
American in the sense of being thoroughly loyal to his
adopted country, and of being always ready, as he always
has been, to discharge all the duties of American citizenship,
even, if necessary, to the shedding of his blood on the
battle-field. But loyalty to the new country need not
quench his love for the old. The two virtues can very well
live in harmony together and I can see no likelihood of
their ever coming into conflict. Might one take a broader
and a higher view of the situation (some no doubt will call
it a mere flight of foolish fancy) and think what the United
States would be to-day, if the Irishman from the beginning
had undertaken to mould the American character instead of
passively receiving its impress? There is no doubt that the
race of the original colonial settlers is fast dying out and
that before very long the Yankee will become as rare as the
Red Indian, on the banks of the Hudson. Who more fitted
to take his place than the Irish Celt who, unlike the Anglo-
American, seems destined to enjoy the freshness and vigour
of perpetual youth? If the Irish immigrant had only
retained his home virtues and his spiritual and religious
ideals, and combined with these virtues and ideals the
energy, the activity, the enterprise, the industry, the grit,
the progressiveness of the American, then you would have
an America that would indeed be the world's glory, and an
Ireland beyond the seas not only in name but in deed. Is
this a mere echo of a fond dream, or may we reckon it
amongst the might-have-beens of the recent past or amongst
the possibilities of the not distant future?

[To be continued.]   M. F. SHINNORS, O.M.I.

ST. ASSICUS

FIRST BISHOP AND PATRON OF THE DIOCESE OF ELPHIN

SCARCE any vestige of any ancient building can now be traced in Elphin or its immediate neighbourhood. The Protestant Church authorities, who so long held absolute sway there, seem to have effectively removed them all. The arx or dun of the noble druid Ono has long since been levelled to the ground. It has been stated that Ono's fort stood where the pound is at present, and that this was also the site of the College of St. Assicus, because the castle of Elphin stood there, and the field lying to the east is called the *Castle garden* in all the leases granted by the Protestant bishops who held it. But this was the site of the residence of some of the Protestant bishops. It was erected by bishop King (1611-38). The castle was delivered into the hands of of the Lord-President of Connaught in 1645 by the Protestant bishop Tilson, who retired to England. His son became Governor of Elphin, and declared for the Parliament. This building, and not Ono's fort or castle, seems to have given its name to Castle-street and Castle Gardens. In my opinion, Ouo's residence and the monastery and college of St. Assicus stood in Abbey Cartron, separated from the pound only by the roadway, and may have given name to that small townland of about thirty acres, even before the Franciscans came to Elphin ; and the Franciscan monastery afterwards stood on the site of the college of St. Assicus, in Abbey Cartron.[1] O'Donovan, in his letters from Elphin, during the progress of the Ordnance Survey in 1837, writes : An Inquisition 27th Elizabeth, finds that the Abbey of Elphin belonged to the Order of St. Dominic, with a church cloister, and dormitory, with the half cartron of land adjacent thereto. This is the land now called Abbey Cartron.

---

[1] By advice of the Saint (Patrick) Assicus introduced here a celebrated college of monks and presided over them. In process of time this became a parish church, and was dedicated to the original founder. About the year 1450, Cornelius, then bishop of the see, with the consent of the canons and inhabitants, granted this church to the Conventual Franciscan Friars, Coenobium Sti Patrioii.—Archdall's *Monasticon*, pp. 609, 610; *Tr. Th.* pp. 89 139.

Archdall and O'Donovan, I believe, are in error when they state that the Dominicans ever had an abbey or cloister in Elphin. Burke, in the *Hibernia Dominicana*, makes no mention of any Dominican foundation in Elphin. The appendix to Fr. Malone's *History of the Church of Ireland* seems to give a full list of monasteries and religious houses from the arrival of the English to the end of the fifteenth century. There is no mention of any Dominican convent in Elphin. D'Alton's *Annals of Boyle* treat of many inquisitions of that date : there is no record of a Dominican Abbey at Elphin. The learned Dr. Boetius Egan, who was bishop of Elphin in the time of Colgan, and whose approbation and signature are prefixed to the autograph of the *Annals of the Four Masters*, in his very full *relatio* written in 1637, gives no Dominican house as having ever been in Elphin. ' Sequitur hic,' he writes, ' completus numerus prioratuum et conventuum, necnon religiosarum mulierum locorum in hac dioecesi situatorum.' He then enumerates Dorean (Derrane), Cluaintuskert, Kilmore, Inchmacrinen, etc., and continues : ' Ordinis S.P. Dominici quinque sunt Prioratus ; scilicet, Prioratus de Roscommon, Prioratus de Tuillsge [Tulsk , Prioratus de Chinseaumbuile (Cloonshan-ville), Prioratus de Balliniduin [Ballindoon], et Prioratus de Sligo. Unicus Conventus ord. Seraphici P.N. Francisci, situatus in civitate Elphinen., estque de Observantia. Omnia praedicta loca, laus Deo, hoc tempore possidentur a Protestantibus, imo et a temporibus ferme regis Henrici VIII.' [1] There is no local tradition in Elphin that a

---

[1] *Spicilegium Ossoriense*. Colgan says, *Trias Thaumaturga, Septima Vita Patricii*, pars. ii., p. 176, note 75 : 'Ailfin is to this day an episcopal See of ample extent in Connaught, of which Boethius Egan of our Order of Friars Minor of the Stricter Observance, a man venerable for his merits, is at this day bishop.' And again, p. 564 : In catalago Ecclesiarum dioecesis Ailfinensis transmisso mihi a Reverendissimo Alfinen. Episcopo, fratri Boetio Aegano, viro plane non tantum de Ordine nostro Seraphico, ex quo ad id munus assumptus est, sed et de tota patria bene merito, reperio S. Brigidam in singulis harum, Ecclesiarum tanquam loci Patronam coli.'

Kilnegoone, in O'Flanagan's country, which O'Donovan, *Four Masters*, vol. iii., p. 448, following the Inquisition of Elizabeth, as quoted by Archdall, p. 610, says belonged to the Dominican Abbey of Elphin, belonged, I have little doubt, to the Franciscan Abbey.

Dominican Convent was ever there. Archdall[1] states that the possessions of the Dominicans were granted to Terence O'Beirne, the same person to whom D'Alton says the possessions of the Franciscans were given. I conclude, therefore, that in the Inquisition quoted by Archdall, a mistake has somehow been made, and Dominic substituted for Francis.

In the Renahan MSS.,[2] in Maynooth College Library, I find the following reference to the foundation of the Franciscans at Elphin : William O'Reilly, the deposed Provincial of the Franciscans, now Vicar of the Observants, petitioned for, and obtained, on the 23rd of April, 1450, license from Nicholas V. to erect a convent for Observants in the province of Tuam; either in Killala, Achonry, or Elphin, in neither of which was there any house of the Order. But, says Wadding, ' it does not appear where it was built. I know there was a convent in Elphin, from the ruins of which the Protestant bishop erected a profane or private house ; but I find no more about it.' On the 16th of October, 1453, the same William O'Reilly, reinstated as Provincial, obtained leave from Nicholas V. to establish a convent of Observants in the city of Elphin. The Bull, *Sacrae religionis*, states that Cornelius, bishop of Elphin, lately gave for this purpose the parish church of St. Patrick, with the consent of his Chapter and of the perpetual Vicar and of the citizens, who also gave certain lands held of the bishop, free from all rent and incumbrance, to be converted to the use of a Convent of Minors to be established. The Bull allows O'Reilly, whom it regularly styles Provincial of Ireland, to erect three or four other convents in the province of Tuam, in such places as he should find convenient. The Bull is directed to the bishop of Clonfert (the bishop of Elphin being at the Curia ; for the Bull says : Nuper venerat frater noster Cornelius Egan). Ware writes:[3] Cornelius, bishop of Elphin, built a monastery for the Minorities at Elphin about 1450, in the place where before stood the parish church of St. Patrick. We have seen that

---

[1] *Monasticon Hibernicon*, p. 610.
[2] Renahan MSS., p. 17.
[3] Ware, *Bishops*, p. 9.

the site of the original church built by St. Patrick and over which he placed St. Assicus, and which became the cathedral church of the diocese of Elphin, was that of the present Protestant church of Elphin, the title of which now is : Ecclesia Catholica Beatae Virginis Mariae.[1] It was a place of great importance after the union of the minor sees of Roscommon, Ardcardne, Drumcliff, and other bishoprics of less note with it, which must have taken place in the twelfth century.

Ware[2] also states that by these unions the see of Elphin was at last esteemed one of the richest of all Ireland, and had about seventy-nine parish churches under it.[3] The Four Masters describe the church as the Great Church in 1235, and speak of the Bishop's Court at Elphin in 1258. It had its dean and chapter at this time, as we learn from the mandate of Innocent IV., dated Lyons, July 3, 1245, to the Archbishop of Tuam, notifying him that the Pope had annulled the election of the provost of Roscommon to the see of Elphin, and ordering him to appoint Archdeacon John, postulatedby Malachy, dean, John and Clare, archdeacons, and Gilbert, treasurer, and to consecrate same.[4]

The question arises : Was it the church erected by St. Patrick, the Great Church, Teampuill-Phadruig, afterwards St. Mary's Church, the cathedral that bishop Cornelius Egan delivered to the Franciscan Friars? It is evident that the church given to the Friars was not the Cathedral of St. Patrick, but the Abbey, as D'Alton calls it. The ruins of the ancient College of St. Assicus, in Abbey Cartron, thus became the Franciscan Convent of Elphin, and was dedicated to the original founder, St. Patrick.[5] We find in the Four Masters

---

[1] In the Elphin *Taxation* of Boniface VIII. (which does not contain the revenue of bishop or chapter), the first item is ' St. Mary of Elphin,' valued at 10s. 8d. ; the third, ' the church of St. Patrick of Elphin,' valued at 8s. 8d. (*Calendar of Documents relating to Ireland*, 1302-7, p. 223.)

[2] *Bishops*, Elphin, p. 9.

[3] *Ibid.*, p. 9. The *Taxation* had 89 churches (one was illegible to the Rolls' editors). The statement in reference to wealth, it has to be admitted, is not borne out by the return : ' sum total of taxation of diocese of Elphin, 69l. 7s. 4d.' (p. 225.)

[4] Theiner, *Monumenta*, etc., p. 44.

[5] *Vide ante*, p. 400.

the entries: 1463, Gilchrist Mac Edigan [Egan] Vicar of
St. Patrick's Church at Elphin, and a canon chorister died.
1488, Cathal Mac Edigan [Egan], Vicar of St. Patrick's
Church, and a canon chorister in Elphin, died. In the
Annals of Duald Mac Firbis, at 1461, we have Muirgeas
[Maurice], William O'Flanagan's son, priest of Shankill, and
the chiefe of the quire in Elphin, quievit and the said kill
or church was burnt in harvest following.

Therefore, after the transfer, the Cathedral of St. Patrick
remained in the possession of the Bishop and his chapter.
Father Hugh Ward, writing in 1630, says : XXI. Elphin.
In the reign of Elizabeth, in 1563, the Protestant bishop of
that see drove out the Friars and did not leave a stone of
the convent standing ; with the materials building a
residence for himself. Wadding also, as we have seen, says[1]
that the Protestant bishop erected a private or profane
house for himself from the ruins of the Franciscan convent
of Elphin. This was certainly not on the site of the ancient
Church of St. Patrick. It is not by any means clear who
the Protestant bishop was who drove out the Franciscans.
I am inclined to think that Ward has made a mistake in the
date.[2] Canon Mannion, parish priest of Elphin, has now in
his possession an ancient chalice with the inscription:
Orate pro anima Aeneae Conry sacerdotis qui me fieri
fecit ad usum Conventus Sti. Francisci de Elfin. Anno
Dni. 1670—from which it appears that, as in Boyle
the Cistercians, so in Elphin the Franciscans, long kept
watch and ward over the site of their abbey, hoping in vain
for better times. The Conrys or O'Mulconrys, of Cloonahee,
near Elphin, were the hereditary Ollavs of Sil-Murray, or the
Connaught O'Conors and their co-relatives. In the church
built on the site presented by Ono, was preserved from the
time of St. Patrick the chief relic of Connaught, namely,
the Buacach-Patraig, Patrick's cap or mitre. In the *Annals
of the Four Masters*, anno 1406, it is recorded that in a
battle fought in that year at Geashill, King's County, this

[1] Wad., tom. xii. 187. Reg. 589.
[2] Lynch says in his MS. Hist.: The first attempt at introducing a
Protestant prelate into the (Elphin) see was made in 1583, when the Lord
Deputy chose a certain McKeever to fill the see.

relic was taken from the English. 'Besides the loss of
their men,' says MacGeoghegan's translation of the *Annals
of Clonmacnoise*, 'they also lost one of the relics of
St. Patrick, which before remained at Elfyn, until it was
lost by them that day, which was computed to be the
chiefest relicke of all Connaught.' Ware says :—

Elphin, or as others write it Elfin, is situated on a rising
ground in a pleasant and fertile soil. St. Patrick built the
Cathedral Church there about the middle of the fifth century,
near a little river flowing from two fountains, and set Asic, a
monk, over it, who was a great admirer of penance and austerity ;
and by him consecrated bishop, who afterwards filled it with
monks. He died in Rath-cung in Tirconnell, where he was also
buried. Some say that this Assic (the correct form) was a most
excellent goldsmith, and by his art beautified the Cathedral with
six pieces of very curious workmanship.[1]

The *little river* of Ware and the *spring* of the *Tripartite*
and O'Flaherty, are the present stream from St. Patrick's
Well; and the two fountains were no more than two
fissures in the *Ail* out of which two tiny streams flowed
separately for a short distance, when they united. This is
the case to the present time. The water flowing from the
spot where the *Ail* stood is conveyed in two covered drains
as far as the water-shed. The original fissures in the rock
did not contain much water at any time ; and, as described
by a nonogenarian who had drawn water from it, the *ail*
was a large rock considerably raised over the surface of the
surrounding earth, and in its centre or between its shafts,
were the fissures or crannies from which sprang the *clear*
water that produced the rivulet. This celebrated rock,
which, together with the crystal stream that flowed from
it, has given a name to the most ancient diocese of
Connaught, was shattered to pieces by the application
of blasting powder, by Rev. William Smith, Protestant
Vicar-General of Elphin, between the years 1820 and 1830.
Owing to this vandalism, there is now no trace of the
Ail-finn or Rock of the Clear Spring. It is a mistake to
say that, when it was broken, the *Ail* stood several perches

---

[1] Ware, *Bishops*, Elphin, p. 9.

from the present St. Patrick's Well at Elphin. It stood close
beside the well. I have seen the roots or the part of the
rock beneath the surface of the earth which had been dug to
erect a new fountain over the well. I have also seen portion
of a stone crucifix, dug up at the same time, which once had
stood over the Holy Well of St. Patrick and St. Assicus (and
had doubtless been also shattered by the men of England),
now in possession of the Very Rev. Canon Mannion,
parish priest of Elphin. O'Flaherty, in his *Ogygia*,[1] says
that a person predicted the falling of this stone on a certain
day, and that it fell on that day [Wednesday], 9th of October,
1675. But there were two remarkable stones in Elphin,
one over St. Patrick's Well, and the other in the middle of
the town. Near Elphin is the townland of Lahausk, *i.e.*
Leacht h As[i]c ; flag-stone of Assic. The tradition is that
the place was so called, because St. Assicus, in the course
of his missionary labours, broke his leg on a flag there.

It remains to deal with the attempt to identify Assicus
or Assic with Tassach, who administered the viaticum to
St. Patrick. The accessible authorities for Tassach are :
   (1.) Irish Hymn of Fiac on St. Patrick :—

> Tassach remained with him (Patrick),
> When he gave Communion to him :
> He said that soon Patrick would go (die),—
> The word of Tassach was not false.

Tassach is glossed : 'namely, wright of Patrick . . .
Raholp, by Downpatrick, to the east, is his church.'[2]
   (2.) The Calendar of Aengus :—

> April the 14th :
> The royal-bishop Tassach
> Gave, when he came [to visit the dying Saint],
> The body of Christ, the King truly strong,
> With [*i.e.* in] Communion to Patrick.

---

[1] Lapis hic, ut obiter adnotem, nostris his diebus anno nimirum reparatae
salutis humanae 1675, nono die Octobris in terram prostratus decidit ; et quod
magis admirandum est, non defuit, qui eodem die, ac hora qua corruit,
ruiturum praedixit, testesque statuo horae praemonitos ad prospiciendum
oculis collabentem adscivit. *Ogygia*, Pars iii. cap. lxxix.,'pp. 375, 376. There
is no tradition in Elphin regarding this marvellous story.

[2] Stokes, p. 410 (text); p. 424 (gloss).

The fourth line of the quatrain is glossed—*i.e.*, it is the body of Christ that was Communion for him.[1] The gloss adds :—Tassach is venerated in Raholp in Lecale, in Ulster ; *i.e.*, wright and bishop of Patrick was Tassach, and this is the feast of his death.

(3.) The imperfect *Martyrology of Tallaght*, a copy of the short recension of the so-called *Hieronyman Martyrology*, with native saints added to each day (*Book of Leinster*, page 358 fg.), XVIII. Kal. Mai. ; the first Irish name is Sancti Tassagi.

(4.) The List of Irish saints who were bishops, in the *Book Leinster*, page 365 : Nomina episcoporum Hibernensium incipiunt: the sixth name is Tassach.

(5.) The Drummond Kalendar : XVIII. Kal. Mai : Apud Hiberniam, Sanctus Episcopus et Confessor Tassach hoc die ad Christum migravit.[2]

Dr. Todd[3] thought that Assicus was identical with Tassach, who administered the Viaticum to St. Patrick. That is, he took Tassach to be equivalent to Da(th) Assac[b], the *da* or *do* (*thy*) being the prefix of affection applied to saints. Whether Tassach, the saint's name, like Tassach, the name of king Laeghaire's father-in-law,[4] was composed of the inseparable particle *do* and Assach is beside the present purpose. But that *do*, thy, was a factor is disproved, in the first place, by the historical fact that this adjective of reverential affection applied to names of saints is of post-Patrician origin ; secondly, by phonology, for Assic with *t* for *do* (*da*) before the vowel would be Tassic ; Assach, with the same, Tassach. Here consequently we find two radical differences : (1) the final *i* and *a;* (2) c *hard* (=k) and guttural ch : as, for instance, in Patraic and Muiredach. Accordingly, the *Tripartite* and *Book of Armagh* distinguish Assicus and Tassach most clearly.

The earliest instance of the confusion is perhaps in a

---

[1] *Lebar Breac*, lithographed edition, page 85.
[2] Stokes's *Tripartite*.
[3] *The Book of Obits and Martyrology of the Cathedral Church of the Holy Trinity, commonly called Christ Church, Dublin*, edited by J. J. Croithwaite, A.M., and Rev. James Henthorne Todd, D.D. Introduction, page xiii.
[4] *Tripartite*, p. 506, Stokes's edition.

synopsis inserted in the Third Part of the *Tripartite*, as follows: Na cerda oc denam nammias ocus na menistreach ocus na cailech n-altora i.e. Tassach ocus Essu ocus Bite. The artizans a-making the patens and the service-sets[1] and the altar-chalices, namely, Tassach and Essu and Bite. But the value of this may be readily estimated from the fact that the writer was so ignorant as to distinguish *menstir* (= paten and chalice) from paten and chalice. From this the error passed into other Patrician memoranda. Thus, a List of St. Patrick's Household added to the *Tripartite* in one of the two known MSS. (and copied, minus the final clause, of which anon, into the *Books of Leinster*,[2] and *Lecan*,[3] and *Lebar Breac*,[4]) has *A tri cerdi: Essu ocus Bite ocus Tassach*—His three wrights: Essu and Bite and Tassach. A document so circumstantial and so widely diffused demands a brief examination, which is all the more necessary, as the Rolls' editor has annotated it only to the extent of a date that is erroneous by no less than eighteen years. Omitting the names of the persons, we have (in the original order): bishop, priest, brehon [a bishop], champion, psalm-singer, *chamberlain, bell-ringer*, cook, brewer [a priest], chaplain, two *waiters* [priests], charioteer, fire-woodman [a priest], cowherd, three smiths, three wrights and three embroidresses,—in all, sixteen offices, with four-and-twenty officials.

Passing over the dubious functionaries, whose names we give in italics (Stokes' translations of Colgan's Latin random renderings), a Catalogue that assigns a judge (brehon) to the National Apostle is palpably of a piece with the famous Patrician *Commission of Nine* for the reform of the Brehon Laws,—a myth that (to show our progress in historical

---

[1] Stokes, p. 250. Dr. MacCarthy has shown (*Transactions R.I.A.*, 1889, pp. 185, 194) that *menstir*, translated by Stokes credence-tables, is = ministerium, service-set, i.e., chalice and paten, and that the true reading is *Na cerda oc denum na menistrech : idon, nammias ocus na cailech n-altora*—the artizans a-making the service-sets ; namely, the patens and the chalices of the altar.

[2] Lithographed edition, p. 353d; given in Stokes's ed. of the *Tripartite*, p. 266.

[3] O'Donovan : *IV.* MM., vol. i, at A.D. 448.

[4] Lith. ed., p. 220b; in Stokes's ed., p. 574.

critcism), notwithstanding Lanigan's scathing exposure,[1] is still believed amongst us. The fraud is not far to seek in its origin. It was suggested, as appears from the diagram and description of Tara banquetting hall, given in the *Book of Leinster*,[2] and reproduced in Petrie's *History and Antiquities of Tara Hill*,[3] by the domestic arrangements of the native regal establishments. Why should the spiritual ruler lack the suitable counterpart of what befitted the temporal?

The unerring test of Chronology reveals the post-Patrician date of the patchwork. The *cook* is Aithgein of Bodoney[4] (in Strabane barony, co. Tyrone). Now, according to a perfectly reliable authority, the *Genealogies of* [Irish] *Saints*,[5] Aihgein, was sixth in descent from Colla the Stammerer (one of the three Collas who razed Emania, or Navan Fort, near Armagh city, about A.D. 350). Applying the rule of thirty years to a generation, we thus find the patron of Bodoney flourished in the second quarter of the sixth century, whilst St. Patrick, as we know, died in the last decade of the fifth, a difference of some five and twenty years! In its original form, accordingly, the Catalogue cannot date much higher than A.D. 530.

The motive is revealed in the closing paragraph. 'And those are the complement legally entitled[6] to be in the retinue (literally, *unity*) of Joseph, and that is the complement legally entitled to be at the table of the king of Cashel, down from the time of Felim, son of Criffan, king of [Desmond and Thomond] the two provinces of Munster, and so on.' The *complement* in question was the suite allowed to the Primate, when going by permission of the king, on provincial circuit, to enforce the *Law of Patrick*, that is, to exact cess in money and kind. According to the

[1] *E. H. I.*, vol. i., p. 171.
[2] Lith. ed., p. 29.
[3] Page 197.
[4] *Both-domnaig, tugurium-dominici* (i.e. *ecclesiae*: for the authorities, see *Annals of Ulster*, ed. MacCarthy, vol. iii., pp. 486-7).
[5] *Book of Leinster*, p. 347f; *Book of Ballymote*, pp. 216f, 217a.
[6] *Dlegar*. See under *Dligid* in Atkinson's recently issued Index to the Brehon Laws.

Book of the Angel, fabricated before 808,[1] the number was to be fifty, exclusive of those who followed from other reasons ; including such persons, one hundred !

Fifteen years later, A.D. 823, the *Law* was *promulgated* in Munster by the above-named Felim (820-847),—the event alluded to in the text. Among the *insignia* of St. Patrick carried around on such visitations was the *Book of Armagh.* The interesting query immediately suggests itself: Did Primate Artri (823-833), in accordance with the angelic ordinance recorded therein, obtain bed and board for fifty of an entourage and fifty others ? ' Nothing of the kind,' declares in effect our redactor, who writes during the primacy of Joseph (927-936),[2] ' then, as now, the unattached were excluded to a man ; the quota entertained amounted, all told, to no more than five-and-twenty.' And, albeit not entered in the *Book of Armagh* (the *maor,* or custodian, took ample precaution as to that), the drastic limitation obtained equal, perhaps indeed wider, circulation as an Appendix to the other and better known Patrician document in the native tongue, the *Tripartite Life.* Widely as they diverge, the two enactments are at one in their unique presentment of national character : public hospitality, they will have us believe, was meted out by rigid rule to churchmen in Christian Ireland ! *Arcades ambo :* the Momonian falsary fitly pairs off with his congener, the Ultonian.

The origin of the mistake is quite obvious. The compiler or compilers of the List lived when *do, thy,* was being prefixed to saints' names, and consequently took Tassach to be T'Assach = T'Assic.

Two instances remain, in which the patron of Raholp is confounded with the first bishop of Elphin,—the glosses already given on the hymn of Fiac and on the

---

[1] This is the date of the transcription of the *Book of Armagh,* in which the pretended revelation to St. Patrick is contained. See the whole text and the first published translation of the (Latin) original by Dr. MacCarthy in Father Coleman's edition of Stuart's *Historical Memoirs of the City of Armagh* (Dublin, 1900), pp. 449-454.

[2] According to Stokes, he ' flourished A.D. 945 ' ! (p. 267). For similar instances of his historical lore, see the *Introduction* to the *Annals of Ulster,* pp. xcix.-c.

Calendar of Aengus. The first is of the eleventh century; the second, of the fifteenth. In the present case, they are accordingly devoid of importance.

Colgan observed[1] that the Natalis of Assicus, under that name, cannot be found in the Irish martyrologies, although the name is thus written in the *Acts of St. Patrick*; and, to account for this omission, supposed that he was identical with Assanus, whose feast occurs on the 27th of April, according to the *Martyrology of Donegal*. Yet, in the *Martyrology of Tallaght*, which he had under his hand, it is the second name given under April the 26th, disguised as *Isaac*, which Dr. Matthew Kelly,[2] of Maynooth (clarum et venerabile nomen), all but succeeded in rightly amending. His reading is 'Assach'; the true lection is As[s]ic. The transposition of the vowels (*cf*. Falertus for Felartus),[3] and the error of a day may be attributed to the fact that the compiler belonged to south-east Leinster. As to the omission from the (metrical) *Calendar of Aengus* (end of eighth, and beginning of ninth, century), the only other ancient martyrology which Colgan possessed, suffice it to say that the bard preferred to commemorate foreign saints. For instance, at April 26th, the *Tallaght Martyrology* has six Irish names; the *Calendar* selects the first saint of the day, the martyr Grillus. At April 27th, the former gives four natives; the latter, the first foreign name, Alexander, abbot of Rome.[4]

The investigation of the most reliable authorities regarding St. Assicus, first bishop and patron of Elphin, affords

---

[1] *Tria. Taumaturg.*, Vita Sexta S. Patricii, n. 122, p. 114.

[2] *Calendar of Irish Saints*, etc., by the Rev. Matthew Kelly, D.D., of Maynooth (Dublin, 1857), p. 2,—a little work worth its weight in gold. It is a transcript of the native names in the *Tallaght Martyrology*, made whilst the MS. (the *Book of Leinster*) contained all but the final folio.

The collation of what is extant was entrusted by De Rossi to his fellow-editor, Duchesne, for the edition of the Hieronyman Martyrology in the November *Acta Sanctorum*. The latter, however, contented himself with requesting the reader to blame *him* for neglecting to undertake the labour of a few days!

It is grateful to me to record that Dr. Kelly of Maynooth has shown us the way to the identification of Assicus in the Martyrologies.

[3] See I. E. RECORD, April, 1902, p. 300.

[4] Stokes's ed., p. 70.

fresh proof that the closer the study of our ancient and
authentic documents, the more evident becomes the truth
of the popular traditions respecting the lives of our native
saints.[1]

J. J. KELLY.

---

[1] I have to express my grateful acknowledgment to Rev. B. Mac Carthy,
D.D., for his verifications of native references. By this distinguished Irish
scholar the equation Isaac (in the *Martyrology of Tallaght*) = As[s]io had
been independently discovered, when he found that the first partial elucidation
of the name of the patron of Elphin belongs to Dr. Kelly of Maynooth.

I hope Dr. Mac Carthy may be prevailed upon to give us an edition of the
Tripartite; restoring the text, pointing out the additions and dates of same,
and supplying notes on persons, places, and illustrative matter. He has shown
that he possesses a thorough and scholarly knowledge of the ancient *Patrician
Documents*, and it would be of great advantage to our Irish Church, in view of
the labours of Protestant writers on these records, to have a thoroughly
reliable edition of the *Tripartite* from a competent Catholic scholar. In the
absence of such editions of the original materials, it is vain to hope for real
progress in our Ecclesiastical History.

I have pleasure in also thanking the Very Rev. Canon Mannion, P.P., for
local information and valuable references regarding Elphin.

FÉNELON—II

LOUIS XIV., after a stormy youth, came in early middle life under the influence of Madame de Maintenon. This remarkable woman, who throughout her long career preserved a spotless reputation, first became known to him as the governess of his natural children. During his visits to them he gradually came to recognise her devotedness to her young charges, and her prudence and good sense. In her company he found rest from the cares of court and the quarrels of his mistresses. She was, indeed, a beauty herself, but of the reserved and stately type, and she was his senior by three years. Even the poor injured Queen, far from being jealous of the new favourite, was grateful for her good offices. 'Providence,' she said, 'has raised up Mme. de Maintenon to bring my husband back to me.' And certainly she succeeded in winning Louis to a more regular life. When the Queen died suddenly in 1683, Mme. de Maintenon's position became still more important. A year later the King secretly married her, and henceforth, though never acknowledged as Queen, she reigned over France. Among her little circle of pious courtiers were the Duke and Duchess of Beauvillier, already known to us, and these took care to introduce their friend, the Abbé de Fénelon, to the great lady.

Fénelon was at this time in the very prime of life. It would have been hard to find a more brilliant specimen of abbé-courtier of the best type—polished, scholarly, and devout. He had already become known as a spiritual director of persons in high station, for which function his knowledge of the world, as well as his sincere piety, admirably fitted him. Those who entrusted their consciences to his keeping found him kind and sympathetic, and were all the more captivated, especially the lady penitents, because his spirituality was high-flown and his

method autocratic. Mentor in *Télémaque* gives us some
notion of his system. As long as the young hero is sub-
missive to the counsels of his preceptor, all goes well;
when he acts of himself or in opposition he comes to grief.
Mme. de Maintenon never chose Fénelon for her confessor:
perhaps she thought him too clever and too masterful. But
she had a high opinion of his judgment, and constantly
consulted him about her own spiritual affairs and about her
darling foundation, the School of Saint-Cyr. ' Read M. de
Fénelon's exhortations of surrender to the will of God and
willing acceptance of all sorts of duties,' she wrote soon
after making his acquaintance, ' I have never seen anything
more tender, more sterling, more free ; his spirit of devotion
is, indeed, the right one.' We have still a number of his
spiritual letters to her, containing much sound advice as to
her conduct in her difficult station. Among these is one in
answer to her request that he would tell her her faults.
We priests know well how delicate a task it is to comply
with such a request : it is much to the credit of both that
Fénelon wrote plainly to the inquiring lady.

The Convent of Saint-Cyr was a community of ladies
devoted to the education of young girls, daughters of the
poorer nobility.[1] As the scheme was based upon Fénelon's
Education des Filles, it was but natural that the Foundress
should frequently consult him in the management of it.

> Submit yourself simply to the Abbé de Fénelon and Mgr. de
> Chartres [she says to one of her future nuns (1691)]. I always
> give in to the opinion of those two saints. Accustom yourself to
> live by their rule ; but do not spread the abbé's maxims among
> such as have no taste for them. . . . As for Mme. Guyon,
> you extol her excessively ; we must be satisfied with keeping her
> to ourselves. It would not do for her, any more than for me, to
> direct our ladies. It would expose her to fresh persecution.

The lady here mentioned played such an important part
in Fénelon's subsequent career that a short account of her
must now be given.

---

[1] There is a delightful account of it given in Horace Walpole's letter to
George Montagu, September 17, 1769.

Jeanne Marie de la Mothe was born in 1648. She
wished to become a nun, but was married, when only fifteen
years of age, to Jacques Guyon, a man of great wealth,
much her senior. At twenty-eight she was left a widow,
and was henceforth able to lead her own life. From infancy
she had always been in weak health ; she was of a nervous
hysterical temperament, extremely sensitive, always feeling
the victim of persecution. Amidst her physical sufferings
and domestic worries she found consolation in prayer. But
hers was not ordinary prayer. It was a sort of ecstasy in
which her soul abandoned itself to God, without any word
or act on her part—completely passive under His divine
influence. This, to her mind, was the true state of perfection : it included all, or rather superseded all, the virtues,
making us indifferent to heaven or hell. This happy state
she must communicate to others. It is described at length
in her book : *Moyen Court et très Facile de faire Oraison.*
Being young and attractive, rich and clever, she speedily
made disciples. At first she fixed on Geneva as the scene
of her labours. There was in that city a convent of the
Nouvelles Catholiques, an institution already known to us
in connection with Fénelon. A certain Père Lacombe, a
Barnabite, was completely won over by her at this time,
and accompanied her in her many wanderings. At Geneva,
Turin, Grenoble, Marseilles, Alessandria, Genoa, and
Vercelli, the pair were received with enthusiasm. But in
each place a reaction soon set in : the ecclesiastical
authorities found it necessary to interfere and put a stop to
her extraordinary opinions and practices. When Lacombe
was summoned to Paris, his patroness followed him. The
two were charged with heresy : Lacombe was imprisoned
for life at Lourdes, and Mme. Guyon was shut up in a
convent (1688). It might be thought that her career was
now at an end. However, a saintly lady, Mme. de
Miramion, interested herself in the case, and brought it
under the notice of Mme. de Maintenon, who procured the
release of the unhappy *détenue.* Immediately after regaining
her freedom she resumed the propagation of her views. A
friend who had known her from childhood, the Duchess de

Béthune, took her up once more and introduced her to
Fénelon and Mme. de Maintenon.

Fénelon must often have heard of Mme. Guyon at the
Paris convent of the *Nouvelles Catholiques*, but he does not
seem to have seen her until after her release. She herself
tells the story of their first meeting. It was at the Duchess
de Béthune's country villa. The two travelled back to Paris
together, in company with a maid of the duchess. 'At
once,' says Mme. Guyon in her ecstatic style, 'I was forcibly
and sweetly taken up [*occupée*] with him. It seemed to me
that our Lord joined him with me very closely and more
than He had done in the case of anyone else.' Fénelon,
however, does not appear to have been equally impressed.

I felt [she goes on to say], that this first interview did not
satisfy him : he did not relish me. As for me I felt a something
which urged me on to pour out my heart into his, but I found no
response on his part. . . . I was in pain for eight whole
days : after that I found myself united to him without any
obstacle.

We should like to have Fénelon's account of this episode,
but his letters to her have been destroyed. Five or six years
later he wrote : ' It is true that I have seen her at Mme. de
Charost's, and once or twice besides in good society, and
that I was impressed by her, but I have given her no
introductions.'

Let us go to the château of Marly-le-roi one day in the
autumn of the year 1690. In Mme. de Maintenon's own
private salon a small group of devotees is assembled. The
Duke and Duchess of Chevreuse are there, and the Duke
and Duchess of Beauvillier ; and the Duchess of Béthune
has come, bringing with her Mme. Guyon, who looks
charming in her nun-like costume. Their talk is very
different from that in vogue at other salons of the day. How
well his Majesty was looking on his name-day ! Why do
not those poor Protestants come over at once and not force
him to be severe with them ? How can they resist the
eloquence of the good Père Bourdaloue ? Those wicked
Jansenists are the ones who should be most severely
punished. 'Ah!' breaks in Mme. Guyon, 'if they only

knew the true method of prayer !' And then she discourses
sweetly on the Spouse in the Canticles and the pure
love of God. All are hushed and listen with rapture.
But stop! M. de Fénelon is announced. There is a
little flutter among the duchesses : a fresh flush comes over
Mme. Guyon's inspired face ; and the stately hostess herself
beams radiantly as her favourite abbé makes his bow.
How is the dear little duke? Did M. l'Abbé hear Père
Bourdaloue's great sermon? What? Prefer Monsieur de
Meaux? And, he : What news of the Chanoinesse? Is she
still doubtful about her vocation? She must be careful;
high spirituality is not meant for all. And then he, too,
discourses with equal fervour, but with more judgment and
learning, of the maxims of the saints.

Alas! *Vanitas vanitatum!* Pass over a few years, and
Mme. Guyon is shut up in the Bastille ; Fénelon is in exile
at Cambrai, humbled to the dust by his mighty brother of
Meaux ; Mme. de Maintenon writes that she has lost all
faith in him ; and he, on his side, deplores her jealousy, her
prejudices, and her love of intrigue. *Vanitas vanitatum, et
omnia vanitas!*

5

It often happens that men of very dissimilar talents and tastes
are attracted together by their very dissimilitude. They live in
intimacy for a time, perhaps a long time, till their circumstances
alter, or some sudden event comes to try them. Then the peculiarities of their respective minds are brought into action, and
quarrels ensue which end in coldness or separation. This contrast
of character leading, first, to intimacy, and then to differences, is
interestingly displayed, though painfully, in one passage of the
history of Basil and Gregory : Gregory the affectionate, the tender-
hearted, the man of quick feelings, the accomplished, the eloquent
preacher ; and Basil, the man of firm resolve and hard deeds, the
high-minded ruler of Christ's flock, the diligent labourer in the
field of ecclesiastical politics. . . . Both were men of classical
taste ; both were special champions of the Catholic creed ; both
were skilled in argument, and successful in their use of it ; both
were in the highest place in the Church.[1]

Though Mme. Guyon was a welcomed member of the

---

[1] Newman, *Church of the Fathers*, chap. iii.

THE IRISH ECCLESIASTICAL RECORD

little *coterie* over which Fénelon presided, her views were not altogether acceptable to all the members of it. Mme. de Maintenon, as we have seen, thought these should not be recommended indiscriminately, and least of all, to the young pupils of Saint-Cyr. Fénelon, too, had written: ' I would, above all, keep pious women and the sisters of a community away from books on high spirituality.' But the ' Chanoinesse,' Mlle. de Maizonfort, who was Mme. Guyon's cousin, and whose religious vocation had been decided by Fénelon, precipitated matters at Saint-Cyr. There the nuns talked of nothing but pure love and holy indifference ; and the lay-sisters, instead of doing their work, spent their time in reading Mme. Guyon's books. The Foundress grew alarmed. Her influence over her darling institution was being undermined, and her favourite Abbé seemed to be succumbing to the wiles of the charmer. And then, again, the king could not stand Mme. Guyon and her ravings.

I have had a copy of *L'Explication des Cantique des Cantiques* for two months [wrote Mme. de Maintenon in May, 1694]. There are some involved passages, some instructive, and some which I do not in any way approve. L'Abbé de Fénelon tells me that the highest form of devotion is to be found in the *Moyen Court*. . . . I have begged Mme. Nôtre Supérieure to forbid our ladies to have these books in their hands in future. Such reading is too strong for them ; they must have milk suited to their age. Mme. Guyon edifies them, nevertheless. I have asked her to discontinue her visits ; but I cannot forbid them to read letters from one of such piety and virtue.

It was in the preceding May (1693) that Mme. Guyon had been forbidden Saint-Cyr. At Fénelon's instigation she then appealed to Bossuet. To his judgment she submitted all her published works, and also many MSS. which had never seen the light, including her life and her commentaries on some of the books of the Old and New Testaments. After mature examination his decision was entirely against her teaching. Naturally such a result did not satisfy her. She asked that in a matter of such grave importance, two other judges should be associated with him, viz., the Bishop of Châlons (M. de Noailles) and

M. Tronson, the Superior-General of the Sulpicians, to examine into her conduct and doctrine. This was granted, but the inquiry was restricted to the latter. The judges met at Issy in 1694, and continued their sittings until the following March. The result was the same as before: Mme. Guyon's writings were condemned. Thirty-four articles summing up the orthodox teaching were drawn up by the judges and were accepted by Mme. Guyon. Meantime, at Christmas, Mme. de Maintenon had obtained for Fénelon the rich Abbey of S. Valéry, and a few weeks later the Archbishopric of Cambrai. The new prelate was consecrated in July (1695) by Bossuet and de Noailles, in the Chapel of Saint-Cyr, in the presence of the Foundress and her pupils and friends. All seemed to have ended happily: Mme. Guyon's influence was destroyed; Saint-Cyr and Fénelon were safe.

But a difficulty arose. Bossuet was composing a work entitled *Introduction sur les États d'Oraison*, as a commentary on the articles of Issy. Fénelon was asked to give it his approval, but absolutely declined; the book, he said, attacked Mme. Guyon personally, and that he could never do. In a lengthy *Mémoire* intended for Mme. de Maintenon's perusal, he explained that Bossuet attributed to Mme. Guyon all sorts of impious doctrines which he himself could not find in her writings; that, moreover, he (Fénelon) had esteemed and encouraged her at the very time when she was said to have taught these abominations, and that, therefore, he could not defame her without defaming himself. These explanations did not satisfy his friends. They were shocked that he should be still so devoted to his *amie*,' and began to tremble for his orthodoxy. ' I have seen our friend (Fénelon),' writes Mme. de Maintenon, October 7, 1696; ' we have had a great discussion. . . . I wish I was as faithful and devoted to my duties as he is to his *amie*. Bossuet, of course, obtained for his *Etats d'Oraison* the hearty approbation of the Archbishop of Paris (M. de Noailles) and the Bishop of Chartres (M. Godet des Marais). It was arranged that the work should be published in the spring of 1697 ; but before it could come out Fénelon was first in the field with his *Explication des Maximes des Saints sur la Vie Intérieure.*[1]

Hitherto the contest between these two great ecclesiastics had been of a semi-private character; now it was to be fought out before the eyes of the world. Well might Fénelon say that they, the champions of the Faith, had become the laughing stock of the infidels and the sorrow of the faithful. Even now, as we run our eye along the rows of their works, we cannot but lament that so much of their time, their energy, and their temper was wasted in this miserable strife. Before we go into the merits of the case itself, we must first consider the human elements which had so large a share in its origin and in its development. Four persons play a prominent part in the story—Mme. de Maintenon and Mme. Guyon, Fénelon and Bossuet. At first the famous Bishop of Meaux is patronising towards his brilliant young friend, the Abbé-Supérieur of the *Nouvelles Catholiques*, and helps to obtain for him the post of preceptor to the king's grandson. This office brings Fénelon into close friendship with the lady whom Louis XIV. has lately made his wife. Next enters Mme. Guyon on the scene with her fascinating fervour; and spiritually captivates the susceptible Abbé, the youngest member of the group. Mme. de Maintenon is warned of this lady's influence and opinions. At the wish of the other three, Bossuet is called in. He decides against the seductress, and calls upon Fénelon to approve of the condemnation. But Fénelon is no longer the simple Abbé: he is Archbishop of Cambrai, Prince of the Holy Roman Empire, and a Duke of France. He resents the overbearing manner in which he is addressed by a mere bishop; and he cannot help feeling for the poor victim, his devoted friend, whom he is called upon to crush. He flatly refuses, and hence arises 'a discussion, so that they departed one from another.' If two Apostles, 'men of like passions' (ὁμοιοπαθεῖς) with ourselves, could disagree over the conduct of a weaker brother, we cannot wonder at the sad dispute between the Archbishop of Cambrai and the Bishop of Meaux.

---

[1] The story of the controversy is well told by Card. de Bausset, *Histoire de Fénelon*, tome I.

But what was it all about? It was the old contest
between poetry and prose, romance and reason, sentiment
and common sense. All of these have their place in devotion;
and the greatest writers on the mystical life have especially
insisted on the importance of the contemplative and ecstatic
states of the soul. But it is plain that such phenomena
must be exceptional, and that the treatment of them must
require the greatest care. Just about the time when
Fénelon first met Mme. Guyon, the doctrine of a Spanish
priest, named Molinos, had been condemned at Rome. He
had taught (1) that perfect contemplation is a state in which
the soul neither reasons nor reflects upon God or upon itself,
but merely receives passively the impression of heavenly
light, without exercising any act of love or adoration, or any
other act of Christian piety. This state of inaction and
absolute inattention he called *Quietude*. (2) In this state of
perfect contemplation the soul desires nothing—not even
eternal salvation ; it fears nothing—not even eternal damna-
tion ; it feels no other sentiment but complete abandonment
to the good pleasure of God. (3) A soul which has reached
this state of perfect contemplation is dispensed from receiving
the sacraments and practising good works; all acts and
exercises of Christian piety become indifferent ; the most
criminal imaginations affect only the sensitive part of the
soul without staining the soul itself, and they are completely
outside the higher part in which the understanding and the
will reside. From these three principles Molinos drew the
conclusion that a soul in this state ceased to be guilty in
God's sight even when abandoning itself to the foulest
crimes. Mme. Guyon entirely rejected this last inference ;
but she taught that even ordinary souls might be conducted
to a state of perfection in which a continuous and unchangeable act of contemplation dispensed them from all other acts
of religion. Fénelon merely held the possibility of an habitual
state of pure love, from which were excluded as so many
imperfections all explicit acts of the other virtues, even the
desire of heaven or fear of hell. He rejected Molinos' system
and the views attributed to Mme. Guyon ; but he considered
that in condemning her, Bossuet had struck at genuine

mysticism, the teaching of St. Francis of Sales, St. John of
the Cross, and St. Theresa. It was to defend these that the
Maximes was written.

At once a storm raged round the *États d'Oraison* and
the *Maximes*. But on one point opinions were not divided ;
all agreed that in logic and style Fénelon was no match for
his great rival. Bossuet sent his book to the Sovereign
Pontiff, and was rewarded by a commendatory letter from
Innocent XII. (May 6, 1697). This was the more significant,
because only nine days earlier Fénelon had appealed to the
solemn judgment of the Holy See. A little later he asked
the king's permission to go to Rome to defend his cause in
person. Not only was his request refused, but he was
peremptorily commanded to betake himself to Cambrai, and
remain in his diocese until further orders (August 1).

The cause was now *sub judice*. It might have been
hoped that both parties would keep silence until the decision
was given; but both continued to write with increasing bitterness. And here the chief blame must' rest on Bossuet's
shoulders. Not satisfied that public opinion, as well as
ecclesiastical authority, was on his side, he seemed resolved
to crush and humiliate his opponent. He who had always
been so dignified and courteous in his discussions with
Jansenists, and even with Protestants, had now no such
consideration for a distinguished ornament of his own
Church, once his disciple and friend. His *Rélation sur le
Quietisme* made reconciliation impossible. In his *États
d'Oraison* he had condemned Mme. Guyon's teaching
without mentioning her name, and he had been careful
to avoid all reflections on her conduct. Fénelon, however,
had pointed out that if she taught what was attributed to
her she deserved to be burnt : he had refused his approbation because he believed her to be blameless. Very well,
replied Bossuet in his *Rélation*, let us see what her conduct
has been ; and, quoting from Mme. Guyon's private MSS.,
entrusted to him by herself, and from Fénelon's *Mémoire*, he
tells some queer stories about her, and gives specimens of
her esoteric spirituality quite sufficient to destroy her
reputation for sanctity. She had, indeed, repented and

retracted, and, therefore, though her writings were impious, she herself no longer deserved condemnation. ' No,' says Bossuet, in a scathing passage—

Your *amie* did not deserve ' to be burnt with her books,' for the simple reason that she herself condemned them. Your *amie* was not even 'a monster upon earth'; she was only an ignorant woman, dazzled by a specious spirituality, deceived by her directors and applauded by a man of your importance ; she condemned her error as soon as some one took the trouble to instruct her. This avowal could give nothing but edification to the Church, and deter from her books those persons who had been led astray by them. The Archbishop of Cambrai could not but approve of conduct so just—but he had too much at heart the fear of defaming his *amie* and of ' defaming himself.' What he calls defaming his *amie* is to understand her books in their natural sense, as his confrères have done, and as everyone else has done who has condemned them. He would not let his friends think that he had put such bad books into their hands—that is what he meant ' by defaming himself.' . . . . His real fear is not about ' defaming himself,' but about acknowledging that he was wrong. This is not defaming one's self : this is to do one's self honour and to restore one's injured reputation. Is it such a great misfortune to have been deceived by an *amie* ? The Archbishop of Cambrai takes good care to have it said in Rome that he hardly knows Mme. Guyon. What strange conduct ! At Rome he is ashamed of this *amie* : here in France, where he dare not say that she is unknown to him, he will not let her books be branded ; he makes himself responsible for them though their author has herself already condemned them.

In spite of all its qualifications the *Maximes des Saints* contains both Mme. Guyon and Molinos . . . and when I say that the work of an ignorant female visionary and the work of M. de Cambrai are of one and the same stamp, I am only saying what is, after all, self-evident. . . .

I am careful not to impute to the Archbishop of Cambrai any other purpose than that which is revealed by his own writings, by his book, by his answers, and by the course of admitted facts—it is surely enough, and more than enough, to be the open protector of her who foretells and purposes the seduction of the whole universe. If this be considered too strong language to use against a woman whose errors have gone to the verge of craziness, I grant it—if that craziness is not downright fanaticism : if the spirit of seduction is not at work in that woman : if that Priscilla has not found her Montanus to defend her.

' M. de Meaux's book is making a great stir,' write Mme. de Maintenon to Card. de Noailles (June 29, 1698) :

'The facts are within everybody's grasp. Mme. Guyon's follies are most amusing. The book is short, lively, and well put together. People lend it to each other, snatch it out of each other's hands, and devour it.' This from the once devoted patroness of Fénelon and Mme. Guyon! No wonder that his few faithful friends thought him crushed beyond hope. No reply seemed possible; both the archbishop and his protégée had been convicted out of their own mouths. But it is dangerous to press a beaten enemy too hard. Had Bossuet confined himself to argument, his position would have been unassilable, but his insolence laid him open to attack, and Fénelon's *Réponse à la Rélation de M. de Meaux* is one of the ablest rejoinders ever written. He begins by pointing out that Bossuet has now descended to personalities—a sure sign that he has been beaten on the points of doctrine. Moreover, to support these attacks he has stooped to reveal the most private documents, even those almost as sacred as the seal of confession. But Fénelon knew well that though such a proceeding is universally acknowledged to be base, yet the more private the evidence the more likely it is to be believed. He, therefore, goes on at once to deal with the main charge : his relations with Mme. Guyon. You have dared to call us the new Priscilla and the new Montanus, he says, and yet how have *you* behaved towards her? how have you behaved towards me ? After a prolonged examination, after keeping her at Meaux for six months, you have certified that you 'are satisfied with her conduct, and have continued to her the participation in the holy sacraments just as [you] found her when she came to [you]'; you have declared 'that [you] have not found her implicated in any way in the abominations of Molinos, or others condemned at other times, and that [you] have not meant to include her in the mention made of them in your ordonnance.' It was at your dictation that she wrote :—'I have none of the errors explained in the said Pastoral [Bossuet's own], having always had the intention of writing in a most Catholic sense, not understanding at that time that what I wrote could have any other.' This after a thorough examination of all her most private

writings ; whereas Fénelon solemnly denied that he had
ever read any of them. She had often spoken to him about
her extraordinary revelations, but he had treated them as
illusions ; and she herself had followed the rule of St. John
of the Cross in such matters, viz., never to dwell upon them
at all, and she had written them down only in obedience to
her half-crazy director, Lacombe. She is no Priscilla on
your own showing ; but if she is, who is the real Montanus?
If you believed me to be a real Montanus in league with
a real Priscilla, how could you consecrate me to the holy
office of Bishop ? It was not I who wished to be consecrated
by you—it was you who insisted on overcoming all difficulties
in order to consecrate me.[1] There is much more in this
style dealing with the various questions raised in the
Rélation. Then Fénelon concludes :

> If M. de Meaux has any further documents to bring against
> me I beg him not make a half-secret of them (worse than com-
> plete publication), and I entreat him to send them all to Rome.
> I have no fear, thank God, for anything that may be communicated
> and legally examined. . . . If he believes me to be so impious
> and such a hypocrite, it is his duty to make use of every proof in
> his possession. As for me I cannot keep from calling Him to
> witness Whose eyes enlighten the most profound darkness, and
> before Whom we must all soon appear. He knows, He Who reads
> our hearts, that I am attached only to Him and to His Church. and
> that I beseech unceasingly in His presence that He would bring
> back peace, and put an end to the scandal, that He would restore
> the pastors to their flocks, and that He would grant to M. de
> Meaux as many blessings as He has been pleased to bestow
> crosses upon me.

The *Réponse* had an even greater success than the
Rélation. In Rome, as well as in Paris, it produced a
complete revolution in his favour. Bossuet replied with
Remarques sur la Réponse de M. de Cambray, and Fénelon
rejoined with *Réponse aux Remarques*; but the merits of the
controversy may well be judged by the *Rélation* and the

---

[1] The ceremony was to take place at Saint-Cyr. Could Bossuet be senior
consecrator with the bishop of the diocese as his assistant ?

original *Réponse.* There is, however, one passage in the second *Réponse* well worth quoting :—

This fanatic [Montanus] had enticed from their husbands two women, who followed him about; he delivered them up to a false inspiration, which was a veritable possession by the Evil One. He himself was possessed as well as these women ; and it was while he was in a transport of diabolical fury, which seized him and Maximilla, that they both strangled themselves. Such is the man, the horror of all ages, to whom you compare your brother-bishop, ' the dear, life-long friend whom your bear in your bosom '; and you take it amiss that he complains of the comparison. No, Monseigneur, I do not complain ; I am grieved, and it is for you.

Meantime the affair was proceeding in Rome. After prolonged discussion the commissioners appointed by the Pope were equally divided in opinion. Fénelon now felt confident that he should escape censure. He ventured to write once more to Mme. de Maintenon (November, 1698), assuring her of his continued 'respect, attachment, and gratitude.' 'None of the crosses,' he says, 'which have been laid upon me is so heavy as that of having caused you so much displeasure.' We have no evidence that any answer was vouchsafed to this pathetic epistle. We know that Louis XIV. was furious at his probable acquittal. A fresh examination was ordered by the Pope, this time to be made by the Cardinals, and at length it was decided that the *Maximes* must be condemned. After the Papal Brief had been drawn up, but just before it was published, Louis addressed to the Pope a *Mémoire* of more than usual insolence, demanding an immediate and definite decision. This document, it is sad to relate, was from the pen of Bossuet himself.[1]

On the Feast of the Annunciation, 1699, Fénelon was about to ascend the pulpit of his cathedral to preach on the great mystery of the day. A letter was put into his hands. In it he read that the Holy See had condemned his *Maximes* as containing propositions which were rash,

---

[1] See his letter to his nephew, March 16, 1699,

scandalous, and offensive to pious ears. There was only
time for a few moments of recollection, and then he entered
the pulpit. Already the news had spread among the vast
congregation. Amidst such expressions of sympathy from
them as the sacred occasion permitted, he delivered a discourse far different from that which he had prepared and they
had expected. And yet he found in the sublime story of the
Incarnation the subject and the example which he needed.
He spoke to them of perfect submission to superiors, and he
pointed out that it was the most exalted of creatures who
had said *Ecce ancilla Domini : fiat mihi secundum verbum
tuum*. A fortnight later he issued a *mandement* to his
diocese.

We adhere to the Brief [he says] both with regard to the text
of the book and the twenty-three propositions, simply, absolutely,
and without any reserve. Hence we condemn both the book and
the twenty-three propositions precisely in the same form and with
the same qualifications simply, absolutely, and without any
reserve. Moreover, we forbid, under the same penalties, all the
faithful of our diocese to read the book or keep it in their
possession.

He also wrote to the Pope in similar terms, and received
a touching reply. It is melancholy to have to record that
his enemies, and chief among them Bossuet and Mme. de
Maintenon, found this submission insufficient.

How could I believe [the latter wrote] in the sincerity of this
submission when I could not see the prelate becoming, like
St. Paul, a preacher of the faith which he had assailed ? I only
believe in conviction of error when I see it attacked as fiercely as
it has formerly been upheld.

Those who are inside the Church think that such submission is easy : those who are outside think it impossible.
The present writer had occasion to take a small part on
the losing side in a recent controversy. He can, therefore,
speak with some authority on the subject, and he can assure
both parties that submission is extremely difficult and yet
can be sincere. When a man has made the best use of his
powers in forming his opinion ; when that opinion has had
the ardent support of some of the greatest names ; when in

the course of discussion he has had good reason to believe
that he has by no means been worsted; when, too, he has
been a witness of the human passions inseparable from all
human contentions—then, indeed, it is hard to acknowledge
that his adversaries were right and that he was wrong. Yet
this acknowledgment can be perfectly sincere. A Catholic
knows very well that his own private judgment is not the
sole rule of his belief. He has the teaching of the Sovereign
Pontiff to look to, a teaching which is guided by the Spirit
of Truth. Hence, when his own opinion is in conflict with
the solemn judgment of the Holy See he does not hesitate
as to which must give way. It is not to the adversaries'
arguments or wiles that he yields, but to Divine authority.

> Non me tua fervida terrent
> Dicta, ferox : Dî me terrent, et Jupiter hostis.

When Fénelon's *mandement* was published at Louvain,
the censor prefixed to it the fine quotation from Tacitus :
Pro quo exemplum quærimus, id olim pro exemplo erit. And
so it came to pass that a simple country priest, at the end
of the nineteenth century, was helped, in no small degree,
to make his submission by the shining example of François
de Fénelon, the noble Archbishop of Cambrai.

6. It is time that we should follow Fénelon to his diocese,
and see how he spent the last twenty years of his life. In
those old days a courtier-bishop looked upon his diocese as
a land of exile, and took care to spend there as little of his
time as possible. When Fénelon was appointed to Cambrai
he declared that he was about to enter upon ' a life of cease-
less slavery in a foreign land.' Nevertheless, he resolved to
reside there at least three-quarters of the year. His banishment from court (August, 1696) compelled him to remain
all the year round.

When we consider the life of a bishop under the old
regime, we must bear in mind that his position was far
different from that of his successors at the present day. At
that time he was the leading personage in the city and in
the surrounding country. His wealth and his domains,
his feudal and political rights made him a high and
mighty *seigneur*. This was especially true in the case of a

diocese like Cambrai. The archbishop was a prince of the Holy Roman Empire, and a duke in the kingdom of France, with a revenue of 200,000 livres. Fénelon's familiarity with court life would, naturally, fit him to fill with dignity this high post. On the other hand, his polished and refined character exposed him to many a shock from the rude rustic habits of his Flemish clergy and people. He seems, however, to have adapted himself so well to their ways that in a few years he became popular among them. His episcopal duties were admirably performed. He made his visitations regularly, and put down abuses with that mixture of firmness and gentleness which is already familiar to us in his story. In the matter of patronage he was careful to prevent outsiders from securing the best benefices. We have already examined his views with regard to the treatment of Protestants. He was especially shocked at any cases of hypocritical conformity, and put a stop to them by obtaining for such persons permission to reside in the foreign part of his diocese. His treatment of the Jansenists was severe, Flanders being at that time their stronghold. There is something incongruous in one who had himself been condemned, persecuting others for their heterodox views. But in this, as in many other of the incidents of Fénelon's life, we see the human frailty of his character. The *Nouveau Testament* of the Oratorian Quesnel had been approved by Card. de Noailles, and had been defended by Bossuet. When the Bull *Unigenitus* appeared (1713), Fénelon exclaimed : ' One hundred and one propositions condemned! What a disgrace for the approvers of such a book ! ' And he insisted that the approvers themselves should be condemned. This last remark shows that the two great prelates were never really reconciled. Bossuet died on April 12, 1704. A few months later his secretary, Le Dieu, visited Cambrai, and called on the archbishop. He gives us an interesting picture of the everyday life of the prelate, a mixture of personal simplicity and official splendour. After supper the conversation turned on Bossuet's death.

They asked me [writes the secretary], whether he had been conscious and had received the Sacraments. But the prelate

partioularly wished to know who had prepared him for death. I
believe that in putting this question he thought that M. de Meaux
on his deathbed had need of sound advice and of a person of
authority, after having taken part in so many important and
delicate affairs. In all our talk the Archbishop did not say a
single word in praise of M. de Meaux.

However, we have Fénelon's own assurance that he
prayed heartily (*de bon cœur*) for ' feu M. de Meaux.'

The loss of the battle of Oudenarde (1708) brought the
war into the neighbourhood of Cambrai. Then it was that
the archbishop proved himself the true father of his clergy
and people. The country priests were reduced to beggary
and were quite unable to pay the extraordinary imposts
levied upon them.[1] The archbishop took upon himself the
whole of this burden. Next year, after the disaster of
Malplaquet, Cambrai was filled with fugitives flying before
the advance of the victorious allies. Fénelon fed vast
numbers of them at his own expense. His palace was
turned into a barrack ; his seminary into a hospital. Even
the captive enemy benefited by his generosity to such an
extent that Marlborough and Prince Eugene spared his
estates from pillage, and those also which he specially pleaded
for. The spiteful Saint-Simon relates that the archbishop's
reputation was greatly enhanced by his conduct, and that
Louis XIV. himself, though so prejudiced against him,
was grateful for his services.

It seemed that, after his long years of exile from the
court, he was about to be received once more into favour.
In April, 1711, his enemy, the Dauphin, Bossuet's former
pupil, was carried off by a sudden illness, and the Duke of
Burgundy was summoned to share in the government of the
realm. Beauvillier and Chevreuse, and especially Fénelon,
at once became persons of importance. It was known that
the archbishop had the greatest influence over the new

---

[1] It is commonly asserted that the clergy before the Revolution paid no
taxes. They did not, indeed, pay the ordinary taxes, but they gave to the
State a *don gratuit* levied in their own assemblies ; and besides, they frequently
contributed in other ways. Thus, before the summoning of the States-
General, the annual contribution of the clergy amounted to 25,000,000 francs.
See *Revue des Questions Historiques*, July, 1890.

Dauphin, and would be entrusted with the highest offices in the event of a demise of the crown. Fénelon now corresponded regularly with his former pupil. Moreover, at the instigation of Beauvillier and Chevreuse, he drew up a plan of government for the future king. This work was entitled *Tables de Chaulnes*, from the name of the place where the conferences of the three friends used to be held. It does not, of course, go so far as the principles of 1789 ; better still, it lays down principles which, if carried out, might have prevented all the excesses of the Revolution. His plan is based upon the rights of the people and the duties of the king ; a thorough reform of the court ; the summoning of the States-General ; the freedom of the Church from government interference. In his *Examen de Conscience des Devoirs de la Royauté*, he attacks the whole of the policy of Louis XIV.—and especially war, of which he himself had seen the terrible consequences. Everything now seemed to point to the speedy commencement of a reign full of promise of peace and prosperity for France. Louis was past eighty ; his grandson was not yet thirty, and Fénelon, the trusted counsellor, just sixty. All these bright hopes were dashed to the ground by the mysterious death of the young prince (February 16, 1712).

Once more Fénelon had to fall back upon the consolations of sincere piety, his duties, and his books. His life-long friends, Chevreuse and Beauvillier, who had stood by him in his darkest days, did not long survive their royal pupil. At the death of the latter (August, 1714) he wrote to the widowed duchess : 'We shall soon find him again whom we have lost. . . He whom we can no longer see, is closer to us than before ; we meet him continually in our common centre, God.' A few weeks later he met with a serious accident while out on an episcopal visitation. On New Year's day he was attacked by fever. For six days he was in agony, and at last expired peacefully on the morning of January 7, 1715.

His life had been in his own eyes a double failure : the king had banished him from court, the Pope had condemned his book. And yet it is that failure which has endeared him

to posterity. Had he retained the royal favour he might
have become a Wolsey or a Richelieu, but we should not
have had the model archbishop devoted to his clergy and
his flock. Had his book been approved we should have lost
a most striking example of submission. Such lives as
Fénelon's reconcile many a man of light and leading to bear
with patience the bitterest of all pangs—to feel capable of
doing much and yet to be allowed to do nothing.[1]

T. B. SCANNELL.

GLIMPSES OF IRISH COLLEGIATE LIFE IN PARIS IN THE SEVENTEENTH AND EIGHTEENTH CENTURIES

IN a former paper (March, 1902) the present writer gave
an account of the languages in use amongst Irish
ecclesiastical students in Paris in the eighteenth century.
In the present paper he purposes to give some further
details concerning Irish collegiate life in Paris in the seventeenth and eighteenth centuries especially in its economic
aspect In this respect it may be of interest to inquire :
1. What preparation was made for the journey to the
continent, and how it was accomplished? 2. How the
maintenance of students was provided for? 3. What was
the character of the schools frequented by Irishmen?
4. How their vacations were spent, and 5. What was the
status of the Superiors of the College? On these points
the records which have come down to us are meagre, but the
information they contain is not unworthy of being preserved.

I

What then was the preparation made by students
for the journey to the continent, and how was it accomplished? Here ecclesiastical students found themselves
face to face with a threefold difficulty. The first arose
from the laws which made it penal to go abroad for

---

[1] 'Εχθίστη δὲ ὀδύη ἐστὶ τῶν ἐν ἀνθρώποισι αὕτη, πολλὰ φρονέοντα μηδενὸς κρατέειν (HEROD, ix. 16.)

the purpose of education; the second arose from want of
means, and the third from the inconvenience of the journey
itself. To escape the penalties of the law they were obliged
to lay aside every mark of the ecclesiastical state. The
better to conceal their purpose some travelled under assumed
names; others, like Patrick Joseph Plunkett, so late as
1764, became articled as apprentices to merchants, and
travelled as if on the business of their masters.[1]

The second difficulty was to provide means to defray the
expense of the journey. To meet this difficulty many
aspirants to the ecclesiastical state were promoted to priesthood before their departure from Ireland. Where some
remnant of ecclesiastical benefices still existed they were
appointed to parishes. But they were required to make
their studies as soon as possible. Thus for instance, a
decree of a Provincial synod of Armagh, held in 1670,
ordered young priests ordained within the previous six
years to go to make their studies under penalty of
being deprived of their parishes. Meantime they were
authorized to absent themselves for five years and to retain
a portion of the revenues of their parishes to defray the
expenses of their education. In other cases young priests
were invited by some of the senior clergy to officiate
in their parishes; and an appeal was made to the people to
contribute towards the expenses of their education.[2] In the
latter case as in the former they were required to set out for
the continent as soon as possible. Sometimes it was found
necessary to urge their departure. We find an instance of
this in a resolution of the Chapter of Armagh, presented to
the Primate, Dr. Blake, towards the close of the eighteenth
century. It was couched in the following terms :—

We see with sorrow, my Lord, that two of the three ordained
last year have remained at home from their studies, to the great

---

[1] Cogan's *Diocese of Meath*, vol. iii., p. 1.

[2] Statuimus et ordinamus ut omnes juniores sacerdotes qui a sexennio
ordinati sunt, studia prosequi cogantur privatione beneficiorum si parochias
habeant; concedimus iis licentiam substituendi alios sacerdotes ab ordinario
approbatos, et ad quinquennium emolumentum quod paciscantur cum substi-
tuto, et quod ordinario justum videbitur, annue accipiendi ; et si nullas
parochias habeant ab aliis adjuventur.—*Statut. Armac.*, n. 21, Renehan's
Collections, p. 153.

loss of not having in proper time a sufficient supply for the diocese, and contrary to your Grace's positive orders to them, we therefore recommend your Grace (in order to hinder the like inconvenience for the future) to direct an order to be given to every young priest along with his letters of ordination; and an exeat, a suspension from saying Mass in Ireland to be incurred, *ipso facto*, after so many days, weeks, or months, as your Grace will judge it convenient to appoint for their leaving the kingdom, and we further request your Grace, to discourage any priest or Community boy [1] that will return to this diocese, except in case of sickness, and that properly attested, before he finishes his regular course, and has proper attestations of good conduct from his superiors; and that if any should return, to oblige him to go back again without any benefice or promotion.[2]

In the eighteenth century burses were founded for the education of ecclesiastics, and in some instances, the founders made provision for the travelling expenses of students. In the M'Mahon Foundation there was a provision of this kind. That foundation made in 1710 was ratified and interpreted in 1714, by Dr. Hugh M'Mahon, Bishop of Clogher, and nephew of the founder. In the deed of ratification the following passage occurs :—

As the Province of Ulster is the most over-run in the whole kingdom by Scotch Presbyterians, who occupy town and country, and exterminate the natives, there are few parents capable of paying the travelling expenses of their children. In consequence, subjects the most talented, and who would have a right to enjoy the foundation in preference to all others, cannot avail themselves of it, for want of means to travel, a circumstance which would frustrate the intention of the founder, who, not being aware of the state of things, ordered that one hundred livres should be given to each occupant of a burse when returning to Ireland. Hence the better to fulfil the intention of the will it is better to divide the one hundred livres into two equal portions. Fifty livres shall be sent to Ireland to defray the travelling expenses of boys who shall be nominated to the burses, and the Sieurs Administrators shall be good enough to forward that sum when they shall be called on by the nominators. The other fifty shall serve for the return, and shall be granted only to such as are capable of serving the mission, and are willing to do so according to what is laid down in the fifth article.[3]

---

[1] The official title of the Junior division of the Irish College in Paris was ' Communitas Clericorum Hibernorum.'
[2] Resolution of the Chapter of Armagh, 1764.—Renehan's *Collections, Archbishops*, p. 108.
[3] Extract from the terms of the M'Mahon Foundation.

When young men were fully provided with means to travel there still remained the difficulty of the journey, by no means an imaginary one, in an age when steamboats and railways were unknown. Some students sailed from Cork or Dublin direct to France ; others crossed through England. Two instances may be mentioned of the manner in which the journey was performed. One is that of Thomas Lewis O'Beirne. In 1768 O'Beirne, who had already been a student in Paris, went to Ireland on account of his health. On his return, some time later, it is stated that he made the journey from Holyhead to London on foot. On the way he is said to have made, in a wayside inn in Wales, the acquaintance of an English nobleman, who afterwards offered him the position of secretary. O'Beirne accepted the appointment, was led into the Protestant society, and subsequently became a pervert.[1] The second instance is that of Rev. Charles O'Donnell, afterwards Bishop of Derry. The account of his journey to Paris in 1777, extracted from his diary, is as follows[2] :—

July, 1777. Invoice of things put into my saddle-bags at the Rev. Dr. M'Davitt's house, near Strabane :—Nine shirts of fine linen marked C.D. ; six ditto of a coarse kind, eight stocks, nine pair of stockings, two pair of breeches, two flannel waistcoats, one French grammar, two Irish hymn-books, two pocket-handkerchiefs, six pair of ruffled sleeves.

Left Strabane, July 8th ; slept that night at Augher, at Widdow Duggan's ; second night at Castleblayney. Third day to Drogheda. Stayed there two nights. Supped and took breakfast with the ladies of the nunnery. Became acquainted with Father Burrell, and some gentlemen besides. Fourth day of my journey went to Dublin on the stage coach. Stayed there two nights. Took the packet-boat to Liverpool at five o'clock afternoon. Had a pleasant view of the country going down the Liffey, the hill of Howth to the left hand, and the Wicklow mountains to the right, which we had in view next morning, likewise Holyhead ; sailed down the Welsh coast, and arrived at Liverpool on 16th at 8 p.m. Took a slight view of the docks, which were well supplied with ships. Saw also the floodgates, drawbridges, with some other curiosities. The most pleasing view was that of the Exchange from which the whole town can be seen.

---

[1] *Sham Squire*, pp. 212-15.
[2] *Brief Memoirs of the Bishops of Derry*, by the Rev. James M'Laughlin, P.P., pp. 63, 64.

That evening [the next we presume after his arrival] I took my seat in the Liverpool fly and set out for London at five o'clock. Drove all night. Dined at Lichfield, about 100 miles from Liverpool, a country village not very large, but remarkable for an ancient church adorned with three spires, and a great many pictures of saints or other religious people, as they seemed to me to be, set up in places outside the church all made for them. Supped that night at Meridon, about thirty miles off. Went by Coventry, St. Alban's and Highgate. From thence to London where I arrived at eight o'clock, p.m., on the 19th day of the month. Stayed there two nights, having heard Mass in Lincoln Field Chapel. Saw the Royal appartments in the King's palace. Took an outside passage on the Dover stage, being anxious to see the country. Went out by the Queen's Head Inn. Eight miles from London to Rochester, a long narrow town, but with few streets, having the Thames running through the middle. From thence to Canterbury, twenty-five miles, to Dover fifteen miles; seventy-three miles from London to Dover. The country seemed very productive, beans, wheat, hops, no flax or potatoes, but great quantities of brush or wood.

That day the rain fell prodigiously. We had very little pleasure on the journey, but very wet skins for our curiosity. That night we slept at Dover.

Entered the College of the Lombards on the 26th July, 1777.

Thus at the end of the eighteenth century eighteen days were spent in making a journey which can now be made in twenty-four hours.

II

The feelings of young men arriving in Paris for the first time must have been of joy mingled with anxiety. The perils and fatigues of the journey were over but dangers and anxieties no less serious remained. Like the celebrated Boussard, Chancellor of the University (A.D. 1518), they might say that they had come to a city the most celebrated in the world for its vices and its learning.[1] They had to seek a home and means of support. At first they lived as boarders at one of the University Colleges, or at lodgings in the city, while frequenting the schools as externs. After a time the liberality of M. de l'Escalopièr, Baron de St. Just, provided them with a residence of which Messingham speaks in terms of eulogy.[2]

---

[1] Veni adolescens natus annos decem et septem ad Parisiorum civitatem illam inclytam toto, vitiis et literis, cantatissimam orbe.

[2] Obscuro satis loco manentes alumnorum paucitate incognitos ad magnificam domum ab ipso translatos, auctis mediis et alumnorum numero, ad communem notitiam deductos.—Messingham, Florelegii, S. Hib., Preface.

At a later period the Lombard College became their residence ; but, as will be seen by the appeal which we give below,[1] even that establishment was found insufficient, and until between 1730 and 1740 some Irish students were compelled to seek lodgings in the city.

But let us now proceed to give some details concerning the expense of their support, and how it was provided for. The students were composed of two categories, viz., priests ordained before leaving home and young men not yet in orders. As we shall see later on, 400 francs a year was considered sufficient for the support of a student in the seventeenth

[1] AUX PERSONNES PIEUSES ET ZÉLÉES POUR LE SOULAGEMENT DE LEURS FRÈRES EN JÉSUS CHRIST

Le Collège de Lombards où Louis XIV. a permis aux Irlandais de s'etablir, n'a pas assez de logement pour contenir tous les prêtres et tous les jeunes Etudiants de cette Nation, qui viennent á Paris commencer ou achever leurs études.

Les superieurs majeurs de ce Collège ont jugé qu'il etait necessaire d'y faire un nouveau corps de logis, qui pût contenir sous un même toit, et sous une même discipline ce qu'il y a de Prêtres et d'Etudiants Irlandais repandus dans les differents quartiers de cette capitale.

Toute jeunesse qui n'est pas disciplinée fait ordinairement de mauvaises études. Elle prend souvent dans le monde des impressions contraires á sa vocation. Les Prêtres même y courent risque d'alterer l'esprit de leur état. La dissipation est inseparable de gens qui sont occupés de se procurer le necessaire, et n'entraine que trop souvent le dérèglement. Quand les Ecclesiastiques Irlandais de Paris se trouveront rassemblés dans une même maison tous ces inconvenients disparaitront. L'on espère par là soulager leurs besoins et faciliter leurs études.

Les Catholiques d'Irlande, qui depuis les Revolutions de Angleterre ont toujours regardé la France comme leur principal refuge, osent se flatter que la Nation Française, si zélée pour le maintien et la conservation de la Religion, si genereuse envers les Etrangers, surtout envers les Irlandais ne se dementirá pas en cette occasion.

Les Irlandais ne s'etendiront point ici sur les obligations qu'ils ont dejá á la France. Il suffit de dire qu'elle est le principal instrument dont Dieu s'est servi pour conservér la Foi in Irlande : En effet c'est à Paris que la plupart des Ecclesiastiques de cette Nation desolée viennent puiser les lumières, la sainteté et le courage necessaires pour remplir leur ministère et qu'ils se mettent en etat d'etre reèllement et selon Dieu, utiles á la mission, et á leur Patrie. Dieu a beni cet ouvrage.

Une triste experience nous apprend, que partout où la Foi est persecutée, elle s'eteint presquè en moins d'un siecle, ou passe á une autre nation, sans laisser aucune trace de sa lumiére chez le people qu'elle abandonne. C'est ainsi qu'en Suede l'erreur ; le schisme en Moscovie, en Asie l'infidélite ont eteint jusqu'au nom de Catholique.

Cependant la Foi pure telle que tous les Chretiens l'ont reçu de Jesus Christ, par le ministère de ses Apotres et de leurs successeurs, subsiste encore en Irlande. Apres deux siecles de persecution le plus grand nombre de ses habitants est encore Catholique. La Hierarchie Ecclesiastique s'y maintient. La rigeur des Lois, la privation des Biens, l'exclusion des Charges et des Dignitiés sont de vains obstacles. La foi y est toujours la plus forte. Et cette

and in the beginning of the eighteenth century. The priests received stipends for their masses. The stipend was usually a franc. By means of these stipends, they were able to provide themselves with at least absolute necessaries. They purchased their own furniture, and, as we learn from a memorandum drawn up by them about 1736, they paid their accounts to the Econome of the College once a week.[1] Besides the priests there were also the

constance est un miracle, dont la Providence ne fournit aucun example dans l'histoire Ecclesiastique.

C'est pour se mettre en etat de soutenir une œuvre si digne de la coopération de tous les Fideles que les Irlandais invitent aujourd'hui les Français à les secourir dans la depense, qu'ils ont à faire non seulement pour leur nouveau batiment mais encore pour la réédification de leur chapelle, qui tombe en ruines, et qu'ils ne peuvent se dispenser de demolir incessament.

Les Prieres sont la seule recompense que puissent attendre des Chretiens, et que des Protres puissent offrir ; surtout quand il s'agit des bienfaits entre une nation genereuse et florissante et un peuple humble et persecuté.

Les Irlandais ne cesseront donc de prier Dieu pour leur Bienfaiteurs et pour la France leur seconde Patrie. Ils n'ont j'amais pu lui temoignor assez la juste reconnaissance, qu'ils leur doivent pour l'asyle qu' Elle accorde au Roi Jacques. Ce qu'ils purent faire dans le temps fut de venir au nombre de quarante cinq mille hommes se joindre aux Français pour combattre les ennemis communs, lorsque toute l'Europe etait ligné contre Louis XIV de triomphante memoire.

Le souvenir que la France à bien vouler conserver des batailles de la Marseilles, de Luzata, et d'Almanza, des sieges du Namur, Charleroi, Barcelone, etc., et enfin du choc de Cremoné et de quelques autres occasions où les Irlandais firent leur devoir, est si flatteur pour eux, qu'ils n'ont pas de regret au sang repandu à son service, et qu'ils sont encore prêts a verser pour Elle tout ce qu'il leur en reste. Les Ecclesiastiques prieront, les laiques combattront.

ETAT PRESENT DU COLLEGE DES LOMBARDS

Ce College est à present composé de quatre vingt dix personnes y compris les quatre Proviseurs, le Prefet des Clercs et les domestiques.

Ce grand nombre n'a d'autre ressource fixe pour subsister que dix huit cent livres de Rentes, mais la Providence est infinie.

Quoniam eleemosyna a morte liberat, et ipsa est quae purgat peccata, et facit invenire misericordiam et vitam aeternam. (Tob. xii. 9.)

L'aumone delivre de la mort, et c'est elle qui efface lespechés et qui fait trouver la misericorde et la vie Eternelle. (Tob xii. 9.)

Ceux qui auront la charite de contribuer quelque chose à cette pieuse entreprise auront la bonté de s'addresser à Monsieur l'Abbé de Vaubrun l'un des Superieurs majeurs ; il demeure à l'Hotel d'Estrees, rue de Grenelle, Faubourg St. Germain. Il a deja fait des avances tres considerable pour ce batiment qui coutera plus de 80,000 livres.

Les personnes charitables qui voudront contribuer à cette bonne œuvre pourront aussi s'adresser à Monsieur Bourk, demeurant au Collège des Lombards, Provisour et Procureur du dit College.—*Receuil des pieces*, Mazarin Library, A 15,422, undated. M. Bourk was Provisor from 1728 to 1734.

[1] On one occasion, when some were in arrears, the Econome looked the door of the refectory, and when the priests assembled for supper they found the door shut against them.—*Memoire pour les Pretres*, Arch. Nat., M 147.

junior students. These again may be divided into three classes. Some amongst them had means of their own, and paid a pension; others were supported by burses founded by benefactors; and others again, in the eighteenth century, were supported at the expense of the College.

At the close of the seventeenth and beginning of the eighteenth century the value of a burse was 400 livres. The Maginn Foundation amounted to 2,500 livres, and six students were supported on it. In like manner the annual revenue of the Molony Foundation, made in 1701 for the support of six students at the College of Clermont, and subsequently transferred to the Irish College was 2,500 livres. In some other foundations the amount 400 livres is expressly mentioned. It may be of interest to inquire what such a burse entitled a student to receive. On this point some of the acts of foundation enter into minute details. The terms of the Foundation Bannan are as follows :—

Pour laquelle somme de quatre cent livres, la dite communauté sera obligée, de nourir, chauffer, eclairer, blanchir, entretenir d'habits, de linge de lit, et de livres d'études, dans le dite communante à Paris, et non ailleurs, un etudiant qui sera nommé par qui il sera dit cy-après.

The terms of the Duffy Foundation are no less detailed :—

Les sujets admis en la dite communauto en vertu des presentes, y seront nourris, logés, blanchis, et entretenus d'habits, linge, bas, souliers, livres de classes, generalement de tout ce qui sera necessaire pour un étudiant pendant le cour de ses études, jusqu' et compris la Licence, s'il en est jugé capable ; et jusqu'à ce qu'il ait reçu l'ordre de prêtrise dans le dite communaute.

Again, in the Foundation Farely, it was stipulated :—

Lorsqu'ils auront été reçu dans la dite communauté ; ils y seront nourris comme les autres etudiants, ils y seront entretenus, modestement et honnetement d'habits, linge, et autres hardes : on leur fera blanchir leur linge, et ils seront fournis de livres de classe, papier, encre, et plumes, et généralement tout ce qui sera necessaire pour leur nourriture, leur entretien et leurs études.

In the Foundation O'Keeffe it is laid down that the bursars shall be treated as follows :—

Il leur sera fourni une nourriture saine, viande, pain, boisson, soit vin, ou bière, et en outre ils seront, blanchis, chauffés et entretenus modestement et honnetement d'habits, bas, souliers, chapeaux, linge, livres, papiers, et généralement de tout ce qui leur sera necessaire pour leur nourriture et leurs etudes.

In the Maher Foundation made in the Irish Jesuit College at Poitiers, the terms were these :—

Que, les dits boursiers seront nourris tant en santé qu'en maladie ; et qu'il leur sera fourni tous les ans un habit conforme á leur état et convenable á un prêtre, ainsi que le linge, le chapeau, les souliers, la chandelle, le bois, le blanchissage, et les frais necessaires pour le barbier.[1]

A burse then of the annual value of 400 francs provided for the maintenance of a student for the entire year. At the close of the eighteenth century 400 livres was no longer considered sufficient, and when the Poitiers burses were transferred to Paris the sum allocated for the support of a student was 600 livres.

Besides the bursars there were other students some of whom paid a pension, and some were educated gratis. The amount of the pension, as may be gathered from the following letter of Dr. Kearney (A.D. 1788), was moderate :—

The only method for pensioners [he writes] would be to have them pay a round sum all at once. For a boy who begins his philosophy nothing less than sixty guineas can at present be taken, and one-third more for a boy who would begin his troisième. What I shall call for, then, to be fixed by his Grace of Paris, is that each pensioner shall give, on his arrival here, at once, at least fifty guineas if he begins in philosophy and about seventy if he begins in troisième. Dividing that sum between the number of years they are to spend in the house from the beginning of their classes, they will only have paid at the rate of 200[2] livres yearly.

Other students again were educated gratis. The qualifications necessary to entitle a young man to this privilege, are thus set forth in a letter of Dr. Plunket :—

He [the student] must be of an age not too advanced for troisième, that is fifteen, sixteen, or seventeen, or thereabouts. In this supposition he will be received gratis, as soon as he shall win a premium in the university. Should this happen the first year, he will have nothing at all to pay during the course of his studies. At anyrate Dr. Kelly admits him for ten pounds a year until his application is crowned with the above-mentioned success.[4]

---

[1] *Recueil des ouvrages de M. le President Roland.* Paris, 1783, p. 644.
[2] 200 livres equals about £8.
[3] Cogan's *Diocese of Meath*, vol. iii. pp. 125, 128.
[4] Letter of Dr. Plunket, A.D. 1775. Cogan's *Meath*, vol. iii. p. 7.

The maintenance of students received gratis was derived from pious foundations made for the general purposes of the College and not destined for the exclusive benefit of a particular diocese or family. These details, arid though they are, serve to throw light on the manner in which the education of the Irish clergy was provided for in the eighteenth century They also show that when offerings for Masses became rarer at the approach of the Revolution, and when the price of provisions increased in years of scarcity, it is not to be wondered at, that the two Irish Colleges in Paris suffered severely and contracted debts.[1]

III

Such, from an economic point of view, was the condition of Irish ecclesiastical students in Paris in the seventeenth and eighteenth centuries. Let us now follow these into the schools. The priests usually devoted two years to the study of philosophy, three to theology and one to preparation for pastoral work. The junior clerics, in many cases, began in the grammar classes and then passed on to philosophy and theology. The more talented were allowed to remain for two years after their baccalaureat to prepare for their Licence.

A word, therefore, on the character of the schools frequented by them may not be uninteresting. The first of the university schools frequented by the Irish students was the Collège Montaigu. The students of that College were divided into two categories, viz., the rich, who paid a pension, and the poor, who were supported on the College foundation. The latter formed a community canonically organised. This community was divided into four sections. Each section rose at midnight for a week at a time, in turn, to recite the Divine Office. The other sections rose at 8 a.m. for prayer.

For some years after the foundation of the College the students received no breakfast, but were permitted to take their place amongst the poor at the door of the neighbouring

---

[1] *Irish College in Paris*, 1578-1901, pp. 54, 57.

Carthusian monastery, where they received an alms. At a later period a piece of bread only was given them in the College. Advent was observed as rigorously as Lent, and each Friday throughout the year was a fast-day. The statutes of the College prescribed that the meals should be frugal, and that they were not undeserving of that appellation may be inferred from the menu, which was as follows :—

Les prêtres seuls auront l'usage de vin, mais in petite quantité, c'est á dire, une pinte sera partagée entre trois, et il y aura un quart d'eau. Chacun aura pour entrée la trentième d'un livre du heurre ou des pommes cûites, ou des pruneaux. Cela sera suivi d'une soupe aux legumes sans graisse, avec un demi-hareng ou un œuf á chacun des jeunes ecoliers, et aux theologiens unhareng entier, ou deux œufs, ce qui sera suivi d'un peu de fromage ou fruits. On aura grand soin des malades. On leur permettra l'usage de la viande, mais avant toutes choses, en entrant á l'infirmaire ils se confesseront.

The rigorous discipline of the Montaigu College was celebrated, and parents used to bring their refractory children to a sense of their duty by threatening to send them to that establishment.[1]

This *régime* continued until 1683, when an effort was made to mitigate its severity, but without success. In 1744 the Parliament of Paris interfered, and dispensed the students from rising at night for the recitation of the Office, and authorised the use of flesh meat.

The earliest batch of Irish students, with Rev. John Lee at their head, entered this College in 1578, and so late as 1681 many Irishmen continued to attend it for lectures. It is worthy of mention that an Irishman, Rev. Richard Ferris, was Econome of the Collège Montaigu in 1789. The Marquis Lally Tollendal, in a confidential note to the Minister of the Interior in 1811, in which he recommends the appointment

---

[1] The author of *Gargantua* thus satirises it: ' Ne pensez pas que j'ai mis mon fils au collège qu'on nomme Montagut. Mieux l'eusse voulu le mettre entre les guenaux des saints Innocents pour l'enorme cruauté que j'y cognu (connu). Car trop (beaucoup) mieux sont traités les forcés (forcats) entre les Maures et les Tartares, les meurtriers en la maison criminelle, voire certes les chiens en votre maison que ne sont ces malotrus au dit collège : et si j'etais roi de Paris, le diable m'emporte, si je ne mettrais le feu dedans et ferais bruler et principal et regent qui endurent cette inhumanite devant leur yeux.— Rabelais, *Gargantua*. Apud de Gaulle, *Hist. de Paris*, etc., vol. il., p. 429.

of Dr. Ferris as Superior of the Irish College, thus enumerates his qualifications : 'Doctor of the Sorbonne, Licentiate of Laws, Advocate in Parliament, Promoter-General of the Diocese and Deputy of the Clergy of Amiens, Procurator of the Nation d'Allemagne, Member of the Tribunal of the University, and Procurator Syndic for life at the College of Montaigu.'   He adds that Dr. Ferris had refused to take the constitutional oath, and had been deprived in consequence of his office as Econome.

Another college frequented by Irish students was that of Boncour, where Dr. Molony, of Killaloe, was professor in the early years of the seventeenth century. The College of Boncour was distinguished for its discipline, the course of studies extended over seven years, and the sermons addressed to the students were delivered in the Latin language.

During the seventeenth and eighteenth centuries the Irish priests of the Lombard College attended the Collège des Grassins for lectures in Philosophy. In a former paper[1] an account has been given of that ancient establishment and of the connexion of Irishmen with it. About 1708 its financial position became embarrassed, but a member of the family of the founder came to its aid. Its former prosperity was restored, and it continued to flourish until it perished with the University itself in 1793.

The junior clerics attended lectures in Classics and Philosophy at the College of Plessis, otherwise called Plessis-Sorbonne. Its discipline and the merit of its professors earned for that College a high rank in the University. It sustained, says De Gaulle,[2] its reputation to the end, and there was no College in the University in which scholastic discipline was better observed, or which produced a greater number of distinguished men.

Besides the colleges just mentioned, Irishmen also frequented the College of Navarre. According to the author just cited, of all the University establishments, the College of Navarre had the most complete course of studies,

[1] I. E. RECORD, Nov., 1901.   [2] Hist. de Paris, vol. ii., pp. 436-37.

comprising the Humanities, Philosophy, and Theology. It was styled the 'Ecole de la noblesse française et l'honneur de l'Universite.' With none of the University Colleges were Irishmen more intimately connected. Dr. Michael Moore, who had already been professor there, became its Principal in 1702. Rev. James Wogan was Professor of Philosophy at Navarre in 1730. There, too, Rev. John Plunkett was Professor of Theology in 1740. Dr. Patrick Plunkett held the same chair in 1782, and Rev. Peter Flood in 1789.[1]

Amid such surroundings Irishmen made their studies. Their success in the schools is testified to by the degrees which they won, and the professorships to which some of them were promoted. Even French satirists, by their reference to Irish dialectic skill, pay a tribute to their reputation in the schools. Elsewhere we have quoted the verses of Santeul, and of Rulhieres.[2] Lesage, too, and Montesquieu mention them. The former puts the following words into the mouth of one of his heroes :—

Jè m'appliquai á la logique qui m'apprit á raisonner beaucoup. J'aimais tant la dispute que j'arretais les passans connus et inconnus pour leur poser des arguments. Je m'adressais quelquefois á des figures hibernoises, qui ne demandaient pas mieux ; et il fallait alors nous voir disputer. Quels gestes, quelles grimaces, quelles contortions. Nos yeux etaient pleins de fureur et nos bouches ecumantes, on nous devoit plutot prendre pour des possidés que pour des philosophes.[3]

In his edition of Lesage, in 1825, M. le Comte de Chateauneuf thus refers to this passage :—

C'etait surtout á Paris que l'on rencontrait ces figures hibernoiscs, venus d'Irlande avec le Roi Jacques Stuart, et signalées aussi dans les lettres persanes. Quand Lesage les place á Oviedo, c'est une première preuve qui si le lieu de la scène est en Espagne, l'original des tableaux est le plus- souvent en France.[4]

---

[1] Dr. Flood, Dr. Aherne, and Dr. Plunkett, Professor Emeritus, professors at Navarre ; Dr. Ferris, Procurator at the Montaigu College, and MacMahon, Professor at Louis le Grand, refused the Constitutional oath in 1789, and were deprived of their position. On the list of University Professors, who acted in the same way the names Delahogue and Anglade occur.—Jourdain, *Hist. de l'Univer*, ed. 1866. vol. i., p. 486.

[2] *Irish College in Paris*, 1578-1901. pp. xi.-18.

[3] Le Sage, *Gil Blas*, liv. i., c. i., p. 7.　　[4] Loc. cit.

Montesquieu above alluded to, speaks thus :—

Il y a des quartiers ou l'on voit comme une melée noire et epaisse de ces sortes de gens . . Ils se nourrissent de distinctions. Ils vivent de raisonments obscurs et fausses consequences. Ce metier où l'on devrait mourir de faim ne laisse pas de rendre. On a vu une nation entière chasée de son pays, traverser les mers pour s'etablir en France, n'emportant avec elle pour parer aux necessités de la vie, qu'un redoutable talent pour la dispute.[1]

IV

But how, it may be asked, did they spend their vacations? Here we have no data to guide us. Only in 1769 do we find mention of a country house. At that date Dr. Kelly purchased a house and garden at Ivry, which from that period to the outbreak of the Revolution served as a vacation residence for students and professors. To this residence Dr. Marky thus refers in a letter to Dr. Plunket, dated 9th August, 1779 :—

Flood is in a fair way to finish himself—and so intent is he upon it, that he chooses rather to stay vegetating and poring over his books in Paris, than spend the vacation with us at Ivry, where he might certainly read as much as any reasonable pounder would desire. . . . Our garden has done its duty extremely well. We have plenty of fruit. The melons have succeeded tolerably.[2]

The Superiors themselves seldom returned to Ireland. Father Donlevy mentions that in 1742 he had been absent from his native country for over thirty-one years. They generally spent their vacations in France, and strange as it may seem to those of the present day it was considered a restorative in illness to go to take the waters at Passy.

When the course of studies was completed the young priests were obliged to return to the mission in Ireland. In the seventeenth, and in the earlier years of the eighteenth century, the homeward journey was beset with dangers' Priests landing in Ireland were liable to imprisonment and to banishment. Even at the close of the eighteenth century there remained the fatigue and inconvenience of the journey. The expense too was not inconsiderable. But

---

[1] Lettre 36.
[2] Cogan, *Hist. of the Diocese of Meath*, vol. iii., p. 16.
[3] *Irish College in Paris*, 1578-1901, p.p. 21-44.

provision for this was made in the case of some. Thus to the the M'Mahon bursars fifty livres, to the Farely bursars three hundred livres and to the O'Keefe bursars a competent sum was assigned by the terms of those foundations for that purpose.

V

Having seen what was the condition of the students let us now proceed to consider what was the status of the Superiors of the College.

By the statutes of the Lombard College the Superiors were required to be graduates of the University of Paris. This qualification was so indispensable that in 1716, the Rector of the University having learned that the students of the Province of Munster purposed to elect as their Provisor a priest who was not a graduate, issued a mandate forbidding them to elect anyone who was not at least a Master of Arts in the University. The mandate was obeyed, and the Abbé Fogarty, Doctor of Theology, was elected provisor for Munster.[1]

Being graduates, the Superiors were members of the Nation d' Allemagne, and as such took part in the affairs of the University. Many of them filled the office of Procurator of that Nation; and in that capacity they had a vote in the election of the Rector of the University. One of the most interesting and important of the Rectorial elections was that held in 1739, in which the Abbé Pierre Armand Rohan de Ventadour was elected. The youthful and noble Rector succeeded at a critical moment in inducing the University to withdraw its appeal and accept the Bull Unigenitus. One of the four electors on this occasion was Dr. Farely,[2] Principal of the Lombard College. After 1730 the University registers of the Nation d'Allemagne are missing, and from that period it is more difficult to give a full list of Irish Procurators. But many Irishmen continued to hold that office down to 1790, nor was there any drawing off from the University either on the part of the Superiors or the students until the University ceased to exist.

But what, it may be asked, was the income of the Provisors?

---

[1] Jourdain, *Hist. de l'Université de Paris.* Ed. 1866: vol. i., p. 319.
[2] Jourdain, *ibid.,* vol. i. p. 368. There were two of the name. Dr. Farley, senior, died in 1736.

Here we have no very precise documents to guide us. The first Provisors, Dr. Maginn and Dr. Kelly, were benefactors rather than salaried officers of the College. In his *Notes Confidentielles* to the Minister of the Interior, Lally Tollendal states that the salaries of the Superiors of the College previous to the Revolution, did not exceed 400 livres. No doubt they had board and lodging and Mass stipends. In some cases, too, the founders of burses assigned an annual sum of 50 or 60 or 100 livres to the Provisor under whose care a burse was placed to indemnify him for the expense and trouble of administration.

But while filling the office of Provisor, some of the Superiors held professorships in the University. Dr. Plunket, for instance, and Dr. Flood, were Royal Professors of Theology in the College of Navarre. When established in 1659 by Louis XIV. the salary of the Royal professorship at that College was fixed at 900 livres, and soon after it was increased to 1,000 livres.

In the faculty of Arts, as we learn from Jourdain,[1] that at the end of the eighteenth century, the salary of a professor of Philosophy or Rhetoric from all sources was 2,400 francs, that of a professor of troisième 2,200 francs, and of a professor of quatrième and cinquième 2,000 francs. After twenty years service they were entitled to retire with a pension of 1,400 francs. A supplement of 300 was granted to the twenty senior *emeriti.* The salary of a professor of Theology in the University Colleges at the same period was probably equal to that of a professor of Philosophy.

Outside college and university life the Superiors of the Irish College were not without acquaintances. Some amongst them had relatives amongst the officers of the Irish Brigade, and some of them like Dr. Maginn and Dr. Kelly were known at Court. Just at the outbreak of the Revolution the Abbé O'Brien, one of the officials of the College, held the office of chaplain at one of the country houses of the King's brother. Others were favourably known to members of the French Episcopate. The Abbé Kearney before his appointment as Superior of the College had been

---

[1] *Hist. de l'Université,* ed. 1866, vol. i, p. 474.

nominated Vicar-General of the diocese of Tarbes, and Dr. Walsh was for some time Vicar-General of Clermont in the early years of the nineteenth century. The Superiors, therefore, though not affluent, occupied a position of influence and honour.

But to one of them, Dr. Charles Kearney, more than a passing notice is due. Charles Kearney entered the College as a boy in 1762. In 1772 his name occurs amongst the signatories of the deed of Donation by Dr. Kelly. He was then a sub-deacon. At a latter period he took his degree, and in 1783 he was appointed Superior of the Collège rue de Cheval Vert. We have elsewhere given some account of the administration of Dr. Kearney.[1] To the confidential report above mentioned of the Marquis Lally Tollendal to the Minister of the Interior, dated 12th March, 1811, we are indebted for additional interesting information regarding him.

Dr. Kearney, says the Marquis, could not see anyone in distress without opening his purse to relieve him, and when his own was empty that of the College. During the Revolution he permitted Frenchmen to deposit their title deeds in the College as being a place under the protection of International Law. He also provided many British subjects with means to escape from Paris and thus save their lives. Moreover he was associated with M. Gavroi, the Abbé Edgeworth, M. de Vauvilliers, and M. Swinburne, first page of the Queen, in a plan for the escape of Louis XVI.[2] A vessel was engaged, and in readiness at Havre, to take the King to England; a boat was waiting on the Seine to bring him to Havre. But Louis would not consent to depart without the Queen. It was found impossible to contrive means for the evasion of both together, and in consequence the project was abandoned.

---

[1] *The Irish College in Paris*, 1578-1901, pp. 56-67.

[2] Il ne pouvait voir un être souffrant sans lui ouvrir sa bourse, et quand elle etait vide celle du college. Il avait concouru avec M. Garvoi, l'Abbé Edgeworth, M. de Vauvilliers, M. Swinburne, primier page de la Reine, et autres à unprojet d'evasion pour l'infortuné Louis XVI. Le vaisseau etait acheté et en panne au Havre, la barque qui devait y conduire a longtemps attendu la funeste indecision et le plus funeste refus de ce trop malheureux Prince. On ne pouvait, on ne voulait se charger que du Roi seul, et le Roi ne voulait partir sans la Reine.—Notes Confidentielles de Lally Tollendal, sur l'administration des collèges irlandais, anglais et ecossais; reunis dans tout Empire francais, aux Arch. Nat. H³. 2561.

Meanwhile Dr. Kearney continued to reside at the College. On 12th August, 1792, a band of men armed with clubs, sabres, and muskets, broke into the College, the students saved themselves by leaping over the walls into the neighbouring gardens and streets. The cry, 'Seize the Citizen Kearney, alive or dead,' resounded on all sides. Dr. Kearney, however, succeeded in making his escape. About this time the papers and other property of the Superiors of the College were put under seals by the Revolutionary Government. But a mob, headed by Truchon, surnamed Longuebarbe, broke into the College, snatched the keys from the official in charge of the seals, and ransaked the whole house. Dr. Kearney again returned, and Mass continued to be said in the College until 17th May, 1793. Soon after that date Dr. Kearney was arrested and cast into prison. He was tried by a Revolutionary tribunal. Amongst the documents produced against him one was a letter from an English colonel, referring to the part Dr. Kearney had taken in the plan for the escape of Louis XVI. to England; another was a letter from the Duke of FitzJames, thanking him for the aid he had given to British subjects, whereby they were enabled to save their lives and escape to their native country. He was detained in prison for three years, partly at the Luxembourg, and partly in the Temple. Of that period he spent thirty-six days in a *cachot* or dongeon, whence he was told he would come forth only to be led to the scaffold. When all hope seemed lost, his liberation came from a quarter whence it was to be least expected. Years before he had befriended Camille Desmoulins, then a poor student at the Collège Louis Legrand. Learning that his former benefactor was in danger Camille Desmoulins interfered in his behalf, saved him from the scaffold, and restored him to liberty.

On his return to the College, Dr. Kearney let it for a period of nine years to the Abbé M'Dermott, while he

---

[1] These facts are given by Lally Tollendal as taken from the ' declarations authentiques du guardien des scellés, du commissaire du police, des maires adjoints de l'arrondissement.'

himself continued to reside in Paris, and supported himself by giving lessons.

After the Peace of Amiens Dr. Walsh was appointed Administrator of the Irish Foundations. He obliged the Abbé M'Dermott to give up possession of the College, and opened it to students under his own management. Dr. Kearney remained in Paris, where he was befriended by many, and amongst his benefactors was the Queen of Holland. In 1820 he was again appointed Rector of the College, and held that office until his death in 1824. His funeral obsequies were celebrated in the College. Many French ladies and gentlemen, whom he had befriended during the Revolution, assisted at the ceremony, after which he was laid to rest in the vault beneath the chapel, along with Dr. Laurence Kelly, Dr. Michael Cahill, and Rev. Donal M'Mahon.

In bringing these remarks and papers to a close one may be permitted to apply to him the concluding words of the panegyric of Dr. Michael Moore :—

Supersedeo, plura dicere, satis non deseruisse quidem, sed delimasse me arbitror qualis in vos fuerit venerabilis senex, ut nostri muneris fuisse censeatur, hos qualescumque flores ejus sepulchro injicere, et piis Rectorii viri manibus pacem aeternam adprecari.[2]

PATRICK BOYLE, C.M.

[1] Summarised from the *Notes Confidentielles* of Lally Tollendal.
[2] From the oration of M. Delaval on Dr. Moore, Paris, 1726, Regist. 40 de la Nation d'Allemagne.

ϻotes anὸ Queries

LITURGY

MAY CANDIDATES VALIDLY INVEST THEMSELVES WITH SCAPULAR?

Rev. Dear Sir,—A question has been raised by one of the fathers engaged here in giving a mission, as to the conditions of valid investiture in the Confraternity of Our Lady of Mount Carmel. The father thinks that he read in the I. E. Record some time within the years 1894-98, a decision that the priest who receives into the confraternity may validly invest with the scapular, by simply getting the candidates to put on the scapular themselves after (that is) he has blessed the scapulars and read the other required prayers. The negative of this opinion finds more favour with the rest of the fathers, who think that the priest must *invest* each candidate *individually*.

His reverence has requested me to write direct to the editor of the I. E. Record. T. C.

We cannot find in any number of the I. E. Record the decision referred to. There are two articles on the subject of scapulars—one in the number of September, 1890, page 845, and the other in that of October, 1901, page 311. In both of these articles it is supposed that the investiture must be performed by the *hand of the priest*, though the question of the validity of the other mode of investiture is not expressly raised. Beringer also[1] has : ' Ensuite on en impose un a chaque fidèle en particulier,' etc. The same author, in another place,[2] does expressly raise the question of the validity of the investiture described by our correspondent and decides against it, except there be a special Apostolic Indult authorizing it :—

' Enfin en ce qui concerne la reponse du General des Carmes

---

[1] Vol. i., p. 398, k.   [2] Vol. ii., Append. 11, p. 31.

. . . elle n'a nul rapport avec la question presente (de la formule au pluriel) : elle regarde les cas où l'on distribuait d'abord les scapulaires à tous et où l'on recitait ensuite la formule d'imposition au pluriel, pendant que *chacun s'imposait le scapulaire à lui-même.* Le General des Carmes avait bien raison de dire que de telles impositions *sont nulles et de nulle valeur,* si l'on n'a point un indult spécial de Rome.'

It is plain that the invalidity arises from the self-investiture and not from the use of the plural form, because, at the end of the same page the author holds most distinctly the validity of the plural form :—

' Il n'est donc plus possible de révoquer en donte la validite et la licéité de l'imposition du scapulaire à plusieurs personnes, en récitant une seule fois la formule au pluriel.'

We are not aware of any recent decision opposed to this teaching.

P. O'LEARY.

DOCUMENTS

ENCYCLICAL OF HIS HOLINESS POPE LEO XIII.[1]

EX ACTIS LEONIS XIII. ET E SECRETAR. BREVIUM
LEO XIII, INEUNTE 25 ANNO AB INCOEPTO S. PONTIFICATU, DESCRIBIT
PERSECUTIONES OLIM ET NUNC CONTRA ECCLESIAM EXORTAS, EX
QUIBUS QUAMPLURIMA MALA EXSURGUNT IN CIVILI SOCIETATE,
ETC.

LETTRE APOSTOLIQUE DE SA SAINTETÉ LE PAPE LÉON XIII À TOUS
LES PATRIARCHES, PRIMATS, ARCHEVÊQUES ET EVÊQUES DU
MONDE CATHOLIQUE

LÉON XIII PAPE

VÉNÉRABLES FRÈRES SALUT ET BÉNÉDICTION APOSTOLIQUE.

Parvenu à la vingt-cinquième année de Notre Ministère apostolique, et étonné Nous-même de la longueur du chemin qu'au milieu d'âpres et continuels soucis Nous avons parcouru, Nous Nous sentons tout naturellement porté à élever Notre pensée vers le Dieu à jamais béni, qui, parmi tant d'autres faveurs a bien voulu Nous accorder un Pontificat d'une durée telle qu'on en rencontre à peine quelques-uns de pareils dans l'histoire. C'est donc vers le Père de tous les hommes, vers Celui qui tient dans ses mains le mystérieux secret de la vie, que s'élance, comme un impérieux besoin de Notre cœur, l'hymne de Notre action de grâces. Assurément, l'œil do l'homme ne peut pas sonder toute la profondeur des desseins de Dieu, lorsqu'il a ainsi prolongé au delà de toute espérance notre vieillesse ; et ici Nous ne pouvons que Nous taire et l'adorer. Mais il y a pourtant une chose que Nous savons bien, c'est que s'il Lui a plu, et s'il Lui plaît de conserver encore Notre existence, un grand devoir Nous incombe : vivre pour le bien et le développement de son Epouse immaculée, la Sainte Eglise, et, loin de perdre courage en face des soucis et des peines, lui consacrer le restant de Nos forces jusqu'à Notre dernier soupir.

Après avoir payé le tribut d'une juste reconnaissance à notre

---

[1 This Encyclical was not composed in Latin, but was issued simultaneously in Italian and in French. We give the French official text.—ED. I. E. RECORD.]

Père céleste, à qui soient honneur et gloire pendant toute l'éternité, il Nous est très agréable de revenir vers vous par la pensée et de vous adresser la parole, à vous, Vénérables Frères, qui, appelés par l'Esprit Saint à gouverner des portions choisies du troupeau de Jésus-Christ, participez par cela même avec Nous aux luttes et aux triomphes, aux douleurs et aux joies du ministère des Pasteurs. Non, elles ne s'évanouiront jamais de Notre mémoire, les nombreuses et remarquables preuves de religieuse vénération que vous Nous avez prodiguées au cours de Notre Pontificat, et que vous multipliez encore avec une émulation pleine de tendresse dans les circonstances présentes. Intimement uni à vous déjà par Notre devoir et par Notre amour paternel, ces témoignages de votre dévouement, extrêmement chers à Notre cœur, Nous y ont attaché encore, moins pour ce qu' ils avaient de personnel en ce qui Nous regarde, que pour l'attachement inviolable qu'ils dénotaient à ce Siège Apostolique, centre et soutien de tous les autres sièges de la catholicité. S' il a toujours été nécessaire qu'aux divers degrés de la hiérarchie ecclésiastique tous les enfants de l'Eglise se tinssent jalousement unis dans les liens d'une charité réciproque et dans la poursuite des mêmes desseins, de manière à ne former qu'un cœur et qu' une âme, cette union est devenue de nos temps plus indispensable que jamais. Qui peut ignorer en effet l'immense conjuration de forces hostiles qui vise aujourd'hui à ruiner et à faire disparaître la grande œuvre de Jésus-Christ, en essayant, avec un acharnement que ne connaît plus de limites, dans l'ordre intellectuel, de ravir à l' homme le trésor des vérités célestes, et, dans l'ordre social, de déraciner les plus saintes, les plus salutaires institutions chrétiennes ? Mais tout cela, vous en êtes, vous-mêmes, frappés, tous les jours, vous qui Nous avez plus d'une fois exprimé vos préoccupations et vos angoisses, en déplorant la multitude de préjugés, de faux systèmes et d' erreurs qu'on sème impunément au milieu des foules. Que de pièges ne tend-on point de tous côtés aux âmes croyantes ? Que d'obstacles ne multiplie-t-on pas pour affaiblir et, autant que possible, pour annihiler la bienfaisante action de l'Eglise ? Et, en attendant, comme pour ajouter la dérision à l'injustice, c'est l' Eglise elle-même qu' on accuse de ne pas savoir recouvrer sa vertu antique, et d'être impuissante à endiguer le torrent de passions débordées qui menace de tout emporter !

Nous voudrions bien vous entretenir, Vénérables Frères, d'un sujet moins triste et qui fût en harmonie plus grande avec

l'heureuse circonstance qui Nous incline à vous parler. Mais rien
ne comporte un pareil langage, ni les graves épreuves de l'Eglise,
qui appellent avec instance un prompt secours, ni les conditions
de la société contemporaine qui, déjà fortement travaillée au point
de vue moral et matériel, s'achemine vers des destinées encore
pires par l'abandon des grandes traditions chrétiennes : une loi de
la Providence, confirmée par l'histoire, prouvant qu'on ne peut
pas porter atteinte aux grands principes religieux, sans ébranler
en même temps les bases de l'ordre et de la prospérité sociale.
Dans ces circonstances, pour permettre aux âmes de reprendre
haleine, pour les réapprovisionner de foi et de courage, il Nous
paraît opportun et utile de considérer attentivement, dans son
origine, dans ses causes, dans ses formes multiples, l'implacable
guerre, que l'on fait à l'Eglise, et, en dénonçant les funestes
conséquences, d'en assigner les remèdes. Que Notre parole résonne
donc bien haut, quoiqu'elle doive rappeler des vérités affirmées
d'autres fois déjà ; qu'elle soit entendue non seulement par les fils
de l'unité catholique, mais encore par les fils de l'unité catholique,
mais encore par les dissidents et même par les infortunés qui
n'ont plus la foi ; car ils sont tous enfants du même Père, tous
destinés au même bien suprême, qu'elle soit accueillie enfin comme
le testament qu' à la faible distance où Nous sommes des portes
de l'éternité Nous voulons laisser aux peuples comme un présage
du salut que Nous désirons pour tous.

De tout temps, la Sainte Eglise du Christ a eu à combattre et
à souffrir pour la vérité et pour la justice. Instituée par le divin
Rédempteur lui-même pour propager dans le monde le règne de
Dieu, elle doit conduire, aux clartés de la loi évangélique, l'humanité
déchue vers ses immortelles destinées c'est-à-dire la faire entrer en
possession des biens sans fin que Dieu nous a promis, à la hauteur
desquels, nos seules forces ne nous permettent pas de monter :
céleste mission dans l'accomplissement de laquelle elle ne pouvait
que se heurter aux innombrables passions reçues de l'antique
déchéance et de la corruption qu'elle a engendrée, orgueil, cupidité,
amour effréné des jouissances matérielles, vices et désordres qui
en découlent et qui ont tous rencontré dans l'Eglise le frein le
plus puissant.

Le fait de ces persécutions ne doit pas nous étonner ; ne nous
ont elles pas été prédites par le Divin Maître et ne savons-nous
pas qu'elles dureront autant que le monde ? Que dit en effet le
Sauveur à ses disciples, lorsqu'il les envoya porter le trésor de sa

doctrine à toutes les nations ? Personne ne l'ignore : 'Vous serez poursuivis de ville en ville, à cause de mon nom, vous serez haïs, méprisés, vous serez traduits devant les tribunaux et condamnés aux derniers des châtiments.' Et pour les encourager à supporter de telles épreuves il se donna lui-même en example : ' Si le monde vous hait, sachez qu'il m'a haï avant vous, tout le premier.' *Si mundus vos odit, scitote quia me priorem vobis odio habuit.*[1] Voilà les joies, voilà les récompenses qu'ici-bas le Divin Sauveur nous promet.

Quiconque juge sainement et simplement des choses ne pourra jamais découvrir la raison d'une pareille haine. Qui donc le divin Redempteur avait-il jamais offensé, ou en quoi avait-il démérité ? Descendu sur cette terre sous l'impulsion d'une charité infinie, Il y avait enseigné une doctrine sans tache, consolatrice et on ne peut mieux faite pour unir fraternellement tous les hommes dans la paix et dans l'amour. Il n'avait convoité ni les grandeurs de ce monde, ni ses honneurs et n'avait usurpé sur le droit de personne : bien au contraire, on l'avait vu infiniment compatissant pour les faibles, pour les malades, pour les pauvres, pour les pécheurs et pour les opprimés ; en sorte qu'Il n'avait passé dans la vie que pour semer á pleines mains parmi les hommes ses divins bienfaits. Ce fut donc un pur excès de malice de la part de ces hommes, excés d'autant plus lamentable qu'il était plus injuste, et suivant la prophétie de Siméon, le Sauveur devint le signe de la contradiction sur cette terre *Signum cui contradicetur.*[2]

Faut-il s'étonner dès lors si l'Eglise catholique qui est la continuatrice de la mission divine de Jésus-Christ et l'incorruptible gardienne de sa vérité, n'a pas pu échapper au sort du Maître ? Le monde ne change pas ; à côté des enfants de Dieu, se trouvent toujours les séides du grand ennemi du genre humain, de celui qui, rebelle au Très-Haut dès le principe, est appelé dans l'Evangile la prince de ce monde. Et voilà pourquoi, en face de la loi divine et de qui la lui présente au nom de Dieu, ce monde sent bouillonner et se soulever en lui, dans un orgueil sans mesure, un esprit d'indépendance auquel il n'a aucun droit ! Ah ! que de fois, avec une cruauté inouïe, avec une impudente injustice et pour la perte évidente de toute la société, que de fois, dans les époques les plus agitées, les ennemis de l'Eglise ne se sont-ils pas formés en colonnes profondes pour renverser l'œuvre divine !

---

[1] Io. xv. 18.   [2] Luc. ii. 34.

Un genre de persécution restait il sans succès ? ils essayaient d'un autre. Pendant trois grands siècles, l'Empire romain, abusant de la force brutale, parsema toutes ses provinces des cadavres de nos martyrs et empourpra de leur sang chacune des mottes de terre de cette ville sacrée. Puis l'hérésie, tantôt sous un masque et tantôt le visage à découvert, recourut aux sophismes et à des artifices perfides, afin de briser l'harmonie de l'Eglise et son unité. Comme une tempête dévastatrice, se déchaînèrent ensuite, du nord les barbares, et du midi l'Islamisme, laissant partout derrière elle des ruines dans un immense désert. Ainsi se transmettait de siècle en siècle le triste héritage de haine sous lequel l'Epouse du Christ était accablée. Alors vint un césarisme, soupçonneux autant que puissant, jaloux de la grandeur d'autrui, quelque développement qu'il eut d'ailleurs donné à la sienne, et qui se reprit à livrer d'incessants assauts à l'Eglise pour faire main basse sur ses droits et pour fouler aux pieds sa liberté. Le cœur saigne à voir cette Mère si sovent assiégée par les angoisses et par d'inexprimables douleurs ! Cependant, triomphant de tous les obstacles, de toutes les violences et de toutes les tyrannies, elle plantait toujours, de plus en plus largement ses tentes pacifiques, elle sauvait du désastre le glorieux patrimoine des arts, de l'histoire, des sciences et des lettres, et, en faisant, pénétrer profondément l'esprit de l'Evangile dans toute l'étendue du corps social, elle créait de toutes pièces la civilisation chrétienne, cette civilisation à qui les peuples, soumis à sa bienfaisante influence, doivent l'équité des lois, la douceur des mœurs, la protection des faibles, la piété pour les pauvres et pour les malheureux, le respect des droits et de la dignité de tous les hommes et, par là même, autant du moins que cela est possible au milieu des fluctuations humaines, ce calme dans la vie sociale qui dérive d'un accord sage entre la justice et la liberte.

Ces preuves de la bonté intrinsèque de l'Eglise sont aussi éclatantes et sublimes qu'elles ont eu de durée. Et cependant, comme au moyen-âge et durant les premiers siècles, dans des temps plus voisins du nôtre, nous voyons cette Eglise assaillie, d'une certaine façon au moins, plus durement et plus douloureusement que jamais. Par suite d'une série de causes historiques bien connues, la prétendue Réforme leva au XVIᵉ siècle l'étendard de la révolte, et, résolue à frapper l'Eglise en plein cœur, elle s'en prit audacieusement à la Papauté ; elle rompit le lien si précieux de foi et d'autorité, qui, centuplant bien souvent la force, le

prestige, la gloire, grâce à la poursuite harmonieuse des mêmes
desseins, réunissait tous les peuples sous une seule houlette et un
seul pasteur, et elle introduisait ainsi dans les rangs chrétiens un
principe funeste de lamentable désagrégation.

Ce n' est pas que Nous prétendions affirmer par là que dès le
début même du mouvement on eût en vue de bannir le principe
du christianisme du sein de la société ; mais, en refusant d'une
part de reconnaître la suprématie due Siège de Rome, cause
effective et lien de l'unité, et en proclamant de l'autre le principe
du libre examen, on ébranlait, jusque dans ses derniers fonde-
ments, le divin édifice et on ouvrait la voie à des variations
infinies, aux doutes et aux négations sur les matières les plus
importantes, si bien que les prévisions des novateurs eux-mêmes
furent dépassées.

Le chemin était ouvert : alors surgit le philosophisme orgueil-
leux et railleur du XVIII° siècle, et il va plus loin. Il tourne en
dérision le recueil sacré des Ecritures et rejette en bloc toutes les
vérités divinement révélées, dans le but d' en arriver finalement
à déraciner de la conscience des peuples toute croyance religieuse
et à y étouffer jusqu'au dernier souffle l' esprit chrétien. C' est
de cette source que découlèrent le rationalisme et le panthéisme,
le naturalisme et le matérialisme ; systèmes funestes et délétères
qui réinstaurèrent, sous de nouvelles apparences, des erreurs
antiques déjà victorieusement réfutées par les Pères et par les
Docteurs de l'Eglise, en sorte que l'orgueil des siècles modernes,
par un excès de confiance dans ses propres lumières, fut frappé de
cécité et, comme le paganisme, ne se nourrit plus que de rêveries,
même en ce qui concerne les attributs de l'âme humaine et les
immortelles destinées qui constituent son privilège glorieux.

La lutte contre l'Eglise prenait ainsi un caractère de gravité
plus grande que par le passé, non moins à cause de la véhémence
des attaques qu'à cause de leur universalité. L' incrédulité contemporaine ne se borne pas en effet à révoquer en doute ou à nier
telle ou telle vérité de foi. Ce qu'elle combat, c'est l' ensemble
même des principes que la révélation consacre et que la vraie
philosophie soutient ; principes fondamentaux et sacrés qui
apprennent à l'homme le but suprême de son passage dans la vie,
qui le maintiennent dans le devoir, qui versent dans son âme le
courage et la résignation et qui, en lui promettant une incorruptible
justice et une félicité parfaite au delà de la tombe, le forment à
subordonner le temps à l' éternité, la terre au ciel. Or, que

mettait-on à la place de ces préceptes, réconforts incomparables fournis par la foi ! Un effroyable scepticisme qui glace les cœurs et qui étouffe dans la conscience toutes les aspirations magnanimes.

Des doctrines aussi funestes n'ont que trop passé comme vous le voyez, ô Vénérables Frères, du domaine des idées dans la vie extérieure et dans les sphères publiques. De grands et puissants états vont sans cesse les traduisant dans la pratique, et ils s'imaginent ainsi faire œuvre de civilisation et prendre la tête du progrès. Et, comme si les pouvoirs publics ne devaient pas ramasser en eux-mêmes et refléter tout ce qu'il y a de plus sain dans la vie morale ils se sont tenus pour affranchis du devoir d'honorer Dieu publiquement, et il n'advient que trop souvent qu'en se vantant de rester indifférents en face de toutes les religions, de fait ils font la guerre à la seule religion instituée par Dieu.

Ce système d'athéisme pratique devait nécessairement jeter, et de fait a jeté une perturbation profonde dans le domaine de la morale ; car, ainsi que l'ont entrevu les sages les plus fameux de l'antiquité païenne, la religion est le fondement principal de la justice et de la vertu. Quand on rompt les liens qui unissent l'homme à Dieu, Législateur souverain et Juge universel, il ne reste plus qu'un fantôme de morale : morale purement civile, ou, comme on l'appelle, indépendante, qui, faisant abstraction de toute raison éternelle et des lois divines, nous entraîne inévitablement et par une pente fatale à cette conséquence dernière d'assigner l'homme à l'homme comme sa propre loi. Incapable dès lors de s'élever sur les ailes de l'espérance chrétienne jusque vers les biens supérieurs, cet homme ne cherche plus qu'un aliment matériel dans l'ensemble des jouissances et des commodités de la vie ; en lui s'allument la soif des plaisirs, la cupidité des richesses, l'âpre désir des gains rapides et sans mesure, doive la justice en souffrir ; en lui s'enflamment en même temps toutes les ambitions et je ne sais quelle avidité fiévreuse et frénétique de les satisfaire, même d'une manière illégitime ; en lui enfin s'établissent en maîtres le mépris des lois et de l'autorité publique et une licence de mœurs qui, en devenant générale, entraîne avec soi un véritable déclin de la société.

Mais peut-être, exagérons-nous les tristes conséquences des troubles douloureux dont nous parlons ? Non, car la réalité est là, à notre portée et elle ne confirme que trop nos deductions. Il est manifeste en effet que, si on ne les raffermit pas au plus tôt les bases mêmes de la société vont chanceler et qu' elles entraîneront dans leur chute les grands principes du droit et de la morale éternelle.

C'est de là que proviennent les graves préjudices qu' ont eu à souffrir toutes les parties du corps social à commencer par la famille. Car, l' état laïque, sans se souvenir de ses limites, ni du but essentiel de l' autorité qu' il détient, a porté la main sur le lien conjugal pour le profaner, en le dépouillant de son caractère religieux ; il a entrepris autant qu' il le pouvait sur le droit naturel qu' ont les parents en ce qui concerne l' éducation des enfants ; et dans plusieurs endroits, il a détruit la stabilité du mariage, en donnant à la licencieuse institution du divorce une sanction légale. Or, chacun sait les fruits que ces empiétements ont protés : ils ont multiplié au delà de toute expression des marriages ébauchés seulement par de honteuses passions et par suite se dissolvant à bref délai, ou dégénérant, tantôt en luttes tragiques, tantôt en scandaleuses infidélités ! Et Nous ne disons rein des enfants, innocente descendance qu'on néglige, ou qui se pervertit, ici au spectacle des mauvais exemples des parents, et là sous l'effet du poison que l'état, devenu officiellement laïque, lui verse tous les jours.

Avec la famille l'ordre social et politique est, lui aussi, mis en danger, surtout pas les doctrines nouvelles, qui, assignant à la souveraineté une fausse origine, en ont corrompu par là même la véritable idée. Car si l'autorité souveraine découle formellement du consentement de la foule et non pas de Dieu, principe suprême et éternel de toute puissance, elle perd aux yeux des sujets son caractère le plus auguste, et elle dégénère en une souveraineté artificielle qui a pour assiette des bases instables et changeantes, comme la volonté des hommes dont on la fait dériver. Ne voyons-nous pas aussi les conséquences de cette erreur dans les lois ? Trop souvent en effet, au lieu d'être la *raison écrite*, ces lois n' expriment plus que la puissance du nombre et la volonté prédominante d' un parti politique. C'est ainsi qu' on caresse les appétits coupables des foules et qu'on lâche les rênes aux passions populaires, même lorsqu'elles troublent la laborieuse tranquillité dos citoyens, sauf à recourir ensuite, dans les cas extrêmes, à des répressions violentes où l' on voit couler le sang.

Les principes chrétiens répudiés, ces principes qui sont si puissamment efficaces pour sceller la fraternité des peuples et pour réunir l'humanité tout entière dans une sorte de grande famille, peu à peu prévalu dans l'ordre international un système d'égoïsme jaloux, par suite duquel les nations se regardent mutuellement, sinon toujours avec haine, du moins certainement avec la défiance qui anime des rivaux. Voilà pourquoi dans leurs entreprises elles sont facilement entraînées à laisser dans l'oubli les grands principes de la moralité et de la justice, et la protection des faibles et des opprimés. Dans le désir qui les aiguillonne d'augmenter indéfiniment la richesse nationale, les nations ne regardent plus que l'opportunité des circonstances, l'utilité de la réussite et la tentante fortune des faits accomplis, sûres que personne ne les inquiètera ensuite au nom du droit, et du respect qui lui est dû. Principes funestes, qui ont consacré, la force matérielle, comme la loi suprême du monde, et à qui l'on doit imputer cet accroissement progressif et sans mesure des préparatifs militaires, ou cette paix armée comparable aux plus désastreux effets de la guerre, sous bien des rapports au moins.

Cette confusion lamentable dans le domaine des idées a fait germer au sein des classes populaires l'inquiétude, le malaise et l'esprit de révolte, de là une agitation et des désordres fréquents qui préludent à des tempêtes plus redoutables encore. La misérable condition d'une si grande partie du menu peuple, assurément bien digne de relèvement et de secours, sert admirablement les desseins d'agitateurs pleins de finesse, et en particulier ceux des factions socialistes, qui, en prodiguant aux classes les plus humbles de folles promesses, s'acheminent vers l'accomplissement des plus effrayants desseins.

Qui s'engage sur une pente dangereuse roule for cément jusqu'au fonde de l'abîme. Avec une logique qui a vengé les principes, s'est donc organisée une véritable association de criminels. D'instincts tout à fait sauvages, dès ses premiers coups, elle a consterné le monde. Grâce à sa constitution solide et à ses ramifications internationales, elle est déjà en mesure de lever partout sa main scélérate, sans craindre aucun obstacle et sans reculer devant aucun forfait. Ses affiliés, répudiant toute union avec la société, et rompant cyniquement avec les lois, la religion et la morale, ont pris le nom d'*anarchistes* ; ils se proposent de renverser de fond en comble la société actuelle, en employant tous les moyens qu'une passion aveugle et sauvage peut suggérer. Et, comme la société reçoit l'unité et la vie de l'autorité qui la gouverne, c'est contre l'autorité tout d'abord que l'anarchie

dirige ses coups. Comment ne pas frémir d'horreur, autant que
d'indignation et de pitié, au souvenir des nombreuses victimes
tombées dans les dernières années, empereurs, impératrices, rois,
présidents de républiques puissantes, dont l'unique crime con-
sistait dans le pouvoir suprême dont ils étaient investis ?

Devant l'immensité des maux qui accablent la société et des
périls qui la menacent, Notre devoir exige que Nous avertissions
une fois encore les hommes de bonne volonté, surtout ceux qui
occupent les situations les plus hautes, et que Nous les conjurions,
comme Nous le faisons en ce moment, de réfléchir aux remèdes
que la situation exige et, avec une prévoyante énergie, de les
appliquer sans retard.

Avant tout, il faut se demander quel sont ces remèdes et en
scruter la valeur. La liberté et ses bienfaits, voilà d'abord ce que
Nous avons entendu porter jusques aux nues ; en elle, on exaltait
le remède souverain, un incomparable instrument de paix féconde
et de prospérité. Mais les faits ont lumineusement démontré
qu'elle ne possédait pas l'efficacité qu'on lui prêtait. Des conflits
économiques, des luttes de classes s'allument et font éruption de
tous les côtés, et l'on ne voit pas même briller l'aurore d'une vie
publique où le calme régnerait. Du reste, et chacun peut le
constater, telle qu'on l'entend aujourd'hui, c'est à dire indis-
tinctement accordée à la vérité et à l'erreur, au bien et au mal, la
liberté n'aboutit qu'à rabaisser tout ce qu'il y a de noble, de saint,
de généreux, et à ouvrir plus largement la voie au crime, au
suicide et à la tourbe abjecte des passions.

On a soutenu aussi que le développement de l'instruction, en
rendant les foules plus polies et plus éclairées, suffirait à les
prémunir contre leurs tendances malsaines et à les retenir dans
les limites de la droiture et de la probité. Mais une dure réalité
ne nous fait-elle pas toucher du doigt chaque jour à quoi sert une
instruction que n'accompagne pas une solide instruction religieuse
et morale ? Par suite de leur inexpérience et de la fermentation
des passions, l'esprit des jeunes gens subit la fascination des
doctrines perverses. Il se prend surtout aux erreurs qu'un jour-
nalisme sans frein ne craint pas de semer à pleines mains et
qui, en dépravant à la fois l'intelligence et la volonté, alimentent
dans la jeunesse cet esprit d'orgueil et d'insubordination, qui
trouble si souvent la paix des familles et le calme des cités.

On avait mis aussi beaucoup de confiance dans les progrès de
la science. De fait, le siècle dernier en a vu de bien grands, de

bien inattendus, de bien marveilleux assurément. Mais est-il si
vrai que ces progrès nous aient donné l'abondance de fruits, pleine
et réparatrice, que le désir d'un si grand nombre d'hommes en
attendait ? Sans doute, le vol de la science a ouvert de nouveaux horizons à notre esprit, il a agrandi l'empire de l'homme sur
les forces de la matière et la vie dans ce monde s'en est trouvée
adoucie à bien des égards. Néanmoins tous sentent, et beaucoup
confessent que la réalité n'a pas été à la hauteur des espérances.
On ne peut pas le nier, quand on prend garde à l'état des esprits
et des mœurs, à la statistique criminelle, aux sourdes rumeurs qui
montent d'en bas et à la prédominance de la force sur le droit.
Pour ne point parler encore des foules qui sont la proie de la
misère, il suffit de jeter un coup d'œil, même superficiel, sur le
monde, pour constater qu'une indéfinissable tristesse pèse sur
les âmes et qu'un vide immense existe dans les cœurs.
L'homme a bien pu s'assujettir la matière, mais la matière n'a
pas pu lui donner ce qu'elle n'a pas, et aux grandes questions qui
ont trait à nos intérêts les plus élevés, la science humaine n'a pas
donné de réponse ; la soif de vérité, de bien, d'infini, qui nous
dévore, n'a pas été étanchée, et ni les joies et les trésors de la
terre, ni l'accroissement des aises de la vie n'ont pu endormir
l'angoisse morale au fond des cœurs. N'y a-t-il donc qu'à
dédaigner ou à laisser de côte les avantages qui découlent de
l'instruction, de la science, de la civilisation et d'une sage
et douce liberté ? Non certes ; il faut au contraire les tenir
en haute estime, les conserver et les accroître comme un
capital de prix ; car ils constituent des moyens qui de leur
nature sont bons, voulus par Dieu lui-même et ordonnés par
l'infinie sagesse au bien de la famille humaine et à son profit.
Mais il faut en subordonner l'usage aux intentions du Créateur et
faire en sorte qu'on ne les sépare jamais de l'élément religieux,
dans lequel réside la vertu, qui leur confère, avec une valeur particulière leur véritable fécondité. Tel est le secret du problème.
Quand un être organique dépérit et se corrompt, c'est qu'il a cessé
d'être sous l'action des causes qui lui avaient donné sa forme et
sa constitution. Pour le refaire sain et florissant, pas de doute
qu'il ne faille le soumettre do nouveau à l'action vivifiante de ces
mêmes causes. Or la société actuelle, dans la folle tentative
qu'elle a faite pour échapper à son Dieu, a rejeté l'ordre surnaturel
et la révélation divine ; elle s'est soustraite ainsi à la salutaire
efficacité du Christianisme, qui est manifestement la garantie la

plus solide de l'ordre, le lien le plus fort de la fraternité et l'inépuisable source des vertus privées et publiques.

De cet abandon sacrilège est né le trouble qui la travaille actuellement. C'est donc dans le giron du Christianisme que cette société dévoyée doit rentrer, si son bien-être, son repos et son salut lui tiennent au cœur.

De même que le Christianisme ne pénètre pas dans une âme sans l'améliorer, de même il n'entre pas dans la vie publique d'un peuple sans l'ordonner. Avec l'idée d'un Dieu qui régit tout, qui est sage, infiniment bon et infiniment juste, il fait pénétrer dans la conscience humaine le sentiment du devoir, il adoucit la souffrance, il calme les haines et il engendre les héros. S'il a transformé la société païenne, et cette transformation fut une résurrection véritable, puisque la barbarie disparut à proportion que le Christianisme s'étendit, il saura bien de même, après les terribles secousses de l'incrédulité remettre dans le véritable chemin et réinstaurer dans l'ordre les Etats modernes et les peuples contemporains.

Mais tout n'est point là : le retour au Christianisme ne sera pas un remède efficace et complet, s'il n'implique pas le retour et un amour sincère à l'Eglise une, sainte, catholique et apostolique. Le Christianisme s'incarne en effet dans l'Eglise catholique, il s'identifie avec cette société spirituelle et parfaite, souveraine dans son ordre, qui est le corps mystique de Jésus-Christ, et qui a pour chef visible le Pontife Romain, successeur du Prince des Apôtres. Elle est la continuatrice de la mission du Sauveur, la fille et l'héritière de sa rédemption ; elle a propagé l'Evangile et elle l'a défendu au prix de son sang ; et, forte de l'assistance divine et de l'immortalité qui lui ont été promises, ne pactisant jamais avec l'erreur, elle reste fidèle au mandat qu'elle a reçu de porter la doctrine de Jésus-Christ à travers ce monde et, jusqu'à la fin des siècles, de l'y garder dans son inviolable intégrité.

Légitime dispensatrice des enseignements de l'Evangile, elle ne se révèle pas seulement à nous comme la consolatrice et la rédemptrice des âmes ; elle est encore l'éternelle source de la justice et de la charité, et la propagatrice en même temps que la gardienne de la liberté véritable et de la seule égalité qui soit possible ici-bas. En appliquant la doctrine de son divin Fondateur, elle maintient un sage équilibre et trace de justes limites entre tous les droits et tous les privilèges dans la société. L'égalité qu'elle proclame ne détruit pas la distinction des différentes classes sociales ; elle la veut intacte, parce qu'évidemment la nature même les requiert. Pour faire obstacle à l'anarchie de la raison émancipée de la foi et abandonnée à elle-même, la liberté qu'elle donne ne lèse ni les droits de la vérité, parce qu'ils sont supérieurs à ceux de la liberté, ni les droits de la justice, parce qu'ils sont supérieurs à ceux du nombre et de la force, ni les droits de Dieu, parce qu'ils sont supérieurs à ceux de l'humanité.

Au foyer domestique, l'Eglise n'est pas moins féconde en bons effets. Car non seulement elle résiste aux artifices que l'incrédulité met en œuvre pour attenter à la vie de la famille, mais elle prépare encore et elle sauvegarde l'union et la stabilité conjugale, dont elle protège et développe l'honneur, la fidélité, la sainteté. Elle soutient en même temps et elle cimente l'ordre civil et politique, en apportant d'une part une aide efficace à l'autorité, et de l'autre, en se montrant favorable aux sages réformes et aux justes aspirations des sujets ; en imposant le respect des Princes et l'obéissance qui leur est dûe et en défendant les droits imprescriptibles de la conscience humaine, sans jamais se lasser. Et c'est ainsi que grâce à elle les peuples soumis à son influence n'ont rien eu à craindre de la servitude, parce qu'elle a retenu les princes sur les pentes de la tyrannie.

Parfaitement conscient de cette efficacité divine, dès le commencement de Notre Pontificat, Nous Nous sommes soigneusement appliqué à mettre en pleine lumière et à faire ressortir les bienfaisants desseins de l'Eglise et à étendre le plus possible, avec le trésor de ses doctrines, le champ de son action salutaire.

Tel a été le but principaux actes de Notre Pontificat, notamment des Encycliques sur *philosophie chrétienne*, sur la *liberté humaine*, sur le *mariage chrétien*, sur la *franc-maçonnerie*, sur les *pouvoirs publics*, sur la *constitution chrétienne des Etats*, sur le *socialisme*, sur la *question ouvrière*, sur les *devoirs des citoyens chrétiens* et sur d'autres *sujets* analogues. Mais le vœu ardent de Notre âme n'a pas été seulement d'éclairer les intelligence ; Nous avons voulu encore remuer et purifier les cœurs, en appliquant tous nos efforts à faire refleurir au milieu des peuples vertus chrétiennes. Aussi ne cessons-nous pas de prodiguer les encouragements et les conseils pour élever les esprits jusqu'aux biens impérissables et pour les mettre ainsi à même de subordonner le corps à l'âme, le pèlerinage terrestre à la vie céleste et l'homme à Dieu.

Bénie par le Seigneur, Notre parole a pu contribuer à raffermir les convictions d'un grand nombre d'hommes, à les éclairer davantage au milieu des difficultés des questions actuelles, à stimuler leur zele et à promouvoir les œuvres les plus variées. C'est surtout pour le bien des classes déshéritées que ces œuvres ont surgi et continuent à surgir encore dans tous les pays, parce qu'on a vu s'y raviver cette charité chrétienne qui a toujours trouvé au milieu du peuple son champ d'action le plus aimé. Si la moisson n'a pas été plus abondante, Vénérables Frères, adorons Dieu, mystérieusement juste, et supplions-le en même temps d'avoir pirié de l'aveuglement de tant d'âmes auxquelles peut malheureusement s'appliquer l'effrayante parole de l'apôtre : *Deus huius saeculi excaecavit mentes infidelium, ut non fulgeat illis illuminatio evangelii gloriae Christi.*[1]

Plus l'Eglise Catholique donne d'extension à son zèle pour le bien moral et matériel des peuples, plus les enfants des ténèbres se lèvent haineusement contre elle et recourent à tous les moyens, afin de ternir sa beauté divine et de paralyser son action de vivifiaute réparation. Que de sophismes ne propagent-ils pas, et que de calomnies ! Un de leurs artifices les plus perfides consiste à redire sans cesse aux foules ignorantes et aux gouvernements envieux que l'Eglise est opposée aux progres de la science, qu'elle est hostile à la liberté, que l'Etat voit ses droits usurpés par elle et que la politique est un champ qu'elle envahit à tout propos. Accusations insensées, qu'on a mille fois répétées et qu'ont mille fois réfutées aussi la saine raison, l'histoire et avec elles, tous ceux qui ont un cœur honnête et ami de la vérité.

L'Eglise, ennemie de la science et de l'instruction? Ah ! sans doute elle est la vigilante gardienne du dogme révélé ; mais c'est cette vigilance elle-même qui l'incline à protéger la science et à favoriser la saine culture de l'esprit ! Non ! en ouvrant son intelligence aux révélations du Verbe, vérité suprême de qui émanent originairement toutes les vérités, l'homme ne compromettra jamais, ni en aucune manière, ses connaissances rationnelles. Bien au contraire les rayonnements qui lui viendront du monde divin donneront toujours plus de puissance et de clarté à l'esprit humain, parce qu'ils le préserveront dans les questions les plus importantes, d'angoissantes incertitudes et de mille erreurs. Du reste dix-neuf siècles d'une gloire, conquise par le catholicisme dans toutes les branches du savoir, suffisent amplement à réfuter cette calomnie. C'est à l'Eglise catholique qu'il faut faire

---

[1] II. Cor. iv. 4.

remonter le mérite d'avoir propagé et défendu la sagesse chrétienne, sans laquelle le monde serait encore gisant dans la nuit des superstitions païennes et dans une abjecte barbarie. A elle, d'avoir conservé et transmis aux générations les précieux trésors des lettres et des sciences antiques ; à elle, d'avoir ouvert les premières écoles pour le peuple et d'avoir créé des Universités qui existent encore et dont le renom s'est perpétué jusqu'à nos jours. A elle enfin, d'avoir inspiré la littérature la plus haute, la plus pure et la plus glorieuse, en même temps qu'elle rassemblait sous ses ailes protectrices les artistes du génie le plus élevé.

L'Eglise, ennemie de la liberté ? Ah ! comme on travestit l'idée de liberté, qui a pour objet un des dons les plus précieux de Dieu, quand on exploit son nom pour en justifier l'abus et l'excès ! Par liberté, que faut-il entendre ? L'exemption de toutes les lois, la délivrance de tous les freins, et, comme corollaire, le droit de prendre le caprice pour guide dans toutes les actions ? Cette liberté, l'Eglise la réprouve certainement, et tous les cœurs, honnêtes la réprouvent avec elle. Mais salue-t-on dans la liberté la faculté rationnelle de faire le bien, largement, sans entrave et suivant les règles qu'a posées l'éternelle justice ? Cette liberté, qui est la seule digne de l'homme et la seule utile à la société, personne ne la favorise, ne l'encourage et ne la protège plus que l'Eglise. Par la force de sa doctrine et l'efficacité de son action, c'est cette Eglise en effet qui a affranchi l'humanité du joug de l'esclavage, en prêchant au monde la grande loi de l'égalité et de la fraternité humaine. Dans tous les siècles, elle a pris en mains la défense des faibles et des opprimés contre l'arrogante domination des forts ; elle a revendiqué la liberté de la conscience chrétienne en versant à flots le sang de ses martyrs ; elle a restitué à l'enfant et à la femme la dignité et les prérogatives de leur noble nature, en les faisant participer, au nom du même droit, au respect et à la justice, et elle a largement concouru ainsi à introduire et à maintenir la liberté civile et politique au sein des nations.

L'Eglise, usurpatrice des droits de l'Etat, l'Eglise, envahissant le domaine politique ? Mais l'Eglise sait et enseigne que son divin Fondateur a ordonné de rendre à César ce qui est à César et à Dieu ce qui est à Dieu et qu'il a ainsi sanctionné l'immuable principe de la perpétuelle distinction des deux pouvoirs, tous les deux souverains dans leur sphère respective : distinction féconde et qui a si largement contribué au développement de la civilisation chrétienne. Etrangère à toute pensée hostile, dans son esprit de charité, l'Eglise ne vise donc qu'à marcher parallélement aux pouvoirs publics pour travailler sans doute sur le même sujet, qui est l'homme, et sur la même société, mais par les voies et dans le dessein élevé que lui assigne sa mission divine. Plût à Dieu que son action fut accueillie sans défiance et sans soupçon : car les innombrables bienfaits dont nous avons parlé plus haut ne feraient que se multiplier. Accuser l'Eglise de visées ambitieuses, ce n'est donc que répéter une calomnie que ses puissants ennemis ont plus d'une fois employée du rest comme prétexte pour masquer eux-mêmes leur propre tyrannie. Et loin d'opprimer, l'histoire l'enseigne clairement, quand on l'étudie sans préjugés, l'Eglise, comme son divin Fondateur, a été le plus souvent au contraire la victime de l'oppression et de l'injustice. C'est que sa puissance réside, non pas dans la force des armes, mais dans la force de la pensée et dans celle de la vérité.

C'est donc sûrement dans une intention perverse qu'on lance contre l'Eglise de semblables accusations. Œuvre pernicieuse et déloyale, dans la poursuite de laquelle va, précédant tous les une secte ténébreuse, que la société porte depuis de longues années dans ses flancs et qui, comme un germe mortel y contamine le bien-être, la fécondité et la vie. Personnification permanente de la révolution, elle constitue une sorte d société retournée, dont le but est d'exercer une suzeraineté occulte sur la société reconnue et dont la raison d'être consiste entièrement dans la guerre à faire à Dieu et à son Eglise. Il n'est pas besoin de la nommer, car à ces traits, tout le monde a reconnu la franc-maçonnerie, dont Nous avons parlé d'une façon expresse dans Notre Encyclique ' *Humanum genus* ' du 20 avril 1884, en denonçant ses tendances délétères, ses doctrines erronées et son œuvre néfaste. Embrassant dans ses immenses filets la presque totalité des nations et se reliant à d'autres sectes qu'elle fait mouvoir par des fils cachés, attirant d'abord et retenant ensuite ses affiliés par l'appât des avantages qu'elle leur procure, pliant les gouvernants à ses desseins, tantôt par ses promesses et tantôt par ses menaces, cette secte est parvenue à s'infiltrer dans toutes les classes de la société. Elle forme comme un état invisible et irresponsable dans l'état legitime. Pleine de l'esprit de Satan qui, au rapport de l'Apôtre, sait au besoin se transformer en ange de lumière,[1] elle met en avant un but humanitaire

---

[1] II. Cor. ix. 14.

mais elle sacrifie tout à ses projets sectaires ; elle proteste qu'elle n' a aucune visée politique, mais elle exerce en réalité l'action la plus profonde dans la vie législative et administrative des états ; et tandis qu'elle professe en paroles le respect de l'autorité et de la religion elle-même, son but suprême (ses propres statuts en font foi) est l'extermination de la souveraineté et du sacerdoce, en qui elle voit des ennemis de la liberté.

Or, il devient de jour en jour plus manifeste que c'est à l'inspiration et à la complicité de cette secte qu'il faut attribuer en grande partie les continuelles vexations dont on accable l'Eglise et la recrudescence des attaques qu'on lui a livrées tout récemment. Car, la simultanéité des assauts dans la persécution qui a soudainement éclaté en ces derniers temps, comme un orage, dans un ciel serein, c'est-à-dire sans cause proportionnée à l'effet ; l'uniformité des moyens mis en œuvre pour préparer cette persécution, campagne de presse, réunions publiques, productions théâtrales ; l'emploi dans tous les pays des mêmes armes, calomnies et soulèvements populaires, tout cela trahit bien vraiment l'identité desseins et le mot d'ordre parti d'un seul et même centre de direction. Simple épisode du reste qui se rattache à un plan arrêté d'avance et qui se traduit en actes sur un théâtre de plus en plus large, afin de multiplier les ruines que nous avons énumérées précédemment. Ainsi veut-on surtout restreindre d'abord, exclure complètement ensuite l'instruction religieuse, en faisant des générations d'incrédules ou d'indifférents ; combattre par la presse quotidienne la morale de l'Eglise, ridiculiser enfin ses pratiques et profaner ses fêtes sacrées.

Rien de plus naturel dès lors que le sacerdoce catholique qui a précisément pour mission de prêcher la religion et d'administrer ses sacrements, soit attaqué avec un particulier acharnement : en le prenant pour point de mire, la secte veut diminuer aux yeux du peuple son prestige et son autorité. Déjà, son audace croissant d'heure en heure et en proportion de l'impunité dont elle se croit assurée, elle interprète malignement tous les actes du clergé, elle le soupçonne sur les moindres indices et elle l'accable des plus basses accusations. Ainsi de nouveaux préjudices s'ajoutent à ceux dont ce clergé souffre déjà, tant à cause du tribut qu'il doit payer au service militaire, grand obstacle à sa préparation sacerdotale, que par suite de la confiscation du patrimoine ecclésiastique que les fidèles avaient librement constitué dans leur pieuse générosité.

Quant aux Ordres religieux et aux Congrégations religieuses, la pratique des conseils évangéliques faisait d'eux la gloire de la société autant que la gloire de la religion : ils n'en ont paru que plus coupables aux yeux des ennemis de l'Eglise, et on les a implacablement dénoncés au mépris et à l'animosité de tous. Ce Nous est ici une douleur immense que de devoir rappeler les mesures odieuses, imméritées et hautement condamnées par tous les cœurs honnêtes dont tout récemment encore les religieux ont été les victimes. Rien n'a pu les sauver, ni l'intégrité de leur vie restée inattaquable même pour leurs ennemis ; ni le droit naturel qui autorise l'association contractée dans un but honnête, ni le droit constitutionnel qui en proclame hautement la liberté ; ni la faveur des peuples, pleins de reconnaissance pour les services précieux rendus aux arts, aux sciences, à l'agriculture, et pour une charité qui déborde sur les classes les plus nombreuses et les pauvres de la société. Et c'est ainsi que des hommes, des femmes, issus du peuple, qui avaient spontanément renoncé aux joies de la famille pour consacrer, au bien de tous, dans de pacifiques associations, leur jeunesse, leurs talents, leurs forces, leur vie elle-même, traités en malfaiteurs comme s'ils avaient constitué des associations criminelles, ont été exclus du droit commun et proscrits, en un temps où partout on ne parle que de liberté !

Il ne faut pas s'étonner que les fils les plus aimés soient frappés, quand le Père lui-même, c'est-à-dire le Chef de la catholicité, le Pontife Romain, n'est pas mieux traité. Les faits sont bien connus. Dépouillé de la souveraineté temporelle et privé par le fait même de l'indépendance qui lui est nécessaire pour accomplir sa mission universelle et divine, forcé dans cette Rome elle-même qui lui appartient de se renfermer dans sa propre demeure, parce qu'un pourvoir ennemi l'y assiège de tous les côtés, il a été réduit, malgré des assurances dérisoires de respect et des promesses de liberté bien précaires, à une condition anormale, injuste, et indigne de son haut ministère. Pour Nous, Nous ne savons que trop les difficultés qu'on lui suscite à chaque instant, en travestissant ses intentions et en outrageant sa dignité. Aussi la preuve est-elle faite et elle devient de jour en jour plus évidente : c'est la puissance spirituelle du Chef de l'Eglise elle-même que peu à peu on a voulu détruire, quand on a porté la main sur le pouvoir temporel de la Papauté. Ceux qui furent les vrais auteurs de cette spoliation n'ont du reste pas hésité à le confesser.

A en juger par les conséquences, ce fait est non seulement un fait impolitique, mais encore une sorte d'attentat antisocial; car les coups qu'on inflige à la religion sont comme autant de coups portés au cœur même de la société.

En faisant de l'homme un être destiné à vivre avec ses semblables, Dieu dans sa Providence avait aussi fondé l'Eglise et, suivant l'expression biblique, il l'avait établie sur la montagne de Sion, afin, qu'elle y servît de lumière et qu'avec ses rayons fécondants elle fit circuler le principe de la vie dans les multiples replis de la société humaine, en lui donnant des règles d'une sagesse céleste, grâce auxquelles celle-ci pourrait s'établir dans l'ordre qui lui conviendrait le mieux. Donc, autant la société se de l'Eglise, part considérable de sa force, autant elle déchoit ou voit les ruines se multiplier dans son sein, en séparant ce que Dieu a voulu uni.

Quant à Nous, Nous ne Nous sommes jamais lassé, toutes les fois que l'occasion nous en a été offerte, d'inculquer ces grandes vérités, et Nous avons voulu le faire une fois encore et d'une manière expresse dans cette circonstance extraordinaire. Plaise à Dieu que les fidèles s'en trouvent encourages et instruits à faire converger plus efficacement vers le bien commun tous leurs efforts et que, mieux éclairés, nos adversaires comprennent l'injustice qu'ils commettent, en persécutant la mère la plus aimante et la bienfaitrice la plus fidèle de l'humanité.

Nous ne voudrions pas que le souvenir des douleurs présentes abattît dans l'âme des fidèles la pleine et entière confiance qu'ils doivent avoir dans l'assistance divine : car Dieu assurera à son heure et par ses voies mystérieuses le triomphe définitif. Quant à Nous, quelque grande que soit la tristesse qui remplisse Notre cœur, Nous ne tremblons pas néanmoins pour les immortelles destinées de l'Eglise. Comme Nous l'avons dit en commençant, la persécution est son partage, parce qu'en éprouvant et en purifiant ses enfants par elle, Dieu en retire des biens plus hauts et plus précieux. Mais en abandonnant l'Eglise à ces luttes, il manifeste sa divine assistance sur elle, car il lui ménage des moyens nouveaux et imprévus, qui assurent le maintien et le développement de son œuvre, sans que les forces conjurées contre elle parviennent à la ruiner. Dix-neuf siècles d'une vie écoulée dans le flux et le reflux des vicissitudes humaines nous apprennent que les tempêtes passent, sans avoir atteint les grands fonds.

Nous pouvons d'autant plus demeurer inébranlables dans la

confiance, que le présent lui-même renferme des symptômes bien faits pour nous empêcher de nous troubler. Les difficultés sont extraordinaries, formidables, on ne saurait le nier : mais d'autres faits, qui se déroulent sous nos regards, témoignent en même temps que Dieu remplit ses promesses avec une sagesse admirable et avec bonté. Pendant que tant de forces conspirent contre l'Eglise et qu'elle s'avance, privée de tout secours, de tout appui humain, ne continue-t-elle pas en effet à poursuivre dans le monde son œuvre gigantesque et n'étend-elle pas son action parmi les nations les plus différentes et sous tous les climats ? Non, chassé qu'il en a été par Jésus-Christ, l'antique prince de ce monde ne pourra plus y exercer sa domination altière comme jadis, et les efforts de Satan nous susciteront bien des maux sans doute, mais ils n'aboutiront pas à leur fin. Déjà une tranquillité surnaturelle, due à l'Esprit Saint qui couvre l'Eglise de ses ailes et qui vit dans son sein, règne, non pas seulement dans l'âme des fidèles, mais encore dans l'ensemble de la catholicité ; tranquillité qui se développe avec sérénité, grâce à l'union toujours de plus en plus étroite et dévouée de l'Episcopat avec ce siège apostolique et qui forme un merveilleux contraste avec l'agitation, les dissensions et la fermentation continuelle des sectes qui troublent la paix de la société. Féconde en innombrables œuvres de zèle et de charité, cette union harmonieuse existe aussi entre les Evêques et leur clergé. Elle se retrouve enfin entre le clergé et les laïques catholiques, qui, plus serrés et plus affranchis de respect humain que jamais, se réveillent et s'organisent avec une émulation généreuse, afin de défendre la cause sainte de la religion. Oh ! c'est bien là l'union que Nous avons recommandée si souvent et que Nous recommandons de nouveau encore, et Nous la bénissons, afin qu'elle se développe de plus en plus largement et qu'elle s'oppose, comme un mur invincible, à la fougueuse violence des ennemis du nom divin.

Rien de plus naturel dès lors, que, semblables aux surgeons qui germent au pied de l'arbre, renaissent, se fortifient et se multiplient les innombrables associations que Nous voyons avec joie fleurir de nos jours dans le sein de l'Eglise. On peut dire qu'aucune forme de la piété chrétienne n'a été laissée de côté qu'il s'agisse de Jésus-Christ lui-même et de ses adorables mystères ou de sa divine Mère, ou des Saints dont les vertus insignes ont le plus brillé. En même temps, aucune des variétés de la charité n'a été oubliée, et c'est de tous les côtés qu'on a rivalisé de zèle, pour instruire chrétiennement la jeunesse, pour assister les malades, pour moraliser le peuple et pour voler au secours des classes les moins favorisées. Avec quelle rapidité ce mouvement se propagerait et combien ne porterait-il pas des fruits plus doux, si on ne lui opposait pas les dispositions injustes et hostiles auxquelles il va si souvent se heurter !

Le Dieu qui donne à l'Eglise une vitalité si grande dans les pays civilisés où elle est établie depuis de longs siècles déjà, veut bien nous consoler par d'autres espérances encore. Ces espérances, c'est au zèle des missionaires que nous les devons. Sans se laisser décourager par les périls qu'ils courent, par les privations qu'ils endurent et par les sacrifices de tout genre qu'ils doivent s'imposer, ils se multiplient et conquièrent à l'Evangile et à la civilisation des pays entiers. Rien ne peut abattre leur constance, quoiqu'à l'exemple du Divin Maître ils ne recueillent souvent que des accusations et des calomnies pour prix de leurs infatigables travaux.

Les amertumes sont donc tempérées par des consolations bien douces et, au milieu des luttes et des difficultés qui sont Notre partage, Nous avons de quoi rafraîchir Notre âme et espérer. C'est là un fait qui devrait suggérer d'utiles et sages reflexions à quiconque observe le monde avec intelligence et sans se laisser aveugler par la passion. Car il prouve que, comme Dieu n'a pas fait l'homme indépendant en ce qui regarde la fin dernière de la vie et comme il lui a parlé, ainsi il lui parle encore aujourd' hui dans son Eglise, visiblement soutenue par son assistance divine, et qu'il montre clairement par là où se trouvent le salut et la vérité. Dans tous les cas, cette éternelle assistance remplira nos cœurs d'une espérance invincible : elle nous persuadera qu'à l'heure marquée par la Providence et dans un avenir qui n'est pas très éloigné la vérité, déchirant les brumes sous lesquelles on cherche à la voiler, resplendira plus brillante et que l'esprit de l'Evangile versera de nouveau la vie au sein de notre société corrompue et dans ses membres épuisés.

En ce qui Nous concerne, Vénérables Frères, afin de hâter l'avénement du jour des miséricordes divines, Nous ne manquerons pas, comme d' ailleurs Notre devoir Nous l'ordonne, de tout faire pour défendre et développer le règne de Dieu sur la terre. Quant à vous, votre sollicitude pastorale Nous est trop connue pour que Nous vous exhortions à faire de même. Puisse seulement la flamme ardente qui brûle dans vos cœurs se transmettre de plus en plus dans le cœur de tous vos prêtres ! Ils se trouvent en contact immédiat avec le peuple : ils connaissent parfaitement ses aspirations, ses besoins, ses souffrances, et aussi les pièges et les séductions qui l'entourent. Si, pleins de l'esprit de Jésus-Christ et se maintenant dans une sphère supérieure aux passions politiques, ils coordonnent leur action avec la vôtre, ils réussiront sous la bénédiction de Dieu à accomplir des merveilles : par la parole ils éclaireront les foules, par la suavité des manières ils gagneront tous les cœurs, et en secourant avec charité ceux qui souffrent, ils les aideront à améliorer peu à peu leur condition.

Le Clergé sera fermement soutenu lui-même par l'active et intelligente collaboration de tous les fidèles de bonne volonté. Ainsi, les enfants qui ont savouré les tendresses maternelles de l'Eglise l'en remercieront dignement, en accourant vers elle pour défendre son honneur et ses gloires. Tous peuvent contribuer à ce devoir si grandement méritoire : les lettrés et les savants, en prenant sa défense dans les livres ou dans la presse quotidienne, puissant instrument dont nos adversaires abusent tant ; les pères de familles et les maîtres, en donnant une éducation chrétienne aux enfants ; les magistrats et les représentants du peuple, en offrant le spectacle de la fermeté des principes et de l'intégrité du caractère, tous en professant leur foi sans respect humain. Notre siècle exige l'élévation des sentiments, la générosité des desseins et l'exacte observance de la discipline. C'est surtout par une soumission parfaite et confiante aux directions du Saint Siège que cette discipline devra s'affirmer. Car elle est le moyen le meilleur pour faire disparaître ou pour atténuer le dommage que causent les opinions de parti lorsqu'elles divisent, et pour faire converger tous les efforts vers un but suprérieur, le triomphe de Jésus-Christ dans son Eglise.

Tel est le devoir des catholiques. Quant au succès final, il dépend de Celui qui veille avec sagesse et amour sur son épouse immaculée et dont il a été écrit : *Jesus Christus heri, et hodie ipse et in saecula.*[1]

C'est donc vers Lui qu'en ce moment Nous laissons monter encore Notre humble et ardente prière ; vers Lui qui, aimant d'un amour infini l' errante humanité, a voulu s'en faire la victime expiatoire dans la sublimité du martyre ; vers Lui qui assis, quoique invisible, dans la barque mystique de son Eglise peut seul apaiser la tempête, en commandant au déchaînement des flots et des vents mutinés.

---

[1] Ad Hebr. xlii. 8.

Sans aucun doute Vénérables Fères, vous supplierez volontiers
ce divin Maître avec Nous, afin que les splendeurs de la lumière
céleste éclairent ceux qui, plus peut-être par ignorance que par
malice, haïssent et persécutent la religion de Jésus-Christ, et aussi,
afin que tous les hommes de bon vouloir s'unissent étroitement et
saintement pour agir : Puisse le triomphe de la vérité et de la
justice être ainsi hâté dans ce monde, et sur la grande famille
humaine se lever doucement des jours meilleurs, des jours de
tranquillité et de paix.

Qu'en attendant, gage des faveurs divines les plus précieuses,
descende sur Vous, et sur tous les fidèles confiés à vos soins la
bénédiction que Nous Vous donnons de grand cœur.

Donné à Rome, près Saint Pierre, le 19 Mars de l'année 1902,
de Notre Pontificat la vingt-cinquième.

LÉON XIII PAPE.

**RESOLUTIONS OF THE STANDING COMMITTEE OF THE IRISH
ARCHBISHOPS AND BISHOPS ON EMIGRATION AND ITS
REMEDIES**

At a meeting of the Standing Committee of the Archbishops and Bishops of Ireland, held at University College,
Dublin, on Tuesday, April 15, 1902, his Eminence Cardinal
Logue in the chair, the following resolutions were unanimously adopted :—

1. The population of Ireland having decreased by a quarter of
a million of inhabitants within the last ten years, and by little
short of four millions within the last half century, we cannot but
regard this continued depletion with feelings of deep anxiety for
the fortunes of our race in their own country.

We, therefore, deem it a pressing duty to publicly discourage
the ruinous outflow of our people from their own country, where
Providence has provided sufficient room for them, if only they
were employed in cultivating Irish land and engaged in the
manufacturing and industrial occupations that should find place
in every city, town, and village of Ireland.

Apart from what we cannot but regard as the radical causes of
the depopulation of Ireland, we consider it utterly reckless on the
part of the vast majority of male emigrants to the United States
and Canada to quit Ireland in the present condition of the
American labour market. Many young Irishmen are wasting

their lives in idleness, and are driven to seek help from public charity far away from home and relatives, in American towns and cities. And many female emigrants, too, have learned to regret that they ever abandoned their Irish homes, attracted by some bright vision beyond the Atlantic.

2. We have seen with satisfaction the efforts made by the Congested Districts Board to have large grazing tracts broken up and distributed amongst the tillers of the soil, and we look to a wider extension of these operations as a most effectual means of stemming the tide of emigration.

3. We consider that the promotion of suitable industries in town and country and the establishment of factories along the numerous rivers of Ireland would also powerfully contribute to the same all-important end.

4. We desire to impress upon our people the duty of practically encouraging Irish manufactures and industries by purchasing Irish-made goods, and thus causing Irish money to circulate in its proper channels.

We appeal with confidence to the clergy throughout the country to use their influence by emphasising these few practical points in their public addresses to their flocks.

Signed on behalf of the meeting,

✠ Michael Cardinal Logue, *Chairman.*

✠ John, Bishop of Clonfert, ⎫
✠ Richard Alphonsus, Bishop ⎬ *Secretaries.*
   of Waterford and Lismore, ⎭

RESOLUTIONS OF THE STANDING COMMITTEE OF THE IRISH ARCHBISHOPS AND BISHOPS ON THE LICENSING QUESTION

We think it right to insert on the present occasion the resolutions of the Standing Committee on the Licensing Question that were passed on the 21st of January last As our attention was not specially called to these resolutions they somehow escaped our notice at the time they were passed :—

That we, the Standing Committee of the Archbishops and Bishops of Ireland, view with deep concern and sorrow the continued multiplication, in town and country, of licences for the sale of intoxicating drink, and deplore the reckless facility with which the licensing authorities have been granting these licences, and perpetuating what we deem a grave abuse.

That as pastors of our flocks, we appeal to the licensing authorities of the country to abstain from granting new licences, and to take every legitimate opportunity of reducing the number of existing licences until it has been brought within reasonable limits.

That we look forward with feelings of alarm to the disastrous consequences, spiritual and material, of this multiplication of centres of temptation to excessive drinking unless promptly and effectually checked by an awakened healthy public opinion.

That we call upon our clergy to earnestly co-operate, in season and out of season, in creating and fostering a sound and enlightened public policy upon this licensing question, as well as upon the widespread evil of intemperance, which, as a canker, is fast praying upon the social and industrial life of our country, and blighting domestic peace, happiness, and prosperity.

(Signed)

✠ MICHAEL Cardinal LOGUE, *Chairman.*

✠ JOHN, Bishop of Clonfert,
✠ RICHARD ALPHONSUS, Bishop of } *Secretaries.*
Waterford and Lismore,

NOTICES OF BOOKS

MARIAE CORONA : CHAPTERS ON THE MOTHER OF GOD AND
HER SAINTS. By the Rev. P. A. Sheehan, D.D.,
author of ' My New Curate,' etc. Published for the
'Catholic Truth Society of Ireland' by Browne and
Nolan, Limited. 1902.

WE are particularly happy to call attention to this excellent
collection of papers in honour of the Blessed Virgin, which, whilst
they will promote ardent devotion to Our Lady during the month
of May, will at the same time give the reader a beautiful insight
into the inner life of a popular clerical ' litterateur.' The papers
we notice have been secured by the Catholic Truth Society of
Ireland, and we trust they may become even more popular than
any of Dr. Sheehan's previous works. We confess that we have
great hopes that good results will follow from the diffusion of
books of this kind, which are pious without being dull, fresh and
readable in form, enlivened here and there by touches of genuine
feeling, and lifted above the commonplace by the experience, the
sympathy and cultivated taste of the writer. The book appears
most appropriately before the month of May. May it serve its
devout purpose well and encourage the ' Catholic Truth Society
of Ireland' to circulate other books of the same kind.

J. F. H.

HOW TO REASON : THE A B C OF LOGIC REDUCED TO
PRACTICE. By Rev. Richard C. Bodkin, C.M. Browne
& Nolan, Dublin. 1s.

A VERY readable and useful little book. It is not an exhaustive
or elaborate treatise on the subject ; it rather aims at being
practical. It is intended mainly for those who have neither the
time nor the opportunity to read an extensive course of Logic, and
to those, we think, it will strongly recommend itself.

The section dealing with Propositions and Syllogisms has been
treated with great simplicity and yet with considerable skill.
While excluding all those minutiae, that are so apt to puzzle and
discourage the beginner, the author has managed to omit little
that was either necessary or important. To render his treatment

more practical he has subjoined a chapter on Logical Analysis,
in which one gets an idea of how some of the principles and rules
of Logic are to be employed for the end for which they were
intended.

We were pleased to notice the special importance attached to
Definition in the book. For the sake of that chapter alone, we
would wish it fell into the hands of many of our countrymen who
waste so much time in heated discussions about subjects on which
they have often rather hazy ideas.

We congratulate the author on his work. He has endeavoured
to popularize a very dry subject, and his attempt has been
successful. We recommend the book to those who are
anxious to have some working knowledge of the principles and
rules of Logic. It will enable them to profit by their reading. It
will give them a facility in analyzing any speech, essay, or book,
and it will aid them considerably in estimating the value of the
opinions whether scientific, political, or economic, with which they
are every day brought into contact.

C. J. F.

DERRIANA: ESSAYS AND OCCASIONAL VERSES. Chiefly
relating to the Diocese of Derry. By the Most Rev.
Dr. O'Doherty, Bishop of Derry. Dublin: Sealy,
Bryers and Walker; also Gill and Son. 1902.

As most of the essays published in this volume already
appeared in our own pages they require neither commendation
nor any prolonged notice from us. We have merely to discharge
the very pleasant duty of informing our readers that these valuable
papers have been collected and published in a single volume by
his Lordship the Bishop of Derry. This, we are sure, will be
welcome news to all who are in any way connected with the
Diocese of Derry; but interest in the work will not be confined to
them. The papers on Redmond O'Gallagher and Sir Cahir
O'Doherty are of national importance, and are both very valuable
contributions to history. At the end of the volume his Lordship
has added a number of poems composed on various occasions, but
takes care to inform us that they were written in far off college
days, and consequently bear the marks of juvenility. He quotes
Cardinal Newman to the effect that ' life is not long enough to
do more than our best, whatever that may be; that they who are
ever taking aim make no hits; that they who never venture never

gain; that to be for ever safe is to be for ever feeble; and that to do some substantial good is a compensation for much incidental imperfection.' We do not see any necessity for such an elaborate apology; for the verses are much better thanm any of the effusions that have acquired popularity in our time. If Dr. O'Doherty is the only occupant of the Episcopal bench who has written verses he has at all events only continued a tradition that was long honoured in the Irish Church. The Irish bishop, who is now the Patron Saint of the city of Ghent, was the most accomplished poet of the seventh century. The lines he wrote on the tomb of St. Bavo of Ghent were pronounced by the late Cardinal Pitra the best that come down to us from his time. Another Iirsh Bishop who ruled the diocese of Fiesole in the ninth century not only wrote verses but gave lessons in metre to his disciples. Donatus, like Livinus, had tasted of the Castalian spring. The poems of the modern Irish bishop are inspired by the same religious spirit that moved the ancient ones. The themes are similar; and although the Bishop's fame, particularly in his diocese of Derry, will not have to depend upon his verses, we are sure that, insignificant though he may think them, they will help to perpetuate his memory and commend his virtues to generations who may forget the schools he has erected and the churches he has built.

J. F. H.

[We are reluctantly compelled to hold over till June the reply of Mr. Vesey Hague to Father Fitzsimons' criticism in our last issue. The publication of the Papal Encyclical, which could not be delayed, has also crushed out other contributions. We think it only fair to Mr. Hague, however, to say that he has met his opponent without delay and remains unmoved by a criticism which he regards as entirely beside the mark.—ED. I. E. RECORD.]

"Ut Christiani ita et Romani sitis." " As you are children of Christ, so be you children of Rome."
Ex Dictis S. Patrocii. In Libro Armacano. fol. 9.

The Irish Ecclesiastical Record

A Monthly Journal, under Episcopal Sanction.

Thirty-fifth Year]
No. 414.   **JUNE, 1902.**   [Fourth Series
     Vol. XL

Nihil Obstat.
GIRALDUS MOLLOY, S.T.D.
Censor Dep.
Imprimatur.
✠ GULIELMUS.
Archiep. Dublin.,
Hiberniae Primas

BROWNE & NOLAN, Limited
Publishers and Printers, 24 & 25
NASSAU STREET, DUBLIN.

. . PRICE ONE SHILLING . .

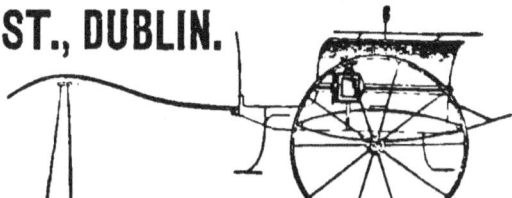

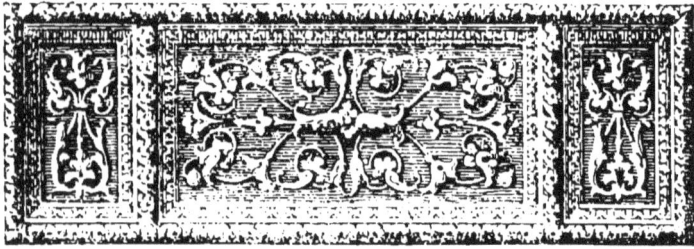

THE RELIGIOUS MIND OF A GERMAN STUDENT

PERCHED on the summit of a deeply-wooded hill by the Rhine, not many miles from Bonn, stands the ruined castle of Roland, the Paladin of Charlemagne. In the olden times, when the taper or the torch was burning in every chamber after nightfall, it must have looked like some great lanthorn aglow with ruddy panes. Many a time must the massive walls have shook with the noise of revelry, and many a time must the guests in the banquet-hall have heard their songs repeated by the careless fisher on the river far beneath, as he drifted down stream with idle sail. The distant mountains, too, could tell us many a story of those wondrous days. Often were they startled from their slumbers by the echoes of the magic horn when Roland, hot upon the chase, flung out a wild call to the laggard huntsmen of his train. In the middle of the rapid river below lies a long, narrow island, riding like a ship at anchor. The large building towards the centre is the convent where Roland's bride sought shelter when the news came that he had fallen in the battle of the Pyrenees. Here, too, he found her on his sad return, recognising her voice amongst the whole choir of sisters at the singing of some vesper hymn. Away on the other side of the river rise the Seven Mountains, with many a patch of bare red rock peeping through a scanty robe of vineyard and pine forest. Drachenfels stands nearest to us, and then come Petrusberg, the Mount of Olives, and the rest. Somewhere here, on the river's brink, is the rock from which Lorelei, the Siren of the Rhine, lured many a bark to ruin with the witchery of her song.

One day, some two years ago, I found myself in a chamber of the ancient castle. I drew back a little space from the outer wall, so as to make a ruined window serve as a frame for the landscape. Was it not fitting, I thought, that such a region, so rich in natural beauty and in stories of the grey old time, should be bordered all around with the rough lines of that very window from which, mayhap, the lonely Roland listened to the voices from the cloister? The blue shade, dark upon the river, but verging into misty white along the distant mountains, enriching all things along the Rhine valley with a peculiar lustre, was absent that day. The sky was black with electric clouds; the lightning quivered down in silver streams upon the earth, hushed for an instant, and then the very rock on which I stood trembled to the roar of the thunder. I had just made up my mind to seek shelter in some house down in the valley, when I heard the shuffle of footsteps behind me and, as I thought, some muttered words from the *Œdipus Coloneus*, where the chorus stand gazing with terror on a similar scene. I recognised my chance companion as one whom I had seen at lecture. Perceiving that his look was friendly, I introduced myself to him, with the very sensible informality of the German student.[1] We descended the steep path together, and reached a little cottage on the outskirts of a wood, just in time to escape the downpour which marked the end of the thunderstorm.

The friendship, begun in this rather romantic fashion, lasted whilst I remained at the university. We found that our lines of reading lay in the same direction, and moreover by working together we soon realised that, owing to the

---

[1] In England two students may sit side by side for three whole terms or more, and never think of breaking silence until some common friend has introduced them. In Germany one goes up to another, makes a quick bow, jerks out his surname; the other does likewise, and the pair are introduced.

very great disparity of the methods in which we had each
been trained, one could give the other assistance of some
value.   Karl von Ellenfels was a delightful companion.
He had brought back from the army a stiffness of bearing
and a precision of movement which somehow seemed to
consort admirably with his rapid, steel-trap style of
speaking.   He was full of legendary lore.   He knew all the
Rhine sagas by heart, though he thought little of their
antiquity.   He was a tireless reader not only in his own
subject, but in general literature besides.   This is, in fact,
the very reason why I have masked him with a pseudonym :
I was afraid lest his busy eyes might chance upon these
pages, and that he might chide me for dragging him before
the gaze even of a stranger people, especially as I have
altered his words by insertion and omission, partly through
lapse of memory, partly because I wished to darken the
lines a little here and there, and so make a clearer portrait.
I make no doubt he will recognise the features, in spite of
the trifles which I have touched in to make the picture
represent his comrades as well as himself.

I found him in his rooms one evening, poring over some
ancient tome.   The lamp was shaded so as to leave his
thoughtful face but dimly visible.   He looked very like the
pictures of the High German doctor, deep in the study of
Paracelsus.   If only a crucible and some phials stood upon
the table, he might have been searching for the philosopher's
stone or the secret of life.   A pair of swords hung crossed
upon the wall, and on each side of them, two or three pistols,
for our friend had been through more than half a dozen
duels and loved to make open profession of his martial
character.   In a corner stood a murderous-looking but really
very harmless blunderbuss, which he used in place of Indian
clubs.   He was smoking a long pipe, with a flexible stem,
the bowl of which rested on the table, and the smoke, too
listless for cones or vortex-rings, drifted upward, wrapping
his face round in a thin veil of cloud.   He often said, quite
seriously, and, indeed, I heard many other Germans say
the same, that a close study of the classical authors, without
the aid of nicotine, was injurious to the health : one had to

give such close attention to a host of minutiæ that the nervous system required something to soothe it.

That evening we worked through the seventh idyll of Theocritus. After a hot dispute as to whether it contained any clear proof as to the poet's birthplace, I rose to go, suggesting that he need not pay me a return visit on the following day, as it was Sunday, and he might have other matters to attend to. This innocent remark was the key that opened his mind.

'The fact of the matter is, though nominally a Protestant, I really have no religion. Perhaps it's from reading so much classics; at all events, I have come to regard your account of the origin of the world, the fall of man, the deluge, and soforth, as so many fables not one whit more credible than the stories about Prometheus, Deucalion and Pyrrha, and all that other tangle of myth and deliberate invention. For my own part, if I were to make a selection of theocracies, I should prefer the ancient German system to all others. I should prefer to believe in Wôdan, Donar, Tiu, and that goddess whose name Tacitus translates Isis.' This seemed to me so utterly ridiculous that I could not conceal my merriment. He confessed, with a smile, that he did not mean his reference to the long-forgotten German gods to be taken quite seriously. ' Still,' he continued, ' I do find something attractive about the way in which our ancestors worshipped. They did not immure their gods in temples, nor did they consider themselves competent to represent them in image of wood or stone. Each divinity was identified in some mysterious way with the spirit of the groves and glades set apart in its honour. What's this Tacitus says? Yes. Here are the words in the ninth chapter of his *Germania :* ' Ceterum Germani) nec cohibere parietibus deos neque in ullam humani oris speciem adsimulare ex magnitudine caelestium arbitrantur; lucos ac nemora consecrant deorumque nominibus appellant secretum illud quod sola reverentia vident.' [1] And as for the moral side our people stood in the highest place, as

---

[1] H. von E. knows quite well that the commentators have rubbed all the gilding off his theory.

the same writer tells us. We haven't their religious system in its completeness; but if we had, I shouldn't be surprised to find that their moral code was almost as noble as yours. . . . Yes, I *have* read the New Testament, and never read the Gospels without being deeply touched by the gentle life, the dignity and the kindness of the Saviour. But still the religion is of Jewish origin. . . . I mean that the ceremonial worship, and soforth, are Jewish, or, at all events, that is my impression. No doubt the moral code is almost perfection, simply because it is nothing more than the natural law, or the social law, as I prefer to call it.

'I met a co-religionist of yours some time ago. We had some conversation about these subjects. It was too friendly to be called a controversy, and I suppose it wasn't learned enough to be called a discussion. At all events, in the course of some remarks, he explained that you believe in the existence of a Providence, whose ministers are often guardian spirits, a Providence which watches with an intense love over the life of man, which notes every thought that arises in his mind, every impulse born within his will, which counts every throb of his heart, and whose whole endeavour is to bring him after death to the home of the angels. He told me that that same beneficent Power held the whole world in the embrace of His love, and that without Him the sparrow did not fall from the roof, nor the blade of grass tremble in the wind. He appealed to me to bow down before that Being and ask of it light to see the way. My imagination was fascinated for a little by all that these thoughts suggested, and it seemed to me as if the world were peopled with white-robed angels that watched over all things lifeless and living, over the sea with all its changes, the flowers of the forest, over man himself with his joys and sorrows. But when I wished to pray, I found that I could not. However beautiful the thought, I had no real faith in such a Being or His ministering spirits. He might as well have asked me to pray to Jupiter or Mercury.

'I hope you're not offended at my running on in this way. I am afraid, you must think it strange, to hear what you consider almost self-evident truths treated with such scant respect.'

There was, I admit, some ground for these last remarks. However, I could scarcely suspect von Ellenfels of insincerity; so I thought it better to hear him out.

Before proceeding further with his self-revelation he fetched a note-book from a shelf, and read in it for a few moments with great care. The sequel will show, what I could have well deemed incredible, that he had gained some acquaintance with matters which I had always thought very far removed from the threshold of theology or philosophy.

'Well,' he said, closing his book, 'to pass on to something quite different. . . . By the way, I'd be obliged to you if you'd just let me talk. I know you will find it hard to keep yourself from breaking in on me. But just let me tell you to-night how I stand; let me show you my mind, and you can take me up some other night and give me as sound a drubbing as you please, although, I warn you, the blows won't be all on one side. If you wish, I'll let you have this note-book; so that you'll have every chance of making a successful onslaught. . . . Well, to pass on. There's the great difficulty about reconciling human liberty with divine omniscience and divine omnipotence. I have read Scheeben and some other theologian of your school—I forget his name, it's here in this book somewhere—on these questions. I must admit that I'm fairly satisfied about the omniscience. I think your people have answered that fairly well; but they seem to have broken down utterly on the other difficulty. There appear to be two chief attempts at solving it. How is this you call those two schools? Yes, quite so— Thomists and Molinists. Very well. The Thomists say, don't they, that man is moved by God, that he infallibly does what God moves him to, but that he is moved freely. Now, what, in the name of common sense, could any man call that but the merest quibbling? The other explanation is not a bit better. It seems to be a principle in your theology that there is no being unsupported by the hand of God, and that men's actions require that divine support or concurrence as much as the men themselves. Now, how does the other explanation fit in with this? It says that the ultimate determination of the will is somehow independent of this

concurrence; and then, if you say to them: but isn't that
determination an act, and for that matter isn't it the most
important of all acts, and oughtn't it require concurrence
as much, at the very least, as any other act? they answer
you blandly that that ultimate determination is a mere
non-ens. Wortspiel und Ausrede ! (quibble and subterfuge).
Why can't you face the situation honestly? Admit that
there is a difficulty, but that there is no explanation.
Surely the initial difficulty is preferable to the new difficulties raised by either of these systems.[1] As for myself, I see
no reason whatever for believing that the human will is free.
I have dipped into one or two of your philosophical books.
I hope you find them more interesting than I do. I feel
inclined at times to a belief in destiny, but have not satisfied
myself as to the evidence. I don't want to go into the matter
to-night, as I have so much else of greater moment to say.
Enough for the present to observe, that what I call destiny
is a peculiar grouping of causes, which produces results in
the moral order, as strikingly symmetrical as the formation
of crystals in the order of inert matter. By the way,
I read, a good while ago, that the words, "conticuere
omnes," were found on a wall in Pompeii. Could the
fingers that traced those words have moved at the dictate
of a mere chance, blind to what lay beyond the present
hour? Surely it was a prophecy of the silence of death
which fell upon the city on the day when the anger of
Vesuvius covered it from human eyes. All were silent with
the silence of the grave.[2]

'But, now, let me come to another point. You remember a few days ago when we were doing the *Phædo*, or,
rather, some extracts from it, we discussed the arguments
for the spirituality of the human soul, or, to put it in my

---

[1] H. von E. seems to think that we are committed to one or other of the
two systems. If he had read his authorities more carefully he would have
found that there are theologians who take his view of the question, although
they do not present it with such heat nor depreciate the solutions laudably
attempted by others.

[2] There seems to be some lapse in logic here. However, one may gather
that H. von E. is not a materialist of the ordinary kind. His words appear
to me to hold out a hope, that he may some day exchange the notion of this
lifeless power, for that of a personal omnipotent Being.

own way, for the existence of a human soul. I was struck
by the arguments you used, but at the same time, was hardly
convinced by them. Taking the principal argument, I
conceive it to be something like this: the mind perceives
abstract ideas, such as justice, virtue, and so on, but nothing
material like the eye or the hand could perceive or touch
things, like virtue or justice, which have no extension, no
property which could make them felt by the senses, therefore, the power which perceives these ideas must, like the
ideas, be devoid of extension, and like them be independent
of matter. Now, it strikes me that that is one of those
proofs, just a little too clever to be true. How do you
know but that these abstract ideas are nothing more than
confused pictures of just acts, or virtuous acts, as the case
may be?[1] And then, not content with telling us about the
human soul, you volunteer a whole lot of statements about
the lower animals. You tell us that they have no powers
of reasoning, reflection, no such thing as volition. What
can you really know about them? You cannot enter into
their consciousness and come out again and tell us what
you found there. One would imagine, from what your people
say, that they had occupied in turn all the cages of the zoo.
You say that they show no signs of reasoning, and if I or a
naturalist tells you of some wonderful thing done by a horse
or dog you account for it by saying it was simply an accident
or coincidence, or that the act of reasoning in the case was
ab extra not *ab intra*.[2] It appears to me, that you come to
study philosophy with a lot of conclusions ready made,
and that you so fix your principles and so order your methods
as to produce the very conclusions you require. Still you

---

[1] This is an appeal to consciousness: do we, as a matter of fact, when we
conceive the idea of justice, have before our minds a confused blending of a
number of just acts of which we have had experience? Is not our idea quite
distinct from these? When a man sees a number of bodies fall to the ground,
he arrives at a general formula called the law of gravitation. Is this law a
confused picture of a number of objects falling to the ground? Is it not
rather a kind of formula like the abstract idea which includes not only the
phenomena actually observed, but all similar phenomena as well?

[2] Some of our philosophers may, perhaps, have exposed themselves to
this charge. At all events, H. von E. forgets that a great many of our
adversaries who approach this question with the pre-conceived notion that
there is *no* essential difference between man and the lower animals, are just
as deserving of his censure.

are very far beyond Kant, Hegel and all that rout, who seem
so often to write as though they enjoyed a special license to
be nonsensical.[1] Your philosophy, as you said to me a few
days ago, squares best with the findings of common sense,
simply because,though occasionally the caricaturists, you are,
in the main, the faithful interpreters of the divine Aristotle.[2]

' Then as to immortality. Well, some philosophers—I
don't know whether they are of your school or not—are
honest enough to admit that there is no argument to prove it.
Others, however, say that the universal belief in immortality
is a proof that there is such a thing, because the fact that
such a belief is universal proves that it comes from human
nature itself ; in other words, it was implanted in human
nature by its Author.   Now, what is the use of this kind of
argument?   Didn't the whole world believe at one time that
the earth was flat, and don't they still believe in ghosts and
fairies ?[3] Of course, I know that there is another argument,
which, indeed, hardly pretends to be an argument.   It puts
us the question : Can we believe that the grave is the limit
of life? Can we believe that the friends we loved, the
friends who, perhaps, died for us, will be separated from us
for ever?   I wish I could believe it were so. You often think
poor fellows like myself are merely posing when we talk like
this ; but you'd very soon change your mind if you but felt
the sharpness of the grief that pierced me through when I
heard of my father's death.   They brought him home dead
one day from the forest, where he had been hunting, with
the blood trickling from a ghastly wound in his forehead.

---

[1] A faithful report of the words used. H. von E. was the only German
non-Catholic whom I heard speak in this strain of German philosophy.

[2] H. von E. was later on considerably impressed when I reminded him,
first, that the Catholic Church alone claims to be the sole infallible teacher,
and secondly, that our philosophers, who, according to his own assertion, start
by assuming the truth of Catholic dogma, and who make their philosophy fit
in with their religion, yet produce, as the result of all this, a philosophy which
harmonises so admirably with the verdicts of common sense.

[3] There is no use in discussing the immortality of the soul with one who
denies its simplicity and spirituality.   If he admitted the simplicity and
spirituality, he should also admit, that it could not be destroyed after death
except by the direct interference of God. Such an interference would, however, be altogether out of the question according to H. von E.'s philosophical
principles.   The remaining portion of the paragraph deals with an argument
which, as far as I am aware, is not looked upon by anyone as conclusive.

. . . Let me draw a veil over what followed. Enough to
tell you that I realised then for the first time, in the cruel-
lest of all ways, that I had lost the faith[1] of my childhood ;
I felt that my father and I were separated for ever. The
night that would never end had fallen on him before he
had time to say a single word of farewell. I struggled,
but struggled in vain, with the voice of reason. Faith was
vanquished and reason triumphed, and I was left more
lonely than I thought man could ever be. . . . I can scarcely
recall the train of reasoning which passed through my mind.
As far as I remember it was something like this : Friend-
ships are often dissolved by difference of opinion and other
causes, and are, therefore, perishable, and, just like our
perishable bodies, why should not nature fix a certain limit
for their existence ? Moreover, granted the truth of all that
religion teaches, what guarantee have we that we shall meet
our friends again ? For, are there not more mansions than
one in that other world of yours ? And, again, look at the
many instances of friendship between, let us say, man and the
lower animals ! What could be more touching than the story
of the dog that died of grief on its master's grave ? Or the
story of the war-horse that stood by its fallen master and
defended him fiercely against the human jackals of the
battle-field ? And yet true friendship of this kind is supposed to end with the grave ! If it does, and I grant that
it does, what greater reason is there for saying that men,
who may not love one another with the intensity or loyalty
of these dumb creatures, are to be accorded the privilege of
continuing their friendship after death ?

'There are some other points I wanted to speak of.
They're not exactly religious difficulties ; they're rather
criticisms of the attitude of the Catholic Church towards
science and of her general influence on human character.
She seems to be always at loggerheads with the scientists.
At the present day every reasonable man accepts the theory
of evolution.'

Here I could not help interjecting the remark that

[1] H. von F., we may charitably suppose, never had any faith.

very recently Fleischmann of Erlangen, a scientist of high standing, had written a most damaging critique of evolution, and that the only way in which Haeckel could reply to him was to accuse him of dishonest intentions.

'Well, at all events, evolution is more probable than non-evolution. Look at it in this way : we see certain resemblances between the various species of animals. How are you going to account for them? Surely all the resemblances cannot be due to chance! Take our own subject and you will find a parallel case:—We see certain resemblances, very close and far-reaching, between French, Italian, and Spanish, and we argue therefrom that these languages grew from a common stock, which we know historically to be a fact. So, too, we see similar resemblances between the other Indo-European languages, and we trace them all back to five or six sources, such as Latin, Celtic, Slavonic, and so on. Between these chief languages we find resemblances as before, and we conclude without any historical evidence that they all sprang from some one primitive language. Similarly we can trace many of the Asiatic languages back to a common fountainhead. Should I be wrong, then in saying that not only do all the languages of the world spring from, let us say, forty or fifty parent stems, but that these parent stems themselves may have grown from a common root?[1] Your theologians, at all events, would gladly accept such a supposition simply because it accorded with the Bible narrative. But the evidence for evolution is of a similar kind exactly. Of course, it is not an absolute certainty. . . . I mean rather that if one wants to make out a case against it, there is abundant material at hand. Still, the unprejudiced man admits evolution of race, just as he admits evolution of language.'[2]

'Now for that other point I was speaking of. I have always heard, and I know it to be a fact, that Catholics are

---

[1] Philology is not yet sufficiently advanced to offer an opinion on this point.

[2] The doctrine of evolution is no doubt looked upon with disfavour by the Church. Our position is this: evolution has not yet been proved, we are therefore not certain of its truth ; we are certain of our religious belief, and we think, so far at all events, that evolution does not well accord with our belief. We cling to what we are sure of, calmly awaiting the final verdict of science.

wanting in energy and push. I do not know how things
are in your country. Here, at all events, the poorest section
of the population is Catholic. Nearly all the great business
houses are Protestant (*Evangelisch*). Most of the great
Government positions are filled by Protestants.[1] Your
people drive our vans, dig our fields, and carry our letters.
In this very town of Bonn—a so-called Catholic town—
although the Protestants are but one-third of the population,
their valuation is equal to that of the Catholics.[2] This often
struck me as very strange. Can it be that Catholicity has
a numbing effect on the faculties, or does it teach that we
ought to think nothing of thrift and hard work?

'But in spite of all that I've said, you needn't look on
me as a zealous opponent of Christianity. I subscribe myself a Protestant, although I am not really such, and in public,
at all events, I will say nothing to give offence to those who
believe themselves to be my co-religionists. Not taking
account of the Socialists, I look on Germany as divided into
two great and almost equal sections—the Catholic and the
Protestant. When I say almost equal, I mean that the
number of real Protestants is not much greater than the
number of real Catholics. Of course, there are a great many
like myself, perhaps one-third[3] of those professing Protestantism, who have no religion, but take the Protestant
side, simply because they look upon Catholicity as anti-
German, inasmuch as the centre of the religion is outside
Germany. It would not do for them to form a distinct party
as that might strengthen the Catholics and the Socialists.
In any case, we are not in favour of the spread of irreligion.
We think that the people require religion to make them
contented, to make them honest, peaceful, truthful, and in
general to observe their social obligations. So you need not
be in the least afraid that, by and by, when I am a teacher
or professor, I shall instruct my pupils in the doctrines
of unbelief. At the same time, you needn't build up any

---

[1] Simply because Protestants are unduly favoured.
[2] I have no means of checking this. I believe he altogether exaggerates
the strength of Protestantism.
[3] A mere guess.

ingenious argument [1] from the admissions I have made, about
the effect of religion on the vulgar mind. I look on the
human race as still very imperfect. We are still little more
than children. And as you give children toys of all kinds to
amuse them, and as you invent bugbears to frighten them
and make them good, so too you hold up before the vulgar
mind the threat of a future judgment, of rewards and punishments, to save them from sinning against the common good.
By and by when the race becomes perfect, it will look back
at all this as so much fiction, devised, when the world was
young, by the cunning minds of a few men, wise before their
time. . . .' [2]

We passed through the window, down a flight of steps
into the garden. It was pleasant to sit awhile in the cool
night air with the sounds of distant music wooing the ear.
My companion, whose recent words had made him more
thoughtful than usual, remained silent for many minutes,
barely rousing himself to bid me welcome to the fair retreat
in the words of his *Coloneus*, half-abstractedly uttered:
' Stranger . . . thou hast come to earth's fairest home, even
to our white Colonus ; where the nightingale, a constant
guest, trills her clear note in the covert of green glades,
dwelling amid the wine-dark ivy and inviolate bowers rich in
berries and fruit, unvisited by sun, unvexed by wind of any
storm. . . . And fed of heavenly dew, the narcissus flowers
morn by morn with fair clusters . . . and the crocus blooms
with golden beam.' And, as it chanced, there *was* a nightingale in the heart of a great chestnut-tree, fluting its silver
melodies to the sleeping songsters of the day. The lilac and
the laburnum and a flowering tree whose name eludes my
memory, supplied the place of the olive and the vine. Still
the words of the pagan writer jarred upon my ear. It was a

---

[1] A reference, of course, to the moral argument.
[2] This doctrine about the development of the human race has been often
stated, but no proof has ever been vouchsafed. The great progress, made in
physical science during the last two hundred years, has suggested the possibility of a similar development in the intellectual and moral orders. If we
appeal to the testimony of history, Plato and Aristotle, and the saints of the
early Church can hardly be regarded as mere half-developed imperfections in
comparison with the prodigies of the present era.

relief to gaze for a little space into God's Open Book, and
after all I had heard, to make new acts of faith in His
existence, and of love for His watchful care. My companion,
I felt, in spite of a keen intellect and a stainless character,
had quenched his light, if, indeed, it was ever burning, and
was groping in the dark. For him, even the voice of Nature
had lost more than half its meaning.[1]

M. Sheehan, M.A., D.Ph.

THE RISE AND PROGRESS OF HIGHER CRITICISM

THE SUPPLEMENT THEORY

WHEN men of good-will that unfortunately have either
no faith or no infallible guide, attempt to write on
the origin and meaning of Scripture or on kindred subjects,
it is no wonder they fall into error. They cannot avoid it
sooner or later, try as they may. Gladstone is an instance
of the second class. What, then, can be looked for when
rationalists that neither believe Scripture nor respect it, put
forward their theories about its origin? What shall be done
with this dry wood? Rationalists disregard all authority
and discard all tradition. Each of them is his own prophet,
and each of them has his theory. Hence the multitude of
errors. We come now to those that are classed under the
name of the Supplement-Hypothesis. This is the third
phase in the rapid development of the rationalistic treatment of Scripture. It owes its existence to the erroneous
notion that in the Pentateuch there are two distinct consti-
tuents, viz., a continuous narrative in which God's name is
Elohim, and a series of annotations to it, or a ' supplement,'
in which God is called Jehovah. The great advocate of this
hypothesis, Tuch, states the case thus : ' Not Genesis alone,

---

[1] The above article was written long before the articles of Mr. Harrison
or Sir Henry Thompson appeared in the *Fortnightly Review*, and, therefore
was not been in any sense inspired by them.

but the whole Hexateuch, has as its basis an historical composition in which God is called Elohim.' Tuch and his associates hold also that the J passages were added to the E document by the man who wrote them, or, in critical parlance, that the Jehovist is the Supplementer.

There is no difficulty in understanding how a theory of this kind was invented, and how, false though it be, it at once became popular. Intrinsically it was simply the result of a reaction in critical circles against the extravagancies of the Fragment-Hypothesis. As long as Vater and the other representatives of the second stage of higher criticism found occupation in proving that Astruc's theory was not radical enough, things went on well with them. The attention of their rationalist followers was confined to this one point. It was, indeed, easy to show by experiment that their own theory applied critical principles to the analysis of the Pentateuch with more relentless consistency than had been attempted hitherto. There could be no doubt whatever that the Fragment-Hypothesis was a far more powerful solvent than the old Documentary one; for instance where Astruc had made out thirteen elements, Vater discovered thirty-eight.

But at length even those rationalist disciples began to see that the Fragment-Hypothesis went too far; it carried the process of dissolution and disintegration to extremes; chapters and verses of Scripture were divided and subdivided into alleged heterogeneous fragments, till men grew tired and began to inquire where the process was to stop. The residuum of its analysis was almost too minute to be visible. Vater and Hartmann had overreached themselves; but this was not their only discomfiture. When they were asked to account, if they could, for the harmony of design, the beautiful unity, and the perfect arrangement of every part, in the Pentateuch, they had no answer to give. Their theory was destructive; it was not constructive. The audiences in Halle and Berlin must have felt it very unsatisfactory to be put off with the magisterial evasion, that the books of Moses were the mere outcome of a fortuitous concurrence of a multitude of short passages, and half-verses, and stray words. It presumably occurred to many of the university students that this *dictum* bore a suspicious resemblance to the atomic theory of the origin of the world propounded by Leucippus and Democritus, of which Cicero said that it would not explain the existence of even one page of Ennius.

Hence, the Supplement-Hypothesis which promised to account satisfactorily for the unity and the symmetry of the Pentateuch was eagerly welcomed. It is not, however, certain which of the critics invented this hypothesis. Holzinger, who has evidently taken great pains to investigate its origin says that it appears for the first time in this remark of De Wette's 'there runs throughout Genesis and the first chapters of Exodus a sort of epic poem which serves as the foundation of the whole. It is older than most of the fragments, and, in a certain sense, it is the original to which the fragments are attached as explanatory supplements.'[1] This was merely an *obiter dictum* quite unconnected, or, rather, quite inconsistent with the Fragment-Hypothesis which regarded the books in question as made up of independent pieces. But as we saw[2] De Wette gave up the Fragment Theory of which he had long been a strenuous supporter, and these words may be taken to indicate the change in his opinion. He did not, however, follow up the idea. Neither did Stähelin's book, *Kritische Untersuchungen über die Genesis,* Basel, 1830, lead to the formation of the new theory, though Kittel, another critic, believes it did, and of course launches into a panegyric of Stähelin for the benefit he conferred upon mankind. True, Stähelin rejected the Fragment-

---

[1] 'Durch die Genesis und den Anfang des Exodus zieht sich ein ursprüngliches Ganzes, eine Art von epischem Gedicht, welches früher als fast alle übrigen Stücke und von diesen gleichsam das Original, der Urkundensammlung uber diesen Teil der Geschichte als Grundlage gedient hat, auf welche die übrigen als Erlauterungen und Supplemente aufgetragen sind.'—*Beiträge,* ii. s. 28.

Cornill, one of the most learned rationalists at the present day, who has paid special attention to the history of higher criticism, also says in his *Einleitung* that De Wette had a faint notion of the Supplement-Hypothesis, and was favourably inclined to it, but that van Bohlen was the first to speak clearly about it.

[2] I. E. RECORD, February, 1902, p. 130.

Hypothesis, but he reverted to the old Documentary one. What has procured for Stähelin a front place amongst the founders of higher criticism was his bold opposition to Ewald's reasons for his rejection of the Fragment-Hypothesis, and, still more, his drastic examination of Ewald's own system. We mean, of course, Ewald's first system, which will be described presently. Here it is enough to say that his reviewing the *Kritische Untersuchungen* was the occasion of Ewald's abandoning a position true in itself, but badly defended by him. With the introduction of the Supplement-Hypothesis, literary criticism began to revive. It was Stähelin's work in this department that completed what had been undertaken by Eichhorn and others. He thoroughly examined the linguistic and grammatical peculiarities of Genesis, and devoted special attention to the style, etc., of the 'Jehovist.' To Stähelin's statements very little has been added since. We Catholics know that all this labour was thrown away. Stähelin's energies were spent in a bad cause. *Mutatis mutandis*, his futile attempts remind us of the never-ending toil of the Jewish rabbis who pored after their own fashion over every consonant and vowel in the law, not aware that the Messiah had come. But they did this in mistaken zeal, they believed in the Old Testament, whereas Stähelin acted out of opposition to it. Stähelin's own attempt to account for the Pentateuch was just as insane as that of the rationalists he differed from. He was of opinion that the redaction of the Pentateuch in its present form (together with the book of Joshua in its present form, Judges *minus* the appendix, and the original sources of 1 Samuel[1]) dated from the time of Saul. It might be the work of Samuel, or of one of his disciples. But the basis of it was a history from the creation to the taking possession of

---

[1] Readers must have noticed ere now the rather frequent employment of the Protestant nomenclature of some of the inspired books as well as some of the persons mentioned in them. For instance, ' Joshua, 1 Samuel, Chronicles, Isaiah, Hezekiah.' An explanation may be looked for, and it is easy to give it. The retention of these names serves to mark the passages in which they respectively occur as belonging to rationalists, the subject of whose criticism is thus expressed in their own terminology. But the terminology is not adopted. In the refutation of the rationalists, as readers may observe, the Catholic names are used, *e.g.*, ' Josue, 1 Kings, Paralipomenon,' etc.

Canaan, which contained a great part of Genesis, the greater part of the middle books, and the geographical portions of Joshua. This book was written under the early Judges. The paramount result of, or the great momentous inference from, all Stähelin's critical investigations was, that nothing in the Pentateuch is of Mosaic origin !

Descending now to particulars, Stähelin asserted that part of Genesis was made up of two documents, an Elohist and a Jehovist, both of which aimed at showing the greatness and dignity of the Israelites, by relating the history of their ancestors. The Elohist document which was written in the reign of Saul had also in view the secondary object of establishing the people's right to Palestine, while in a similar way the Jehovist document which belongs to the time of David lays stress upon the inferiority of the Gentiles and their rightful subjection to the Jews.

The compiler of our Genesis combined the twofold scope of both documents : he was a harmonizer, or redactor. When the two sources narrated the same event, he either reproduced word for word the account that suited him, or else wrote a composite narrative ; in some passages, the sources are laid under contribution equally ; in other passages one of them predominates. When, however, in the two sources one identical occurrence is referred respectively to different times or different places, he represents it as if it really happened twice. This is done by means of short interpolations which have the desired effect of making it appear that an occurrence was repeated.[1]

---

[1] A person that has not looked into the pages of the rationalist commentators, can hardly form an idea of the multifarious, occupations of the Redactor. If in an Elohist passage, ' Jehovah ' occurs, or *vice versa* ; if a verb or adverb that ought, according to higher criticism, be the exclusive property of the Elohist, occur in a Jehovist verse, or *vice versa*—if the theory won't work ; the ' Redactor' accounts for it all. But did he ever exist ? Professor Green gives the following description of the case for the Jehovist :—' A hypothetical personage who has to be represented by turns as artless and artful, as an honest reporter and a designing interpolator, as skilful and a bungler, as greatly concerned about conformity of style and thought in some passages—of which he is wholly regardless in others, and of whose existence we have no other evidence than that afforded by these contradictory allegations respecting him, can scarcely be said to have his reality established.'—*The Higher Criticism of the Pentateuch.*

In this last foolish and irreverent remark, Stähelin presumably alludes to the narrative about a king, Abimelech (Genesis xx. and xxvi. 8-11), and similar passages, technically called 'doublets.' If he believed Scripture, he would have learned that there was two monarchs of that name. Indeed Abimelech may, as Pharao or Cæsar, have not been a personal appellation, but a dynastic title. But however this may be, contrary to Scripture, and of course without the possibility of proof, Stähelin has the audacity to assert that the two narratives refer to one event.

Though his foolish fancies, to call them by a mild name, and the fancies of the other critics are seriously and minutely described in these pages, our readers will not think that any importance is attached to them, intrinsically considered. Neither will our readers think them deserving of detailed refutation. To make use of a familiar example, the ecclesiastical historian takes pains to describe accurately the absurd systems of the early Gnostics, for, inasmuch as they are a unique phase of religious error, they have a right to a place in his work, while in themselves they are nothing more than a tissue of grotesque blasphemies. The historian, however, does not feel that he is called upon to refute them all minutely ; they refute themselves. So, too, here : it is useful for ecclesiastics to know exactly what Stähelin and the other leaders of higher criticism have taught, and ecclesiastics can then for themselves disprove all the wicked notions.

We said above that Stähelin's book had the effect of making Ewald give up his early belief and his first system and this is the place to say what the object of that belief was—nothing less than the unity of the Pentateuch. When only nineteen years of age Ewald attracted the attention of all Germany by the consummate learning he displayed in his criticism of the systems of Vater and De Wette. In his *Enleitung*[1] Keil says that he gave a death-blow to the Fragment-Hypothesis. Its supporters had judged an Oriental book by the canons of European literature ; but

---

[1] Page 62, 2nd ed.

Ewald showed by examples that the respective methods of composition were widely dissimilar. His great knowledge of Arabic literature supplied him with numerous instances of sub-titles in one and the same book, of frequent repetitions, circumlocutions, etc. If all these did not militate against the unity of an Arabic work, why should the twelve Toledoth (or sections beginning with 'These are the *generations*') and apparent repetitions and displacements be considered a conclusive argument against the unity of the Pentateuch? What Ewald commenced, Ranke completed. Keil, who was one of the so-called 'orthodox Protestants,' or firm supporters of the traditional origin of the Pentateuch, remarks that Ranke's intrinsic proof of its unity buried the Fragment-Hypothesis and put it out of sight for ever.

But to return to Ewald. Against the old Document Theory he demonstrated to evidence that the two divine names (Elohim and Jehovah) are not marks indicative of two sources of information, and he brought forward numerous instances to show that the names are nowhere employed indifferently, but of deliberate choice ; that the context determines which one is to be used, and that each of the names is generally found in connection with certain characteristic words and phrases. This was Ewald's first system or theory to explain the phenomenon that had engaged the attention of scholars ever since the publication of Astruc's *Conjectures*. Here again Ewald's intimate acquaintance with the Hebrew text, and with the comparative syntax of the Semitic languages, stood him in good stead. Just as he had done when refuting the Fragment-Hypothesis, he showed that in the Pentateuch numerous *minutiæ* indicate unity of plan and identity of authorship, and that numerous archaisms and idioms distinguish the work itself from all others. Hence, concluded Ewald, where perfect harmony reigns, there cannot have been such an origin as Astruc or Eichhorn imagine.

But Ewald at length retracted all this in a review of Stähelin's book which he published in the *Studien u. Kritiken*, 1831. In this sense it may be true to say that Stähelin was the originator of the Supplement-Hypothesis,

viz. :—because his book became the occasion of Ewald's
accepting part of his assertions and of developing something
like the new theory. This is a very slender claim to the
honour and glory of being a leader among unbelievers, yet
it is painful to see how the higher critics dispute about
it. Ewald's view now was that the basis of the whole
Pentateuch (for Genesis was not to be separated from
the following books) was an historical work which reaches
from the creation of the world to the death of Moses, and
even to the conquest of Chanaan by Josue. It can be recognised by its well-defined plan and also by its simple and
beautiful style.[1] It uses Elohim as the name for God.
This is the earliest continuous narrative, and, so to speak,
the oldest stratum of the Pentateuch, though in some places
pieces still older are found imbedded in it, e.g., the Decalogue
and the Book of the Covenant (Exodus xx. 22, xxiii.). At
a later period when literary activity had increased, another
historical work was composed, which also contained extracts
from ancient documents, e.g., Genesis xiv. It took quite a
different view of the past, was richer in legends, and aimed
at a more elaborate and ornamental style of description.
As the living memory of events was gradually lost in the
course of time, the manner of representing them gained in
originality and freedom, for instance, even in the history of
the patriarchs, the name 'Jehovah' is used without the
slightest embarrassment. The author read the religious
ideas of his own time into the records of antiquity. (In the
next article the drift of this remark of Ewald's will be
explained at length.) Passages from this Jehovist narrative
were incorporated into the other, but they were so deftly
interwoven, that the Elohist source remained throughout
the groundwork or warp of the history. It might be thought
that the Jehovist passages now preserved in the Pentateuch
never had an independent existence, never formed part
of a homogeneous whole, but Ewald will not admit the

---

[1] It is as well to know that the critics of the present day, e.g., Baudissin,
Cornill, Westphal, Spurrell, Wellhausen, Driver, all agree that this document
is written in a stiff, lawyerlike manner, and that this very characteristic mode
of expression enables them to recognise it with certainty, wherever it appears.
Thus does one erroneous system contradict the other.

probability of such a conjecture, because, he says, they have a character of their own and they differ too much from the Elohist to permit our imagining that they were originally written in connection with it. These additions to the 'Elohimschrift' are not of the nature of notes. With regard to the 'Redactor' or editor who combined both these sources of information in the manner just described, Ewald declares that he is a third personage, distinct from the two authors. He did his work well ; the Jehovist passages are inserted not at random but with admirable discretion and skill. He makes use in some places of other sources, and here and there he adds connecting links in order to bind more closely the different passages. Ewald ends his critique by saying that the appearance of unity which the Pentateuch presents is due chiefly to the original arrangement of the Elohist document.

From this summary it is evident that Ewald does not hold the Supplement-Hypothesis: though some of his assertions are considered by certain critics as in reality the principles from which the hypothesis may be logically deduced. Ewald stands alone, no one agrees with him throughout. Indeed, the following rationalists differ from him on the essential point, by identifying the Supplementer with the Jehovist. Bleek, who, as we saw,[1] abandoned the Fragment Theory, now opposed Ewald, because it appeared to him that the utter absence of any connection, as he considered, between the Jehovah passages, was a clear and convincing proof that no Jehovist history, such as Ewald postulated, had ever existed. It also appeared to him that several of the J passages—whether in their original or in their revised form : i.e., after they had left the Redactor's hands—were, in the first instance, composed with reference to the E document, because they were essentially supplementary and explanatory. Moreover, they were added by the author of Genesis, and of the following books.[2] Hence.

---

[1] I. E. RECORD, February, 1902, page 140.
[2] This modification, for such it really was, of the Document-Hypothesis, once so popular, was now accepted with one limitation by van Bohlen. He asserted that the Elohist document had not been revised, or worked over twice.

the Jehovist is the Supplementer. Besides his own contributions, he added statements taken from other sources, but it would be impossible for us at the present day to determine either the nature of these sources, or the number and extent of the statements derived from them. Deuteronomy, the latest of the books, has an independent origin : its compiler combined a composition of his own, with one by the Jehovist, in which, however, he made considerable alterations. This was done in the first half of the seventh century, or, to speak more definitely, in the early part of the reign of Manasses (697-642 A.C.).

Next in the succession of higher critics comes Tuch, the 'classic writer,' as he is styled of the Supplement Theory school. He begins by making the stereotyped remark that not only in Genesis, but throughout the remainder of the Pentateuch, two documents are distinguishable by their respective use of Elohim and Jehovah as the name of God.[1] The E is the fundamental document, and it describes the events of the whole period whose history is contained in the Pentateuch. The present plan and arrangement of the Pentateuch is derived from the E; the whole legislation is taken from it, and so are the outlines and the leading features of the historical parts. The Jehovist, who at times uses the name Elohim, is the Supplementer. 'No connected

---

but that an editor or 'diaskeuast' had gathered these ancient pieces and inserted them into his recension. He was followed by Tuch (*Studien u. Kritiken*, 1835), who applied this theory to Genesis, and then by Stähelin (*Kritische Untersuchungen über den Pentateuch*, 1843), who extended the theory to the three middle books. It is worth remembering that Stähelin said he found in the legislation of these books the nucleus of the Elohist document. The new idea was hailed as a wonderful discovery by De Wette, von Lengerke, Knobel, and Delitzsch. On one point, however, the critics did not agree, viz., whether Deuteronomy (with the exception of xxxii. 48-52, and xxxiv. 1-9, which they all ascribed to the Elohist) was the work of the Jehovist or Supplementer ('the author of the second legislation,' Stähelin calls him), or of a third person, the 'Deuteronomist,' who inserted his own composition into that of the Supplementer, after having transferred the two passages about the death of Moses which were mentioned above, from the end of the Book of Numbers to the places they now occupy in Deuteronomy. Stähelin maintained the first notion ; Tuch, von Lengerke, De Wette held the second.

[1] The opposite notion, viz., that this mark of difference ceases at Exodus vi. 2-8 is universally accepted by rationalists at the present day. See any one of the critics. According to Strack, Ewald deserves the credit of this discovery.

passage of his is extant, what belongs to him is at present
so interwoven with the background of the Pentateuch
that it is only supplementary to it. In fact, it is only in this
relation that the J possesses either purpose or coherency.
Where E's information is meagre, J's is full.' Just as
Ewald, Tuch perceives in the employment of the name
Jehovah before the time of Moses, a different view of
antiquity from that taken by the Elohist, and an inaccurate
view, viz., that the true religion of Israel was the primitive
one. The human race did not start with monotheism.
(This is one of the most diabolical ideas of the higher
critics. We shall see it fully worked out when we come
to Wellhausen and his followers). The same tendency to
interpret the past by the present is visible also in J's
description of civilization. It may be added that, both in
language and in style of composition E and J differ.
Granting, just for the sake of discussion, that J was originally
an organic whole, a literary work properly so called, then
the Redactor made alterations in the passages which he
took from J, and he added passages of his own. Tuch however
insists that the supposition of the Redactor being a distinct
individual not only calls for one writer more than the data
either need or allow, but that it creates a difficulty. Besides,
even if it were not so certain as it is, it is simpler—and this
consideration, in Tuch's opinion, settles the matter—to say
that it was the Jehovist gave the book its present form.
The style of the Pentateuch throughout shows that both E
and J depended on written documents. This is acknowledged in matters of history, and is evident to every attentive
observer in matters of legislation (E). Tuch is certain that
E and J were written in the time of the Kings and in the
land of Chanaan. They were known not only to the writer
of Deuteronomy, but also to the earlier prophets. Descending at last to particulars, Tuch informs the world at large
that the E document, which has not a word about the
temple, but which describes the tabernacle from eyesight,
must belong to the reign of Saul; while the J one, or the
Supplementer's, which presupposes a new Jehovah cult
that to him is the chief object of interest, must have been

written some time subsequently. As, however, the centralization of worship in Jerusalem had not yet been introduced, this series of annotations cannot have been added to the E later than the time of Solomon. In Tuch's system there is the deadly virus of that 'higher criticism' which has done incalculable harm to the souls of many; but the consideration of some of its points—such as monotheism not being the primitive religion, centralization, etc.—will be more conveniently treated of in connection with Wellhausen's system, in which all these notions are completely developed.

In 1840 De Wette renounced for ever the Fragment-Hypothesis;[1] *i.e.*, with one exception; for he continued to hold that in the two chief sources several fragments of even greater antiquity were preserved, and adopted the new

---

[1] What De Wette says on the origin of the Pentateuch, in the seventh and last edition of his *Einleitung* (pp. 193, 194) must be taken as the expression of his final opinion. He says there: ' Die Hypothese, dass der Pentateuch aus einzelnen Stücken von zweifelhaften ursprünglichen Zusammenhange zusammengestellt worden, ist nunmehr mit Recht aufgegeben, da wir gesehen haben dass die Urschrift Elohim ein ganzes gebildet hat, und der Jehovist fast durchdeg denselben schriftstellerischen Charakter bewahrt. An jener Hypothese ist nur so viel wahr, dass der Elohist einige ältere Stücke in sein Werk aufgennomen zu haben scheint, und auch unter den Jehovistichen Bestandtheilen manche älter seyn mögen. Wegen des einheitlichen Charakters der jehovistichen Bestandtheile, bei dem Mangel eines sie verbindeten Planes ist es auch nicht wahrscheinlich, dass sie ehedem eine Schrift für sie gebildet, welche der Sammler mit der Urschrift E. zusammengearbeitet hätte. Das Warscheinlichste vielmehr ist, dass der Jehovist durch Bearbeitung und Vermehrung jener Urschrift den vier ersten Büchern ihre heutige Gestalt gegeben hat, nur dass nach seiner Redaction die Elohistichen Bestandtheile des 5 B. Moses und Vielleicht 5 Moses xxxi. 14-22 dash 4 Buch schlossen. Späterhin schob dann der Deuteronomist seine Ermahnungsreden, die neue Gesetzgebung, und die Verpflictung auf das Gesetz ein, und setzte die Schlusstheile des 4 Büches ans Ende.'

In his *Founders of Higher Criticism* (p. 32) Cheyne speaks thus of De Wette:—' His views on the composition of the Pentateuch are of a highly provisional character. He hovers between the Fragment and the Document-Hypothesis, and, though he is evidently not hopeless of reconciling them, he cannot form a distinct theory of his own.' And (p. 50): ' Extensive and useful as his critical work is, we cannot say that it is worthy of the epoch-making opener of the historical criticism of the Pentateuch. In definite literary and historical results it is comparatively poor. And this remark applies to all De Wette's critical writings, alike on the Old Testament and on the New. In both departments of study he began with scepticism and negativism, and as a rule fails to attain to positive conclusions, much less to assured historical synthesis. And the reason is that he has a theory of criticism which, though not unsound, is incomplete.' N.B.—Cheyne himself is a thorough rationalist.

theory. He now agreed with Tuch that the Jehovist was
the author of the additions to the E document; but, in
opposition to Stähelin, he distinguished between the Jehovist
and the Deuteronomist. The Deuteronomist, who belonged
to a later period, added to the Jehovistic rescension the
warnings which he ascribes to Moses, the new legislation, and
the exhortations to observe the law. The original E document, apart from its own quotations, on the one hand, and
the additions subsequently made to it on the other, belongs
at the earliest to the reign of Jeroboam I. (937-915). The
Jehovist wrote at a time when prophecy had reached a very
high degree of perfection. Genesis xxvii. 40 (Isaac's prophecy
about Edom) would indicate the reign of Jehoram II.
(851-843), King of Judah. We may observe, in passing, that
this highly ' critical ' remark of De Wette's is intended to
imply, presumably with a sneer, that the ' alleged ' prophecy
was contemporary with the event it referred to. This being a
first principle of high criticism, no rationalist would demean
himself by giving a reason for his holding it. The first trace
of the Deuteronomist's existence that De Wette can discover
is the finding of the book of the law under Josiah (640-609) !
So the tale ended. Von Lengerke and the elder Delitzsch
accepted this partly original system of De Wette's, but, of
course, with some modifications, just to show that they had
as much right to be ' higher critics ' as he could lay claim to.
Lengerke assigned the E document to the beginning of
Solomon's reign, and the J to the Assyrian period. Delitzch
had his own equally true and equally creditable opinion, but
afterwards he changed it for the two Elohist-theory, Priestly
code, etc. While these rationalists were putting the oldest
books of Scripture through permutations enough to delight
the heart of an algebraician, Ewald, whom Holzinger proudly
styles ' der Vater der Erganzungshypothese,' had seen fit also
to alter his theory. He disclaimed any sympathy with the
Supplement-Hypothesis and its attempts to solve the Pentateuchal problem ' in the simplest way possible.' Instead of
it he now put forward what Delitzsch has happily called
' the crystallization hypothesis.' It was in reality nothing
more than the development of an idea which Ewald had

always held, viz., that in the first four books of the Pentateuch there were many passages assignable neither to E nor J.

The elaborate analysis of the sources whence these passages were derived is to be found in the prolegomena to Ewald's *History of Israel*, a well-known work which contains a veritable mine of philological lore in its abundant notes, but which in point of archæology and comparative chronology has long since been superseded. What however in it concerns us now is its introductory part, and in particular the sections of this which give the authorities made use of in the history, together with copious notices of them, literary, critical and biographical. Every relevant detail connected with these personages is stated with that conscientious thoroughness and completeness which is characteristic of a German professor's knowledge of the literature of his subject. And at the same time, all this is done with such tranquil ease and calm confidence, that a reader whose educational outfit had been supplied exclusively by magazines and periodicals of a certain class, by non-Catholic works on Scripture, etc., and who knew only that Ewald was reported to be a man of prodigious erudition and the greatest Orientalist of his day, would be led to repose implicit faith in his statements. Whatever Ewald wishes to say is said so dogmatically, that the uneducated individual we have been contemplating would certainly think he had some reason for saying it. Such a person would naturally make some reflections such as these :— ' Though I have never heard of these books, the famous Göttingen Professor of Scripture has read them all, and he evidently knows who wrote them, and when and where these authors lived, and it is by means of this recondite information that he is enabled to throw such new and unexpected light on the history of Israel. All the magazines I read are loud in their praise of his book, so its contents shall henceforth be part of my mental system.' Yet if a person who knew only from what he heard as a child that the Pentateuch was written by Moses, spoke in this fashion, he would be surrendering so much truth at the bidding of an impertinent rationalist. Ewald was great as a linguist and

grammarian, but not as a commentator or a historian: in
this he resembles Huxley and Mivart, men learned in their
own departments where they ought to have remained, but
fond of excursions into theology about which they knew
nothing, and where they failed. How can men that have not
faith, speak rightly about the things of God? Every line
in the imaginary books discoursed about by Ewald, exists in
the real books which the Jewish and then the Christian
Church has guarded for more than thirty centuries. There
is nothing new in the introduction to his history of Israel,
except the arbitrary divisions and combinations of the
Inspired Word, the pseudo-chronology and the list of hypothetical authors, those airy nothings to whom Ewald would
fain give a local habitation and a name. None of them was
ever mentioned in Scripture, tradition, or profane history:
no trace of even one of them, or even of any work written
by one of them, is to be found in all antiquity—but,
never mind, ' higher criticism ' will call them from the vasty
deep. Ewald is intimately acquainted with their works, of
course he was all but personally acquainted with themselves.
and only circumstances over which he had no control prevented him from actually looking over the shoulder of the
Redactor while that estimable old gentleman was combining
his selections from their works, and fusing them into one
composition, which ignorant people will persist in attributing to Moses.

1. Let us open the ' Introduction.' First of all we are
shown by Ewald ' The Great Book of Origins.' (At present,
if you please, the correct name for it is ' the Hexateuch.' It
is co-extensive with the Pentateuch and Josue.) In it, the
Professor informs us, the only passages from the pen of
Moses are the Decalogue, a few poems, and some legal
axioms or short *formulæ* for the use of judges. None of the
more lengthy laws, none of the numerous series of enactments, were written by him. The Great Book contains also
some fragments of very early date ; for instance, the list of
encampments in Numbers xxxiii.; the enrolments, Numbers
i.-iv.; the battle of the allied kings and the meeting of
Abraham and Melchizidech, Genesis xiv., etc.

2. The Book of the Wars of Jehovah. It is referred to
in Numbers xxi. 14. The song of triumph (Exodus xv.
1-18), chanted by the people after the passage through the Red
Sea, probably belonged to this book; so, too, did Joshua
xiv. 18.

3. The Biography of Moses, written about a century
after his death. Only two passages, both of them about his
relations with Jethro (Exodus iv. 8 and xviii.) can be
referred with certainty to it.

4. The Book of the Covenants.[1] This is the most
ancient of the historical books, properly so called. It is
Elohist throughout, and its name is due to the description
of the covenant made between Elohim and Israel, ' in the
sublimest passage of the history' (Exodus xxiv.), and of the
covenants made between Jacob and Laban (Genesis xxxi.
41-54), Abimelech and Isaac (xxvi. 28-31), and Abimelech
and Abram (xxi. 22-30). Between the ratifications of all
these covenants a very remarkable resemblance exists.
The work itself began with the history of Abram, and
contained what are now fragments in Genesis, from ch. xi.
on ; in Exodus, among other passages, the collection of laws
xxi. 2, xxii. 19—i.e., a part of what is now often called ' the
Book of the Covenant '[2]—and fragments in Numbers, Josue,
and Judges. It must have been written in the latter half of
the period of the Judges, or, to speak more particularly, in

---

[1] Error reproduces itself in another form. Spinoza, who had hold that
Esdras was the author of the Pentateuch, had granted to Moses the authorship of the Book of the Wars of the Lord (Exodus xvii. 14), of the Book of
the Covenant (Exodus xx. 22, 23), and of some Book of the Law, which was
the foundation of the alleged legislation.

[2] It may not be superfluous to direct some readers' attention to the point
that this book of Ewald's is quite distinct from the 'Book of the Covenant '
or 'Bundesbuch ' (xxi. 22, xxiii.), which later critics are so fond of talking about.
Of course, the assumed independent existence of either book is equally
chimerical. Ewald's 'Book der Bündnisse' may have suggested to his pupil,
Wellhausen, the idea of the 'Vierbundesbuch ' (Quatuor Foederum Liber), the
symbol of which is Q; but Wellhausen's Q is substantially the E, or the
'Grundschrift.' He himself says: 'Ich habe für die s. g. Grundschrift das
Zeichen Q gewählt als Abkürzung für Vierbundesbuch (quatuor) welchen
Namen ich als den passendsten für sie vorschlage.' Wellhausen's four
covenants, all differing from those selected by Ewald, are the following :—
1. Between God and our first parents (Genesis i. 28-30). 2. Between God and
Noah (ix. 1-17). 3. Between God and Abraham (xvii.). 4. Between God and
Israel (Exodus vi. 2 ff).

the time of Sampson (*a Danite*), as may be inferred from
its words now preserved in Genesis xlix. 16.[1] 'Dan shall
judge his people as one of the tribes in Israel.'

5. The Book of Origins. It is the first to contain legislation in detail, and it is Elohist (or uses Elohim to designate
God) up to God's manifestation of Himself to Israel (Exodus
vi. 2-8), after which it is Jehovist as a rule. It was written
within the first twelve years of Solomon's reign by a priest
who intended to set forth the origins of what existed in his
time, chiefly with a view to religion. He began his work
with a description of the creation of the world, and he
concluded it with a short narrative of the building of
Solomon's temple (Kings viii. 11), now somewhat altered.

Ewald thus states his arguments for the date which he
assigns to the Book of Origins [1] :—

Here it is said among other things that Abraham, and likewise
Sarah and Jacob, shall become ' a multitude of nations, and that
kings shall come out of them.' Now, why should the blessing
be so defined and limited to something so special and seemingly
so casual as that kings should descend from the Patriarchs? and
how is it that such a conception of the divine promise is found
only in the demonstrable fragments of this book, and in no other?
This question can never be answered, but by maintaining that the
work belongs to the first period of the rising monarchy which
advanced the true prosperity of Israel, when, in the full sense of
the words, ' a multitude of nations ' assembled round the throne
of the far-ruling king of Israel, and Israel, after the dismal days
of dissolution and weakness, could boast with a new pride that it
possessed 'kings.' . . . We are brought nearer to a result by
a passage on the kings of Edom, in Genesis xxxvi., closely connected with the above-mentioned declarations. When about to
enumerate the series of the kings of Edom, the author finds
occasion to add that they reigned before there reigned any king in
in Israel. There was then a king in Israel at the time he wrote
this ; and the words excite in us the feeling that he half-envied
Edom for having enjoyed far sooner than Israel the blessing of an
united and well-regulated kingdom. But, further, not only is the
last enumerated king in this series described as if the narrator
had known him exactly as one of the kings of Israel, but the

---

[1] N.B.—A *soi-disant* prophecy, according to Ewald.
[2] *History of Israel*, English translation, p. 75, ff.

enumeration of the kings is followed (v. 40-43) by that of the chieftains of Edom, as if after the monarchy the country had returned to the rule of chiefs; this sounds quite as if David had already vanquished the last king of Edom and put the country again under mere chieftains. The Hadad, descended from the blood of the kings of Edom, who at David's conquest fled, very young, to Egypt, may have been a grandson of Hadad, the last king, as the grandson frequently bears the grandfather's name.

But the exactest indication of the period of composition of this work is to be sought in the dedication of the temple of Solomon, 1 Kings viii. 1-11. The account, as we have it, has, indeed, indubitably passed through the hands of a subsequent reviser, who must have altered or added much of it: yet it preserves the clearest traces of having been originally composed by the historian whose work we are here considering; so that we cannot but allow that the author must have finished his work after the great event of the dedication of the temple of Solomon. The main proofs of this assertion are: the use of the word 'nasbi,' v. 1, and of the expression 'col adath Ishrael hannodim halaiw' (all the congregation of Israel, that were assembled unto him) v. 5, which all have the peculiar air of the Book of Origins; the perfect harmony of v. 7, ff. with Exodus xxv. 13, ff. 20; xxxvii. 9; Numbers iv. 6, ff; and on the contrary the discrepancy between these descriptions and 1 Kings vi. 23-27; lastly, the remarkable agreement of v. 10 ff. with Exodus xl. 34, ff., the weight of which cannot be made apparent till we treat of the Mosaic time.[1]

Wherever a section begins with the explanation of the origin of any important tribe or family, the author always puts as a kind of title the words, 'These are the origins;' and where the family of the first man, and consequently the proper commencement of this whole work on the history of mankind begins, it is said, 'This is the origin of man.' And, in fact, it can hardly be doubted that in accordance with this superscription, the work bore the short title of 'The Book of Origins.'[2]

This extract is rather long, but it is given in order that our readers may have the opportunity of judging for themselves the strength of the arguments on which Ewald relies.

---

[1] *History of Israel*, page 80.

[2] Toledoth is the Hebrew for 'origins,' 'generations.' There are in Genesis ten ' Toledoth ' sections, or sections commencing with the words; ' These are the generations,' viz. (of heaven and earth). ii. 4; (of Adam) v. 1; (of Noe) vi. 9; (of the sons of Noe) x. 1; (of Sem) xi. 10; (of Thare) xi. 27; (of Ismael) xxv. 12; (of Isaac) xxv. 19; (of Esau) xxxvi. 1; (of Jacob) xxxvii. 2.

Could any more futile and illogical be conceived? His first one tacitly assumes the impossibility of prophecy, and consequently involves a *petitio principii*. The Book of Origins says that there will be kings of Jacob's line, therefore, concludes Ewald, it must have been written at a time when there were already kings in Israel. The fundamental axiom of rationalistic exegesis which underlies this mode of reasoning is directly opposed to the statements in the Book of Origins and to all similar statements in Scripture, for which ostensibly Ewald professes respect. Considerable portions of Scripture, and in the Old Testament all the more important parts, are based on the fact of revelation and prophecy: if they are impossible, those parts of Scripture, and by implication the remaining parts too, are done away with. So much for Ewald's theory. Yet, after all, it cannot be said that he is inconsistent, because considered in itself neither Scripture in general nor the Book of Origins in particular is the object of his belief and respect: but only Scripture and the Book of Origins as edited and commented on by Ewald. The English translator of his *History of Israel*, Russell Martineau, says, with perfect truth. in his own introduction : ' Niebuhr and Ewald do not believe the history as it is told; they tell it as they believe.' Of course, this is intended for high praise. Russell means that as Niebuhr took a critical and philosophical view, *e.g.*, of the story about Numa Pompilius, so did Ewald of ' the legends of Israel.' This is, indeed, only too manifest in the history itself ; for instance, the chapter on the Levitical instructions comes after the chapter on the monarchy.

In the next place it may be observed that in this argument, Ewald has resorted to a favourite trick of the higher critics. He adroitly appropriates all the texts (Genesis xvii. 6, 16; xxxv. 11) that mention royal descendants of Abraham and Jacob; then he triumphantly challenges his opponents to quote another. In the present instance this was child's play to Ewald, he knew there were only three such passages; but even where there is need of collecting fifty or a hundred instances of the recurrence of a word or of a phrase, and of being certain that every single instance has been extracted

before the opponent is called on to produce an additional
one if he can, this piece of jugglery can be done with the
assistance of a Concordance; it costs only a little time, and
it is found to be highly effective when the critic has to do
with uninitiated readers. They are surprised, and, at the
same time, deeply impressed by his informing them that a
Hebrew verb is employed eighty-three times, and only by
J; that it is, in fact, one of J's characteristic words; or,
again, that a Hebrew adverb is the exclusive property of the
second Elohist, or that a certain construction will never be
found outside the Priestly code, or that genealogies are a
sure mark of P. In the last case, for instance, how could it
be otherwise? All the genealogies in these books have been
enumerated accurately, not one has been overlooked; and
when the list is complete every genealogy is labelled 'P.'
So, too, here Ewald takes the three texts; then he asks is it
not wonderful that *all* the texts referring to kings descended
from Jacob should be in the Book of Origins (which he has
previously so constructed that it includes the three), and
then he infers that the book must really exist. Of course,
if the texts are part of a book, and are not to be found
outside the Book of Origins, then it follows that it is
a reality. If the exegetical juggler is allowed to beg
the premises, he will in return make you a present of the
conclusion.

The same remark applies to what Ewald says about his
Book of Origins (see the end of extract). He first collected
all the passages in Genesis that commence with the formula
'These are the generations' (or origins, *i.e.*, *Toledoth;* see
the twelve passages, *supra*, p. 511). He then directed
attention to the significant fact, that his Book of Origins, or
of generations, always uses these words as a title of its
sections. Was it not wonderful? Ewald's second argument is
that the mention of kings that ruled in Edom before there was
a king of Israel, shows that the author of Genesis xxxvi. 31
was contemporary with an Israelite monarch. Now if Ewald
is acting in good faith, if he sincerely considers his inference
to be correct, we can only say that he betrays his ignorance
of a Hebrew idiom. At the sametime it must be confessed

that such an excuse for the author of a masterly work on
Hebrew grammar is by no means satisfactory. But however
this may be, the word used in the text, *lipnei* = ' before,'
implies no affirmation such as Ewald attempts to make out.
It implies nothing whatever. It tells us only this, that
during a certain period, while there was no monarch in
Israel, the Edomites had kings. It gives no information
about subsequent times, neither does it warrant any inference
regarding them. So far as the Hebrew word *lipnei* informs
us, we could not say that there ever was an Israelite monarch.
Let us take a parallel instance with which we are all familiar.
It occurs in St. Matthew i. 18—' Antequam convenirent,
inventa est in utera habens de Spiritu Sancto.' Helvidius
and other opponents of our Blessed Lady's virginity quoted
the evangelist, or rather misquoted him, to prove their
blasphemous assertion. But St. Jerome who knew Hebrew
replied:—' Quod autem dicitur ; antequam convenirent ; non
sequitur ut postea convenerint ; sed Scriptura, quod factum
non sit ostendit.' The answer to Ewald's objection also is
non sequitur. Of course Moses knew that there were to be
kings in Israel ; not only did he record the predictions referred
to above, but he mentions the future fact (Deuteronomy,
xxviii. 86), and legislates accordingly (*ib.* xvii. 14-20). Another
unwarranted inference of Ewald's is that the author of Genesis
xxxvi. 31, almost envied Edom, her kings ; but let this pass.
It is, however, necessary to remark that several grammatical
peculiarities in the passages are missed, or ignored by Ewald.
There is, as (Archbishop) Smith points out so well in his work
on the Pentateuch, neither a plural nor a collective noun (*king*
or *kings*) that might imply an existing dynasty ; there is
no concrete expression, no definite article, no historical
tense, to point to any event, past, present, or to future.
The Hebrew phrase is as abstract as it could be. In bar-
barous Latin ' ante regnare regem in Israel ' would be
an equivalent. The Septuagint renders it well : προ του
βασιλευσαι βασιλεα εν Ισραηλ (E). Ewald is wrong, too, in
concluding that the passage appears to imply that after the
monarchy the land of Edom had returned to the rule of
chiefs. There is absolutely nothing to justify this inference.

What is in the passage, Ewald does not mention; and what
is not in the passage even virtually, he talks about. He could
have seen in Exodus xv. 15 that the chiefs or 'Alluphim '
were the contemporaries of a king. Smith makes it very
probable that the Alluphim were the hereditary nobility
descended from Esau, and the electors of the king. (See
also Knabenbauer). Lastly, there is nothing to show that
the Hadad who fled into Egypt (3 Kings xi. 14 was the
grandson of the Hadad spoken of in Genesis xxxvi. 35. The
identity of name is no proof. So far as that goes he might
as well have been the twentieth in descent, and Scripture
shows he was far removed.

Ewald's last objection is a masterpiece of higher criticism and another *petitio principii.* The chimerical Book
of Origins contains the description of the dedication of
Solomon's temple simply and solely because Ewald is pleased
to put 3 Kings viii. 1-11 into it. Is it not wonderful? His
book would also include a description of the dedication of
the second temple, if he chose to insert 1 Esdras vi. 15-17;
and he would have had just as much reason for doing it.

Lastly, as regards what he calls the main proofs of this
assertion, passing by the fact that the Septuagint appear
not to have read *nashi* in verse 1, and that some scholars
regard it as a gloss, we observe that the word also is found
in Ezechiel and Paralipomenon. Why did not Ewald incorporate into his book the passages of these books that
contain the word? It may be observed, too, that the phrase,
col edath Ishrael hannodin hailaw, is used also in the parallel
passage 2 Paralipomenon v. 6. Why is this verse not admitted
into the Book of Origins, seeing that the phrase confessedly
has the peculiar air of that book? In his next proof Ewald
is simply trifling with the intelligence or the patience of his
readers. What support does the perfect harmony between
the statement in 3 Kings and those in Exodus and Numbers
afford to his visionary theory? We read in these passages
that the Cherubim, with outstretched wings, overshadowed
the ark; but surely this argument is not due to the
existence of a Book of Origins. The simple reason is that
one part of Scripture necessarily agrees with another, and

when Solomon is doing what Moses did, what is more natural than that the words of the first description should reappear in the second? Lastly, 3 Kings vi. 23-27, which gives the dimensions of the Cherubim, is quite intelligible in connection with the other passages.

Ewald thus apostrophises the author of the Book of Origins :—

Lofty spirit ! Thou whose work has for centuries not irrationally had the good fortune of being taken for that of thy great hero, Moses himself, I know not thy name, and I divine only from thy vestiges when thou didst live and what thou didst achieve ; but if these, thy traces incontrovertible, forbid me to identify thee with him who was greater than thee, and whom thou thyself dost desire to magnify according to his deserts, then behold that there is no guile in me, nor any pleasure in knowing thee not absolutely as thou art.—(Page 96.)

After this rhapsody Ewald proceeds to describe the other personages on whose word he relies—the so-called ' prophetic narrators.' As used by him the name has not the meaning we attach to it.[1] In Ewald's pages it denotes philosophical historians of a certain kind, writers that take intelligent views of the past and deal freely with their materials, combining them so that they shall convey to ordinary readers the meaning which the historians were the first to perceive in them. Describing their influence, Ewald says :—

But more powerful than anything else was the prophetic conception and treatment of history throughout the entire course of these ages ; and as this prophetic conception has greater freedom to mould the subject matter to its will, the further the field of the narrative is removed from the present time, and the more it has thereby become already the subject of a higher kind of contemplation, it found in the primitive history the most impressionable soil on which it could combine with historical composition. This is the main cause of the great freedom of repeated narration,

---

[1] Our readers will not have forgotten that Ewald rejects prophecy, properly understood. The word ' prophetic,' in a Rationalist's mouth, has no more value than ' inspiration ' and ' revelation ' have. They all have lost their meaning. As regards Ewald's ' prophetic narrators,' they appear to have been invented, consciously or unconsciously, in order to serve as prototypes and precedents for himself. They do not believe the primitive history as it is told ; they tell it as they believe. In this way Ewald obtains the highest possible sanction for his history of Israel.

which so remarkably distinguishes this work from the Book of
Origins and the older books; for all legendary literature will
endeavour more to break through old restraints, and will move
with the greater freedom the oftener it treats the same subject-
matter; but here it was especially the grandeur of prophetic
truths, that declared itself by means of the freer exposition thus
admitted.

Let us now make the acquaintance of these worthies,
about whom Ewald discourses so eloquently.

3. The third narrator, an Ephraimite, who lived either
in the end of the tenth or in the beginning of the ninth
century, A.C., a contemporary of Elijah or of Joel. He uses
Elohim as the name for God in his description of the pre-
Mosaic period; many of the Elohist elements in Genesis
proceed from him, *e.g.*, chapter xx. (sojourn at Gerar),
xxviii. 10-22 (Jacob's dream at Bethel), xxix.-xxxi. (Jacob in
Mesopotamia), and much of the history of Joseph, which he
must have invested with its present charming dress. Also
historical passages in Exodus and Numbers. Ewald gives
the finishing touch to the portrait thus :—

> The third narrator is far removed from the more artistic repre-
> sentation and bolder painting of the fourth narrator, next to be
> mentioned. But this narrator's peculiar pre-eminence consists in
> his uncommonly high and distinct conception of the working of
> the Divine and prophetic spirit. As narrator of the primitive
> history he is the best prophet, just as the author of the Book of
> Origins was the best legislator and national leader.

4. This character makes his debut in the second edition
of Ewald's *Geschichte Israels*. He is credited with Genesis
iii.-xii. 2, 3; xviii., xix. 1-28; xxii. 18; xxvi. 4; xxxii. 11,12;
Exodus xxxii.-xxxiv. He is stated to have employed earlier
narratives largely, to have added much that is new, and to
have revised extraneous matter in a prophetic spirit. Ewald
says :—' If we regard closer the truths which are here forced
upon us, we shall have to confess that they flow from a
height of prophetic activity and advanced national culture
totally foreign to the "Book of Origins."' [1] This narrator is

---

[1] Insane as this is, it is not so mad as the notion of Ewald's pupil,
Wellhausen, and other higher critics of the present day, viz., that the priestly
narrator and the prophetic contradict one another.

rather Jehovist, and he lived about the end of the ninth or
the beginning of the eighth century.

5. The fifth [1] prophetic narrator who is Jehovist from the
first word he writes, was a native of the kingdom of Judah.
He lived in the reign of either Uzziah or Jotham (first half,
or middle of eighth century), and it was he put the narratives
together. He also composed a good deal. With the exception of a few passages noted elsewhere, he wrote the first
four books of Genesis, the end of Deuteronomy, and the book
of Joshua.[2] But his work was subsequently enlarged by
the three Redactors.

Here again with delightful freedom Ewald repudiated one
of his once cherished discoveries; he might well be called
the Henry VIII. of higher criticism. According to the
first edition of his *History of Israel*, the fragment,
Leviticus xxvi. 3-45, must have been inserted by a
descendant of one of the exiled inhabitants of Israel, at
the end of the eighth or beginning of the seventh century
(First Redactor); Deuteronomy i. 1, xxxii. 47, xxxiv. 10-12,
during the second half of the reign of Manasseh, by some
one originally belonging to the kingdom of Judah but
then an exile in Egypt (Second Redactor, who also gave the
book of Joshua its present shape), and lastly the blessings
of Moses, Deuteronomy xxxiii., added probably in the reign of
Josiah (Third Redactor). The second edition of Ewald's
history arranges the origin of Deuteronomy differently. The
author composed it as an independent work of much greater
extent than what now goes by the name because it described
the whole course of the Mosaic history. The Third Redactor
who inserted Deuteronomy xxxiii. united what he retained
of the original Deuteronomy to the other books of the
Hexateuch, and, of course, gave Deuteronomy its final
form.

This eclectic, bizarre group of hypotheses was intended
to be a golden mean between supernaturalism and mythism,
the latter of which Ewald held in particular detestation.
As is well known, he had a supreme and sovereign contempt

---

[1] Fourth, 1st ed.
[2] See in proof, all their J passages.

for German philosophy,[1] Fichte, Schelling, and Hegel being abominations in his eyes. Both Baur and Strauss were Hegelians, both of them leaders of the Tübingen mythical school, and both of them abhorred by Ewald. Not only on Scripture but in politics, was he diametrically opposed to them. He believed that there was an intimate connection between their system of mythical interpretation, and the revolutionary excesses of 1848. He himself was an uncompromising conservative, and in consequence of his political opinions was twice deprived of his chair in Göttingen, first in 1837 and then in 1867 (on the latter occasion, because when Hanover was annexed by Prussia, he would not acknowledge William I. as his king). Ewald all along paid more attention to the Hegelianism of Baur and Strauss than to that of Vatke, because the latter's cumbrous involved style deterred people from reading him and because he had little or no following in the German universities at the time. There cannot, however, be any doubt of Vatke's dependence on Hegel. Westphal, one of the historians of higher criticism, and a critic himself, says :—

On pourrait faire une etude fort interessante sur la parenté philosophique des ouvrages de George et Vatke, avec La Vie de Jesus de Strauss, qui parut la meme annee qu'eux (1835), et dont Ulhorn a dit avec raison qu'elle est née de l'union de la philosophie hegelienne avec la critique.[2]

Ewald's own system gained no adherents, it was represented by himself. This may have been owing to his antagonism to German philosophy. He never tolerated any opposition to his own theories, and he seldom deigned to give a proof for what he said. ' L'interpretation c'est moi.' He was the personification of the dogmatic, autocratic spirit of rationalism. We may mention one act, characteristic of the man. On the occasion of the Vatican Council he addressed to Pius IX. an open letter, published in the newspapers, advising the Pope to turn Protestant.

But to return to the Supplement-Hypothesis. Its period

---

[1] See his *Lehre der Bibel*, vol. ii., p. 45.
[2] *Sources du Pentat.* p. xxi.

of popularity was by this time fast coming to an end. Only
three or four more critics employed it in their respective
attacks on the Pentateuch. The first of them, Knobel
(1861), still maintained that E was the 'Grundschrift' (or
that the passages in which God is called Elohim formed the
basis of the Pentateuch), but he asserted that its author,
who lived in the time of Saul, had incorporated into it some
written documents of an earlier date, *e.g.*, the lists in
Numbers i. and xxxiii. But what Knobel prided himself
on was his discovery in the Pentateuch of a ' Rechtsbuch '
and a 'Kriegsbuch.' It was to no purpose that another very
advanced critic, Kuenen, professor in Leyden, told him that
these books existed only in his imagination. Knobel determined to stake on them his hopes to immortal fame as a
Biblical critic. Of course the ' Rechtsbuch' was nothing
else than an arbitrary selection from the law of Moses,
almost identical with what is now styled the second Elohist
code. Knobel's theory about it was briefly this : The
' Rechtsbusch ' was written after the ' Grundschrift,' from
which it differs in two respects. Its statements are not
entitled to the same respect, and while the ' Grundschrift '
has only theocratic laws, the ' Rechtsbuch ' contains besides
very much social legislation. Its author was a Levite, who
lived in the northern kingdom at a time, as appears from
Number xxiv. 20, and Judges xviii. 30, when Assyria had
already become a great power. Knobel's other 'independent
source of history,' the ' Kriegsbuch, or Book of the Wars,'
was ' discovered,' or invented, in the same way. Knobel
simply put together the numerous passages about the wars
of Jehova. Then he declared that this document is distinguished from both G and R by being the work of a
Jehovist, who lived in the Kingdom of Judah in the reign of
Jehosaphat, and was apparently a Levite. He is the Supplementer. His additions are taken from legends, popular
notions, and from written documents also in his account of
the Patriarchs. But the J document never was an original
and independent composition, all of it has reference to the
E. This is the way the Jehovist worked : He made E the
foundation (on which account, sapiently observes Knobel,

almost the whole of E is extant). In order to supplement
it, he inserted passages taken from the other two sources, a
great many of them being taken from the ' Rechtsbuch, and
only a few from the ' Kriegsbuch.' He preserved the words
of the originals as far as possible, and harmonized the texts
with considerable care and skill. Knobel utterly rejected
Stähelin's indentification of the Jehovist and the Deuteronomist. His theory was that the Deuteronomist had both
the E and J documents before him when writing, and that
he was the last contributor to the Hexateuch, because his
Hebrew shows that he was a contemporary of the prophet
Jeremiah. In England Dean Stanley accepted the Supplement-Hypothesis unreservedly, and Bishop Perowne with
some exceptions. Colenzo also partly held the Supplement-
Hypothesis, but he contributed nothing deserving of notice
to its development. He was a retailer of other rationalists'
opinions. One attempt he can, however, claim as his own;
he was the first to attack the veracity of the ' Grundschrift.'
But this exploit belongs to the history of the Development-
Hypothesis.

Schrader comes next. He proposed to combine the
three Hypotheses (Document, Fragment, Supplement),
especially the first and third, into one harmonious system.
According to Schrader, the Pentateuch is the result mainly
of two documents, one of which was written by the annalist
(first E), the other by the theocratic narrator (second E).
A third writer, the prophetic narrator (or the Jehovist),
treated both texts very freely, and united them at the same
time, making minor additions from written and oral
traditions, as he thought fit. The Jehovist is, therefore,
both Supplementer and Redactor. A fourth writer, the
Deuteronomist, then inserted into this composite work, 'the
Law of Moses ' (Deuteronomy i. 1, xxxi. 12), the nucleus of
which (iv.-xxviii.) was probably an independent treatise;
and from that verse on he revised the original history, which
certainly extended further, and continued it down to the
Babylonian exile. Schrader is good enough to put his
annalistic narrator, of the tribe of Judah, into the early part
of David's reign, some time before the capture of Jebus; the

theocratic narrator who was an Ephraimite, or, at least, belonged to the northern kingdom, into the period 975-950, or soon after the schism of the ten tribes, 977; and the prophetic narrator, who also belonged to the northern kingdom, into the reign of Jeroboam II., 825-800. Deuteronomy was written a short time before the eighteenth year of Josiah by a man who lived to see the misfortunes of the Kingdom of Judah after the death of Josiah (639-608), and was then able to combine all the parts enumerated above. It is a sincere pleasure to be able to say that Schrader subsequently became conscious of the folly of all this, though he did not renounce higher criticism with all its works and pomps.   He adopted   Hupfeld's Development-Hypothesis with some differences.   But what deserves praise, is that he has applied himself to Assyriology, and is now one of the greatest authorities on this most interesting and useful subject.   About four months ago he published part of the third edition of his monumental work, *Die Keilinschriften und das Alte Testament*, the great storehouse of the information afforded by the cuneiform inscriptions in aid of Old Testament exegesis.

As recenty as 1890, Klostermann (who is famous among critics for the word he coined, *Heiligkeitsgesetz* or *Law of Holiness*, as the name for Leviticus xvii.-xxvi.) made an unsuccessful attempt to revive the Supplement-Hypothesis. He would identify the Redactor with the First Elohist. But the Wellhausen theory was too popular, and Klostermann was handled rather severely by a writer in the *Studien und Kritiken*, and by Professor Driver in the *Expositor*.   With him, the ill-starred theory came to an end.

Our readers will have perceived long before this that the Supplement-Hypothesis got its defenders into inextricable confusion.   Every one of them had his own original and pet notions, and every one of them failed.   Welte, the great Catholic exegete, made many unanswerable objections to these absurd theories.   Viewing the Supplement-Hypothesis as a whole, and that is all that can be done here, it is sufficient to point out its two intrinsic and irremediable contradictions.   First, its vaunted 'Grunschrift' is not a continuous narrative, but a series of unconnected statements, as any one that takes the trouble of reading them consecutively may see. Secondly, and still worse, these very E passages frequently refer to or imply what is said only in the J passages. Of course the blame is put on the Redactor ; a paltry subterfuge. It is only making the confusion greater to say that these references, virtual or actual, are Jehovistic interpolations. Once you contradict the authority of the Church and begin to explain the origin of Scripture out of your own head, there is no knowing what you may say.

REGINALD WALSH, O.P.

GREGORIAN MUSIC IN OUR CHURCHES[1]

THE social and moral influence of music in the world is very generally admitted. But while an instrument for good, it may also be an instrument for evil. Beneath its spell the passions are aroused as well as allayed, and hence the psalmist cautions us in our devotion, for God is honoured in the song of His praises, to sing wisely. Long before Christianity had dawned on the world, God was worshipped, and His praises sung, in the music of the Jewish Temple; and we learn, that in the passage of the Red Sea, so memorable in the history of the Israelites, Mary, the sister of Aaron, sang a song with all the women, of praise and thanksgiving to the Lord, ' Let us sing to the Lord for He is gloriously magnified, the horse and his rider He hath thrown into the sea.' At the time of David and Solomon music had reached its highest perfection among the Hebrews, but after the destruction of Jerusalem, the art was discouraged in the synagogues of the Jews, because it was claimed, owing to a passage in one of their prophets, that music should be dispensed with until the coming of the Messiah. Music, however, was still cultivated among the Egyptians, and from them the Greeks drew their inspirations of that art: and to Athens, and pre-Christian Rome, we are indebted for some of our most beautiful melodies in ecclesiastical chant.

The Church has ever encouraged music in her worship, following the precepts of St. Augustine, and the Fathers, who invariably taught that, through the delectation of the ear, men's minds are raised to pious sentiments and affections. Hence we find, everywhere in the Catholic churches, music is an essential or at least an integral part of the devotions, thus following the inspired counsel, ' Sing praises to our God, sing ye: sing praises to our King, sing ye. For God is the King of all the earth: sing ye wisely.'

[1] Read at the International Scientific Catholic Congress, Munich, 1900.

Not only on earth, but in heaven God is worshipped through song, for we learn from that beautiful vision vouchsafed to St. John in the Apocalypse, that singing forms part of the devotion and homage of the celestial mansions, 'and they sung a new canticle.'

Just as language, the immediate origin of song is wrapped in some obscurity. Whether it is purely and at once the gift of God, the imitation of musical sounds in nature, or the outcome of a certain state of feeling, all this opens up a field for much enquiry. That it was originally an imitation of the musical natural sounds, seems a very reasonable view. God is honoured and praised in the musical cadences of nature—'Aquae omnes : serpentes et volucres pennatae : omnis spiritus laudet Dominum : ' and, hence, man in his adoration and praises of the Deity, through the instrumentality of music, should have found a beautiful exemplar in nature. Be this as it may, music in its original state was very simple. When a strain or air was produced that pleased and charmed the listeners, some means had to be adopted to preserve it and serve as a guide to others. This was nothing more than an occasional line or stroke, to indicate the rises and falls of the composition. In the course of ages, it became more complicated, until in the time of St. Ambrose it was found necessary to considerably simplify the system of the Greeks, who were then the great masters. Among the Greeks, as with ourselves, music was regarded as a great accomplishment, and a training therein, as well as in gymnastics, was indispensable in the young Athenian. This was rather a strange admixture. But accomplishments equally opposite, are, not unfrequently, required in the youth of our time. Centring, as they did, so much importance in the art, it was eventually worked up to a science, and as most sciences by continuous improvement and discovery become too complicated for the average intelligence, so too the musical science of the Greeks had to be modified and adapted to the capacity of all. It was the intention of the great saint, that all could take part in the services of the Church.

St. Ambrose adopted four of the principal scales of the

Greeks, and on these all the Church chant was to be formed. In this system, the notes had not any definite length, and the time was regulated by the prosody of the syllable and the spirit of the composition. Ambrosian Chant originally was very simple, but grace notes were subsequently introduced, so that it lost much of its former simplicity and solemn character. At the close of the sixth century St. Gregory founded a more perfect system, based, however, on that of St. Ambrose, the time and method of singing being in both cases the same. St. Gregory adopted eight scales, four more than St. Ambrose, and on these the compositions were to be formed. He also introduced the letters of the Roman alphabet to indicate the musical sounds. We had not then the Solfeggio, which is now so common and so convenient. The syllables do, re, mi, fa, sol, la, si, now so universal in music, in their present form are of recent date, and owe their origin mainly to Guido, of Arezzo, a Benedictine monk of Tuscany. The idea was borrowed from the hymn in honour of St. John the Baptist, written by Paulus Diaconus. It runs :—

> Ut queant laxis,
> Resonare fibris,
> Mira gestorum,
> Famuli tuorum,
> Solve polluti,
> Labii reatum.

The adoption of these syllables became soon very general. In the seventeenth century the syllable bi was added, which was subsequently changed into si. Ut was changed into do by the Italians in the last century, as being more convenient and pleasing in sound. I may observe that the hymn to St. John the Baptist, in the *Breviarium Romanum*, is written thus :—

> Ut queant laxis resonare fibris,
> Mira gestorum, famuli tuorum,
> Solve polluti labii reatum,
> Sancte Joannes.

Le Maire, to whom we are indebted for the addition of si, probably drew his inspiration from the first syllable of the

Sancte, of the last line. These syllables are adopted in Gregorian music, and found most convenient.

In the system of St. Gregory, we have said, the notes are of equal length, and the spirit of the composition and prosody of the syllables regulate the time. This seems to have been subsequently overlooked, and in the *Directorium Chori*, published by Giovanni Guidetti, the pupil of Palestrina, we find the following instructions :—

Haec nota ■ vocatur *brevis :* cui subjecta syllaba ita profertur, ut in currendo tempus unum insumatur. Haec ◆ dicitur *semibrevis* et syllaba quae sub illam cadit, celerius est percurrenda, ut dimidium unius temporis impendatur. Haec altera ◗ quae *longa* est paulo tardius proferenda est, adeo ut in cantu tempus unum et dimidium insumatur.

Notwithstanding so eminent an authority, this rule is not commonly observed in our day, and we are seemingly returning to the days of St. Ambrose and St. Gregory. I subjoin the following from directions in the latest edition of the *Vesperale Romanum :*—

Notae musicae in hoc Vesperali adhibitae sunt triplices : ■ ◆ ◗

Ordinarie nota ◆ dicta *semibrevis* minori temporis spatio profertur quam nota *brevis* ■, *longa* ◗ autem majori. Quae nota *brevis* ■ per se tempus incertum exprimit, ita ut valor ejus syllaba cui incidit definiatur. Valet ergo regula ; Cantabis syllabas sicut pronuntiaveris.

I take it, therefore, that the Gregorian notes, differently from the ordinary staff notation, have not definite time, and that their value is to be estimated by the spirit of the piece, and the prosody of the syllables. The names here given the notes, I might add, are not universally adopted. I have seen the notes written by very eminent authority, *virga, punctum,* and *brevis* respectively, and it is hardly necessary to add that in Plain Chant the name of note, as distinct from any other name, affords no assistance to the performer. A knowledge of the theory of Gregorian music is within the capacity of the dullest. Bearing in mind that the notes have not any fixed time, and that the name of a note is not always an indication of its pitch, we soon come to learn all that is necessary of the Plain Chant. It is well to know that the two clefs, the do and fa clefs, give their name to all the notes on the line on which they fall, and thus serve as a guide to the names of all the others. But this is more theory than practice. A knowledge of the major and minor intervals is important, and, without this, it would be impossible to sing with any very great degree of accuracy. But the great difficulty consists in taking the proper pitch at the inception. Gregorian music is not always sung as it is written, and hence the pitch note must be taken so as to bear in mind the height to which the composition ascends, as well as the extent to which it falls. At the same time the quality and capacity of the voices engaged must also be considered. The ancients, in this matter, had a very wise rule which, so far as it went, was very practical, but hardly covered the whole ground. ' Nunquam cantus nimis basse incipiatur, quod est ululare ; nec nimis alte quod est clamare, sed mediate quod est cantare '; and the *Graduale Romanum* adds : 'Ita ut cantores, aut major pars eorum, acumen et gravitatem cantûs attingere possunt.' The pitch note is also regulated by the mode in which the piece is written ; this proves rather difficult for the average student.

There are eight modes commonly in use, although the number has been extended to fourteen. We should bear in mind, the spirit and intonation of the chant depend on the mode in which the composition is written. This is rarely attended to, and although we have the mode as well as the dominant and final indicated at the beginning of most of our pieces in Plain Chant, seldom any attention is paid to the fact. I might here observe the number of the modes had long been a subject of dispute. The question was even referred to Charlemagne, who decided in favour of eight, but we learn when afterwards requested by the Greeks to change this decision, he decided in favour of twelve. After the example of St. Gregory, the Plain Chant, as we have stated, is written in eight modes ; but the ninth mode does occur in the Psalm, ' In exitu Israel ' when preceded by the antiphon ' nos qui vivimus.' Though irregular, this is one of the most beautifully plaintive and touching of the Psalms.

The mode, therefore, must not be overlooked, and attention to the following lines will be found serviceable in singing :—

> Primum tonum hilarem suaviter tange,
> Secundum flebilem et aerumnosum,
> Tertium acerrimum et severum,
> Quartum amorosum et blandum,
> Quintum jucundum et delectabilem,
> Sextum pium et devotum,
> Septimum querimoniosum,
> Octavum magnanimum et felicem.

We have touched upon the essentials of Plain Chant, and we easily infer how intelligible and simple it is. For this reason, among others, it readily recommends itself to the Church, and is now regarded as the only true ecclesiastical chant. The Popes, from the days of St. Gregory to our own illustrious Pontiff, have recognised and recommended it. The Council of Trent strongly counsels the Gregorian music in the churches, and the decision of the Council was warmly encouraged by Popes Pius V., Gregory XIII., and Paul V. ; and we find that Benedict XIV., in an encyclical, 1749, speaks of this chant as more devotional, and better adapted to the religious tone and spirit of church music. Within recent years we have had very remarkable pronouncements by Pius IX. and Leo XIII., which, while not making it the sole chant of the Church, strongly encourage and recommend it. The views of Pius IX. in the Brief, 1873, *Qui choricis*, and that of Leo XIII., 1878, *Sacrorum Concentuum*, are embodied in a recent decree of the Congregation of Rites. This decree is dated 7th July, 1894, and most warmly encourages pure ecclesiastical chant, and at the same time firmly condemns any unauthorised changes. There can, therefore, no longer be any doubt of the mind of the Church on this matter.

The Plain Chant, as collected and arranged in the *Antiphonarium* of St. Gregory, must ever form the basis of true ecclesiastical chant, and the Church recognises every day more and more, that any serious departure therefrom cannot be an improvement in point of devotion. A rivalry between the theatre and the Church is unmeaning.

The contest is unreasonable, and, at the same time, unequal. The theatre has its prima donna, and the falsetto voice, or the male voice made to take the part of the female, is not capable of fully fulfilling that part. We may take it that Rome is the exemplar in ceremonies and church music. Female voices are not employed, nor are women admitted into the singing choirs in Rome. This custom is gradually spreading, and there is reason to believe it shall eventually become very general. We must also take into account the composition is very much different, and the chant of the *Graduale* or *Vesperale* requires much more solemn treatment. For church music the words are always unchanged, whereas each new year brings something novel, and something that can be wielded and modulated to suit the pitch and capacity of the operatic performer. I have not spoken of the evil effect of an attempt at operatic singing in our churches upon the non-Catholic or agnostic. Instinctively they feel it is not inspired by devotion.

The theory of Gregorian music is very simple, but to sing with effect great practice and adaptability are necessary. Strictly there is no instrumental accompaniment, although there is an adaptation which is not always called into requisition. There is no accompaniment in the Sistine choir, nor in St. Peter's, when the Pope is present, and the Papal choir sings. The difficulty of singing without accompaniment is not to be too lightly overlooked, and can only be attempted in public after considerable practice. Greater numbers, too, are required to make out in volume the want of the accompaniment. But experience shows that, in a small church, six or seven well-trained voices can sing the Mass with good effect, and in very pleasing style. Notwithstanding the objections sometimes raised to Gregorian Chant, it must ever be practised in the Church, for it is the sole chant for the missal, and, properly, the Mass and office for the dead. The High Church Party in England have revived the Plain Chant in their services, feeling, as we do, that it is more devotional and better adapted for congregational singing. Rightly the Gregorian should be sung in unison, but it is also harmonised and sung in parts. This system goes by the name of the 'Falso Bordone.' We have also the system called by the Italians 'Neume d'ornamento,' in which there is an effort to introduce grace notes, or groups of notes to be sung quickly, several to one syllable. This is something of a departure, so that time and again it is necessary for the Holy See to step in and guard against any novelty that might be at variance with the true ecclesiastical chant as constituted by St. Gregory. The system is not, however, condemned.

I may be pardoned, for, even here, making allusion however brief to this remarkable Pontiff, whose name is inseparably associated with Gregorian music, and after whom it takes its name. There have been no fewer than sixteen Popes who took the title of Gregory. Five have been very remarkable : among these is Gregory the Great. This illustrious Pontiff, who must ever have the veneration of the English nation, was born in 540 of a noble Roman family. He held several important civil positions under Justin II., and was even prefect or governor of Rome. This office he held for a considerable time with much *eclat*. He afterwards resigned and became a religious. On the death of his father he became possessed of great wealth, which he freely distributed in founding monasteries. He subsequently became abbot and later Pope. It was about the year 575, while walking the streets of Rome, he beheld some English exposed for sale in the market-place. Struck with their appearance, he exclaimed, ' Non Angli sed angeli '—not English but angels, if they were Christians. He was forthwith seized with the desire of evangelizing that country, and in person. He had even set out some length on the journey when he was recalled by the then Pope, at the many and persistent solicitations of the Romans, who were impatient at the thought of his absence from amongst them. On his elevation to the Papacy he entrusted this office to St. Augustine, who was the immediate apostle of England, and to whom that nation is indebted for the faith. He died in the year 604, rich in honours and graces, and was subsequently canonized. He is, perhaps, best known through the chant of which he is the founder. It is to be regretted the original

Antiphonarium of St. Gregory is nowhere to be found. The earliest record of Plain Chant discoverable is in the monastery of St. Gall, Switzerland, probably of the ninth or tenth century.

I have said, I think, enough on the history and theory of this simplest and most devotional chant of the Church to commend it. A few lessons will suffice to learn all that is essential, while, at the same time, it is the recognised ecclesiastical music. It could be taught in our colleges and schools and practised generally in our churches.

D. F. M'CREA, M.R.I.A

THE IRISH IN THE UNITED STATES

LONG before European governments found it to their interests to watch, study, and imitate the Republic of the West, as they are doing to-day, the Catholic Church in the United States had attracted the attention of the critics and the collectors. The former class found so much weakness and evil tendency in the Catholic body that conscience forced them to give the world warning; the latter witnessed and profited by a generosity which has induced them to call often and early, and to send others as well. At one time the Irish and their descendants practically made up the Catholic body in the United States, and had to bear in consequence the burden of criticism and of contribution to foreign charity. Times have changed in one respect. Other nationalities and their offspring now form part of the Church in America. In another respect unfortunately times have not changed; the Irish and their offspring have still to bear the financial burden, and to endure the shafts of an ill-informed and ill-natured criticism, pouring in from all sides.

For example, the German critics who appealed to Rome in the famous Cahensly troubles, denounced the American bishops for their supposed neglect of the German Catholics in their dioceses, and tried to prove the inferiority of faith and Christian practice among the American Irish. At all times the critics of the province of Quebec, French-Canadian critics, have held up the Irish priesthood of the United States as a suspicious and decadent body, and the French-Canadian priests have tried to prevent emigration of their people by describing the poor quality of Catholicity among the Irish. The French critics who have hounded the memory of Father Hecker and demonstrated to their own imaginations the existence of a great heresy in America, have directed their guns against the English-speaking Catholics, who are of Irish blood for the most part.[1] Finally, visitors of all nationalities have gone home to Europe after observing American Catholics, and have written detailed accounts of the wretched condition of English-speaking Catholics in the United States, while coldly praising the fine external appearance which the Church makes before the American public.

The sum of this criticism can be given in a dozen sentences, of which a number were printed not long ago in this Review ; for the Irish in America is the road to hell ; too many immigrants give up their faith as soon as they arrive in the United States ; this is particularly true of the Irish, who assimilate rapidly with Americans ; Catholic immigrants of other nationalities are protected from contagion by their ignorance of the English tongue ; the Irish, speaking the English tongue, are exposed at once to the contagion of heresy and the corruption of American cities ; they become Americanised, which means to become de-christianised ; the heresy of Liberalism is rampant among American Catholics using the English tongue ; millions have fallen and are falling away from the Church ; the proof of this wholesale apostasy of the past and the present

---

[1] We expressed our own opinion of ' Americanism ' in an article on the Holy Father's Letter to Cardinal Gibbon's when it was written some time ago. We accept responsibility for no other commentary, and we think it only common justice to give an American priest an opportunity of defending his country when it is attacked – Ed. I. E. RECORD.

can be found in the figures of the statisticians ; in particular
the proof of apostasy and desertion among the Irish can be
found in the same resources ; therefore the glamour which
surrounds American labour and American citizenship with
false splendour must be torn away, and behind that veil the
Irish emigrant in the United States will be too often
found Godless, faithless, hopeless, sunk into depths of
social misery and spiritual debasement from which there
is no arising.

This is a rather fierce and precise indictment from critics
who have never been in the country, like the wonderful
critics of France and of Quebec, or have enjoyed our
hospitality for half a year, like most of the others.
Americans listen to this hysterical rhetoric with amusement. Knowing its exaggeration they have not considered
its dangers. Convinced that they are masters of the
situation, proud of their successes, they have not replied
to criticism. They know that the United States is the
greatest country of the world and of history, in a sense
which no European can understand. Explanation will not
do. He must come to this country, live here, and learn its
greatness for himself. American Catholics know also that
their division of the Church Universal takes rank with any
other on the globe in the purity and strength of its faith,
and in the enterprise of the Catholic body. Perhaps the
time has come to take notice of the critics, at least for the
sake of our friends everywhere. It may interest the general
public, also, to learn what value we place on the criticism,
and in what fashion we reply to it among ourselves. It
is only of late that American Catholics have begun to
study themselves and to compare their achievements, their
methods, and their environment with those of their
brethren in other parts of the world. Not only foreign
criticism, but also domestic strife has forced them to
examine into various matters. What is set down in this
essay may be safely accepted as an average opinion, representative of the average American feeling.

Now, let it be observed at the outset, as a most important
factor in the discussion, that all criticism of the Church in

America is directed against the English-speaking Catholics of the United States, which really means the Irish and their descendants. All the others, French, Germans, Canadians, and soforth, protected by the barrier of language, are supposed to have kept the faith in its purity, and to practise it to perfection. The foreign critics find firm support for their contentions among the leaders of the non-English-speaking Catholics ; in fact from these leaders the critics get their arguments and illustrations. It is not necessary to my purpose to explain this curious fact. In answering foreign criticism all critics will be answered.

The general organisation of the Church in America is complete and very satisfactory. The hundred dioceses are ruled by a competent hierarchy, the legislation of the councils works fairly well, and the twelve thousand priests may rank as mission-workers with any. The parochial organisation is probably the best in the world. The American method of work prevails in the working of parishes, the same enterprise, the same adaptation of means to end, the same determination to get thorough results. In city and country parishes the churches are within easy reach of all parishioners, the Masses are numerous, confessions are heard weekly, and oftener, the census of the parish is often taken, the priests keep in touch with the people both to keep up the spirit of faith, and to preserve a sound financial condition. Relationship with the non-Catholic community is very pleasant. In the East generally, and in well-settled parts, the old hatred of Catholics has diminished or died out entirely. The hierarchy and the priesthood, the monks and nuns, are held in esteem. At this moment and for the last twenty years the Church is regarded with deep respect by millions of non-Catholics. The point I wish to make from these statements is the practical and universal organisation of the Church to meet all wants at every point, and the willingness of non-Catholics to let the Church do that work in peace. Because, if what I have just said be true, what becomes of the statements that for Irish emigrants America is the road to hell, too many lose their faith as soon as they arrive,

and lose it because they have not the barrier of a language
to keep them from American corruption? It is impossible
for any Catholic immigrant to escape the Church organisation, no matter to what part of the United States he may
go. The Church and the priest are at his right hand and
his left; the force of universal example is all around him;
the current of Catholic life eddies about church and priest
in the United States. Only one determined to break away
from the fold can possibly escape from immediate and
direct contact with religious activity.

There are no workers superior to the bishops of the
United States. It would take a volume to recount their
labours. For example, in New York city, in the dioceses of
New England, in Philadelphia, Chicago, Detroit, and other
centres of commerce, the bishops have not only provided
for the needs of the English-speaking majority, but have
built churches, and secured priests for ten different
nationalities. In New York Germans, Italians, Poles,
Bohemians, French, French-Canadians, Syrians, Greeks,
Hungarians, and Slavonians have their churches and
priests. How many of the critics have any conception of
the heroic struggle required to found and continue these
parishes? European priests of the nationalities named do
not follow their people into exile, and the bishops have
had to importune for years before they could interest the
bishops of Europe in the work of saving the emigrants. In
the beginning these parishes were maintained by the contributions of the Irish. Many of them are so supported
until this day, for the continental emigrant has no training
in the matter of contributing to the support of a parish.
He will not pay a cent to the Church, until he has learned
the fitness and necessity of American methods. The
establishment of these parishes for Italians and others is
an example of what the bishops have done and are willing
to do that no soul may be lost to the faith. I repeat here
that no immigrant need be a moment without religious
ministration after landing in the United States, unless he
has determined to refuse it.

If then it be true in any case, that too many immigrants

give up their faith as soon as they arrive, the explanation
of apostasy will have to be made by their leaders at home.
The American bishops have provided every opportunity for
them to practise their faith, their religion here is held in
esteem by all, there is no hindrance in practising it, and
even the temptations of the proselytisers are no longer so
indiscriminate and so alluring as in earlier days. Personally
I do not believe there is any foundation for these reckless
statements of wholesale apostasy, even on the part of the
Italians, Bohemians, and others. The Italians seem to be
the most hopeless of all immigrants. They know nothing
of doctrine, have never learned the catechism, and their
whole religious duty consists in getting to church on some
obscure feast day of a national saint. They contribute not
a cent, never go near the sacraments, and are the despair
of their priests. But they are not apostates even in the
presence of temptation. Their faith is in their blood.
However, it is not much to the credit of their pastors in
Italy that millions should grow up in ignorance of the
simplest doctrines, ignorance as dense and complete as ever
was. Let me add that the complaints against all classes of
immigrants on this score of ignorance are increasing on
every side. I have not investigated them, but I have the
declarations of nearly a hundred rectors that this ignorance
of Christian doctrine, of the little catechism, among Irish,
Italian, and other immigrants, is simply astounding, if one
admits that the priests of Europe are doing their simplest
duty. Can it be that this lack of common training accounts
for the supposed apostasy of so many immigrants, an
apostasy all the more terrible that the circumstances make
it needless and useless?

In answer to the statement of speedy apostasy on the
part of the immigrant, I have shown its unlikelihood from
two facts, the readiness of the Church to meet the immigrant,
and the lack of temptation from the sects. If ignorance is
the parent of apostasy in this case, the responsibility
remains in Europe. The statement of Irish apostasy so
bristles with possible answers that one is embarrassed in a
choice. Let me take the explanation given above, that the

Irish fall away speedily from the faith because the barrier
of a foreign language is not present to keep them from
American contagion. Does a language keep any Christian
from the contagion of heresy? We have battled on that
question here for twenty years. It is the contention of the
German pastors, of the French-Canadian pastors, of the
Polish pastors that only through the special language will
they ever be able to keep the faith in their people. This
belief brought about the Cahensly riot in the Church. If it
be true, then the Germans and Canadians and Poles will all
lose their faith, for in spite of their pastors they learn the
vernacular, forget the paternal tongue, and fight to get
away from all things German, Canadian, and Polish. The
children of the immigrants are American to the core, they
want to be American in speech, habit, association; they are
weary of the bonds thrown around them by their pastors,
and they break away as soon as they can. The defenders
of Cahenslyism have been at pains to explain their contention that a German or Frenchman who gives up his
language also gives up his faith, while the Irish in the
same conditions have held to the faith. Their explanation
is that English is the language of the Irish immigrant,
and opposition to Protestantism a factor in his training;
whereas the German, Canadian, and Italian have been
brought up in Catholic surroundings, and the adoption of
the English tongue and American citzenship together,
bringing him into social intimacy with Protestants, is very
apt to lead him into apostasy.

This explanation is to the point here, since it contains
the admission that the Irish do not lose their faith because
they speak the English language. I also maintain that
apostasy in other races does not spring from their adoption
of the English tongue. The steady use of the German
language among the Lutherans in the United States has
not saved them from the ravages of American rationalism:
neither has their native tongues saved the Jews from the
same pestilence. However, there is no need to discuss
this point further. Enough has been said to show that the
power of a language to act as a barrier against corruption

is disputed. There is no doubt whatever of the power of a
language to keep brethren apart when they should be
working together in harmony. The Catholics of the United
States are divided one against another according to language.
It is easier for a Catholic German or Canadian to marry
with agnostics and Protestants than to form alliance with
the Irish Catholic of the next parish. This is a result of
the language barrier which has been entirely overlooked in
the public discussions of past years.

The barrier of language is supposed to act against the
corruption of the cities and to hinder that Americanisation
which is declared to be dechristianisation for the immigrant.
I deny the corruption of the cities, and the fact that to
become an American means to become an infidel. Very
likely the critics have been reading the balderdash of the
reform journals, the crazy declarations of Parkhurst, and
the lies of Mr. Smalley in the London *Times*. These
sources are all discredited in the United States. It is
unnecessary to defend the great cities of our land. From
every point of view they are superior to anything that
Europe has to show in city administration, with perhaps
two or three exceptions. Certainly on the score of public
morality no city of America has ever yet sunk to so low
a level as the capitals of Europe. This is not saying they
are without fault. Undoubtedly there is too much wickedness in them, but to find it one must have determination,
and to seek earnestly and wilfully in the secret places.
While on the other hand these same cities are so well
provided with the things of religion, the current of life sets
so strongly towards priest, church, and school, that the
immigrant need never expose himself to the corruption
which hides in the purlieus. The most splendid examples
of Christian life are to be found in the cities: the Church
has made in them her finest showing, and won her best
triumphs. The leakage is least among the city populations
from any cause. This is a well-known fact. What then
becomes of the charge of corruption? Parkhurst, Smalley,
and the politicians are not authorities on anything.

When the critics have the Catholic Americans under

consideration they explain everything nowadays with the word *Americanism*. It has not yet occurred to them that we might retort more effectively with the term, *Europeanism*, a word which to us means much more, because there is a fact behind it, than *Americanism* means to the critics of Europe. Why should the process of Americanisation for the immigrant result of necessity in dechristianisation? The United States is Christian in the Protestant sense at least, and one-fifth of its population is Christian in the Catholic sense. It is truly a Christian land, although the old religion has begun to decay. We are at a loss here to know just what process stands in the imagination of the critics as Americanisation. Do they forget that three-fourths of American Catholics are native born? What is this Americanisation! For an immigrant to become an American involves only a residence of a few years in the country, and the taking of the oath of naturalisation. He may be said to be Americanised when he has fairly shaken off the shackles of Europeanism, shackles that have bound will and intellect for four centuries in terrible bonds, and has begun to appreciate the unutterable freedom of American life. What that freedom is none may analyse, none describe. It is so new and so delightful a thing in the world that no name has yet been found for it.

Critics make a grave mistake when they consign the Christianity of the United States to the limbo of agnosticism. Disintegration of the sects is going on, but another century will still see here a strong, old-fashioned belief in the Divinity of Christ. The leaders of American thought have, indeed, betrayed their people; editors, novelists, essayists, historians, university professors, scientists, and some preachers have all gone the agnostic way. Literature, philosophy, science, politics, shut out Christianity; but the people are still Christian in feeling, in thought, in expression. And in spite of the declarations so frequent in the mouths of the irresponsible on this subject, the consensus of opinion leaves the United States still Christian. Upon what grounds, then, do the critics make. Americanisation downright apostasy to agnosticism?

Bottled moonshine, as Carlyle would name it, is the

proper phrase for the vaporings of travellers in America.
Of course they provide figures for their statements, as one
provides anchors for balloons. The last appeal for the confirmation of all these wild assertions must necessarily be to
the statistics, and to the figures the critics appeal with
ridiculous confidence. They have been careful to state that
statistics concerning the Church in the United States are
only approximations. They have not been so particular in
stating that the statistics of apostasy do not exist. Their
inferences and figures on this point are simply approximations based upon approximations! There are no statistics
of character, of scientific value, on the Church in America.
We all know how the *Catholic Directory* makes up its items
and summaries. Pastors furnish the chancery office of the
diocese with the figures of their parishes, and the chancellor
sends a summary to the editor of the *Directory*. Three
months after the year begins the *Directory* makes its
appearance with as many imperfections and as numerous
blunders as one could desire. This year the Catholic
population is given as 10,000,000 in round numbers. To
my mind this estimate is from three to five millions out of
the way. What can be expected from statistics made up in
diocesan fashion?

The critic accepts these figures, and then proceeds to
argue in this manner:—4,000,000 of people left Ireland in
the last sixty years; by this time there should be at least
10,000,000 of Irish Catholics in the United States, and the
other Catholic races should be 10,000,000 more, but the
entire Catholic body is only 10,000,000; therefore 10,000,000
souls have fallen away. How the shade of Mulhall must
smile at this manipulation of imaginary figures! The Irish
emigrant went to Canada, South America, Australia, and New
Zealand, though the majority of emigrants settled in the
United States. In that period of sixty years a hundred factors,
of which no account is taken by the critic, played their part
in the history of the exiles. The disasters of emigration, the
scattering of relatives, the distress of settling in new conditions, the early hardships, the catastrophe of the Civil War,
all had their influence, and a very large influence, in hinder-
ing the natural increase of a fruitful people. These facts

have no place in the estimate of the critic. However, not
to draw out this discussion interminably, let it be said that
there are no reliable statistics concerning the Church in this
country, from which sound inferences might be made ; that
there are no statistics whatever for apostasy ; and that the
critics have not shown themselves competent to handle even
the poor statistics accidentally provided. What becomes
then of this vast structure of inference raised amid tears and
sobs over the unhappy fate of imagined millions ?

Undoubtedly there has been a heavy leakage from the
Church in the United States, and no one is more sensible of
the fact than the mission priest. He encounters daily the
children of the apostate, of the indifferent, of the lost. We
are preparing even now to investigate that leakage of the
past and present ; but until a scientific study has been made
of the subject we deny to anyone the right to invent figures
concerning a matter of which no one knows anything
definite. In presenting these figures the critics of all nationalities have had but one aim : to prove how wretchedly the
Irish and their descendants, that is the English-speaking
Catholics, have upheld the faith in the United States.
Yet the people who truly know the situation know well that
the enterprising faith, the missionary faith, which nobly and
effectively presents the Gospel to the American world, the
faith which builds the fort, and organises the foray, the
aggressive faith which wakes up outsiders to inquiry,
belongs exclusively to the Irish and their children ; or to
put it more generously, to the English-speaking Catholics
of the country. The Germans, the French, the Canadians
of Quebec, the Poles, are shut up in their language, their
Europeanism, which is nearly as offensive here as at home,
and much more harmful. Their contribution to progress is
criticism of their hard-working neighbours. It is they who
invented the term 'Americanism,' to conceal their own
deficiencies, and who have helped the foreign contingent
on the Continent in the attack on their English-speaking
brethren. They are determined to fix upon us the reproach
of heresy, an ancient game of decadent theologians, which
cannot be played in this country except at the risk of the
decadents.

I hear their intonations in the phrases, 'glamour of American labour,' and 'glamour of American citizenship.' I recognise their spirit in the two sentences, 'America is the road to hell for the Irish emigrant,' and 'Godless, faithless, hopeless, sunk into depths of social misery and spiritual debasement from which there is no arising.' These are the charges and sentiments which the American Episcopate, with a few German exceptions, unsparingly denounced in their protest to the Pope against the Cahensly memorials. They are positive slanders, known as such to all men of America. The conditions of labour here are not celestial, but by comparison with labour conditions in Europe they *are* celestial. American citizenship enjoys the usual deficiencies of human inventions, but by comparison with average citizenship in any other known land it is nearly divine. These expressions will surely sound bombastic to the European ear. I cannot help that. I state the common conviction of the unprejudiced and experienced. This country is the divinely-appointed political teacher of the world. It is a step forward in the progress of government. Americans have no reason to grow conceited over it, since God produced it, not the fathers of the Revolution.[1]

I can appreciate the grief of Irish leaders over the loss of their people, that mournful out-pouring of the best blood of a nation to enrich the fields of the stranger. But if that must continue no other place can compare with the United States as a home for the emigrants. Here the Irish exiles have won their finest and most enduring triumphs. On this grand stage they have proved to the world, and particularly to the English world, their capacity to rule in politics, in business, in manufactures, in war, and in letters. Not only have they built up the faith in the whole country, they have also helped by their lavish contributions to build it anew in other countries. I have no desire to boast, or to minimize the good work of others, but only to show that the various achievements of the Irish emigrant could not

---

[1] " Sed quanquam haec vera sunt, tamen error tollendus nequis hinc sequi existimet petendum ab America exemplum optime ecclesiae status : aut universe licere vel expedire rei civilis reique sacrae distractas esse dissociatasque, more Americano, rationes: Leo XIII. in Letter " *Longinqua Oceani Spatia.*"— ED. I. E. RECORD.

have been won by a race half apostate, easily overcome by temptation, as the critics would have us believe. The loss of her people Ireland can prevent only by great changes in her economic condition. Misrepresentation of this country will not do. It was tried in Canada, but it did not hinder half a million French-Canadians from settling in New England. The world is pouring into the United States, and even Canada cannot hold its natural increase. Few return to their ancient seats. Why? Because they secure here what is not to be got at home, readier money and a greater variety of opportunity.

Before Canada, Italy, Sweden, Ireland, and all the other countries whose people emigrate to the United States, can stop the flow of emigration, they must make home more profitable to their people, perhaps I might say more endurable. Undoubtedly they can diminish the flow by a good statement of the hardships of emigration. These have proved fatal to thousands. America has become for the European poor a fairy land of prosperity. When this dream meets the cold facts it vanishes into bitter disappointment. One does not pick up work here for the asking any more. It is difficult in the changed conditions of the last twenty years for the immigrant to get a grip. The French settle in the manufacturing towns, the Germans go to the farms, the Irish fix themselves doggedly in the great cities. They take what is offered, what they can get, and often stay where they land. The condition of the less capable becomes wretched, they drift into hopelessness, the saloon takes their small earnings, and in time they join the submerged tenth of the population. Their fate has furnished the critics with dreadful examples. But the true morals of their story is that the emigrants should consider change carefully, study the matter soberly, make shrewd preparations, and not let go of the bird in the hand until quite sure of the two in the bush. It is a point worth considering by the Irish leaders that the letters sent home from America by the successful boy and girl to parent and friend are the real promoters of Irish emigration.

JOHN TALBOT SMITH.

CATHOLIC DISABILITIES

THE abortive attempt recently made in the English Courts to revive the yet remaining proscriptive enactments existing on the statute book against Catholics in these countries naturally directs attention to the present state of the law upon this subject, and suggests the question as to how far the personal liberty of the professors of that faith is liable to be interfered with. It is the settled belief of a large number of well meaning but not well informed persons, that *qua* Catholic, no disability, actual or possible, attaches to one and that every remnant of the old spirit of persecution and proscription has been legislatively removed and that there exists upon the statute book nothing to warrant the feeling that Catholics, as such, have any reason to complain of the laws. A little light upon this subject may therefore not be entirely uninteresting. The charter of Catholic liberties in England and Ireland will practically be found within the four corners of the 10 Geo. IV., c. 7, entituled 'An Act for the Relief of His Majesty's Roman Catholic subjects,' which received the Royal assent on the 13th of April, 1829. This is what is popularly known as the Catholic Emancipation Act, which was largely due to the agitation successfully and ably led by Daniel O'Connell.[1]

The first section of the Emancipation Act deals with

---

[1] The effect of the Act of 1829 had often come up in the course of cases dealing with bequests to the several Orders, and was sought to be availed of in a recent case of *Roche* v. *M'Dermot*, I. R. 1 (1901), where a bequest ' to the Rector of the Jesuits at Mungret in aid of the school there for the training of pupils intended for the Church ' was held not to be invalid as contrary to the policy of the Act (10 Geo. IV., c. 7). In his judgment the Master of the Rolls, with characteristic fairness, stated—' I have very often said that it appears to me to be a crying injustice that a system of law depending upon religious disabilities should be enforced in this branch of the Courts in reference to property and used as an engine for the purpose of defeating the otherwise lawful intentions of testators when it was not directly intended for that purpose and when the enactments themselves have been allowed to become a dead letter for the last eighty-two years. It is said that this College at Mungret is illegal ; that the institutions of the Jesuits are illegal ; that the members are liable to indictment for misdemeanour by reason of their very existence in this country. There is no statesman or public person dreams of putting this law into force directly, and in the only way specifically contemplated it is to the Judges of the Chancery Division to apply and enforce it in relation to questions of property and questions of charities otherwise perfectly

Acts relating to oaths and declarations against 'Transubstantiation and the Invocation of the Saints and the Sacrifice of the Mass,' and renders them no longer necessary to enable a Catholic to sit in Parliament or to enjoy certain offices, franchises, and civil rights.

The second section renders it lawful for any peer or member of the House of Commons to sit and act as such upon taking and subscribing the following oath instead of the oaths of allegiance, supremacy, and abjuration :—

I, A. B., do sincerely promise and swear that I will be faithful and bear true allegiance to His Majesty King George the Fourth, and will defend him to the utmost of my power against all conspiracies and attempts whatever which shall be made against his Person, Crown, and Dignity ; and that I will do my utmost endeavour to disclose and make known to His Majesty, His Heirs and Successors, all treasons and traitorous conspiracies which may be formed againt Him and Them ; and I do faithfully promise to maintain, support and defend, to the utmost of my power, the succession of the Crown which succession by an Act intituled 'An Act for the further limitation of the Crown and better securing the Rights and Liberties of the Subject ' is and stands limited to the Princess Sophia, the Electress of Hanover and the Heirs of her body being Protestants ; hereby utterly renouncing and abjuring any obedience or allegiance unto any other Person claiming or pretending a Right to the Crown of this Realm : And I do further declare that it is not an article of my Faith and that I do renounce, reject and abjure the opinion that Princes excommunicated or deprived by the Pope or any other authority of the See of Rome may be deposed or murdered by their subjects or by any person whatsoever : And I do declare that I do not believe that the Pope of Rome or any other Foreign Prince, Prelate, State or Potentate, had or ought to have any Temporal or Civil Jurisdiction, Power, Superiority or Pre-eminence directly or indirectly within the Realm.   I do swear that I will defend to the utmost of my Power the settlement of Property within this Realm as established by the laws : And I do hereby

legal and praiseworthy and thus indirectly to enforce a law which never is and can now be directly enforced.'

Yet, although the policy of the Act is no longer approved of, and is really repugnant to latter-day notions of English toleration, this relic of the age of bigotry and proscription is left upon the statute books—an insult to Catholics and their beliefs ; and although incapable of active administration it is retained to irritate by its presence and insult by its continuance.

In a series of learned articles which appeared in the I. E. RECORD during the past few years the Archbishop of Dublin clearly and concisely pointed out how the Act has worked injustice to Catholics and deprived Catholic Charities of moneys left to them by generous testators, whose gifts under the provisions o the Emancipation Act were declared to be invalid and ineffective.

disclaim, disavow and solemnly abjure any intention to subvert the present Church Establishment, as settled by Law within this Realm : And I do solemnly swear that I never will exercise any Privilege to which I am or may become entitled, to disturb or weaken the Protestant Religion or Protestant Government in the United Kingdom : And I do solemnly, in the presence of God, profess, testify and declare that I do make this declaration and every part thereof, in the plain and ordinary sense of the words of this Oath without any evasion, equivocation or mental reservation whatsoever. So help me God.

The oaths of allegiance, supremacy, and abjuration referred to in the above were formerly prescribed by the statutes 30 Chas. II., stat. 2, the 13 Will. III., c. 6, and 1 Geo. I., stat. 2, c. 13, and were required to be taken by every member of Parliament. They were the oaths to which O'Connell objected and which he refused to take. By the Catholic Emancipation Act, as was seen, the above oath was substituted, but by the 21 and 22 Vic., c. 48, one oath for Protestant members was substituted for the oaths of allegiance supremacy, and abjuration, and by the 29 and 30 Vic., c. 19, a single oath was prescribed for members of Parliament of all religious denominations which, by the 31 and 32 Vic., c. 72, is now in the following form :—

I, ———, do swear that I will be faithful and bear true allegiance to Her Majesty Queen Victoria, Her heirs and successors, according to law. So help me God.

It will be seen that up to 1868 the oath of 1829 endured, and that a Catholic was compelled to take it. More enlightened and tolerant views, however, prevailed, and this restraint was removed, but a review of the other provisions of the Emancipation Act will show that many irritating and annoying disabilities still attach to the profession of the Catholic faith, which, if not enforced at the instance of a prejudiced Protestant, yet exist upon the statute book, and are enforceable by the Crown, and are an insult to the religion of a majority of the Irish people. The Emancipation Act consists of forty sections and a schedule. I have referred already to Sections 1 and 2, and I will only here epitomise some of the others in their order. Section 3 deals with the name of the Sovereign for the time being to be used in the oath. Section 4 makes no Roman Catholic

capable of sitting or voting until he has taken the oath.
Section 5 provides that Roman Catholics may vote at
elections and be elected on taking the oath. Section 6 enacts
that the oath shall be administered in the same manner as
former oaths. Section 7 regulates the form of administering
the oath. Section 8 enables a Catholic to be a member in
Scotland (which I believe he never was yet). Section 9
disqualifies a Roman Catholic priest from sitting in the
House of Commons. Section 10 enables Roman Catholics
to hold civil and military offices under the Crown with
certain exceptions. Section 12 states that nothing therein
contained shall extend or be construed to extend to enable
any person professing the Roman Catholic religion to hold
or exercise the office of Guardians and Justices of the United
Kingdom, or of Regent of the United Kingdom, under whatever name, style, and title such office may be constituted;
nor to enable any person otherwise than as he is now by law
enabled, to hold or enjoy the office of Lord High Chancellor,
Lord Keeper, or Lord Commissioner of the Great Seal of
Great Britain or Ireland, or the office of Lord Lieutenant or
Lord Deputy, or other Chief Governor or Governors of
Ireland, or his Majesty's High Commissioner to the General
Assembly of the Church of Scotland. The law still endures
preventing a Roman Catholic from being a Lord Chancellor
in England, or from being in Ireland a Lord Lieutenant
or a Privy Councillor who, as a Lord Justice, may act in the
absence of the Lord Lieutenant. An Unitarian, or a Jew, or
an atheist may be such, or one of any form of belief or unbelief, except a Catholic. Since the disability was removed as
respects the office of Lord Chancellor in Ireland two of that
faith have been Lord Chancellors, namely, Lord O'Hagan and
the Right Hon. Lord Chancellor Nash, but the existence of
the disability in regard to the office in England is said to have
prevented Mr. Gladstone from appointing to that position
Lord Russell of Killowen, and obliged him instead to select
and appoint a lawyer of the Jewish persuasion, the late Lord
Herschell; a Catholic may be Governor-General of Canada
or Governor of any of the Colonies, or dependences of the
Crown. A Catholic may be, and Lord Ripon was, Viceroy
of India, but he may not be Lord Lieutenant of Ireland.

By the 9th section no Roman Catholic priest may sit in Parliament, the words being :—

No person in holy orders in the Church of Rome shall be capable of being elected to serve in Parliament as a member of the House of Commons, and if any such person shall be elected as aforesaid such office shall be void, and if any person being elected to serve in Parliament as a member of the House of Commons shall, after his election, take or receive orders in the Church of Rome, the seat of such person shall immediately become void, etc.

The professed ministers of any and every other Church may sit in Parliament except the clergy of the Established Church, because it is such, and they are practically regarded as civil servants in that respect. Methodist ministers, Congregationalist, Presbyterian, Baptist, in fact a minister of the many forms of religious belief in England have sat and may sit as representatives in Parliament, but the Roman Catholic priest cannot sit there because of his religion alone. The same disability attaches to him as a member of any public elective board. A Catholic priest may not be a member of a County or District Council, a Board of Guardians or a Town Board. He may not be a Justice of the Peace. It is not that the Catholic priests are desirous of seeking such honours, but whether anxious for them or not they should not be disqualified simply and solely on account of their being priests— a sacred profession which should not have attached to it in a Christian country a disadvantage and disability not incident to any other religion. All through the Act we find every means taken that ingenuity could devise to still brand the Catholic religion with proscription and disability and insult its professors in every way possible. The day has passed, we should hope, when there was a foolish dread of Catholicism, and surely it might be allowed the same liberty and civil privileges which persons of other religions or of none enjoy without interference.

The 24th section of the Emancipation Act enacts that:—

If any Roman Catholic ecclesiastic, or any member of any of the orders, communities, or societies hereinafter mentioned shall, after the commencement of this Act, exercise any of the rites or ceremonies of the Roman Catholic religion, or wear the habits of his order, save within the usual places of worship of the Roman Catholic religion, or in private houses, such ecclesiastic or other person shall, being thereof convicted by due course of law, forfeit for every such offence the sum of fifty pounds.

The followers and professors of every other belief may wear the distinctive dress of that religion with impunity. A Mahomedan may so go about, a Parsee or a Brahmin, a Buddist or a Chinese priest may walk our streets in his distinctive garb, a Salvation Army man may strut or swagger along in his uniform, but it is not permissible for Catholic clergymen to appear in public in any religious dress. Why should this exclusive restriction attach to Catholics, as such, and the prohibition be continued against them alone?

The other sections of the Act up to the 27th are of no immediate interest or relevancy to the question under discussion, but that one is of importance in connection with the recent prosecution and the attempt then and there made, without avail as it turned out, to enforce it. And it reads as follows :—

XXVII. And whereas Jesuits and members of other religious orders, communities, and societies of the Church of Rome, bound by monastic and religious vows, are resident within the United Kingdom, and it is expedient to make provision for the gradual suppression and final prohibition of the same therein. Be it therefore enacted that every Jesuit and every member of any other religious order, community, or society of the Church of Rome, bound by monastic or religious vows, who, at any time of the commencement of the Act, shall be within the United Kingdom, shall deliver to the Clerk of the Peace of the County, or place where such person shall reside, or to his deputy, a notice or statement, in the form, and containing the particulars required to be set forth in the schedule to the Act annexed . . . . and in case any person shall offend he shall forfeit and pay to His Majesty for every calendar month during which he shall remain in the United Kingdom without having delivered such notice or statement as hereinbefore required, the sum of fifty pounds.'

The particulars required in the return are the name of the party, his age, place of birth, name of the order, community, or society, whereof he is a member, name and usual residence of the next immediate superior of the order, community, or society, usual place of residence of the party.

By section 29 :—

If any Jesuit or member of any such religious order, community, or society, as aforesaid (that is every member of a religious order, community, or society of the Church of Rome, bound by monastic or religious vows) shall, after the commencement of this Act, come into this realm, he shall be deemed and taken to be guilty of a misdemeanour, and being thereof lawfully convicted, shall be sentenced and ordered to be banished from the United Kingdom for the term of his natural life.

By section 30 it is provided that :—

In case any natural born subject of this realm being at the time of the commencement of this Act a Jesuit, or other member of any such religious order, community, or society, as aforesaid, shall, at the time of the commencement of this Act, be out of the realm, it shall be lawful for such person to return or come into this realm, and upon such his return or coming into the realm, he is hereby required within the space of six calendar months after his first returning or coming into the United Kingdom, to deliver such notice or statement to the Clerk of the Peace, or the county, or place where he shall reside, or his deputy, for the purpose of being so registered and transmitted as hereinbefore directed, and in case any such person shall neglect or refuse so to do, he shall, for such offence, forfeit and pay to His Majesty for every calendar month during which he shall remain in the United Kingdom, without having delivered such notice or statement, the sum of fifty pounds.

By section 31 :—

A license in writing may be granted to any one of His Majesty's principal Secretaries of State, being a Protestant, granting permission to any Jesuit to come in and remain for such period as he may think proper not exceeding six months ; and they can be revoked before the expiration of the period if thought proper, and the person so licensed shall within twenty days depart from the United Kingdom, or if he do not he shall be deemed guilty of a misdemeanour and liable to be banished for the term of his natural life.

By section 32 :—

A return of such licenses shall be laid before Parliament.

By section 33 :—

In case any Jesuit or member of any such religious order shall, after the commencement of this Act, within any part of this United Kingdom admit any person to become a regular ecclesiastic, or brother, or member of any such religious order, community, or society, or be aiding or consenting thereto, or shall administer or cause to be administered, or be aiding or assisting in the administration or taking any oath, vow, or engagement purporting or intended to bind such religious order, community, or society, every person offending in the premises in England or Ireland shall be deemed guilty of a misdemeanour and in Scotland shall be punished by fine and imprisonment.

And by section 34 :—

In case any person shall, after the commencement of this Act, within any part of this United Kingdom be admitted or become a Jesuit or brother or member of any other such religious order, community, or society, as aforesaid, such person shall be taken to be guilty of a misdemeanour, and being lawfully convicted shall be sentenced and ordered to be banished from the United Kingdom for the term of his natural life.

And by section 35 :—

In case any person sentenced and ordered to be banished under the provisions of the Act shall not depart from the United Kingdom within 30 days after the pronouncing of such sentence and order it shall be lawful for His Majesty to cause such person to be conveyed to such place out of the United Kingdom as His Majesty by advice of his Privy Council shall direct.

By section 36 :—

If any offender who shall be so sentenced and ordered to be banished in manner aforesaid shall, after the end of three calendar months from the time of such sentence or order hath been pronounced, be at large within any part of the United Kingdom without some lawful cause, every such offender being so at large as aforesaid on being thereof lawfully convicted, shall be transported to such place as shall be appointed by His Majesty for the term of his natural life.

There is a proviso in section 37 that nothing in the Act shall extend or be construed to extend in any manner to affect any religious order, community, or establishment consisting of females bound by religious or monastic vows.

The remaining sections provide that penalties may be recovered as a debt due to his Majesty by information to be filed by the Attorney-General in the Exchequer Court.

Such are the laws at present existing and capable of being enforced against Catholic religious orders in Great Britain and Ireland—showing that legally they reside in the country by sufferance, and that the badge of proscription is still on their religion. It would be only fair that Catholics should be no longer subjected to such insults as are to be found in those laws, and that the English people should carry out to their logical conclusion their boasted love of personal liberty, and remove from their statute books restrictive laws worthy of a byegone age of persecution and ignorant prejudice, and no longer compatible with the sense of freedom now understood to be enjoyed. In these days of progress, enlightenment, and liberty, it would be well for the English people to clear their statute books of laws which are indefensible in principle and so obsolete and opposed to the spirit of the times that no one but the most fanatic dreams of their enforcement. Yet they remain an insult to the persons and beliefs against which they were directed originally. Either the laws are necessary or they are not, and when by universal consent they are no longer needed, or are ever likely to be, it is full time to remove these disabilities and have them no longer attach to the Catholic religion alone. When every other form of belief and practice is tolerated there seems no reason for continuing to have those penal provisions against Catholics exclusively as part of the laws of the Kingdom, and until and unless they are removed Catholics cannot be considered as in the enjoyment of the full privileges of citizenship and subjects of equal consideration with the rest of the community. Catholics with reason complain of the words used in the Coronation Oath, and they may, with equal grounds of justice, complain of the provisions of the Emancipation Act which still find themselves upon the statute book—innocuous possibly so far as their being applied no doubt, but insulting so long and as long as they form part of the laws of the country.

That the Act is not wholly inoperative and obsolete as is asserted by the apologists for its continuance as part of the laws of the realm and might be made, in the hands of a prejudiced and narrow-minded person, an instrument of irritating annoyance not to say of oppression, is evident from the proceedings before the English Courts recently. The case of the *King* v. *Kennedy*, as fully reported in the *Times Law Reports* 18, page 557, is instructive reading. An attempt was made to enforce the Act against some Jesuit priests, and Mr. Kennedy, a London Police Magistrate, was asked to grant a summons. He refused to do so on the main grounds that the Act was obsolete and was not enforceable by an individual. An appeal was taken from his decision, and last month (April) it came before the Divisional Court, consisting of the Lord Chief Justice (Lord Alverstone), Mr. Justice Darling and Mr. Justice Channing. The case

was fully argued on both sides, and the 'note' recording
the decision reads as follows :—

Upon an information under section 34 of the Roman Catholic
Relief Act, 1829, against certain persons charging them with
having been admitted and become Jesuits within the United
Kingdom, the Magistrate in the exercise of his discretion refused
to grant a summons taking into consideration the fact that the
penalties imposed by the Act had never been put in force, that the
object of the Act was to get the Jesuits out of the country and
not to punish criminally individual Jesuits, and that it was a
matter in which, in the circumstances, proceedings should be
instituted by the Crown and not by a private individual. Upon a
mandamus to the Magistrate to hear and determine the application
for a summons the Court refused to interfere with the exercise of
the Magistrate's decision.

The judgment of the Lord Chief Justice is very interesting in this matter, and the concluding sentences explain
the grounds of his decision :—

But in such a case as this he thought the Magistrate might
take into his consideration that the fact of his refusal of the
summons would not prevent the preferring of an indictment.
The fact was that this was a very special Act. No practice had
arisen under it which could be regarded as *expositio contemporanea*
of it and therefore the considerations the Magistrate should apply
to it were necessarily different from those arising in an ordinary
case. In his opinion it would be no legal bar to proceedings under
the Act that they were taken by a private prosecutor ; and if the
Magistrate had proceeded upon the ground that proceedings could
not be taken by a private individual he thought he would have been
wrong. But he came to the conclusion that the real substance of the
matter was that the Magistrate exercised his discretion. The Court
ought not therefore to interfere and the rule must be discharged.

It is clear from this that if the magistrate in the first
instance had not exercised the discretion vested in him in
the broadminded and liberal manner he did, but had granted
the summons, that other consequences might have ensued.
The Court, on appeal, decided, not that he did right absolutely
in the matter and that therefore his decision was not capable
of being reversed, but that he exercised his discretion and
having done so they would not interfere with such exercise of
discretion. The Act remains capable in the hands of a narrow
and prejudiced Justice of being oppressively used and turned
into an instrument of irritable and irritating interference
with Catholic civil liberty.   RICHARD J. KELLY.

Notes and Queries

THEOLOGY

CAN AN 'UNAPPROVED' PRIEST ABSOLVE FROM VENIAL SINS?

REV. DEAR SIR,—Some time ago I happened to say Mass on the first Friday of the month in a country church. A number of persons who were 'making the nine Fridays' requested me to hear their confessions before Mass. No other priest was available, and they were very unwilling to interrupt the series of their nine first Friday Communions. I had neither jurisdiction nor approbation in the place. However, I heard the confessions, absolved those who had to confess only venial sins or mortal sins already remitted, and admitted them to Communion. I did so on the ground that it is at least a probable opinion that jurisdiction and approbation are necessary only for the absolution of mortal sins not yet sacramentally remitted. Was I justified in hearing the confessions, and for the reason assigned?

NEO-CONFESSARIUS.

There may be room, as we shall see, for doubt about the *validity* of the absolutions given; but regarding their *lawfulness* there can be no second opinion. It would be certainly unlawful, in the circumstances described, for a priest without approbation or jurisdiction to attempt to absolve even from venial sins, or from mortal sins already directly remitted in the Sacrament of Penance.

I. Our correspondent, as well as his penitents on this occasion, seems to have been under the impression that confession and absolution before each of the nine communions are essential conditions of this devotion of the nine Fridays. We are not aware that this view is well-founded. No doubt, those who are burdened with the guilt of mortal sin, not yet directly remitted in the Sacrament of Penance, must receive sacramental absolution before they approach the Holy Eucharist. But, on the one hand, there is nothing, *per se*, to prevent persons who are not burdened with mortal sin from receiving communion without going to confession. And, on the other hand, it would seem that the promises attached to this devotion of the nine Fridays are asserted to be contingent, not on nine confessions and communions, but on nine communions merely. If, therefore, the persons following this devotion had been previously instructed to take this view, or if our correspondent could have prudently enlightened them, the subsequent difficulty regarding the validity and lawfulness of the absolutions could not well have arisen.

II. Towards the end of his letter our correspondent seems to claim that it is probable that a priest requires *no* jurisdiction to absolve from venial sins and from sins already sacramentally remitted. This theory found some supporters among the older theologians. In modern times it is universally rejected ; and rightly, because, in the Sacrament of Penance, the remission of sin is effected *per modum judicii*, and, therefore, it always presupposes jurisdiction. Very probably our correspondent does not mean what his words seem to convey. No one now thinks of holding that any sin —mortal or venial—can be sacramentally remitted without jurisdiction. What many theologians did teach, and what our correspondent possibly had in mind, was that *every* priest *at his ordination* received jurisdiction to absolve from venial sins and mortal sins already sacramentally remitted.

III. Assuming, for the moment, that the opinion just referred to is probable, and that the absolutions given by our correspondent were *valid*, were they also lawful? No, they were certainly *unlawful*. For Innocent XI., 12th February, 1679, expressly forbade bishops to allow priests to absolve even from venial sins without approbation. 'Non permittant [Episcopi] ut venialium confessio fiat simplici sacerdoti non approbato ab Episcopo aut ordinario.' And though it may be contended that this decree of Innocent XI. did not *eo ipso* deprive priests (*simplices sacerdotes*) of any jurisdiction that they may be supposed to have got at their ordination, yet universal custom and the authority of theologians make it quite certain that, at the present time, the

prohibition insisted on by Innocent XI. is everywhere in
force. It follows, therefore, that our correspondent was
not justified in absolving even from venial sins.

IV. Were the absolutions *valid* though unlawful? On
this point authorities are divided. Some hold, and rightly,
we think, that, at his ordination, a priest receives no jurisdiction whatever—not even over venial sins.[1] For, as they
contend, it would be unreasonable to assume that the Church
grants a jurisdiction which, since the time of Innocent XI ,
at all events, she forbids the priest to use.[2] Others, however,[3]
maintain that, in ordination, priests still receive power to
absolve from venial sins and mortal sins already sacramentally remitted ; that Innocent XI. directly, or through the
bishops, forbade the exercise of this power to unapproved
priests, but that the jurisdiction itself was not withdrawn.
According to this opinion, which is supported by Ballerini,[4]
Noldin,[5] and Genicot,[6] among recent writers, the absolutions
given by our correspondent to penitents confessing only
venial sins or mortal sins already sacramentally remitted,
would have been valid.

In view of the fact that the validity of such absolutions
was commonly admitted by the older theologians, and that
it is still upheld by modern writers of repute, we do not
venture to call that opinion improbable which asserts
that a *simplex sacerdos* can *validly* absolve from venial
sins or mortal sins already directly remitted in the
Sacrament of Penance.

V. Lastly, we may remark that our correspondent does
not state how he provided for the possibility that some of
those who presented themselves for confession might have
mortal sins to confess. Did he, before hearing any of the
confessions, give such persons a general warning that he
could do nothing for them? Or, did he hear the confessions
of all and dismiss these persons without absolution? Either

---

[1] *Conf.* Lehmkuhl, *Theol. Moralis*, ii., n. 370.
[2] *Conf.* St. Alphonsus, *De Poenitentia*, n. 542.
[3] *Vid., v.g.,* Suarez, *Disp.* 26, sect. 5, n. 2, 10 ; Lugo, *Disp.* 18, n. 44.
[4] *Opus Theol. Morale.* v.. n. 555.
[5] *De Sacramentis*, n. 336.
[6] *Theol. Moralis*, ii., n. 329.

course would be surrounded by difficulties that in themselves should have restrained our correspondent from hearing *any* confessions on the occasion referred to.

ABSOLUTION FROM EPISCOPAL RESERVED CASES

Rev. Dear Sir,—Absolution from Papal censures and reservations in cases of urgent necessity has been rendered comparatively easy by the modification of the law in 1886. But episcopal cases are of much more frequent occurrence, and give confessors more trouble. May a confessor follow the Papal method of procedure in regard to episcopal cases? Has there been any special legislation in this matter in Ireland?   J. B.

The procedure introduced in 1886 for the purpose of providing for cases of urgent necessity applied to Papal cases only. Of course it is competent for bishops to adopt a similar method of procedure in reference to their own reserved cases. How far individual bishops in Ireland may have adopted the Roman practice we are not in a position to state.

D. Mannix.

LITURGY

THE FIRST OF THE PAPAL PRAYERS AFTER MASS

The *Ephemerides Liturgicae* of February, 1902, p. 110, announces that there has been a new issue of the Papal Prayers after Mass. Two slight changes have been made in the first Prayer. 'Joseph' has been substituted for 'Josepho.' This is more in accordance with Liturgical precedent, the indeclinable form of the name being always used to designate the Spouse of the Blessed Virgin.

The second change is in the conclusion, 'eundem' being introduced before 'Christum.' This, too, is more in keeping with precedent. For instance, in the Missal the two first of the '*Orationes diversae*' have precisely the same mention of Our Lord as the Papal Prayer—'Intercessio Sanctae Dei Genitricis Mariae,' and 'Intercedente . . . Dei Genitrice Maria'—and conclude 'Per eundem,' etc. The same is true of the 'Concede, misericors Deus'—the Prayer of the 'Ave, Regina,' and all similar prayers.

The *Ephemerides* states that it has authority for declaring that either the old or new version may be used. Of course, no change should be made without the sanction of the bishop of the diocese.

THE 'ORATIO IMPERATA LOCI'

REV. DEAR SIR,—Is the *Oratio imperata loci* to be said by a bishop celebrating *in Aliena Dioecesi* ?

It is. A bishop says Mass as a simple priest, except in so far as a different arrangement is made expressly by the Rubrics or the Decrees of the Roman Congregations. A priest saying Mass *in aliena dioecesi*, must say the *Oratio imperata loci*, according to a Decree of the Sacred Congregation of Rites, 5 Mar., 1898 :—

. . . Postulatum fuit.

Utrum Sacerdotes alienae Dioecesis obligentur etiam ad dicendam Orationem praescriptam ab Episcopo loci, ubi celebrant; an potius sint liberi ab hac Oratione imperata ?

Et Sacra Rituum Congregatio . . . proposito dubio respondendum censuit.

'Affirmative, ad primam partem; Negative, ad secundam.'[1]

'ME INDIGNO SERVO TUO'

REV. DEAR SIR,—Does a bishop, celebrating *in Aliena Dioecesi* say in the Canon ' *Et me Indigno Servo Tuo* ' ?

The Rubric is :—

' Si celebrans est Episcopus . . . Omissis praedictis verbis, eorum loco dicit : Et me indigno servo tuo.'[2]

There is no exception made, De Herdt, Martinucci, Bernard, Vavasseur, etc., simply make the general statement of the Rubric. Merati expressly says :—

' Sed hic notandum occurrit, quod non solum Episcopi et Superiores Praelati sed etiam Cardinales propter dignitatis eminentiam, ubicunque celebrent, orant pro seipsis, non pro loci Episcopo, . . . Sicut igitur Episcopi non orant pro aliis Episcopis, etc.'[3]

O'Callaghan teaches the same.[4]

---

[1] Dec. Authen. [2] Rit. Celeb., Tit. viii., n. 2. [3] In Gav. De Can. Minae.
[4] *Sacred Cerem. of Low Mass*, p. 129.

PLENARY INDULGENCE ON FIRST FRIDAY

REV. DEAR SIR,—What is the authority for the statement in the *Ordo*, p. viii., that a Plenary Indulgence may be gained on the first Friday of every month?—Yours etc.,

SACERDOS.

The authority is that of the Raccolta of 1898 approved by Pope Leo XIII. We give the English version of the 'New Raccolta,'[1] which is a faithful translation of the Italian.

'His Holiness, Leo XIII., by a rescript of the S. Congr. of Indulgences, Sept. 7, 1897, has granted to the faithful who, on Friday, after Confession and Communion, shall meditate for some time upon the infinite goodness of the Sacred Heart of Jesus, and pray according to the intentions of the Sovereign Pontiff.

'A PLENARY INDULGENCE, on the first Friday of every month.

'AN INDULGENCE OF SEVEN YEARS AND SEVEN QUARANTINES on all the other Fridays of the year.'

The Decree of Sept. 7, 1897, referred to above is as follows :—

Guillaume Pifferi, Evêque de Porphyre, prosterné aux pieds de Votre Sainteté, fait humblement la demande qui suit: Les Pontifes Romains ont déjà accordé une indulgence plénière pour le premier Vendredi de chaque mois, á tous les membres de la Confrérie du Sacré-Cœur de Jésus : et dans le désir d'accroître encore davantage cette dévotion, on supplie Votre Sainteté de vouloir bien étendre la même indulgence à tous les fidèles, qui le premier Vendredi de chaque mois, sans appartenir à la susdite Confrérie, aprés s'être confessés et avoir communié, méditeront un peu sur la bonté infinie due Sacré-Cœur de Jésus, et prieront selon les intentions de Votre Sainteté ; en outre, de vouloir bien leur accorder une indulgence partielle de sept années et sept quarantaines pour tous les autres vendredis suivants du mois.

C'est la grâce, etc.

SSmus. Dnus. Noster Leo PP. XIII. benigne annuit pro gratia in omnibus juxta preces. Præsenti in perpetuum valituro absque ulla Brevis expeditione. Contrariis quibuscumque non obstantibus.

Datum Romæ, ex Secretaria S. Congregationis Indulgentiis et SS. Reliquiis præpositæ, die 7 Septembris, 1897.

Fr. H. M. Card. GOTTI, *Praef.*
Pro R. P. D. A. Arch. ANTINOEN., *Secret.*
JOSEPH M. Can. COSELLI, *Subst.*

P. O'LEARY.

[1] Page 214.

CORRESPONDENCE

ETHICS AND RELIGION—A REJOINDER

120, PEMBROKE-ROAD,
DUBLIN, 3rd April, 1902.

REV. DEAR SIR,—In the current issue of the I. E. RECORD there appears, under the signature of Rev. Simon Fitzsimons, an article entitled ' Shall we Return to Pagan Ethics ? ' which purports to be a criticism, not to say a refutation, of certain views concerning the relation between Ethics and Religion which I had the honour to lay before the readers of that journal in the issue dated September of last year. I am glad of the opportunity of offering something by way of vindication and elucidation of the views I formerly advanced, and which subsequent reflection has only tended to confirm, however much I may regret the fact that my able and courteous critic should have curiously misapprehended the purport of my argument, and so compelled me to devote a considerable portion of my rejoinder to personal explanation instead of expanding and developing my original conception. To the latter task, I hope, however, with your kind permission, to be able to address myself before very long.

In the first place, then, Father Fitzsimons's argument is a good example of what logicians call *ignoratio elenchi*. He refutes positions which I never maintained, and quietly ignores the avowed purpose of my paper and the conception of ethical theory for which I contended. The very title of his reply is misleading. I put forward no plea for a return to 'pagan ethics' in Father Fitzsimons's sense of the words. By pagan ethics he understands the positive morality (or immorality) of Greece and Rome, and he points out at great length—what surely needed no telling—that the Greeks and Romans did some things which the enlightened moral consciousness of Father Fitzsimons rightly condemns. But of all this there was no question in my paper. I was concerned solely with the theoretical basis of morality, what Kant calls the metaphysic of morals, and the point of my appeal to the scientific moralists of Greece—and *not*, be it noted, to the standard of morality prevalent among the Greeks at large [1]—was, that by

---

[1] If I cared to argue *ad hominem*, I might well urge against Fr. Fitzsimons that the average standard of morality in Greece was at least as high as that

confining themselves to the purely rational or philosophic basis of human conduct they were able to give a coherent account of the principles upon which all morality is in the last analysis founded.

Again, Father Fitzsimons assumes that I was speaking of the moralist in his hortatory function as engaged in moral persuasion, as a preacher, in fact. Nevertheless, I expressly declared (page 213) that 'the hortatory function of the moralist is limited in the extreme'; and the whole drift of my argument tended to shew that I was treating of the theoretical as distinguished from the practical side of Ethics. Indeed I took occasion to point out at the start that the question I was discussing was at bottom 'a question of method,' though none the less important on that account. I tried to shew (what I am convinced is the fact) that Catholic Ethics, so far as theory is concerned, is in a hopeless muddle. Father Fitzsimons replies by pointing out that Ethics, as I conceive it, will not be effective in making men moral. I doubt this, for reasons which will appear in a moment, but meantime is that any answer to my contention ? In fact, throughout his long and rambling paper, Father Fitzsimons never once grapples with the real question at issue. I asserted that morality and religion must be kept distinct and separate, basing my argument on the facts (which I endeavoured to prove), first, that Ethics as currently formulated furnishes no real *rationale* of human conduct, and, secondly, that such *rationale* may be discovered if we keep to the purely rational or philosophic standpoint, as did for example Aristotle, who for that very reason was able to work out a consistent Theory of Ethics. Now, as to the *de facto* unsatisfactory condition of Catholic Ethics (or if he pleases of the metaphysic of morals which passes current amongst Catholics) Father Fitzsimons

---

which prevails in modern 'Christian' communities. Surely the morals of Athens in the time of Pericles compare very favourably with those of modern London, Paris, or Chicago ? On this point I am glad to find myself in agreement with such an authority as Mr. A. W. Benn, every line of whose article on the 'Ethical Value of Hellenism' in the current (April) number of the *International Journal of Ethics* my own studies lead me to endorse. The subject is not one that can be fittingly pursued in the pages of the I. E. Record, and I must content myself with referring Fr. Fitzsimons to Mr. Benn's paper for some facts which may induce him to modify his sweeping condemnation of Greek morality. I may add, however, that in this connection, in addition to his crass misconception of Epicurean Ethics, Fr. Fitzsimons has been guilty of at least one error of fact. So far is Epictetus from being, as Fr. Fitzsimons asserts, an apostle of 'free love ' that he preaches the same standard of conjugal fidelity as was recommended by Plato, (*cf. Laws*, 839-40), and moreover inculcates ante-nuptial chastity for men as well as for women. (See especially, *Encheirid*, xxxiii. 8.)

has not a word to say. The fact is, indeed, beyond dispute. And if Father Fitzsimons is dissatisfied with the remedy I propose, and which, I would again remind him, is a remedy which would leave practical issues exactly as they stand, why does he give us no hint of a better? With regard to the second point, Father Fitzsimons is more explicit, and waxes quite triumphant over his exposure of my 'insanities' and 'inconsistencies.' I contended that on the assumption that the doctrine of Eudaemonism is well-founded, a consistent body of ethical theory may be worked out, and Father Fitzsimons proceeds to enquire what kind of happiness is to constitute the goal of human activity. Writing in a Catholic magazine, and having just made profession of my adherence to Aristotelianism, I should have thought the sense in which I understood the word would have been obvious enough. If Father Fitzsimons wishes for more definite information, I am willing to tell him that I am entirely of the 'pagan' Aristotle's mind when he declares[1] that ἡ θεωρία τὸ ἄριστον καὶ ἥδιστον and that, with the equally 'pagan' author of the Eudemian Ethics I conceive the end of man to be τὸν θεὸν θεραπεύειν καὶ θεωρεῖν[2]—to glorify God and enjoy Him for ever. But even this assurance is quite beside the point. For stated abstractly and in the baldest way, my view comes to this, that morality (rightness or wrongness) is an attribute of human actions regarded in their relation to an end, this end being vaguely designated 'happiness,' and morality being thus regarded as the 'felicific' character of certain classes of actions. Surely this abstract relation of means to an end is intelligible in itself, and may be applied without further ado to human conduct in such a way as to afford a starting-point for ethical theory, leaving the concrete conception of the end to be more fully determined by means of subsequent inquiry. Similarly, the casuistical question as to what is right and what is wrong, cannot 'be settled dogmatically in advance,' though this does not prevent us from conceiving of the abstract notion of morality in the sense explained above. In this way the 'inconsistency' of which Father Fitzsimons makes so much (page 327) disappears. The other 'amusing inconsistency' referred to on the preceding page is easily explained. In the first quotation the word morality is equivalent to what I may call positive morality, and the statement made therein is easily verified. In the third, I speak of

---

[1] *Met.* xii. 7, 1072b. 4. [2] *Eth. End.* 1249b. 20.

moral *precepts*, which on my shewing are, of course, purely religious affairs. As to the second, I should have thought that Father Fitzsimons would have been the first to appreciate the distinction between 'religion' and 'true religion.'

From all this it will be plain, I imagine, that in writing my paper I had no desire to cry up the 'paganism' or 'agnosticism' of which Father Fitzsimons speaks so glibly. It appears, indeed, upon examination, that he completely fails to apprehend the theoretical problem which occasioned my remarks. The truth is that Father Fitzsimons himself in the article which he has done me the honour to devote to the discussion of my views affords a glaring instance of the prevailing confusion of theoretical and practical standpoints towards the dissipation of which I laboured, apparently in vain, in the first instance. As a priest, Father Fitzsimons is interested in the preaching and practice of morality, and believing that unless enforced by an appeal to religious sanctions his preaching is likely to bear little fruit, he is scandalised at the notion of a non-religious theory of ethics, without at all understanding what it is that the moral philosopher has to do, or why the appeal to religious conceptions is quite foreign to his purpose. And having no arguments to bring against the conception of Ethics here advocated, Father Fitzsimons is perforce driven to adopt the cheap and rather obvious device of labelling it with the opprobrious titles of 'paganism' or 'agnosticism.' Thus, too, for no apparent reason, Father Fitzsimons is pleased to assert that I am 'a utilitarian in disguise,' and, presumably to avoid the vagueness of which I am supposed to be guilty, he is so bold as to describe the exact form of utilitarian doctrine which I embrace, and to proclaim me a disciple of Mr. Herbert Spencer! I do not profess to be able to discover how Father Fitzsimons reaches this conclusion, but it certainly affords 'amusing' evidence of the completeness of his failure to grasp my position. An adherent of the 'greatest happiness' principle I most emphatically am not. Utilitarian in a certain sense I may be, but so and in the same sense are Aristotle and S. Thomas Aquinas, company good enough for me, if not for my kindly critic.

There is one further point upon which Father Fitzsimons lays great stress, and to which, in conclusion, I must briefly refer. Dealing with an *obiter dictum* in the course of my paper to the effect that the continuous spread of agnosticism tends to render the recognition of a non-religious ethic every day of more importance,

Father Fitzsimons proceeds to take me severely to task, and he
constantly returns to the subject throughout his lengthy criticism.
But what, after all, would Father Fitzsimons have? Does he
mean to deny the fact that religion is no longer the potent factor
in men's lives that it once was, or that agnosticism, or atheism, or
indifference (the name is of small moment) really is continuously
on the increase? Here in Ireland, where the old faith is still
lively as of yore, one might be pardoned for doubting these facts,
but in the United States, whence Father Fitzsimons hails, the case
is different. Let Father Fitzsimons read, for example, the Pope's
recent Encyclical, and then deny (if he can) that agnosticism
is making strong headway amongst the so-called Christian nations.
We may deplore the fact as we will; but that does not alter it or
minimise its importance. Now, assuming that morality, as currently understood, is inextricably bound up with religion whether
natural or positive (and as to this, of course, Father Fitzsimons
and myself are quite at one), then it seems to me plain that the
spread of irreligion will inevitably tend to bring about the decay of
all morality. 'So much the worse, then,' Father Fitzsimons
would exultingly declare, 'for those who, from whatsoever cause,
relinquish dogmatic beliefs.' I cannot but think that the
'conspicuous absence of Christianity,' which Father Fitzsimons
deplores in my paper, is far more 'conspicuous' in his own
callous and bigoted attitude. Father Fitzsimons is quite content
to leave 'agnostics' to their own devices; mere immorality is
thus a matter of indifference to him. And yet One who spoke with
authority, in telling us that He came to save not the just but
sinners, has deprecated in advance the attitude Father Fitzsimons
so warmly professes. Putting the question on a lower plane, is it
to the interest of humanity at large that men who abandon
Religion should be driven by Religion's adherents to abandon
morality as well? And would Father Fitzsimons seriously deny,
in the name of orthodox Christianity, that there is a true natural
morality common to all men, Catholic, Protestant, and 'agnostic'
alike—a natural light that enlighteneth every man who cometh
into the world? Does he not recognise a distinction between justice
and injustice founded on natural reason, and a notion of right and
wrong immanent in every conscience? Can he forget that free-will
itself has its roots in reason: *totius libertatis radix est in ratione
constituta?* If Catholic theology considers natural and rational
ethics to be practically insufficient without divine assistance, it

nevertheless regards it as necessary and fundamental. It is on the basis of reason and conscience that faith is built; the 'reign of grace' for S. Thomas and Bossuet, as for Leibniz, is the complement of the 'reign of nature.' This admitted, a philosophy of morals, such as I endeavoured to sketch in outline, is demonstrably possible, independently of all religious profession, and the statement is supported by the highest religious authorities themselves. The working out of the metaphysical basis of such natural morality is the business of the moral philosopher as distinguished from the preacher or practical moralist, and it would be a good thing for ethical theory if those whose concerns are wholly practical, and who have but scant conception of the subtle and complex philosophic issues which have to be mooted in the formulation of such theory, would be content to leave to the moral philosopher the discussion and criticism of notions with which they have no immediate concern.

It remains to speak of the dilemma on the horns of which Father Fitzsimons endeavours to pin my argument (page 322), and which might at first sight appear formidable. In reality, however, its plausibility results from the failure to distinguish between the metaphysic of morals and practical efforts towards moral persuasion. What I maintained, and despite Father Fitzsimons's criticism, still maintain, is, that ethical theory can, and indeed must, be formulated quite apart from all religious considerations, though it may be allowed that as a practical matter the counsels of the moralist find useful reinforcement in the appeal to religious sanctions. It is plain, therefore, to all who allow any validity to metaphysical enquiry, that to clear up the philosophic basis of all moral action is not 'superfluous' even for 'those who cling to religion.' It is, perhaps, natural for Father Fitzsimons, in his eagerness to come to practical conclusions, to minimise the importance of the philosophic propaedeutic to ethics; his underestimation need not, however, greatly concern those who have the interest of scientific theory at heart.—I remain, Rev. and dear Sir, your obedient servant,

W. VESEY HAGUE, M.A., B.L.

DOCUMENT

GREGORIAN MUSIC IN OUR CHURCHES

[DECREE REFERRED TO IN THE ARTICLE ON 'GREGORIAN MUSIC.']

What St. Augustine and other fathers have frequently taught with regard to the beauty and utility of ecclesiastical chant, viz., that through the delectation of the ear it should be the means of raising the mind to pious affections,[1] that the Roman Pontiffs, in the exercise of their authority, have always considered it their duty to carry it out perfectly and in its entirety. Hence Gregory the Great devoted so much attention to this department of the Catholic liturgy, and took such pains with it that the sacred chants even borrowed their name from him. However, in process of time, other Pontiffs, conscious that the dignity of divine worship should be duly maintained, following in the footsteps of their immortal predecessor, continually took care not only to restore the Gregorian Chant to its received and most approved form of rhythm, but also to reduce it to a better and more suitable typical form. Notably after the decrees and regulations of the Council of Trent, and the emendation, by the precept and authority of Pius V., of the Roman Missal, which was most diligently examined, the solicitude of Gregory XIII., Paul V., and others for the promotion of the liturgical chant became daily more marked, for they considered it most desirable and important that, to preserve the beauty of the liturgy intact, the uniformity of the chants should everywhere correspond with the uniformity of the rites. In this matter the efforts of the Apostolic See were considerably strengthened by entrusting the *Graduale*, which had been carefully examined and provided with simpler' melodies, to Giovanni ' Perluigi da Palestrina, in order that it might be improved and beautified by him. Now, he learnedly performed his task, and in a way worthy of a man zealous in the discharge of his duty; and such was the industry of this celebrated master

Confess. l. x. cap. 33 n. 3.

that the reform of the liturgical chant was satisfactorily carried out, the genuine characteristics being preserved in accordance with the most judicious standards. By the desire of the Pontiffs this highly important work was then undertaken by distinguished disciples of Perluigi da Palestrina, following his excellent training and principles, in order that it might be printed at the Medicæan Press in Rome. Nevertheless it was reserved for our age to crown these attempts and efforts ; for Pius IX., of holy memory, being most anxious to bring about in a favourable way the unity of liturgical chant, appointed in Rome a special commission of men exceedingly skilled in Gregorian Chant, selected by the Congregation of Rites, and under its guidance and auspices ; and submitted to its examination the edition of the *Graduale Romanum* formerly printed at the Medicæan Press, and approved by the Apostolic Brief of Paul V. This edition had so far been prepared in a very servicable manner, but was now revised with like diligence and the] introduction of suitable emendations, in accordance with standards prescribed by the commission ; and Pius IX. repeatedly expressed his entire satisfaction, not hesitating to declare it authentic by Brief dated May 30th, 1873, the purport of which is as follows :—' We particularly commend this edition of the said *Graduale Romanum* to the Most Rev. Ordinaries and to all who have the care of sacred music. We do this the more earnestly because We are anxious that as in other things pertaining to the sacred liturgy, so also in the chant, one and the same system should be observed, in all places and dioceses, as is used by the Roman Church.' Our Most Holy Father Pope Leo XIII. deemed it important to confirm and extend the approbation of his predecessor by a decree ; for by Apostolic Brief dated November 15th, 1878, he gave a special commendation to the new edition of the first part of the *Antiphonarium*, containing the day hours, which was excellently and intelligently revised, as might be expected from erudite musicians, by those deputed by the Sacred Congregation of Rites ; and, wisely addressing the bishops and all cultivators of sacred music, he made use of these words : ' We therefore, approve of the aforesaid edition, which has been revised by men well skilled in ecclesiastical chant, and deputed by the Congregation of Sacred Rites ; and declare it authentic, and strongly recommend it to the Most Rev. Ordinaries and to others who have the care of sacred music, Our main purpose being that, in all places and dioceses, as in other cases pertaining to the sacred liturgy, so also in the chant, one and the same system should be observed, as is used by the Roman Church.'

But just as, after the Pontifical Brief of Pius IX. respecting the *Graduale*, many controversies arose and obstacles were raised, with the object of throwing doubt on the approbation itself, on account of which the Congregation of Sacred Rites, on the 14th of April, 1877, found it to be a duty to defend the authenticity of the edition, and to confirm it by its decision, so, too, after the Apostolic Brief of Leo XIII., instead of an end being put to contention, some persons thought themselves at liberty to neglect the ordinances and decrees in regard to ecclesiastical chant approved by the theory and practice of the Roman Liturgy. In fact, after the appearance of the Choral Books of the Church, and after the whole matter had been brought to a successful issue, disputes increased; and at a congress of cultivators of liturgical chant, held at Arrezo in the year 1882, the severe censures passed filled with grief those who, rightly and properly, think that as regards the uniformity of the ecclesiastical chant, the Apostolic See is alone to be obeyed. Moreover, as those who had contended about this matter at Arrezo not only published their resolutions or requests, but even brought them in set form before our Most Holy Father Leo XIII., the Holy Father, moved by the importance of the matter, and with the view of consulting for the unity and dignity of the sacred chants, especially the Gregorian Chant, referred these resolutions or requests to the examination of a special body of cardinals of the Congregation of Rites, selected by himself. After carefully weighing everything, and having obtained the opinions of eminent men, they, without any hesitation, decided to decree as follows :—' The resolutions or requests emanating from the Congress of Arezzo last year, and laid before the Apostolic See, in reference to bringing back the liturgical Gregorian Chant to ancient tradition, cannot, as they are worded, be received or approved of ; for, although it always has been, and ever will be, open to cultivators of ecclesiastical chant, for the sake of erudition, to inquire as to the ancient form of that chant and its various phases, just as learned men, in a very praiseworthy manner, have been accustomed to discuss and investigate the ancient rites of the Church and other parts of the sacred liturgy, nevertheless that form alone of Gregorian Chant is to-day to be regarded as authentic and legitimate which has been ratified and confirmed, in accordance with the regulations of the Council of Trent, by Paul V., Pius IX., of holy memory, and our Most Holy Father Leo XIII., and by the Sacred Congregation of Rites, in the edition recently brought out, which alone contains the form of chant used by the Roman Church. Therefore, respecting its authenticity and legitimate character, there can be no further doubt or question among those who sincerely wish to respect the authority of the Apostolic See.'

However, in these latter years, owing to various causes, the old difficulties have again appeared, and there have been fresh disputes, by which it has been sought to invalidate or to assail vigorously the genuineness of the edition itself and of the chant contained therein. There were also some who inferred, from the earnestness with which the Supreme Pontiffs Pius IX. and Leo XIII. had commended uniformity in ecclesiastical chant, that all other forms of the chant, even when long in use in particular churches, were entirely forbidden. In order to remove these doubts, and to prevent all ambiguity for the future, his Holiness decided to refer the matter to an ordinary meeting of all the cardinals of the Congregation of Sacred Rites; and they in sessions held on the 7th and 12th of June last, having again gone into all the points, and maturely weighted others submitted to them, unanimously decided as follows:—'The enactments of Pius IX., of holy memory, in the Brief *Qui choricis*, dated May 30th, 1873; of our Most Holy Father Leo XIII. in the Brief *Sacrorum Concentuum*, dated November 15th, 1878; and the aforesaid prescriptions of the Sacred Congregation of Rites, hold good.' As regards the liberty, however, according to which particular churches can retain a form of chant legitimately introduced and still in use, the same Congregation exhorts all local Ordinaries and other cultivators of ecclesiastical chant, for the preservation of uniformity in the chant, to take care to adopt the aforesaid edition in the sacred liturgy, though, in accordance with the prudent mode of acting on the part of the Apostolic See, it does not insist upon its adoption in every church.

The undersigned Cardinal Prefect of the Sacred Congregation of Rites having faithfully related all this to our Most Holy Father Leo XIII., his Holiness, on the 7th of July, 1894, ratified and confirmed the decree of the same Sacred Congregation, and ordered it to be published.

CAJETANUS Card. ALOISI-MASELLA, *S.R.C. Praefectus.*

L. ✠ S.

ALOISIUS TRIPEPI, *S.R.C. Secretarius.*

NOTICES OF BOOKS

STUDIA SINAITICA. Cambridge University Press.

THE importance of this series can hardly be overrated. The contents of the ten volumes already published are of exceedingly great value to the student of Liturgy or of Scripture, as well as to the Orientalist. Even a cursory glance through the pages reveals some of the many treasures of the library of the ancient monastery of St. Catherine's, Sinai. A few years ago a Doct. Phil., in a continental university of world-wide fame, expressed his astonishment that England possessed ladies competent to decipher and to annotate Syriac and Arabic texts, and we are sure that all who read these volumes will share the professor's admiration of the scholarship displayed by the two editors, Mrs. Lewis and Mrs. Gibson.

I. The first number contains a descriptive Catalogue of the Syriac MSS. in the Sinai Monastery—where liturgical, Scriptural, hagiological and homiletic literature are well represented. This volume gives in photographic facsimile some pages of these MSS., including the Palestinian Lectionary. (Several pages of other MSS. are photographed in the succeeding numbers.) Besides this, there is an Appendix containing quite a number of valuable fragments. Among them, perhaps the most interesting to the Biblical student ar_ the fragment of what is probably the oldest Arabic version of the New Testament, and a fragment of a Greek MS. (seventh century?) in which the concluding verses of St. Mark's Gospel occur in the form of a double alternative, known to us from Codex L. (*i.e.* Regius). The double alternative here spoken of is what we call the Long Conclusion (Deuterocanonical part, v. 9-20), and the Short Conclusion which is found with it in some MSS., and in the margin of the Harkleian Syriac. St. Jerome mentions (*contra Pelagium*, ii., 15) that it was found also in some Greek MSS.

II. An Arabic version of the Epistles to the Romans, Corinthians, Galatians, and a part of that to the Ephesians. The MS. belongs to the ninth century, but there is evidence to show that the version is still older. While on the whole it is remarkably faithful, it is clear that some idiomatic turns in Greek were unintelligible to the translator. The present edition in which wherever necessary modern orthography is substituted for the obsolete and difficult forms of the original, will be found very useful by students of Arabic. In her preface, Mrs. Gibson mentions that this codex contains also an Arabic version of Ecclesiasticus. Let us hope that it will be published in some number of the *Studia Sinaitica*. This is not too much to desire, considering that Mrs. Gibson, and her equally learned sister, Mrs. Lewis, were the first to bring to Europe a leaf of the original Hebrew of this inspired book, which St. Jerome read, but which no living person thought he would ever see before the surprising discovery of 1896 was announced. Now that about half of the long-lost Hebrew text has been recovered, it would be most interesting to compare the Arabic version with it.

III. Catalogue of the Arabic manuscripts. There are more than six hundred in the library, and all these are enumerated and their contents indicated. The Scripture codices come first, then martyrologies and other liturgical books, followed by homilies of the Fathers (among whom we notice that St. John Chrysostom, St. Basil and St. Ephrem are favourites), and lastly numerous lives of Saints, etc.

IV. A tract of Plutarch : ' On the advantage to be derived from one's enemies.' It is edited with translation and notes by Professor Nestle of Maulbronn, to whom we owe a similar edition of the Syriac version of Eusebius, a compendious Syriac grammar, etc. This tract of Plutarch is but one of the number of philosophical writings in Greek which had such a charm for the Syrians. Not only various works of Aristotle, but moral treatises and, in particular, collections of the pithy sayings of the philosophers were most popular. The interesting tract before us has been altered and improved with a view to making its contents still more acceptable to Christian readers.

V. Apocrypha Sinaitica. Seven are given, the first of which the ' Anaphora Pilati,' one of the numerous sequels to the Acta Pilati (or Gospel of Nicodemus), is the account of the miracles and death of our Divine Lord, alleged to have been sent by Pilate to the Emperor Tiberius. We all know that St. Justin and then Tertullian refer to an official report of such a kind, so there can be no doubt of its existence at one time, but it must have been very different from the apocryphal document which now usurps the name. In this one there is indeed nothing contrary to the Gospel history, nor unworthy of the subject, but it is nevertheless the work of a Christian who combined details taken from the

Evangelists with imaginary embellishments. The Greek text of which the Sinaitic Syriac is a version was considered by Tischendorf to belong to the second century, whereas Battifol would assign it to the fourth. An old Armenian version was published in the Mechitarist pediodical, Vienna, 1894. Mrs. Gibson gives three recensions (Syriac and Arabic). This work is followed in her volume by the Recognitions of Clement (Arabic: two versions, *Sinai* and *British Museum*, which differ considerably). This apocryphal tale is one of those proscribed by Pope St. Gelasius. Everyone knows that it gets its name from Clement's recognizing his parents and his brothers. The account of the Saint's martyrdom, which in the B. M. codex follows the Recognitions, contains three interesting episodes, the truth of which is vouchsafed for elsewhere: the miracle of Socinius, and that of the submerged boy, in the ancient frescoes of San Clemente, Rome,[1] and the miracle of the lamb indicating where water would be found, in the Roman Breviary (Nov. 23). The 'Preaching of Peter' and the remaining three legends contained in this volume bear the characteristic marks of orthodox apocrypha.

VI. If we are not mistaken, to most readers this will be the most interesting number of the whole series, which is saying a great deal. Eusebius tells us that before the capture of Jerusalem the Jewish Christians quitted the doomed city and retired across the Jordan to Pella. A Vatican evangeliarium, written either in Antioch or Jerusalem (A.D. 1030), is believed to represent the use of this ancient community. There was also in Egypt at some unknown period a colony of Palestinian Christians to whom we owe the Lectionary (from Genesis, Kings, Amos, and Acts), which has been published by Margoliouth under the title of 'The Liturgy of the Nile.' Then there are the fragments preserved in London, St. Petersburg, and Oxford, that have been published by Land, Gwilliam, Burkitt, and Stenning. Now comes the MS. owned by Mrs. Lewis, which contains more lessons than do all the previous publications put together. A unique interest attaches to the dialect which the Palestinian Lectionary exhibits. As the erudite editor observes, 'It is generally conceded that the dialect is probably that which our Lord spoke, and that which bewrayed St. Peter.' Those acquainted with Syriac will find its study most interesting, though of course they will have to take an

---

[1] See Rev. J. Mullooly, O.P., *St. Clement and his Basilica.*

additional step in order to acquire a knowledge of its peculiarit es It will not however be difficult for them to do so with the assistance provided here. There are notes by Nestle, and a glossary by Mrs. Gibson. Nestle adds critical notes on the underlying Greek text, *i.e.*, that from which the lessons were translated. He maintains that each lesson was translated for this Lectionary, and that it did not previously form part of a complete version, either of the Old or of the New Testament. His argument is that some passages which occur more than once differ; they must therefore be either different translations of one Greek text, or translations of different Greek texts. Gwilliam and Stenning are, however, of the opposite opinion. They think that several of the lessons which they edited belong to the sixth century, because the use of Lectionaries began in the seventh. In the Old Testament the present Lectionary rests on a text dependent on that of Origen. The arrangement of the Lectionary is that proper to the Byzantine rite. There are lessons for Sundays, Christmas, Theophany (Epiphany), Ash Wednesday, Fridays in Lent, Holy Week, Easter Week, etc., and a Hymn in honour of SS. Peter and Paul.

VII. An Arabic version of the Acts of the Apostles (from vii. 37) and of the Catholic Epistles, with a treatise on the Triune Nature of God (Arabic), together with its translation by Mrs. Gibson. The editor says the MS. is the most ancient specimen of Arabic calligraphy to be found in the Sinai library (eighth or ninth century). Mrs. Gibson also mentions that Dr. Gwynn of T.C.D. came to the conclusion that the Acts and the three longer Epistles (St. James, 1 St. Peter, and 1 St. John) were translated from the Peshitta, and the remaining four Epistles from the unrevised Philoxenian. The treatise on the Trinity is orthodox, that is all that can be said in its praise. It does not display any profound theological knowledge, the author was neither an Athanasius nor an Ephrem. Indeed the greater part of the treatise consists of a summary of Bible History. It is noticeable that the writer puts twelve hundred years between Noe and Abraham, thus exceeding the Septuagint (even its highest variant).

VIII. Apocrypha Arabica. The first is the so-called Book of the Rolls. We read in its introductory paragraph 'this is the sixth of Clement's books treasured up in the city of Rome since the time of the Apostles.' The spurious Apostolic Constitutions are sometimes reckoned as the sixth, but they are quite unlike this Book of the Rolls, so, too, is Mgr. Rahmani's second book, in his lately published *Testamentum D.N.J.C.* The book before us bears a general resemblance to the first book of the Tübingen Ethiopic MS. published by Dillman in the *Göttinger gelehrten Anzeigen*, 1858. It contains a rapid sketch of history (chronology often incorrect) from Adam to the Blessed Virgin. We notice in it the interesting statement, that the ark rested on the Kurdish mountains. The Chaldean Genesis (line 142) says that the ship went aground on the mountains of Nizir—which according to some authorities is a chain of hills lying at the foot of the Kurdish mountains. An Assyrian tablet (Records of the past X.) puts Nizir in the land of Gutium, *i.e.*, east of Ninive. On the other hand, the Peshitta and St. Ephrem would indicate Jebel Judi as the mountain in question. The second apocryphal work printed in this volume refers to Aphikia, the alleged wife of Siracides. There is nothing noteworthy in this fanciful tale except the anachronism it contains. The story of Cyprian and Justa (Arabic and Greek) is interesting.

IX. Select narratives of holy women from the Syro-Antiochene or Sinai Palimpsest.

X. Translations by Agnes Smith Lewis. We should like to be able to treat of these lives in detail, but we have already taken up much valuable space. Suffice it then to say that Mrs. Lewis' admirable Introductory Notes give full information about these servants of God—Thecla, Eugenia, Pelagia, Mary, Euphrosyne, Onesima, Drusis, Barbara, Mary, Irene, Euphemia, Sophia and Justa (with an appendix containing Theodosia, Theodota and Susanna)—all of whom, with the exception apparently of Onesima, are honoured by the Greek or by the Latin Church, or by both. Ornamental additions have in some cases been added to the facts of history, indeed the ' Acta Pauli et Theclae ' were proscribed by Pope St. Gelasius.

R. W.

THE LIVES OF THE POPES OF THE EARLY MIDDLE AGES. By Rev. H. K. Mann. London: Kegan Paul. 1902.

IT has often been said that the lives of the Roman Pontiffs are the best compendium of the ecclesiastical history of their respective times. So true indeed is this, that we always find that from their biographies most light is thrown on the great events that have happened during the many centuries of the Church's existence. How much for instance has been made clear and intelligible by Pastor's *Lives of the Popes* ?

What Pastor has accomplished for Martin V. and his successors, Father Mann is now doing for the Popes down to the period at which Pastor begins. It will be a boon to have an uninterrupted, or almost uninterrupted, series. The first volume of Father Mann's work contains the history of no less than twelve Popes, from St. Gregory the Great (590-604) to St. Eugenius I. (654-657). As St. Gregory was by far the greatest man of his time, of his life it is especially true that it reflects as a mirror the chief contemporary events in Christendom. We could, indeed, hardly get a better view of the state of things in the last part of the sixth century and the beginning of the seventh than that which we find in Father Mann's pages on the subject. As might be expected, his style is more flowing than Pastor's. This elegance, however, has not been secured at the cost of accuracy and thoroughness. On the contrary, the volume before us bears evidence of the close and careful study of all the best sources of information, such as the *Liber Pontificalis*, the *Regesta Romanorum Pontificum*, etc.

We hope that it will be widely read, for as Leo XIII. said when the author presented him with a copy, ' Bisogna far conoscere i Papi.'   F. R.

[We are compelled to hold over various questions in Theology and Liturgy till next month. In reply to several questions regarding attendance at the King's Coronation in Westminster Abbey, and the dispensation from fast and abstinence on the same occasion, we must refer our correspondents to approved authors, and if they still have any doubts, to their respective Ordinaries.— ED. I. E. RECORD.]